# CAS

# THE BOOK OF PROFESSIONAL STANDARDS FOR HIGHER EDUCATION 2003

Third Edition
Major Revision

**Theodore K. Miller, Ed.D.**
CAS Publications Editor
Emeritus Professor
The University of Georgia

**Council for the Advancement of Standards
in Higher Education**

**Washington, DC**

# *The CAS Book of Professional Standards for Higher Education 2003*
## *3rd Revised Edition*

**Library of Congress Cataloging-in-Publication Data**

Miller, Theodore K., 1932-
    The CAS Book of Professional Standards in Higher Education 2003
    Includes bibliographic references.

    ISBN 1-58328-032-4
    1. Student Affairs. 2. Student Services. 3. Professional Standards
    4. Advising, 5. Counseling, 6. Higher Education, 7. Learning Assistance

Interior Design: Ted K. Miller, Athens, GA
Cover Design: Carol Ripley, HBP, Hagerstown, MD
Printing and Binding: HBP, Printing, Graphics & Information Services, Hagerstown, MD

This book is a revision of The *CAS Book of Professional Standards for Higher Education 1997, 1999, 2001.*

# CAS

## Council for the Advancement of Standards in Higher Education

### *The Book Of Professional Standards For Higher Education* 2003

### Table of Contents

# CAS

## COUNCIL for the ADVANCEMENT
## of STANDARDS in HIGHER EDUCATION

### *CAS* President's Letter to the Profession

The standards and guidelines for practice listed in this edition of *The Book of Professional Standards for Higher Education* are all new. Standards and guidelines for several functional areas have been added since the publication of the 2001 version and all standards and guidelines have been updated to include new general standards. General standards are applicable in all educational programs and services in higher education and they have been modified from earlier versions to reflect explicit examples of student learning and development outcomes that should help any practitioner interested in assessing student learning to conduct meaningful evaluation studies. The new general standards also include advancements in thinking about institutional effectiveness and quality in higher education.

Representatives of 32 currently active professional associations now embody the CAS Board of Directors and they collectively believe that these new standards represent a significant step forward for educators and policy makers seeking to understand the effects of college on students. These standards and guidelines are up to date on vital issues in education and they bring concreteness to educational practice that should help any educator striving to improve practice. The representatives to the CAS Board of Directors craft these standards and guidelines in concert with multiple experts from many fields of practice and study and represent the collective wisdom of hundreds of professionals in higher education. Board members work diligently to bring widely diverse viewpoints from their respective professional associations and institutions of higher learning in the U. S. and Canada to a level of consensus about threshold criteria for excellent educational practice that is rare if not unique in educational practice.

On behalf of the outstanding educators who serve on the CAS Board of Directors, I commend this new educational resource to all higher education practitioners and scholars. We hope that you will use it to shape and to evaluate your practice, to guide your own professional development, to assist in institutional accreditation, and to shape your own scholarly inquiries into the effects of the use of CAS standards and guidelines in practice. We invite you to use these standards and guidelines in any manner that will help you to be a more effective educator and we invite your feedback and your personal involvement in our efforts to constantly improve this service to professionals in higher education.

Don G. Creamer
CAS President
Professor and Coordinator,
Higher Education and Student Affairs
Department of Educational Leadership
and Policy Studies
College of Human Sciences and Education
Virginia Tech
Blacksburg, VA 24061-0302
June 2003

# EDITOR'S NOTE

As this major revision of *The CAS Book of Professional Standards for Higher Education* nears completion, I am especially aware of what a distinct honor and privilege it has been for me to edit and guide the evolution of the *CAS Blue Book* during its four iterations over the past seven years Since 1979 I have had the pleasure of working with one of the most diverse, diligent, and dedicated groups of higher education professionals one can imagine. As the Council for the Advancement of Standards in Higher Education's (CAS) founding president and more recently its Editor of Publications, I have been involved in a unique and historical process. During the past decade and a half, CAS has established itself as the premier professional body dedicated to the development and promulgation of programmatic standards and guidelines that undergird the learning and development of college and university students. As my tenure on the CAS Board of Directors and my representational efforts on behalf of both the American College Personnel Association (ACPA) and the Southern Association of College Student Affairs (SACSA) comes to a close in 2004, and after 25 years of sometimes difficult but always enjoyable effort on behalf of student learners, I have experienced an exceptional opportunity to serve in the higher education arena and to learn from the many professional colleagues with whom I have had the honor of working.  CAS, along with ACPA and SACSA, have honored me by providing ample opportunity to be of service and I am forever in their debt for the trust placed in me to represent them in various ways. There can be no doubt that the rewards have far outnumbered the labor, time, and energy expended on behalf of important CAS initiatives, many resulting directly from the wonderful people with whom I have collaborated. One could not fairly ask for more.

Perhaps the most signal transformation to evolve in higher education in recent years is the increasingly evident interaction between student affairs and academic affairs as they have subtly, but clearly, begun to collaborate to establish educational environments that are intentionally conducive to enhanced student learning and development. Although CAS cannot take credit for the philosophical and paradigmatic shifts increasingly in evidence, the Council has clearly been influential in the shifts currently underway. Prior to the CAS initiative, most student support practitioners had little more than native intuition and best guesses to guide their work with students. Today, there is an expanding body of professional knowledge and complementary standards available to guide practice and upon which to base personal, professional, and programmatic development. The CAS contribution has focused on the development and promulgation of standards and it has provided a nexus where student needs and the collective interests and talents of professional associations can connect for the betterment of student learning and development. The CAS initiative is truly unique and it is with pleasure that the CAS consortium of professional associations presents the 2003 revised edition of the CAS book of professional standards for the edification of us all.

This edition presents one new set of standards, Conference and Events Programs, a revised academic preparation standard, and 28 revised functional area standards. A significant part of the revisions represents an increased emphasis on student learning and development outcomes and the importance of their assessment in all arenas. In regard to the final copy editing of the manuscript, I want to thank Tamara Miller Bowden, of Auburn University, who was extremely helpful in cleaning up the kinks and typos from the penultimate version.

CAS is a consortium of professional associations that exists for purposes of promoting quality programs and services for college and university students. The CAS initiative continues and this book is a reflection of the Council's important work.

Ted K. Miller
Professor Emeritus
The University of Georgia
Athens, Georgia
August  2003

# PROLOGUE

This 2003 edition of *The Book of Professional Standards for Higher Education,* often referred to as the *CAS Blue Book* or the *CAS Book of Standards*, is the fifth iteration of professional standards generated and promulgated by the Council for the Advancement of Standards in Higher Education (CAS). This edition, which will be in effect through 2005, contains 26 previously published but recently revised functional area standards, all of which have incorporated a new set of "general standards" into them. Included in addition are three standards that have recently undergone major revision including the master's level preparation program standards and the Alcohol, Tobacco, and other Drug Programs and Disability Services functional area standards. One totally new standard, Conference and Events Programs, appears for the first time in this edition as well. Readers will note that newly generated CAS standards increasingly focus attention on higher education functions that transcend traditional student affairs organizational structures. Although the CAS standards development initiative continues to emphasize programs and services in support of student learning and development, increased attention is being paid to other educational functions essential to institutional effectiveness that may be less inclusive of direct student contact or support. This expanded CAS vision reflects an increased emphasis on developing standards to guide professional practice throughout the whole of higher education.

CAS was established nearly a quarter century ago for purposes of developing and promulgating standards of professional practice to guide higher education practitioners and their institutions, especially in regard to work with college students. Currently, the CAS Board of Directors is composed of delegates from 32 professional higher education associations in the United States and Canada. These organizations represent a full range of not-for-profit corporations concerned with student learning and development, many of which identify with the field of student affairs. In addition to the functional area practice standards, CAS has adopted and promulgated a set of master's level academic program standards to guide the graduate education of student affairs entry level administrators. Included in this publication are the standards and guidelines for 29 functional areas along with a description of their historical evolutions and contextual settings.

As institutions of higher learning face new challenges, they often require faculty and staff members to implement their educational responsibilities in new and different ways. Approaches and strategies that were previously successful often need to be amended as institutions and programs evolve and student populations and characteristics change. Consequently, both educational and developmental needs brought to campus by students may change over time, requiring new and different approaches for those needs to be met effectively. As institutions and their constituents change, so to must the vehicles that guide practice within the shifting culture. As new developments occur that result in previously unrecognized or newly identified student needs, institutional support services and programs must change likewise. In light of these factors, each CAS standard must be viewed as a living document that will shift over time as it reflects an evolving function. Consequently, users of the CAS standards must anticipate that the standards will change as demands shift and transitions occur.

The Council for the Advancement of Standards in Higher Education, a name adopted in 1992 to reflect the expanded context of the Council's higher education focus, was originally established in 1979 as a not-for-profit corporation called the Council for the Advancement of Standards for Student Services/Development Programs. Impetus for its existence was encouraged by a movement on the part of several national associations to develop accreditation standards for academic programs that prepare counselors and counselor educators. This movement, which culminated in the establishment of the Council for the Accreditation of Counseling and Related Educational Programs (CACREP) in 1980, provided the American College Personnel Association (ACPA) with impetus to create a set of preparation standards for use in master's level college student affairs administration programs. Rather than promulgating these standards as its own, ACPA sought out other professional associations interested in the development of standards for student affairs preparation and practice. The National Association of Student Personnel Administrators (NASPA) indicated an interest in the project and the two associations jointly issued invitations to a meeting of interested professional associations. Seven student affairs oriented organizations sent representatives to the exploratory meeting held in Alexandria, Virginia in June 1979. This meeting resulted in the creation of an inter-association consortium for purposes of developing and promulgating professional standards to guide both student affairs practice and academic preparation of those who administer student support programs and services. A subsequent organizational meeting in September 1979 resulted in the establishment of CAS as a not-for-profit corporate consortium of 11 charter member associations (see Appendix A).

Today, after 24 years of collaboration and a name change to reflect its expanded interests, the Council for the Advancement of Standards in Higher Education is composed of 32 member associations, and has generated and promulgated 29 sets of functional area standards and guidelines and one set of master's level academic preparation program standards for college student affairs administration.

## CAS Mission

The Council was founded to implement several profession-wide initiatives, with emphasis on the development and promulgation of professional standards. As CAS evolved, its *raison d'être* shifted as well. The following reflects the contemporary CAS mission.

1. To establish, adopt, and disseminate unified and timely professional standards to guide student learning and development support programs and services and related higher education initiatives.
2. To promote the assessment and improvement of higher education services and programs through self-study, evaluation, and the use of CAS standards.
3. To establish, adopt, and disseminate unified and timely professional preparation standards for the education of student affairs practitioners.
4. To promote the assessment and improvement of professional preparation graduate programs for student affairs administrators through the use of CAS standards for assessment, evaluation, and self-study purposes.
5. To advance the use and importance of professional standards among practitioners and educators in higher education.
6. To promote and encourage public and private higher education systems and institutions to focus attention on the assurance of quality in all educational endeavors.
7. To promote inter-association efforts to address the issues of quality assurance, student learning and development, and professional integrity in higher education.

As these purposes imply, CAS exists to accomplish several complementary tasks. A primary purpose of the Council is to provide a forum in which representatives from higher education organizations can meet and interact for purposes of seeking consensus on the fundamental principles of "best practice" that can lead to enhanced professional standards. The CAS initiative provides a forum wherein all voices can be heard in the creation of timely and useful standards to guide contemporary practice. This approach encourages the establishment of viable linkages among professional associations, most of which focus on highly specialized functions. This professional collaboration results in the creation of standards that represent a profession-wide perspective rather than a narrow and limited viewpoint.

Not only does the CAS initiative provide a vehicle for the development of functional area and academic preparation standards, but it also provides a well recognized and credible profession-wide entity to publish and promulgate standards and encourage and educate practitioners to apply the standards effectively in their work with students. Further, and of special significance, the CAS consortium speaks with a single voice that bridges numerous specialty areas and can represent the profession-at-large on matters concerning professional standards and quality assurance.

## CAS Rationale

As appears obvious in retrospect, CAS was created as a direct response to the emerging profession's need to establish standards to guide both practice and preparation. By the 1960s, the felt need for a profession-wide entity to speak as one voice for all was very apparent. An initial attempt to establish such a spokesbody, the Council of Student Personnel Associations in Higher Education (COSPA), was mounted in the late 1960s by 10 student affairs associations. This consortium is best remembered for its promotion of an enlightened approach to student affairs practice reflected in a statement published in 1972 by its Commission of Professional Development entitled

"Student Development Services in Post-Secondary Education" (Rentz, 1994). Unfortunately, COSPA was dissolved in 1976, largely as a result of member disillusionment resulting from unresolved political issues.

CAS was established on a comparable consortial basis to that of the COSPA for an equally important, though less ambitious, purpose. Whereas COSPA was intended to function on a full range of professional issues, from the outset, CAS sought to avoid politicization and be driven by agreed upon values rather than special interests. Consequently, the purposes and objectives of CAS are highly focused, which tends to protect the Council from internal strife resulting from member disagreement about its designated purpose and the processes used to accomplish its mission.

Although some may question the value of CAS's existence, it is virtually assured that without CAS working collaboratively and speaking collectively on behalf of practitioners and their functional area specialties, there would be no profession-wide criteria of good practice such as the CAS standards. In effect, CAS desires to represent every college and university educator and functional area specialist who deems the learning and development of students of all ages, heritages, and life-styles to be to be the essence of higher education.

Although some professional associations or inter-association collectives may endeavor unilaterally to establish standards of good practice for student support services, their products and models will inevitably fail to become part of the educational culture unless viewed as an enhancement to the educational interests of students. In other words, credibility within the whole of higher education is more effectively gained through collective action than through narrowly defined initiatives of individuals or associations. For standards of professional practice to be truly viable, they must reflect the interests and values of multiple professional organizations and the functional areas they champion. CAS strives to provide this collaborative avenue to establishing thoughtful, balanced, and achievable standards upon which all can rely.

**Foundations for Standards and Guidelines**

The initial CAS publication, *CAS Standards and Guidelines* (CAS, 1986), was based on the premise that student support practitioners needed access to a comprehensive and valid set of criteria to judge support program quality and effectiveness. Further, it was viewed as essential that those standards represent best practices that any college or university program can reasonably achieve.

From the CAS perspective, virtually all functional areas of practice, no matter how specialized, have identifiable commonalties with other functions. For example, an institution's admission, academic advising, campus activities, and career services programs, although established to accomplish clearly different purposes, will each benefit from establishing a written mission statement that is compatible with the mission of the host institution. Although the specific purpose of each functional area will vary, having a clearly defined mission that articulates each program's primary and secondary purposes and objectives is essential. Likewise, the same is true for human, fiscal, physical, and technological resources; legal responsibilities; campus and community relations; ethical consider-ations; and program evaluation among others. Consequently, CAS has incorporated a number of common criteria that have relevance for each and every functional area, no matter what its primary focus. These common criteria are referred to as "general standards" and will be found in all functional area standards along with criteria that attend to specialized aspects. These general standards are designed to overcome the "silo effect" so common throughout higher education wherein autonomous administrative units, programs, and services function as if the territorial imperative were viable. In effect, the general standards make the CAS standards highly utilitarian and promote inter-departmental, inter-program, and inter-service cooperation and collaboration. Users are encouraged to view the CAS standards and guidelines as vehicles that interconnect administrative units. Because what these various functional units have in common (e.g., educational purpose, student learning, and develop-ment) often exceeds their differences, the effective practitioner will find that collaboration between and among units can enhance the educational environment in many important ways.

All CAS standards use the auxiliary verbs "**must**" and "shall." Which appear in" bold print so that users can quickly identify them. As previously noted, all functional areas have specialty standards in addition to the general standards. Specialty standards are essential to accomplishing a support program's purpose and appear in **bold print** as do the general standards.

CAS standards are constructed to represent criteria that every higher education institution and its student support programs should be expected and able to meet with the application of reasonable effort and diligence. Although the standards are carefully worded for easy understanding, it is sometimes helpful to amplify them by providing additional information to facilitate the user's ability to interpret them accurately. Also, when programs are organizationally mature, there is need to provide users with additional criteria that may be used to make good programs even better. Conse-quently, as a supplement to its standards, CAS has established"" guidelines" designed to clarify and amplify the standards. Guidelines may be used to guide enhanced practice when a program has previously achieved high levels of effectiveness. Guidelines use the auxiliary verbs "should" and "may" and are printed in lightface type with smaller font to distinguish them from the standards.

In summary, CAS functional area standards and guidelines are basic statements that should be achievable by any program in any higher education institution when adequate and appropriate effort, energy, and resources are applied. Further, standards reflect a level of good practice generally agreed upon by the profession-at-large. In addition to the standards, guidelines are incorporated into each functional area to amplify and explain the standards and to guide enhanced practice. This dual presentation is most helpful because functional area programs in both early and advanced stages of development can use the CAS standards to good purpose. Most important is the fact that the CAS standards have been conceived and developed via a profession-wide process that can assure continuity and consistency of practice among all higher education institutions. In addition, each set of standards is reviewed on a five year staggered basis to assure currency and determine need for revision. When found wanting, the standard is submitted to a CAS committee for revision.

## CAS Applications

The CAS standards and guidelines were established for institutions' student support programs and services to use for program development, program self-study, and staff development purposes. Although the standards have utility for institutional and program accreditation purposes, CAS has not sought to establish its own accrediting process. Rather, CAS takes the position that individualized institutional and program "self-regulation" is the preferred route to program quality and effectiveness. There is little doubt that CAS standards have utility for complementing regional or specialty accreditation self-studies. At this juncture, however, CAS views its profession-wide role as one to develop and promulgate professional standards to guide practice and to educate practitioners in the appropriate use of its standards.

## CAS Role in Professional Practice

The professional role of the Council for the Advancement of Standards in Higher Education has become increasingly important during the past quarter century. The first order of business was to develop and promulgate professional standards of practice and preparation for student affairs and student support programs and services. However, CAS is viewed by many as an important professional development vehicle as well. CAS user surveys designed to determine how CAS influenced professional practice and the use of CAS materials were most revealing and are summarized below.

Many practitioners indicated that CAS standards are important because they speak to the issues of institutional change as practitioners struggle to meet the needs of ever changing student constituent bodies, not only in numbers but in age, gender, race, ethnicity, ability, and long term goals as well. One respondent shared the perspective that

". . . as each campus has examined it's own situation, and looked to it's peers for ideas, the CAS standards have guided not only implementation but review and evaluation. Most of this work was done in expansionary times. Now as we regroup, downsize, retrench, whatever institutions name it, we need to have some means by which to measure what we do. The CAS standards, in all of the functional areas, serve as an excellent tool to begin that process. They are flexible without being vague, broad without being limitless, and ideal for what we constantly face in higher education, change."

One comment that reflected the value of the CAS initiative for entry-level professionals was most telling.

"I can easily imagine that the standards would provide indispensable guidance for some of our younger or less experienced colleagues in graduate education. It must be like having a consultant's report at your finger tips that attests, 'Do at least this much well, and you will find success in your program'."

This suggests that the CAS standards have great utility for providing a foundation for practice to which all college student service providers can aspire. It also suggests that academic preparation programs and new staff development orientation programs would be enhanced by incorporating the CAS standards as an essential part of their content.

The CAS enterprise has led to a number of spin-offs in that some professional groups have expanded on the standards to meet sometimes highly specific professional needs. One example is in the area of learning assistance. As one respondent noted,

"No sooner than the first "Learning *Assistance Program Standards* were published, we were already talking about how to build upon that work. Whereas the CAS standards addressed broad basic elements that are essential to a comprehensive learning assistance program, practitioners in the field expressed interest in obtaining similar statements that addressed pedagogical components as well."

Consequently, the National Association for Developmental Education [NADE] responded to the challenge by creating

"NADE Guides." These documents emulated the CAS standards assessment model and addressed the specific functions of tutoring services, adjunct instructional programs, developmental coursework, and the teaching/learning process. This developmental activity led to inter-association cooperation among learning assistance and developmental education organizations and paved a path for communication and collaboration in the revision of the CAS *Learning*

*Assistance Program Standards* that follow in Part 2 of this volume. As the respondent noted,

"I can think of no other project that has generated, nurtured, and advanced such inter-association collaboration. I see the CAS standards as being a major force in consolidating a diverse profession."

A related comment was made by a close observer of CAS initiatives.

"I have two general observations. First, CAS has filled a void that no other organization could accomplish. A network has been established to mutually equip the student affairs profession with standards of performance. Second, the CAS effort has attracted increased attention and offered increased value over the years. A genuine service has been provided to the academy by helping and guiding all students toward achieving holistic development."

Another respondent noted the value and utility of the CAS standards to a specific functional area in a mid-sized public institution.

"The CAS standards were an excellent guide to use in assessing and improving the progress and success of our career center. They outlined expectations and served as a model in striving to achieve high quality services for the college community."

Another CAS sponsored survey was initiated in Spring 2000 and directed by Jan L. Arminio at Shippensburg University. CAS surveyed over 5,000 individual members from 22 CAS member associations. Of those responding, 62.5% had heard of CAS (i.e., 85 percent of responding vice presidents; 67% of functional area directors, 66% of new professionals, and 31% of faculty members). Participants in the study were asked if they measured learning outcomes and if so was there a connection between CAS standards and positive learning outcomes. Forty-one percent stated that there was a connection, 28% said there was a vague or indirect connection, 2% stated there was no connection, and 19% were unsure. Of those who stated that CAS has positively influenced their programs, 27% believed CAS positively influenced programs through assessing current programs, 22% in expanding current programs, 13% through clarifying mission and goals, 10% by justifying current programs, 8% by emphasizing student and staff training, 5% as a guide for new programs, and 4% to influence budget programs. Eighty-two percent of vice presidents and associate vice presidents for student affairs stated that CAS standards were positively associated with learning outcomes. A member of NACA noted, "CAS has closed the loop in student activities advising to see if student leaders learn or do not."

Numerous other observations about CAS standards were elicited as were comments describing how CAS standards were being used. Some of the more salient comments follow.

"They (CAS standards) serve as a wonderful reminder of what we should be doing."

"CAS standards remain in a high visibility location on my desk—a clear reminder of what I need to accomplish every day to adequately contribute to quality of campus life."

"I believe they (CAS standards) are so important in our everyday work and push myself to review them every year as I set goals for the new year."

"The CAS standards assisted me in redeveloping our departmental mission statement in 1993 and in 2000. I also used the CAS standards to plan and implement a professional development session for my campus."

"CAS is a great staff builder and long term strategy builder. We've learned a great deal about our perspectives (+ or - ) by using the assessment pieces."

"We have adapted the CAS standards to produce an outcome determinative model. This model allows us to link outcomes directly to program quality, service delivery, and resource allocation."

"We have evaluated our CAS preparation program using the standards. The process was time consuming, but the information gained through the process was invaluable. Likewise the instrument (Preparation SAG) was very useful as a guide during collection of data for distribution to our assessment team and external reviews."

"I have found the CAS standards very helpful when creating or expanding a program. We can use them as rationale for budget requests."

"Our assessment has helped us clarify our strengths and weaknesses. It also provides a nice communication tool for our adjunct faculty to ensure that they are clearly aware of our CAS expectations."

"We have found them invaluable, especially with program reviews and accreditation visits."

" Makes you qualify and quantify services and information in areas such as diversity, ethics, and legal responsibility."

"In self-assessment, you get intra-office perceptions of work areas."

"It is a great introduction for emerging professionals."

In regard to CAS publications, more respondents had read the 1997 edition of *The CAS Book of Professional Standards for Higher Education* than either the 1986 or the 1999 editions or any of the CAS functional area self-assessment guides (SAGs). Most respondents noted that they used the 1997 CAS Book of Standards as their primary guide, closely followed by one or more of the functional area SAGs.

Practitioners from nine different professional associations reported that they had used the Housing Program SAG, which was determined to be the most commonly accessed CAS SAG by survey respondents.

There was evidence that CAS is not only used in traditional student affairs functions (such as housing and residence life, campus activities, fraternity and sorority advising) but across institutions. For example, there were 77 participants in the study who were faculty members. Thirty-eight percent had heard of CAS and of those, 22% were members of the National Association of Developmental Educators (NADE) and 18% of the American College Personnel Association (ACPA).

Future study is needed to answer other important questions about the influence of CAS and its initiatives. In an article to be published in the *College Student Affairs Journal* (in press) Don G. Creamer offers several research questions that need to be addressed related to CAS Standards.

1. What is the level of use of CAS Standards by functional area and geographical area?
2. What is the type and frequency of use of CAS Standards and Guidelines?
3. How do CAS Standards shape professional practice?
4. What is the role of CAS in shaping educational programs and services?
5. Do practitioners perceive that the use of CAS Standards and Guidelines improves their performance?
6. Does CAS benefit professionals' learning and development?
7. Are programs and services that meet CAS Standards and Guidelines more effective in meeting learning goals than those that do not?
8. How does professional practice influenced by CAS in turn influence student learning?

There can be little doubt that the CAS initiative has been fruitful during its two-and-a- half-decade existence. Although there is much work yet to do, especially in the standards education arena, the Council for the Advancement of Standards in Higher Education has made a professional difference and is prepared to continue its important efforts toward professionalizing student support services.

**Recent Developments**

Probably the most significant and potentially influential CAS initiative was the recently completed and adopted revision of the CAS general standards that appear in each functional area standard. Not only were the general standards revised, but they incorporated a new, major emphasis on student learning and development. The Program component, Part Two, of each functional area standard, now includes a table of 16 relevant student learning and development outcome domains designed to guide practitioners in their attempts to both emphasize and assess student learning and development. The example assessment indicators included in the table are intended to help practitioners identify behaviors that reflect student achievement in the various domains. This new student learning and development outcome domain emphasis will facilitate the program self-study process in the area of program assessment and evaluation.

# *CAS* **Context**

A standard to guide practice is an essential characteristic of any established profession. It is essential during the evolution of a mature profession that a relevant set of standards be developed and promulgated by and for those working in that arena. The Council for the Advancement of Standards in Higher Education (CAS) was founded in 1979 as a profession-wide entity to establish standards to guide practice by student affairs, student development, and student support service providers employed by institutions of higher learning. Currently, 32 professional associations claim membership in CAS, representing nearly 100,000 higher education service providers. This book provides 29 functional area standards for use by the profession at large. This CAS Book Of Standards represents the fifth major iteration of CAS standards, the first having been published under the auspices of the American College Testing Program (CAS, 1986).

During the twentieth century, college and university student support programs evolved from a few faculty members being assigned part-time to attend to students' needs beyond the classroom to the establishment of institutional divisions designed to complement the educational goals of academic affairs. Further, contemporary student support programs employ many full-time, well qualified staff members, most with highly specialized knowledge and skills in accompaniment with advanced degrees. There is little doubt that the complexity of the student support services enterprise has increased as organizational structures have expanded. It is largely in response to the increased complexity of role, function, and purpose that the CAS standards were developed. As the field matured and the responsibilities of its practitioners expanded, a complementary need for accountability increased. It is no longer feasible, let alone desirable, for practitioners to function on the basis of best guesses or intuition when creating environments conducive to student learning and development. Likewise, practitioners have demanded that standards be developed to guide the quality of practice. The CAS functional area standards and guidelines have been developed to meet these important professional needs. CAS was created as a bellwether for the profession at large. To ensure cross-fertilization of theories, research, and application strategies from the field as a whole, knowledgeable representatives from its member associations bring to the table the most current thinking in the functional areas they represent and champion. This commitment to collaboration among functional area specialties ensures that no single component will dominate the foundations that underlie the generation,

revision, and presentation of each CAS standard. Although the standards reflect a broad range of interests, they are clearly value driven. Underlying them is a set of fundamental principles upon which CAS was founded and by which it is guided.

## CAS Guiding Principles

The fundamental principles that undergird the work of CAS and guide its initiatives are organized into five categories. They were derived from theories and conceptual models implicit within human development, group dynamics, student learning, organizational management, and higher education administration that inform the work of student affairs administrators, student development educators, and student support service providers.

### Students and Their Institutions

The initial eight principles are concerned with how students learn and the environmental conditions that institutions need to emphasize for learning and development to occur. The first four principles were derived from the 1938 and 1949 editions of the Student Personnel Point of View (Miller & Prince, 1976, p.4) and reflect fundamental "truths" upon which the CAS Standards and Guidelines are based. Principles five through eight reflect institutional perspectives that complement the student focused viewpoint. When combined, these principles represent the presuppositions upon which student support programs and services are founded.

- The student must be considered as a whole person.
- Each student is a unique person and must be treated as such.
  The student's total environment is educational and must be used to achieve full development.
- Students seek higher education in responsible ways and will, when encouraged to do so, access appropriate educational resources when they are provided, made known, and relevant to students' felt educational and developmental needs.
- Institutions of higher learning are purposeful and function as social and cultural resources to provide opportunities for students to learn and develop in holistic ways.
- The primary responsibility for learning and development rests with the student.
- Institutions of higher learning reflect the diversity of the societies and cultures in which they exist.
- Institutions are responsible for creating learning environments that provide a choice of educational

opportunities and challenge students to learn and develop while providing support to nurture their development.

Each CAS functional area standard was created to inform practitioners about the criteria that represent fundamental levels of programmatic and organizational application that must be met if institutions of higher learning are to facilitate effectively student learning and development.

In effect, when a college or university provides programs and services that meet or exceed the CAS criteria, the institution will have effectively implemented an intentional educational environment conducive to the learning and development of its students. It is important to note that the CAS standards do not dictate that students, individually or collectively, must conform to a prescribed standard of involvement or behavior. Rather, they call for institutions and student support programs to meet a standard of programmatic and organizational efficiency and effectiveness sufficient to provide opportunity and encouragement for students to grow, develop, and achieve individual potentials. The institution and its educational programs are social resources that provide citizens opportunities to expand their horizons and capacities to serve society. The CAS standards have been developed and promulgated from a profession-wide point of view to provide institutions with a relevant, reasonable, and achievable set of voluntary professional standards.

**Diversity and Multiculturalism**

Issues of diversity in institutions of higher education are often fraught with dissension and discord. The CAS standards affirm the importance of recognizing the existence of diversity and considering its influence when creating and implementing educational and developmental initiatives. In an increasingly complex and shrinking global environment, it is essential that students learn to function effectively and justly when exposed to alternative ideas, beliefs, values, physical and mental abilities, sexual orientations, lifestyles, and cultures that differ from their own. To do otherwise would be to perpetuate a world in which contention and strife predominate, to the detriment of all. Two principles in this regard are embedded in the CAS standards.

• Recognizing the ubiquitous nature of human diversity, institutions are committed to eliminating barriers that impede student learning and development, attending especially to establishing and maintaining diverse human relationships essential to survival in a global society.

• Justice and respect for differences bond individuals to community; and thus education for multicultural awareness and positive regard for differences is

essential to the development and maintenance of a health engendering society.

The CAS standards call for institutions of higher learning and their student support programs to recognize the increasingly diverse societies to be served and the importance of enhancing students' capacities to function effectively within the context of constantly shifting environments and opinions. Both individuals and institutions may experience discomfort with the demands imposed on them by multiple viewpoints, cultures, and characteristics but they must learn to acknowledge diversity and appreciate its potential for enhancing the importance and viability of the higher education enterprise. CAS recognizes that the spirit of affirmative action is inherent in the delivery of effective student support services and that discrimination against any student population or employment category is inimical to belief in the dignity of the individual. This proposition is fundamental to student development theory and its applications to practice. The CAS standards reinforce the fact that those responsible for creating educational environments need to be open to and accepting of differences, and to recognize how such environments are important for enhancing the quality of the education provided and the learning achieved. Further, the standards consistently call for personnel whose ethnic and racial characteristics reflect those of the institution's constituencies. In addition, all students must have access to the educational and co-curricular resources available to the academic community at large; no student, for any reason, should be denied access to them.

**Organization, Leadership, and Human Resources**

The CAS standards reflect the belief that form follows function. Consequently, the structure of an organization should mirror the purposes for which it was established. It is essential that institutions, programs, and services be based on a mutually determined, clearly and publicly stated, and well understood purpose. Without a clearly defined mission, an institution and its programs are virtually rudderless and will ultimately founder. Unmistakably defined lines of authority must be drawn, detailed duties and job responsibilities described, and policies and procedures established to guide the desired processes. Those who lead and administer programs of student support must remember that because theory without practice is empty, and practice without theory is blind, it is essential that the theory embraced be connected to the purposes sought in pursuit of quality practice. Three basic principles concerned with these factors also underlie the CAS standards.

- Capable, credible, knowledgeable, and experienced leadership is essential for institutional success; organizational units are most successful when their missions and outcome expectations are effectively documented and understood by all concerned.
- Effective programs and services require well-qualified staff members who understand and support the student learning and development outcomes the programs are intended to promote.
- Student learning and personal development will be enhanced when staff members at all levels of responsibility possess appropriate, relevant, and adequate educational preparation and practical experience.

CAS standards do not prescribe organization or administrative structures to which institutions and programs are expected to adhere. CAS is guided by the belief that every institution is unique and must establish the frame of administrative reference most appropriate to its particular mission. Consequently, avoiding prescription, the standards provide fundamental criteria that practitioners can use to judge the effectiveness of their current or projected structures. For example, certain crucial elements clearly are essential to functional success including employing leaders who possess viable visions of how and what is to be achieved and are suitably positioned for access to the highest administrative levels. Leaders and staff members alike must possess effective managerial skills, be properly titled, and be well qualified by both education and experience. This is essential for maintaining quality programs and services that will effectively accomplish the program's stated objectives. Under-educated and under-experienced staff members, good intentions notwithstanding, will virtually always fail to accomplish the program's objectives over the long term.

## Health Engendering Environments

Institutional environments of quality combine educational philosophies and values in conjunction with adequate physical facilities, human resources, and fiscal support to create positive input on the education and development of students. Seeking to reflect this important integration of components, the CAS standards provide both criteria against which programs and services can be tested and guidelines to explain and amplify the standards for effective application. The establishment of effective, health generating environments is an important aspect of the CAS standards.

- Student support and developmental programs and services prosper in benevolent environments that provide students with appropriate levels of challenge and support.

The primary purpose of education has always been to promote change, both in individuals and in society. College and university student support programs are primarily educational enterprises. Clearly, the Student Learning Imperative (ACPA, 1996) prevails throughout each CAS functional area standard because an important purpose of the standards is to provide criteria that can be used to judge a program's capacity and effectiveness in creating learning and development opportunities. The establishment of educational environments conducive to student learning and development is essential if an institution of higher learning is to achieve its educational purposes.

## Ethical Considerations

A major component in each CAS standard incorporates the fundamental ethical expectations to which all student support practitioners must adhere to ensure fair and equitable practice. Just as a mission statement is essential to provide programs with direction, ethical standards are essential to guide the behavior of staff members in ways that enhance the overall integrity of both the program and its host institution.

- Because special mentoring relationships exist between students and those who facilitate their learning and development, support service providers must exemplify impeccable ethical behavior in both their professional relationships and personal lives.

As an essential task of every profession's emergence, it establishes and codifies ethical standards to guide the behavior of its members. The CAS standards provide the essential ethical foundations upon which to build humane, ethical practice. Without a clearly defined code of ethics, support service staff members would have little or no guidance for establishing and maintaining a reasonable level of effective moral and ethical behavior. The best of intentions are insufficient if they are not founded on a solid ethical base that can be understood and acknowledged by all concerned.

## Putting CAS Standards To Work

CAS standards and guidelines are conceived and crafted with care to be instructive and useful to practitioners and educational leaders. Based upon professional judgment and societal expectations, they include principles that are fundamental to student learning and development and guidelines for practice for particular student support functions. For each set of standards and guidelines, CAS provides a Self-Assessment Guide (SAG) that includes a comprehensive self-study process for program evaluation. Seven basic steps to using a SAG are suggested for implementing a functional area self-study. Following, in summary form, is the recommended self-study process.

1. *Establish and Prepare the Self-Assessment Team*
   Division and functional area leaders need first to determine the functional area or areas to be evaluated. It is desirable to involve the full staff in the initial planning stage of the self-study process; including classified and technical staff members and knowledgeable students and faculty members when feasible. This approach provides opportunity for shared ownership in the evaluation. A representative group of three to five members, including one or more knowledgeable individuals from outside the area under review, should be selected to compose the primary self-study team. Initially, the team should familiarize itself with the relevant CAS functional area standard by examining it carefully before making individual or group judgments. It is important that all members come to understand and interpret the standard in similar fashion. This may require team training to ensure that members' interpretive differences are resolved before initiating the study process. Likewise, ground rules for the study should be established and agreed upon. Team members should realize and accept that disagreement is natural, healthy, and probably inevitable, but the resulting debates will usually strengthen the team's ultimate consensus on the matter.

2. *Initiating the Self-Study*
   It is suggested that team members use the CAS Functional Area Self-Assessment Guide (SAG) to implement the self-study. When used, the initial step is for members to rate the criterion measures individually, and then collectively to make judgments about how well the program meets the criteria. The SAG provides a 4-point scale from Not Met to Fully Met for rating the criterion measures, which reflect the essence of the standards. Once the team completes the initial rating process and arrives at a consensus on the ratings, It should respond to a series of questions posed in the SAG that are designed to stimulate summary thinking and to facilitate interpretation of the ratings. Next, the team should identify aspects of program performance that exceeded the criterion and is viewed by the team as excellent, features that were found to be satisfactory, and aspects that were judged weak and in need of remediation.
   Following the rating and review procedure, it is desirable for the study team to invite the full staff to review and discuss the team's interim assessment of program compliance with the standards. This approach

provides opportunity to inform all staff members of the team's evaluation and permits all staff members to explore together how well the program appears to be accomplishing its stated purpose. Through this process, team members may be exposed to alternative interpretations of the study results-to-date and obtain additional insight into the program from the perspective of others.
   In some instances, especially when a program is mature and aspires to levels of quality and effectiveness that exceed the basic standards, the study team may decide to treat one or more of the guideline statements as a standard for self-study purposes. For example, a functional area guideline might include the statement
   "facilities should include a private office where individual consultations can be held." The study team may decide that this guideline statement, which is not a CAS standard compliance requirement, should be treated as a standard for purposes of their self-study. If so decided, a criterion measure statement such as "private office space is available for staff members to use for consultation purposes" would be inserted as a criterion measure to be rated along with the measures included in the SAG and treated as a standard rather than as a guideline for testing the program against the criteria.

3. *Identify and Summarize Evaluative Evidence*
   Judging the program by rating it against the standard's criterion measures and identifying program strengths and weaknesses does not represent a completed self-study. Rather, the process requires documentation of the evidence that supports each criterion measure rating. The character of such documentary evidence may be quantitative, qualitative, or, most typically, a combination of the two. For example, quantitative measures might include the staff-to-student ratio for a given activity, an analysis of the cost effectiveness of a given activity, or the results of a developmental task assessment of student learning and development outcome achievement. Qualitative documentation, on the other hand, might include notes on the process used to develop the program's mission or outcome objectives or structured interviews with students. Essential documentation includes relevant publications [e.g., student and staff handbooks), program descriptions (e.g., career decision-making workshop outlines), program evaluation data (e.g., program assessment results), institutional data (e.g., student profiles), and self-study initiated research (e.g., student survey or focus group results). No self-study can be considered complete without relevant data and related documentation to support and validate the team's judgments. These data can be collected over

time and stored in a database for self-study purposes. Such data also have utility for preparing annual reports.

4. *Identify Discrepancies*

Study team members should compare their ratings and interpretations of program characteristics, accomplishments, strengths, and shortcomings against the criteria expressed in the standard. Further, the study team should carefully review each criterion measure and related practice that the study team rated as Not Done, Unsatisfactory, or wherein rated discrepancies of two or more were noted. A specific rationale should be prepared for each shortcoming identified.

When discrepancies are noted between the assessment criteria and actual practice, it is possible to identify existing operational problems that need resolution. For example, each standard calls for the existence of a program mission statement consistent with the nature and goals of the institution. If the program has no written mission statement or an outdated one, then the discrepancy between the standard and actual program practice clearly calls for the creation of a current, relevant program mission statement that is consistent with the institution's mission.

5. *Determine Appropriate Corrective Action*

The self-study team should describe in detail the adjustments that need to be implemented for the program to achieve the quality and effectiveness to which it aspires. For example, returning to reflections on the status of the program mission, the action required would call for program staff members to draft a statement delineating the goals they believe are agreed upon, circulate them for review and comment, and then prepare and disseminate a final program mission statement to guide the program and its services. An important point to note in regard to corrective action is the importance of subdividing the overall task into manageable parts that can be accomplished in step-by-step fashion. Trying to revise a total functional area in one step is neither a desirable nor an effective approach to program development. It is important that the study team list specific actions identified in the self-study that require implementation. It is also desirable to set priorities on the list by order of importance, need, and achievability of the desired change.

6. *Recommend Special Actions for Program Enhancement*
   *Even excellent programs can be further refined to provide more desirable and effective outcomes. Action in this regard is particularly relevant for*

*programs in which self-study team members identified selected guidelines calling for enhanced functioning. Unless staff members are satisfied with meeting basic standards only, additional initiatives can be implemented to enhance program quality and effectiveness. This can be accomplished by listing each specific action identified in the self-study that would enhance and strengthen services and set priorities among them for follow-up purposes.*

7. *Prepare an Action Plan*

As the self-study process comes to fruition, it is important for staff members to identify and establish priorities to influence the program's future directions. This represents a process of comparing past performance with desired outcomes and can best be accomplished by carefully reviewing the actual self-study process that was conducted to ensure that all relevant program issues are addressed. The post-self-assessment action plan should acknowledge the program's strengths as well as its shortcomings as it moves toward establishing a strategic approach for correcting deficiencies and initiating enhancements. The primary goal of this final step is to identify and set priorities for future actions and directions, after comparing past performance with the outcomes to which the program aspires.

The process for preparing a final program action plan consists of preparing a comprehensive action plan for implementing program changes, identifying resources (i.e., human, fiscal, physical) that are essential to program enhancement, establishing dates by which specific actions are to be completed, identifying responsible parties to complete the action steps, and setting tentative start-up date for initiating a subsequent self-study.

For those interested in obtaining additional information and training on the self-assessment process described above, CAS has prepared an e-learning program that is incorporated into the CAS Standards CD ROM referred to on the order form on the back pages of this book.

**Other Uses of the CAS Standards**

In addition to program self-assessment, the CAS standards have great utility for staff development and academic preparation purposes among others.

**Staff Development**

Staff members can study the various criteria to determine how well they and their colleagues are implementing the standards in their daily work with students. A comprehensive staff development program, using one of the functional area standards and guidelines as a training device, may require from six to twelve hours of meeting time during which staff members share responsibility for leading discussions about the standard's various components. This approach is particularly valuable when a program self-study is in the offing. In such an instance, staff members can both learn how CAS standards can be used to guide and influence good practice and provide a vehicle for implementing a program self-study. Training staff members before conducting a self-study typically produces a more comprehensive and valuable program evaluation.

## Academic Preparation

The CAS standards have another valuable educational function when used as a resource in formal academic preparation programs, especially in an introductory course concerned with student support functions common to institutions of higher learning. The 29 CAS functional area standards and their accompanying contextual statements, presented in Part 2 of this book, provide an excellent primer for those entering the fields of student affairs and higher education administration. The contextual statements summarize the roles and functions of key program and service units, their primary purposes, historical perspectives, and relevant resources available to explore the areas in greater detail. These succinct summary statements provide an introduction for those unfamiliar with the areas under study. The CAS standards provide an in depth description of the characteristics common to and expected of the various functional areas.

For students who desire to examine a given functional area in greater detail or participate in a practicum, internship, or externship experience, the CAS Self-Assessment Guide (SAG) provides a unique resource for obtaining a comprehensive understanding. Each functional area SAG includes the standards, guidelines, and criterion measures that can be used to judge the level of compliance a program exhibits in regard to the standards. Using a SAG, students can readily identify a program's strengths and shortcomings. Further, the SAG has utility as a vehicle for both students and supervisors to use for examining together and discussing the various components of the area under study. For learning the basics of student support functions, there is no better information available than that provided by the CAS standards and the complementary Self-Assessment Guides that operationalize the various standards.

## Credibility

Any profession and its practitioners must exhibit a reasonable level of credibility if it is to survive.

Professional entities lacking user confidence will be at best underutilized and may ultimately disappear. In effect, credibility is essential to the existence of all service agencies, including those associated with higher education. Through publication of and adherence to standards of professional practice, institutions seek to assure potential student users and the general public of their competence and credibility. Both laypersons and professionals alike attribute credibility to programs, professions, and institutions that meet stringent standards; compliance with such standards demonstrates that quality is present.

Various means have been established to ensure quality assurance. Institutional and academic program credibility is typically established through accreditation, a voluntary process by which agencies encourage and assist institutions and their sub-units (e.g., colleges, schools, departments, and programs) to evaluate and improve their programs and services (Eaton, 2001). The institutions and programs that voluntarily meet or exceed acceptable standards of quality and effectiveness are made public by the accrediting body. It is not uncommon for institutions not possessing accreditation status to be denied federal aid or other resources available to accredited institutions. Graduates of non-accredited institutions may be denied admission to graduate schools and/or certain employment opportunities. Accreditation is intended to assure the public that an institution and its programs do indeed provide quality education.

However, the general public cannot be assured that individuals who have diplomas, certificates, or degrees from accredited institutions and programs are, in fact, effective practitioners. Consequently, various structures have been established by professional and governmental oversight agencies to judge the professional qualifications of service providers in education, health, and social service areas.

Three primary methods have been established to enable individuals to document their professional qualifications: registry, certification, and licensure. CAS, which is a consortium of higher education professional associations, focuses minimal attention on these credentialing options, although some have encouraged CAS to expand its focus into registry and certification, which are often initiated by non-governmental professional bodies. Licensure, on the other hand, is largely the province of governments. For instance, licenses based on generally comparable criteria are required of physicians, psychologists, and lawyers in all states; counselors, morticians, and engineers, on the other hand, require licenses in only some states and are judged by diverse criteria from state to state. A recent employment criterion trend in some states has been to require college counselors and psychologists to be licensed in order to be eligible for employment. Although not yet fully tested in the courts, such initiatives are likely to increase during the coming decades.

As demand for accountability in higher education increases, so too does demand for practitioner accountability. There may come a day when higher education will need to establish professional eligibility criteria for student support staff members or face the prospect of having external agencies, such as state, federal, or provincial governments, set the criteria for them. CAS and other professional bodies may be called on to join the discussion. CAS currently endorses self-regulation as the most viable approach to program accountability, calling for each institution to initiate a program of self-assessment for its student support programs, services, and personnel. Whether student support units are administratively assigned to student affairs, academic affairs, business affairs, or elsewhere in the organizational hierarchy, CAS encourages program review and evaluation on a continuing basis using the CAS standards. From this perspective, self-regulation becomes a preferred strategy to establish and maintain credibility. When deemed appropriate and desirable, the various functional areas could invite representatives from peer institutions to review their self-assessment reports as part of the validation process. Self-regulation requires institutions and their leaders to establish their own policies and procedures for institutional assessment and evaluation and to adhere to them when evaluating quality and effectiveness. Thus, through continuing assessment, institutions can compile and maintain in databases the internal documentation required by regional accrediting bodies and governmental oversight agencies. Self-regulation provides institutions and their student support programs with tools to achieve and evidence quality assurance. In effect, if institutions accept responsibility for initiating meaningful and well considered assessment processes and procedures, there is less likelihood that external oversight agencies, governmental or otherwise, will seek to do so.

### *CAS* Initiatives

The Council for the Advancement of Standards in Higher Education was established as a profession-wide collaborative body to develop and promulgate professional standards and to inform those responsible for providing higher education with information about how to use standards effectively. CAS functional area standards were created as living, evolving documents. The Council established a five-year review program to ensure that each standard undergoes regular review and updating. Protocols to guide the development of new and the revision of existing standards are in place

and appear in Appendix E. These protocols identify the processes, participants, and procedures used by CAS to create and review its standards. Completion of a typical standard review takes approximately one year from initiation to Board adoption. It takes slightly longer to complete a new standard because an initial draft must be written before the CAS review process can be initiated. Because of the complex and often laborious nature of standards development, the process is very time consuming. Historically, by the time a functional area standard has undergone the long and arduous development and review, the CAS Board of Directors has nearly always been unanimous in its decision to adopt a new or revised standard.

### Applying *CAS* Standards

In addition to its primary purpose to develop and promulgate professional standards, CAS takes seriously its responsibility to inform and educate the higher education community and the public about the importance of professional standards and their utility for institutional and program self-assessment. Over the years, CAS Board members have represented the Council in numerous conferences, workshops, and instructional activities designed to inform members of the higher education community about CAS initiatives and instruct practitioners in using the standards. Most of the 32 CAS member associations have periodically included CAS related presentations and training workshops in their conference programs. On several occasions, CAS representatives have made presentations at the annual American Association of Higher Education Assessment Forum and in 2002 CAS was represented at the European Association of Institutional Research in Prague. Likewise, CAS has sponsored a series of assessment workshops designed to instruct higher education personnel in the use of CAS standards in combination with regional accrediting criteria when implementing institutional accreditation self-studies.

Many student service leaders and faculty members have used the CAS standards to enhance institutional program development and as instructional tools to inform staff members and graduate students about the nature and characteristics of the various functional areas

### Example Applications

Following is a summary of examples of how CAS standards have been applied in practice and for purposes of professional staff development.

From an institutional perspective, many practitioners view the CAS standards as a staple for conducting comprehensive program reviews. One institution's policy requires that a standard external to the institution be used to implement periodic comprehensive program reviews. Because CAS standards are readily available, easily understood, and simple to use, they are often the standard of choice for administrative unit reviews. The fact that operational versions of the standards in the form of CAS Self-Assessment Guides (SAGs) are also available has increased both the availability and ease with which the standards can be used for program review purposes. In addition, the very presence of the CAS standards typically informs practitioners that professional practice is neither ad hoc nor layman's work. Rather, it consists of the application of the collective wisdom of the profession and is subject to assessment and regulation.

From a programmatic perspective, the CAS standards have special utility, especially for emerging student support areas. For example, educators responsible for guiding programs of learning assistance and developmental education tend to exhibit strong commitment to promoting the use of professional standards in their ranks. Many leaders in this arena literally "invented" their programs and learned from each other what worked best to produce quality outcomes. During the past decade, the CAS Learning Assistance Programs Standards and Guidelines has become a shared document among learning assistance practitioners. Leaders in this arena have indicated that the CAS standards provided a common ground to unite those responsible for ensuring that students received the special attention and support they needed to be successful.

From another program-specific perspective, two important uses of the standards in addition to the self-assessment function were identified; one as a guide for initiating new programs and the other for advocacy. On virtually a weekly basis, the National Clearinghouse for Commuter Programs (NCCP) receives requests from institutions desiring to establish on-campus commuter programs. Most practitioners interested in such initiatives fail initially to comprehend the scope of the functions essential to a comprehensive program. Often, the initiator is interested in establishing a particular type of program (e.g., peer mentoring, orientation for commuters) or service (e.g., off-campus housing referral, commuter newsletter). When such requests are made, the CAS standards are readily available as a professionally sanctioned tool that provides guidance to those interested in providing support for such populations.

Advocacy was a second use noted, because it is often helpful when consulting with colleagues about student support programs to make a case for broadening the administrators' understanding of what is required to meet the basic essentials. All too often, campus administrators tend to limit their initial thinking about a new program to relatively mundane issues such as access, and not to think in terms of how a new program could help students become better integrated into the campus community or enhance their learning and development. There can be little doubt that the CAS standards have great utility for opening institutional leaders' eyes to the importance of comprehensive programming and grasping a broader view.

From another professional association perspective, the Association of Fraternity Advisors [AFA] discovered that standards can be extremely beneficial in relating association purpose to the broader mission of higher education and those of various institutions. Association leaders determined that when colleagues utilized the CAS standards to establish or reorganize various student support services, the very existence of those program changes were not challenged because the standards provided a recognized level of credibility that did not exist prior to the availability of the CAS standards.

From the perspective of graduate education, many programs have integrated the CAS standards into their curricula. Often, the concept of quality assurance is quite vague to graduate students, especially at the master's level. However, the idea of applying standards to practice is more concrete and students can quickly come to understand the role, function, and utility of professional standards. Thus, even beginning students can undertake the process of engaging in the professional interests of self-regulation and improvement. Many college student affairs academic programs have incorporated the CAS standards into their practicum and internship experiential components. Students complete a "mini-self-study" of the functional areas to which they are assigned as part of their practical field-work experiences. This not only ensures that future practitioners know about the existence of the CAS standards, but also provides them with direct experience that enhances their ability to put the standards into practice as they move into entry level positions.

The CAS standards provide an important tool that expresses to students, faculty, and administrators alike the complex and vital nature of student support programs and services and their relationship to student learning and development. There are ample indications within higher education that there exists a lack of understanding about the importance of creating supportive, health engendering environments for students as an important condition that enhances the higher education experiences. Over the years, those providing students with basic educational support services have often been viewed as secondary or supplemental participants in achieving the academic mission, rather than integral to it. The creation of clearly articulated professional standards has gone far to deepen the understanding of faculty and administrative colleagues and their confidence in the valuable educational and developmental role that student support service providers offer students. There is little doubt that the CAS standards have impacted higher education in many positive ways. In addition to the functional area standard and guideline statements presented herein, CAS publishes 29 operational standards in Self-Assessment Guide (SAG) format. These guides are available in print. CD ROM, and web-based formats. The SAGs are designed for practitioners to use for program evaluation purposes, including self-studies. Each CAS standard is presented in a format that lists individual criterion measures with a rating scale used to judge the extent to which a program is in compliance with the various criteria. Every functional area standard has a complementary SAG for practitioners to use for assessment and evaluation purposes. Order information for CAS publications is located in the back of this book and can be found at www.CAS.edu.

## *CAS* Preamble

Let us raise a standard to which the wise and honest can repair.   George Washington, 1787

### The *CAS* Purpose

The Council for the Advancement of Standards in Higher Education (CAS) develops and promulgates standards that enhance the quality of a student's total learning experience in higher education. CAS is a consortium of associations in higher education whose representatives achieve consensus on the nature and application of standards that guide the work of practitioners. CAS derives its authority from the prestige and traditional influence of its member associations and from the consensus of those members in establishing requirements for high-quality practice.

The CAS philosophy is grounded in beliefs about excellence in higher education, collaboration between teacher and learner, ethics in educational practice, student development as a major goal of higher education, and student responsibility for learning. Taken together, these beliefs about practice shape the vision for all CAS endeavors.

The beliefs about excellence require that all programs and services in institutions of higher education function at optimum level.

The beliefs about collaboration require that learning be accomplished in concert by students and educators.

The beliefs about ethics require that all programs and services be carried out in an environment of integrity and high ideals.

The beliefs about student development require that the student be considered as a whole person in the context of a diverse population and a diversity of institutions, that outcomes of education be comprehensive, and that the total environment be structured to create opportunities for student involvement and learning.

The beliefs about responsibility require that the institution recognize the rights and responsibilities of students as its citizens and that it provide an array of resources and learning opportunities that enable students to exercise their responsibility to take full advantage of them.

CAS collectively develops, examines, and endorses standards and guidelines for program and service areas in higher education. The CAS approach to ensuring quality educational experiences is anchored in the assumption that its standards and guidelines can be used in a variety of ways to enhance institutional quality. They can, for example, be used for design of programs and services, for determination of the efficacy of programs, for staff development designed to enhance the skills of those providing professional services, for programmatic self-assessment to assure institutional effectiveness, and for self-regulation purposes.

### Background

The Council for the Advancement of Standards in Higher Education was established in 1979 as the Council for the Advancement of Standards for Student Services/Development Programs, a consortium of professional associations representing student affairs practitioners committed to assuring quality programs and services for students. Members of nearly 32 established professional associations have directed their interests, talents, and resources to develop and promulgate professional standards and guidelines based on state-of-the-art thinking about educational programs and services. From the beginning, CAS has employed an open process of consensus-building among the representatives of member associations as the primary tool for producing its standards and guidelines.

The Council published the original set of 16 functional area standards and the academic preparation standards in 1986, with a grant from American College Testing (ACT). In 1988, CAS developed a Self-Assessment Guide (SAG) for each set of functional area standards to facilitate program assessment and evaluation. Each SAG is an operational version of a functional area standard designed to provide practitioners with a detailed instrument for self-assessment.

The Council's current name and expanded mission were adopted in 1992, to be inclusive of all programs for students in higher education, including those serving undergraduate, graduate, traditional, and nontraditional students. CAS now oversees the development of standards for new service areas and the systematic review and periodic revision of existing standards and guidelines.

## The CAS Approach to Self-Regulation and Self-Assessment

Self-regulation is an internally motivated and directed institutional process devoted to the creation, maintenance, and enhancement of high-quality programs and services. CAS believes this approach is preferable to externally motivated regulation, because those within an institution generally have the clearest perceptions of its mission, goals, resources, and capabilities. The essential elements of self-regulation include:

Institutional culture that values involvement of all its members in decision making,

• Quality indicators that are determined by the institution,

• Use of standards and guidelines in quality assurance,

• Collection and analysis of data on institutional performance, and

• Commitment to continuing improvement that presupposes freedom to explore and develop alternative directions for the future.

The success of self-regulation depends on mutual respect between an institution and its members. Within the self-regulated institution, individual accomplishments are valued, goals are based on shared vision, systems are open and interactive, processes are carried out in a climate of mutual trust and caring, conflicts are mediated in the best interests of the entire community, and achievements are recognized and rewarded. Such an environment stimulates individual and group initiatives and fosters self-determination of goals. In a self-regulating environment, members identify quality indicators in consultation with a variety of internal and external constituencies and stakeholders, including professional associations.

These indicators may include professionally derived standards, such as those of CAS, which comprise the views of many professional practitioners and professional associations. Self-regulation relies on the willingness and capacity of the organization to examine itself meticulously, faithfully, and reliably, and then to assemble the pertinent results of that examination into coherent reports that constituents can comprehend and use. Such reports are essential for recording the evidence assembled in self-study, for displaying synthesis and analysis of information, for fostering the broad participation of members in the self-regulation process, and for registering benchmark results and conclusions for future reference.

Finally, the self-regulation process relies on the institution's capacity to modify its own practices as needed. A culture that supports self-regulation must operate in a climate that permits members to make independent choices among reasonable alternatives. These choices constitute a commitment to constant improvement of educational practices and of the health of the organization.

Approved by CAS Board Of Directors
November 18, 1994
Washington, DC

## References

American College Personnel Association (ACPA). (March/April 1996). Special issue: The student learning imperative. Journal of College Student Development 37(2). Whole issue.

Council for the Advancement of Standards (CAS). (1986). CAS standards and guidelines for student service/development programs. Iowa City: American College Testing Program.

Council of Student Personnel Associations in Higher Education. (1994; 1972). Student development services in post-secondary education (pp. 428-447). In A. L. Rentz (Ed.), Student affairs: A profession's heritage. Washington, D. C.: American College Personnel Association.

Creamer, D. G. (Spring, 2003).. Research needed on the use of CAS standards and guidelines. *Journal of College Student Affairs, 22*:2. Pp 109-124.

Eaton, J. S. (March/April 2001). Regional accreditation reform: Who is served? Change Magazine. Pp. 39-45.

Miller, T. K., & Prince, J. S. (1976). *The future of student affairs: A guide to student development for tomorrow's higher education.* San Francisco: Jossey-Bass.

# The Role of the *CAS* General Standards in *CAS* Functional Area Standards and Guidelines

The Council for the Advancement of Standards in Higher Education (CAS) was established in 1979 as a consortium of professional associations whose members championed student learning and development in a variety of functional areas. From the outset, CAS identified its primary mission as the development and promulgation of professional standards that higher education practitioners could use to guide, develop, and assess programs and services. By 1986, with a repayable grant from the American College Testing Program (ACT), CAS had created 16 sets of functional area standards and published them in the first *CAS Blue Book*. It was clear by the time of the initial publication that there were a number of characteristics common to all functional areas, commonalties that demanded inclusion in all current and future CAS standards. As a result, a set of *boiler plate*, *General Standards* were devised that CAS Board members unanimously agreed were relevant to all the student learning and development programs championed by CAS member associations. As the CAS General Standards evolved over the years, the Council consistently held to the principle that the fundamental commonalities underlying student learning and development are of the essence and must be maintained within the context of all CAS standards.

The most recent major revision of the General Standards was adopted by the CAS Board of Directors in 2002. A significant feature of this revision was the increased emphasis placed on achievable, observable, and assessable outcomes associated with student learning and development. Earlier versions of the CAS General Standards included a list of developmental domains (e.g., intellectual growth, effective communication, realistic self-appraisal, clarified values, career choices, leadership, and meaningful interpersonal relationships among others) for functional area programs to consider in their educational efforts. The 2002 revision, however, reaffirmed and reinforced the importance of the specified outcome domains by building into the General Standards a stated expectation that all functional area programs must place emphasis on identifying relevant learning outcomes and assessing their achievement by students.

Those who use CAS standards for program evaluation, development, and enhancement will note the importance of the 16 specified outcome domains and the fact that they are viewed as highly desirable for all functional areas to pursue. To facilitate assessment of the various outcome domains, the General Standards include a table listing the 16 domains along with examples of assessment indicators that can be used to guide the assessment process. The indicators represent observable student behaviors that practitioners can use to judge learning and developmental achievement. In effect, the General Standards recognize the potential educational impact that functional area programs can have upon student learning and development and expect them to emphasize and influence that learning as a significant part of their missions. It is anticipated that over time the student learning and development emphases among student support programs and services will increase and that ultimately these programs that currently complement formal academic learning will become coordinate in status as a recognized aspect of student learning and development.

Although the CAS General Standards were not designed to stand alone, they are presented here to remind and inform educators about the commonalities that exist among the many student support programs and services throughout the realm of higher education. There can be little doubt that if those who lead and practice in such programs combine their collective powers to make an educational difference in the lives of the students they serve, the resulting educational trust will carry student support programs and services to new heights of achievement for all concerned.

# *CAS* General Standards
## Revised and Adopted October 2002

## Part 1: MISSION

Each program and service in higher education must incorporate student learning and student development in its mission. The program and service must enhance overall educational experiences. The program and service must develop, record, disseminate, implement and regularly review its mission and goals. Mission statements must be consistent with the mission and goals of the institution and with the standards in this document. The program and service must operate as an integral part of the institution's overall mission.

## Part 2: PROGRAM

The formal education of students consists of the curriculum and the co-curriculum, and must promote student learning and development that is purposeful and holistic. Programs and services must identify relevant and desirable student learning and development outcomes and provide programs and services that encourage the achievement of those outcomes.

Relevant and desirable outcomes include: intellectual growth, effective communication, realistic self-appraisal, enhanced self-esteem, clarified values, career choices, leadership development, healthy behaviors, meaningful interpersonal relationships, independence, collaboration, social responsibility, satisfying and productive lifestyles, appreciation of diversity, spiritual awareness, and achievement of personal and educational goals.

Each program and service must provide evidence of its impact on the achievement of student learning and development outcomes. The table below offers examples of evidence of achievement of student learning and development.

Programs and services may use the examples that follow or identify other more germane indicators.

### Student Learning & Development Outcome Domains

### Intellectual Growth
Examples of Achievement Indicators
Produces personal and educational goal statements; Employs critical thinking in problem solving; Uses complex information from a variety of sources including personal experience and observation to form a decision or opinion; Obtains a degree; Applies previously understood information and concepts to a new situation or setting; Expresses appreciation for literature, the fine arts, mathematics, sciences, and social sciences

### Effective Communication
Examples of Achievement Indicators
Writes and speaks coherently and effectively; Writes and speaks after reflection; Able to influence others through writing, speaking or artistic expression; Effectively articulates abstract ideas; Uses appropriate syntax; Makes presentations or gives performances

### Enhanced Self-Esteem
Examples of Achievement Indicators
Shows self-respect and respect for others; Initiates actions toward achievement of goals; Takes reasonable risks; Demonstrates assertive behavior; Functions without need for constant reassurance from others

### Realistic Self-Appraisal
Examples of Achievement Indicators
Articulates personal skills and abilities; Makes decisions and acts in congruence with personal values; Acknowledges personal strengths and weaknesses; Articulates rationale for personal behavior; Seeks feedback from others; Learns from past experiences

### Clarified Values
Examples of Achievement Indicators
Articulates personal values; Acts in congruence with personal values; Makes decisions that reflect personal values; Demonstrates willingness to scrutinize personal beliefs and values; Identifies personal, work and lifestyle values and explains how they influence decision-making

### Career Choices
Examples of Achievement Indicators
Articulate career choices based on assessment of interests, values, skills and abilities; Documents knowledge, skills and accomplishments resulting from formal education, work experience, community service and volunteer experiences; Makes the connections between classroom and out-of-classroom learning; Can construct a resume with clear job objectives and evidence of related knowledge, skills and accomplishments; Articulates the characteristics of a preferred work environment; Comprehends the world of work; Takes steps to initiate a job search or seek advanced education

### Leadership Development
Examples of Achievement Indicators
Articulates leadership philosophy or style; Serves in a leadership position in a student organization; Comprehends the dynamics of a group; Exhibits democratic principles as a leader; Exhibits ability to visualize a group purpose and desired outcomes

## Healthy Behavior
### Examples of Achievement Indicators
Chooses behaviors and environments that promote health and reduce risk; Articulate the relationship between health and wellness and accomplishing life long goals; Exhibits behaviors that advance a healthy community

## Meaningful Interpersonal Relationships
Examples of Achievement Indicators
Develops and maintains satisfying interpersonal relationships; Establishes mutually rewarding relationships with friends and colleagues; Listens to and considers others' points of view; Treats others with respect

## Independence
Examples of Achievement Indicators
Exhibits self-reliant behaviors; Functions autonomously; Exhibits ability to function interdependently; Accepts supervision as needed; Manages time effectively

## Collaboration
Examples of Achievement Indicators
Works cooperatively with others; Seeks the involvement of others; Seeks feedback from others; Contributes to achievement of a group goal; Exhibits effective listening skills

## Social Responsibility
Examples of Achievement Indicators
Understands and participates in relevant governance systems; Understands, abides by, and participates in the development, maintenance, and/or orderly change of community, social, and legal standards or norms; Appropriately challenges the unfair, unjust, or uncivil behavior of other individuals or groups; Participates in service/volunteer activities

## Satisfying and Productive Lifestyles
Examples of Achievement Indicators
Achieves balance between education, work and leisure time; Articulates and meets goals for work, leisure and education; Overcomes obstacles that hamper goal achievement; Functions on the basis of personal identity, ethical, spiritual and moral values; Articulates long-term goals and objectives

## Appreciating Diversity
Examples of Achievement Indicators
Understands ones own identity and culture. Seeks involvement with people different from oneself; Seeks involvement in diverse interests; Articulate the advantages and challenges of a diverse society; Challenges appropriately abusive use of stereotypes by others; Understands the impact of diversity on one's own society

## Spiritual Awareness
Examples of Achievement Indicators
Develops and articulates personal belief system; Understands roles of spirituality in personal and group values and behaviors

## Personal and Educational Goals
Examples of Achievement Indicators
Sets, articulates, and pursues individual goals; Articulate personal and educational goals and objectives; Uses personal and educational goals to guide decisions; Understands the effect of one's personal and education goals on others

**Programs and services must be (a) intentional, (b) coherent, (c) based on theories and knowledge of learning and human development, (d) reflective of developmental and demographic profiles of the student population, and (e) responsive to needs of individuals, special populations, and communities.**

## Part 3: LEADERSHIP
**Effective and ethical leadership is essential to the success of all organizations. Institutions must appoint, position and empower leaders within the administrative structure to accomplish stated missions. Leaders at various levels must be selected on the basis of formal education and training, relevant work experience, personal skills and competencies, relevant professional credentials, as well as potential for promoting learning and development in students, applying effective practices to educational processes, and enhancing institutional effectiveness. Institutions must determine expectations of accountability for leaders and fairly assess their performance.**

**Leaders of programs and services must exercise authority over resources for which they are responsible to achieve their respective missions.**

**Leaders must . . .**
- **articulate a vision for their organization**
- **set goals and objectives based on the needs and capabilities of the population served**
- **promote student learning and development**
- **prescribe and practice ethical behavior**
- **recruit, select, supervise, and develop others in the organization**
- **manage financial resources**
- **coordinate human resources**
- **plan, budget for, and evaluate personnel and programs**
- **apply effective practices to educational and administrative processes**
- **communicate effectively**
- **initiate collaborative interaction between individuals and agencies that possess legitimate concerns and interests in the functional area**

**Leaders must identify and find means to address individual, organizational, or environmental conditions that inhibit goal achievement.**

Leaders must promote campus environments that result in multiple opportunities for student learning and development.

Leaders must continuously improve programs and services in response to changing needs of students and other constituents, and evolving institutional priorities.

## Part 4: ORGANIZATION & MANAGEMENT

Guided by an overarching intent to ensure student learning and development, programs and services must be structured purposefully and managed effectively to achieve stated goals. Evidence of appropriate structure must include current and accessible policies and procedures, written performance expectations for all employees, functional workflow graphics or organizational charts, and clearly stated service delivery expectations.

Evidence of effective management must include use of comprehensive and accurate information for decisions, clear sources and channels of authority, effective communication practices, decision-making and conflict resolution procedures, responsiveness to changing conditions, accountability and evaluation systems, and recognition and reward processes. Programs and services must provide channels within the organization for regular review of administrative policies and procedures.

## Part 5: HUMAN RESOURCES

The program and service must be staffed adequately by individuals qualified to accomplish its mission and goals. Within established guidelines of the institution, programs and services must establish procedures for staff selection, training, and evaluation; set expectations for supervision, and provide appropriate professional development opportunities. The program and service must strive to improve the professional competence and skills of all personnel it employs.

Professional staff members must hold an earned graduate degree in a field relevant to the position they hold or must possess an appropriate combination of educational credentials and related work experience.

Degree or credential-seeking interns must be qualified by enrollment in an appropriate field of study and by relevant experience. These individuals must be trained and supervised adequately by professional staff members holding educational credentials and related work experience appropriate for supervision.

Student employees and volunteers must be carefully selected, trained, supervised, and evaluated. They must be trained on how and when to refer those in need of assistance to qualified staff members and have access to a supervisor for assistance in making these judgments. Student employees and volunteers must be provided clear and precise job descriptions, pre-service training based on assessed needs, and continuing staff development.

Each organizational unit must have technical and support staff members adequate to accomplish its mission. Staff members must be technologically proficient and qualified to perform their job functions, be knowledgeable of ethical and legal uses of technology, and have access to training. The level of staffing and workloads must be adequate and appropriate for program and service demands.

Salary levels and fringe benefits for all staff members must be commensurate with those for comparable positions within the institution, in similar institutions, and in the relevant geographic area.

Programs and services must institute hiring and promotion practices that are fair, inclusive, and non-discriminatory. Programs and services must employ a diverse staff to provide readily identifiable role models for students and to enrich the campus community.

Program and services must create and maintain position descriptions for all staff members and provide regular performance planning and appraisals.

Programs and services must have a system for regular staff evaluation and must provide access to continuing education and professional development opportunities, including in-service training programs and participation in professional conferences and workshops.

## Part 6: FINANCIAL RESOURCES

Each program and service must have adequate funding to accomplish its mission and goals. Funding priorities must be determined within the context of the stated mission, goals, objectives and comprehensive analysis of the needs and capabilities of students and the availability of internal or external resources.

Programs and services must demonstrate fiscal responsibility and cost effectiveness consistent with institutional protocols.

## Part 7: FACILITIES,TECHNOLOGY, and EQUIPMENT

Each program and service must have adequate, suitably located facilities, adequate technology, and equipment to support its mission and goals efficiently and effectively. Facilities, technology, and equipment must be evaluated regularly and be in compliance with relevant federal, state, provincial, and local requirements to provide for access, health, safety, and security.

## Part 8: LEGAL RESPONSIBILITIES

Staff members must be knowledgeable about and responsive to laws and regulations that relate to their respective responsibilities . Staff members must inform users of programs and services and officials, as appropriate, of legal obligations and limitations including constitutional, statutory, regulatory, and case law; mandatory laws and orders emanating from federal, state/provincial and local governments; and the institution's policies.

Staff members must use reasonable and informed practices to limit the liability exposure of the institution, its officers, employees, and agents. Staff members must be informed about institutional policies regarding personal liability and related insurance coverage options.

The institution must provide access to legal advice for staff members as needed to carry out assigned responsibilities.

The institution must inform staff and students in a timely and systematic fashion about extraordinary or changing legal obligations and potential liabilities.

## Part 9: EQUITY and ACCESS

Staff members must ensure that services and programs are provided on a fair and equitable basis. Facilities, programs and services must be accessible. Hours of operation and delivery of and access to programs and services must be responsive to the needs of all students and other constituents. Each program and service must adhere to the spirit and intent of equal opportunity laws.

Policies and practices of programs and services must not discriminate on the basis of age, color, disability, sex, national origin, race, religious creed, sexual identity, and/or veteran status. Exceptions are appropriate only where provided by relevant law and institutional policy.

Consistent with their mission and goals, programs and services must take affirmative action to remedy significant imbalances in student participation and staffing patterns.

As the demographic profiles of campuses change and new instructional delivery methods are introduced, institutions must recognize the needs of students who participate in distance learning for access to programs and services offered on campus. Institutions must provide appropriate services in ways that are accessible to distance learners and assist them in identifying and gaining access to other appropriate services in their geographic region.

## Part 10: CAMPUS and EXTERNAL RELATIONS

Programs and services must establish, maintain, and promote effective relations with relevant individuals, campus offices, and external agencies.

## Part 11: DIVERSITY

Within the context of each institution's unique mission, diversity enriches the community and enhances the collegiate experience for all; therefore, programs and services must nurture environments where commonalties and differences among people are recognized and honored.

Programs and services must promote educational experiences that are characterized by open and continuous communication that deepens understanding of one's own identity, culture, and heritage, and that of others. Programs and services must educate and promote respect about commonalties and differences in their historical and cultural contexts.

Programs and services must address the characteristics and needs of a diverse population when establishing and implementing policies and procedures.

## Part 12: ETHICS

All persons involved in the delivery of programs and services must adhere to the highest principles of ethical behavior. Programs and services must develop or adopt and implement appropriate statements of ethical practice. Programs and services must publish these statements and ensure their periodic review by relevant constituencies .

Staff members must ensure that privacy and confidentiality are maintained with respect to all communications and records to the extent that such records are protected under the law and appropriate statements of ethical practice. Information contained in students' education records must not be disclosed without written consent except as allowed by relevant laws and institutional policies. Staff members must disclose to appropriate authorities information judged to be of an emergency nature, especially when the safety of the individual or others is involved, or when otherwise required by institutional policy or relevant law.

All staff members must be aware of and comply with the provisions contained in the institution's human subjects research policy and in other relevant institutional policies addressing ethical practices and confidentiality of research data concerning individuals.

Staff members must recognize and avoid personal conflict of interest or appearance thereof in their transactions with students and others.

Staff members must strive to insure the fair, objective, and impartial treatment of all persons with whom they deal. Staff members must not participate in nor condone any form of harassment that demeans persons or creates an intimidating, hostile, or offensive campus environment.

When handling institutional funds, all staff members must ensure that such funds are managed in accordance with established and responsible accounting procedures and the fiscal policies or processes of the institution.

Staff members must perform their duties within the limits of their training, expertise, and competence. When these limits are exceeded, individuals in need of further assistance must be referred to persons possessing appropriate qualifications.

Staff members must use suitable means to confront and otherwise hold accountable other staff members who exhibit unethical behavior.

Staff members must be knowledgeable about and practice ethical behavior in the use of technology.

## Part 13: ASSESSMENT and EVALUATION

Programs and services must conduct regular assessment and evaluations. Programs and services must employ effective qualitative and quantitative methodologies as appropriate, to determine whether and to what degree the stated mission, goals, and student learning and development outcomes are being met. The process must employ sufficient and sound assessment measures to ensure comprehensiveness. Data collected must include responses from students and other affected constituencies.

Programs and services must evaluate periodically how well they complement and enhance the institution's stated mission and educational effectiveness.

Results of these evaluations must be used in revising and improving programs and services and in recognizing staff performance.

# THE ROLE of ACADEMIC ADVISING
## *CAS* Standards Contextual Statement

Academic advising is an essential element of a student's collegiate experience. It evolves from the institution's culture, values, and practices and is delivered in accordance with these factors. Academic advising is one of the few endeavors universal to all college and university students and plays a significant role in their education. Advising practice draws from various educational and human development strategies and theories (e.g., teaching and counseling, the psychology of learning, communication studies, theories of decision making and information transfer, and story telling as a mechanism for understanding human experience).

Academic advising was long the purview solely of faculty who accepted the responsibility in earnest. However, with the advent of electives into the curriculum, academic advising has been delivered also by professional, full-time staff members outside the faculty tenure track structure as well as by graduate and undergraduate students. Today's academic advising is well supported by contemporary computing technologies, particularly in activities such as registration, information dissemination, and auditing of student progress in meeting degree requirements.

Academic advising is one of the very few institutional functions that connect all students to the institution. As higher education curricula become increasingly complex and as educational options expand, pressure to make the educational experience as meaningful as possible for students has increased as well. Higher education, in turn, has responded with renewed attention to the need for quality academic advising.

The establishment of the National Academic Advising Association (NACADA) following the first national conference on advising in 1977 was a significant turning point in according recognition to those in higher education who consider their work in academic advising as purposeful and unique. Today, NACADA is flourishing with membership numbering more than 5200 and national and regional meetings attracting more than 4000 participants annually during the 1990s. Responding to the growing need for ethical principles to guide advising practice and to enable all academic advisors to examine their behavior within a professional framework, NACADA developed a Statement of Core Values that was last revised in 1994.

Academic advising became a significant category in the professional literature during the 1980s, and this trend has continued during the past decade; for example, see Gordon's chapter in 'Teaching Through Academic Advising: A Faculty Perspective (Reinarz & White, 1995) and Current Practices In Academic Advising: Final Report On ACT's Fifth National Survey Of Academic Advising (Habley & Morales, 1998). NACADA publishes a monograph series that examines various aspects of advising. Additional resources, including annotated bibliographies, are available from the Clearinghouse on Academic Advising. Information about NACADA's publications, as well as a link to the Clearinghouse, can be located electronically via the NACADA web site on the World Wide Web. The NACADA Executive Office is an excellent source of general information as well.

Academic advising has been described as a crucial component of all students' experiences in higher education. Within this context, students can find meaning in their lives, make significant decisions about the future, be supported to achieve to their maximum potential, and access all that higher education has to offer. When practiced with competence and dedication, academic advising can enhance retention rates. In an age often characterized by impersonality and detachment, academic advising provides a vital personal connection that students need and frequently seek.

## References, Readings and Resources

Cramer, G. L., & Childs, M. W. (eds.) (1996). Transforming academic advising through the use of information technology,

Monograph No. 4. Manhattan, KS: National Academic Advising Association

Frost, S. H. (1991). Academic advising for student success: A system of shared responsibility. ASHE-ERIC Higher Education Report No. 3. Washington, DC: The George Washington University.

Glennen, R. E., & Vowell, F. N. (eds.) (1995). Academic advising as a comprehensive campus process, Monograph No. 2. Manhattan, KS: National Academic Advising Association.

Gordon, V. N. (1994). Academic advising: An annotated bibliography. Westport, CT: Greenwood Press.

Habley, W.R., and Morales, R.H. (eds.). (1998). Current practices in academic advising: Final report on ACT's fifth national survey of academic advising, Monograph No. 6. Manhattan, KS: National Academic Advising Association

Reinarz, A. G., & White, E. R. (eds.) (1995). Teaching through academic advising: A faculty perspective. San Francisco: Jossey-Bass.

Upcraft, M. L., & Cramer, G. L. (eds.) (1995). First-year academic advising: Patterns in the present *pathways to the future,* Monograph No. 18. Columbia, SC: National Resource Center for the Freshman Year Experience and Students in Transition.

Winston, R. B., Jr., Ender, S. C., & Miller, T. K. (eds.) (1982). *Developmental approaches to academic advising.* New Directions for Student Services, No. 17. San Francisco: Jossey-Bass.

Winston, R. B., Jr., Miller, T. K., Ender, S. C., Grites, T. J., & Associates (1984). *Developmental academic advising: Addressing students educational, career, and personal needs.* San Francisco: Jossey-Bass.

Clearinghouse on Academic Advising, 110 Enarson Hall, The Ohio State University, Columbus, OH 43210.

National Academic Advising Association, 2323 Anderson Avenue, Manhattan, KS 66502-2912; (785) 532-5717; Fax: (785) 532-7732; Web Page: www.ksu.edu/nacada

# ACADEMIC ADVISING
## CAS STANDARDS and GUIDELINES

## Part 1. MISSION

The academic advising program (AAP) must incorporate student learning and student develop in its mission. The AAP must develop record, disseminate, implement and regularly review its mission and goals. Mission statements must be consistent with the mission and goals of the institution and with the standards in this document.

The primary purpose of the AAP is to assist students in the development of meaningful educational plans that are compatible with their life goals.

The institution must have a clearly written statement of philosophy pertaining to academic advising which must include program goals and expectations of advisors and advisees. The program must operate as an integral part of the institution's overall mission.

The ultimate responsibility for making decisions about educational plans and life goals rests with the individual student. The academic advisor should assist by helping to identify and assess alternatives and the consequences of decisions.

Institutional goals for academic advising should include . . .
- development of suitable educational plans
- clarification of career and life goals
- selection of appropriate courses and other educational experiences
- interpretation of institutional requirements
- enhancement of student awareness about educational resources available (e.g., internship, study abroad, honors, and learning assistance programs)
- evaluation of student progress toward established goals
- development of decision-making skills
- reinforcement of student self-direction
- referral to and use of institutional and community support services
- collection and distribution of data regarding student needs, preferences, and performance for use in making institutional decisions and policy

## Part 2. PROGRAM

The formal education of students is purposeful, holistic, and consists of the curriculum and the co-curriculum. The academic advising program (AAP) must identify relevant and desirable student learning and development outcomes and provide programs and services that encourage the achievement of those outcomes.

Reasonable and desirable outcomes include: intellectual growth, effective communication, realistic self-appraisal, enhanced self-esteem, clarified values, career choices, leadership development, healthy behaviors, meaningful interpersonal relations, independence, collaboration, social responsibility, satisfying and productive lifestyles, appreciation of diversity, spiritual awareness, and achievement of personal and educational goals.

The AAP must assist students in overcoming educational and personal problems and skill deficiencies. The program must provide evidence of its impact on the achievement of student learning and development outcomes.

Programs and services may use the examples that follow or identify other more germane indicators.

### Student Learning & Development Outcome Domains

#### Intellectual Growth
Examples of Achievement Indicators
Produces personal and educational goal statements; Employs critical thinking in problem solving; Uses complex information from a variety of sources including personal experience and observation to form a decision or opinion; Obtains a degree; Applies previously understood information and concepts to a new situation or setting; Expresses appreciation for literature, the fine arts, mathematics, sciences, and social sciences

#### Effective Communication
Examples of Achievement Indicators
Writes and speaks coherently and effectively; Writes and speaks after reflection; Able to influence others through writing, speaking or artistic expression; Effectively articulates abstract ideas; Uses appropriate syntax; Makes presentations or gives performances

#### Enhanced Self-Esteem
Examples of Achievement Indicators
Shows self-respect and respect for others; Initiates actions toward achievement of goals; Takes reasonable risks; Demonstrates assertive behavior; Functions without need for constant reassurance from others

#### Realistic Self-Appraisal
Examples of Achievement Indicators
Articulates personal skills and abilities; Makes decisions and acts in congruence with personal values; Acknowledges personal strengths and weaknesses; Articulates rationale for personal behavior; Seeks feedback from others; Learns from past experiences

## Clarified Values

Examples of Achievement Indicators

Articulates personal values; Acts in congruence with personal values; Makes decisions that reflect personal values; Demonstrates willingness to scrutinize personal beliefs and values; Identifies personal, work and lifestyle values and explains how they influence decision-making

## Career Choices

Examples of Achievement Indicators

Articulate career choices based on assessment of interests, values, skills and abilities; Documents knowledge, skills and accomplishments resulting from formal education, work experience, community service and volunteer experiences; Makes the connections between classroom and out-of-classroom learning; Can construct a resume with clear job objectives and evidence of related knowledge, skills and accomplishments; Articulates the characteristics of a preferred work environment; Comprehends the world of work; Takes steps to initiate a job search or seek advanced education

## Leadership Development

Examples of Achievement Indicators

Articulates leadership philosophy or style; Serves in a leadership position in a student organization; Comprehends the dynamics of a group; Exhibits democratic principles as a leader; Exhibits ability to visualize a group purpose and desired outcomes

## Healthy Behavior

Examples of Achievement Indicators

Chooses behaviors and environments that promote health and reduce risk; Articulate the relationship between health and wellness and accomplishing life long goals; Exhibits behaviors that advance a healthy community

## Meaningful Interpersonal Relationships

Examples of Achievement Indicators

Develops and maintains satisfying interpersonal relationships; Establishes mutually rewarding relationships with friends and colleagues; Listens to and considers others' points of view; Treats others with respect

## Independence

Examples of Achievement Indicators

Exhibits self-reliant behaviors; Functions autonomously; Exhibits ability to function interdependently; Accepts supervision as needed; Manages time effectively

## Collaboration

Examples of Achievement Indicators

Works cooperatively with others; Seeks the involvement of others; Seeks feedback from others; Contributes to achievement of a group goal; Exhibits effective listening skills

## Social Responsibility

Examples of Achievement Indicators

Understands and participates in relevant governance systems; Understands, abides by, and participates in the development, maintenance, and/or orderly change of community, social, and legal standards or norms; Appropriately challenges the unfair, unjust, or uncivil behavior of other individuals or groups; Participates in service/volunteer activities

## Satisfying and Productive Lifestyles

Examples of Achievement Indicators

Achieves balance between education, work and leisure time; Articulates and meets goals for work, leisure and education; Overcomes obstacles that hamper goal achievement; Functions on the basis of personal identity, ethical, spiritual and moral values; Articulates long-term goals and objectives

## Appreciating Diversity

Examples of Achievement Indicators

Understands ones own identity and culture. Seeks involvement with people different from oneself; Seeks involvement in diverse interests; Articulate the advantages and challenges of a diverse society; Challenges appropriately abusive use of stereotypes by others; Understands the impact of diversity on one's own society

## Spiritual Awareness

Examples of Achievement Indicators

Develops and articulates personal belief system; Understands roles of spirituality in personal and group values and behaviors

## Personal and Educational Goals

Examples of Achievement Indicators

Sets, articulates, and pursues individual goals; Articulate personal and educational goals and objectives; Uses personal and educational goals to guide decisions; Understands the effect of one's personal and education goals on others

**The AAP must be (a) intentional, (b) coherent, (c) based on theories and knowledge of teaching, learning and human development, (d) reflective of developmental and demographic profiles of the student population, and (e) responsive to the special needs of individuals.**

**The AAP must identify environmental conditions that may negatively influence student academic achievement and propose interventions that may neutralize such conditions.**

**The academic advisor must review and use available data about students' academic and educational needs, performance, aspirations, and problems.**

The AAP must assure that academic advisors collaborate in the collection of relevant data about students for use in individual academic advising conferences. Individual academic advising conferences must be available to students each academic term.

Through private, individual conferences with students, the academic advisors should provide assistance in refining goals and objectives, understanding available choices, and assessing the consequences of alternative courses of action. Course selection, understanding and meeting institutional requirements, and providing clear and accurate information regarding institutional policies, procedures, resources, and programs may be carried out individually or in groups.

The academic status of the student being advised should be taken into consideration when determining caseloads. For example, first year, undecided, under prepared, and honors students may require more advising time than upper division students who have declared their majors.

**Academic advising caseloads must be consistent with the time required for the effective performance of this activity.**

When determining workloads it should be recognized that advisors may work with students not officially assigned to them and that contacts regarding advising may extend beyond direct contact with the student.

**The AAP must provide current and accurate advising information to academic advisors.**

Supplemental systems for the delivery of advising information, such as on-line computer programs, may be employed.

Referrals to appropriate institutional or community support services should be made as needed.

The academic advising program should make available to academic advisors all pertinent research (e.g., about students, the academic advising program, and perceptions of the institution).

## Part 3. LEADERSHIP

Effective and ethical leadership is essential to the success of all organizations. Institutions must appoint position and empower academic advising program (AAP) leaders within the administrative structure to accomplish stated missions. Leaders at various levels must be selected on the basis of formal education and training, relevant work experience, personal skills and competencies, relevant professional credentials, as well as potential for promoting learning and development in students, applying effective practices to educational processes, and enhancing institutional effectiveness. Institutions must determine expectations of accountability for leaders and fairly assess their performance.

AAP leaders must exercise authority over resources for which they are responsible to achieve their respective missions.

AAP leaders must . . .
- **articulate a vision for their organization**
- **set goals and objectives based on the needs and capabilities of the population served**
- **promote student learning and development**
- **prescribe and practice ethical behavior**
- **recruit, select, supervise, and develop others in the organization**
- **manage financial resources**
- **coordinate human resources**
- **plan, budget for, and evaluate personnel and programs**
- **apply effective practices to educational and administrative processes**
- **communicate effectively**
- **initiate collaborative interaction between individuals and agencies that possess legitimate concerns and interests in the functional area**

AAP leaders must identify and find means to address individual, organizational, or environmental conditions that inhibit goal achievement. Leaders must promote campus environments that result in multiple opportunities for student learning and development.

AAP leaders must continuously improve programs and services in response to changing needs of students and other constituents, and evolving institutional priorities.

## Part 4. ORGANIZATION and MANAGEMENT

The academic advising program (AAP) must be structured purposefully and managed effectively to achieve its stated goals. Evidence of effective management must include use of comprehensive and accurate information for decisions, clear sources and channels of authority, effective communication practices, decision-making and conflict resolution procedures, responsiveness to changing conditions, accountability and evaluation systems, and recognition and reward processes. The program must strive to improve the professional competence and skills of all personnel it employs.

The AAP must provide channels within the organization for regular review of administrative policies and procedures.

The design of the AAP must be compatible with the institution's organizational structure and its students' needs. Specific advisor responsibilities must be clearly delineated, published, and disseminated to both advisors and advisees.

In some institutions, academic advising is a centralized function, while in others, it is decentralized, with a variety of people throughout the institution assuming responsibilities. Whatever system is used, students, faculty advisors, and professional staff should be informed of their respective advising responsibilities.

## Part 5. HUMAN RESOURCES

The academic advising program (AAP) must be staffed adequately by individuals qualified to accomplish its mission and goals. Within established guidelines of the institution, the program must establish procedures for staff selection, training, and evaluation; set expectations for supervision, and provide appropriate professional development opportunities. The program must strive to improve the professional competence and skills of all personnel it employs.

Academic advisors must hold an earned graduate degree in a field relevant to the position held or must possess an appropriate combination of educational credentials and related work experience.

Degree or credential-seeking interns must be qualified by enrollment in an appropriate field of study and by relevant experience. These individuals must be trained and supervised adequately by professional staff members holding educational credentials and related work experience appropriate for supervision.

Student employees and volunteers must be carefully selected, trained, supervised, and evaluated. They must be trained on how and when to refer those in need of assistance to qualified staff members and have access to a supervisor for assistance in making these judgments. Student employees and volunteers must be provided clear and precise job descriptions, pre-service training based on assessed needs, and continuing staff development.

The AAP must have technical and support staff members adequate to accomplish its mission. Staff members must be technologically proficient and qualified to perform their job functions, be knowledgeable of ethical and legal uses of technology, and have access to training. The level of staffing and workloads must be adequate and appropriate for program and service demands.

Salary levels and fringe benefits for all AAP staff members must be commensurate with those for comparable positions within the institution, in similar institutions, and in the relevant geographic area.

The AAP must institute hiring and promotion practices that are fair, inclusive, and non-discriminatory. AAP must employ a diverse staff to provide readily identifiable role models for students and to enrich the campus community.

AAP must create and maintain position descriptions for all staff members and provide regular performance planning and appraisals.

The AAP must have a system for regular staff evaluation and must provide access to continuing education and professional development opportunities, including in-service training programs and participation in professional conferences and workshops.

The institution must designate a specific individual to direct the AAP. The director must possess either an earned graduate degree or equivalent combination of academic and educational experience, previous experience as an academic advisor, and knowledge of the literature of academic advising. The director must be skilled in fiscal management, personnel selection and training, conceptualization, planning and evaluation tasks.

Academic advisors should have an understanding of student development; a comprehensive knowledge of the institution's programs, academic requirements, majors, minors, and support services; a demonstrated interest in working with and assisting students; a willingness to participate in pre-service and in-service workshops and other professional activities; and demonstrated interpersonal skills.

Sufficient personnel should be available to meet students' advising needs without unreasonable delay. Advisors should allow an appropriate amount of time for students to discuss plans, programs, courses, academic progress, and other subjects related to their educational programs.

Academic advising personnel may be organized in various ways. They may be full-time or part-time professionals who have advising as their primary function or may be faculty whose responsibilities include academic advising. Paraprofessionals (e.g., graduate students in practice, interns, or assistants) or peer advisors may also assist advisors.

Support personnel should maintain student records, organize resource materials, receive students, make appointments, and handle correspondence and other operational needs. Technical staff may be used in research, data collection, systems development, and special projects.

Technical and support personnel should be carefully selected and adequately trained, supervised, and evaluated.

## Part 6. FINANCIAL RESOURCES

**The academic advising program (AAP) must have adequate funding to accomplish its mission and goals. Funding priorities must be determined within the context of the stated mission, goals, objectives and comprehensive analysis of the needs and capabilities of students and the availability of internal or external resources.**

**The AAP must demonstrate fiscal responsibility and cost effectiveness consistent with institutional protocols.**

Special consideration should be given to providing funding for training and development of advisors, particularly those for whom the advisory function is part-time and/or secondary assignment.

Financial resources should be sufficient to provide high quality print and non-print information for students and training materials for advisors. Also, there should be sufficient resources to promote the academic advising program.

## Part 7. FACILITIES, TECHNOLOGY, EQUIPMENT

**The academic advising program (AAP) must have adequate, suitably located facilities, adequate technology, and equipment to support its mission and goals efficiently and effectively. Facilities, technology, and equipment must be evaluated regularly and be in compliance with relevant federal, state, provincial, and local requirements to provide for access, health, safety, and security.**

**The AAP must assure that technology-assisted advising includes appropriate approvals, consultations, and referrals.**

Computing equipment and access to local networks, student data bases, and the Internet should be available to academic advisors.

Privacy and freedom from visual and auditory distractions should be considerations in designing appropriate facilities.

## Part 8. LEGAL RESPONSIBILITIES

**Academic advising program (AAP) staff members must be knowledgeable about and responsive to laws and regulations that relate to their respective responsibilities. Staff members must inform users of programs and services and officials, as appropriate, of legal obligations and limitations including constitutional, statutory, regulatory, and case law; mandatory laws and orders emanating from federal, state/provincial and local governments; and the institution's policies.**

**Academic advisors must use reasonable and informed practices to limit the liability exposure of the institution, its officers, employees, and agents. Academic advisors must be informed about institutional policies regarding personal liability and related insurance coverage options.**

The institution must provide access to legal advice for academic advisors as needed to carry out assigned responsibilities and must inform academic advisors and students, in a timely and systematic fashion, about extraordinary or changing legal obligations and potential liabilities.

## Part 9. EQUITY and ACCESS

**Academic advising program (AAP) staff members must ensure that services are provided on a fair and equitable basis. Facilities, programs, and services must be accessible. Hours of operation and delivery of and access to programs and services must be responsive to the needs of all students and other constituents. The AAP must adhere to the spirit and intent of equal opportunity laws.**

**The AAP must be open and readily accessible to all students and must not discriminate except where sanctioned by law and institutional policy. Discrimination must especially be avoided on the bases of age; color, creed; cultural heritage; disability; ethnicity; gender identity; nationality; political affiliation, religious affiliation, sex, sexual orientation; or economic, marital, social, or veteran status.**

**Consistent with the mission and goals, the AAP must take affirmative action to remedy significant imbalances in student participation and staffing patterns.**

**As the demographic profiles of campuses change and new instructional delivery methods are introduced, institutions must recognize the needs of students who participate in distance learning for access to programs and services offered on campus. ☐Institutions must provide appropriate services in ways that are accessible to distance learners and assist them in identifying and gaining access to other appropriate services in their geographic region.**

## PART 10. CAMPUS & EXTERNAL RELATIONS

**The academic advising program (AAP) must establish, maintain, and promote effective relations with relevant individuals, campus offices, and external agencies.**

Academic advising is integral to the educational process and depends upon close working relationships with other institutional agencies and the administration. The academic advising program should be fully integrated into other processes of the institution.

For referral purposes, the academic advising program should provide academic advisors a comprehensive list of relevant external agencies, campus offices, and opportunities.

## Part 11. DIVERSITY

Within the context of the institution's unique mission, diversity enriches the community and enhances the collegiate experience for all; therefore, the academic advising program (AAP) must nurture environments where similarities and differences among people are recognized and honored.

The AAP must promote educational experiences that are characterized by open and continuous communication that deepens understanding of one's own identity, culture, and heritage, and that of others. The AAP must educate and promote respect about commonalties and differences in their historical and cultural contexts.

The AAP must address the characteristics and needs of a diverse population when establishing and implementing policies and procedures.

## Part 12. ETHICS

All persons involved in the delivery of the academic advising program (AAP) must adhere to the highest principles of ethical behavior. The AAP must develop or adopt and implement appropriate statements of ethical practice. The AAP must publish these statements and ensure their periodic review by relevant constituencies.

Ethical standards or other statements from relevant professional associations should be considered.

AAP staff members must ensure that privacy and confidentiality are maintained with respect to all communications and records to the extent that such records are protected under the law and appropriate statements of ethical practice. Information contained in students' education records must not be disclosed without written consent except as allowed by relevant laws and institutional policies. Staff members must disclose to appropriate authorities information judged to be of an emergency nature, especially when the safety of the individual or others is involved, or when otherwise required by institutional policy or relevant law.

All AAP staff members must be aware of and comply with the provisions contained in the institution's human subjects research policy and in other relevant institutional policies addressing ethical practices and confidentiality of research data concerning individuals.

AAP staff members must recognize and avoid personal conflict of interest or appearance thereof in their transactions with students and others.

AAP staff members must strive to ensure the fair, objective, and impartial treatment of all persons with whom they deal. Staff members must not participate in nor condone any form of harassment that demeans persons or creates an intimidating, hostile, or offensive campus environment.

When handling institutional funds, all AAP staff members must ensure that such funds are managed in accordance with established and responsible accounting procedures and the fiscal policies or processes of the institution.

AAP staff members must perform their duties within the limits of their training, expertise, and competence. When these limits are exceeded, individuals in need of further assistance must be referred to persons possessing appropriate qualifications.

AAP staff members must use suitable means to confront and otherwise hold accountable other staff members who exhibit unethical behavior.

AAP staff members must be knowledgeable about and practice ethical behavior in the use of technology.

## Part 13. ASSESSMENT and EVALUATION

The academic advising program (AAP) must conduct regular assessment and evaluations. The AAP must employ effective qualitative and quantitative methodologies as appropriate, to determine whether and to what degree the stated mission, goals, and student learning and development outcomes are being met. The process must employ sufficient and sound assessment measures to ensure comprehensiveness. Data collected must include responses from students and other affected constituencies.

The program must evaluate periodically how well they complement and enhance the institution's stated mission and educational effectiveness.

Results of these evaluations must be used in revising and improving the program in recognizing staff performance.

# THE ROLE of COLLEGE ADMISSION PROGRAMS
## *CAS* Standards Contextual Statement

"When any scholar is able to read Tully or such like classical Latin author *ex tempore*, and make and speak true Latin in verse and prose *suo (ut aiunt) Marte*, and decline perfectly the paradigms of nouns and verbs in the Greek tongue, then may he be admitted into College, nor shall any claim admission before such qualifications." Statutes of Harvard, 1646 (Goodchild & Wechsler, 1989)

This statement describes the first criteria for admission established by the founders of the first educational institution in the New World. When America's first colonial colleges were founded, their primary mission was similar English tradition of providing liberal education and professional study for young men of intellectual and financial ability. Admission focused on identifying and admitting young men for the ministry. However, as other colleges were subsequently founded, chartered, and funded, their missions changed to address changes in student needs, ages, religions, social class, and proximity to campus.

Against the backdrop of American higher education's 350 year history, the role of admissions professionals and the process of admission today might best be understood by considering two competing forces: service to the institution and service to prospective students. In general, the job of admission professionals is to help students understand the process of transition to college, admission criteria, and the competitiveness of their credentials. These tasks are typically accomplished through personal interactions, group presentations, publications, and other recruitment and counseling strategies.

The admission professional must also have a firm understanding of the institution's mission, enrollment goals, fiscal priorities, and student and departmental needs. When performing well, the successful admissions professional serves a vital role establishing good matches between students and institutions. Just as changes in demographics, finances, laws, and shifts in the competitiveness of their credentials have affected prospective college students, the role of the admission officer has also changed over time, from the functions suggested by titles such as registrar, counselor, dean and director, marketer, and recruiter to that of enrollment manager.

In general, admission professionals . . .
* provide information and assistance to prospective students, families, and secondary school counselors on the academic, financial, and co-curricular offerings of their institutions

* evaluate the academic and personal qualifications of applicants
* develop, implement, and coordinate the institution's strategic marketing or recruitment plans
* work with the college faculty and administration to develop, implement, and evaluate enrollment policies and goals for the institution
* establish cooperative relationships with secondary school counselors and other relevant constituencies
* work in concert with other campus offices to ensure that students are not only recruited but retained and eventually graduate.

The admission professional today is faced with many challenges: diverse students and student needs, high college costs, limited financial aid, and intense competition for students. They must also apply new technologies to deliver messages about the institution. The more than 3,000 post-secondary institutions in the US have admission policies ranging from "open-admission" to highly competitive and selective. Similarly, the hundreds of thousands of applicants present varying ability levels, financial concerns, personal challenges, and academic interests, and admission officers must be prepared to serve them all Admission offices must have appropriate and adequate staff, policies, and skills in human relations to manage their important roles.

As the new century approaches, admission professionals recognize the benefits of cooperating with other student affairs professionals to enhance students' educational experiences. During the past decade, enrollment management models have been developed to bring greater sophistication to efforts to recruit, retain, educate, and graduate students. On today's campuses, models for admission offices may include such areas as admissions, recruitment or outreach, financial assistance, orientation, housing, and academic advising—all reporting to a central administrator. Enrollment management assumes the establish-ment of activities based on understanding of market research, student impact research, and organizational theory. Enrollment management paradigms are viewed as on-going processes that can enable college and university administrators to exert greater influence over factors that shape their enrollments. Clearly, today's admission professionals must continue to respect students and their need for quality counseling and support throughout the whole admission process, while they also address institutional expectations. The *Admission Program Standards and Guidelines* that follow have been designed to facilitate the admission professional's response to these increasingly complex demands.

### Recommended Readings and Resources

Goodchild, L. F., & Wechsler, H. W. (eds.) (1989). The statutes of Harvard, 1646. *ASHE Reader on The History of Higher Education*. pp. 89-90. Needham Heights, MA: Ginn Press.

American Association of Collegiate Registrars and Admissions Officers. (1997). *The college admission handbook*. Washington, DC: Author.

American Association of Collegiate Registrars and Admissions Officers (AACRAO), The College Entrance Examination Board (CEEB), The Educational Testing Services (ETS), and the National Association of College Admission Counselors (NACAC). (1995). *Challenges in college admissions: A report of a survey of undergraduate admissions policies, practices, and procedures*. Washington, DC: Authors.

Fetter, J. (1995) *Questions and admissions: Reflections on 100,000 admissions decisions at Stanford*. Stanford, CA: Stanford University Press.

Hossler, E. & Litten, L. (1993). *Mapping the higher education landscape*. New York: The College Entrance Examination Board.

Loeb, J. (1992). *Academic standards in higher education*. New York: The College Entrance Examination Board.

National Association for College Admission Counseling. (1993). *Achieving diversity: Strategies for the recruitment and retention of traditionally underrepresented students*. Alexandria, VA: Author.

American Association of Collegiate Registrars and Admission Officers (AACRAO) One Dupont Circle, NW, Suite 330, Washington, DC 20036-1171 202-293-9161; 202-872-8857 (fax). http://www.reg.uci.edu/aacrao Publisher of *College and University*.

The College Board
45 Columbus Avenue, New York, NY 10023
212-713-8000; http://www.collegeboard.org
Publisher of *The College Review*

The National Association for College Admission Counseling (NACAC)
1631 Prince Street, Alexandria, Virginia 22314-2818
703-836-2222; 703-836-8015 (fax);
http://www.nacac.com
Publisher of the *Journal of College Admission*

The National Association of Graduate Admissions Professionals (NAGAP)
Joanne Nagy, President
Associate Dean The Graduate School
University of Wisconsin-Madison
500 Lincoln Drive, 231 Bascom Hall
Madison, WI 53706-1380; 608-262-6509
Publisher of the *NAGAP Journal*
www.nagap.org

# ADMISSION PROGRAMS

## *CAS* STANDARDS and GUIDELINES

## Part 1. MISSION

The admission program (AP) must incorporate student learning and development in its mission. The program must enhance overall educational experiences and must develop, record, disseminate, implement and regularly review its mission and goals. Mission statements must be consistent with the mission and goals of the institution and with the standards in this document. The AP must operate as an integral part of the institution's overall mission.

Admission programs must . . .

- address the abilities needs and expectations of prospective students as they move from secondary to postsecondary education, from one postsecondary institution to another, or as they return from a period of non-enrollment to formal learning

- establish, promulgate, and implement admission criteria that accurately represent the mission, goals, and purposes of the institution, and that accommodate the abilities, needs, and interests of potential students

- reflect the mission, goals, policies, procedures, facilities, and characteristics of the parent institution, and must be compatible with the ability of the institution to bring adequate resources to bear upon the relevant needs and aspirations of all students accepted for enrollment

- develop and regularly review institutional goals for admission with appropriate individuals within the institution; such goals must be consistent with good admission practices and with the nature and mission of the institution

Generally, in higher education, the terms *admission, admission program*, and *admission counselor* refer respectively to the processes, the agencies, and the institutional agents involved in the many activities that are related to the formal entry of students into postsecondary institutions. These generally include recruitment, counseling, selection, enrollment, orientation, advisement, and retention of students. In practice, institutions may establish separate agencies to provide these programs and services.

Admission programs should provide or ensure personalized counseling that is responsive to the needs and expectations of each prospective student and his or her family, with particular attention given to the transition process.

Admission criteria should also reflect a variable approach which includes the student's academic record (e.g., grade point average, test scores, class rank), personal characteristics, and extracurricular involvement.

## Part 2. PROGRAM

The formal education of students consists of the curriculum and the co-curriculum, and must promote student learning and development that is purposeful and holistic. The admission program (AP) must identify relevant and desirable student learning and development outcomes and provide programs and services that encourage the achievement of those outcomes.

Relevant and desirable outcomes include intellectual growth, effective communication, realistic self-appraisal, enhanced self-esteem, clarified values, career choices, leadership development, healthy behaviors, meaningful interpersonal relationships, independence, collaboration, social responsibility, satisfying and productive lifestyles, appreciation of diversity, spiritual awareness, and achievement of personal and educational goals.

The AP must provide evidence of its impact on the achievement of student learning and development outcomes.

The AP may use the examples that follow or identify other more germane indicators.

### Student Learning & Development Outcome Domains

### Intellectual Growth
**Examples of Achievement Indicators**
Produces personal and educational goal statements; Employs critical thinking in problem solving; Uses complex information from a variety of sources including personal experience and observation to form a decision or opinion; Obtains a degree; Applies previously understood information and concepts to a new situation or setting; Expresses appreciation for literature, the fine arts, mathematics, sciences, and social sciences

### Effective Communication
**Examples of Achievement Indicators**
Writes and speaks coherently and effectively; Writes and speaks after reflection; Able to influence others through writing, speaking or artistic expression; Effectively articulates abstract ideas; Uses appropriate syntax; Makes presentations or gives performances

## Enhanced Self-Esteem

**Examples of Achievement Indicators**

Shows self-respect and respect for others; Initiates actions toward achievement of goals; Takes reasonable risks; Demonstrates assertive behavior; Functions without need for constant reassurance from others

## Realistic Self-Appraisal

**Examples of Achievement Indicators**

Articulates personal skills and abilities; Makes decisions and acts in congruence with personal values; Acknowledges personal strengths and weaknesses; Articulates rationale for personal behavior; Seeks feedback from others; Learns from past experiences

## Clarified Values

**Examples of Achievement Indicators**

Articulates personal values; Acts in congruence with personal values; Makes decisions that reflect personal values; Demonstrates willingness to scrutinize personal beliefs and values; Identifies personal, work and lifestyle values and explains how they influence decision-making

## Career Choices

**Examples of Achievement Indicators**

Articulate career choices based on assessment of interests, values, skills and abilities; Documents knowledge, skills and accomplishments resulting from formal education, work experience, community service and volunteer experiences; Makes the connections between classroom and out-of-classroom learning; Can construct a resume with clear job objectives and evidence of related knowledge, skills and accomplishments; Articulates the characteristics of a preferred work environment; Comprehends the world of work; Takes steps to initiate a job search or seek advanced education

## Leadership Development

**Examples of Achievement Indicators**

Articulates leadership philosophy or style; Serves in a leadership position in a student organization; Comprehends the dynamics of a group; Exhibits democratic principles as a leader; Exhibits ability to visualize a group purpose and desired outcomes

## Healthy Behavior

**Examples of Achievement Indicators**

Chooses behaviors and environments that promote health and reduce risk; Articulate the relationship between health and wellness and accomplishing life long goals; Exhibits behaviors that advance a healthy community

## Meaningful Interpersonal Relationships

**Examples of Achievement Indicators**

Develops and maintains satisfying interpersonal relationships; Establishes mutually rewarding relationships with friends and colleagues; Listens to and considers others' points of view; Treats others with respect

## Independence

**Examples of Achievement Indicators**

Exhibits self-reliant behaviors; Functions autonomously; Exhibits ability to function interdependently; Accepts supervision as needed; Manages time effectively

## Collaboration

**Examples of Achievement Indicators**

Works cooperatively with others; Seeks the involvement of others; Seeks feedback from others; Contributes to achievement of a group goal; Exhibits effective listening skills

## Social Responsibility

**Examples of Achievement Indicators**

Understands and participates in relevant governance systems; Understands, abides by, and participates in the development, maintenance, and/or orderly change of community, social, and legal standards or norms; Appropriately challenges the unfair, unjust, or uncivil behavior of other individuals or groups; Participates in service/volunteer activities

## Satisfying and Productive Lifestyles

**Examples of Achievement Indicators**

Achieves balance between education, work and leisure time; Articulates and meets goals for work, leisure and education; Overcomes obstacles that hamper goal achievement; Functions on the basis of personal identity, ethical, spiritual and moral values; Articulates long-term goals and objectives

## Appreciating Diversity

**Examples of Achievement Indicators**

Understands ones own identity and culture. Seeks involvement with people different from oneself; Seeks involvement in diverse interests; Articulate the advantages and challenges of a diverse society; Challenges appropriately abusive use of stereotypes by others; Understands the impact of diversity on one's own society

## Spiritual Awareness

**Examples of Achievement Indicators**

Develops and articulates personal belief system; Understands roles of spirituality in personal and group values and behaviors

## Personal and Educational Goals

**Examples of Achievement Indicators**

Sets, articulates, and pursues individual goals; Articulate personal and educational goals and objectives; Uses personal and educational goals to guide decisions; Understands the effect of one's personal and education goals on others

**The AP must be (a) intentional, (b) coherent, (c) based on theories and knowledge of learning and human development, (d) reflective of developmental and demographic profiles of the student**

population, and (e) responsive to needs of individuals, special populations, and communities.

**Admission programs must . . .**

• **provide programs and services designed to establish, meet, and maintain desired enrollment**

• **promote and maintain integrity, timeliness and accuracy in program delivery**

• **promote deliberate educational planning opportunities for all relevant constituencies**

• **provide oral and written information for all relevant constituencies**

• **promote and provide equal access to all eligible prospective students interested in and capable of pursuing an education at the institution**

**Admission priorities, preferences, and objectives must be stated clearly in the formal admission policies and procedures of the institution. This statement must be easily obtainable by individuals seeking admission.**

Not every student is suited for a particular postsecondary institution. Proper student-institutional matches are a major factor in the persistence of students toward graduation.

The distribution of current and complete information is an important priority for admission offices. Students and parents require comprehensive information on admission policies, requirements and procedures, as well as on institutional program offerings, selection criteria, acceptance decisions and financial aid opportunities. All admission personnel should be well informed and able to share such information in a variety of contexts in the interest of deliberate planning.

All admission professional staff members should be expected to perform the admission counseling function.

This includes the following activities and interventions . . .

• assistance and direction of students engaged in the admission process to encourage an appropriate match between student interests and available postsecondary opportunities

• acquisition and dissemination of timely, accurate and relevant information regarding postsecondary opportunities, curriculum choices, and future educational plans

• promotion and development of individual problem-solving practices by students

• referral of students to appropriate institutional or other resources in response to particular needs

• encouragement of students toward deliberate choices and realistic expectations regarding institutional and personal standards of performance

• effective work with students of different levels of ability

• acknowledgment and positive use of proper interest in the student on the part of high school counselors, faculty, administrators, and students' families

• facilitation of proper exchange of non-restricted information among high schools, postsecondary institutions, families, students, and others involved in the admission process

• encouragement of students to engage in effective life planning

• provision of opportunities for a personal interview to students who are being considered for enrollment where appropriate

• making available to prospective students information regarding financial aid opportunities and deadlines; standard financial aid forms should be available through the admission office as well as through any financial aid office

• providing to students who are offered admission information about academic advising and counseling, and student orientation programs and activities. Any other information regarding student services which may enhance success at the institution should be provided.

The admission program may be accomplished through practices which may include but are not limited to:

• recruitment, marketing and public relations activities (e.g., high school visits, college fairs, direct mail campaigns, publications, alumni relations and assistance, dissemination of admission and financial aid information)

• admission counseling (e.g., evaluation of student credentials, selection, and notification)

• pre-enrollment counseling (e.g., academic advisement and orientation)

• establishment of institutional policies regarding advanced placement, prior college level credit, or credit for equivalent experience.

## Part 3. LEADERSHIP

**Effective and ethical leadership is essential to the success of all organizations. Institutions must appoint, position and empower admission program (AP) leaders within the administrative structure to accomplish stated missions. AP leaders at various levels must be selected on the basis of formal education and training, relevant work experience, personal skills and competencies, relevant professional credentials, as well as potential for promoting learning and development in students, applying effective practices to educational processes, and enhancing institutional effectiveness. Institutions must determine expectations of accountability for leaders and fairly assess their performance.**

**AP leaders must exercise authority over resources for which they are responsible to achieve their respective missions.**

**The designated leader must . . .**

- articulate a vision for the organization
- set goals and objectives based on the needs and capabilities of the population served
- promote student learning and development
- prescribe and practice ethical behavio
- recruit, select, supervise, and develop others in the organization
- manage financial resources
- coordinate human resources
- plan, budget for, and evaluate personnel and programs
- apply effective practices to educational and administrative processes
- communicate effectively
- initiate collaborative interaction between individuals and agencies that possess legitimate concerns and interests in the functional area

AP leaders must identify and find means to address individual, organizational, or environmental conditions that inhibit goal achievement. Leaders must promote campus environments that result in multiple opportunities for student learning and development. AP leaders must continuously improve programs and services in response to changing needs of students and other constituents, and evolving institutional priorities.

## Part 4. ORGANIZATION and MANAGEMENT

Guided by an overarching intent to ensure student learning and development, admission program (AP) must be structured purposefully and managed effectively to achieve stated goals. Evidence of appropriate structure must include current and accessible policies and procedures, written performance expectations for all employees, functional workflow graphics or organizational charts, and clearly stated service delivery expectations.

Evidence of effective management must include use of comprehensive and accurate information for decisions, clear sources and channels of authority, effective communication practices, decision-making and conflict resolution procedures, responsiveness to changing conditions, accountability and evaluation systems, and recognition and reward processes. AP must provide channels within the organization for regular review of administrative policies and procedures.

The institution must appoint or designate a senior admission officer. This officer must be positioned in the institutional organization so that the needs of students and the operations of admission are both well-represented and advocated at the highest levels of administration.

The specific title and lines of accountability may vary among institutions in light of particular settings and institutional needs. Selection of the chief admission officer should be based on personal characteristics as well as formal training.

The chief admission officer should be able to develop advocate, and implement a statement of the mission goals and objectives for the admission program on campus.

The chief admission officer should create an effective system to manage the programs, services, and personnel of the admission office. He or she should plan, organize, staff, lead, and regularly assess programs. The leader should also be able to coordinate the admission program with other institutional services and with institutional development activities.

The chief admission officer should attract and select qualified staff members who are capable of making informed decisions about policies, procedures, personnel, budgets, facilities and equipment. He or she should assume responsibility for program and staff development, assessment, and improvement.

Administrative policies and organization structures should be written, properly disseminated and posted, and modified when necessary.

Admission programs, policies, and procedures should minimally include:
- an organizational chart which depicts areas of accountability and reporting relationships for units and personnel as appropriate
- job descriptions that accurately reflect the duties and responsibilities for all admission program personnel
- clearly stated criteria used in the decision making process for admission to the institution and the source of authority for the criteria employed
- steps for appealing, evaluating, or revising policies and procedures

## Part 5. HUMAN RESOURCES

The admission program (AP) must be staffed adequately by individuals qualified to accomplish its mission and goals. Within established guidelines of the institution, the program must establish procedures for staff selection, training, and evaluation; set expectations for supervision, and provide appropriate professional development opportunities. The AP must strive to improve the professional competence and skills of all personnel it employs.

AP professional staff members must hold an earned graduate degree in a field relevant to the position they hold or must possess an appropriate combination of educational credentials and related work experience.

36

Degree or credential-seeking interns must be qualified by enrollment in an appropriate field of study and by relevant experience. These individuals must be trained and supervised adequately by professional staff members holding educational credentials and related work experience appropriate for supervision.

Student employees and volunteers must be carefully selected, trained, supervised, and evaluated. They must be trained on how and when to refer those in need of assistance to qualified staff members and have access to a supervisor for assistance in making these judgments. Student employees and volunteers must be provided clear and precise job descriptions, pre-service training based on assessed needs, and continuing staff development.

Each organizational unit must have technical and support staff members adequate to accomplish its mission. AP staff members must be technologically proficient and qualified to perform their job functions, be knowledgeable of ethical and legal uses of technology, and have access to training. The level of staffing and workloads must be adequate and appropriate for program and service demands.

Salary levels and fringe benefits for all AP staff members must be commensurate with those for comparable positions within the institution, in similar institutions, and in the relevant geographic area.

AP must institute hiring and promotion practices that are fair, inclusive, and non-discriminatory. The program must employ a diverse staff to provide readily identifiable role models for students and to enrich the campus community.

AP must create and maintain position descriptions for all staff members and provide regular performance planning and appraisals.

AP must have a system for regular staff evaluation and must provide access to continuing education and professional development opportunities, including in-service training programs and participation in professional conferences and workshops.

The admission office must be provided with or have designated adequate and qualified professional staff to fulfill the mission of the agency and to implement all aspects of the program.

*PROFESSIONAL STAFF*

The chief admission officer should be an experienced and effective manager and have substantial work experience in admission-related employment.

Professional staff members should be competent to provide assistance to the prospective student and to work effectively to assist each student with his or her educational goals. This assistance may include, but should not be limited to, the following . . .

- ethical and objective presentation of the institution's programs and opportunities; careful and concerned analysis of each student's goals
- establishment of a clear understanding of likely student-institution compatibility
- responsible decision-making in the selection of an institution
- knowledgeable guidance and counseling on all admission issues and concerns; interpretation of tasks and statistical data
- explanation of and placing in a proper context any relevant governmental policy or practice on education

The professional staff should be knowledgeable in the areas of marketing, financial aid, and testing, and should demonstrate knowledge and sensitivity to the needs of traditionally under-represented students and students with a special talent. Activities in these special areas of concern should contribute positively to the reputation of the institution and its position in the higher education marketplace.

Admission staff members should be specifically trained to articulate the institution's unique and essential aspects. Training should be supplemental to formal outside training. While no specific timeline is prescribed, a minimum of two weeks' specialized training is recommended. Included in this training should be . . .

- a thorough tour of the campus
- familiarization with the college catalog, all academic programs, freshman and transfer admission policies, and all service and social aspects of the institution
- systematic orientation to relevant other facets of the institution
- familiarization with clerical and financial aid operations

Institutions should provide ongoing opportunities for career-related information and professional growth to the entire admission staff. This process will promote effective admission services and encourage the continued involvement of admission personnel in the field. Numerous avenues promote professional growth. These include inservice workshops, membership and participation in professional organizations, and the development of an admission library. A library should include current scholarly literature, research findings, trade journals, and newspapers.

Continuing education is essential for all admission officers. It is important to be alert to changes in the field and to be able to integrate changes into daily practice when appropriate. Every admission officer should be . . .

- willing to seek out and implement new ideas
- able to translate new ideas into practical methods for improving the overall operation of the admission function

- willing to seek out and use new conceptual frameworks and equipment that bring information to students more clearly and effectively
- aware of relevant developments in the broad context of formal education and able to incorporate these developments in his or her work

For formal training in preparation for professional admission work, suggested areas for graduate work include student services administration and higher education management. Additional course work may include computer literacy, research and statistical methods, counseling, enrollment management, legal issues relating to admission and higher education, leadership skills, transcript evaluation and public relations.

*CLERICAL AND SUPPORT STAFF*

Support staff members such as administrative assistants, transcript evaluators, and office assistants, should possess the academic background, experience, personal interest, and competence necessary for effective performance of their responsibilities. Support staff should be skilled in interpersonal communications, public relations, referral techniques, and dissemination of information.

Training in procedures, policies, and good office practices should be included in the employment orientation for clerical and support staff. Such training will promote a consistent presentation of the institution and dependable performance of staff.

An annual admission staff workshop to plan and review admission programs is recommended. Topics and components of the workshop may include current issues in college admission, team development, marketing, computer operations, and financial aid issues and status.

## Part 6. FINANCIAL RESOURCES

**Admission programs (AP) must have adequate funding to accomplish its mission and goals. Funding priorities must be determined within the context of the stated mission, goals, objectives, and comprehensive analysis of the needs and capabilities of students, and the availability of internal or external resources.**

**AP must demonstrate fiscal responsibility and cost effectiveness consistent with institutional protocols.**

**The admission program budget must be properly prepared, clearly detailed and defined, continually monitored and adequately funded for full program support.**

The institution must prescribe policies governing . . .
- **in-kind consideration in lieu of cash payment, reimbursement, or remuneration for approved admission related activity or participation**

- **any necessary external contractual agreements (e.g., professional consultation fees, special mailings)**
- **travel, accommodations, and all expenditures authorized for recruitment purposes; reimbursements for out-of-pocket expenses**

Institutions should provide support for an admission program that offers prospective students ample opportunities to:
- inquire about the entrance requirements and nature of the institution
- inquire about and receive counseling regarding the institution's admission process; apply for admission; and, where appropriate
- receive financial aid information and forms
- be interviewed as applicants for admission
- receive assistance in orientation and academic advisement

Institutional admission offices should be able to respond in a timely manner to requests for information, literature, programs and services upon the request of prospective students.

## Part 7. FACILITIES, TECHNOLOGY, EQUIPMENT

**Admission programs (AP) must have adequate, suitably located facilities, adequate technology, and equipment to support its mission and goals efficiently and effectively. Facilities, technology, and equipment must be evaluated regularly and be in compliance with relevant federal, state, provincial, and local requirements to provide for access, health, safety, and security.**

Sufficient office space should be allocated for confidential interviews and counseling, processing of all relevant documents, files, and staff supervision.

Office space should be adequate and properly equipped for the secure and confidential storage of student records as appropriate.

Security measures, facilities, and equipment appropriate for handling cash or negotiable paper should be provided when necessary.

The admission office should be readily accessible to prospective students, parents and others who have need for admission services or personnel.

Special concern for providing readily accessible and nearby parking, or the availability of convenient public transportation is strongly recommended.

Campus maps and highly visible signage that will assist visitors and prospective students to locate the admission office are strongly recommended.

## Part 8. LEGAL RESPONSIBILITIES

**Admission program (AP) staff members must be knowledgeable about and responsive to laws and regulations that relate to their respective responsibilities . Staff members must inform users of programs and services and officials, as**

appropriate, of legal obligations and limitations including constitutional, statutory, regulatory, and case law; mandatory laws and orders emanating from federal, state/provincial and local governments; and the institution's policies.

AP staff members must use reasonable and informed practices to limit the liability exposure of the institution, its officers, employees, and agents. Staff members must be informed about institutional policies regarding personal liability and related insurance coverage options.

The institution must provide access to legal advice for AP staff members as needed to carry out assigned responsibilities and must inform AP staff and students in a timely and systematic fashion about extraordinary or changing legal obligations and potential liabilities.

Admission counselors must be aware of the legal and ethical limits and standards relevant to their professional roles, and perform any counseling or guidance functions accordingly.

## Part 9. EQUITY and ACCESS

Admission Programs (AP) staff members must ensure that services and programs are provided on a fair and equitable basis. Facilities, programs and services must be accessible. Hours of operation and delivery of and access to programs and services must be responsive to the needs of all students and other constituents. AP must adhere to the spirit and intent of equal opportunity laws.

The AP must be open and readily accessible to all students and must not discriminate except where sanctioned by law and institutional policy. Discrimination must especially be avoided on the bases of age; color, creed; cultural heritage; disability; ethnicity; gender identity; nationality; political affiliation, religious affiliation, sex, sexual orientation; or economic, marital, social, or veteran status.

Consistent with their mission and goals, programs and services must take affirmative action to remedy significant imbalances in student participation and staffing patterns.

All admission publications and forms must clearly state students' rights and responsibilities in the admission process. Admission practices must be congruent with the institution's policies on Equal Opportunity, Access, and Affirmative Action.

Admission publications must reflect relevant institutional policies.

As the demographic profiles of campuses change and new instructional delivery methods are introduced, institutions must recognize the needs of students who participate in distance learning for access to programs and services offered on campus. □Institutions must provide appropriate services in ways that are accessible to distance learners and assist them in identifying and gaining access to other appropriate services in their geographic region.

## Part 10. CAMPUS and EXTERNAL RELATIONS

Admission Programs (AP) must establish, maintain, and promote effective relations with relevant individuals, campus offices, and external agencies.

Admission documents used by academic advising and counseling, orientation, housing, counseling, testing, the office of records and international student services must be accurate and handled with confidentiality.

Institutional organizational functions and constituencies linked to admission typically include financial aid, student development, student activities, athletics, student accounts, academic support, counseling, career planning and placement, the registrar, records, the faculty, the alumni, and institutional advancement. Residents of the larger community in which the institution is located may also have special interests regarding institutional admission practices.

Students with special needs should be identified and referral made to the appropriate office. Special needs may include those with learning disabilities, physical handicaps, deficiencies in certain academic skills, and those who come from educationally disadvantaged backgrounds. Financial aid and admission decisions should be made independently. However, the financial aid office should have access to appropriate information in the student's admission file. After financial aid has been allocated, the admission office should have access to information regarding the amount and characteristics of the financial aid award. Admission decisions should be based on the establishment or a match between the student's needs and the characteristics of the institution. A student's apparent ability to pay for the services of the institution should not affect the admission decision.

## Part 11. DIVERSITY

Within the context of each institution's unique mission, diversity enriches the community and enhances the collegiate experience for all; therefore, admission program (AP) must nurture environments where commonalties and differences among people are recognized and honored.

Admission programs must promote educational experiences that are characterized by open and continuous communication that deepens understanding of one's own identity, culture, and heritage, and that of others. Programs must educate and promote respect about commonalties and differences in their historical and cultural contexts.

AP must address the characteristics and needs of a diverse population when establishing and implementing policies and procedures.

## Part 12. ETHICS

All persons involved in the delivery of admission program (AP) must adhere to the highest principles of ethical behavior. Programs must develop or adopt and implement appropriate statements of ethical practice. AP must publish these statements and ensure their periodic review by relevant constituencies .

AP staff members must ensure that privacy and confidentiality are maintained with respect to all communications and records to the extent that such records are protected under the law and appropriate statements of ethical practice. Information contained in students' education records must not be disclosed without written consent except as allowed by relevant laws and institutional policies. AP staff members must disclose to appropriate authorities information judged to be of an emergency nature, especially when the safety of the individual or others is involved, or when otherwise required by institutional policy or relevant law.

All AP staff members must be aware of and comply with the provisions contained in the institution's human subjects research policy and in other relevant institutional policies addressing ethical practices and confidentiality of research data concerning individuals.

AP staff members must recognize and avoid personal conflict of interest or appearance thereof in their transactions with students and others. Further, staff members must strive to ensure the fair, objective, and impartial treatment of all persons with whom they deal. Staff members must not participate in nor condone any form of harassment that demeans persons or creates an intimidating, hostile, or offensive campus environment.

When handling institutional funds, all AP staff members must ensure that such funds are managed in accordance with established and responsible accounting procedures and the fiscal policies or processes of the institution.

AP staff members must perform their duties within the limits of their training, expertise, and competence. When these limits are exceeded, individuals in need of further assistance must be referred to persons possessing appropriate qualifications. Likewise, staff members must use suitable means to confront and otherwise hold accountable other staff members who exhibit unethical behavior.

AP staff members must be knowledgeable about and practice ethical behavior in the use of technology.

As professional members of the institution's staff, admission personnel must receive compensation in the form of a fixed salary, rather than commissions or bonuses on the number of students recruited or enrolled.

Admission officers must ensure timely and fair administration of policies regarding: admission decisions; proper notification; wait-listing; evaluating student competencies, credentials, and prior credits and confidentiality in keeping with federal and state laws.

Promotional publications, written communications, and presentations must . . .
- state entrance requirements clearly and precisely
- include a current and accurate admission calendar
- provide precise information on opportunities for financial aid
- offer accurate and detailed information regarding special programs
- include realistic descriptions, illustrations, and photographs of the campus and community

Development of admission criteria must be centered on the probability of academic success. When evaluating applicants, particularly those with special talents, admission officers must be guided by their best judgment and should make exception to established admission policies only after a thorough and prudent evaluation of all relevant circumstances including where appropriate, consultation with relevant other agencies.

In some cases applicants may possess outstanding talent in drama, music, athletics, art, or other areas. These students might not meet all established criteria for academic success. However, in some cases a special talent can motivate a student to perform well in a secondary school program. Where this is possible, admission officers are encouraged to acknowledge the special talent when evaluating the applicant.

In some cases, the applicants may possess special needs. For instance, students with learning disabilities or those from academically disadvantaged backgrounds might be admitted. Ethical practices would insist that the appropriate support services be available for these students if they are admitted.

**Any comparisons made between or among institutions must be based on accurate and appropriate data. General comments of a disparaging nature about other institutions must be avoided.**

## Part 13. ASSESSMENT and EVALUATION

**Admission Programs (AP) must conduct regular assessment and evaluations. Programs must employ effective qualitative and quantitative methodologies as appropriate, to determine whether and to what degree the stated mission, goals, and student learning and development outcomes are being met. The process must employ sufficient and sound assessment measures to ensure comprehensiveness. Data collected must include responses from students and other affected constituencies.**

**AP must evaluate periodically how well they complement and enhance the institution's stated mission and educational effectiveness.**

**Results of these evaluations must be used in revising and improving programs and services and in recognizing staff performance.**

Each institution should require that its admission offices, programs, and staff be evaluated regularly. This evaluation should determine the effectiveness of services to students and their families, achievement of departmental and institutional goals and direction toward more efficient cost-effective operations. The periodic study of needs, interests, and expectations of prospective and current students and others served by the program may be conducted in conjunction with these evaluations. Data collected from the study should be used to determine the effectiveness of institutional admission policies and programs. Marketing and recruitment techniques used by the admission officer should be regularly reviewed.

# THE ROLE of ALCOHOL, TOBACCO, and OTHER DRUG PROGRAMS
## *CAS* Standards Contextual Statement

Abuse of alcohol and other drugs has historically been a major concern for institutions of higher education. Many colleges and universities have employed professional staff members to administer campus-based alcohol, tobacco, and other drug programs directed at prevention of associated problems. Most of these programs were initially established to respond to student needs, but increasingly are being developed to serve the entire campus, including faculty, staff and their families. Campus administrators are now recognizing that the behaviors of all community members affect the nature of the problem and that efforts at education and prevention must be addressed to the whole college community. There has been a national movement to broaden the prevention efforts to include both the individual and the environmental approach.

Major factors that helped focus attention on the problems of alcohol and other drug abuse include

- 1981 creation of the Inter-Association Task Force on Alcohol and Other Substance Issues, a consortium of professional associations
- 1984 creation of National Collegiate Alcohol Awareness Week
- 1985 promulgation of Guidelines for Beverage Alcohol Marketing on College and University Campuses
- 1986 passage by Congress of the Drug Free School and Communities Act and the establishment of the FIPSE (Fund for the Improvement of Post-Secondary Education) grant program for IHEs
- 1987 establishment by the US Department of Education of the Network of Colleges and Universities Committed to the Elimination of Drug and Alcohol Abuse, now called The Network: Addressing Collegiate Alcohol and Other Drug Issues.
- 1990 development of Standards and Guidelines for Alcohol and Drug Programs by the Council for the Advancement of Standards in Higher Education
- 1993 establishment of the Higher Education Center by the US Department of Education
- 2003 NIAAA College Drinking Report

Alcohol, Tobacco, and Other Drug Programs (ATODP) play an important role in challenging individual behaviors detrimental to the maintenance of civility in an increasingly complex microcosm of society, the college campus. ATODP staff members serve as counselors, advisers, educational programmers, change agents, and collaborators for many campus constituencies exploring appropriate venues to discuss, formulate, and educate campus

groups about program mission and philosophy; policy enforcement; intervention strategies; treatment, referral, and support groups; healthy alternative activities; resource needs; target population needs; and appropriate assessment, evaluation, and research efforts. The professional staff member who is primarily responsible for the ATODP program generally serves as its campus spokesperson and must also handle public relations issues.

The institution's chief administrative office and all other campus leaders must support a comprehensive campus ATODP for it to be effective. Those who voice support for these programs must view the problems as solvable and believe that confronting the problems created by alcohol and other drug abuse is a major responsibility facing educational institutions. Any effective strategy to combat these issues must emphasize the necessity for individual action, choice, and assumption of responsibility.

## Recommended Readings and Resources

Anderson, D.S., & Milgram, G.G. (1996). *Promising practices: Campus alcohol strategies.* George Mason University (Topical areas comprising policies and implementation, assessment and evaluation, training, peer-based initiatives, environmental and targeted strategies, enforcement, curriculum, awareness and information, support and intervention services, and staffing and resources.).

Coombs, R.H., & Ziedonis, D. (1995). *Handbook on drug abuse prevention: A Comprehensive strategy to prevent the abuse of alcohol and other drugs.* Boston: Allyn & Bacon.

Wechsler, H., Dowdall, G., Davenport, A., & Castillo, S. (July, 1995). Correlates of college student binge drinking. *American Journal of Public Health*, 85, 7.

*Journal of Drug Education*: Baywood Publishing Co., Inc., P.O. Box 337, Amityville, NY 11701

The U.S. Department of Education's Higher Education Center publications, www.edc.org/hec

AMA Office of Alcohol & Other Drug Abuse www.ama-assn.org/ama/pub/category/3337.html

BACCHUS and GAMMA Peer Education Network www.bacchusgamma.org

National Clearinghouse for Alcohol and Drug Information (NCADI) www.health.org

National Institute of Drug Abuse (NIDA) www.drugabuse.gov

National Institute on Alcohol Abuse and Alcoholism (NIAAA) www.collegedrinkingprevention.gov

# ALCOHOL, TOBACCO, and OTHER DRUG PROGRAM
## *CAS* STANDARDS and GUIDELINES

For the purpose of this document the term "alcohol, tobacco, and other drug use or abuse" includes (a) the illegal use of alcohol, tobacco, prescription medications and other drugs and (b) the high-risk use and/or abuse of alcohol, tobacco, prescription medications, over-the-counter medications and nutritional supplements.

## Part 1. MISSION

The alcohol, tobacco, and other drugs program (ATODP) must incorporate student learning and student development in its mission. The program must enhance overall educational experiences. The program must develop, record, disseminate, implement and regularly review its mission and goals. Mission statements must be consistent with the mission and goals of the institution and with the standards in this document. The program must operate as an integral part of the institution's overall mission.

The goals of ATODP must . . .

- acknowledge and mitigate the inherent risks to the total community associated with alcohol, tobacco, and other drug use
- develop, disseminate, interpret, and support the enforcement of campus regulations that are consistent with institutional policies and local, state/provincial, and federal law
- promote healthy choices concerning the use of alcohol, tobacco, and other drugs, emphasizing the elimination of illegal use, high-risk behavior, harmful use, and related violence
- promote a safe, healthy, and learning conducive environment
- define ATODP policies and practices for prevention, education, training, intervention, evaluation, referral and treatment
- develop shared ownership of the issue by involving all entities of the campus community including governing boards, administrators, faculty and staff members, students, and community leaders
- protect the legal rights of students

## Part 2. PROGRAM

The formal education of students consists of the curriculum and the co-curriculum, and must promote student learning and development that is purposeful and holistic. The alcohol, tobacco, and other drugs program (ATODP) must identify relevant and desirable student learning and development outcomes and provide programs and services that encourage the achievement of those outcomes. **The programs must provide evidence of student learning and development outcomes.**

**Relevant and desirable outcomes include: intellectual growth, effective communication, realistic self-appraisal, enhanced self-esteem, clarified values, career choices, leadership development, healthy behaviors, meaningful interpersonal relations, independence, collaboration, social responsibÄlity, satisfying and productive lifestyles, appreciation of diversity, spiritual awareness, and achievement of personal and educational goals.**

**The program must provide evidence of its impact on the achievement of student learning and development outcomes.**

The program may use the examples that follow or identify other more germane indicators.

### Student Learning & Development Outcome Domains

### Intellectual Growth
<u>Examples of Achievement Indicators</u>

Produces personal and educational goal statements; Employs critical thinking in problem solving; Uses complex information from a variety of sources including personal experience and observation to form a decision or opinion; Obtains a degree; Applies previously understood information and concepts to a new situation or setting; Expresses appreciation for literature, the fine arts, mathematics, sciences, and social sciences

### Effective Communication
<u>Examples of Achievement Indicators</u>

Writes and speaks coherently and effectively; Writes and speaks after reflection; Able to influence others through writing, speaking or artistic expression; Effectively articulates abstract ideas; Uses appropriate syntax; Makes presentations or gives performances

### Enhanced Self-Esteem
<u>Examples of Achievement Indicators</u>

Shows self-respect and respect for others; Initiates actions toward achievement of goals; Takes reasonable risks; Demonstrates assertive behavior; Functions without need for constant reassurance from others

### Realistic Self-Appraisal
<u>Examples of Achievement Indicators</u>

Articulates personal skills and abilities; Makes decisions and acts in congruence with personal values; Acknowledges personal strengths and weaknesses; Articulates rationale for personal behavior; Seeks feedback from others; Learns from past experiences

## Clarified Values

Examples of Achievement Indicators

Articulates personal values; Acts in congruence with personal values; Makes decisions that reflect personal values; Demonstrates willingness to scrutinize personal beliefs and values; Identifies personal, work and lifestyle values and explains how they influence decision-making

## Career Choices

Examples of Achievement Indicators

Articulate career choices based on assessment of interests, values, skills and abilities; Documents knowledge, skills and accomplishments resulting from formal education, work experience, community service and volunteer experiences; Makes the connections between classroom and out-of-classroom learning; Can construct a resume with clear job objectives and evidence of related knowledge, skills and accomplishments; Articulates the characteristics of a preferred work environment; Comprehends the world of work; Takes steps to initiate a job search or seek advanced education

## Leadership Development

Examples of Achievement Indicators

Articulates leadership philosophy or style; Serves in a leadership position in a student organization; Comprehends the dynamics of a group; Exhibits democratic principles as a leader; Exhibits ability to visualize a group purpose and desired outcomes

## Healthy Behavior

Examples of Achievement Indicators

Chooses behaviors and environments that promote health and reduce risk; Articulate the relationship between health and wellness and accomplishing life long goals; Exhibits behaviors that advance a healthy community

## Meaningful Interpersonal Relationships

Examples of Achievement Indicators

Develops and maintains satisfying interpersonal relationships; Establishes mutually rewarding relationships with friends and colleagues; Listens to and considers others' points of view; Treats others with respect

## Independence

Examples of Achievement Indicators

Exhibits self-reliant behaviors; Functions autonomously; Exhibits ability to function interdependently; Accepts supervision as needed; Manages time effectively

## Collaboration

Examples of Achievement Indicators

Works cooperatively with others; Seeks the involvement of others; Seeks feedback from others; Contributes to achievement of a group goal; Exhibits effective listening skills

## Social Responsibility

Examples of Achievement Indicators

Understands and participates in relevant governance systems; Understands, abides by, and participates in the development, maintenance, and/or orderly change of community, social, and legal standards or norms; Appropriately challenges the unfair, unjust, or uncivil behavior of other individuals or groups; Participates in service/volunteer activities

## Satisfying and Productive Lifestyles

Examples of Achievement Indicators

Achieves balance between education, work and leisure time; Articulates and meets goals for work, leisure and education; Overcomes obstacles that hamper goal achievement; Functions on the basis of personal identity, ethical, spiritual and moral values; Articulates long-term goals and objectives

## Appreciating Diversity

Examples of Achievement Indicators

Understands ones own identity and culture. Seeks involvement with people different from oneself; Seeks involvement in diverse interests; Articulate the advantages and challenges of a diverse society; Challenges appropriately abusive use of stereotypes by others; Understands the impact of diversity on one's own society

## Spiritual Awareness

Examples of Achievement Indicators

Develops and articulates personal belief system; Understands roles of spirituality in personal and group values and behaviors

## Personal and Educational Goals

Examples of Achievement Indicators

Sets, articulates, and pursues individual goals; Articulate personal and educational goals and objectives; Uses personal and educational goals to guide decisions; Understands the effect of one's personal and education goals on others

**The ATODP must be (a) intentional, (b) coherent, (c) based on theories and knowledge of learning and human development, and evidence-based prevention and public health models (d) reflective of developmental and demographic profiles of the student population, (e) collaborative with related campus and community agencies, and (f) responsive to needs of individuals, special populations and communities.**

**The ATODP must involve students, faculty members, staff, and community constituents to reduce heavy and high-risk use of alcohol, tobacco, prescription medication and other drugs.**

**The ATODP must include environmental management strategies,** institutional policies, enforcement strategies, bi-annual review, community collaboration, training and education, assistance and referral, and student leadership

**ATODP staff members must serve as positive role models for ethical and healthy behaviors.**

Because faculty and staff members' behaviors often serve as models for students, resources should be available on-campus to assist supervisors in dealing with employees who exhibit high risk behavior related to alcohol, tobacco, and other drugs.

**The ATODP must develop and provide education on policies, laws, prevention, intervention and treatment resources, and training for students, including student organizations.**

The ATODP education and training program should address the cultural and economic context in which society promotes and condones alcohol, tobacco, and other drug use, including traditions and rituals conducive to high-risk drinking. Other topics may include: legal, physiological, psychological, and social aspects and effects of alcohol, tobacco, and other drug use, abuse, and dependency; high-risk uses of alcohol; risk factors for groups including risk factors for groups as identified through assessment; differences between actual student use and perceptions of student use; and the impact of alcohol, tobacco, and other drug use related to physiological and behavioral differences linked with gender. Techniques and protocols for identifying and referring students with problems to appropriate campus entities should also be included.

The ATODP should develop, provide, and advocate strategies that model practical applications of prevention theories and research results, including environmental approaches, risk reduction approaches, social norms approaches, student assistance programs, curricular infusion projects, development of on-campus task forces, and the development of campus and community coalitions.

The ATODP should provide training for faculty and staff members in identifying, intervening, and referring students with alcohol, tobacco, and other drug problems.

The ATODP should use public health prevention strategies that are evidenced-based and have demonstrated effectiveness in reducing heavy and high-risk drinking and other drug use in college populations.

The ATODP should advocate for incorporating alcohol, tobacco, and other drugs information within relevant courses and expanding campus library holdings.

**The ATODP must provide access to support services for students with alcohol or other drug related concerns.**

Student involvement in assistance services may be voluntary upon self-initiation or referral, or mandatory upon referral by judicial authorities or other entities.

The student assistance services program should include confidential individual assessment for students to explore and evaluate their attitudes, perceptions, and behaviors; the consequences, risk factors, and relationship to alcohol or other drugs; and make decisions based on the student's individual situation.

Student assistance services should provide, with peer involvement, a coordinated system across the campus for intervention and referral services for students. This system should include training programs on alcohol abuse and other drug use and referral skills.

Student assistance services should identify and maintain contacts with campus and community entities that offer effective treatment, education, and support to students, family members, and friends. Such services may include structured education and counseling sessions for individuals and groups; community service work; disability support services; self-help groups such as Alcoholics Anonymous, Narcotics Anonymous, Al-Anon and Adult Children of Alcoholics; support groups; and detoxification and inpatient therapy.

## Part 3. LEADERSHIP

**Effective and ethical leadership is essential to the success of all organizations. Institutions must appoint, position, and empower leaders within the administrative structure to accomplish stated missions. Leaders at various levels must be selected on the basis of formal education and training, relevant work experience, personal skills and competencies, relevant professional credentials, as well as potential for promoting learning and development in students, applying effective practices to educational processes, and enhancing institutional effectiveness. Institutions must determine expectations of accountability for leaders and fairly assess their performance.**

**Alcohol, tobacco, and other drugs program (ATODP) leaders must exercise authority over resources for which they are responsible to achieve their respective missions.**

**ATODP leaders must . . .**

(a) **articulate a vision and mission statement for their program**

(b) **gather relevant data and review current literature**

(c) **set goals and objectives based on the needs and capabilities of the population served that will enhance program and institutional effectiveness**

(d) **promote student learning and development**

(e) **develop strategic, operational, and resource utilization plans and policies**

(f) **prescribe and practice ethical behavior**

(g) **recruit, select, supervise, and develop others in the program**

(h) manage financial resources

(i) coordinate human resources

(j) plan, budget for, manage, and evaluate personnel and programs

(k) apply effective practices in educational and administrative processes

(l) communicate effectively

(m) initiate collaborative interaction between the program and individuals or agencies that possess legitimate concerns and interests in the ATODP

(n) ensure compliance with all institutional, state/provincial, and federal regulations and policies

(o) advocate for the advancement of the ATODP in the institution

ATODP leaders should provide institutional leaders with information on ATODP issues on their campus to engender support.

ATODP leaders must institute processes that improve programs and services in response to changing needs of students and other constituents, and evolving institutional priorities.

ATODP leaders must promote campus environments that result in multiple opportunities for student learning and development.

ATODP leaders must identify and find means to address individual, organizational, or environmental conditions that inhibit goal achievement.

## Part 4. ORGANIZATION & MANAGEMENT

Guided by an overarching intent to ensure student learning and development, the alcohol, tobacco, and other drugs program (ATODP) must be structured purposefully and managed effectively to achieve stated goals. Evidence of appropriate structure must include current and accessible policies and procedures, written performance expectations for all employees, functional work flow graphics or organizational charts, and clearly stated service delivery expectations.

Evidence of effective management must include use of comprehensive and accurate information for decisions, clear sources and channels of authority, effective communication practices, decision-making and conflict resolution procedures, responsiveness to changing conditions, accountability and evaluation systems, and recognition and reward processes. The ATODP must provide channels within the organization for regular review of administrative policies and procedures.

The ATODP director or coordinator must be placed within the institution's organizational structures so as to be able to promote cooperative interaction with appropriate campus and community entities and to develop the support of high-level administrators.

The scope and structure of the ATODP should be defined by the size, nature, complexity, and philosophy of the institution.

The ATODP should maintain an advisory board, preferably appointed by the executive officer, comprised of knowledgeable members of the campus and community, for advice and support on polices and programs.

The ATODP must collaborate in the development of policies to . . .

• maintain consistency with federal, state/provincial, and local laws and regulations

• promote an educational, social and living environment free from the abuse of alcohol, tobacco, legal drugs, and the use of illegal drugs

• define geographic jurisdictions and demographic characteristics of popula-tions to whom policies pertain

• define individual and group behaviors and group activities that are prohibited both on campus property and at off-campus events controlled by the institution

• specify the potential consequences for using or possessing, distributing or manufacturing different amounts and/or categories of alcohol, tobacco, and other drugs

• establish protocols and procedures for the involvement of campus law enforcement, campus judicial programs, and other campus entities

• establish protocols and procedures for referring individuals with alcohol, tobacco, or other drug problems to appropriate sources for assistance

• define campus procedures on the availability and marketing of alcoholic beverages, if permitted

• define appropriate procedures for any permitted use of alcohol or tobacco

## Part 5. HUMAN RESOURCES

The alcohol, tobacco, and other drugs program (ATODP) must be staffed adequately by individuals qualified to accomplish its mission and goals. Within established guidelines of the institution, programs and services must establish procedures for staff selection, training, and evaluation; set expectations for supervision, and provide appropriate professional development opportunities. The program and service must strive to improve the professional competence and skills of all personnel it employs.

**Professional staff members who provide clinical services must hold an earned graduate degree or appropriate license in a field relevant to the position description or must possess an appropriate combination of educational credentials and related work experience.**

The ATODP should be supervised by professional staff members who have earned a master's degree from an accredited institution in fields of study such as health education, student services/development, psychology, social work, counseling, education, public health, or other appropriate health-related area, and who have relevant training and experience. Such training and experience should include prevention and intervention, assessment and treatment issues and strategies, and supervised work with older adolescents and adults of all ages.

**The ATODP prevention specialist must hold a minimum of a bachelor's degree in a related field and have relevant training and experience.**

Training and experience should include an understanding of prevention and intervention strategies as well as work experience with college students.

**Degree or credential seeking interns, or others in training, must be qualified by enrollment in an appropriate field of study and by relevant experience. These individuals must be trained and supervised adequately by professional staff members holding educational credential and related work experience appropriate for supervision.**

**Student employees and volunteers must be carefully selected, trained, supervised, and evaluated. They must be trained on how and when to refer those in need of assistance to qualified staff members and have access to a supervisor for assistance in making these judgments. Student employees and volunteers must be provided clear and precise job descriptions, pre-service training based on assessed needs, and continuing staff development.**

**The ATODP must have support and technical staff members adequate to accomplish its mission. Staff members must be technologically proficient and qualified to perform their job functions, be knowledgeable of ethical and legal uses of technology, and have access to training. The level**

of staffing and workloads must be adequate and appropriate for program and service demands.

**Salary levels and fringe benefits for all staff members must be commensurate with those for comparable positions within the institution, in similar institutions, and in the relevant geographic area.**

**ATODP must institute hiring and promotion practices which are fair, inclusive, and non-discriminatory. Programs and services must employ a diverse staff to provide readily identifiable role models for students and to enrich the campus community.**

**ATODP must create and maintain position descriptions for all staff members and provide regular performance planning and appraisals.**

**The ATODP must have regular systems of staff selection and evaluation, and must provide access to continuing education and professional development opportunities, including in-service training programs and participation in professional conferences and workshops.**

The ATODP should provide training on problem recognition and referral procedures for professional and support staff, pre-professionals, and paraprofessionals.

## Part 6. FINANCIAL RESOURCES

**The alcohol, tobacco, and other drugs program (ATODP) must have adequate funding to accomplish its mission and goals. Funding priorities must be determined within the context of the stated mission, goals, objectives, and comprehensive analysis of the needs and capabilities of students and the availability of internal and external resources.**

**The ATODP must demonstrate fiscal responsibility and cost effectiveness consistent with institutional protocols.**

The institution should provide sufficient baseline funding for the ATODP so that staff members may spend the majority of their time on planning, programming, providing services, and evaluation rather than on seeking new or continuing funding sources.

## Part 7. FACILITIES, TECHNOLOGY, EQUIPMENT

**The alcohol, tobacco, and other drugs program (ATODP) must have adequate, suitably located facilities, adequate technology and equipment to support its mission and goals efficiently and effectively. Facilities, technology, and equipment must be evaluated regularly and be in compliance**

with relevant federal, state/provincial, and local requirements to provide for access, health, safety, and security.

Facilities for the ATODP should support a range of services, including prevention, education, assessment, intervention, programming, and a resource center.

Office space should be physically separate from human resources, campus security, and judicial programs.

Facilities and furnishings should ensure secure confidential files.

The ATODP should be provided facilities that ensure confidentiality and a location in which students, faculty, and staff might access and read information on alcohol, tobacco, and other drugs.

The ATODP should possess, or have access to, equipment and services such as audio-visual equipment and services, printing services, campus and community media resources, and computers.

## Part 8. LEGAL RESPONSIBILITIES

Alcohol, tobacco, and other drugs program (ATODP) staff members must be knowledgeable about and responsive to law and regulations that relate to their respective responsibilities. Staff members must inform users of programs and services and officials, as appropriate, of legal obligations and limitations including constitutional, statutory, regulatory, and case law; mandatory laws and orders emanating from federal, state/provincial and local governments; and the institution's policies.

Staff members must use reasonable and informed practices to limit the liability exposure of the institution, its officers, employees, and agents. ATODP staff members must be informed about institutional policies regarding personal liability and related insurance coverage options.

The institution must provide access to legal advice for staff members as needed to carry out assigned responsibilities.

ATODP staff members must be aware of and seek advice from the institution's legal counsel on: privacy and disclosure of student information and parental notification.

The institution must inform staff and students, in a timely and systematic fashion, about extraordinary or changing legal obligations and potential liabilities.

## Part 9. EQUITY AND ACCESS

Alcohol, tobacco, and other drugs program (ATODP) staff members must ensure that services and programs are provided on a fair and equitable

basis. ATODP must be accessible. Hours of operation and access to programs must be responsive to the needs of all students and other constituents. The ATODP must adhere to the spirit and intent of equal opportunity laws.

The ATODP must be open and readily accessible to all students and must not discriminate except where sanctioned by law and institutional policy. Discrimination must be avoided on the bases of age; color; creed; cultural heritage; disability; ethnicity; gender identity; nationality; political affiliation; religious affiliation; sex; sexual orientation; or social, economic, marital, or veteran status.

Consistent with its mission and goals, the ATODP program must take affirmative action to remedy significant imbalances in student participation and staffing patterns.

As the demographic profiles of campuses change and new instructional delivery methods are introduced, institutions must recognize the needs of students who participate in distance learning for access to programs and services offered on campus. Institutions must provide appropriate services in ways that are accessible to distance learners and assist them in identifying and gaining access to other appropriate services in their geographic region.

## Part 10. CAMPUS and EXTERNAL RELATIONS

The alcohol, tobacco, and other drugs program (ATODP) must establish, maintain, and promote effective relations with relevant campus offices, community agencies and leaders and other external agencies.

The ATODP must gather and disseminate information to the campus community, including students, their parents, staff, and faculty on alcohol, tobacco, and other drug problems, risk reduction strategies, resources and related topics.

The ATODP must maintain effective working relationships with various campus offices and community groups and agencies to promote a healthy environment in which the use or abuse of alcohol and use of other drugs does not interfere with the learning, performance, or social aspects of college life,

These campus offices may include senior administrators; medical services; health promotion and prevention services; counseling; law enforcement and safety; judicial programs; residential life; campus information and visitor services; fraternity and sorority life; athletics; student and other campus media; disability support services, student activities offices and student organizations; academic departments; personnel services; and community relations and public affairs. Community agencies may include relevant local, state/provincial, and federal agencies and authorities such as the state liquor store control authority, state alcohol agency, the office of highway traffic safety, mayor and council, neighborhood associations, faith community, family, parents or guardians, school systems, area health care and treatment providers, support groups, as well as representatives from the local chamber of commerce and the hospitality industry.

The ATODP should engage the campus and community in the issues of access and availability of alcohol, tobacco, and other drugs, and in the enforcement of the law.

**The ATODP must work with campus and community resources to encourage staff members to utilize appropriate screening protocols.**

## Part 11. DIVERSITY

Within the context of the institution's unique mission, diversity enriches the community and enhances the collegiate experience for all; therefore, the alcohol, tobacco, and other drugs program (ATODP)must nurture environments where commonalities and differences among people are recognized and honored.

The ATODP must promote cultural educational experiences that are characterized by open and continuous communication that deepens understanding of one's own identity, and promote respect about commonalities and differences in their historical and cultural contexts.

The ATODP must address the characteristics and needs of a diverse population when establishing and implementing policies and procedures.

## Part 12. ETHICS

All persons involved in the delivery of alcohol, tobacco, and other drugs program (ATODP) must adhere to the highest principles of ethical behavior. The ATODP must develop or adopt and implement statements of ethical practice. The programs must publish these statements and ensure their periodic review by relevant constituencies.

ATODP staff members must ensure that privacy and confidentiality is maintained with respect to all communications and records to the extent that such records are protected under the law and appropriate statements of ethical practice.

Information contained in students' educational records must not be disclosed without written consent except as allowed by relevant laws and institutional policies. Staff members must disclose to appropriate authorities information judged to be of an emergency nature, especially when the safety of the individual or others is involved, or when otherwise required by institutional policy or relevant law.

All staff members must be aware of and comply with the provisions contained in the institution's human subjects research policy and in other relevant institutional policies addressing ethical practices and confidentiality of research data concerning individuals.

Staff members must recognize and avoid personal conflict of interest or appearance thereof in their transactions with students and others.

Staff members must strive to insure the fair, objective, and impartial treatment of all persons with whom they deal. Staff members must not participate in any form of harassment that demeans persons or creates an intimidating, hostile, or offensive campus environment.

When handling institutional funds, ATODP staff members must ensure that such funds are managed in accordance with established and responsible accounting procedures and the fiscal policies or processes of the institution.

Staff members must perform their duties within the limits of their training, expertise, and competence. When these limits are exceeded, individuals in need of further assistance must be referred to persons possessing appropriate qualifications.

Staff members must use suitable means to confront and otherwise hold accountable other staff members who exhibit unethical behavior and must be knowledgeable about and practice ethical behavior in the use of technology.

## Part 13. ASSESSMENT and EVALUATION

Alcohol, tobacco, and other drugs program (ATODP) must conduct regular assessment and evaluations. ATODP must employ effective qualitative and quantitative methodologies as appropriate, to determine whether and to what degree the stated mission, goals, and student learning and development outcomes are being met. The process must employ sufficient and sound assessment measures to ensure comprehensiveness. Data collected must include responses from students and other affected constituencies.

The ATODP must evaluate periodically how well they complement and enhance the institution's stated mission and educational effectiveness. Results of these evaluations must be used in revising and improving programs and services and in recognizing staff performance.

The ATODP must assess systematically the following campus factors:
- attitudes, beliefs, and behaviors regarding alcohol, tobacco, and other drug use, abuse, and dependency
- consequences of alcohol, tobacco, or other drug use or abuse upon social skills; academic and work performance; property damage; policy violations; health, counseling, and disciplinary caseloads; and other indicators of problems
- perceptions of campus alcohol, tobacco, and other drug use norms
- features of the environment that abet high-risk alcohol use, tobacco, and other drug use marketing and promotion that promotes heavy or underage consumption of alcohol; inconsistent enforcement of campus policy and community law; lack of availability of alcohol-free social and recreational options on campus and in the surrounding community

The ATODP should assess the norms, behaviors, and behavioral consequences of specific focus populations.

The ATODP and other campus entities must exchange general and non-confidential assessment results of mutual application and benefit.

# THE ROLE of CAMPUS ACTIVITIES
## *CAS* Standards Contextual Statement

One of the first noted formal campus organizations established for the purpose of bringing students together (primarily for debating important issues of the day) was the Oxford Union founded in 1823. The Union's clubs also provided educational opportunities beyond the classroom, through such group activities as discussions of literature and poetry and involvement in hobbies and recreational activities. Today, numerous clubs and organizations (hundreds on some campuses) offer students opportunities to learn through their involvement in campus life.. There is little debate now that the collegiate experience involves what occurs outside the classroom and that a college education includes more than what goes on in the classroom.

Campus activities is the combined efforts of clubs and organizations established for and/or by students, including, but not limited to, governance, leadership, cultural, social, diversity, recreational, artistic, political and religious activities. Many of these efforts focus on programs that serve to educate, develop, or entertain club, organization, or group members, their guests, and the campus community.

Theory of involvement contends that the amount of energy—both physical and psychological—that students expend at their institution positively affects their development during college. Students who are involved in campus life also devote considerable energy to their academic programs, spend considerable time on campus, participate actively in student organizations, and interact frequently with other students. Campus activities is one of the vehicles for involving students with the institution.

Though students' efforts are the backbone of campus activities, campus activity advisors serve as the catalysts for these efforts. They plan and implement training for student leaders and group members to assist them in attaining their goals, primarily regarding working with others; provide continuity for student clubs and organizations from year to year; educate students about institution policy, related legal matters, and fiscal responsibility; mediate conflicts between individuals and groups; encourage innovation and responsibility in program implementation; provide opportunities to practice leadership and organizational skills; integrate knowledge gained in the classroom with actual practice; and instruct about ethics, diversity, and other critical values.

The role of campus activity advisors is certainly linked to the quality of a student's involvement experience and thus a student's development. The CAS Standards and Guidelines that follow offer direction for campus activity advisors to create quality campus activity programs that are engaging, developmental, and experiential.

## References, Readings, and Resources

Boatman, S. (1997). Leadership programs in campus activities. *The management of campus activities.* Columbia, SC: National Association of Campus Activities Education Foundation.

Cuyjet, M. J. (1996). Program development and group advising. In S. R. Komives & D. B. Woodward, Jr. (Eds.), *Student services: A handbook for the profession* (3rd ed., pp. 397-414). San Francisco: Jossey-Bass.

Julian, F. (1997). Law and campus life. *The management of student activities.* Columbia, SC: National Association for Campus Activities.

Meabon, D., Krehbiel, L., & Suddick, D. (1996). Financing campus activities. *The management of student activities.* Columbia, SC: National Association for Campus Activities.

Metz, N. D. (1996). *Student development in college unions and student activities.* Bloomington, IN: Association of College Unions International

Nejman, M. R. (1995). *Diversity, student activities, and their roles in community colleges: Developing an effective program to achieve unity through diversity.* Columbia, SC: National Association for Campus Activities.

Roberts, D. C. (2003). Community Building and Programming. In S. R. Komives & D. B. Woodard (Eds.), *Student Services: A handbook for the profession* (4th ed.) (pp. 539-554). San Francisco: Jossey Bass.

Skipper, T. L. & Argo, R. (Eds.). (2003). *Involvement in campus activities and the retention of first-year college students.* Columbia, SC: National Resource Center for the First-Year Experience & Students in Transition and National Association of Campus Activities.

American College Personnel Association, Commission for Students, Their Activities and Their Community. One Dupont Circle, N.W., Suite 300, Washington, DC 20036-1110. (202) 835-2272.

Association of College Unions International (ACUI), One City Center. 120 W. Seventh Street, Suite 200, Bloomington, IN 47404-3925

National Association for College Activities. 13 Harbison Way, Columbia, SC 29212-3401. (803) 732-6222. Web Page: www.naca.org

# CAMPUS ACTIVITIES PROGRAM
## *CAS* Standards and Guidelines (2002)

## Part 1. MISSION

The campus activities program (CAP) must incorporate student learning and student development in its mission. The CAP must enhance overall educational experiences. The CAP must develop, record, disseminate, implement and regularly review its mission and goals. Mission statements must be consistent with the mission and goals of the institution and with the standards in this document. The CAP must operate as an integral part of the institution's overall mission.

The CAP must complement the institution's academic programs. The purposes must enhance the overall educational experiences of students through development of, exposure to, and participation in social, cultural, multicultural, intellectual, recreational, community service, and campus governance programs.

Campus activities programs should provide environments in which students and student organizations are afford opportunities and are offered assistance to . . .
- participate in co-curricular activities; participate in campus governance
- develop leadership abilities
- develop healthy interpersonal relationships; use leisure time productively
- explore activities in individual and group settings for self-understanding and growth
- learn about varied cultures and experiences, ideas and issues, art and musical forms, and
styles of life
- design and implement programs to enhance social, cultural, multi-cultural, intellectual, recreational, community service, and campus governance involvement; comprehend institutional policies and procedures and their relationship to individual and group interests and activities; and learn of and
use campus facilities and other resources

Campus activities programs should be planned and implemented collaboratively by students, professional staff, and faculty. Such programs should reflect the institution's ideals and should serve to achieve its goals. These programs especially serve to enhance the appropriate recruitment and retention of students, to strengthen campus and community relations, and to reinforce accurate images of the institution. Programs should be comprehensive and should reflect and promote the diversity of student interests and needs, allowing especially for the achievement by students of a sense of self-worth and pride.

## Part 2. PROGRAM

The formal education of students consists of the curriculum and the co-curriculum, and must promote student learning and development that is purposeful and holistic. The campus activities program (CAP) must identify relevant and desirable student learning and development outcomes and provide programs and services that encourage the achievement of those outcomes.

Relevant and desirable outcomes include intellectual growth, effective communication, realistic self-appraisal, enhanced self-esteem, clarified values, career choices, leadership development, healthy behaviors, meaningful interpersonal relationships, independence, collaboration, social responsibility, satisfying and productive lifestyles, appreciation of diversity, spiritual awareness, and achievement of personal and educational goals.

The CAP must provide evidence of its impact on the achievement of student learning and development outcomes.

The program may use the examples that follow or identify other more germane indicators.

### Student Learning & Development Outcome Domains

### Intellectual Growth
Examples of Achievement Indicators
Produces personal and educational goal statements; Employs critical thinking in problem solving; Uses complex information from a variety of sources including personal experience and observation to form a decision or opinion; Obtains a degree; Applies previously understood information and concepts to a new situation or setting; Expresses appreciation for literature, the fine arts, mathematics, sciences, and social sciences

### Effective Communication
Examples of Achievement Indicators
Writes and speaks coherently; Writes, speaks, and listens effectively; Writes and speaks after reflection; Able to influence others through writing, speaking or artistic expression; Effectively articulates abstract ideas; Uses appropriate syntax; Makes presentations or gives performances

### Enhanced Self-Esteem
Examples of Achievement Indicators
Shows self-respect and respect for others; Initiates actions toward achievement of goals; Takes reasonable risks; Demonstrates assertive behavior; Functions without need for constant reassurance from others

## Realistic Self-Appraisal
Examples of Achievement Indicators
Articulates personal skills and abilities; Makes decisions and acts in congruence with personal values; Acknowledges personal strengths and weaknesses; Articulates rationale for personal behavior; Seeks feedback from others; Learns from past experiences

## Clarified Values
Examples of Achievement Indicators
Articulates personal values; Acts in congruence with personal values; Makes decisions that reflect personal values; Demonstrates willingness to scrutinize personal beliefs and values; Identifies personal, work and lifestyle values and explains how they influence decision-making

## Career Choices
Examples of Achievement Indicators
Articulates career choices based on assessment of interests, values, skills and abilities; Documents knowledge, skills and accomplishments resulting from formal education, work experience, community service and volunteer experiences; Makes the connections between classroom and out-of-classroom learning; Can construct a resume with clear job objectives and evidence of related knowledge, skills and accomplishments; Articulates the characteristics of a preferred work environment; Comprehends the world of work; Takes steps to initiate a job search or seek advanced education

## Leadership Development
Examples of Achievement Indicators
Understands that leadership is a process rather than a position; Acknowledges that leadership is relational; Understands that everyone has a leadership capacity; Engages in the leadership process in increasing levels of quality and quantity; Analyzes contexts that influence the leadership process (i.e., characteristics of self and others, society, organizations); Relates insights to the application of the leadership process; Recognizes the ethical components of leadership;

## Healthy Behavior
Examples of Achievement Indicators
Chooses behaviors and environments that promote health and reduce risk; Articulate the relationship between health and wellness and accomplishing life long goals; Exhibits behaviors that advance a healthy community

## Meaningful Interpersonal Relationships
Examples of Achievement Indicators
Develops and maintains satisfying interpersonal relationships; Establishes mutually rewarding relationships with friends and colleagues; Listens to and considers others' points of view; Treats others with respect

## Independence
Examples of Achievement Indicators
Exhibits self-reliant behaviors; Functions autonomously; Exhibits ability to function interdependently; Accepts supervision as needed; Manages time effectively

## Collaboration
Examples of Achievement Indicators
Works cooperatively with others; Seeks the involvement of others; Seeks feedback from others; Contributes to achievement of a group goal; Exhibits effective listening skills

## Social Responsibility
Examples of Achievement Indicators
Understands and participates in relevant governance systems; Understands, abides by, and participates in the development, maintenance, and/or orderly change of community, social, and legal standards or norms; Appropriately challenges the unfair, unjust, or uncivil behavior of other individuals or groups; Participates in service/volunteer activities

## Satisfying and Productive Lifestyles
Examples of Achievement Indicators
Achieves balance between education, work and leisure time; Articulates and meets goals for work, leisure and education; Overcomes obstacles that hamper goal achievement; Functions on the basis of personal identity, ethical, spiritual and moral values; Articulates long-term goals and objectives

## Appreciating Diversity
Examples of Achievement Indicators
Understands ones own identity and culture. Seeks involvement with people different from oneself; Seeks involvement in diverse interests; Articulates the advantages and challenges of a diverse society; Challenges appropriately abusive use of stereotypes by others; Understands the impact of diversity on one's own society

## Spiritual Awareness
Examples of Achievement Indicators
Develops and articulates personal belief system; Understands roles of spirituality in personal and group values and behaviors

## Personal and Educational Goals
Examples of Achievement Indicators
Sets, articulates, and pursues individual goals; Articulates personal and educational goals and objectives; Uses personal and educational goals to guide decisions; Understands the effect of one's personal and education goals on others

The CAP must be (a) intentional, (b) coherent, (c) based on theories and knowledge of learning and human development, (d) reflective of developmental and demographic profiles of the student population, and (e) responsive to needs of individuals, special populations, and communities.

Campus activities must include social, cultural, multicultural, intellectual, recreational, governance, leadership, group development, campus and community service, and entertainment programs. Effective administrative support and individual and group advising must be provided.

The CAP should be based on valid indicators of student needs and interests, such as results of needs assessment surveys, research findings, professional literature, and judgments of professionals.

The CAP should be of broad scope, inclusive of all educational domains for student learning and development. Representative programming includes activities that:

- reinforce classroom instruction and complement academic learning
- offer instruction and experience in social skills and social interactions
- provide opportunities for individual participation in group membership and leadership
- develop citizenship through participation in campus and community affairs
- foster campus and community inter group participation in common concerns and interests
- promote physical and psychosocial well being
- stimulate the cultural, intellectual, and social life of the campus community
- promote understanding of people of varied cultures and ethnic backgrounds
- raise awareness about and address the needs of women, persons with disabilities and other special populations
- develop and disseminate activities calendars, organizational directories, student handbooks, and other materials on public events
- foster meaningful interactions between students and members of the faculty, administration, and staff

The CAP should be promoted and produced according to professional practices and protocols. They should blend into the fabric of the institution, adding richness and texture to on going and integral functions. Programs may evolve from student self governing bodies which may conduct a wide variety of activities and services, including executive, judicial, legislative, business functions, and educational programs consistent with institutional values and mission.

The CAP may involve recruiting, negotiating, and contracting with performers by students. Entertainment should reflect the values stated in the campus activities mission statement. Admission fees for activities should be maintained at levels that encourage wide spread student attendance at events. Policies should discourage hospitality requirements allowing for the provision of alcohol for entertainers. A constituency based advisory system should be in place for activities planning, execution, and evaluation.

## Part 3. LEADERSHIP

Effective and ethical leadership is essential to the success of all organizations. Institutions must appoint, position and empower campus activities program (CAP) leaders within the administrative structure to accomplish stated missions. CAP leaders at various levels must be selected on the basis of formal education and training, relevant work experience, personal skills and competencies, relevant professional credentials, as well as potential for promoting learning and development in students, applying effective practices to educational processes, and enhancing institutional effectiveness. Institutions must determine expectations of accountability for leaders and fairly assess their performance.

CAP leaders must exercise authority over resources for which they are responsible to achieve their respective missions.

CAP leaders must:

- articulate a vision for their organization
- set goals and objectives based on the needs and capabilities of the population served
- promote student learning and development
- prescribe and practice ethical behavior
- recruit, select, supervise, and develop others in the organization
- manage financial resources
- coordinate human resources
- plan, budget for, and evaluate personnel and programs
- apply effective practices to educational and administrative processes
- communicate effectively
- initiate collaborative interaction between individuals and agencies that possess legitimate concerns and interests in the functional area

CAP leaders must identify and find means to address individual, organizational, or environmental conditions that inhibit goal achievement.

CAP leaders must promote campus environments that result in multiple opportunities for student learning and development.

CAP leaders must continuously improve programs and services in response to changing needs of students and other constituents, and evolving institutional priorities.

54

## Part 4. ORGANIZATION and MANAGEMENT

**Guided by an overarching intent to ensure student learning and development, the campus activities program (CAP) must be structured purposefully and managed effectively to achieve stated goals. Evidence of appropriate structure must include current and accessible policies and procedures, written performance expectations for all employees, functional workflow graphics or organizational charts, and clearly stated service delivery expectations.**

**Evidence of effective management must include use of comprehensive and accurate information for decisions, clear sources and channels of authority, effective communication practices, decision-making and conflict resolution procedures, responsiveness to changing conditions, accountability and evaluation systems, and recognition and reward processes. CAP must provide channels within the organization for regular review of administrative policies and procedures.**

The administrative leader of campus activities programs normally is responsible to the chief student affairs officer.

## Part 5. HUMAN RESOURCES

**The campus activities program (CAP) must be staffed adequately by individuals qualified to accomplish its mission and goals. Within established guidelines of the institution, CAP must establish procedures for staff selection, training, and evaluation; set expectations for supervision, and provide appropriate professional development opportunities. The program must strive to improve the professional competence and skills of all personnel it employs.**

**CAP professional staff members must hold an earned graduate degree in a field relevant to the position they hold or must possess an appropriate combination of educational credentials and related work experience.**

Professional staff members should be qualified by experience and formal graduate studies including at least a master's degree in college student affairs, higher education administration, or a related program. Graduate studies should include courses in the behavioral sciences, management, recreation, student affairs, student development, and research techniques. Institutions may require particular training and experience appropriate to serving distinctive campus populations and specialized campus or community needs.

The primary functions of full time professional staff members include the administration and coordination of campus activities programs; assessment of student interests and needs; planning, implementing, and evaluating programs for students; advising student groups; and advising student self governance organizations.

Depending upon the scope of campus activities programs, the activities staff may include an activities director, a program coordinator, organization and program advisors, orientation and leadership specialists, and a financial officer.

At least one professional staff member should be assigned to be responsible for campus activities programs at each institution. Qualifications of campus activities staff members include:
• ability to collaborate with faculty, administrative, staff colleagues, students and all other constituencies
• capacity to interpret student concerns and interests to the campus community
• expertise in the developmental education of students
• skill to create and deliver programs, activities, and services to students and to student groups
• skill for promoting student leadership
• capability of serving as a role model of ethical behavior
• commitment to professional and personal development
• knowledge of group dynamics and abilities to work effectively with groups

**Degree or credential-seeking interns must be qualified by enrollment in an appropriate field of study and by relevant experience. These individuals must be trained and supervised adequately by professional CAP staff members holding educational credentials and related work experience appropriate for supervision.**

**Student employees and volunteers must be carefully selected, trained, supervised, and evaluated. They must be trained on how and when to refer those in need of assistance to qualified staff members and have access to a supervisor for assistance in making these judgments. Student employees and volunteers must be provided clear and precise job descriptions, pre-service training based on assessed needs, and continuing staff development.**

Individuals such as part time professionals, graduate assistants, practicum and internship students, hourly wage employees, and volunteers may support full time professional staff and assist with campus activities programs.

**The CAP must have technical and support staff members adequate to accomplish its mission. CAP staff members must be technologically proficient and qualified to perform their job functions, be knowledgeable of ethical and legal uses of technology, and have access to training. The level of staffing and workloads must be adequate and appropriate for program and service demands.**

Salary levels and fringe benefits for all CAP staff members must be commensurate with those for comparable positions within the institution, in similar institutions, and in the relevant geographic area.

The CAP must institute hiring and promotion practices that are fair, inclusive, and non-discriminatory. Programs and services must employ a diverse staff to provide readily identifiable role models for students and to enrich the campus community.

The CAP must create and maintain position descriptions for all CAP staff members and provide regular performance planning and appraisals.

The CAP must have a system for regular staff evaluation and must provide access to continuing education and professional development opportunities, including in-service training programs and participation in professional conferences and workshops.

Thorough training should be provided for student employees and volunteers to enable them to carry out their duties and responsibilities and to enhance their personal experiences with campus activities programs. Appropriate training should be offered for all staff members. Training in leadership, organizational planning, ethical decision making and communication skills should be emphasized. Staff members should develop resourcefulness, empathy, openness to serving a diverse student population, and creativity.

Joint ventures in staff development should be encouraged by colleagues in allied programs such as recreational sports, residence halls programming, and special programs for students of traditionally under represented groups and international students, regardless of whether they are administratively connected with campus activities programs.

Student participation in campus activities should be encouraged. Students should be trained in leadership concepts and skills, organizational development, ethical behavior, and other skill training particular to distinctive programming requirements, such as contracting for entertainment. Training should emphasize mutual sensitivity, recognizing diverse and special student or community population needs.

## Part 6. FINANCIAL RESOURCES

The campus activities program (CAP) must have adequate funding to accomplish its mission and goals. Funding priorities must be determined within the context of the stated mission, goals, objectives, and comprehensive analysis of the needs and capabilities of students and the availability of internal or external resources.

The CAP must demonstrate fiscal responsibility and cost effectiveness consistent with institutional protocols.

Methods for collecting and allocating fees must be clear and equitable. The authority and processes for decisions relevant to campus activities fees must be clearly established and funds be spent consistent with established priorities.

Funds for campus activities programs may be provided through state appropriations, institutional budgets, activities fees, user fees, membership and other specialized fees, revenues from programming or fund raising projects, grants, and foundation resources. Funds may be supplemented by income from ticket sales, sales of promotional items, and individual or group gifts consistent with institutional policies.

Students who have fiscal responsibility must be provided with information and training regarding institutional regulations and policies that govern accounting and handling of funds.

Adequate funding should be available for CAP including social, cultural, multicultural, intellectual, recreational, and campus governance programs.

Authority for decisions relevant to campus activities fees should rest in large part with students. Because of the amounts of money generated by campus activities and because of the transience of the student population, good business practice dictates that reasonable safeguards be established to ensure responsible management of and accounting for the funds involved. Student organizations may be required to maintain their funds with the institution's business office in which an account for each group is established and where bookkeeping and auditing services are provided. When possible, it is recommended that processes be established to permit individual student organizations to keep account of their own business transactions. Within this framework, the campus activities office works collaboratively with student organizations on matters of bookkeeping and budgeting, and other matters of fiscal accountability, including contract negotiations, consistent with institutional practices.

Mandatory activities fees normally are initiated by a vote of the student body. The fees, once approved through institutional processes, may be managed and allocations distributed by representative student governing bodies or by another allocations board or committee.

Finance committees of student organizations or student governments should work collaboratively with staff members to establish campus activities fees and priorities. Students and staff members should share responsibility for budget development and implementation according to mutually established program priorities. Specialized fees, generally applicable to college unions and residence halls governing groups and administered by their representative governing bodies, can be considered as part of the overall funding of the range of student activities available. In addition, professional staff members should educate students about the basics of financial management.

## Part 7. FACILITIES, TECHNOLOGY, EQUIPMENT

The campus activities program (CAP) must have adequate, suitably located facilities, adequate technology, and equipment to support its mission and goals efficiently and effectively. Facilities, technology, and equipment must be evaluated regularly and be in compliance with relevant federal, state, provincial, and local requirements to provide for access, health, safety, and security.

Facilities should be located conveniently and designed with flexibility to serve the wide variety of functions associated with campus activities. Appropriate facilities, accessible to all clients, should be provided including student organization offices and adequately equipped public performance spaces.

The CAP may occur in college unions. [See Standards and Guidelines for College Unions.] In addition to their traditional programming, social and service facilities, unions typically house campus activities programs, student organization offices, and related meeting and work and storage rooms. Campus activities functions also may take place in the residence halls, recreation centers, fraternity and sorority houses, sports facilities, and other campus locations. Staff and student space should be designed to encourage maximum interaction among students and between staff members and students.

## Part 8. LEGAL RESPONSIBILITIES

Campus activities program (CAP) staff members must be knowledgeable about and responsive to laws and regulations that relate to their respective responsibilities. CAP staff members must inform users of programs and services and officials, as appropriate, of legal obligations and limitations including constitutional, statutory, regulatory, and case law; mandatory laws and orders emanating from federal, state/provincial and local governments; and the institution's policies.

CAP staff members must use reasonable and informed practices to limit the liability exposure of the institution, its officers, employees, and agents. Staff members must be informed about institutional policies regarding personal liability and related insurance coverage options.

The institution must provide access to legal advice for CAP staff members as needed to carry out assigned responsibilities. Further, the institution must inform CAP staff and students in a timely and systematic fashion about extraordinary or changing legal obligations and potential liabilities.

## Part 9. EQUITY and ACCESS

Campus Activity Program (CAP) staff members must ensure that services and programs are provided on a fair and equitable basis. Facilities, programs, and services must be accessible. Hours of operation and delivery of and access to programs and services must be responsive to the needs of all students and other constituents. The CAP must adhere to the spirit and intent of equal opportunity laws.

The CAP must be open and readily accessible to all students and must not discriminate except where sanctioned by law and institutional policy. Discrimination must especially be avoided on the bases of age; color, creed; cultural heritage; disability; ethnicity; gender identity; nationality; political affiliation, religious affiliation, sex, sexual orientation; or economic, marital, social, or veteran status.

Consistent with their mission and goals, the CAP must take affirmative action to remedy significant imbalances in student participation and staffing patterns.

As the demographic profiles of campuses change and new instructional delivery methods are introduced, institutions must recognize the needs of students who participate in distance learning for access to programs and services offered on campus. Institutions must provide appropriate services in ways that are accessible to distance learners and assist them in identifying and gaining access to other appropriate services in their geographic region.

## Part 10. CAMPUS and EXTERNAL RELATIONS

The campus activities program (CAP) must establish, maintain, and promote effective relations with relevant individuals, campus offices, and external agencies.

The campus activities program should encourage faculty and staff members throughout the campus community to be involved in campus activities. Faculty members should serve as valuable resources related to their academic disciplines, especially as lecturers, performers, artists, and workshop facilitators. Faculty and staff members who serve as administrative advisors may work directly with organizations in program and leadership development and should be supported by the activities staff. Faculty, staff members, and administrators external to the program or institution may be important resources for activities programs. Faculty and staff members, administrators, and students may serve together on advisory boards to provide leadership for important initiatives.

Campus activities programs are highly visible to persons on and off campus and may be influential in forming public opinion about the institution and creating a positive environment for both communities. Cooperation between governmental and social organizations and campus activities programs on matters of mutual community concern strengthens the institution's role in the community, expands the resources available to both communities, and provides valuable developmental opportunities for students.

## Part 11: DIVERSITY

**Within the context of each institution's unique mission, diversity enriches the community and enhances the collegiate experience for all; therefore, the campus activities program (CAP) must nurture environments where commonalties and differences among people are recognized and honored.**

**The CAP must promote educational experiences that are characterized by open and continuous communication that deepens understanding of one's own identity, culture, and heritage, and that of others. The CAP must educate and promote respect about commonalties and differences in their historical and cultural contexts.**

**The CAP must address the characteristics and needs of a diverse population when establishing and implementing policies and procedures.**

**The CAP must provide educational activities that sensitize all constituencies to an appreciation and understanding of cultural diversity among people. Activities programs must emphasize self assessment and personal responsibility for improving intercultural relations.**

**The CAP must provide educational programs that help students of traditionally under represented groups identify their unique needs, set appropriate goals, and learn how to achieve them. All students must be oriented to the culture of the institution. The program must give special attention to students from traditionally under represented groups to ensure their best chances of success.**

## Part 12. ETHICS

**All persons involved in the delivery of the Campus Activities Program (CAP) must adhere to the highest principles of ethical behavior. The CAP must develop or adopt and implement appropriate statements of ethical practice. The program must publish these statements and ensure their periodic review by relevant constituencies .**

Applicable statements may include principles and standards pertaining to:
- civil and ethical conduct

- accuracy of information (i.e., accurate presentation of institutional goals, services, and policies to the public and the college or university community, and fair and accurate representation in publicity and promotions)
- conflict of interest
- role conflicts
- fiscal accountability
- fair and equitable administration of institutional policies; effective disclosure of and respect for relevant civil and criminal law
- student involvement in related institutional decisions
- free and open exchange of ideas through campus activities programs
- fulfillment of contractual arrangements and agreements

**CAP staff members must ensure that privacy and confidentiality are maintained with respect to all communications and records to the extent that such records are protected under the law and appropriate statements of ethical practice. Information contained in students' education records must not be disclosed without written consent except as allowed by relevant laws and institutional policies. CAP staff members must disclose to appropriate authorities information judged to be of an emergency nature, especially when the safety of the individual or others is involved, or when otherwise required by institutional policy or relevant law.**

**All CAP staff members must be aware of and comply with the provisions contained in the institution's human subjects research policy and in other relevant institutional policies addressing ethical practices and confidentiality of research data concerning individuals.**

**CAP staff members must recognize and avoid personal conflict of interest or appearance thereof in their transactions with students and others.**

**CAP staff members must strive to ensure the fair, objective, and impartial treatment of all persons with whom they deal. Staff members must not participate in nor condone any form of harassment that demeans persons or creates an intimidating, hostile, or offensive campus environment.**

**When handling institutional funds, all CAP staff members must ensure that such funds are managed in accordance with established and responsible accounting procedures and the fiscal policies or processes of the institution.**

**CAP staff members must perform their duties within the limits of their training, expertise, and competence. When these limits are exceeded,**

individuals in need of further assistance must be referred to persons possessing appropriate qualifications.

CAP staff members must use suitable means to confront and otherwise hold accountable other staff members who exhibit unethical behavior.

CAP staff members must be knowledgeable about and practice ethical behavior in the use of technology.

## Part 13. ASSESSMENT and EVALUATION

The campus activities program (CAP) must conduct regular assessment and evaluations. The CAP must employ effective qualitative and quantitative methodologies as appropriate, to determine whether and to what degree the stated mission, goals, and student learning and development outcomes are being met. The process must employ sufficient and sound assessment measures to ensure comprehensiveness. Data collected must include responses from students and other affected constituencies.

The CAP must evaluate periodically how well they complement and enhance the institution's stated mission and educational effectiveness.

Results of these evaluations must be used in revising and improving programs and services and in recognizing staff performance.

Campus activities programs should be evaluated regularly and the findings should be disseminated to appropriate campus agencies and constituencies. Evaluation procedures should yield evidence relative to student success and retention, the achievement of program goals, quality and scope of program offerings, responsiveness to expressed interests, program attendance and effectiveness, cost effectiveness, quality and appearance of facilities, equipment use and maintenance, and staff performance. Data sources should include students, staff, alumni, faculty, administrators, community members, and relevant documents and records. Instrumentation and methods should be scientifically designed and implemented. Records of program evaluations should be maintained in the office of the administrative leader of campus activities programs and should be accessible to planners of subsequent programs.

# The Role of Campus Information and Visitor Services
## *CAS* Standards and Guidelines

The development of campus information and visitor services has been a direct result of the increasing diversity, size, complexity and specialization of institutions of higher learning during the 20th century. This pattern has been particularly seen on campuses in the United States and has necessitated the establishment of information centers to address the many informational needs of campus communities. Often these centers have evolved into, or have been combined with, visitor services to become comprehensive gateway operations providing entry points to institutions for visitors, prospective students, alumni, and other community members. The common objective of campus information and visitor services is to bring people and campus services and resources together through increased accessibility to information.

Some of the earliest examples of visitor services and centers include the establishment in 1951 of the Visitor Center at the U.S. Military Academy at West Point and the creation of the Visitor Information Center at the University of California at Berkeley in 1965. Historically, the majority of these programs originated as extensions of institutional recruitment activities and efforts. The earliest example of specialized information and referral services on a campus can be traced to the 1970 establishment of the Campus Assistance Center at the University of Wisconsin-Madison. Specialized information and referral programs were often established as information and rumor control efforts responding to the rapid expansion of campuses, and increasing lack of trust in traditional institutional communication methods. By providing inquirers with the information and services they needed, or referring them to the appropriate resources when necessary, these programs were quickly judged to be very useful in providing improved communication within the campus community and improving the quality of campus life. These early campus information and visitor service programs quickly became permanent campus operations with philosophies focused on access and individualized service. During this early period, many of the programs established clear guidelines for assisting inquirers

in a friendly, sensitive manner and assuring appropriate confidentiality. Campus information and visitor services programs have had a profound impact on their campus communities through their commitment to the principle of providing inquirers with clear, concise, thorough and nonjudgmental information and referrals in the most welcoming environment possible.

By the late 1980s, the increasing need for accountability, outreach, and service to the broader campus community resulted in an increase in the number of campus information and visitor services operations. Institutional accessibility to appropriate and timely information is a critical component in reaching instructional, research and outreach priorities. For many constituents, especially during downtimes—evenings, weekends and breaks—campus information and visitor services become the physical embodiment of an institution. Increasing emphasis on quality improvement and service within the higher education community has been another driving force in the growing number of campus information and visitor services. The increasing importance of computer-mediated (e.g., web and email) and mass communication (e.g., radio and cable television) in the provision of information by institutions, and the resulting need for support services that can assure the accuracy and relevance of rapidly expanding information, have also increased the importance of campus information and visitor services. By having access to an easily available and credible information and visitor service, inquirers are assisted in making well-informed choices, planning wise courses of action, and taking advantage of the available and/or unique resources of the institution and the surrounding community.

These standards and guidelines provide a framework for excellence in the provision of campus information and visitor services (CIVS). CIVS is the process of linking people who have campus-related questions to appropriate resources. Also, the process assists institutional planning by providing feedback to service providers and discovering gaps and duplication in campus programs and services. CIVS provide information to an inquirer in response to a direct request for such information. Inquiries comprise anything related to the campus community, such as directions to a campus building or event; how to contact a department, faculty or staff member; whom to contact or where to go for issues of a personal nature, to resolve a problem, or to apply for admission. Inquirers may be current students, staff, faculty, alumni, prospective students and their families, other visitors, or anyone needing information about the institution. CIVS serve as a gateway to the institution, providing one-on-one information to inquirers within and about the campus. When a direct answer is not possible, then referral is made, with careful attention to: the needs of the inquirer, assessment of appropriate resources and response modes, identification of programs and services capable of meeting those needs, provision of sufficient information about each program and service to help inquirers make informed choices, location of alternative resources when services are unavailable, and actively llinking the inquirer to needed services when necessary.

## References, Readings, and Resources

Hefferlin, J. B. L. (1971). Information Services for Academic Administration. San Francisco: Jossey-Bass.

Alliance of Information and Referral Systems (undated). Out of the Shadows: Information and Referral Bringing People and Services Together. Seattle, Washington: Author.

Alliance of Information and Referral Systems. (undated). The ABC's of I & R: A Self-Study Guide for Information and Referral Staff. Seattle, Washington: Author.

Collegiate Information and Visitor Services Association (CiVSA), Rutgers - The State University of New Jersey Campus Information Services, 542 George Street New Brunswick, New Jersey. 08901. (732) 932-9342; (732) 932-9359 (fax); Publisher of The Welcomer. Web Site: www.civsa.org

# Campus Information and Visitor Services
## *CAS* Standards and Guidelines

## Part 1. MISSION

The overall mission of campus information and visitor services (CIVS) is to facilitate access to the institution by providing accurate information and appropriate referrals. CIVS is a primary point of access to the institution. By providing comprehensive contact information and general descriptions for many aspects of the institution, CIVS must meet the introductory informational needs of the campus community: students, faculty, staff, prospective students and their family members, alumni and general visitors. To accomplish this mission, CIVS must:
- provide accurate information and referrals
- provide a welcoming environment
- be readily accessible
- emphasize personal communication and interaction

CIVS must have a strong commitment to student learning and development, contributing generally to institutional and other agency missions, and because students are an integral part of mission delivery. This commitment must be reflected in its mission statement and demonstrated through quality supervision, staff development, and performance appraisals.

CIVS must incorporate student learning and student development in its mission. CIVS must enhance overall educational experiences. The service must develop, record, disseminate, implement, and regularly review its mission and goals. Mission statements must be consistent with the mission and goals of the institution and with the standards in this document. CIVS must operate as an integral part of the institution's overall mission.

## Part 2. PROGRAM

Campus information and visitor services (CIVS) must be responsive to the needs and interests of students, faculty, staff, alumni, prospective students, and other inquirers.

A broad array of information and services must be available to ensure that accurate resources are provided in a timely manner that accommodates the needs of inquirers.
These services may include telephone or other electronic means of contact, or a walk-in facility, such as a visitor or information center, in which the inquirer has one-to-one, human contact and easy access to information resources such as catalogs, calendars, booklets, schedules, fliers, maps, books, and brochures.

Multiple media approaches must be used to provide information.
Such approaches may include signage, maps, 24-hour recorded telephone information, emergency assistance, and up-to-date web-site listings and e-mail.

The formal education of students consists of the curriculum and the co-curriculum, and must promote student learning and development that is purposeful and holistic. CIVS must identify relevant and desirable student learning and development outcomes and provide programs and services that encourage the achievement of those outcomes.

Relevant and desirable outcomes include: intellectual growth, effective communication, realistic self-appraisal, enhanced self-esteem, clarified values, career choices, leadership development, healthy behaviors, meaningful interpersonal relationships, independence, collaboration, social responsibility, satisfying and productive lifestyles, appreciation of diversity, spiritual awareness, and achievement of personal and educational goals.

CIVS must provide evidence of its impact on the achievement of student learning and development outcomes.
The CIVS may use the examples that follow or identify other more germane indicators.

### Student Learning & Development Outcomes Domains

### Personal and Educational Goals
Examples of Achievement Indicators:
    Effectively utilizes information and referral services to identify options for successful pursuit of individual goals; Can clearly articulate personal, professional and educational goals and objectives; Uses personal, professional and educational goals to guide decisions; Understands the effect of one's personal, professional and educational goals on others and the impact of these goals on decision making

### Effective Communication
Examples of Achievement Indicators:
    Effectively articulates needs and concerns; Writes and speaks coherently and effectively; Writes and speaks after reflection; Able to effect others through writing,

speaking and the information and referral role; Effectively articulates and clarifies ambiguous ideas; Uses appropriate syntax; Makes presentations or performance. Effectively utilizes active listening skills.

## Leadership Development
Examples of Achievement Indicators:
Takes steps to utilize information and referral services to identify and explore available leadership development resources; Articulates leadership philosophy or style; Serves in a leadership position within a work environment; Comprehends the dynamics of a group; Exhibits democratic principles as a leader; Exhibits ability to visualize a group purpose and desired outcomes

## Independence
Examples of Achievement Indicators:
Utilize information and referral resources to make informed and considered decisions that enhance self-reliance; Exhibits self-reliant behaviors; Functions autonomously; Exhibits ability to function interdependently; Accepts guidance and supervision as needed; Manages time effectively

## Enhanced Self-Esteem
Examples of Achievement Indicators:
Takes reasonable risks; Learns from past experience, informational requests and referrals; Shows self-respect and respect for others; Demonstrates appropriate assertive behavior; Functions without need for constant guidance, supervision or reassurance from others

## Realistic Self-Appraisal
Examples of Achievement Indicators:
Articulates personal skills, abilities and understanding; Makes good choices based on available information and knowledge and acts in congruence with personal values; Open to informational guidance and referrals from others; Acknowledges personal strengths and weaknesses; Open to feedback from others; Can assess knowledge and skills and understands role and responsibilities within organizational contexts

## Collaboration
Examples of Achievement Indicators:
Works cooperatively with others to identify and meet information and referral needs; Seeks feedback from others to make informed decisions; Works cooperatively with others in accomplishing goals and tasks; Seeks the involvement of others; Contributes to achievement of group mission and goals; Exhibits effective listening skills

## Career Choices
Examples of Achievement Indicators:
Takes steps to utilize information and referral services to identify and explore available educational and career assistance resources; Articulates the characteristics of a preferred work environment; Articulates career choices based on assessment of interests, values, skills and abilities; Comprehends the world of work; Documents knowledge, skills and accomplishments resulting from formal education, work experience, community services and volunteer experiences; Makes the connections between classroom and out-of-classroom learning

## Intellectual Growth
Examples of Achievement Indicators:
Can articulate personal and educational goal statements; Uses complex information from a variety of sources including personal experience, information and referral contact, and observation to form a decision or opinion; Employs critical thinking in problem solving; Applies previously understood information and concepts to a new situation or setting

## Social Responsibility
Examples of Achievement Indicators:
Utilizes information and referral resources to clarify community, social and legal standards or norms; Utilizes information and referral services to identify available service/volunteer activities and options: Appropriately challenges unfair, unjust, or uncivil behavior of other individuals or groups;
Understands and participates in relevant governance systems; Uses proper channels and methods to encourage change and understanding within complex bureaucratic structures and organizations

## Clarified Values
Examples of Achievement Indicators:
Articulates personal values; Makes decisions that reflect personal values; Acts in congruence with personal values; Demonstrates willingness to scrutinize personal beliefs and values; Identifies personal, work and lifestyle values and is aware of how they influence decision-making

## Appreciating Diversity
Examples of Achievement Indicators:
Seeks out information and referral resources to assist in better understanding ones own identity and culture; Effectively utilizes information and referral resources to seek involvement with diverse interests and people different from oneself;
Appropriately challenges abusive use of stereotypes by others; Articulates the advantages and challenges of a diverse community

## Meaningful Interpersonal Relationships
Examples of Achievement Indicators:
Listens to and considers others' points of view; Develops and maintains satisfying interpersonal relationships; Establishes mutually rewarding relationships with friends and colleagues; Treats others with courtesy and respect

## Satisfying and Productive Lifestyles

Examples of Achievement Indicators:

Effectively utilizes information and referral resources to identify and find solutions to problems and issues that hamper goal achievement; Articulates long-term goals and objectives; Seeks out services, programs and resources that are congruent with personal identity, ethical, spiritual and moral values;

Effectively contributes to an organization through the appropriate application of personal, ethical, spiritual and moral values

## Healthy Behavior

Examples of Achievement Indicators:

Takes steps to utilize information and referral services to identify and explore available choices that promote health and reduce risk;

Exhibits behaviors and habits that advance a healthy organization and community

**CIVS must be (a) intentional, (b) coherent, (c) based on theories and knowledge of learning and human development, (d) reflective of developmental and demographic profiles of the student population, and (e) responsive to needs of individuals, special populations, and communities.**

**CIVS must provide specific information and referral to existing campus programs or, when such programs do not exist, actively link inquirers to alternative community and other programs that can meet their specific needs.**

**CIVS programs must be easily accessible to assist inquirers in making well-informed choices, plan wise courses of action, and take advantage of available institutional resources.**

**CIVS must develop and maintain an accurate information retrieval and delivery system of available campus and community resources. This system must be updated regularly to ensure timeliness, accuracy, and comprehensiveness of information. CIVS must be available at locations and times that meet the needs of the inquirers.**

**CIVS must provide feedback to appropriate campus officials regarding conditions that may negatively influence an inquirer's interaction with the institution and propose interventions to remedy such conditions.**

Feedback topics may include statistics, data analysis, relevant documentation of service use (identifying unmet needs, gaps, and services duplication), and inquirer characteristics.

**CIVS must strive to assist inquirers in friendly, caring, sensitive and non-judgmental manner** and provide clear, concise information. **CIVS must protect the privacy of individuals within the campus community from inappropriate inquiry.**

**CIVS must establish and maintain a planned program of activities to increase campus and community awareness of its services, mission, goals, and objectives.**

Campus information and visitor services may include a campus visitor center, a campus information center, a campus tour program, broadcast services, campus outreach, and student recruitment programs. Information and services may include . . .

- campus orientation and tour programs
- display and presentation space
- broadcast and electronic informational resources and support
- visitor reception space including appropriate support services and facilities adequate in size and scope to meet the volume of inquirers to be assisted

CIVS should be a principal provider of structure and content to the institution's on-line information systems.

A range of information should be provided to inquirers, including brief responses, such as names or phone numbers, as well as details about an organization's policies and procedures.

Program activities may include . . .

- participation in training programs of other offices and departments
- provision of printed materials such as brochures, posters, directional information and exhibits
- public service announcements
- hosting orientation tours
- information-based web site
- role as a resource for other campus and community support services

## Part 3. LEADERSHIP

**Effective and ethical leadership is essential to the success of all organizations. Institutions must appoint, position and empower campus information and visitor services (CIVS) leaders within the administrative structure to accomplish stated missions. CIVS leaders at various levels must be selected on the basis of formal education and training, relevant work experience, personal skills and competencies, relevant professional credentials, as well as potential for promoting learning and development in students, applying effective practices to educational processes, and enhancing institutional effectiveness. Institutions must determine expectations of accountability for leaders and fairly assess their performance.**

**CIVS leaders of programs and services must exercise authority over resources for which they are responsible to achieve their respective missions.**

CIVS leaders must . . .
- articulate a vision for their organization
- set goals and objectives based on the needs and capabilities of the population served
- promote student learning and development
- prescribe and practice ethical behavior
- recruit, select, supervise, and develop others in the organization
- manage financial resources
- coordinate human resources
- plan, budget for, and evaluate personnel and programs
- apply effective practices to educational and administrative processes
- communicate effectively
- initiate collaborative interaction between individuals and agencies that possess legitimate concerns and interests in the functional area

CIVS leaders must identify and find means to address individual, organizational, or environmental conditions that inhibit goal achievement.

CIVS leaders must promote campus environments that result in multiple opportunities for student learning and development. Likewise, leaders must continuously improve programs and services in response to changing needs of students and other constituents, and evolving institutional priorities.

## Part 4. ORGANIZATION and MANAGEMENT

Campus information and visitor services (CIVS) is most effective in an atmosphere of staff teamwork and continuous improvement.

Guided by an overarching intent to ensure student learning and development, CIVS must be structured purposefully and managed effectively to achieve stated goals. Evidence of appropriate structure must include current and accessible policies and procedures, written performance expectations for all employees, functional workflow graphics or organizational charts, and clearly stated service delivery expectations.

Evidence of effective management must include use of comprehensive and accurate information for decisions, clear sources and channels of authority, effective communication practices, decision-making and conflict resolution procedures, responsiveness to changing conditions, accountability and evaluation systems, and recognition and reward processes. CIVS must provide channels within the organization for

regular review of administrative policies and procedures.

CIVS must have well developed policies regarding the type, breadth and currency of information contained in the information retrieval and delivery system. The information retrieval and delivery system used by campus information and visitor services must be organized according to a standardized search system. The information system must have the capacity to accept changes in a very short time frame for information that may change in between regularly scheduled updates.
Policies for the information retrieval and delivery system should include, but not be limited to, responsiveness to inquirers and proximity of the resource to the campus.

CIVS must develop and maintain accurate, up-to-date resource files that include information on available campus resources and procedures for verifying accuracy.
Informational resources should be profiled to include . . .
- legal name, common name, and acronym address (i.e., room, building name, street, city, zip code)
- email address
- telephone number, fax number, hours and days of service
- type and description of service(s) provided
- population(s) served
- date of last update
- internet address
- eligibility guidelines
- intake procedures
- required documents
- cost
- waiting period for service
- contact person
- auspices (i.e., city, state, private, social service, campus)

CIVS must establish and use a system of collecting and organizing inquirer data for appropriate referral and feedback to the campus community.
Campus information and visitor services should pursue meaningful research to review and improve programs and services. Members of the campus community should be involved in the review of these findings, as well as in the design and governance of campus information and visitor services. Students, faculty, staff, and appropriate external agencies should be involved through committees, councils, and boards.

## Part 5. HUMAN RESOURCES

Campus information and visitor services (CIVS) must be staffed adequately by individuals qualified to accomplish its mission and goals. Within established guidelines of the institution, CIVS must establish procedures for staff selection, training, and evaluation; set expectations for supervision, and provide appropriate professional development opportunities. CIVS must strive to improve the professional competence and skills of all personnel it employs.

Continuing staff development experiences should include in-service training programs, professional conferences, workshops, and other continuing education activities.

CIVS staff positions must be filled based on a defined set of qualifications such as level of education, work experience, and personal characteristics (for example, integrity, communication skills, and leadership ability).

Professional staff members must hold an earned graduate degree in a field relevant to the position description they hold or must possess an appropriate combination of education and experience.

CIVS must intentionally seek to employ qualified students, paraprofessional employees, and recruit volunteers to assist in carrying out programs and services.

Degree or credential-seeking interns must be qualified by enrollment in an appropriate field of study and by relevant experience. These individuals must be trained and supervised adequately by professional staff members holding educational credentials and related work experience appropriate for supervision.

Student employees and volunteers must be carefully selected, trained, supervised, and evaluated. They must be trained on how and when to refer those in need of assistance to qualified staff members and have access to a supervisor for assistance in making these judgments. Student employees and volunteers must be provided clear and precise job descriptions, pre-service training based on assessed needs, and continuing staff development.

CIVS must have technical and support staff members adequate to accomplish its mission. Staff members must be technologically proficient and qualified to perform their job functions, be knowledgeable of ethical and legal uses of technology, and have access to training. The level of staffing and workloads must be adequate and appropriate for program and service demands.

A formal training program must be required for all staff, especially those who will be providing direct service.

Training programs should include experiences for initial employee orientations as well as on-the-job training, in-service group training, and individualized training based on employee needs.

Staff-training programs should include . . .
- strategies for understanding campus and community resources
- information retrieval, delivery and data collection
- overview of mission, vision, role, purpose, function, structure, policies, and procedures
- student development theory and practice
- customer service and basic communication skills such as interviewing, listening, empathy, clarification and problem solving; overcoming communication barriers (e.g., hearing impaired, speakers of English as a second language)

Salary levels and fringe benefits for all CIVS staff members must be commensurate with those for comparable positions within the institution, in similar institutions, and in the relevant geographic area.

CIVS must institute hiring and promotion practices that are fair, inclusive, and non-discriminatory. CIVS must employ a diverse staff to provide readily identifiable role models for students and to enrich the campus community. Every CIVS staff member must be expected to show respect for all inquirers.

CIVS must create and maintain position descriptions for all staff members and provide regular performance planning and appraisals.

CIVS must have a system for regular staff evaluation and must provide access to continuing education and professional development opportunities, including in-service training programs and participation in professional conferences and workshops.

Periodic formal written evaluations of CIVS staff must be conducted and kept on record.

## Part 6. FINANCIAL RESOURCES

Campus information and visitor services (CIVS) must have adequate funding to accomplish its mission and goals. Funding priorities must be determined within the context of the stated mission, goals, objectives, and comprehensive analysis of the needs and capabilities of students and the availability of internal or external resources.

CIVS must demonstrate fiscal responsibility and cost effectiveness consistent with institutional protocols.

Institutional funds for campus information and visitor services should be allocated on a permanent basis.

In addition to institutional commitment of general funds, other funding sources may be considered including state appropriations, federal resources, fees and generated revenue, local community funding, donations, and contributions.

Financial resources should be sufficient to provide high quality print and electronic information.

## Part 7. FACILITIES, TECHNOLOGY and EQUIPMENT

Campus information and visitor services (CIVS) must have adequate, suitably located facilities, adequate technology, and equipment to support its mission and goals efficiently and effectively. Facilities, technology, and equipment must be evaluated regularly and be in compliance with relevant federal, state, provincial, and local requirements to provide for access, health, safety, and security.

CIVS must play an active role in the design and decision making process for campus signage.

The CIVS facility should include space for confidential interviewing, display for materials, visitor reception, and information and referral operations. State-of-the-art telephone and computer capability should also be included.

The CIVS facility should be accessible to and by public transportation and be at a location that can best represent the "front door" of the institution.

## Part 8. LEGAL RESPONSIBILITIES

Campus information and visitor services (CIVS) staff members must be knowledgeable about and responsive to laws and regulations that relate to their respective responsibilities. Staff members must inform users of programs and services and officials, as appropriate, of legal obligations and limitations including constitutional, statutory, regulatory, and case law; mandatory laws and orders emanating from federal, state/provincial and local governments; and the institution's policies.

CIVS staff members must use reasonable and informed practices to limit the liability exposure of the institution, its officers, employees, and agents. Staff members must be informed about institutional policies regarding personal liability and related insurance coverage options.

The institution must provide access to legal advice for CIVS staff members as needed to carry out assigned responsibilities.

The institution must inform CIVS staff and students in a timely and systematic fashion about extraordinary or changing legal obligations and potential liabilities.

## Part 9. EQUITY and ACCESS

Campus information and visitor services (CIVS) staff members must ensure that services and programs are provided on a fair and equitable basis. Facilities, programs and services must be accessible. Hours of operation and delivery of and access to programs and services must be responsive to the needs of all students and other constituents. CIVS must adhere to the spirit and intent of equal opportunity laws.

CIVS must be open and readily accessible to all students and must not discriminate except where sanctioned by law and institutional policy. Discrimination must especially be avoided on the bases of age; color, creed; cultural heritage; disability; ethnicity; gender identity; nationality; political affiliation, religious affiliation, sex, sexual orientation; or economic, marital, social, or veteran status.

Consistent with their mission and goals, CIVS must take affirmative action to remedy significant imbalances in student participation and staffing patterns.

As the demographic profiles of campuses change and new instructional delivery methods are introduced, institutions must recognize the needs of students who participate in distance learning for access to programs and services offered on campus. □Institutions must provide appropriate services in ways that are accessible to distance learners and assist them in identifying and gaining access to other appropriate services in their geographic region.

## Part 10. CAMPUS and EXTERNAL RELATIONS

Campus information and visitor services must establish, maintain, and promote effective relations with relevant individuals, campus offices, and external agencies.

CIVS should collaborate closely with campus offices and external agencies to ensure accuracy, timeliness, and reliability of information being provided to inquirers.

When appropriate, inquirers should be referred to other resources, and staff may actively participate in this linking process. This referral process is often integrated with information dissemination, intervention, and advocacy. Inquirers should be encouraged to re-contact the campus information and visitor service if additional information or assistance is needed.

Within institutional guidelines, CIVS should intervene and advocate for inquirers when information is inaccurate or misleading and/or inquirer needs have not been addressed satisfactorily. Follow-up on more complex problem situations should occur to determine the extent to which inquirer needs have been met.

## Part 11. DIVERSITY

Within the context of each institution's unique mission, diversity enriches the community and enhances the collegiate experience for all; therefore, campus information and visitor services (CIVS) must nurture environments where commonalties and differences among people are recognized and honored.

CIVS must promote educational experiences that are characterized by open and continuous communication that deepens understanding of one's own identity, culture, and heritage, and that of others. CIVS must educate and promote respect about commonalties and differences in their historical and cultural contexts.

CIVS must address the characteristics and needs of a diverse population when establishing and implementing policies and procedures.

## Part 12. ETHICS

All persons involved in the delivery of campus information and visitor services (CIVS) must adhere to the highest principles of ethical behavior. CIVS must develop or adopt and implement appropriate statements of ethical practice. CIVS must publish these statements and ensure their periodic review by relevant constituencies .
Ethical standards or other statements from relevant professional associations should be considered.

CIVS staff members must ensure that privacy and confidentiality are maintained with respect to all communications and records to the extent that such records are protected under the law and appropriate statements of ethical practice. Information contained in students' education records must not be disclosed without written consent except as allowed by relevant laws and institutional policies. Staff members must disclose to appropriate authorities information judged to be of an emergency nature, especially when the safety of the individual or others is involved, or when otherwise required by institutional policy or relevant law.

All CIVS staff members must be aware of and comply with the provisions contained in the institution's human subjects research policy and in other relevant institutional policies addressing ethical practices and confidentiality of research data concerning individuals.

CIVS staff members must recognize and avoid personal conflict of interest or appearance thereof in their transactions with students and others.

CIVS staff members must strive to ensure the fair, objective, and impartial treatment of all persons with whom they deal. Staff members must not participate in nor condone any form of harassment that demeans persons or creates an intimidating, hostile, or offensive campus environment.

When handling institutional funds, all CIVS staff members must ensure that such funds are managed in accordance with established and responsible accounting procedures and the fiscal policies or processes of the institution.

CIVS staff members must perform their duties within the limits of their training, expertise, and competence. When these limits are exceeded, individuals in need of further assistance must be referred to persons possessing appropriate qualifications.

CIVS staff members must use suitable means to confront and otherwise hold accountable other staff members who exhibit unethical behavior.

CIVS staff members must be knowledgeable about and practice ethical behavior in the use of technology.

## Part 13. ASSESSMENT and EVALUATION

Campus information and visitor services (CIVS) must conduct regular assessment and evaluations. CIVS must employ effective qualitative and quantitative methodologies as appropriate, to determine whether and to what degree the stated mission, goals, and student learning and development outcomes are being met. The process must employ sufficient and sound assessment measures to ensure compre-hensiveness. Data collected must include responses from students and other affected constituencies.

CIVS must evaluate periodically how well they complement and enhance the institution's stated mission and educational effectiveness.

Results of these evaluations must be used in revising and improving programs and services and in recognizing staff performance. CIVS must

collect inquirer

and customer use
planning activities,
and identification of
services.
the extent to which
ion retrieval skills. All
n and visitor services
ropriate institutional

# The ROLE of CAREER SERVICES
## *CAS* Standards Contextual Statement

The first evidence of assistance in career services dates to the 19th century, when commercial employment agencies began to place graduates of the nation's teacher training programs. Over 200 such agencies existed by the late 1800s. By the turn of the century, an increasing number of institutions had begun to realize their responsibility to help graduates find jobs. When the first institutional appointment and placement services were established, faculty members typically took responsibility for them on part-time bases. Soon, many institutions established programs staffed by full-time "appointment secretaries. By 1920, approximately 75 percent of the nation's normal schools had established placement services. As a direct result of the increasing number of college-sponsored placement services, the number of external agencies decreased.

The first professional associations focusing on job placement for college graduates, the National Institutional Teacher Placement Association and the National Association of Appointment Secretaries, were both established in 1924. The former organization, in 1927, evolved into the American Association for Employment in Education (AAEE) while the latter became the American College Personnel Association (ACPA) in 1931. In addition, others concerned with business and industrial placement established the Eastern College Personnel Association and; by the 1940s, seven other regional associations had been formed.

A forerunner to a comprehensive national association, the Association of School and College Placement, was formed in 1940. This group published the'*School and College Placement* magazine, now known as the *Journal of Career Planning & Employment*. The association's function was broadened in 1953 and its name changed to the College Placement Publications Council. The association's name was changed again in 1956 to the College Placement Council (CPC) and then in 1995 it became the National Association of Colleges and Employers (NACE). The current name encompasses both membership constituencies—college career services and human relations staffing offices—and emphasizes the important connection between campus and career.

Following World War II, the economy exploded and employers sought the nation's college graduates to meet expanding needs. By the mid-1950s, on-campus recruiting of college graduates had reached its apex with over 65 percent of the current career services centers having been established between 1947 and 1960. Over the years, the function of these offices shifted from solely providing placement activities to providing a broad range of career activities. Accordingly, this shift was reflected by office name changes from the'"placement office," to the "career planning and placement office," to the currently popular "career services center."

Today, the majority of colleges and universities have career services centers. Their services often include career classes and job fairs; computer career guidance programs; counseling and credentialing services; employment bulletins; faculty/departmental programs; internships; interviewing and job-searching programs; on-campus recruiting and outreach programs; referral services; and résumé development programs and services.

In recent years, the greatest change in the field has been the increasing use of technology in the delivery of career services. As we progress into the 21st century, it is clear that college and university career services centers will be seeking new ways of using technology to better serve students and other stakeholders in career planning and employment activities.

### References, Readings, and Resources

Allen, C. (Spring 1997). The paperless office: becoming paperless is a bonus. *Journal of Career Planning & Employment, 57,* (3), pp. 24-31.

Bryant, B. J. (Ed.). (August 2003). *The job search handbook for educators.*

Columbus: American Association for Employment in Educational.

Bryant, B. J. (August 2003). *The job hunter's guide: services and career fairs for educators,* Columbus: American Association for Employment in Educational.

Bryant, B. J. (Ed.). (2003). *Educator supply and demand research report.* Columbus: American Association for Employment in Educational.

Gysbers, N. C., & Associates (1994). *Designing careers.* San Francisco: Jossey-Bass.

Herr, E. L., Rayman, J. R., and Garis, J. W. (1993). *Handbook for the college and university career center.* Westport, CT: Greenwood Press.

McDaniels, C., & Gysbers, N. C. (1992). *Counseling for career development.* San Francisco: Jossey-Bass.

Nagle, R., and Bohovich, J. (Summer, 2000). Career services in the year 2000. *Journal of Career Planning & Employment, 60*, (4), pp. 41-44, 46-47.

Nagle, R. (Summer 2001). Facilities, finances, and staffing: Key findings from NACE's 2001 career services survey. *Journal of Career Planning & Employment*, 61, (4), pp. 21-26.

Rayman, J. R. (Ed.) (1993). *The changing role of career services.* San Francisco: Jossey-Bass.

The 1998 NACE Career Services Survey (Spring, 1999). *Journal of Career Planning & Employment, 59,* (3), pp. 41-44, 58-61, 63.

National Association of Colleges and Employers (NACE). 62 Highland Avenue, Bethlehem, PA 18017. Phone: (610) 868-1421. Fax: (610) 868-0208. Web Site. www.naceweb.org

American Association for Employment in Education (AAEE). 3040 Riverside Drive, Suite 125, Columbus, OH 43221. Phone: 614/485-1111. Fax: 614/485-9609. E-mail: aaee@osu.edu. Web Site: www.ub-careers.buffalo.edu/aaee/

American College Personnel Association, Commission on Career Development, One Dupont Circle, Suite 300, Washington, DC 20036-1110. Phone: 202/835-2272. Fax: 202/296-3286: e-mail contact address: <info@acpa.nche.edu> Web Site. www.acpa.nche.edu

# CAREER SERVICES
## *CAS* Standards and Guidelines

## Part 1. MISSION

The primary mission of career services (CS) is to assist students and other designated clients through all phases of their career development.

In addition, the mission of CS is . . .

- to provide leadership to the institution on career development concerns
- to develop positive relationships with employers and external constituencies
- to support institutional outcomes assessment and relevant research endeavors

CS must incorporate student learning and student development in its mission. CS must enhance overall educational experiences. CS must develop, record, disseminate, implement, and regularly review its mission and goals. Mission statements must be consistent with the mission and goals of the institution and with the standards in this document. CS must operate as an integral part of the institution's overall mission.

The stated mission should include helping students and other designated clients . . .

- to develop self-knowledge related to career choice and work performance by identifying, assessing, and understanding their competencies, interests, values, and personal characteristics
- to obtain educational and occupational information to aid career and educational planning and to develop an understanding of the world of work
- to select personally suitable academic programs and experiential opportunities that enhance future educational and employment options
- to take personal responsibility for developing job-search competencies, future educational and employment plans, and career decisions
- to gain experience through student activities, community service, student employment, research or creative projects, cooperative education, internships, and other opportunities
- 'to link with alumni, employers, professional organizations, and others who can provide opportunities to develop professional interests and competencies, integrate academic learning with work, and explore future career possibilities
- to prepare for finding suitable employment by developing job-search skills, effective candidate presentation skills, and an understanding of the fit between their competencies and both occupational and job requirements
- to seek desired employment opportunities or entry into appropriate educational, graduate, or professional programs

CS must promote a greater awareness within the institution of the world of work and the need for and nature of career development over the life span.

Because of the expertise and knowledge on career-related matters, CS should be involved in key administrative decisions related to student services, institutional development, curriculum planning, and external relations.

## Part 2. PROGRAM

The formal education of students consists of the curriculum and the co-curriculum, and must promote student learning and development that is purposeful and holistic. Career services (CS) must identify relevant and desirable student learning and development outcomes and provide programs and services that encourage the achievement of those outcomes.

Relevant and desirable outcomes include: intellectual growth, effective communication, realistic self-appraisal, enhanced self-esteem, clarified values, career choices, leadership development, healthy behaviors, meaningful interpersonal relationships, independence, collaboration, social responsibility, satisfying and productive lifestyles, appreciation of diversity, spiritual awareness, and achievement of personal and educational goals.

CS must provide evidence of its impact on the achievement of student learning and development outcomes.

The program may use the examples that follow or identify other more germane indicators.

### Student Learning & Development Outcome Domains

### Intellectual Growth

Examples of Achievement Indicators

Produces personal and educational goal statements; Employs critical thinking in problem solving; Uses complex information from a variety of sources including personal experience and observation to form a decision or opinion; Obtains a degree; Applies previously understood information and concepts to a new situation or setting; Expresses appreciation for literature, the fine arts, mathematics, sciences, and social sciences

## Effective Communication
Examples of Achievement Indicators

Writes and speaks coherently and effectively; Writes and speaks after reflection; Able to influence others through writing, speaking or artistic expression; Effectively articulates abstract ideas; Uses appropriate syntax; Makes presentations or gives performances

## Enhanced Self-Esteem
Examples of Achievement Indicators

Shows self-respect and respect for others; Initiates actions toward achievement of goals; Takes reasonable risks; Demonstrates assertive behavior; Functions without need for constant reassurance from others

## Realistic Self-Appraisal
Examples of Achievement Indicators

Articulates personal skills and abilities; Makes decisions and acts in congruence with personal values; Acknowledges personal strengths and weaknesses; Articulates rationale for personal behavior; Seeks feedback from others; Learns from past experiences

## Clarified Values
Examples of Achievement Indicators

Articulates personal values; Acts in congruence with personal values; Makes decisions that reflect personal values; Demonstrates willingness to scrutinize personal beliefs and values; Identifies personal, work and lifestyle values and explains how they influence decision-making

## Career Choices
Examples of Achievement Indicators

Articulate career choices based on assessment of interests, values, skills and abilities; Documents knowledge, skills and accomplishments resulting from formal education, work experience, community service and volunteer experiences; Makes the connections between classroom and out-of-classroom learning; Can construct a resume with clear job objectives and evidence of related knowledge, skills and accomplishments; Articulates the characteristics of a preferred work environment; Comprehends the world of work; Takes steps to initiate a job search or seek advanced education

## Leadership Development
Examples of Achievement Indicators

Articulates leadership philosophy or style; Serves in a leadership position in a student organization; Comprehends the dynamics of a group; Exhibits democratic principles as a leader; Exhibits ability to visualize a group purpose and desired outcomes

## Healthy Behavior
Examples of Achievement Indicators

Chooses behaviors and environments that promote health and reduce risk; Articulate the relationship between health and wellness and accomplishing life long goals; Exhibits behaviors that advance a healthy community

## Meaningful Interpersonal Relationships
Examples of Achievement Indicators

Develops and maintains satisfying interpersonal relationships; Establishes mutually rewarding relationships with friends and colleagues; Listens to and considers others' points of view; Treats others with respect

## Independence
Examples of Achievement Indicators

Exhibits self-reliant behaviors; Functions autonomously; Exhibits ability to function interdependently; Accepts supervision as needed; Manages time effectively

## Collaboration
Examples of Achievement Indicators

Works cooperatively with others; Seeks the involvement of others; Seeks feedback from others; Contributes to achievement of a group goal; Exhibits effective listening skills

## Social Responsibility
Examples of Achievement Indicators

Understands and participates in relevant governance systems; Understands, abides by, and participates in the development, maintenance, and/or orderly change of community, social, and legal standards or norms; Appropriately challenges the unfair, unjust, or uncivil behavior of other individuals or groups; Participates in service/volunteer activities

## Satisfying and Productive Lifestyles
Examples of Achievement Indicators

Achieves balance between education, work and leisure time; Articulates and meets goals for work, leisure and education; Overcomes obstacles that hamper goal achievement; Functions on the basis of personal identity, ethical, spiritual and moral values; Articulates long-term goals and objectives

## Appreciating Diversity
Examples of Achievement Indicators

Understands ones own identity and culture. Seeks involvement with people different from oneself; Seeks involvement in diverse interests; Articulate the advantages and challenges of a diverse society; Challenges appropriately abusive use of stereotypes by others; Understands the impact of diversity on one's own society

## Spiritual Awareness
Examples of Achievement Indicators

Develops and articulates personal belief system; Understands roles of spirituality in personal and group values and behaviors

## Personal and Educational Goals
Examples of Achievement Indicators

Sets, articulates, and pursues individual goals; Articulate personal and educational goals/objectives; Uses personal and educational goals to guide decisions; Understands the effect of one's personal and education goals on others

CS must be (a) intentional, (b) coherent, (c) based on theories and knowledge of learning and human development, (d) reflective of developmental and demographic profiles of the student population, and (e) responsive to needs of individuals, special populations, and communities.

CS must be based on an educational philosophy of teaching career development and related processes. CS must assist students and other designated clients to develop the skills necessary to compete in a rapidly changing, competency-based, global workplace.

Components of the CS must be clearly defined and articulated. To effectively accomplish its purpose, the program must include:
- career counseling
- information and resources on careers and further education
- opportunities for career exploration through experiential learning
- job search services
- services to employers
- consultation and outcomes assessment

CS must be delivered in a variety of formats in recognition of institutional settings, different learning styles, cultural differences, and special needs.

Program components of CS must be designed for and reflective of the career development needs and interests of students and other designated clients; current research, theories, and knowledge of career development and learning; contemporary career services practices and national standards of practice; economic trends, opportunities, and/or constraints; the varying needs and employment practices among small businesses, large corporations, government, and nonprofit organizations; and the priorities and resources of the institution.

CS must work collaboratively with academic divisions, departments, individual faculty members, student services, and other relevant constituencies of the institution to enhance students' career development.

CS must develop and implement intentional marketing strategies and outreach programming to promote awareness and encourage use of the services.

Program goals must be reviewed and updated regularly, and communicated, as appropriate, to students, administrators, faculty, staff, and employers and other constituencies.

CS should disseminate information on the availability, scope, and use of career services through institutional publications, campus media, presentations, outreach, and orientation programs.

*Career Counseling*

The institution must offer career counseling that assists students and other designated clients at any stage of their career development to . . .
- understand the relationship between self-knowledge and career choice through assessment of interests, competencies, values, experience, personal characteristics, and desired lifestyles
- obtain and research occupational, educational, and employment information
- establish short-term and long-term career goals
- explore a full range of career and work possibilities
- make reasoned, informed career choices based on accurate self-knowledge and accurate information about the world of work

Career counseling should . . .
- be available to students throughout their academic experience
- encourage students to take advantage of timely involvement in self-assessment, career decision making and career planning activities
- assist students to assess their skills, values, and interests by reflecting on past experiences
- assist students to integrate self-knowledge into their career planning
- recognize that students' career decision making is inextricably linked to additional psycho-social, personal, developmental and cultural issues and beliefs
- encourage and facilitate students' exploration of career interests through field visits, student employment, cooperative education, internships, shadowing experiences, research or creative projects, and informational interviews with working professionals
- be provided through a variety of formats, such as scheduled appointments, drop-in periods, group programs, career planning courses, outreach programs, and information technology

Career counseling should be offered through career services in order to link students= career exploration and decision making process with access to employers and employment information.

*Information & Resources on Careers and Further Study*

CS must help students and other designated clients to identify and access valid career information for their educational and career planning.

CS should provide information and resources . . .
- to help students assess and relate their interests,

competencies, needs and expectations, education, experience, personal background, and desired lifestyle to the employment market
- for constituent groups on career and employment topics and the ethical obligations of students, employers, and others involved in the employment process
- on current employment opportunities and on employers to ensure that candidates have the widest possible choices of employment
- to help students identify and pursue future educational objectives

## Information and resources must be . . .
- **comprehensive, enabling students and other designated clients to explore the widest range of information**
- **current and reflective of economic, occupational, and workplace trends**
- **accessible to clients**
- **organized in a system that is user-friendly, flexible, and adaptable to change**

The scope of information and resources available to clients should include . . .
- self-assessment and career planning
- occupational and job market information
- options for further study (e.g., community college articulation; graduate and professional school information)
- job search information
- experiential learning, internship, and job listings
- employer information

**Career information, resources, and means of delivery must be compatible with the size and nature of the student population, the career and geographic interests of the students and scope of academic programs. CS must provide access to information and resources on the internet.**

**CS must provide information for students and other designated clients to identify and pursue future educational objectives in the context of lifelong learning.**

### Opportunities for Career Exploration through Experiential Learning

**Experiential learning programs enable students to integrate their academic studies with work experiences and career exploration. The institution must provide experiential learning opportunities.**

Experiential learning includes cooperative education, work-based learning, apprenticeships, student teaching, internships, work-study jobs, and other campus employment, volunteer experiences, service-learning, undergraduate research and shadowing experiences.

**Experiential learning programs administered through CS must . . .**
- **provide students with opportunities to define both learning and career objectives and to reflect**

upon learning and other developmental aspects of their experience
- **help students to identify employers for career development and potential employment**
- **teach students appropriate search and application techniques**
- **support institutional efforts to provide students with additional financial resources for attending college and/or opportunities for obtaining academic credit**
- **ensure adequate site supervision**

Experiential learning programs administered through CS should promote mentor/mentee relationships. When experiential learning opportunities are provided by other departments, CS should work closely with those departments.

### Job Search Services

**Job search services must assist students and other designated clients to . . .**
- **develop job-search competencies**
- **present themselves effectively as candidates for employment**
- **obtain information on employment opportunities, trends, and prospective employers**
- **connect with employers through campus recruitment programs, job listings, referrals, direct application, networking, publications, and information technology**
- **identify relevant career management issues (e.g., gender, age, sexual orientation, dual career, disability, cultural, mental health )**
- **access and effectively use career and employer resources on the internet**

Job search services may include offering site visits; campus recruiting; resume referrals; credential file services; information sessions; meetings with faculty members; pre-recruiting activities; student access to employer information; posting job openings; career and job fairs. Job search service should help students and other designated clients develop skills to uncover hidden job markets germane to their career interests.

**CS must develop and implement marketing strategies that cultivate employment opportunities for students.**

### Services to Employers

**Employers are both vital partners in the educational process and primary customers of career services. CS must offer services to employers that reflect student interests and employer needs.**

Employer services may include: providing employers with information on academic departments and students within legal and policy guidelines; assisting in recruiting student populations; arranging experiential learning options such as shadowing experiences, internships, student teaching, or cooperative education; providing video conference interviewing; creating advertising and promotional vehicles; seeking input through career center advisory board membership; and organizing individual employer recruiting and college relations consultations.

CS must identify the range of employers it will serve (e.g., for profit, government, contract agencies, not-for-profit) and articulate policies that guide its working relationships with each of these constituencies.

CS must . . .

- develop strategic objectives for employer services and job development that yield maximum opportunities for the institution's students and graduates
- inform, educate, and consult with employers on the nature of services provided and student candidates available
- encourage employer participation in programs that meet career and employment needs of students and other designated clients (e.g., career conferences, career and alumni fairs, cooperative education, and internships; career planning courses; classroom presentations)
- develop and maintain relationships with employers who may provide career development and employment opportunities for students
- facilitate employer involvement and communication with faculty, students, and administrators concerning career and employment issues
- promote adherence to professional and ethical standards that model professional and ethical conduct for students
- enhance customer service and continuous improvement by using feedback from employers on key performance indicators and measures of services

CS must provide timely, pertinent information to employers regarding . . .

- the institutional student profile, academic programs and curricula, enrollments, and academic calendar
- class profile according to majors
- recruiting options available to reach targeted students
- policies, procedures, and instructions for using the services
- institutional non-discrimination policies with which employers must comply

CS must treat employers fairly and equitably and must develop policies for working with third-party recruiters and vendors.

*Consultation and Outcomes Assessment*

CS must provide consultative services to employers, faculty members, staff, administrators, students, and designated clients that are timely, knowledgeable, ethical, and responsive to constituent needs.

To develop effective long-term relationships with employers, CS must provide guidance to employers on how to develop effective college relations and recruiting strategies.
CS should provide guidance on . . .

- effective and appropriate strategies for reaching and attracting students
- student needs, issues and developmental perspectives
- cultivating relations with academic departments
- working with student leaders and student clubs and organizations
- timely corporate/organizational presence and participation in on-campus recruiting, fairs, and pre-recruiting
- using appropriate campus resources for visibility
- internship, co-op, and full-time hiring guidelines, processes, and programs
- promoting equal access for all students to all employment opportunities

To support the institution's mission and goals, CS must provide faculty and staff and administrative units with information, guidance, and support on career development and employment issues and linkages with the broader community.'
CS should support faculty and staff and administrative units by . . .

- identifying and disseminating information on employment trends and top employing organizations and co-op and internship sponsors
- provide employer feedback on the preparation of students for jobs, the curriculum and the hiring process
- raising awareness of appropriate ethical and legal guidelines for student referrals
- increasing awareness of career development issues and available resources
- providing and interpreting aggregate data on student learning and career-related outcomes for purposes such as accreditation, marketing, institutional development, and curriculum development

CS must consult with students and student groups regarding policy interpretation, program development, and relationships with employers.

## Part 3. LEADERSHIP

Effective and ethical leadership is essential to the success of all organizations. Institutions must appoint, position, and empower career services (CS) leaders within the administrative structure to accomplish stated missions. Leaders at various levels must be selected on the basis of formal education and training, relevant work experience, personal skills and competencies, relevant professional credentials, as well as potential for promoting learning and development in students, applying effective practices to educational processes, and enhancing institutional effectiveness. Institutions must determine expectations of accountability for leaders and fairly assess their performance.

Leaders must exercise authority over resources for which they are responsible to achieve their respective missions and . . .
- articulate a vision for their organization
- set goals and objectives based on the needs and capabilities of the  population served
- promote student learning and development
- prescribe and practice ethical behavior
- recruit, select, supervise, and develop others in the organization
- manage  financial resources
- coordinate human resources
- plan, budget for, and evaluate personnel and programs
- apply effective practices to educational and administrative processes
- communicate effectively
- initiate collaborative interaction between individuals and agencies that possess legitimate concerns and interests in the functional area

CS leaders must identify and find means to address individual, organizational, or environmental conditions that inhibit goal achievement. And must promote campus environments that result in multiple opportunities for student learning and development. Leaders must continuously improve programs and services in response to changing needs of students and other constituents, and evolving institutional priorities.

If career components are offered through multiple units, the institution must designate a leader or leadership team to provide strategic direction and align career services with the mission of the institution and the needs of the constituencies served.
Leaders should coordinate efforts with other units in the institution providing career components to integrate career services into the broader educational mission. Key constituencies served by each unit should be clearly identified and reflected in the mission and goals of the unit.

CS leaders must be advocates for the advancement of career services within the institution.
Leaders should participate in institutional decisions about career services objectives and policies. CSleaders should participate in institutional decisions related to the identification and designation of clients served. Clients may include students, alumni, community members, and employers. Decisions about clients served should include type and scope of services offered and the fees, if any, that are charged.

## Part 4.  ORGANIZATION and MANAGEMENT
Guided by an overarching intent to ensure student learning and development, career services (CS) must be structured purposefully and managed effectively to achieve stated goals. Evidence of appropriate structure must include current and accessible policies and procedures, written performance expectations for all employees, functional workflow graphics or organizational charts, and clearly stated service delivery expectations.

Evidence of effective management must include use of comprehensive and accurate information for decisions, clear sources and channels of authority, effective communication practices, decision-making and conflict resolution procedures, responsiveness to changing conditions, accountability and evaluation systems, and recognition and reward processes.  CS must provide channels within the organization for regular review of administrative policies and procedures.
Other areas for consideration in determining structure and management of career services should include . . .
- size, nature and mission of the institution
- number and scope of academic-related services
- scope and intent of recruiting services
- philosophy and delivery system for services
- varied delivery methods (e.g., direct contact, technology)
CS should be integrated with, and complementary to, employment-related services.

## Part 5.  HUMAN RESOURCES
Career services (CS) must be staffed adequately by individuals qualified to accomplish its mission and goals. Within established guidelines of the institution, CS must establish procedures for staff selection, training, and evaluation; set expectations for supervision, and provide appropriate professional development opportunities.  CS must strive to improve the professional competence and skills of all personnel it employs.

**Collectively, CS staff members must have the competencies necessary to effectively perform the primary functions. Primary functions are program management and administration; program and event administration; career counseling and consultation; teaching/training/educating; marketing/promoting/outreach; brokering/connecting/linking; and information management.**

The primary functions should include the following core competencies and knowledge domains.

Management and Administration Function
Core Competencies; Needs assessment; program design, implementation and evaluation; strategic and operational planning; program integration and integrity; staffing; staff development and supervision; budget planning and administration; political sensitivity and negotiation skills; synthesize, interpret and report information.
Knowledge Domains: Systems theory; organizational development; research design; statistics; accounting and budgeting procedures; revenue generation; principles; purchasing; staff selection; supervision; performance appraisals; management of information systems; customer service; marketing.

Program and Event Administration Function
Core Competencies: Needs assessment; goal setting; program planning; implementation and evaluation; budget allocation; time management; problem solving; attention to detail.
Knowledge Domains: Systems, logistics, and procedures; project management; customer service.

Career Counseling and Consultation Function
Core Competencies: Needs assessment and diagnosis; intervention design and implementation; test administration and interpretation; counseling; feedback; evaluation; advising; empathy and interpersonal sensitivity; work with individuals and groups; use of career, occupational, and employment information.
Knowledge Domains:
Career development theories; adult development theory and unique issues for special populations; statistics; counseling processes; evaluation of person-job fit; job analysis; career decision making; behavior management; job search, interviews, and resumes.

Teaching, Training, and Educating Function
Core competencies: Needs assessment; program/workshop design; researching, evaluating, and integrating information; effective teaching strategies; coaching; work with individuals and groups; use of technology for delivery of content.
Knowledge Domain: Setting learning objectives; designing curricula and learning resources for specific content areas; experiential learning; career development and job search process; learning styles.

Marketing, Promoting, Outreach Function
Core Competencies: Needs assessment and goal setting; written and interpersonal communication; public speaking; job development; effective use of print, web, personal presentation methods.
Knowledge Domains: Customer service; knowledge of institution and its academic programs; career services; employers and faculty needs and expectations; recruiting and staffing methods, trends.

Brokering, Connecting, and Linking functions
Core Competencies: Organize information, logistics, people, and processes toward a desired outcome; consulting; interpersonal skills.
Knowledge Domains: Systems and procedures; candidate/resume referral; recruiting and experiential learning operations; human resource selection practices.

Information Management
Core Competencies: Organization and dissemination; Storage and retrieval; computing systems and applications; data entry and analysis; acquisition of appropriate career resources; web design.
Knowledge Domains: Library and resources center organization; computer systems and applications; specific electronic management information systems.

**CS professional staff members must hold an earned graduate degree in a field relevant to the position they hold or must possess an appropriate combination of educational credentials and related work experience.**

**Degree or credential-seeking interns must be qualified by enrollment in an appropriate field of study and by relevant experience. These individuals must be trained and supervised adequately by professional staff members holding educational credentials and related work experience appropriate for supervision.**

**Student employees and volunteers must be carefully selected, trained, supervised, and evaluated. They must be trained on how and when to refer those in need of assistance to qualified staff members and have access to a supervisor for assistance in making these judgments. Student employees and volunteers must be provided clear and precise job descriptions, pre-service training based on assessed needs, and continuing staff development.**

Training should include customer service, program procedures, and information and resource utilization.

**CS must have technical and support staff members adequate to accomplish its mission. Staff members must be technologically proficient and qualified to perform their job functions, be knowledgeable of ethical and legal uses of technology, and have access to training. The level of staffing and workloads must be adequate and appropriate for program and service demands.**

Career information facilities should be staffed with persons who have the appropriate competencies to assist students and other designated clients in accessing and effectively using career information and resources. A technical support person or support service should be available to maintain computer and information technology systems for career services.

**Salary levels and fringe benefits for all CS staff members must be commensurate with those for comparable positions within the institution, in similar institutions, and in the relevant geographic area.**

**CS must institute hiring and promotion practices that are fair, inclusive, and non-discriminatory. Programs and services must employ a diverse staff to provide readily identifiable role models for students and to enrich the campus community.**

**CS must create and maintain position descriptions for all staff members and provide regular performance planning and appraisals. CS must have a system for regular staff evaluation and must provide access to continuing education and professional development opportunities, including in-service training programs and participation in professional conferences and workshops.**

**CS professional staff members must engage in continuing professional development activities to keep abreast of the research, theories, legislation, policies and developments that affect career services.**

Staff training and development should be ongoing and promote knowledge and skill development across program components.

**All staff must be trained in legal, confidential, and ethical issues related to career services.**

## Part 6. FINANCIAL RESOURCES

**Career services (CS) must have adequate funding to accomplish its mission and goals. Funding priorities must be determined within the context of the stated mission, goals, objectives, and comprehensive analysis of the needs and capabilities of students, and the availability of internal or external resources.**

**CS must demonstrate fiscal responsibility and cost effectiveness consistent with institutional protocols.**

CD should cultivate employer support of the institution, which may include scholarships and other forms of financial support, in coordination with development office efforts. While outside revenue may be generated to supplement the services it should not replace institutional funding. Revenue generated from employers, vendors, students, and other designated clients should be limited and reasonable to carry out stated objectives.

## Part 7. FACILITIES, TECHNOLOGY, EQUIPMENT

**Career services (CS) must have adequate, suitably located facilities, adequate technology, and equipment to support its mission and goals efficiently and effectively. Facilities, technology, and equipment must be evaluated regularly and be in compliance with relevant federal, state, provincial, and local requirements to provide for access, health, safety, and security.**

**CS must provide: private offices for professional staff in order to perform counseling or other confidential work; support staff work areas; reception and student registration area; career resource center; storage space sufficient to accommodate resources, supplies and equipment; technology resources for students and staff sufficient to support career services functions; access to conference rooms, computer labs and large group meeting rooms; private interview facilities for employers and students to accommodate the scope of the recruiting program; and reception spaces adequate to accommodate on-campus recruiting and career counseling services.**

CS should be in a convenient location for students and employers and project a welcoming, professional atmosphere for its users. A private employer workspace should be available. Parking for visitors should be adequate and convenient.

**Equipment and facilities must be secured to protect the confidentiality, security, and safety of records. Contracts with outside vendors must include adherence to ethics, confidentiality, security, institutional policies, as well as reflect support of career services programs, goals and standards.**

## Part 8. LEGAL RESPONSIBILITIES

**Career services (CS) staff members must be knowledgeable about and responsive to laws and regulations that relate to their respective responsibilities. Staff members must inform users of programs and services and officials, as appropriate, of legal obligations and limitations including constitutional, statutory, regulatory, and case law; mandatory laws and orders emanating from federal, state/provincial and local governments; and the institution's policies.**

**Staff members must use reasonable and informed practices to limit the liability exposure of the institution, its officers, employees, and agents. Staff members must be informed about institutional**

policies regarding personal liability and related insurance coverage options.

The institution must provide access to legal advice for CS staff members as needed to carry out assigned responsibilities and must inform CS staff and students in a timely and systematic fashion about extraordinary or changing legal obligations and potential liabilities.

Career services staff members must be aware of and seek advice from the institution's legal counsel on: privacy and disclosure of student information contained in education records; defamation law regarding references and recommendations on the behalf of students and other designated clients; laws regarding employment referral practices of the career services office and others employed by the institution that refer students for employment; affirmative action regulations and laws regarding programs for special populations; liability issues pertaining to experiential learning programs; laws regarding eligibility to work; laws regarding contracts governing service provided by outside vendors; and laws regarding grant administration.

CS must maintain appropriate records for future work with students and other designated clients.

## Part 9. EQUITY and ACCESS

Career services (CS) staff members must ensure that services and programs are provided on a fair and equitable basis. Facilities, programs and services must be accessible. Hours of operation and delivery of and access to programs and services must be responsive to the needs of all students and other constituents. CS must adhere to the spirit and intent of equal opportunity laws.

To respond to the needs of students and other designated clients, career services should provide services in-person, on-line, via telephone, e-mail, or other formats. CS should be responsive to the needs of all its constituencies through the establishment of office hours, customer service systems and on-line operations.

Career Services must be open and readily accessible to all students and must not discriminate except where sanctioned by law and institutional policy. Discrimination must especially be avoided on the bases of age; color; creed; cultural heritage; disability; ethnicity; gender identity; nationality; political affiliation, religious affiliation, sex, sexual orientation; or economic, marital, social, or veteran status.

CS should ensure that employers who use career services adhere to the word and spirit of equal employment

opportunity and affirmative action. CS staff should make every effort to inform or educate faculty members about issues relevant to discriminatory practices related to their referral of students directly to employers.

Consistent with their mission and goals, programs and services must take affirmative action to remedy significant imbalances in student participation and staffing patterns.

These groups may include traditionally under-represented, disabled, evening, part time, commuter, and international students.

As the demographic profiles of campuses change and new instructional delivery methods are introduced, institutions must recognize the needs of students who participate in distance learning for access to programs and services offered on campus. □Institutions must provide appropriate services in ways that are accessible to distance learners and assist them in identifying and gaining access to other appropriate services in their geographic region.

## Part 10. CAMPUS and EXTERNAL RELATIONS

Career services (CS) must establish, maintain, and promote effective relations with relevant individuals, campus offices, and external agencies.

As an integral function within the institution, CS must develop and maintain effective relationships with relevant stakeholders at the institution and in the community.

To achieve this, CS should develop institutional support for career development and employment programs by . .

- participating fully in campus activities such as faculty organizations, committees, student orientation programs, classroom presentations, academic courses in career planning, and student organization programs
- arranging appropriate programs that use alumni experience and expertise
- establishing cooperative relationships with other offices and services to support the practice of mutual referrals, information exchange, resource sharing, and other program functions
- providing information and reports to the academic administration, faculty and key offices of the institution regarding career services for students, employers, and alumni
- developing informal or formal student, faculty, or employer advisory groups
- encouraging dialogues among employers, faculty members, and administrators concerning career issues and trends for students and graduates

In addition, CS should . . .

- encourage staff participation in and through professional associations and community activities related to career and employment issues (e.g., chambers of commerce, workforce development functions, employer open

houses, workshops, federally mandated one stop centers, school-to-work efforts)
- raise issues and concerns with the legal counsel of the institution regarding compliance with laws as they pertain to employment, recruitment, supervision (e.g., interns)

## Part 11. DIVERSITY

Within the context of each institution's unique mission, diversity enriches the community and enhances the collegiate experience for all; therefore, career services (CS) must nurture environments where commonalties and differences among people are recognized and honored.

CS must promote educational experiences that are characterized by open and continuous communication that deepens understanding of one's own identity, culture, and heritage, and that of others and must educate and promote respect about commonalties and differences in their historical and cultural contexts.

CS must address the characteristics and needs of a diverse population when establishing and implementing policies and procedures.

CS should work in conjunction with the institution's special services and minority organizations to enhance student's awareness and appreciation of cultural and ethnic differences. Collaborating departments and minority organizations should provide educational programs that help minority students, multicultural students, and individuals with disabilities to identify and address their unique needs related to career development and employment. CS should initiate partnerships and collaborative programming with other offices representing specific populations to ensure appropriate service delivery.

## Part 12. ETHICS

All persons involved in the delivery of career services (CS) must adhere to the highest principles of ethical behavior. CS must develop or adopt and implement appropriate statements of ethical practice. CS must publish these statements and ensure their periodic review by relevant constituencies.

Ethical standards or other statements from relevant professional associations should be considered.

CS staff members must ensure that privacy and confidentiality are maintained with respect to all communications and records to the extent that such records are protected under the law and appropriate statements of ethical practice. Information contained in students' education records must not be disclosed without written consent except as allowed by relevant laws and institutional policies. Staff members must disclose to appropriate authorities information judged to be of an emergency nature, especially when the safety of the individual or others is involved, or when otherwise required by institutional policy or relevant law.

All CS staff members must be aware of and comply with the provisions contained in the institution's human subjects research policy and in other relevant institutional policies addressing ethical practices and confidentiality of research data concerning individuals.

CS staff members must recognize and avoid personal conflict of interest or appearance thereof in their transactions with students and others. Staff members must strive to ensure the fair, objective, and impartial treatment of all persons with whom they deal. Staff members must not participate in nor condone any form of harassment that demeans persons or creates an intimidating, hostile, or offensive campus environment.

When handling institutional funds, all CS staff members must ensure that such funds are managed in accordance with established and responsible accounting procedures and the fiscal policies or processes of the institution.

CS staff members must perform their duties within the limits of their training, expertise, and competence. When these limits are exceeded, individuals in need of further assistance must be referred to persons possessing appropriate qualifications.

CS staff members must use suitable means to confront and otherwise hold accountable other staff members who exhibit unethical behavior and must be knowledgeable about and practice ethical behavior in the use of technology.

CS leaders/managers should provide guidance and education on these standards to all persons involved in providing career services, including, but not limited to, entry-level professionals, support staff, student staff, interns, graduate assistants, faculty and staff, employers, service providers, and other administrators.

## Part 13. ASSESSMENT and EVALUATION

Career services (CS) must conduct regular assessment and evaluations. CS must employ effective qualitative and quantitative methodologies as appropriate, to determine whether and to what degree the stated mission, goals, and student learning and development outcomes are being met. The process must employ sufficient and sound assessment measures to ensure comprehensiveness. Data collected must include responses from students and other affected constituencies.

CS must evaluate periodically how well they complement and enhance the institution's stated mission and educational effectiveness.

Career services must conduct regular evaluations to improve programs and services, to adjust to changing client needs, and to respond to environmental threats and opportunities.

In order for institutions to employ comparable methods for evaluation, resources from recognized peers and professional associations should be consulted. CS should collaborate with institutional research units, state agencies, accrediting bodies, and other evaluative groups that generate and assess evaluation information. CS should promote institutional efforts to conduct relevant research on career development, institutional issues such as academic success and retention, student learning outcomes, employment trends, and career interests.

Evaluations should include . . .

- review of the strategic plan, mission, human resources needs, diversity efforts, and other areas covered in this document
- regular feedback from participants on events, programs, and services
- systematic needs assessment to guide program development
- first destination surveys at or following graduation
- employer and student feedback regarding experiential learning programs
- alumni follow-up surveys administered at specific times after graduation
- reports and satisfaction surveys from students and other constituencies interacting with career services such as employers, faculty, and other post-secondary institutions

Results of these evaluations must be used in revising and improving programs and services and in recognizing staff performance.

CS should prepare and disseminate annual and special reports, including career services philosophy, goals and objectives, current programs and services, service delivery information, first destination information, and graduate follow-up information.

# THE ROLE of COLLEGE HEALTH PROGRAMS
## *CAS* Standards Contextual Statement

College health programs have a unique position within institutions of higher learning. Society has become increasingly aware of the impact of health issues on the effectiveness of learning environments. College health programs can play a major role by attending to these critical issues. New partnerships are being forged within institutions so that both clinical and educational concerns become integrated into campus and community practices.

College health programs have a unique opportunity to respond to the new challenges of partnership and integration. The demand for high quality educational programs requires the development of new approaches and strategies. Higher levels of awareness and knowledge are necessary to help students participate in their own health. Armed with these new approaches and operational styles, college health professionals seek to focus proactively on students' health enhancing behaviors and measures that aid student learning in ways that are not limited solely to problems, symptoms, or illnesses.

In the recent NASPA (1998) publication, *Principles of Good Practice for Student Affairs: Statement and Inventory*, student affairs professionals were called upon to be *responsible stewards*. To that end, college health programs have served as stewards of health engendering learning environments. There are more than 3400 institutions of higher education in the United States with approximately 14.3 million students enrolled. By far the majorities (80%) of these students attend campuses that have some organized arrangement for advancing their health. The work of college health programs has always been more than simply providing convenient medical treatment for students. The first college health program focused on public health with mandatory hygiene classes and daily mass exercise routines. With the onset of communicable diseases, Infirmaries were created to isolate students with infectious disease. By the late 1940s when veterans returned and took advantage of the GI Bill, mental health and other counseling services were added while public health and behavioral risk factors returned to the forefront in the sixties and

seventies. In effect, from its beginnings in 1860 when Edward Hitchcock, a physician and professor of hygiene, was charged with advancing the health of students, college health has been an important component of most institutions of higher learning.

In general, the historical reasons for college health programs are as follows . . .

- a call from faculty to create a support system to maintain the student's health for academic studies
- the public health and communicable disease concern of isolation within a compact campus community, prior to the advent of vaccines and antibiotics
- the specialized medical needs of the historically adolescent population, that may differ from the care of adult and pediatric care provided in the surrounding community
- the confidentiality needs of a young adult when establishing a new relationship with parents
- the need for access to treatment for an uninsured population
- a health care financing system did not cover primary care, even when a student was insured

Although some of these historical reasons remain, the financing and delivery of medical care has changed. Managed care as a method of financing health care, focuses on providing primary care as a way of decreasing costs. Therefore, students who are insured are often covered for primary care at a designated in-area facility and may not use these medical services within the college health program. Nevertheless, approximately thirty percent of students are uninsured for any type of medical care. Another effect of this change in financing health care is increased market competition for professionals trained in primary care. Today, the health issues threatening students' academic success are often behavioral rather than risk of infection or disease. Consequently, there is increased emphasis on prevention as opposed to simply treating a condition and on understanding that health behaviors must be considered within a social context. Society's perception of what contributes to the health status of individuals is changing and so must college health programs. A unique challenge for college health programs is the continual change required to meet the charge of being suitable stewards to advance campus health.

College health programs are often, naively, compared to other primary care ambulatory medical services. However, medical services are but one aspect of college health because current public health models emphasize prevention, societal intervention and community, creating a golden gateway for enhanced college health. The most important aspect of a comprehensive college health program is its ability to create and maintain relationships with the larger academic community that emphasize student academic success and the need for a healthy and safe campus community.

The "four leaf clover" model has utility for guiding the structure of college health programs. Although many programs today reflect a "sunflower" model, with a large central focus on treatment and small various pedals attached, the four leaf clover model uses the institution's academic mission as a stem and allows four leaves to overlap as needed to best serve the specifics of the population to be served. The four leaves represent (a) Consumer Services, (b) Counseling Services, (c) Health Promotion and Prevention, and (d) Medical/Clinical Services.

These areas do not necessarily report to the same director and may overlap as in a Venn diagram. Although various program models exist, the model in current use on a given campus is not as important as the assessment and decision process that guided those responsible for the program to select an intentional design for the services offered. Becoming population sensitive" can enhance any model because contrasting the current campus climate with the historical reasons for the program's existence will often facilitate the creation of new and more effective services. Again, the most important aspect of a comprehensive college health program is its ability to create and maintain relationships with the larger academic community that emphasize student academic success and the need for a healthy and safe campus community.

Health promotion and prevention, along with increased reliance on professional counseling, are elements of a comprehensive scope of services. Contemporary campus health programs address health risks pertinent to the population such as depression, alcohol and other drug use and issues surrounding emerging sexuality, as well as physical fitness. They also deal increasingly with racism, sexism and heterosexism behaviors. The impact of gender and relationship problems on health requires services to address sexual harassment and assault, including issues of acquaintance rape. Student populations include a wide diversity of individuals and lifestyles. Colleges must also meet the special needs of the physically and mentally challenged, which creates special challenges and opportunities. As campuses and their health program responds to a broad range of student needs, they also create windows of opportunity that can be used to influence students who will become productive members of a constructive society.

Although institutions differ in size and scope of services, there are universal concepts that impact upon the provision of health promotion, health protection, disease prevention, and clinical care for college students. The CAS standards that follow are based in large measure *on The American College Health Association's Guidelines for a College Health Program*, which complement the standards.

### References, Readings and Resources

American College Health Association. (1996). *College health 2000: A perspective statement in higher education*. Baltimore: Author.

American College Health Association. (1996). *College health 2000: Strategies for the future*. Baltimore: Author.

American College Health Association. (1999). *Guidelines for a college health program*. Baltimore: Author.

American College Health Association. (2001). *Standards of best practice for health promotion in higher education*. Baltimore: Author.

Bridwell, M.W. & Kinder, S.P. (1993). Confronting health issues. In M.J. Barr & Associates (Eds.), *The handbook of student affairs* (pp. 481-492). San Francisco: Jossey-Bass.

Centers for Disease Control and Prevention. (1997). Youth risk behavior surveillance: National College Health Risk Behavior Survey-United

States, *Morbidity & Mortality Weekly Report CDC Surveillance Summary, 46*(6), 1-56.

Christmas, W.A. & Dorman, J.M. (1996). The Storey of college health hygiene: Thomas A. Storey, MD (1875-1943) and the promotion of hygiene. *Journal of American College Health, 45*(1), 27-34.

Grace, T. W. (1997). Health problems of college students. *Journal of American College Health, 45*(6), 243-50.

Jackson, M, Weinstein, H. (1997). The importance of healthy communities of higher education. *Journal of American College Health, 45*(6), 237-241.

Keeling, R.P. (2000). Beyond the campus clinic: A holistic approach to student health. *AAC&U Peer Review, 2*(3), 13-18.

Modeste, N. (1996). *Dictionary of public health promotion and education: Terms and concepts,* Thousand Oaks, CA: Sage.

National Association of Student Personnel Administrators (1998). *Principles of good practice for student affairs.* Washington, DC: Author.

Neinstein, L.S. (in press). *Adolescent health care: A practical guide* (4th ed.). Philadelphia: Lippincott, Williams and Wilkins.

Packwood, W. (1989) *College Student Personnel Services.* Springfield, IL: Charles C. Thomas. 298-365.

Patrick, K. (1988). Student health: Medical care within institutions of higher education. *Journal of the American Medical Association*; 260(22), 3301-3305.

Patrick, K. (Ed). (1992). Principles and practices of student health volume three college health, Oakland, CA: Third Party Publishing Company.

Swinford, P. (in press). Advancing the health of students. *Journal of American College Health.*

Turner, S.H. & Hurley, J.L. (Eds.). (in press). *The history and practice of college health.* Lexington, KY: The University Press of Kentucky.

U.S. Department of Human Services. (2000). *Healthy People 2010. 2nd ed. Understanding and improving health & Objectives for improving health* (Vols. 1-2). Washington, DC: U.S. Government Printing Office.

American College Health Association [ACHA]. ACHA National Office, P.O. Box 28937. Baltimore, MD 21240-8937. (410) 859-1500; Fax (410) 859-1510. http//www.acha.org

American College Personnel Association [ACPA]. ACPA National Office, One Dupont Circle, N.W., Suite 300. Washington, DC 20036-1110. (202) 835-2272; Fax (202) 296-3286. http//www.acpa.nche.edu

Journal of American College Health. Heldref Publications, 1319 Eighteenth Street, N.W., Washington, DC 20036-1802. (202) 296-6267; Fax (202) 296-5149.

National Association of Student Personnel Administrators [NASPA]. NASPA National Office, 1875 Connecticut Ave., N.W., Suite 418. Washington, DC 20009. (202) 265-7500. http//www.naspa.org

# COLLEGE HEALTH PROGRAMS
## *CAS* STANDARDS and GUIDELINES

## Part 1. MISSION

College health programs (CHP) must provide, promote, and support services that integrate individual health, education for health, prevention of disease, clinical treatment for illness, and public health responsibilities consistent with the educational mission of the institution and relevant legal requirements.

The following characteristics exemplify a CHP that is consistent with ever-changing environments of health and the educational mission of the institution . . .

- a wide spectrum of services, that support the overall health of the campus community in its broadest sense integrating primary prevention, public health, clinical, physical, and mental health services
- easy and equal access to services regardless of income level, ability to pay, age, color, disability, gender, national origin, race, religious creed, sexual orientation, gender identity, and/or veteran status
- advocacy for a healthy campus community and providing leadership on policy issues regarding public safety, alcohol and/or other drug use, and other health related risk behaviors
- evidence of measures of quality, such as national accreditation of services
- significant student involvement in advising the program's mission, goals, services, funding and evaluation
- delivery of efficient and effective services based on data and benchmarking

The CHP must incorporate student learning and student development in its mission. CHP must enhance overall educational experiences. CHP must develop, record, disseminate, implement, and regularly review its mission and goals. Mission statements must be consistent with the mission and goals of the institution and with the standards in this document. CHP must operate as an integral part of the institution's overall mission.

## Part 2. PROGRAM

The formal education of students consists of the curriculum and the co-curriculum, and must promote student learning and development that is purposeful and holistic. College health programs (CHP) must identify relevant and desirable student learning and development outcomes and provide programs and services that encourage the achievement of those outcomes.

Relevant and desirable outcomes include: intellectual growth, effective communication,

realistic self-appraisal, enhanced self-esteem, clarified values, career choices, leadership development, healthy behaviors, meaningful interpersonal relationships, independence, collaboration, social responsibility, satisfying and productive lifestyles, appreciation of diversity, spiritual awareness, and achievement of personal and educational goals.

CHP must provide evidence of its impact on the achievement of student learning and development outcomes.

The college health program may use the examples that follow or identify other more germane indicators.

### Student Learning & Development Outcome Domains

### Intellectual Growth

Examples of Achievement Indicators

Produces personal and educational goal statements; Employs critical thinking in problem solving; Uses complex information from a variety of sources including personal experience and observation to form a decision or opinion; Obtains a degree; Applies previously understood information and concepts to a new situation or setting; Expresses appreciation for literature, the fine arts, mathematics, sciences, and social sciences

### Effective Communication

Examples of Achievement Indicators

Writes and speaks coherently and effectively; Writes and speaks after reflection; Able to influence others through writing, speaking or artistic expression; Effectively articulates abstract ideas; Uses appropriate syntax; Makes presentations or gives performances Shows self-respect and respect for others; Initiates actions toward achievement of goals; Takes reasonable risks; Demonstrates assertive behavior; Functions without need for constant reassurance from others

### Enhanced Self-Esteem

Examples of Achievement Indicators

Shows self-respect and respect for others; Initiates actions toward achievement of goals; Takes reasonable risks; Demonstrates assertive behavior; Functions without need for constant reassurance from others

### Realistic Self-Appraisal

Examples of Achievement Indicators

Articulates personal skills and abilities; Makes decisions and acts in congruence with personal values; Acknowledges personal strengths and weaknesses; Articulates rationale for personal behavior; Seeks feedback from others; Learns from past experiences

## Clarified Values

Examples of Achievement Indicators

Articulates personal values; Acts in congruence with personal values; Makes decisions that reflect personal values; Demonstrates willingness to scrutinize personal beliefs and values; Identifies personal, work and lifestyle values and explains how they influence decision-making

## Career Choices

Examples of Achievement Indicators

Articulates career choices based on assessment of interests, values, skills and abilities; Documents knowledge, skills and accomplishments resulting from formal education, work experience, community service and volunteer experiences; Makes the connections between classroom and out-of-classroom learning; Can construct a resume with clear job objectives and evidence of related knowledge, skills and accomplishments; Articulates the characteristics of a preferred work environment; Comprehends the world of work; Takes steps to initiate a job search or seek advanced education

## Leadership Development

Examples of Achievement Indicators

Articulates leadership philosophy or style; Serves in a leadership position in a student organization; Comprehends the dynamics of a group; Exhibits democratic principles as a leader; Exhibits ability to visualize a group purpose and desired outcomes

## Healthy Behavior

Examples of Achievement Indicators

Chooses behaviors and environments that promote health and reduce risk; Articulate the relationship between health and wellness and accomplishing life long goals; Exhibits behaviors that advance a healthy community

## Meaningful Interpersonal Relationships

Examples of Achievement Indicators

Develops and maintains satisfying interpersonal relationships; Establishes mutually rewarding relationships with friends and colleagues; Listens to and considers others' points of view; Treats others with respect

## Independence

Examples of Achievement Indicators

Exhibits self-reliant behaviors; Functions autonomously; Exhibits ability to function interdependently; Accepts supervision as needed; Manages time effectively

## Collaboration

Examples of Achievement Indicators

Works cooperatively with others; Seeks the involvement of others; Seeks feedback from others; Contributes to achievement of a group goal; Exhibits effective listening skill

## Social Responsibility

Examples of Achievement Indicators

Understands and participates in relevant governance systems; Understands, abides by, and participates in the development, maintenance, and/or orderly change of community, social, and legal standards or norms; Appropriately challenges the unfair, unjust, or uncivil behavior of other individuals or groups; Participates in service/volunteer activities

## Satisfying and Productive Lifestyles

Examples of Achievement Indicators

Achieves balance between education, work and leisure time; Articulates and meets goals for work, leisure and education; Overcomes obstacles that hamper goal achievement; Functions on the basis of personal identity, ethical, spiritual and moral values; Articulates long-term goals and objectives

## Appreciating Diversity

Examples of Achievement Indicators

Understands ones own identity and culture. Seeks involvement with people different from oneself; Seeks involvement in diverse interests; Articulates the advantages and challenges of a diverse society; Challenges appropriately abusive use of stereotypes by others; Understands the impact of diversity on one's own society

## Spiritual Awareness

Examples of Achievement Indicators

Develops and articulates personal belief system; Understands roles of spirituality in personal and group values and behaviors

## Personal and Educational Goals

Examples of Achievement Indicators

Sets, articulates, and pursues individual goals; Articulates personal and educational goals and objectives; Uses personal and educational goals to guide decisions; Understands the effect of one's personal and education goals on others

CHP must be (a) intentional, (b) coherent, (c) based on theories and knowledge of learning and human development, (d) reflective of developmental and demographic profiles of the student population, and (e) responsive to needs of individuals, special populations, and communities.

CHP must establish appropriate policies and procedures for responding to emergency situations, especially where facilities, personnel and resources are not equipped to handle emergencies.

CHP must provide an infrastructure to support its services. The program must also create and maintain a network throughout the campus and surrounding communities.

CHP must conform to a general level of acceptable practice, regardless of the size or scope of health services offered at a given institution. In order to render such services to students and others in the college community, the program must meet reasonable standards of clinical services, counseling services, public health education, as appropriate.

In determining the scope of services to be offered, the following guidelines should apply.

- CHP contribute to the overall responsibility of the college for education of students in the areas of lifestyle and behavior that promote physical, psychological, spiritual, and social health.
- The scope and objectives of the program should be planned and outlined according to standard practice utilizing goals and objectives, target populations, assessment strategies and evaluative methodologies.
- The educational goals of CHP should be consistent with nationally and internationally developed health objectives addressing current and future trends, when consistent with college student needs.
- Documented evidence of organized program planning and implementation should be available.
- Educational and promotional materials should be accurate, understandable, and appropriately geared to the college population.
- Should provide outreach educational opportunities to address health and wellness issues.
- Appropriate interdisciplinary health service and interagency collaboration should occur regularly.

In determining the quality of services provided, the following guidelines should apply.

- Services are provided in accordance with standards of professional practice and ethical conduct and with concern for the costs versus benefit to the population
- CHP may have program accreditation and staff certification, and/or licensure, should be obtained where appropriate
- Services should be cost-effective, relevant and designed to address unique campus configurations of service delivery
- Coordination of services to ensure individuals are served appropriately
- The college health program should identify less expensive alternative resources for individuals when appropriate

## Part 3.  LEADERSHIP

Effective and ethical leadership is essential to the success of all organizations. Institutions must appoint, position, and empower college health programs (CHP) leaders within the administrative structure to accomplish stated missions. CHP leaders at various levels must be selected on the basis of formal education and training, relevant work experience, personal skills and competencies, relevant professional credentials, as well as potential for promoting learning and development in students, applying effective practices to educational processes, and enhancing institutional effectiveness. Institutions must determine expectations of accountability for leaders and fairly assess their performance.

Leaders of CHP must exercise authority over resources for which they are responsible to achieve their respective missions.

CHP leaders must . . .

- articulate a vision for their organization
- set goals and objectives based on the needs and capabilities of the  population served
- promote student learning and development
- prescribe and practice ethical behavior
- recruit, select, supervise, and develop others in the organization
- manage  financial resources
- coordinate human resources
- plan, budget for, and evaluate personnel and programs
- apply effective practices to educational and administrative processes
- communicate effectively
- initiate collaborative interaction between individuals and agencies that possess legitimate concerns and interests in the functional area

CHP leaders must identify and find means to address individual, organizational, or environmental conditions that inhibit goal achievement and must promote campus environments that result in multiple opportunities for student learning and development.

CHP leaders must continuously improve programs and services in response to changing needs of students and other constituents, and evolving institutional priorities.

The institution should have a defined governance structure that sets policy and is responsible for the college health program and its operations. The institution is a legally constituted entity in the state(s)/provinces in which it is located and provides services.

## Part 4.  ORGANIZATION and MANAGEMENT

Guided by an overarching intent to ensure student learning and development, college health programs (CHP) must be structured purposefully and managed effectively to achieve stated goals. Evidence of appropriate structure must include current and accessible policies and procedures, written performance expectations for all employees, functional workflow graphics or organizational charts, and clearly stated service delivery expectations.

The structure should be defined by the size, nature, complexity, and philosophy of the institution and by the documented needs of the population it serves.

The program should establish and maintain an advisory board with broad constituent representation, with specific duties and responsibilities for policy, budget, and services, facilities, and resources.

CHP should make initial appointments, reappointments, and assignment or curtailment of clinical privileges based upon a professional review of credentials and as directed by institutional policy and state/provincial law.

**Evidence of effective management must include use of comprehensive and accurate information for decisions, clear sources and channels of authority, effective communication practices, decision-making and conflict resolution procedures, responsiveness to changing conditions, accountability and evaluation systems, and recognition and reward processes. CHP must provide channels within the organization for regular review of administrative policies and procedures.**

CHP should establish criteria and implement a procedure for the credentialing and recredentialing of practitioners.

CHP or institutions should have their own independent process of credentialing. Credentialing of a health care practitioner by another health care organization other than the accrediting organization, such as a hospital, may be utilized as part of an overall independent process of credentialing by the accrediting organization, but is not relied upon exclusively.

CHP should establish and implement a procedure for verifying credentials, as it makes appointments, and assigns or curtails privileges and practices. Practitioner credentialing by another health care organization may be utilized as part of an overall independent process of credentialing.

**The college health program director or coordinator must be placed within the institution's organizational structures so as to be able to promote cooperative interaction with appropriate campus and community entities and to develop the support of high-level administrators.**

## Part 5. HUMAN RESOURCES

**College health programs (CHP) must be staffed adequately by individuals qualified to accomplish its mission and goals. Within established guidelines of the institution, CHP must establish procedures for staff selection, training, and evaluation; set expectations for supervision, and provide appropriate professional development**

opportunities. **CHP must strive to improve the professional competence and skills of all personnel tthe program employs.**

Personnel policies should be established and implemented to facilitate attainment of the mission, goals, and objectives of CHP.

CHP should strive to improve the professional competence and skill, as well as the quality of performance of all personnel it employs.

CHP should provide personnel with convenient access to library services that include materials pertinent to the clinical, educational, administrative, institutional, and research services offered by the college health program.

CHP should provide adequate orientation and training to familiarize all personnel with the appropriate policies, procedures, and facilities.

CHP should encourage participation of personnel in seminars, workshops, and other educational activities pertinent to its mission, goals, objectives, and the professional role.

CHP should accept evidence of participation in relevant external educational programs, when attendance at educational activities is required of professional personnel.

Educational activities should be responsive to the findings of quality improvement findings and to goals for professional education established by recognized professional authorities.

CHP should monitor the use of educational resources available to its professional personnel to assure that activities are relevant to the mission, goals, and objectives of the college health service, and to maintain the licensure and/or certification of professional personnel.

**Professional staff members must hold an earned graduate degree in a field relevant to the position they hold or must possess an appropriate combination of educational credentials and related work experience.**

All professional staff members should have appropriate professional preparation and competencies in both theories and practice.

**Degree or credential-seeking interns must be qualified by enrollment in an appropriate field of study and by relevant experience. These individuals must be trained and supervised adequately by professional staff members holding educational credentials and related work experience appropriate for supervision.**

**Student employees and volunteers must be carefully selected, trained, supervised, and evaluated. Degree or credential-seeking interns must be qualified by enrollment in an appropriate field of study and by relevant experience. These individuals must be trained and supervised adequately by professional staff members holding**

educational credentials and related work experience appropriate for supervision. They must be trained on how and when to refer those in need of assistance to qualified staff members and have access to a supervisor for assistance in making these judgments. Student employees and volunteers must be provided clear and precise job descriptions, pre-service training based on assessed needs, and continuing staff development.

Students may serve as peer health advocates, educators, opinion leaders, or peer counselors with proper training and supervision.

CHP must have technical and support staff members adequate to accomplish its mission. Staff members must be technologically proficient and qualified to perform their job functions, be knowledgeable of ethical and legal uses of technology, and have access to training. The level of staffing and workloads must be adequate and appropriate for program and service demands.

Salary levels and fringe benefits for all CHP staff members must be commensurate with those for comparable positions within the institution, in similar institutions, and in the relevant geographic area.

CHP must institute hiring and promotion practices that are fair, inclusive, and non-discriminatory. CHP must employ a diverse staff to provide readily identifiable role models for students and to enrich the campus community.

Staff members should take part in training sessions about gender, racial, cultural, and ethnic sensitivity and should be aware of campus and community issues and encouraged to participate in events and issues.

Staff members should educate students about health service philosophies, policies, and procedures. They demonstrate a strict regard for confidentiality and project an image of trust when dealing with sensitive information.

CHP must create and maintain position descriptions for all staff members and provide regular performance planning and appraisals.

CHP must have a system for regular staff evaluation and must provide access to continuing education and professional development opportunities, including in-service training programs and participation in professional conferences and workshops.

Specific aspects of the college health program for which staff should be assigned include business and financial management, program delivery, and assessment.

Leaders should involve staff members in designing organizational structure and creating and reviewing policies and procedures that foster health-engendering attitudes and behaviors.

When the staff of a college health program is involved in formal teaching or supervision, policies governing those activities must be consistent with the mission, goals, and objectives of the institution.

When the staff of a college health program is involved in research and publishing, policies governing those activities must be consistent with mission, goals, and objectives of the institution and clinical capabilities of the program.

All staff should be informed of the college health program and institution research policies.

## Part 6. FINANCIAL RESOURCES

College health programs (CHP) must have adequate funding to accomplish its mission and goals. Funding priorities must be determined within the context of the stated mission, goals, objectives, and comprehensive analysis of the needs and capabilities of students, and the availability of internal or external resources.

CHP must demonstrate fiscal responsibility and cost effectiveness consistent with institutional protocols.

The institution should provide sufficient funding for CHP so that staff members may spend the majority of their time on planning, programming, providing services, and evaluation rather than on seeking new or continuing funding sources.

Financial planning and projections should include budget data for both current and long- term expenditures to achieve effective financial planning that includes capital expenditures and deferred maintenance costs.

## Part 7. FACILITIES, TECHNOLOGY, EQUIPMENT

College health programs (CHP) must have adequate, suitably located facilities, adequate technology, and equipment to support its mission and goals efficiently and effectively. Facilities, technology, and equipment must be evaluated regularly and be in compliance with relevant federal, state, provincial, and local requirements to provide for access, health, safety, and security.

CHP must ensure that its facilities, technology, and equipment are accessible for persons with disabilities.

CHP should support a range of activities including prevention, education, intervention, programming, and consultation. A safe, functional and effective environment for students, staff, and others is crucial to providing appropriate services and achieving desired outcomes.

Effective environmental conditions should include . . .
- facilities that comply with applicable federal, state/provincial, and local building codes and regulations, local fire prevention regulations
- necessary facilities, equipment, and procedures to handle clinical emergencies
- [a] regulations prohibiting smoking
- elimination of hazards that might lead to slipping, falling, electrical shock, burns, poisoning, or other trauma
- adequate reception areas, toilets, and telephones
- guest parking
- accommodations for persons with physical disabilities
- adequate lighting and ventilation
- clean and properly maintained facilities
- confidentiality and privacy of services and records
- appropriate urgent care/emergency equipment and supplies readily accessible in all medical services areas
- testing and proper maintenance of equipment
- a system for the proper identification, management, handling, transport, treatment, and disposition of hazardous materials and wastes whether solid, liquid, or gas
- appropriate alternative power sources
- use of technology to improve services and facilities

## Part 8. LEGAL RESPONSIBILITIES

College health program (CHP) staff members must be knowledgeable about and responsive to laws and regulations that relate to their respective responsibilities. CHP staff members must inform users of programs and services and officials, as appropriate, of legal obligations and limitations including constitutional, statutory, regulatory, and case law; mandatory laws and orders emanating from federal, state/provincial and local governments; and the institution's policies.

Staff members must use reasonable and informed practices to limit the liability exposure of the institution, its officers, employees, and agents. Staff members must be informed about institutional policies regarding personal liability and related insurance coverage options.

The institution must provide access to legal advice for CHP staff members as needed to carry out assigned responsibilities and must inform CHP staff and students in a timely and systematic fashion about extraordinary or changing legal obligations and potential liabilities.

CHP must inform the college community of its policies and procedures addressing: individual rights and responsibilities; balancing continuity of care and protection of individual health and safety with the individual rights to confidentiality and privacy; risk management; health insurance; informed consent; and, the access, release, content, and maintenance of individual records in accordance with legal obligations and limitations.

CHP must develop and maintain a program of risk management appropriate to the organization.
Risk management programs should focus on:
- methods by which individuals may be dismissed from care or refused care
- methods of collecting unpaid accounts
- review of all litigation
- review of all deaths, trauma, or adverse events
- communication with the liability insurance carrier
- methods of dealing with inquiries from government agencies, attorneys, consumer advocate groups, reporters, and the media
- methods of addressing the relationships with competing health care organizations
- methods to manage a situation in which a physician becomes incapacitated during a medical or surgical procedure
- the impaired health care worker
- methods for complying with governmental regulations and contractual agreements
- methods for prevention of unauthorized proscribing

## Part 9. EQUITY and ACCESS

College health program (CHP) staff members must ensure that services and programs are provided on a fair and equitable basis. Facilities, programs and services must be accessible. Hours of operation and delivery of and access to programs and services must be responsive to the needs of all students and other constituents. CHP must adhere to the spirit and intent of equal opportunity laws.

College health programs should accommodate the unique needs individual disabilities and should encourage faculty, staff, and other students to develop awareness and sensitivity. Students with disabilities should be encourage to self identify individual needs as soon as possible following admission (pre-matriculation) so that special efforts can be made.

For students with physical disabilities, institutional efforts should normally be made to meet special needs through health programs, housing, food services, and counseling. Whenever possible, the institution should eliminate architectural barriers that create difficulties for students with mobility limitations.

In order to meet the special needs of older students, a college health program may provide those services directly or identify appropriate resources in the community. Such special services may include screening for and monitoring of chronic illnesses.

The CHP must be open and readily accessible to all students and must not discriminate except where sanctioned by law and institutional policy. Discrimination must especially be avoided on the bases of age; color, creed; cultural heritage; disability; ethnicity; gender identity; nationality;

**political affiliation, religious affiliation, sex, sexual orientation; or economic, marital, social, or veteran status.**

Students with special health risks may be identified by information provided on health history or behavioral assessment forms, or through programs of screening, surveillance, and education.

Students with chronic health conditions such as diabetes, epilepsy, HIV disease, and pulmonary or chronic cardiovascular disease, may be identified and informed of support services.

In order to meet the special needs of older students, a college health program may provide those services directly or identify appropriate resources in the community. Such special services may include screening for and monitoring of chronic illnesses.

**Consistent with their mission and goals, CHP take affirmative action to remedy significant imbalances in student participation and staffing patterns.**

**As the demographic profiles of campuses change and new instructional delivery methods are introduced, institutions must recognize the needs of students who participate in distance learning for access to programs and services offered on campus. ▢Institutions must provide appropriate services in ways that are accessible to distance learners and assist them in identifying and gaining access to other appropriate services in their geographic region.**

**CHP must ensure that students are informed about the importance of health insurance and how to make an informed decision based on their needs.**

As a condition of enrollment, the college may require students to provide evidence that they have health insurance coverage.

The student health insurance/benefits program should be available to all eligible students.

## Part 10. CAMPUS and EXTERNAL RELATIONS

**College Health Programs (CHP) must establish, maintain, and promote effective relations with relevant individuals, campus offices, and external agencies.**

**To ensure success, CHP must maintain good relations with students, faculty, staff, alumni, the community at large, contractors, and support agencies.**

CHP staff should participate actively with their institutions in designing policies and practices and developing resources, including health promotion and disease prevention as well as illness treatment approaches, which have direct impacts on the health of the campus population.

Policies on requirements for immunization prior to and during matriculation should be implemented and maintained to assure compliance, protect community health, and meet the needs of students at risk.

CHP should review and assess health aspects of relevant institutional policies and practices addressing health issues such as alcohol and other drug use, eating disorders, sexually transmitted diseases, blood-borne diseases, sexual harassment/assault, suicide and homicide threats, and discrimination of all types.

CHP should review potential health hazards or problems related to academic service/outreach programs.

CHP should identify and utilize community services, whenever appropriate, to build resource networks and educate the community about special health needs of diverse population groups.

## Part 11. DIVERSITY

**Within the context of each institution's unique mission, diversity enriches the community and enhances the collegiate experience for all; therefore, college health programs (CHP) must nurture environments where commonalties and differences among people are recognized and honored.**

**CHP must promote educational experiences that are characterized by open and continuous communication that deepens understanding of one's own identity, culture, and heritage, and that of others. CHP must educate and promote respect about commonalties and differences in their historical and cultural contexts.**

**CHP must address the characteristics and needs of a diverse population when establishing and implementing policies and procedures.**

Every contact should be viewed as an opportunity to recognize and honor diversity and address specific concerns which might impact health problems and quality of life issues for the individual and community.

Students should be provided an environment of caring with an inclusive approach, which is essential for establishing levels of confidentiality, trust, and comfort.

All students should be encouraged to discuss with staff their comfort or discomfort with various approaches in delivery of services.

Individuals should be accepted in a free and open manner and in an atmosphere of mutual respect, in order to encourage candid discussion of the sensitive personal problems. Staff members should demonstrate sensitivity and understanding to students from diverse backgrounds and cultures, in order to provide satisfactory services.

## Part 12. ETHICS

**All persons involved in the delivery of college health program (CHP) services must adhere to the highest principles of ethical behavior. CHP must develop or adopt and implement appropriate statements of ethical practice. CHP must publish**

these statements and ensure their periodic review by relevant constituencies.

CHP staff members must ensure that privacy and confidentiality are maintained with respect to all communications and records to the extent that such records are protected under the law and appropriate statements of ethical practice. Information contained in students' education records must not be disclosed without written consent except as allowed by relevant laws and institutional policies. Staff members must disclose to appropriate authorities information judged to be of an emergency nature, especially when the safety of the individual or others is involved, or when otherwise required by institutional policy or relevant law.

The task of media relations involving individual care status should be assigned to staff members who are well versed in the information that can be released. Staff members should prevent visitors from entering the facility in any manner that would compromise confidentiality.

All CHP staff members must be aware of and comply with the provisions contained in the institution's human subjects research policy and in other relevant institutional policies addressing ethical practices and confidentiality of research data concerning individuals.

Staff members must recognize and avoid personal conflict of interest or appearance thereof in their transactions with students and others.

Conflicts of interest should be avoided such as in athletic medicine; pharmacy services; band in the use of clinical consultants, vendors, and contractors. Products and services should not be promoted for any other reason than the individual's benefit.

CHP staff members must strive to ensure the fair, objective, and impartial treatment of all persons with whom they deal. Staff members must not participate in nor condone any form of harassment that demeans persons or creates an intimidating, hostile, or offensive campus environment.

When handling institutional funds, all CHP staff members must ensure that such funds are managed in accordance with established and responsible accounting procedures and the fiscal policies or processes of the institution.

CHP staff members must perform their duties within the limits of their training, expertise, and competence. When these limits are exceeded, individuals in need of further assistance must be referred to persons possessing appropriate qualifications.

CHP staff members must use suitable means to confront and otherwise hold accountable other staff members who exhibit unethical behavior.

CHP staff members must be knowledgeable about and practice ethical behavior in the use of technology.

All marketing and advertising concerning the college health program must communicate the scope and range of services provided without deception.

College health programs should inform individuals of their basic rights and responsibilities regarding health care and service. Such rights and responsibilities include . . .

- care and service that is competent, considerate and compassionate, recognizes basic human rights, safeguards personal dignity, and respect values and preferences
- provision of appropriate privacy, including protection from access to confidential information by faculty members, staff, and others not responsible for direct health care
- ability to change primary and specialty health care providers
- accurate information regarding competence and capabilities of the college health program
- use of identified methods to express grievances and make suggestions
- information concerning diagnosis, treatment, prognosis and participation in decisions involving health care and service
- individual disclosure of complete and full information on health status which will be treated confidentially and which the individual gives authority to approve or refuse release in compliance with applicable state/federal/provincial laws
- a process for sharing necessary personal health care information with mental health/ counseling/ psychotherapy services and other college professionals on a need-to-know basis

## Part 13. ASSESSMENT and EVALUATION

College health programs (CHP) must conduct regular assessment and evaluations. CHP must employ effective qualitative and quantitative methodologies as appropriate, to determine whether and to what degree the stated mission, goals, and student learning and development outcomes are being met. The process must employ sufficient and sound assessment measures to ensure comprehensiveness. Data collected must include responses from students and other affected constituencies.

A college health program should maintain an active, organized, peer-based, quality management and improvement program that links peer review, quality improvement activities, and risk management in an organized, systematic way.

Periodically, the organization should assess consumer satisfaction with services and facilities provided by the college health program and incorporate findings into quality improvement.

To develop criteria used to evaluate care, staff members should understand, support and participate in programs of quality management and improvement. Data should be collected in an ongoing manner to identify unacceptable or unexpected trends or occurrences.

The quality improvement program should address clinical, administrative, and cost-of-care issues and patient outcomes. Quality improvement activities conducted by specific disciplines should be consistent with the characteristics of the organization's quality improvement program.

**CHP must evaluate periodically how well they complement and enhance the institution's stated mission and educational effectiveness. Results of these evaluations must be used in revising and improving programs and services and in recognizing staff performance.**

# THE ROLE of COLLEGE UNIONS
## *CAS* Standards Contextual Statement

Today's college union is the campus community center, serving students, faculty, administration, staff, alumni, and guests. It is a unifying force that brings together diverse people, provides a forum for divergent viewpoints, and creates an environment where all feel welcome.

The college union—which may refer to an organization, a program, or a building—evolved from the debating tradition of British universities. The earliest college union, founded at Cambridge University in 1815, was literally a "union" of three debating societies. The first US college union was organized at Harvard in 1832; like its British predecessors, it existed primarily for debating purposes. By the late 1800s, the Harvard Union had embraced the concept of being a general club. The first building erected explicitly for union purposes was Houston Hall at the University of Pennsylvania. Built in 1896, it housed lounges, dining rooms, reading and writing rooms, an auditorium, game rooms, and student offices; it was given to the university by the Houston family as a "place where all may meet on common ground."

In the 1930s, the success of civic recreational and cultural centers influenced college union leaders to view the union as the campus counterpart of the "community center," with an educational and recreational mission to perform. The most extensive period of union building construction took place following World War II, as enrollments surged and colleges and universities sought to better fulfill the needs of students and faculty. During the last half of the 20th Century, the college union movement has concentrated on building community, emphasizing its educational mission, and promoting student development and leadership.

Additionally, the contemporary college union offers many services used by all members of the campus community. College unions often include banks, post offices, child care, dining facilities, study lounges, computer labs, bookstores and other services the campus community, and students especially, rely on during the course of the day while they are on campus. In providing these services, the college union allows its community to focus on academic and personal achievement.

The college union provides numerous educationally purposeful activities outside the classroom, which are "key to enhancing learning and personal development," according to *The Student Learning Imperative* (ACPA, 1994). The official *Role of the College Union* states that it is "an integral part of the educational mission of the college." The union contributes to the education of the student body at large through its cultural, educational, social, and recreational programs and by encouraging "self-directed activity, giving maximum opportunity for self-realization." But the union also educates the students involved in its governance and program boards and those it employs. The role statement defines the union as "a student centered organization that values participatory decision making. Through volunteerism, its boards, committees, and student employment, the union offers firsthand experience in citizenship and educates students in leadership, social responsibility, and values." These models of college union governance foster student/staff partnerships that form the foundation for student development and leadership training.

## References and Resources

American College Personnel Association [ACPA] (1994) The student learning imperative. Washington, DC: Author.

Butts, P. F. (1971). *The college union idea*. Bloomington, IN: Association of College Unions International.

McMillan, A., & Davis, N. T. (Eds.) (1989). *College unions: Seventy-five years*. Bloomington, IN: Association of College Unions International.

Metz, N. D. (Ed.) (1996). *Student development in college unions and student activities*. Bloomington, IN: Association of College Unions International.

Metz, N., & Sievers, C. S. (2002). *Student leadership in college unions and student activities*. Bloomington, IN: ACUI.

Mitchell, R. L. (1997). *Metaphors, semaphores and two-by-fours: Reflections on a personal profession*. Bloomington, IN: ACUI.

Maul, S. Y. (1994). *Building community on campus*. Bloomington, IN: ACUI.

Association of College Unions International (ACUI) Central Office, One City Centre, Suite 200, 120 W. Seventh St., Bloomington, IN 47404-3925. (812) 855-8550

*The Bulletin*, ACUI publication, published bimonthly; available from the ACUI Central Office.

# COLLEGE UNION
## *CAS* STANDARDS and GUIDELINES

## Part 1. MISSION

The college union (CU) must incorporate student learning and student development in its mission. The CU must enhance overall educational experiences. The CU must develop, record, disseminate, implement and regularly review its mission and goals. Mission statements must be consistent with the mission and goals of the institution and with the standards in this document. The CU must operate as an integral part of the institution's overall mission.

The primary goals of the CU must be to maintain facilities, provide services, and promote programs that are responsive to student developmental needs and to the physical, social, recreational, and continuing education needs of the campus community.

The CU is a center for the campus community and, as such, is an integral part of the institution's educational environment. The union represents a building, an organization, and a program; it provides services, facilities, and educational and recreational programs that enhance the quality of college life.

Through the work of its staff and various committees the CU can be a "laboratory" where students can learn and practice leadership, programming, management, social responsibility, and interpersonal skills. As a center for the academic community, the union provides a place for increased interaction and understanding among individuals from diverse backgrounds.

To meet its goals, college unions should provide . . .
- food services
- leisure time and recreational opportunities
- social, cultural, and intellectual programs
- continuing education opportunities
- retail stores
- service agencies that are responsive to campus needs
- student leadership development programs and opportunities
- student employment
- student development programs

## Part 2. PROGRAM

The formal education of students consists of the curriculum and the co-curriculum, and must promote student learning and development that is purposeful and holistic. The college union (CU) must identify relevant and desirable student learning and development outcomes and provide programs and services that encourage the achievement of those outcomes.

Relevant and desirable outcomes include: intellectual growth, effective communication, realistic self-appraisal, enhanced self-esteem, clarified values, career choices, leadership development, healthy behaviors, meaningful interpersonal relationships, independence, collaboration, social responsibility, satisfying and productive lifestyles, appreciation of diversity, spiritual awareness, and achievement of personal and educational goals.

The College Union must provide evidence of its impact on the achievement of student learning and development outcomes.

The program may use the examples that follow or identify other more germane indicators.

### Student Learning & Development Outcome Domains

### Social Responsibility

Examples of Achievement Indicators
Understands and participates in relevant governance systems; Understands, abides by, and participates in the development, maintenance, and/or orderly change of community, social, and legal standards or norms; Appropriately challenges the unfair, unjust, or uncivil behavior of other individuals or groups; Participates in service/volunteer activities

### Leadership Development

Examples of Achievement Indicators
Articulates leadership philosophy or style; Serves in a leadership position in a student organization; Comprehends the dynamics of a group; Exhibits democratic principles as a leader; Exhibits ability to visualize a group purpose and desired outcomes

### Collaboration

Examples of Achievement Indicators
Works cooperatively with others; Seeks the involvement of others; Seeks feedback from others; Contributes to achievement of a group goal; Exhibits effective listening skills

### Satisfying and Productive Lifestyles

Examples of Achievement Indicators
Achieves balance between education, work and leisure time; Articulates and meets goals for work, leisure and education; Overcomes obstacles that hamper goal achievement; Functions on the basis of personal identity, ethical, spiritual and moral values; Articulates long-term goals and objectives

## Effective Communication
Examples of Achievement Indicators
> Writes and speaks coherently and effectively; Writes and speaks after reflection; Able to influence others through writing, speaking or artistic expression; Effectively articulates abstract ideas; Uses appropriate syntax; Makes presentations or gives performances

## Meaningful Interpersonal Relationships
Examples of Achievement Indicators
> Develops and maintains satisfying interpersonal relationships; Establishes mutually rewarding relationships with friends and colleagues; Listens to and considers others' points of view; Treats others with respect

## Enhanced Self-Esteem
Examples of Achievement Indicators
> Shows self-respect and respect for others; Initiates actions toward achievement of goals; Takes reasonable risks; Demonstrates assertive behavior; Functions without need for constant reassurance from others

## Independence
Examples of Achievement Indicators
> Exhibits self-reliant behaviors; Functions autonomously; Exhibits ability to function interdependently; Accepts supervision as needed; Manages time effectively

## Realistic Self-Appraisal
Examples of Achievement Indicators
> Articulates personal skills and abilities; Makes decisions and acts in congruence with personal values; Acknowledges personal strengths and weaknesses; Articulates rationale for personal behavior; Seeks feedback from others; Learns from past experiences

## Clarified Values
Examples of Achievement Indicators
> Articulates personal values; Acts in congruence with personal values; Makes decisions that reflect personal values; Demonstrates willingness to scrutinize personal beliefs and values; Identifies personal, work and lifestyle values and explains how they influence decision-making

## Appreciating Diversity
Examples of Achievement Indicators
> Understands ones own identity and culture. Seeks involvement with people different from oneself; Seeks involvement in diverse interests; Articulate the advantages and challenges of a diverse society; Challenges appropriately abusive use of stereotypes by others; Understands the impact of diversity on one's own society

## Intellectual Growth
Examples of Achievement Indicators
> Produces personal and educational goal statements; Employs critical thinking in problem solving; Uses complex information from a variety of sources including personal experience and observation to form a decision or opinion; Obtains a degree; Applies previously understood information and concepts to a new situation or setting; Expresses appreciation for literature, the fine arts, mathematics, sciences, and social sciences

## Personal and Educational Goals
Examples of Achievement Indicators
> Sets, articulates, and pursues individual goals; Articulate personal and educational goals and objectives; Uses personal and educational goals to guide decisions; Understands the effect of one's personal and education goals on others

## Career Choices
Examples of Achievement Indicators
> Articulate career choices based on assessment of interests, values, skills and abilities; Documents knowledge, skills and accomplishments resulting from formal education, work experience, community service and volunteer experiences; Makes the connections between classroom and out-of-classroom learning; Can construct a resume with clear job objectives and evidence of related knowledge, skills and accomplishments; Articulates the characteristics of a preferred work environment; Comprehends the world of work; Takes steps to initiate a job search or seek advanced education

## Healthy Behavior
Examples of Achievement Indicators
> Chooses behaviors and environments that promote health and reduce risk; Articulate the relationship between health and wellness and accomplishing life long goals; Exhibits behaviors that advance a healthy community

## Spiritual Awareness
Examples of Achievement Indicators
> Develops and articulates personal belief system; Understands roles of spirituality in personal and group values and behaviors

**The CU program must be (a) intentional, (b) coherent, (c) based on theories and knowledge of learning and human development, (d) reflective of developmental and demographic profiles of the student population, and (e) responsive to needs of individuals, special populations, and communities.**

**The CU activities and services must be appropriate to the size and diversity of the campus and must provide opportunities for student, staff, and faculty participation, interaction, and collaboration on policy establishment, facility operation, and program activities. The CU must strive to enhance intellectual and behavioral learning.**

The program of college unions includes services, facilities and activity events. The college union should provide, in varying degrees, food services, meeting rooms student and administrative offices an information reception center, lounge(s), a merchandise counter or store, a lobby, public telephones, recreation facilities, and rest rooms.

Additional services and facilities provided by most unions include music listening rooms, table game rooms, space for exhibits, parking facilities, and conference rooms.

The union should include a balanced variety of activities, such as art, performing arts, music, cinematic arts, games and tournaments, outdoor recreation, lecture and literary events, crafts and hobbies, social and dance events, and activities addressing social responsibility and human relations. Program events should be diverse reflecting the richness of the community's cultures.

## Part 3: LEADERSHIP

Effective and ethical leadership is essential to the success of all organizations. Institutions must appoint, position, and empower college union (CU) leaders within the administrative structure to accomplish stated missions. Leaders at various levels must be selected on the basis of formal education and training, relevant work experience, personal skills and competencies, relevant professional credentials, as well as potential for promoting learning and development in students, applying effective practices to educational processes, and enhancing institutional effectiveness. Institutions must determine expectations of accountability for leaders and fairly assess their performance.

CU leaders must exercise authority over resources for which they are responsible to achieve their respective missions and must . . .

• articulate a vision for their organization
• set goals and objectives based on the needs and capabilities of the  population served
• promote student learning and development
• prescribe and practice ethical behavior
• recruit, select, supervise, and develop others in the organization
• manage  financial resources
• coordinate human resources
• plan, budget for, and evaluate personnel and programs
• apply effective practices to educational and administrative processes
• communicate effectively
• initiate collaborative interaction between individuals and agencies that possess legitimate concerns and interests in the functional area

CU leaders must identify and find means to address individual, organizational, or environmental conditions that inhibit goal achievement and must promote campus environments that result in multiple opportunities for student learning and development.

CU leaders must continuously improve programs and services in response to changing needs of students and other constituents, and evolving institutional priorities.

## Part 4. ORGANIZATION and MANAGEMENT

Guided by an overarching intent to ensure student learning and development, the college union (CU) must be structured purposefully and managed effectively to achieve stated goals. Evidence of appropriate structure must include current and accessible policies and procedures, written performance expectations for all employees, functional workflow graphics or organizational charts, and clearly stated service delivery expectations.

Evidence of effective management must include use of comprehensive and accurate information for decisions, clear sources and channels of authority, effective communication practices, decision-making and conflict resolution procedures, responsiveness to changing conditions, accountability and evaluation systems, and recognition and reward processes. The CU must provide channels within the organization for regular review of administrative policies and procedures.

The CU must be organized to maintain its physical plant, to provide for cultural, intellectual, and recreational programming, to operate its business enterprises, and to deliver successfully the services inherent in the union's mission.

A variety of facilities, programs, and services may be incorporated within the building and operation. These include: food service; store and other revenue producing services; leisure time activities; social, cultural, and intellectual activities; building operations; and continuing education.

The CU must involve members of the campus community in its governance and programming structure and in the formulation of necessary union policies.

Operations involve day to-day undertakings such as fiscal controls, maintenance of physical plant and equipment, provision of services supervision of personnel, planning, and public relations.

Involvement of the campus community should include students, faculty, staff, and alumni, as appropriate. Typically such involvement is through advisory, governing, and program boards. These boards might address issues such as (a) facility operating policies related to the use and/or rental of the union by campus and non-campus groups, (b) scheduling of controversial speakers and/or events, (c) budget planning and allocation of funds (d) employment policies, (e) space allocation priority setting, and (f) hours of operation.

## Part 5. HUMAN RESOURCES

**The college union (CU) must be staffed adequately by individuals qualified to accomplish its mission and goals. Within established guidelines of the institution, the CU must establish procedures for staff selection, training, and evaluation; set expectations for supervision, and provide appropriate professional development opportunities. The CU must strive to improve the professional competence and skills of all personnel it employs.**

**CU professional staff members must hold an earned graduate degree in a field relevant to the position they hold or must possess an appropriate combination of educational credentials and related work experience.**

Staff should include persons providing the necessary professional leadership to assume responsibility for the entire union as well as for specific programs.

Desirable qualities of staff members should include: (a) knowledge of and ability to use, management principles, including the effective management of volunteers; (b) skills in assessment, planning, training, and evaluation; (c) interpersonal skills; (d) technical skills; (e) understanding of union philosophy; (f) commitment to institutional mission; and (g) understanding of, and the ability to apply student development theory.

Graduate degrees should be earned in fields relevant to college unions including, but not limited to, student development business administration, higher education administration, and recreation leadership.

**Degree or credential-seeking interns must be qualified by enrollment in an appropriate field of study and by relevant experience. These individuals must be trained and supervised adequately by professional staff members holding educational credentials and related work experience appropriate for supervision.**

Graduate students pursuing advanced degrees in student development, business administration, higher education institutional management, and recreation are among those to whom an internship or practicum in the college union can be valuable. Such experiences should provide a variety of opportunities within the union operation. Graduate assistantships also may allow persons pursuing careers in specific areas of the union field to expand their expertise. Graduate students frequently serve as program advisors or assist operations, recreation or other department supervisors while pursuing advanced degrees. Others such as paraprofessional staff and volunteers, may fulfill specific needs. The union should utilize volunteers in a manner consistent with its mission.

**Student employees and volunteers must be carefully selected, trained, supervised, and evaluated. They must be trained on how and when to refer those in need of assistance to qualified staff members and have access to a supervisor for assistance in making these judgments. Student employees and volunteers must be provided clear and precise job descriptions, pre-service training based on assessed needs, and continuing staff development.**

Student employees and volunteers may be an important part of the union's operation. Their work experience can be an important part of their educational experience as well as a source of income. A thorough training program should be provided for part time student helpers and volunteers and, depending on their assigned duties, might include leadership training, group facilitation skills, and communication skills. Volunteers should be adequately supervised and evaluated.

**The CU must have technical and support staff members adequate to accomplish its mission. Staff members must be technologically proficient and qualified to perform their job functions, be knowledgeable of ethical and legal uses of technology, and have access to training. The level of staffing and workloads must be adequate and appropriate for program and service demands.**

There should be adequate technical and clerical personnel to provide the services and maintain the facilities of the union. Included may be cooks, dishwashers, projectionists, stage hands, maintenance personnel, secretaries, bookkeepers, typists, attendants, receptionists, housekeepers, scheduling clerks, sales clerks, and cashiers.

**Salary levels and fringe benefits for all CU staff members must be commensurate with those for comparable positions within the institution, in similar institutions, and in the relevant geographic area.**

**The CU must institute hiring and promotion practices that are fair, inclusive, and non-discriminatory. The CU must employ a diverse staff to provide readily identifiable role models for students and to enrich the campus community.**

**The CU must create and maintain position descriptions for all staff members and provide regular performance planning and appraisals.**

**The CU must have a system for regular staff evaluation and must provide access to continuing education and professional development opportunities, including in-service training programs and participation in professional conferences and workshops.**

The CU must employ qualified professional, technical, and support staff members who have the ability to meet the varied educational, service, social, leisure, and recreational requirements inherent in the union's mission.

Specific aspects of the union's mission for which staff should be assigned include business operations (e.g., operations, program activities, cultural, recreational, theater, and arts and crafts), and special events.

## Part 6. FINANCIAL RESOURCES

The college union (CU) must have adequate funding to accomplish its mission and goals. Funding priorities must be determined within the context of the stated mission, goals, objectives and comprehensive analysis of the needs and capabilities of students and the availability of internal or external resources.

The CU must demonstrate fiscal responsibility and cost effectiveness consistent with institutional protocols.

The institution's budget commitment to the union should be sufficient to support the achievement of its mission and to provide appropriate services, facilities, and programs deemed necessary to maintain standards and diversity of services commensurate with the image and reputation of the institution.

The union should have adequate financial resources to ensure reasonable pricing of services, adequate programming, adequate staffing, proper maintenance and professional development.

The institution should consider various methods and sources of financial support including, but not limited to: (a) income from sales, services, and rentals; (b) student activities or program fees; (c) fees for operation or debt service; and (d) direct institutional support (e.g., utilities subsidy, salary assistance, cleaning and maintenance, operating subsidy, and membership fees).

## Part 7. FACILITIES, TECHNOLOGY, EQUIPMENT

The College Union (CU) must have adequate, suitably located facilities, adequate technology, and equipment to support its mission and goals efficiently and effectively. Facilities, technology, and equipment must be evaluated regularly and be in compliance with relevant federal, state, provincial, and local requirements to provide for access, health, safety, and security.

The physical plant should be proportional in size to the campus population. Generally a college union should contain approximately 10 square feet of gross space for each student enrolled. Smaller colleges may require more square feet per student; large colleges may require less. Also to be considered is the nature of the student body. Colleges with a large number of commuter and/or part time students or members of a special population might adjust facility requirements accordingly.

## Part 8. LEGAL RESPONSIBILITIES

College union (CU) staff members must be knowledgeable about and responsive to laws and regulations that relate to their respective responsibilities. CU staff members must inform users of programs and services and officials, as appropriate, of legal obligations and limitations including constitutional, statutory, regulatory, and case law; mandatory laws and orders emanating from federal, state/provincial and local governments; and the institution's policies.

CU staff members must use reasonable and informed practices to limit the liability exposure of the institution, its officers, employees, and agents. Staff members must be informed about institutional policies regarding personal liability and related insurance coverage options.

The institution must provide access to legal advice for CU staff members as needed to carry out assigned responsibilities.

The institution must inform CU staff and students in a timely and systematic fashion about extraordinary or changing legal obligations and potential liabilities.

## Part 9. EQUITY and ACCESS

College union (CU) staff members must ensure that services and programs are provided on a fair and equitable basis. Facilities, programs and services must be accessible. Hours of operation and delivery of and access to programs and services must be responsive to the needs of all students and other constituents. The CU program and services must adhere to the spirit and intent of equal opportunity laws.

The CU must be open and readily accessible to all students and must not discriminate except where sanctioned by law and institutional policy. Discrimination must especially be avoided on the bases of age; color, creed; cultural heritage; disability; ethnicity; gender identity; nationality; political affiliation, religious affiliation, sex, sexual orientation; or economic, marital, social, or veteran status.

As the demographic profiles of campuses change and new instructional delivery methods are introduced, institutions must recognize the needs of students who participate in distance learning for access to programs and services offered on campus. Institutions must provide appropriate services in ways that are accessible to distance learners and assist them in identifying and gaining access to other appropriate services in their geographic region.

## Part 10.  CAMPUS and EXTERNAL RELATIONS

The college union (CU) must establish, maintain, and promote effective relations with relevant individuals, campus offices, and external agencies.

The success of the CU is dependent on the maintenance of good relationships with students, faculty, administrators, alumni, the community at large, contractors, and support agencies. Staff members must encourage participation in union program by relevant groups

Each member of the campus community is a potential patron of the union's services, a potential member of the union organization, including its governing board, and a potential participant in the union's programming.

Students are the principle constituency of the union.  Much of the vitality, variety, and spontaneity of the union's activities stem from student boards and committees.

Student government and other groups should have ongoing involvement with the union's programs, services, and operations.

Student publications also may be important for communicating information about union programs. Communications with students should be continuous.

The involvement of faculty, staff, and alumni is essential to the vitality of union programs and services.

Faculty members should be involved in policy making processes and program efforts of the union.

Alumni are potential sources of support and involvement financial and otherwise.

The administrative staff of the institution is important to day to day operations of the union. In some instances important union services such as food, cleaning, repairs, bookstore, or accounting may be administered by a department of the college rather than by union staff; relations with those department heads and their representatives must be cultivated carefully. The support of other student affairs agencies as well as chief campus officials is important.

Technical and clerical staff members can be important as customers, members of the various committees, and members of the governing board.

Positive relations with lessees and contractors, (e.g., barbershops, boutiques, food services, bookstores) require close and continuing attention.

## Part 11.  DIVERSITY

Within the context of each institution's unique mission, diversity enriches the community and enhances the collegiate experience for all; therefore, the College Union (CU) must nurture environments where commonalties and differences among people are recognized and honored.

The CU must promote educational experiences that are characterized by open and continuous communication that deepens understanding of one's own identity, culture, and heritage, and that of others.  The CU must educate and promote respect about commonalties and differences in their historical and cultural contexts.

The CU must address the characteristics and needs of a diverse population when establishing and implementing policies and procedures.

## Part 12.  ETHICS

All persons involved in the delivery of college union (CU) programs and services must adhere to the highest principles of ethical behavior.  The CU must develop or adopt and implement appropriate statements of ethical practice.  The CU must publish these statements and ensure their periodic review by relevant constituencies .

CU staff members must ensure that privacy and confidentiality  are maintained with respect to all communications and records to the extent that such records are protected under the law and appropriate statements of ethical practice. Information contained in students' education records must not be disclosed without written consent except as allowed by relevant laws and institutional policies. Staff members must disclose to appropriate authorities information judged to be of an emergency nature, especially when the safety of the individual or others is involved, or when otherwise required by institutional policy or relevant law.

All CU staff members must be aware of and comply with the provisions contained in the institution's human subjects research policy and in other relevant institutional policies addressing ethical practices and confidentiality of research data concerning individuals.

CU staff members must recognize and avoid personal conflict of interest or appearance thereof in their transactions with students and others.

CU staff members must strive to ensure the fair, objective, and impartial treatment of all persons with whom they deal.  Staff members must not participate in nor condone any form of harassment that demeans persons or creates an intimidating, hostile, or offensive campus environment.

When handling institutional funds, all CU staff members must ensure that such funds are managed in accordance with established and responsible accounting procedures and the fiscal policies or processes of the institution.

CU staff members must perform their duties within the limits of their training, expertise, and competence. When these limits are exceeded, individuals in need of further assistance must be referred to persons possessing appropriate qualifications.

CU staff members must use suitable means to confront and otherwise hold accountable other staff members who exhibit unethical behavior.

CU staff members must be knowledgeable about and practice ethical behavior in the use of technology.

## Part 13. ASSESSMENT and EVALUATION

The college union (CU) must conduct regular assessment and evaluations. The CU must employ effective qualitative and quantitative methodologies as appropriate, to determine whether and to what degree the stated mission, goals, and student learning and development outcomes are being met. The process must employ sufficient and sound assessment measures to ensure comprehensiveness. Data collected must include responses from students and other affected constituencies.

The CU must evaluate periodically how well they complement and enhance the institution's stated mission and educational effectiveness.

Results of these evaluations must be used in revising and improving programs and services and in recognizing staff performance. Evaluation of union facilities, staff, programs, services, and governance must be continuous and must be within the context of the union's mission.

Evaluation may include goal related progress on such considerations as attendance at programs, cash flow, appearance of facilities, and vitality of volunteer groups.

Periodic reports, statistically valid research, and outside reviews should be utilized.

# The Role of Commuter Programs and Services
## *CAS* Standards Contextual Statement

Commuter students, defined as those who do not live in institution-owned housing on campus, accounted for over 80 percent of college students in the US. Commuter students attend virtually every institution of higher education. Their numbers include full-time students who live at home with their parents and fully employed adults who live with their own families and attend college part time. Commuters may live near the campus or far away; they may commute by car, public transportation, walking, or bicycle. They may represent a small minority of students at a private, residential liberal arts college or the entire population of a community college or urban institution.

Regardless of differences in backgrounds and educational goals, commuter students share a common core of needs and concerns such as issues related to transportation that limit the time they spend on campus, multiple life roles, the importance of integrating their support systems into the collegiate world, and developing a sense of belonging on the campus. Whether they attend a predominantly residential or commuter institution, the fact that they commute to college profoundly affects the nature of their educational experience.

Despite the overwhelming numbers of commuter students, the long-standing residential tradition of American higher education has impeded effective, comprehensive institutional response to their presence on campus. Typically, the relationship of commuter students to the institution has been neither understood nor incorporated into the design of policies, programs, and practices. Too often, it has been assumed erroneously that what has worked for residential students will serve commuter students equally well.

To begin to correct the inequities that have been built into policies and programs, institutions must critically and comprehensively examine their practices from the point of view of commuter students. The *CAS Standards and Guidelines for Commuter Student Programs and Services* provide a basis for institutional self-assessment and program development. In addition, because the commuter student population is so diverse and because each institution's commuter population is unique, it is important that each college and university regularly collect data about its commuter students and the nature of their college experience.

The question has arisen about whether the term "commuter" is appropriately applied to students who live in close proximity to the campus. Rather than dwelling on terminology, the standards take the approach that all students should have equitable access to services and engagement opportunities regardless of place of residence.

### References, Readings, and Resources

American College Personnel Association, Commission for Commuter Students and Adult Learners, One Dupont Circle NW, Suite 300, Washington DC 20036. (202) 835-2272. http://www.acpa.nche.edu

Chickering, A.W. *Commuting Versus Resident Students.* San Francisco: Jossey-Bass. 1974.

Jacoby, B., (Ed.) *Involving Commuter Students in Learning.* New Directions for Higher Education #109, 2000.

Jacoby, B., *The Student as Commuter: Developing a Comprehensive Institutional Response.* ASHE-ERIC Higher Education Report No. 7, Washington, DC, School of Education and Human Development, The George Washington University. 1989.

Jacoby, B., and Girrell, K. "A model for improving service and programs for commuter students" (The SPAR Model), *NASPA Journal*, 18:3, Winter 1981.

Schlossberg, N.K., Lynch, A.Q., and Chickering, A.W., *Improving Higher Education Environments for Adults*, Jossey-Bass, 1989.

Stewart, S.S. ed., *Commuter Students: Enhancing Their Educational Experience*, Jossey-Bass, New Directions for Student Services #24, 1983.

National Clearinghouse for Commuter Programs. *Learning About Commuter Students: Resources Within Reach*, 8th ed., 2000.

National Clearinghouse for Commuter Programs. *Serving Commuter Students: Examples of Good Practice*, 5th ed., 1997.

National Clearinghouse for Commuter Programs. *Commuter Perspectives.* (published quarterly).

National Clearinghouse for Commuter Programs, Stamp Student Union, University of Maryland, College Park, MD 20742, (301) 314-5274. www.umd.edu/nccp

# COMMUTER STUDENT PROGRAMS
## *CAS* STANDARDS and GUIDELINES

## Part 1. MISSION

Commuter student programs (CSP) must incorporate student learning and development in its mission. The CSP must enhance overall educational experiences. The program must develop, record, disseminate, implement, and regularly review its mission and goals. Mission statements must be consistent with the mission and goals of the institution and with the standards in this document. The CSP must operate as an integral part of the institution's overall mission.

The CSP must consider and respond to the diverse needs of commuting students and must help these students benefit from the institution's total educational process.

The goals of a CSP must be to . . .
- provide services and facilities to meet physical, personal safety, and educational needs of commuting students based on institutional assessment of their needs
- ensure that the institution provides commuter students equal access to services and facilities
- make available opportunities to assist commuting students in their individual development
- act as an advocate for commuter students.

Commuter students may range from a small minority to the entire student population. The commuting students in any higher educational institution are entitled to the full benefits of the curricular and co-curricular programs and services offered, regardless of their full-time or part-time status, whether they commute from near or far, are day or evening students, are living independently for the first time, or are returning after an extended interruption. Each commuter student is entitled to fair and reasonable access to institutional resources and full administrative support.
CSP should address . . .
- the unique needs of commuter students such as adequate parking, emergency assistance in parking lots, carpool programs, study space in classroom buildings, and mobile food service
- developmental opportunities, such as tutoring for reentry students, assessment of prior experience, social programs for students to meet other students, and support groups for those experiencing major life transitions
- information to faculty and staff regarding commuter students such as lifestyle characteristics, head of household status, marital status, and employment status
To respond to the student as commuter, many colleges and universities create a separate commuter-student area within the student affairs division. When that is the case, the standards outlined here apply. When no specific office is identified for the student as commuter, then all student affairs areas should be evaluated to ensure that quality services and programs exist to meet survival, esteem, and self-actualization needs of commuting students.

## Part 2. PROGRAM

The formal education of students consists of the curriculum and the co-curriculum, and must promote student learning and development that is purposeful and holistic. The commuter student program (CSP) must identify relevant and desirable student learning and development outcomes and provide programs and services that encourage the achievement of those outcomes.

The CSP must be (a) intentional, (b) coherent, (c) based on theories and knowledge of learning and human development, (d) reflective of developmental and demographic profiles of the student population, and (e) responsive to needs of individuals, special populations, and communities.

Relevant and desirable outcomes include: intellectual growth, effective communication, realistic self-appraisal, enhanced self-esteem, clarified values, career choices, leadership development, healthy behaviors, meaningful interpersonal relationships, independence, collaboration, social responsibility, satisfying and productive lifestyles, appreciation of diversity, spiritual awareness, and achievement of personal and educational goals.

The CSP must provide evidence of its impact on the achievement of student learning and development outcomes.
The program may use the examples that follow or identify other more germane indicators.

### Student Learning & Development Outcome Domains

**Intellectual Growth**
Examples of Achievement Indicators
Produces personal and educational goal statements; Employs critical thinking in problem solving; Uses complex information from a variety of sources including personal experience and observation to form a decision or opinion; Obtains a degree; Applies previously understood information and concepts to a new situation or setting; Expresses appreciation for literature, the fine arts, mathematics, sciences, and social sciences

104

## Effective Communication
Examples of Achievement Indicators
Writes and speaks coherently and effectively; Writes and speaks after reflection; Able to influence others through writing, speaking or artistic expression; Effectively articulates abstract ideas; Uses appropriate syntax; Makes presentations or gives performances

## Enhanced Self-Esteem
Examples of Achievement Indicators
Shows self-respect and respect for others; Initiates actions toward achievement of goals; Takes reasonable risks; Demonstrates assertive behavior; Functions without need for constant reassurance from others

## Realistic Self-Appraisal
Examples of Achievement Indicators
Articulates personal skills and abilities; Makes decisions and acts in congruence with personal values; Acknowledges personal strengths and weaknesses; Articulates rationale for personal behavior; Seeks feedback from others; Learns from past experiences

## Clarified Values
Examples of Achievement Indicators
Articulates personal values; Acts in congruence with personal values; Makes decisions that reflect personal values; Demonstrates willingness to scrutinize personal beliefs and values; Identifies personal, work and lifestyle values and explains how they influence decision-making

## Career Choices
Examples of Achievement Indicators
Articulate career choices based on assessment of interests, values, skills and abilities; Documents knowledge, skills and accomplishments resulting from formal education, work experience, community service and volunteer experiences; Makes the connections between classroom and out-of-classroom learning; Can construct a resume with clear job objectives and evidence of related knowledge, skills and accomplishments; Articulates the characteristics of a preferred work environment; Comprehends the world of work; Takes steps to initiate a job search or seek advanced education

## Leadership Development
Examples of Achievement Indicators
Articulates leadership philosophy or style; Serves in a leadership position in a student organization; Comprehends the dynamics of a group; Exhibits democratic principles as a leader; Exhibits ability to visualize a group purpose and desired outcomes

## Healthy Behavior
Examples of Achievement Indicators
Chooses behaviors and environments that promote health and reduce risk; Articulate the relationship between health and wellness and accomplishing life long goals; Exhibits behaviors that advance a healthy community

## Meaningful Interpersonal Relationships
Examples of Achievement Indicators
Develops and maintains satisfying interpersonal relationships; Establishes mutually rewarding relationships with friends and colleagues; Listens to and considers others' points of view; Treats others with respect

## Independence
Examples of Achievement Indicators
Exhibits self-reliant behaviors; Functions autonomously; Exhibits ability to function interdependently; Accepts supervision as needed; Manages time effectively

## Collaboration
Examples of Achievement Indicators
Works cooperatively with others; Seeks the involvement of others; Seeks feedback from others; Contributes to achievement of a group goal; Exhibits effective listening skills

## Social Responsibility
Examples of Achievement Indicators
Understands and participates in relevant governance systems; Understands, abides by, and participates in the development, maintenance, and/or orderly change of community, social, and legal standards or norms; Appropriately challenges the unfair, unjust, or uncivil behavior of other individuals or groups; Participates in service/volunteer activities

## Satisfying and Productive Lifestyles
Examples of Achievement Indicators
Achieves balance between education, work and leisure time; Articulates and meets goals for work, leisure and education; Overcomes obstacles that hamper goal achievement; Functions on the basis of personal identity, ethical, spiritual and moral values; Articulates long-term goals and objectives

## Appreciating Diversity
Examples of Achievement Indicators
Understands ones own identity and culture. Seeks involvement with people different from oneself; Seeks involvement in diverse interests; Articulate the advantages and challenges of a diverse society; Challenges appropriately abusive use of stereotypes by others; Understands the impact of diversity on one's own society

## Spiritual Awareness
Examples of Achievement Indicators
Develops and articulates personal belief system; Understands roles of spirituality in personal and group values and behaviors

## Personal and Educational Goals
Examples of Achievement Indicators
Sets, articulates, and pursues individual goals; Articulate personal and educational goals and objectives; Uses personal and educational goals to guide decisions; Understands the effect of one's personal and education goals on others

Campus scheduling policies must accommodate commuters, including evening students, part-time students, and students who depend on fixed-transportation schedules.

If a commuter student program office exists, it must serve a wide variety of needs and interests, either through direct delivery of essential programs and services or by assisting other offices in meeting those needs.

CSP staff must:

• **assist students with transportation needs and serve as liaison with campus security and municipal transit agencies to communicate commuter needs**

Transportation information and programs such as car pools, intra-campus transit (depending on size), and transport between campus and local community should be available. Provisions should be made for parking; emergency services (including jumper cables, towing service, road aid); and walkway, bike path, and parking lot security.

• **assist students in obtaining housing and dealing with landlord and/or community regulatory agencies**

Off-campus housing programs should assist students in making informed choices about housing, and should include information about available housing, tenancy ordinances, tenants' rights, legal aid information, small claims court, parking, transportation to campus, and special lease provisions and limitations.

• **assist students to acquire needed information and receive accurate referrals**

Information about campus services, programs, and current events should be disseminated in a variety of formats, including calendars, campus and local newspapers and radio stations, telephone hotlines, electronic bulletin boards, fliers, and the World Wide Web. Access to processes such as course registration and advising should be available via computer and telephone as well as in traditional modes.

• **provide for educational, recreational, and social programs consistent with the needs of the diverse commuter population**

Staff members should provide commuter students programs that include daytime social and cultural activities, workshops on relevant topics (e.g., landlord/tenant issues, energy conservation for homes and apartments, banking and personal financial management), activities located in areas off campus that are densely populated by students, and family-oriented activities.

• **encourage representation of the commuter perspective at all appropriate levels of campus planning, budgeting, and governance**

Commuter student advocacy should focus on . . .

• access to comprehensive academic advising, student support services, and sources of information
• recognition of the diverse subgroups of the commuter student population, including students that are older, married, fully employed, part-time, evening, veterans, or those living at home with parents
• fair ratio of fee burden for campus services for resident and commuter students
• fair representation of commuter students in areas of campus employment, internship placement, and financial aid awards
• working with faculty to enhance understanding of the demographic characteristics and unique needs of commuter students
• inclusion of the commuter perspective in community decision making . Examples include transportation route changes and zoning changes

• **provide for institutional research including the variables of residence, proximity to campus, age, and employment status so that institutional planners and decision makers can understand the complexity of the lifestyle of the commuter student**

Research efforts may include demographic studies, needs assessments, environmental assessments, longitudinal studies, and commuter/resident comparisons.

## Part 3. LEADERSHIP

Effective and ethical leadership is essential to the success of all organizations. Institutions must appoint, position, and empower commuter student program (CSP) leaders within the administrative structure to accomplish stated missions. Leaders at various levels must be selected on the basis of formal education and training, relevant work experience, personal skills and competencies, relevant professional credentials, as well as potential for promoting learning and development in students, applying effective practices to educational processes, and enhancing institutional effectiveness. Institutions must determine expectations of accountability for leaders and fairly assess their performance.

CSP leaders must exercise authority over resources for which they are responsible to achieve their respective missions.

CSP leaders must . . .

• **articulate a vision for their organization**
• **set goals and objectives based on the needs and capabilities of the population served**
• **promote student learning and development**
• **prescribe and practice ethical behavior**
• **recruit, select, supervise, and develop others in the organization**

- manage financial resources
- coordinate human resources
- plan, budget for, and evaluate personnel and programs
- apply effective practices to educational and administrative processes
- communicate effectively
- initiate collaborative interaction between individuals and agencies that possess legitimate concerns and interests in the functional area

CSP leaders must identify and find means to address individual, organizational, or environmental conditions that inhibit goal achievement.

CSP leaders must promote campus environments that result in multiple opportunities for student learning and development.

CSP leaders must continuously improve programs and services in response to changing needs of students and other constituents, and evolving institutional priorities.

## Part 4. ORGANIZATION and MANAGEMENT

Guided by an overarching intent to ensure student learning and development, the commuter student program (CSP) must be structured purposefully and managed effectively to achieve stated goals. Evidence of appropriate structure must include current and accessible policies and procedures, written performance expectations for all employees, functional workflow graphics or organizational charts, and clearly stated service delivery expectations.

Evidence of effective management must include use of comprehensive and accurate information for decisions, clear sources and channels of authority, effective communication practices, decision-making and conflict resolution procedures, responsiveness to changing conditions, accountability and evaluation systems, and recognition and reward processes. The CSP must provide channels within the organization for regular review of administrative policies and procedures.

The CSP shall play a principal role in implementing institutional programs developed in response to the assessed needs of commuter students.

The administrative organization of the commuter student program shall be governed by the size, nature, and mission of the institution. Commuter student programs may function as autonomous student services units or may be housed as component units of other student services departments. In either instance, the commuter student program must be organized and administered in a manner that permits its stated mission to be fulfilled.

## Part 5. HUMAN RESOURCES

The commuter student program (CSP) must be staffed adequately by individuals qualified to accomplish its mission and goals. Within established guidelines of the institution, CSP must establish procedures for staff selection, training, and evaluation; set expectations for supervision, and provide appropriate professional development opportunities. The program must strive to improve the professional competence and skills of all personnel it employs.

Professional staff members must hold an earned graduate degree in a field relevant to the position they hold or must possess an appropriate combination of educational credentials and related work experience.

Degree or credential-seeking interns must be qualified by enrollment in an appropriate field of study and by relevant experience. These individuals must be trained and supervised adequately by professional staff members holding educational credentials and related work experience appropriate for supervision.

Student employees and volunteers must be carefully selected, trained, supervised, and evaluated. They must be trained on how and when to refer those in need of assistance to qualified staff members and have access to a supervisor for assistance in making these judgments. Student employees and volunteers must be provided clear and precise job descriptions, pre-service training based on assessed needs, and continuing staff development.

The CSP must have technical and support staff members adequate to accomplish its mission. Staff members must be technologically proficient and qualified to perform their job functions, be knowledgeable of ethical and legal uses of technology, and have access to training. The level of staffing and workloads must be adequate and appropriate for program and service demands.

Salary levels and fringe benefits for all CSP staff members must be commensurate with those for comparable positions within the institution, in similar institutions, and in the relevant geographic area.

**The CSP must institute hiring and promotion practices that are fair, inclusive, and non-discriminatory. The programs must employ a diverse staff to provide readily identifiable role models for students and to enrich the campus community.**

**The CSP must create and maintain position descriptions for all staff members and provide regular performance planning and appraisals.**

**The CSP must have a system for regular staff evaluation and must provide access to continuing education and professional development opportunities, including in-service training programs and participation in professional conferences and workshops.**

The professional staff should consist of individuals whose primary responsibility is to assist commuter students to accomplish their educational, personal, and social goals.

Professional staff should: (a) develop and implement programs and services; (b) counsel students; (c) conduct research and evaluation; (d) advocate for the improvement of the quality of life for students as commuters, and (e) perform developmental educational functions.

Technical and support staff should perform office and administrative functions, including reception, information-giving, problem identification, and referral.

The professional staff should possess the academic preparation, experience, abilities, professional interests, and competencies essential for the efficient operation of the office as charged, as well as the ability to identify additional areas of concern about the commuter student population.

Relevant graduate preparation programs include those in counseling and guidance, student development, and higher education administration.

Some courses of study relevant to professionals working in commuter student services are:
- research methodologies
- the American college student
- history of higher education
- organizational behavior and change
- interpersonal communication
- social psychology
- developmental theory and personality
- the individual and society
- counseling theories and techniques
- environmental assessment
- program evaluation
- the adult learner
- management in higher education.

Staff development is an essential activity if staff members are to remain current and effective in an educational setting. Additional credit courses, seminars, professional conferences, access to published research and opinion, and to relevant other media are examples of staff-development activities.

Pre-professional, practicum, or intern student staff members should come from academic programs in counseling and guidance, student development, higher education administration, or comparable programs, and should be appropriately supervised.

Where student staff members are employed, they should be provided with clear and precise job descriptions, pre service training, and adequate supervision.

In the selection and training of technical and support staff members, special emphasis should be placed on skills in the areas of public relations, information dissemination, problem identification, and referral. A thorough knowledge of the institution and its various offices is important.

## Part 6. FINANCIAL RESOURCES

**The commuter student program (CSP) must have adequate funding to accomplish its mission and goals. Funding priorities must be determined within the context of the stated mission, goals, objectives and comprehensive analysis of the needs and capabilities of students and the availability of internal or external resources.**

**The CSP must demonstrate fiscal responsibility and cost effectiveness consistent with institutional protocols.**

Services that are paid for with student fees should benefit the student population as a whole, and they should be accessible to all students or financed equitably through user fees or in some manner other than through a general fee.

Consideration should be given to an equitable fee burden/ service ratio (i.e., the fees paid for the services delivered). This ratio should be related to the percentage of commuting students in the campus population and should be applied to obvious commuter services such as parking lots, lockers, and to more routine institutional offerings such as library hours, laboratories, recreational facilities, and programs.

## Part 7. FACILITIES, TECHNOLOGY, EQUIPMENT

**The Commuter Student Program (CSP) must have adequate, suitably located facilities, adequate technology, and equipment to support its mission and goals efficiently and effectively. Facilities, technology, and equipment must be evaluated regularly and be in compliance with relevant federal, state, provincial, and local requirements to provide for access, health, safety, and security.**

**The campus must provide adequate free-time facilities for the use of commuter students, including recreational, study, and lounge space; computer work stations; lockers; and eating facilities.**

Because commuter students do not have a residence on campus in which to spend time before, between, and after classes, it is important that a variety of comfortable free-time spaces be specifically designated for commuter student use. These spaces should be in classroom buildings, as well as in college union and student center buildings, and should include individual locker and campus mail facilities.

## Part 8. LEGAL RESPONSIBILITIES

Commuter student program (CSP) staff members must be knowledgeable about and responsive to laws and regulations that relate to their respective responsibilities. Staff members must inform users of programs and services and officials, as appropriate, of legal obligations and limitations including constitutional, statutory, regulatory, and case law; mandatory laws and orders emanating from federal, state/provincial and local governments; and the institution's policies.

CSP staff members must use reasonable and informed practices to limit the liability exposure of the institution, its officers, employees, and agents. CSP staff members must be informed about institutional policies regarding personal liability and related insurance coverage options.

The institution must provide access to legal advice for staff members as needed to carry out assigned responsibilities.

The institution must inform CSP staff and students in a timely and systematic fashion about extraordinary or changing legal obligations and potential liabilities.

## Part 9. EQUITY and ACCESS

Commuter student program (CSP) staff members must ensure that services and programs are provided on a fair and equitable basis. Facilities, programs and services must be accessible. Hours of operation and delivery of and access to programs and services must be responsive to the needs of all students and other constituents. The CSP must adhere to the spirit and intent of equal opportunity laws.

The CSP must be open and readily accessible to all students and must not discriminate except where sanctioned by law and institutional policy. Discrimination must especially be avoided on the bases of age; color, creed; cultural heritage; disability; ethnicity; gender identity; nationality; political affiliation, religious affiliation, sex, sexual orientation; or economic, marital, social, or veteran status.

Consistent with their mission and goals, the CSP must take affirmative action to remedy significant imbalances in student participation and staffing patterns.

As the demographic profiles of campuses change and new instructional delivery methods are introduced, institutions must recognize the needs of students who participate in distance learning for access to programs and services offered on campus. Institutions must provide appropriate services in ways that are accessible to distance learners and assist them in identifying and gaining access to other appropriate services in their geographic region.

## Part 10. CAMPUS and EXTERMAL RELATIONS

Commuter student programs (CSP) must establish, maintain, and promote effective relations with relevant individuals, campus offices, and external agencies.

The commuter service program should maintain a high degree of visibility with the academic units through direct promotion and delivery of services, through involvement with co-curricular programs, and through staff efforts to increase understanding of the special needs of commuting students.

The commuter student program should be actively involved and informed about the activities of other offices whose efforts directly affect commuting students. These include such areas as campus safety and security, transportation and parking, public information, scheduling, and campus switchboard, as well as campus-wide committees that bear on these issues.

Staff should be particularly cognizant that for many commuting students the institution is only one facet of their lives. Many important needs of commuter students are met through interaction with community agencies and services.

The commuter service program should maintain active contacts with various community service agencies such as legal assistance, housing boards, and transportation services.

The commuter student service program should promote involvement in events and activities that may affect commuter students.

## Part 11. DIVERSITY

Within the context of each institution's unique mission, diversity enriches the community and enhances the collegiate experience for all; therefore, commuter student program (CSP) must nurture environments where commonalties and differences among people are recognized and honored.

The CSP must promote educational experiences that are characterized by open and continuous communication that deepens understanding of one's own identity, culture, and heritage, and that of others. The program must educate and promote respect about commonalties and differences in their historical and cultural contexts.

The CSP must address the characteristics and needs of a diverse population when establishing and implementing policies and procedures.

## Part 12. ETHICS

All persons involved in the Commuter Student Program (CSP) must adhere to the highest principles of ethical behavior. The CSP must develop or adopt and implement appropriate statements of ethical practice. The program must publish these statements and ensure their periodic review by relevant constituencies .

CSP staff members must ensure that privacy and confidentiality are maintained with respect to all communications and records to the extent that such records are protected under the law and appropriate statements of ethical practice. Information contained in students' education records must not be disclosed without written consent except as allowed by relevant laws and institutional policies. CSP staff members must disclose to appropriate authorities information judged to be of an emergency nature, especially when the safety of the individual or others is involved, or when otherwise required by institutional policy or relevant law.

All staff members must be aware of and comply with the provisions contained in the institution's human subjects research policy and in other relevant institutional policies addressing ethical practices and confidentiality of research data concerning individuals.

CSP staff members must recognize and avoid personal conflict of interest or appearance thereof in their transactions with students and others.

CSP staff members must strive to insure the fair, objective, and impartial treatment of all persons with whom they deal. CSP staff members must not participate in nor condone any form of harassment that demeans persons or creates an intimidating, hostile, or offensive campus environment.

When handling institutional funds, all CSP staff members must ensure that such funds are managed in accordance with established and responsible accounting procedures and the fiscal policies or processes of the institution.

CSP staff members must perform their duties within the limits of their training, expertise, and competence. When these limits are exceeded, individuals in need of further assistance must be referred to persons possessing appropriate qualifications.

CSP staff members must use suitable means to confront and otherwise hold accountable other staff members who exhibit unethical behavior.

CSP staff members must be knowledgeable about and practice ethical behavior in the use of technology.

## Part 13. ASSESSMENT and EVALUATION

The commuter student program (CSP) must conduct regular assessment and evaluations. CSP must employ effective qualitative and quantitative methodologies as appropriate, to determine whether and to what degree the stated mission, goals, and student learning and development outcomes are being met. The process must employ sufficient and sound assessment measures to ensure comprehensiveness. Data collected must include responses from students and other affected constituencies.

The CSP must evaluate periodically how well they complement and enhance the institution's stated mission and educational effectiveness. Results of these evaluations must be used in revising and improving CSP programs and services and in recognizing staff performance.

# THE ROLE OF CONFERENCE AND EVENT PROGRAMS
## CAS Standards Contextual Statement

Broadly defined, a higher education campus is a community where people gather to learn, share, and discuss issues of interest in an open, non-threatening, and enlightened atmosphere. It is a place where topics important to society are addressed freely in a number of public settings, in addition to the classroom. Campuses are centers for symposia, lectures, concerts, demonstrations, conferences, and other short duration teaching and learning programs attended by people from all walks of life, generations, and education levels. These important institutional events help to identify the campus as a place where spirited scholarly, cultural, social, and athletic activities can freely occur in many forms and at many levels. As institutions become less constrained by physical borders, conferences and events are occurring at off campus locations as well. An administrative unit responsible for developing, coordinating, and marketing on and off campus conferences and events, is typically found at the core this important educational responsibility.

Conference and event programs address a broad range of organizing, hosting, and logistical service needs. Services are provided to a variety of constituents and include activities such as assisting sponsors in program planning and arrangements; managing conference centers; developing conferences in conjunction with faculty and staff members; providing logistical support for summer youth camps; coordinating guest services and special celebrations; scheduling facilities; and organizing donor events, inaugurations, groundbreaking commencements, homecomings, parents weekends, and other traditional gatherings.

Although the portfolios of program responsibilities vary from campus to campus, the common element is helping institutions expand their activities, presence, and influence beyond the traditional roles of faculty, students, and staff. Such programs strive to make the campus a user friendly place for non-traditional students. Conference and events programs enhance diverse campus cultures and the subject matter adds depth and variety to campus dialogue. Such

programs clearly support institutional efforts to function as a center for celebrations and non-traditional educational activities. They also provide venues for free-speech and provide opportunities for people to participate in cultural events, to be exposed to research findings. and to observe what higher education is all about. Conference and event programs often provide activities during periods when fewer students are present to optimize efficient use of campus resources.

Conference and event programs often provide institutions additional sources of revenue and contribute to the availability of faculty and staff member employment. In recent years, many institutions have increased the number of short-term learning opportunities for non-traditional students, both pre-college and professional, whose support service needs vary greatly. Many of the roles associated with student affairs are tailored to the needs of these students through a single conference and event programs office, which serves the special needs of the non-traditional student clientele. The Association of Collegiate Conference and Event Directors–International (ACCED-I) estimates that more than 1,500 U.S. institutions of higher learning have designated offices engaged in some level of conference and event planning activity. Their operations may include overseeing the summer rental of residence halls and classrooms; year-round management of full-service conference centers; coordination of large public events held in campus arenas and stadiums; and procurement of services and facilities at off-campus locations. Today, conference and event staff members provide everything from multi-department coordination of services to academic support services and professional event planning consultation.

In recent decades, a global increase in complex campuses has evolved resulting in a growing need to formalize and standardize conference and event services as well as the establishment of societies for campus conference and event professionals. As these associations matured, the need for professional standards became increasingly apparent. A study of service practices by the

Canadian University and College Conference Officers Association (CUCCOA) culminated in a summary report that called for establishing international standards for practitioners. In 1997 ACCED-I, CUCCOA, the Association of College and University Housing Officers International (ACUHO I), and the British Universities Accommodation Consortium (BUAC), now named VENUEMASTERS collectively agreed on the need for developing professional standards in collaboration with the CAS standards development initiative.

By establishing professional standards in conjunction with CAS, institutional conference and event programs can become increasingly interconnected, forming a basis on which industry-defined service standards may become a reality. The CAS standards and guidelines that follow provide a professional context for the campus conference and event industry that can serve as a useful tool for all who wish to provide conference and event programs in higher education settings.

### Resources
Association of College and University Housing Officers International (ACUHO I)
http://www.acuho.ohio-state.edu/
Association of Collegiate Conference and Event Directors–International (ACCED-I)
http://www.acced-i.com/
Canadian University and College Conference Officers Association (CUCCOA)
http://www.cuccoa.org/
United Kingdom: VENUEMASTERS
http://www.venuemasters.co.uk/

# CONFERENCE and EVENT PROGRAMS
## *CAS* STANDARDS and GUIDELINES

## Part 1. MISSION

The primary mission of conference and events programs (CEP) is to provide on and off campus constituents opportunity and access to educational conferences, workshops, events, and activities that are relevant and complementary to the mission of the institution.

The CEP must incorporate student learning and student development in its mission. CEP must enhance overall educational experiences. CEP must develop, record, disseminate, implement, and regularly review its mission and goals. Mission statements must be consistent with the mission and goals of the institution and with the standards in this document. CEP must operate as an integral part of the institution's overall mission.

The program mission must recognize and accommodate, as appropriate, relevant goals of other campus agencies that are integral providers of important services, or are major users of conference and events services.

## Part 2. PROGRAM

Conference and event programs (CEP) must provide leadership within and for the institution relative to conference and event planning and management.
To accomplish this, the CEP office may . . .
- Serve as a point of contact for multiple campus services
- Provide effective coordination of multiple services
- Collaborate with clients and service providers to assure that programs have a positive and compatible presence in the campus community
- Create opportunities for student affairs and other campus departments to fulfill their programmatic goals for students and other learners
- Create opportunities for campus departments to extend employment for employees during periods outside of the regular academic calendar
- Provide additional revenue derived from campus income-producing facilities and services
- Provide employment and experiential opportunities for students
- Ensure that scheduled and routine campus activities are free from undue interference or interruption by activities related to conferences, events, and similar programs
- Ascertain the appropriateness and compatibility of conferences, events, and similar activities with the institution's mission

- Know, articulate, and exercise state-of-the-art meeting/event planning concepts and procedures
- Provide one-stop access to and coordination of services to planners of conferences, events, and similar gatherings
- Be a knowledgeable source of information about student services, campus facilities, and support services
- Exercise appropriate authority with regard to campus resources necessary to support conferences and events in collaboration with campus service providers, through agreements and memoranda of understanding
- Communicate effectively among campus agencies as to specially scheduled or on-going campus activities that might influence or conflict with planned or potential conferences/events
- Provide clear description of activities on campus events and calendars

The formal education of students consists of the curriculum and the co-curriculum, and must promote student learning and development that is purposeful and holistic. CEP must identify relevant and desirable student learning and development outcomes and provide programs and services that encourage the achievement of those outcomes.

Relevant and desirable outcomes include: intellectual growth, effective communication, realistic self-appraisal, enhanced self-esteem, clarified values, career choices, leadership development, healthy behaviors, meaningful interpersonal relationships, independence, collaboration, social responsibility, satisfying and productive lifestyles, appreciation of diversity, spiritual awareness, and achievement of personal and educational goals.

CEP must provide evidence of its impact on the achievement of student learning and development outcomes.
The program may use the examples that follow or identify other more germane indicators. Student refers to those learners who are enrolled in or attend conferences and events held at the institution.

### Student Learning & Development
### Outcome Domains

#### Intellectual Growth
Examples of Achievement Indicators
Gained new knowledge from exploring divergent learning opportunities by attending a campus conference/event.; evaluated the institution's academic curriculum and decided to enroll in a degree program.

## Effective Communication
Examples of Achievement Indicators
> Continues dialogue after attending a conference/event and views programs and services as a valuable resource of information on a variety of topics; articulate learning outcomes of the conference/event experience; expanded vocabulary and breadth of thinking on a variety of subjects by interacting with institution's faculty and traditionally enrolled students.

## Enhanced Self-Esteem
Examples of Achievement Indicators
> Articulates personal growth as a result of a conference or event experience; was inspired by the community of accomplished and energized thinkers and becomes motivated to participate in open discourse.

## Realistic Self-Appraisal
Examples of Achievement Indicators
> Gained enhanced understanding of self and individual abilities from the conference/event experience; evaluates strengths and abilities through exposure to abundance of disciplines and perspectives that exist in the collegiate environment.

## Clarified Values
Examples of Achievement Indicators
> Gained perspective and insight into personal values and those of persons from other backgrounds and cultures; achieved insight into learning and education and the opportunity to prioritize it in relation to personal values.

## Career Choices
Examples of Achievement Indicators
> Formed opinions and is motivated to take steps toward advanced education and new career possibilities; makes connections between classroom and out-of-classroom learning; discovered alternate career options that a formal education can make possible.

## Leadership Development
Examples of Achievement Indicators
> Uses resources discovered in the academic environment to take action on matters of concern or to resolve perceived problems; learned to lead, and gained confidence in abilities through interaction with a variety of role models encountered in the collegiate community.

## Healthy Behavior
Examples of Achievement Indicators
> Experienced health education and took opportunities to explore healthy ways of life; chooses behavior that constructively affects long-term health

## Meaningful Interpersonal Relationships
Examples of Achievement Indicators
> Sustained acquaintances made during campus conferences and events; Evidences appreciation and respect for others; Developed sustaining relationships with others.

## Working Independently
Examples of Achievement Indicators
> Learned the value of research and was motivated to produce work without unnecessary assistance; took advantage of the wealth of resources available within the collegiate community to enhance personal work efforts.

## Working Collaboratively
Examples of Achievement Indicators
> Shared work responsibilities with others; can articulate benefits gained by working with others; connected with scholars who could help advance effort and achievement.

## Social Responsibility
Examples of Achievement Indicators
> Participated in a larger learning community by attending a campus conference or event; formed viewpoints from exposure to social issues at the forefront of higher education.

## Satisfying and Productive Lifestyles
Examples of Achievement Indicators
> Achieved a productive balance between education, work, personal, and leisure times while taking part in a campus conference or event; evidences a value for holistic learning experiences that incorporate elements of the curriculum and the co-curriculum.

## Appreciating Diversity
Examples of Achievement Indicators
> Achieved insight into other cultures and perspectives by interacting with the variety of students and scholars typically present in an academic community; learned to understand and appreciate lifestyle and cultural differences via the campus living experience.

## Spiritual Awareness
Examples of Achievement Indicators
> Personal beliefs are expressed to others in the campus community; students discover greater openness to spiritual discourse in an academic environment.

## Personal and Educational Goals
Examples of Achievement Indicators
> Comprehends and can define educational and other personal goals; uses the on-campus conference experience to help determine formal education interests; chose to enter the institution as a matriculated student in a program of study.

**CEP must be (a) intentional, (b) coherent, (c) based on theories and knowledge of learning and human development, (d) reflective of developmental and demographic profiles of the student population, and (e) responsive to needs of individuals, special populations, and communities.**

Conference and Event Programs must promote student learning and development through the creation, marketing, and staffing of conferences, events, and similar educational activities.

## Part 3. LEADERSHIP

Effective and ethical leadership is essential to the success of all organizations. Institutions must appoint, position, and empower Conference and event programs (CEP) leaders within the administrative structure to accomplish stated missions. CEP leaders at various levels must be selected on the basis of formal education and training, relevant work experience, personal skills and competencies, relevant professional credentials, as well as potential for promoting learning and development in students, applying effective practices to educational processes, and enhancing institutional effectiveness. Institutions must determine expectations of accountability for leaders and fairly assess their performance.

Leaders of CEP must exercise authority over resources for which they are responsible to achieve their respective missions.

Because of the likely involvement of multiple campus units in the delivery of conference and event services, special attention may be required to properly empower the program leaders to exercise necessary authority over resources.

CEP leaders must:

- articulate a vision for their organization
- set goals and objectives based on the needs and capabilities of the population served
- promote student learning and development
- prescribe and practice ethical behavior
- recruit, select, supervise, and develop others in the organization
- manage financial resources
- coordinate human resources
- plan, budget for, and evaluate personnel and programs
- apply effective practices to educational and administrative processes
- communicate effectively
- initiate collaborative interaction between individuals and agencies that possess legitimate concerns and interests in the functional area

CEP leaders must identify and find means to address individual, organizational, or environmental conditions that inhibit goal achievement.

CEP leaders must promote campus environments that result in multiple opportunities for student learning and development.

CEP leaders must continuously improve programs and services in response to changing needs of students and other constituents, and evolving institutional priorities.

Special attention should be given to the changing needs of conference and event client and service providers and CEP leaders should provide guidance on . . .
- Effective and appropriate strategies for communicating with prospective program participants
- Student needs, issues, and perspectives
- Cultivating relations with academic departments
- Working with student, campus, and academic leaders and organizations
- Efficient and appropriate use of campus resources
- Promoting equal access for all students and program participants

## Part 4. ORGANIZATION and MANAGEMENT

Guided by an overarching intent to ensure student learning and development, Conference and event programs (CEP) must be structured purposefully and managed effectively to achieve stated goals. Evidence of appropriate structure must include current and accessible policies and procedures, written performance expectations for all employees, functional workflow graphics or organizational charts, and clearly stated service delivery expectations.

Evidence of effective management must include use of comprehensive and accurate information for decisions, clear sources and channels of authority, effective communication practices, decision-making and conflict resolution procedures, responsiveness to changing conditions, accountability and evaluation systems, and recognition and reward processes. CEP must provide channels within the organization for regular review of administrative policies and procedures.

CEP must maintain accurate and current documentation on: operational policies and procedures, agreements and memoranda of understanding with service providers, standards of performance and other expectations of service providers, and access provisions for clients with disabilities.

Other areas for consideration in determining structure and management of conference and event offices may include:
- Availability and characteristics of facilities

• Size, nature, and mission of the institution
• Scope of related academic services
• Philosophy and delivery system for services
• Variety of delivery methods being employed or available to the institution
• Degree of integration with academic disciplines and academic service units

## Part 5. HUMAN RESOURCES

Conference and event programs (CEP) must be staffed adequately by individuals qualified to accomplish its mission and goals. Within established guidelines of the institution, programs and services must establish procedures for staff selection, training, and evaluation; set expectations for supervision, and provide appropriate professional development opportunities. CEP must strive to improve the professional competence and skills of all personnel it employs.

CEP staff members must be proficient in effective customer service techniques.

CEP staff members should be knowledgeable about services offered directly, and by relevant campus agencies and facilities such as housing, dining, recreation, parking, and technology services.

CEP professional staff members must hold an earned graduate degree in a field relevant to the position they hold or must possess an appropriate combination of educational credentials and related work experience.

Degree or credential-seeking interns must be qualified by enrollment in an appropriate field of study and by relevant experience. These individuals must be trained and supervised adequately by professional staff members holding educational credentials and related work experience appropriate for supervision.

Student employees and volunteers must be carefully selected, trained, supervised, and evaluated. They must be trained on how and when to refer those in need of assistance to qualified staff members and have access to a supervisor for assistance in making these judgments. Student employees and volunteers must be provided clear and precise job descriptions, pre-service training based on assessed needs, and continuing staff development.

CEP must have technical and support staff members adequate to accomplish its mission. Staff members must be technologically proficient and qualified to perform their job functions, be knowledgeable of ethical and legal uses of technology, and have access to training. The level of staffing and workloads must be adequate and appropriate for program and service demands.

Salary levels and fringe benefits for all CEP staff members must be commensurate with those for comparable positions within the institution, in similar institutions, and in the relevant geographic area.

CEP must institute hiring and promotion practices that are fair, inclusive, and non-discriminatory. Programs and services must employ a diverse staff to provide readily identifiable role models for students and to enrich the campus community.

CEP must create and maintain position descriptions for all staff members and provide regular performance planning and appraisals.

CEP must have a system for regular staff evaluation and must provide access to continuing education and professional development opportunities, including in-service training programs and participation in professional conferences and workshops.

## Part 6. FINANCIAL RESOURCES

Conference and event programs (CEP) must have adequate funding to accomplish its mission and goals. Funding priorities must be determined within the context of the stated mission, goals, objectives, and comprehensive analysis of the needs and capabilities of students, and the availability of internal or external resources.

CEP must demonstrate fiscal responsibility and cost effectiveness consistent with institutional protocols.

Funds to support the CEP, insofar as possible and desirable should be self-generated from fees set at fair market rates.

For self-support programs, when higher than expected revenue in any one-year results in a surplus, CEP should be authorized to establish reserve funds as a buffer against future shortfalls.

## Part 7. FACILITIES, TECHNOLOGY, EQUIPMENT

Conference and Event Programs (CEP) must have adequate, suitably located facilities, adequate technology, and equipment to support its mission and goals efficiently and effectively. Facilities, technology, and equipment must be evaluated regularly and be in compliance with relevant federal, state, provincial, and local requirements to provide for access, health, safety, and security.

Housing, dining, meeting space, athletic, parking and recreation facilities, sufficient to meet the needs of conference programs should be available consistent with agreements among institutional and community agencies.

## Part 8. LEGAL RESPONSIBILITIES

Conference and Event Programs (CEP) staff members must be knowledgeable about and responsive to laws and regulations that relate to their respective responsibilities. CEP staff members must inform users of programs and services and officials, as appropriate, of legal obligations and limitations including constitutional, statutory, regulatory, and case law; mandatory laws and orders emanating from federal, state/provincial and local governments; and the institution's policies.

CEP staff members should inform conference/event planners, participants, institutional staff and students in a timely, systematic, and forthright fashion, about extraordinary or changing conditions, legal obligations, potential liabilities, risks, and security.

CEP staff members must use reasonable and informed practices to limit the liability exposure of the institution, its officers, employees, and agents. Staff members must be informed about institutional policies regarding personal liability and related insurance coverage options.

Although participation in conferences, events and similar activities is a voluntary action, program leaders should monitor liability for wrongful or negligent acts.

The institution must provide access to legal advice for CEP staff members as needed to carry out assigned responsibilities.

The institution must inform CEP staff and students in a timely and systematic fashion about extraordinary or changing legal obligations and potential liabilities.

## Part 9. EQUITY AND ACCESS

Conference and event program (CEP) staff members must ensure that services and programs are provided on a fair and equitable basis. Facilities, programs and services must be accessible. Hours of operation and delivery of and access to programs and services must be responsive to the needs of all students and other constituents. CEP must adhere to the spirit and intent of equal opportunity laws.

The CEP must be open and readily accessible to all students and must not discriminate except where sanctioned by law and institutional policy. Discrimination must especially be avoided on the bases of age; color, creed; cultural heritage; disability; ethnicity; gender identity; nationality; political affiliation, religious affiliation, sex, sexual orientation; or economic, marital, social, or veteran status.

CEP should provide services and information through a variety of appropriate formats including web site, e-mail, in person through office hours, telephone, and individual appointments, and customer service systems with a goal of maximizing one stop shopping.

Consistent with its mission and goals, the conference and event program must take affirmative actions to remedy significant imbalances in student participation and staffing patterns.

Staff members should ensure that program services provided through third parties are offered on a fair and equitable basis.

As the demographic profiles of campuses change and new instructional delivery methods are introduced, institutions must recognize the needs of students who participate in distance learning for access to programs and services offered on campus. □Institutions must provide appropriate services in ways that are accessible to distance learners and assist them in identifying and gaining access to other appropriate services in their geographic region.

## Part 10. CAMPUS & EXTERNAL RELATIONS

Conference and event programs (CEP) must establish, maintain, and promote effective relations with relevant individuals, campus offices, and external agencies.

The program should develop institutional support by . . .

- Establishing cooperative relationships with other offices (in addition to direct service providers) such as alumni, enrollment management, athletics, institutional advancement, communications, public relations, campus information visitor services, to share information, stimulate program opportunities, and to enhance institutional visibility
- Encouraging staff participation in civic and community organizations such as a chamber of commerce or rotary international as well as involvement in professional associations

CEP should adhere to institution-wide processes that systematically involve academic affairs, student affairs, and administrative units such as police, physical plant and business offices.

CEP should collaborate with campus agencies, as appropriate, and meet regularly with service providers to coordinate schedules and facility use, and to review conferences and events under development. CEP should serve as a resource providing professional advice on conference/event-related issues and activities.

## Part 11. DIVERSITY

Within the context of each institution's unique mission, diversity enriches the community and enhances the collegiate experience for all; therefore, conference and event programs (CEP) must nurture environments where commonalties and differences among people are recognized and honored.

CEP must promote educational experiences that are characterized by open and continuous communication that deepens understanding of one's own identity, culture, and heritage, and that of others. CEP must educate and promote respect about commonalties and differences in their historical and cultural contexts.

CEP must address the characteristics and needs of a diverse population when establishing and implementing policies and procedures.
CEP should make reasonable effort to educate the campus community concerning cultural aspects that are unique to individual conferences and events.

## Part 12. ETHICS

All persons involved in the delivery of conference and event programs (CEP) must adhere to the highest principles of ethical behavior. CEP must develop or adopt and implement appropriate statements of ethical practice. CEP must publish these statements and ensure their periodic review by relevant constituencies.
CEP should consider the ethical standards of constituents to whom it provides services and with whom it partners.

CEP staff members must ensure that privacy and confidentiality are maintained with respect to all communications and records to the extent that such records are protected under the law and appropriate statements of ethical practice.
Advice and information disclosed by clients, students, faculty, and staff in the course of conducting business should be considered confidential.

Information contained in students' education records must not be disclosed without written consent except as allowed by relevant laws and institutional policies. CEP staff members must disclose to appropriate authorities information judged to be of an emergency nature, especially when the safety of the individual or others is involved, or when otherwise required by institutional policy or relevant law.

CEP staff members must disclose to appropriate authorities information judged to be of an emergency nature, especially when the safety of the individual or others is involved, or, when otherwise required by institutional policy or relevant law.

All CEP staff members must be aware of and comply with the provisions contained in the institution's human subjects research policy, and in other relevant institutional policies addressing ethical practices and confidentiality of research data concerning individuals.

CEP staff members must recognize and avoid personal conflict of interest or appearance thereof in their transactions with students and others.

CEP staff members must strive to ensure the fair, objective, and impartial treatment of all persons with whom they deal. Staff members must not participate in any form of harassment that demeans persons or creates an intimidating, hostile, or offensive campus environment.

CEP staff members must perform their duties within the limits of their training, expertise, and competence. When these limits are exceeded, individuals in need of further assistance must be referred to persons possessing appropriate qualifications.

SEP staff members must be knowledgeable about and practice the highest principles of ethical behavior in the use of technology.

CEP staff members must use suitable means to confront and otherwise hold accountable other staff members who exhibit unethical behavior.

When handling institutional funds, all CEP staff members must ensure that such funds are managed in accordance with established and responsible accounting procedures, contractual agreements, and the fiscal policies or processes of the institution.

## Part 13. ASSESSMENT AND EVALUATION

**Conference and event programs (CEP) must conduct regular assessment and evaluations. CEP must employ effective qualitative and quantitative methodologies as appropriate, to determine whether and to what degree the stated mission, goals, and student learning and development outcomes are being met. The process must employ sufficient and sound assessment measures to ensure comprehensiveness. Data collected must include responses from students and other affected constituencies.**

**CEP must evaluate periodically how well they complement and enhance the institution's stated mission and educational effectiveness.**

CEP should collaborate with institutional research units to generate data that could project contributions to the local economy, increase student enrollment, or stimulate of additional research or related programs given conference and event activities.

A representative cross-section of appropriate people from campus communities should be involved in reviewing the conference and event program.

CEP should generate and disseminate an annual report identifying overall goals, activities and programs served, financial contributions, regular feedback from participants, and opportunities that contributes to the overall visibility and promotion of the institution.

**CEP must assess and evaluate regularly its effectiveness in providing students with quality learning and development opportunities.**

**Results of these evaluations must be used in revising and improving programs and services and in recognizing staff performance.**

# The Role of Counseling Services
## *CAS* Standards Contextual Statement

College counseling represents the union of several movements in higher education and the integration of a helping profession activity with an educational environment (Dean & Meadows, 1995). However, the collegiate environment has moved beyond the physical realm to also include a virtual one, due in part to the rapid technological advances of our culture. The nature and type of the higher educational environment and its effects on students are important tools for college counselors. Steenbarger (1990) noted that college counseling exemplifies the developmental framework that has produced a history of creative outreach and support work on campuses. College counseling is counseling in context that can best be illustrated through exploring the development of the field and the models that have influenced it. The delivery of counseling services to students in higher education has and is evolving to effectively respond to clientele in an ever-changing environment.

Historically, the role and function of college counseling has changed in response to both external and internal factors. Social needs, political environment, national economy, and changing demographics all exert changing influences to which counseling services must respond. Change also occurs in response to internal factors unique to each campus environment (e.g., location of the counseling center within health services versus an office that combines the counseling center with career services or academic advising). As a result, the breadth and depth of counseling services reflect the intersection of these influences. Davis and Humphrey's (2000) comprehensive work provided a thorough review of the history of college counseling roles and service delivery models, the changing demographics of higher education, and implications for the future. It is critical for counseling services to respond effectively to these factors. With the rapid technological and cultural changes in our society, the counseling profession among other helping professions has put forth standards of practice to meet the ever changing needs of higher education clientele.

As a result of this rich history, the service delivery of college counseling programs varies extensively across the more than 3,400 accredited institutions of American higher education. As a whole, college counseling services largely reflect the vocational, mental health, and student personnel models of counseling (Oetting, et al., 1970; Davis and Humphrey, 2000). Stone and Archer (1990) highlighted the challenges facing the profession and elaborated specific strategies for effectively addressing the needs

in college counseling to ensure high quality services into the next century.

The current challenges are created by external forces including changing ethnic, racial, national, and experiential backgrounds of students; increasing psychological, health, safety, and financial needs of students; increasing competition for resources in higher education; increased emphasis on accountability; new and changing regulations regarding client privacy and the implications of health and mental health care reform (Stone & Archer, 1990; Gallagher & Zhang, 2002; Magoon, 2002). Moreover, the aftermath of 9/11 and other global traumatic events highlight the necessity for college counseling programs to be responsive to unanticipated factors. The level of severity of college students' presenting concerns is much greater than the traditional presenting problems of adjustment issues and individuation that were typically identified in counseling center research from the 1950s through the early 1980s (Pledge, et al., 1998; Heppner, et al., 1994). In the late 1990s and into the 21st century, research indicated that while the level of severity of presenting problems had stabilized, the complexity of problems continued to increase (Benton et al., 2003; Cornish et al., 2000; Pledge et al., 1998). As the severity and complexity of clients' problems expand, it is increasingly important for college counseling professionals to be prepared to work with physicians, community mental health workers, other campus departments, and other health care professionals. An increased focus on retention and outcomes assessment, generated in part by accreditation agencies, has challenged college counseling programs to be more intentional about demonstrating efficacy (Dean & Meadows, 1995).

Based on these challenges, Stone and Archer (1990) stressed a need for counseling centers to (a) clearly define boundaries on the types of problems and degree of severity of those clients for whom the counseling center will provide services and (b) develop and identify extensive referral and outreach services to transition effectively more severe clients with appropriate community resources. At the same time, college counselors strive to maintain the developmental, preventive, and consultative services that are integral to their work. As Stone and Archer (1990) noted, the concepts of working within limits and achieving balance between demands and resources are significant for college counseling services. Archer and Cooper (1998) further recognized the importance of demonstrating to institutions the positive outcomes of helping students maintain psychological health and develop personally in ways that support retention.

Humphrey, Kitchens and Patrick (2000) go one step further to encourage counseling services to expand and embrace the use of interactional and Internet-based technologies for additional service delivery options.

College counseling services work with other student support services to promote students' personal and educational success through activities that complement formal academic programs. College counselors offer remedial, preventive, crisis, outreach, and consultative services, depending on the nature of the campus and students served. Counseling services have changed and adapted over time along with shifts in student demographics. A strong commitment to professional development, whether through conducting research, providing training and supervision, maintaining professional credentials, upholding ethical standards of practice, or actively participating in professional organizations or other scholarly activities, is the catalyst for competent responses to the changing social issues and complex developmental, psychosocial, and mental health concerns of students.

College attendance creates a unique set of circumstances and stresses that can stimulate significant student growth and development, especially when the many student support functions are well coordinated and working together. As students experience change, they often need to address personal issues, work through challenges, and deal with the implications of growth and change. The rapid changes that characterize today's society compounded by the impact of global crisis, catastrophic natural events, and economic decline can exacerbate students' personal and psychological problems (Archer & Cooper, 1998; Davis & Humphrey, 2000). However, students' access to and success in higher education are maximized as counseling services embrace and utilize the medical, technological and psychological advances of the 21st century. The presence and availability of counseling services is an important support for the education and development of the whole person.

The CAS Counseling Services Standards and Guidelines that follow provide college counselors with criteria to develop, enhance, evaluate, and judge the quality of the campus counseling services offered.

### References, Readings, and Resources

Archer, J., Jr., & Cooper, S. (1998). *Counseling and mental health services on campus: A handbook of contemporary practices and challenges.* San Francisco: Jossey-Bass.

Benton, S., Robertson, J., Tseng, W., Newton, F., & Benton, S. (2003). Changes in counseling center client problems across 13 years, *Professional Psychology: Research and Practice, 34,* 66-72.

Cornish, J., Kominars, K., Riva, M., McIntosh, S., & Henderson, M. (2000). Perceived distress in university counseling center clients across a six-year period. *Journal of College Student Development, 41,* 104-109.

Dean, L. A., & Meadows, M. E. (1995). College counseling: Union and intersection. *Journal of Counseling and Development, 74,* 139-142.

Davis, D., & Humphrey, K. (2000). *College counseling: Issues and strategies for a new millennium.* Alexandria, VA: American Counseling Association.

Gallagher, R.P., & Zhang, B. (2002). *National survey of counseling center directors 2002.* Alexandria, VA: International Association of Counseling Services.

Heppner, P., Kivlighan, D., Good, G., Roehlke, H., Hills, H., & Ashby, J. (1994). Presenting problems of university counseling center clients: A snapshot and multivariate classification scheme. *Journal of Counseling Psychology, 41,* 315-324.

Humphrey, K., Kitchens, H., & Patrick, J. (2000). Trends in college counseling in the 21st century. In D. Davis & K. Humphrey, (Eds.) *College counseling: Issues and strategies for a new millennium* (pp.289-305). Alexandria, VA: American Counseling Association.

Magoon, T. (2002). *College and university counseling center directors' 2001-2002 data bank.* College Park, MD: University of Maryland.

Pledge, D., Lapan, R., Heppner, P., Kivlighan, D., and Roehlke, H. (1998). Stability and severity of presenting problems at a university counseling center: A six year analysis. *Professional Psychology: Research and Practice, 29,* 386-389.

Oetting, E. R., Ivey, A. E., & Weigel, R. G. (1970). *The college and university counseling center* (ACPA Monograph No. 11). Washington, DC: American Personnel and Guidance Association.

Sharkin, B. (1997). Increasing severity of presenting problems in college counseling centers: A closer look. *Journal of Counseling and Development, 75,* 275-281.

Steenbarger, B. N. (1990). Toward a developmental understanding of the counseling specialty. *Journal of Counseling and Development, 68,* 435-437.

Stone, G. L., & Archer, J., Jr. (1990). College and university counseling centers in the 1990s: Challenges and limits. *The Counseling Psychologist, 18,* 539-607.

American College Counseling Association (ACCA): http://www.collegecounseling.org

American College Personnel Association (ACPA): http://myacpa.org; Commission VII: Counseling & Psychological Services: http://www.acpa.nche.edu/comms/comm07/com7hmpg.htm/

American Counseling Association (ACA) http://www.counseling.org

American Psychological Association (APA): http://www.apa.org/ and Division 17, Counseling Psychology http://www.apa.org/about/division/div17.html

Association of Counseling Center Training Agents (ACCTA): http://accta.ucsc.edu/

Association of Counselor Education and Supervision (ACES): http://www.acesonline.net/

Association for the Coordination of Counseling Center Clinical Services (ACCCCS): http://www.ksu.edu/counseling/ACCCCS/index.htm

Association of Psychology Postdoctoral and Internship Centers (APPIC): http://www.appic.org/index.html

Association for University and College Counseling Center Directors (AUCCCD): http://www.aucccd.org

Clearinghouse for Structured/Thematic Groups & Innovative Programs, University of Texas at Austin: http://www.utexas.edu/student/cmhc/clearinghouse/index.html

Counseling Center Village: http://ub-counseling.buffalo.edu/ccv.html

International Association of Counseling Services (IACS): An Accreditation Association: http://www.iacsinc.org/

Resources for College Counselors: http://www.tarleton.edu/~counseling/coresour/cores.htm

Workshop Central: http://ub-counseling.buffalo.edu/wc.html

# COUNSELING SERVICES
## *CAS* STANDARDS and GUIDELINES

## 1. MISSION

**Counseling services (CS) must incorporate student learning and student development in its mission. CS must enhance overall educational experiences. CS must develop, record, disseminate, implement and regularly review its mission and goals. Mission statements must be consistent with the mission and goals of the institution and with the standards in this document. CS must operate as an integral part of the institution's overall mission.**

**The mission of CS is to assist students to define and accomplish personal, academic, and career goals. To accomplish the mission, the scope of CS must include . . .**

- **high quality individual and group counseling services to students who may be experiencing psychological, behavioral, or learning difficulties**
- **programming focused on the developmental needs of college students to maximize the potential of students to benefit from the academic environment and experience**
- **consultative services to the institution to help foster an environment supportive of the intellectual, emotional, spiritual and physical development of students**
- **assessment services to identify student needs and appropriate services and referrals.**

A wide variety of counseling, consultative, evaluative, and training functions may be performed by the CS as an expression of its institutional mission.

To effectively respond to the educational needs of the institution and of students, CS should have the following complementary functions:

*Developmental.* The developmental function is to help students enhance their growth. Developmental interventions help students benefit from the academic environment. To do so, the counseling services promote student growth by encouraging positive and realistic self-appraisal, intellectual development, appropriate personal and occupational choices, the ability to relate meaningfully and mutually with others, and the capacity to engage in a personally satisfying and effective style of living.

*Remedial.* The remedial function recognizes that some students experience significant problems, ranging from serious adjustment issues to more severe psychological disorders that require immediate professional attention. This function includes assisting students in overcoming current specific personal and educational problems and, in some cases, remedying current academic skill deficiencies.

*Preventive.* The preventive function is to anticipate environmental conditions and developmental processes that may negatively influence students' well being and initiate interventions that will promote personal adjustment and growth.

While there are basic similarities in the overall goals of various types of institutions, differences in student populations and institutional priorities may affect emphases of functions within individual counseling services. For these reasons, counseling services at two given institutions may emphasize different combinations of personal counseling, academic counseling, career counseling or student development services.

CS should be organized based on institutional characteristics, priorities and organizational structures. Accordingly, not all functions may exist within the same administrative unit. In such cases, coordination among the units is essential to insure a cohesive system of services for students.

## 2. PROGRAM

**The formal education of students consists of the curriculum and the co-curriculum, and must promote student learning and development that is purposeful and holistic. Counseling services (CS) must identify relevant and desirable student learning and development outcomes and provide programs and services that encourage the achievement of those outcomes.**

**Relevant and desirable outcomes include: intellectual growth, effective communication, realistic self-appraisal, enhanced self-esteem, clarified values, career choices, leadership development, healthy behaviors, meaningful interpersonal relationships, independence, collaboration, social responsibility, satisfying and productive lifestyles, appreciation of diversity, spiritual awareness, and achievement of personal and educational goals.**

**CS must provide evidence of its impact on the achievement of student learning and development outcomes.**

The program may use the examples that follow or identify other more germane indicators.

### Student Learning & Development Outcome Domains

### Satisfying and Productive Lifestyles

Examples of Achievement Indicators

Achieves balance between education, work, family, and leisure time; Articulates and meets goals for work, support system, leisure, and education; Overcomes obstacles that hamper goal achievement; Functions on the basis of personal identity, ethical, spiritual and moral values.

## Personal and Educational Goals

Examples of Achievement Indicators

Identifies personal goals for counseling; Recognizes distinction between others' goals and individual goals for psychological health and well-being; Integrates self-knowledge with external feedback for personal decision-making; Understands the effect of one's personal and education goals on others.

## Healthy Behavior

Examples of Achievement Indicators

Chooses behaviors and environments that promote health and reduce risk; Articulates the relationship between health and wellness and accomplishing life long goals; Exhibits behaviors that advance a healthy community

## Enhanced Self-Esteem

Examples of Achievement Indicators

Exhibits self-respect and respect for others; Initiates actions toward achievement of goals; Takes reasonable risks; Demonstrates culturally-appropriate assertive behavior; Functions without need for constant reassurance from others.

## Realistic Self-Appraisal

Examples of Achievement Indicators

Articulates personal skills and abilities; Makes decisions and acts in congruence with personal values; Acknowledges personal strengths and weaknesses; Articulates rationale for personal behavior; Seeks feedback from others and appropriately integrates it into self-appraisal; Learns from past experiences; Exhibits awareness of how he/she is perceived by others.

## Clarified Values

Examples of Achievement Indicators

Articulates personal values; Acts in congruence with personal values; Makes decisions that reflect personal values; Demonstrates willingness to examine and redefine personal beliefs and values; Identifies personal, work and lifestyle values and understands how they influence decision-making

## Independence

Examples of Achievement Indicators

Exhibits culturally-appropriate self-reliant behaviors; Functions autonomously; Exhibits ability to function interdependently; Manages time effectively; Accepts responsibility for psychological health and well-being.

## Meaningful Interpersonal Relationships

Examples of Achievement Indicators

Develops and maintains satisfying interpersonal relationships; Establishes mutually rewarding relationships with friends and colleagues; Listens to and considers others' points of view; Treats others with respect.

## Intellectual Growth

Examples of Achievement Indicators

Articulates personal and educational goals; Integrates knowledge and awareness of personal mental health; Employs critical thinking in problem solving; Uses complex information from a variety of sources including personal experience and observation to form a decision or opinion; Applies previously understood information and concepts to a new situation or setting.

## Effective Communication

Examples of Achievement Indicators

Writes and speaks coherently and effectively; Writes and speaks after reflection; Effectively articulates abstract ideas.

## Spiritual Awareness

Examples of Achievement Indicators

Develops and articulates personal belief system; Understands roles of spirituality in personal and group values and behaviors.

## Appreciating Diversity

Examples of Achievement Indicators

Understands ones own identity and culture; Seeks involvement with people different from oneself; Seeks involvement in diverse interests; Appropriately challenges abusive use of stereotypes by others; Understands the impact of diversity on one's own experience.

## Collaboration

Examples of Achievement Indicators

Works cooperatively with others; Seeks the involvement of others; Seeks feedback from others; Exhibits effective listening skills; Demonstrates reciprocal empathic responding in group work; Appropriately supports and challenges group members according to group norms; Engages appropriately when in psycho-educational workshop settings.

## Career Choices

Examples of Achievement Indicators

Articulates career choices based on assessment of interests, values, skills and abilities; Articulates the characteristics of a preferred work environment; Comprehends the world of work; Sets career goals that reflect self-awareness.

## Social Responsibility

Examples of Achievement Indicators

Understands, abides by, and participates in the development, maintenance, and/or orderly change of community, social, and legal standards or norms; Appropriately challenges the unfair, unjust, or uncivil behavior of other individuals or groups; Recognizes and accepts responsibility for how his/her behavior impacts others and the environment.

## Leadership Development
Examples of Achievement Indicators
Articulates leadership philosophy or style; Comprehends the dynamics of a group; Exhibits ability to visualize a group purpose and desired outcomes; Recognizes strengths and limitations of group members; Respectfully promotes group involvement and ownership of desired outcomes.

**Programs and services must be (a) intentional, (b) coherent, (c) based on theories and knowledge of learning and human development, (d) reflective of developmental and demographic profiles of the student population, and (e) responsive to needs of individuals, special populations, and communities.**

**To effectively fulfill its mission counseling services must provide the following services either directly, through referral, or in collaboration . . .**
- **Individual counseling or psychotherapy in areas of personal, educational, career development/vocational choice, interpersonal relationships, family, social, and psychological issues**
- **Group interventions (e.g., counseling, psychotherapy, support) to help students establish satisfying personal relationships and to become more effective in areas such as interpersonal processes, communication skills, decision-making concerning personal relation-ships and educational or career matters, and the establishment of personal values**
- **Psychological testing and other assessment techniques to foster client self-understanding and decision making**
- **Outreach efforts to address developmental needs and concerns of students**
- **Counseling support to help students assess and overcome specific deficiencies in educational preparation or skills**
- **Psychiatric consultation, evaluation, and support services for students needing maintenance or monitoring of psychotropic medications**
- **Crisis intervention and emergency coverage**
- **Staff and faculty professional development programs**

In those cases where other campus agencies address similar issues, such as career counseling and educational counseling, CS should establish cooperative relationships and maintain appropriate mutual referrals. In those cases where specialized and needed expertise is not available within counseling services, staff members should make full and active use of referral resources within the institution and the local community.

CS should play an active role in interpreting and, when appropriate, advocating for addressing the needs of students to administration, faculty and staff of the institution. CS can provide a needed perspective for campus administrative leaders, reflecting an appropriate balance between administrative requirements and the special needs and interests of students. CS should interpret the institutional environment to students and intervene to either improve the quality of the environment or facilitate the development of better interactions between the student and environment. CS should be sensitive to the needs of traditionally under-served and special populations.

CS may engage in research that contributes to knowledge of student characteristics and needs and evaluation of student outcomes in its programs. CS may assist students, faculty and staff members who conduct individual research on student characteristics or on the influence of specific student development activities.

CS should provide consultation, supervision, and in-service professional development for faculty members, administrators, staff and student staff members, and paraprofessionals.

Training and supervision of paraprofessionals, practicum students, and interns is an appropriate and desirable responsibility of CS.

## 3. LEADERSHIP
**Effective and ethical leadership is essential to the success of all organizations. Institutions must appoint, position, and empower counseling service (CS) leaders within the administrative structure to accomplish stated missions. CS Leaders at various levels must be selected on the basis of formal education and training, relevant work experience, personal skills and competencies, relevant professional credentials, as well as potential for promoting learning and development in students, applying effective practices to educational processes, and enhancing institutional effectiveness Institutions must determine expectations of accountability for leaders and fairly assess their performance.**

**Leaders of CS must exercise authority over resources for which they are responsible to achieve their respective missions.**

**CS leaders must . . .**
- **articulate a vision for their organization**
- **set goals and objectives based on the needs and capabilities of the population served**
- **promote student learning and development**
- **prescribe and practice ethical behavior**
- **recruit, select, supervise, and develop others in the organization**
- **manage financial resources**
- **coordinate human resources**
- **plan, budget for, and evaluate personnel and programs**
- **apply effective practices to educational and administrative processes**

- communicate effectively
- initiate collaborative interaction between individuals and agencies that possess legitimate concerns and interests in the functional area

CS leaders must identify and find means to address individual, organizational, or environmental conditions that inhibit goal achievement.

CS leaders must promote campus environments that result in multiple opportunities for student learning and development.

CS leaders must continuously improve programs and services in response to changing needs of students and other constituents, and evolving institutional priorities.

## 4. ORGANIZATION and MANAGEMENT

Guided by an overarching intent to ensure student learning and development, Counseling Services (CS) must be structured purposefully and managed effectively to achieve stated goals. Evidence of appropriate structure must include current and accessible policies and procedures, written performance expectations for all employees, functional workflow graphics or organizational charts, and clearly stated service delivery expectations.

Evidence of effective management must include use of comprehensive and accurate information for decisions, clear sources and channels of authority, effective communication practices, decision-making and conflict resolution procedures, responsiveness to changing conditions, accountability and evaluation systems, and recognition and reward processes. CS must provide channels within the organization for regular review of administrative policies and procedures.

Because the functions of CS are essential to the overall mission of an institution, their value and impact should be clearly articulated to the campus and their placement within the organizational structure should be such that it facilitates significant interaction with unit heads in academic and student affairs.

CS should function independently of units directly responsible for making decisions concerning students' official matriculation status, such as judicial actions, academic probation, and admissions or re-admissions actions.

## 5. HUMAN RESOURCES

Counseling services (CS) must be staffed adequately by individuals qualified to accomplish its mission and goals. Within established guidelines of the institution, CS must establish procedures for staff selection, training, and evaluation; set expectations for supervision, and provide appropriate professional development opportunities. CS must strive to improve the professional competence and skills of all personnel it employs.

Counseling functions must be performed by professionals from disciplines such as counseling and clinical psychology, counselor education, psychiatry, and clinical social work, and by others with appropriate training, credentials, and supervised experience.

CS professional staff members must hold an earned graduate degree in a field relevant to the position they hold or must possess an appropriate combination of educational credentials and related work experience.

Degree or credential-seeking interns must be qualified by enrollment in an appropriate field of study and by relevant experience. These individuals must be trained and supervised adequately by professional staff members holding educational credentials and related work experience appropriate for supervision.

Student employees and volunteers must be carefully selected, trained, supervised, and evaluated. They must be trained on how and when to refer those in need of assistance to qualified staff members and have access to a supervisor for assistance in making these judgments. Student employees and volunteers must be provided clear and precise job descriptions, pre-service training based on assessed needs, and continuing staff development.

Salary levels and fringe benefits for all CS staff members must be commensurate with those for comparable positions within the institution, in similar institutions, and in the relevant geographic area.

CS must institute hiring and promotion practices that are fair, inclusive, and non-discriminatory. CS must employ a diverse staff to provide readily identifiable role models for students and to enrich the campus community.

CS must create and maintain position descriptions for all staff members and provide regular performance planning and appraisals. CS must have a system for regular staff evaluation and must provide access to continuing education and

**professional development opportunities, including in-service training programs and participation in professional conferences and workshops.**

CS should maintain an in-service and staff development program which includes supervision, case presentations, research reports, and discussion of relevant professional issues. Institutional budgetary support should be available to provide for in-service and professional development activities.

**The director of counseling services must have an appropriate combination of graduate course work, formal training, and supervised experience.**

The director of CS should have a doctoral degree in counseling psychology, clinical psychology, counselor education or other related discipline from an accredited institution with a minimum of a master's degree in such areas. The director should hold or be eligible for state licensure or certification where such exists or should pursue such credentials. It is highly desirable that the director has a minimum of three years experience as a staff member or administrator in counseling services within higher education. The director should have received supervision (either pre- or post-doctoral) in counseling within higher education.

The director should have the ability to interact effectively with administrators, faculty and staff members, students, colleagues and community members and should possess all the general qualifications of a counseling staff member.

The responsibilities of the director should include . . .

- overall administration and coordination of counseling activities
- coordination, recruitment, training, supervision, development and evaluation of counseling and support staff personnel
- preparation and administration of budget
- preparation of annual reports
- provision of counseling information and services to students, faculty and staff in accordance with the mission of CS and the institution, to the community
- evaluation of services
- provision of consultation/leadership in policy formation and program development
- education of staff members regarding legal issues in mental health, medicine and higher education, as well as legal issues governing the delivery of counseling services.

**Counseling staff members must have an appropriate combination of graduate course work, formal training, and supervised experience.**

The minimum qualification for counseling staff members should be a master's degree from a regionally accredited institution in a relevant discipline such as counseling psychology, clinical psychology, counseling and personnel services, mental health counseling, and clinical social work, with a supervised practicum/internship at the graduate level, preferably in the counseling of students within a higher education setting or should be appropriately supervised until they can transfer their skills to this setting.

Counseling staff members should hold, or be eligible for, state or provincial licensure or certification in their chosen discipline (e.g., counseling, psychology, social work), where such exists.

Counseling staff members should have appropriate course work and training in psychological assessment, theories of personality, abnormal psychology or psychopathology, career development, multicultural counseling, legal and ethical issues in counseling, and learning theory. Counseling staff members should keep abreast of current research, including outcome research. Counseling staff members should also demonstrate knowledge of technology, leadership, organization development, consultation, and relevant federal, regional, and state/provincial statutes.

In cases where counseling staff members are responsible for the supervision of colleagues or graduate interns, the counseling staff members should have doctoral degrees or hold degrees commensurate with those being supervised.

Counseling staff members should participate in appropriate professional organizations and should have the budgetary support to do so. Counseling staff members should be encouraged to participate in community activities related to their profession.

Practicum students and interns, as well as paraprofessional assistants, may perform, under supervision, such counseling functions as are appropriate to their preparation and experience.

**The level of CS staffing must be established and reviewed regularly with regard to service demands, enrollment, user surveys, diversity of services offered, institutional resources, and other mental health and student services that may be available on the campus and in the local community.**

In addition to providing direct services, it is important that staff time be allowed for preparation of interviews and reports, updating institutional information, research, faculty and staff contacts, staff meetings, training and supervision, personal and professional development, consultation, and walk-in and emergency counseling interventions, in accordance with individual staff members' qualifications and task assignments. Similarly, teaching, administration, research, and other such responsibilities should be identified as relevant staff functions.

**CS must have technical and support staff members adequate to accomplish its mission. CS staff members must be technologically proficient and qualified to perform their job functions, be knowledgeable of ethical and legal uses of technology, and have access to training. The level of staffing and workloads must be adequate and appropriate for program and service demands.**

**Clerical staffing must be sufficient to provide receptionist, secretarial, technology-related, and testing support necessary for the effective**

functioning of the services such that professional staff members spend the preponderance of their time on professional duties.

Clerical employees who deal directly with students should be carefully selected, since they play an important role in the students' impressions of the counseling services and often must make some preliminary client-related decisions.

## 6. FINANCIAL RESOURCES

Counseling services (CS) must have adequate funding to accomplish its mission and goals. Funding priorities must be determined within the context of the stated mission, goals, objectives, and comprehensive analysis of the needs and capabilities of students and the availability of internal or external resources.

CS must demonstrate fiscal responsibility and cost effectiveness consistent with institutional protocols.

## 7. FACILITIES, TECHNOLOGY, EQUIPMENT

Counseling services (CS) must have adequate, suitably located facilities, adequate technology, and equipment to support its mission and goals efficiently and effectively. Facilities, technology, and equipment must be evaluated regularly and be in compliance with relevant federal, state, provincial, and local requirements to provide for access, health, safety, and security.

CS must maintain a physical and social environment that facilitates optimal functioning and insures appropriate confidentiality.

When feasible, CS should be physically separate from administrative offices, campus police, and judicial units.

Individual offices for counseling staff members should be provided and appropriately equipped and soundproof.

Counseling offices should be designed to accommodate the functions performed by counseling staff members.

There should be a reception area that provides a comfortable and private waiting area for clients.

CS should maintain or have ready access to professional resource materials.

When counseling services include a career development unit, there should be a resource center that holds institutional catalogs and occupation and career information.

An area suitable for individual and group testing procedures should be available.

CS should maintain, or have ready access to, group meeting space.

CS should maintain equipment that is capable of providing modern technical approaches to treatment and record keeping and have access to equipment for research and media presentations.

CS with training components should have adequate facilities for recording, and direct observation.

## 8. LEGAL RESPONSIBILITIES

Counseling Services (CS) staff members must be knowledgeable about and responsive to laws and regulations that relate to their respective responsibilities. CS staff members must inform users of programs and services and officials, as appropriate, of legal obligations and limitations including constitutional, statutory, regulatory, and case law; mandatory laws and orders emanating from federal, state/provincial and local governments; and the institution's policies.

CS staff members must use reasonable and informed practices to limit the liability exposure of the institution, its officers, employees, and agents. Staff members must be informed about institutional policies regarding personal liability and related insurance coverage options.

The institution must provide access to legal advice for CS staff members as needed to carry out assigned responsibilities.

The institution must inform CS staff and students in a timely and systematic fashion about extraordinary or changing legal obligations and potential liabilities.

## 9. EQUITY and ACCESS

Counseling Services (CS) staff members must ensure that services and programs are provided on a fair and equitable basis. CS facilities, programs and services must be accessible. Hours of operation and delivery of and access to programs and services must be responsive to the needs of all students and other constituents. CS must adhere to the spirit and intent of equal opportunity laws.

CS must be open and readily accessible to all students and must not discriminate except where sanctioned by law and institutional policy. Discrimination must especially be avoided on the bases of age; color, creed; cultural heritage; disability; ethnicity; gender identity; nationality; political affiliation, religious affiliation, sex, sexual orientation; or economic, marital, social, or veteran status.

Consistent with their mission and goals, CS must take affirmative action to remedy significant imbalances in student participation and staffing patterns.

As the demographic profiles of campuses change and new instructional delivery methods are introduced, institutions must recognize the needs of students who participate in distance learning for access to programs and services offered on campus. ▯Institutions must provide appropriate services in ways that are accessible to distance learners and assist them in identifying and gaining access to other appropriate services in their geographic region.

## 10. CAMPUS & EXTERNAL RELATIONS

Counseling services (CS) must establish, maintain, and promote effective relations with relevant individuals, campus offices, and external agencies.

It is desirable that CS develop close cooperation with campus referral sources and with potential consumers of counseling services consultations. CS should also work closely with all other segments of the institution whose goal is the promotion of psychological, emotional, and career development.

CS should work closely with the chief student affairs and chief academic affairs administrators to insure the meeting of institutional goals and objectives.

Within the campus community, CS should establish close cooperation with career services, academic advising, special academic support units (e.g., reading and study skills programs, learning assistance programs) and specialized student services (e.g., services for students with disabilities, international and minority students, TRIO programs, women, veterans, returning adult students).

CS should establish relationships with a wide range of student groups (e.g., student government; gay, lesbian, bisexual, transgender groups; fraternities and sororities) to promote visibility and serve as a resource to them.

CS should establish and maintain a close working relationship with student health services as counseling staff members are often called upon to refer clients for medical concerns or hospitalization, or to serve as consultants to, or to seek consultation from, health services professionals.

CS should foster relationships with academic units and with campus professionals in admissions, registrar's office, student activities, athletics, and residence halls, where appropriate.

CS should establish effective relationships with the institutional legal counsel and the legal staff of relevant professional organizations in order to effectively respond to pertinent legal issues and precedents which underlie the delivery components of CS.

Where adequate mental health resources are not available on campus, CS must establish and maintain close working relationships with off-campus community mental health resources.

CS should have procedures for the referral of students who require counseling beyond the scope of the program.

As the demographic makeup of our campuses change and new instructional delivery methods are introduced, institutions should recognize that students who are at a distance from a physical campus may still need access to the range of counseling functions. Institutions should provide services in ways that are accessible to such learners and assist them in identifying and accessing appropriate services in their own geographic region.

## 11. DIVERSITY

Within the context of each institution's unique mission, diversity enriches the community and enhances the collegiate experience for all; therefore, counseling services (CS) must nurture environments where commonalties and differences among people are recognized and honored.

CS must promote educational experiences that are characterized by open and continuous communication that deepens understanding of one's own identity, culture, and heritage, and that of others. CS must educate and promote respect about commonalties and differences in their historical and cultural contexts.

CS must address the characteristics and needs of a diverse population when establishing and implementing policies and procedures.

## 12. ETHICS

All persons involved in the delivery of counseling services (CS) must adhere to the highest principles of ethical behavior. CS must develop or adopt and implement appropriate statements of ethical practice. CS must publish these statements and ensure their periodic review by relevant constituencies .

CS staff members must recognize and avoid personal conflict of interest or appearance thereof in their transactions with students and others. Staff members must strive to ensure the fair, objective, and impartial treatment of all persons with whom they deal.

When handling institutional funds, all CS staff members must ensure that such funds are managed in accordance with established and responsible accounting procedures and the fiscal policies or processes of the institution.

CS staff members must be knowledgeable about and practice ethical behavior in the use of technology.

CS staff members must not participate in nor condone any form of harassment that demeans persons or creates an intimidating, hostile, or offensive campus environment.

CS staff members must perform their duties within the limits of their training, expertise, and competence. When these limits are exceeded, individuals in need of further assistance must be referred to persons possessing appropriate qualifications.

CS staff members must use suitable means to confront and otherwise hold accountable other staff members who exhibit unethical behavior.

CS staff members must conform to relevant federal, state/provincial, and local statutes which govern the delivery of counseling and psychological services.

CS staff members must be familiar with and adhere to relevant ethical standards in the field, including those professional procedures for intake, assessment, case notes, termination summaries and the preparation, use, and distribution of psychological tests.

Client status and information disclosed in individual counseling sessions must remain confidential, unless written permission to divulge the information is given by the student.

Clients must be made aware of issues such as the limits to confidentiality during intake or early in the counseling process so they can participate from a position of informed consent.

Consultation regarding individual students, as requested or needed with faculty and other campus personnel, is offered in the context of preserving the student's confidential relationship with the counseling services. Consultation with parents, spouses, and public and private agencies that bear some responsibility for particular students may occur within the bounds of a confidential counseling relationship.

When the condition of a client is indicative of clear and imminent danger to the client or to others, counseling staff members must take reasonable personal action that may involve informing responsible authorities, and when possible, consulting with other professionals. In such cases, counseling staff members must be cognizant of pertinent ethical principles, state/provincial or federal statutes, and local mental health guidelines that stipulate the limits of confidentiality.

Information should be released only at the written request or concurrence of a client who has full knowledge of the nature of the information that is being released and of the parties to whom it is released. Instances of limited confidentiality should be clearly articulated. The decision to release information without consent should occur only after careful consideration and under the conditions described above.

CS must maintain records in a confidential and secure manner while specifying procedures to monitor access, use, and maintenance of the records.

CS staff members must ensure that privacy and confidentiality are maintained with respect to all communications and records to the extent that such records are protected under the law and appropriate statements of ethical practice. Information contained in students' education records must not be disclosed without written consent except as allowed by relevant laws and institutional policies. CS staff members must disclose to appropriate authorities information judged to be of an emergency nature, especially when the safety of the individual or others is involved, or when otherwise required by institutional policy or relevant law.

All CS staff members must be aware of and comply with the provisions contained in the institution's human subjects research policy and in other relevant institutional policies addressing ethical practices and confidentiality of research data concerning individuals.

## 13. ASSESSMENT and EVALUATION

Counseling services (CS) must conduct regular assessment and evaluations. CS must employ effective qualitative and quantitative methodologies as appropriate, to determine whether and to what degree the stated mission, goals, and student learning and development outcomes are being met. The process must employ sufficient and sound assessment measures to ensure comprehensiveness. Data collected must include responses from students and other affected constituencies.

CS must evaluate periodically how well they complement and enhance the institution's stated mission and educational effectiveness. Results of these evaluations must be used in revising and improving programs and services and in recognizing staff performance.

# THE ROLE OF DISABILITY SUPPORT SERVICES
## *CAS* Standards Contextual Statement

Beginning in 1973 with the passage of Section 504 of the Rehabilitation Act "no otherwise qualified individual with a disability shall, solely by reason of his/her disability, be excluded from the participation in, be denied the benefits of, or be subjected to discrimination under any program or activity of a public entity". As the result of this legislation, colleges and universities receiving Federal funds were required to provide nondiscriminatory access to programs and facilities for individuals with disabilities. Additionally, the Americans with Disabilities Act of 1990 (the ADA) reinforced and broadened this legislation to include public entities such as restaurants, hotels, stores, transportation and communication systems.

As colleges and universities worked to interpret the laws and design services appropriate to the mission of individual campuses, disability services were often housed in student affairs. As a result, many of the earliest service providers were re-assigned from student life, counseling, advising, or the Dean of Students' office. Additionally, other campuses chose to house the office in affirmative action or in an academic department such as psychology, counseling, special education or education. Many universities and colleges looked to each other to help define the growing need for services. Thus the field of "disability services" evolved.

From the middle 1980's through 2000 most campuses experienced a growing number of students (with disabilities) who disclosed disabilities and requested reasonable accommodations. The courts increasingly heard cases that involved interpretation of the laws to further define who was a "qualified individual with a disability" and what determined a "reasonable and appropriate accommodation". In response to the growth , a uniquely challenged and experienced cadre of professional disability service providers sought professional development from organizations such as the Association on Higher Education and Disability (AHEAD) in order to understand and respond to the needs.

Services for students with disabilities have become an integral component of institutions of higher education. Universities still are challenged by whether to house disability services in student affairs or academic affairs, what types of degrees and backgrounds are required to direct and coordinate disability services and what is still a "reasonable accommodation". However, what is clear is that the offices are typically viable components of a campus, are visible to others, have their own financial resources, and staff. Students with disabilities are more aware of their rights, are better prepared to enter higher education, and are often better advocates for themselves than they were 20 years ago. Promoting disabilities as part of diversity has ensured that others are educated as well.

### References, Readings and Resources

American Council on Education (1994).*Educating students with disabilities on campus: Strategies of successful projects*. Washington, DC: Author.

American Council on Education. (1995). *College freshmen with disabilities: A triennial statistical profile*. Washington, DC: Author.

*Disability Compliance for Higher Education Newsletter*. Dan Gephart, Managing Editor, LRP Publications, Horsheim, PA.

Heyward, S. M. (1996). *Frequently asked questions: Postsecondary education and disability*. Cambridge, MA: Heyward, Lawton and Associates.

Kroeger, S., & Schuck, J. (Eds.) (1993). *Responding to disability issues in student affairs*, no. 64. New Directions For Student Services. San Francisco: Jossey-Bass.

Latham, J. D., & Latham, P. H. (1996). *Documentation and the law for professionals concerned with ADD/LD and those they serve*. Washington, DC: JKL Communications.

Ryan, D, & McCarthy, M. (Eds.) (1994). *A student affairs guide to the ADA and disability issues*, Monograph 17. Washington, DC: National Association of Student Personnel Administrators.

Walling, L. L. (ed.) (1996). *Hidden abilities in higher education: New college students with disabilities*. Monograph series no. 21, National Resource Center for the Freshman Year Experience and Students in Transition. Columbia, SC: University of South Carolina.

Association on Higher Education and Disability (AHEAD), U. of Mass. Boston, 100 Morrissey Blvd, Boston, MA. 02125-3393 (V) 617-287-3880; (f) 617-287-3881; (t) 617-287-3882; www.ahead.org

Disability Compliance for Higher Education: Newsletter published monthly by LRP Publishers, http://www:lrp.com/

HEATH Resource Center , National Clearinghouse on Postsecondary Education housed at the George Washington University, www.heath-resource-center.org

*Journal of Postsecondary Education and Disability*. Association on Higher Education and Disability, Boston, Mass.

U.S. Department of Education - Office for Civil Rights (OCR) www.ed.gov/offices/OCR

U.S. Department of Justice – ADA Home Page www.usdoj.gov/crt/ada/adahom1.htm

# DISABILITY SUPPORT SERVICES
## CAS STANDARDS and GUIDELINES

## Part 1. MISSION

The primary mission of disability support services (DSS) is to ensure equal access for students with disabilities to all curricular and co-curricular opportunities offered by the institution.

In addition, the mission of DSS must . . .

- **Provide leadership to the campus community to enhance understanding and support of DSS**
- **Provide guidance to the campus community to ensure compliance with legal requirements for access**

Relevant legal requirements may vary among governmental jurisdictions but would include minimally for US institutions the requirements defined under Section 504 of the Rehabilitation Act of 1973, and the Americans with Disabilities Act of 1990.

- **Establish a clear set of policies and procedures that define the responsibilities of both the institution and the person eligible for accommodations**

DSS must develop, record, disseminate, implement, and regularly review its mission and goals. Mission statements must be consistent with the mission and goals of the institution and with the standards in this document. In addition, DSS must operate as an integral part of the institution's overall mission.

DSS mission and purpose must incorporate student learning and student development in its mission. The program must enhance overall educational experiences.

To accomplish its mission, DSS must . . .

- **Ensure that qualified individuals with disabilities receive reasonable and appropriate accommodations so as to have equal access to all institutional programs and services regardless of the type and extent of the disability**
- **Possess a clear set of policies and procedures**
- **Inform the campus community about the location of disability services, the availability of equipment and technology helpful to those with disabilities, and identification of key individuals within the institution who can provide services to students with disabilities**
- **Define and describe the procedures for obtaining services and accommodations**
- **Provide guidance and training for institutional staff and faculty members in the understanding of disability issues**

Institutional staff and faculty members should be educated about the stereotypes surrounding people with disabilities as well as appropriate protocols and language.

- **Advocate for equal access, accommodations, and respect for students with disabilities within the campus community**

## Part 2. PROGRAM

The formal education of students consists of the curriculum and the co-curriculum, and must promote student learning and development that is purposeful and holistic.

Disability support services (DSS) must be (a) intentional, (b) coherent, (c) based on theories and knowledge of learning and human development, (d) reflective of developmental and demographic profiles of the student population, and (e) responsive to the needs of individuals, special populations, and communities.

If a formal DSS program does not exist, it must be the responsibility of the institution to ensure that the primary mission is accomplished, either through the direct delivery of essential programs and services by the person(s) designated by the institution as the point of contact for students or by assisting other offices in meeting those needs.

DSS must identify relevant and desirable student learning and development outcomes and provide programs and services that encourage the achievement of those outcomes. Such outcomes include: intellectual growth, effective communication, realistic self-appraisal, enhanced self-esteem, clarified values, career choices, leadership development, healthy behaviors, meaningful interpersonal relations, independence, collaboration, social responsibility, satisfying and productive lifestyles, appreciation of diversity, spiritual awareness, and achievement of personal and educational goals.

DSS must provide evidence of its impact on the achievement of student learning and development outcomes.

The program may use the examples that follow or identify other more germane indicators.

**Student Learning & Development
Outcome Domains**

## Intellectual Growth

Examples of Achievement Indicators

Produces personal and educational goal statements; Employs critical thinking in problem solving; Uses complex information from a variety of sources including personal experience and observation to form a decision or opinion; Obtains a degree; Applies previously understood information and concepts to a new situation or setting; Expresses appreciation for literature, the fine arts, mathematics, sciences, and social sciences

## Effective Communication

Examples of Achievement Indicators

Writes and speaks coherently and effectively; Writes and speaks after reflection; Able to influence others through writing, speaking or artistic expression; Effectively articulates abstract ideas; Uses appropriate syntax; Makes presentations or gives performances

## Enhanced Self-Esteem

Examples of Achievement Indicators

Shows self-respect and respect for others; Initiates actions toward achievement of goals; Takes reasonable risks; Demonstrates assertive behavior; Functions without need for constant reassurance from others

## Realistic Self-Appraisal

Examples of Achievement Indicators

Articulates personal skills and abilities; Makes decisions and acts in congruence with personal values; Acknowledges personal strengths and weaknesses; Articulates rationale for personal behavior; Seeks feedback from others; Learns from past experiences

## Clarified Values

Examples of Achievement Indicators

Articulates personal values; Acts in congruence with personal values; Makes decisions that reflect personal values; Demonstrates willingness to scrutinize personal beliefs and values; Identifies personal, work and lifestyle values and explains how they influence decision-making

## Career Choices

Examples of Achievement Indicators

Articulate career choices based on assessment of interests, values, skills and abilities; Documents knowledge, skills and accomplishments resulting from formal education, work experience, community service and volunteer experiences; Makes the connections between classroom and out-of-classroom learning; Can construct a resume with clear job objectives and evidence of related knowledge, skills and accomplishments; Articulates the characteristics of a preferred work environment; Comprehends the world of work; Takes steps to initiate a job search or seek advanced education

## Leadership Development

Examples of Achievement Indicators

Articulates leadership philosophy or style; Serves in a leadership position in a student organization; Comprehends the dynamics of a group; Exhibits democratic principles as a leader; Exhibits ability to visualize a group purpose and desired outcomes

## Healthy Behavior

Examples of Achievement Indicators

Chooses behaviors and environments that promote health and reduce risk; Articulate the relationship between health and wellness and accomplishing life long goals; Exhibits behaviors that advance a healthy community.

## Meaningful Interpersonal Relationships

Examples of Achievement Indicators

Develops and maintains satisfying interpersonal relationships; Establishes mutually rewarding relationships with friends and colleagues; Listens to and considers others' points of view; Treats others with respect

## Independence

Examples of Achievement Indicators

Exhibits self-reliant behaviors; Functions autonomously; Exhibits ability to function interdependently; Accepts supervision as needed; Manages time effectively

## Collaboration

Examples of Achievement Indicators

Works cooperatively with others; Seeks the involvement of others; Seeks feedback from others; Contributes to achievement of a group goal; Exhibits effective listening skills

## Social Responsibility

Examples of Achievement Indicators

Understands and participates in relevant governance systems; Understands, abides by, and participates in the development, maintenance, and/or orderly change of community, social, and legal standards or norms; Appropriately challenges the unfair, unjust, or uncivil behavior of other individuals or groups; Participates in service/volunteer activities

## Satisfying and Productive Lifestyles

Examples of Achievement Indicators

Achieves balance between education, work and leisure time; Articulates and meets goals for work, leisure and education; Overcomes obstacles that hamper goal achievement; Functions on the basis of personal identity, ethical, spiritual and moral values; Articulates long-term goals and objectives

## Appreciating Diversity

Examples of Achievement Indicators

Understands ones own identity and culture. Seeks involvement with people different from oneself; Seeks involvement in diverse interests; Articulate the advantages and challenges of a diverse society; Challenges appropriately abusive use of stereotypes by others; Understands the impact of diversity on one's own society

## Spiritual Awareness
Examples of Achievement Indicators
Develops and articulates personal belief system; Understands roles of spirituality in personal and group values and behaviors

## Personal and Educational Goals
Examples of Achievement Indicators
Sets, articulates, and pursues individual goals; Articulate personal and educational goals and objectives; Uses personal and educational goals to guide decisions; Understands the effect of one's personal and education goals on others

**Institutions must make effective use of existing administrative structures and resources to avoid unnecessary duplication of services and to ensure that all campus offices and services have as a part of their mission the responsibility to meet the needs of persons with disabilities.**

Depending on the institution, students with disabilities should be served within a decentralized system, with a central office providing those services not provided elsewhere on campus.

**DSS must identify environmental conditions that negatively influence persons with disabilities and propose interventions that are designed to ameliorate such conditions.**

**The institution must regularly evaluate the campus for physical access. Maps and signage must reflect accessible routes, handicapped parking, building accessibility, entrances and restroom facilities. Parking and transportation must comply with applicable accessibility regulations and laws.**

**The major components of DSS, each of which must be clearly identified to the campus and to the potential and current users of the services, include:**

### • A procedure for disclosure.
Persons with disabilities should be given the opportunity to self-disclose to a disability services provider who is trained to evaluate the information and who understands and respects the confidentiality of the individual.

Each person requesting services should be screened during an intake interview, should have documentation from a qualified professional, and should ensure that the service provider receives the documentation. The documentation should be current, state a diagnosis, and give evidence to support the impact of the disability and its effect on the academic or work environment. A referral list of qualified and competent professionals should be maintained for students who need more current or new documentation.

### • Direct assistance to persons with disabilities.
Services to qualified individuals should ensure equal access and also meet the requirements as required by current law and institutional policy. The actual services provided will vary among institutions based on the specific disability and on the location of services provided by other campus offices or the community. Staff members provide for accommodations that assist persons with disabilities in the accomplishment of educational, personal, social, and work goals.

Examples of accommodation can include testing accommodations, readers, scribes, interpreters, note takers, brailed materials, screen magnification systems, text-to-speech, screen reading, voice dictation, and/or optical character recognition systems.

### • Consultation to the campus community
DSS should act as a consultant and advocate to the campus community in ensuring physical and programmatic access to all institutional resources. This would include collaboration with faculty members about teaching and testing techniques for academic departments. DSS should work to ensure equal access to electronic communication and distance learning materials as well as access to print.

### • Advising, counseling, and support for persons with disabilities
DSS should assist individuals in devising strategies to adjust to and succeed in higher education. When strategies include reasonable accommodations, the program should provide information about how to acquire them.

### • Professional and community education
DSS should offer training and educational activities to faculty members, staff, and students and other community members that promotes understanding, awareness, and advocacy.

### • Dissemination of Information
Information should include access issues, accommodations, and legal rights of persons with disabilities to the campus community. Information regarding the laws, the procedures for receiving services, documentation guidelines, and other related policies should be made readily available in both print and electronic formats. Additionally, general information about location, available hours, contact information, and procedures should be made widely available especially in institutional print and electronic publications including, but not limited to, course schedules, catalogs, bulletins, recruitment materials, student and faculty handbooks, and residence life publications. On-line information about DSS should be accessible with the use of assistive technology and must provide appropriate links to other useful services such as financial aid, admissions, residence life, security, parking, and campus information.

### • Collaboration on institutional safety policies and procedures
The program should collaborate with appropriate campus offices and community agencies on the development and dissemination of safety, evacuation, and other emergency response plans.

Maps and signage must reflect accessible routes, handicapped parking, building accessibility, entrances and restroom facilities. The institution must regularly evaluate the physical access of the campus. Parking and transportation must comply with applicable accessibility regulations and laws.

## Part 3. LEADERSHIP

Effective and ethical leadership is essential to the success of all organizations. Institutions must appoint, position, and empower leaders within the administrative structure to accomplish stated missions. Leaders at various levels must be selected on the basis of formal education and training, relevant work experience, personal skills and competencies, relevant professional credentials, as well as potential for promoting learning and development in students, applying effective practices to educational processes, and enhancing institutional effectiveness. Institutions must determine expectations of accountability for leaders and fairly assess their performance.

Leaders of disability support services (DSS) must exercise authority over resources for which they are responsible to achieve their respective missions.

Leaders must . . .
- articulate a vision for their organization
- set goals and objectives based on the needs and capabilities of the population served that will enhance organizational and institutional effectiveness
- promote student learning and development
- prescribe and practice ethical behavior
- recruit, select, supervise, and develop others in the organization
- manage financial resources
- coordinate human resources
- plan, budget for, and evaluate personnel and programs
- apply effective practices in educational processes
- communicate effectively
- initiate collaborative interaction between individuals and agencies that possess legitimate concerns and interests in the DSS
- advocate for needs of students with disabilities

Leaders of the DSS must keep abreast of current litigation, interpretation of case law, changes in the field of medicine and diseases, changes in documenting disabilities, and trends in the field of secondary special education and use this information to advise their institutions and community how to best respond and react to these changes. Also, leaders must be informed of best practices within the field of disability services. Leaders must address individual, organizational, or environmental conditions that inhibit goal achievement.

Leaders of DSS must promote campus environments that result in multiple opportunities for student learning and development. Leaders must improve programs and services continuously in response to changing needs of students and other constituents, and evolving institutional priorities.

## Part 4. ORGANIZATION and MANAGEMENT

Guided by an overarching intent to ensure student learning and development, disability support services (DSS) must be structured purposefully and managed effectively to achieve stated goals. Evidence of appropriate structure must include current and accessible policies and procedures, written performance expectations for all employees, functional workflow graphics or organizational charts, and clearly stated service delivery expectations.

Evidence of effective management must include use of comprehensive and accurate information for decisions, clear sources and channels of authority, effective communication practices, decision-making and conflict resolution procedures, responsiveness to changing conditions, accountability and evaluation systems, and recognition and reward processes. Programs and services must provide channels within the organization for regular review of administrative policies and procedures.

DSS must be situated within the administrative structure to develop and direct program activities effectively. Adequate staff, funding, and resources must be provided.

Such services normally function within divisions of student affairs or academic affairs. The services should involve advisory bodies which include students, faculty and staff members with disabilities.

## PART 5. HUMAN RESOURCES

Disability support services (DSS) must be staffed adequately by individuals qualified to accomplish its mission and goals.

Within established guidelines of the institution, DSS must establish procedures for staff selection, training, and evaluation; set expectations for supervision, and provide appropriate professional development opportunities. Programs and services must strive to improve the professional competence and skills of all personnel it employs.

Professional staff members must hold an earned graduate degree in a field relevant to the position they hold or must possess an appropriate combination of educational credentials and related work experience.
Designated staff members may serve as practicum instructors or intern supervisors.

Degree or credential-seeking interns must be qualified by enrollment in an appropriate field of study and by relevant experience. These individuals must be trained and supervised adequately by professional staff members who hold credentials appropriate for supervision.

DSS must have technical and support staff members adequate to accomplish its mission. Staff members must be technologically proficient and qualified to perform their job functions, be knowledgeable of ethical and legal uses of technology, and have access to training. The level of staffing and workloads must be adequate and appropriate for program and service demands.

Salary levels and fringe benefits for all staff members must be commensurate with those of comparable positions within the institution, in similar institutions, and in the relevant geographic area.

DSS must institute hiring and promotion practices that are fair, inclusive, and non-discriminatory. Programs and services must ensure a diverse staff to provide readily identifiable role models for students and to enrich the campus community.
Staff assignments should take into account the benefits of employing persons with disabilities.

Sign language and oral interpreters must have appropriate qualifications,
including appropriate coursework and certification.

Student employees and volunteers must be carefully selected, trained, supervised, and evaluated. They must be trained on how and when to refer those in need of assistance to qualified staff members and have access to a supervisor for assistance in making these judgments. Student employees and volunteers must be provided clear and precise job descriptions, pre-service training based on assessed needs, and continuing staff development.

Administrative and support staff must be provided with disability awareness training and possess knowledge and understanding of the needs of persons with disabilities. DSS must create and maintain position descriptions for all staff members and provide regular performance appraisals.

DSS must have a system for regular staff evaluation and must provide access to continuing education and professional development opportunities, including in-service training programs and participation in professional conferences and workshops.

## Part 6. FINANCIAL RESOURCES

Disability support services (DSS) must have adequate funding to accomplish its mission and goals. Priorities must be determined within the context of the stated mission, goals, objectives, and comprehensive analysis of the needs and capacities of students and the availability of internal or external resources.

DSS must demonstrate fiscal responsibility and cost effectiveness consistent with institutional protocols.
DSS should be funded as a separate institutional budget item. The institution must provide appropriate funding to carry out its stated mission and goals.

The allocation of financial resources must be adequate to meet the obligations of the institution under relevant national, state, provincial, and local laws.
In addition to normal budget categories, the DSS program may have unusual budgetary requirements that can vary from term to term. These may include readers, interpreters, and special equipment such as a TTY/TDD (telephone communication devices for the deaf), screen readers, voice synthesizers, reading machines, device for enlarging print, Braille capabilities, additional technology to provide accommodated exams, and variable speed tape recorders. The institution is not obligated to provide personal equipment such as wheelchairs, hearing aids, or prosthetics. The number and nature of the devices can be determined based on the population of persons with disabilities requesting services.
The decision of whether to purchase mandated devices should not be weighed against competing departmental needs, such as additional computers or staff. Funding for disability accommodations should come from a centralized institutional source rather than from any one individual department.

## Part 7. FACILITIES, TECHNOLOGY, EQUIPMENT

Disability Support Services (DSS) must have adequate, suitably located facilities, adequate technology, and equipment to support its mission and goals efficiently and effectively. Facilities, technology, and equipment must be evaluated regularly and be in compliance with relevant federal, state, provincial, and local requirements to provide for access, health, safety, and security.

Distance learning programs and institutional websites must be constructed to provide full access to persons with disabilities.

Facilities available to DSS units should include . . .

- offices and programmatic spaces within an accessible facility
- private offices for conducting intake interviews, counseling, or other meetings of a confidential nature
- private and quiet space for tape recording materials, and scribing or taking exams
- a receptionist area with accessible counter heights and TTY/TDD
- storage area to ensure the confidentiality of records
- conference room and training space adequate to accommodate persons in wheelchairs
- nearby availability of accessible rest rooms, water fountains, elevators, and corridors
- adequate handicapped parking convenient to the facility
- coat racks and bulletin boards
- warning devices such as strobe/buzzer fire alarms for emergencies.

## Part 8. LEGAL RESPONSIBILITIES

Disability support services (DSS) staff members must be knowledgeable about and responsive to laws and regulations that relate to their respective responsibilities. Staff members must inform users of programs and services and officials, as appropriate, of legal obligations and limitations including constitutional, statutory, regulatory, and case law; mandatory laws and orders emanating from federal, state/provincial and local governments; and the institution's policies.

DSS staff members must use reasonable and informed practices to limit the liability exposure of the institution, its officers, employees, and agents. Staff members must be informed about institutional policies regarding personal liability and related insurance coverage options.

The institution must provide access to legal advice for staff members as needed to carry out assigned responsibilities.

Staff members must be aware of and seek advice from the institution's legal counsel on privacy and disclosure of student information contained in educational records, defamation law regarding references and recommendations on behalf of students, affirmative action laws, protective health information laws, and regulations regarding programs and liability issues pertaining to sponsored programs.

The institution must inform staff and students, in a timely and systematic fashion, about extraordinary or changing legal obligations and potential liabilities. Higher education institutions must adhere to the law in appointing a disability compliance officer.

The DSS staff must, in conjunction with legal counsel, work to develop policies, procedures, and guidelines as required under relevant disability laws.

Interpretation of the laws and their application to the campus should be a coordinated effort with institutional legal counsel.

## Part 9. EQUITY and ACCESS

Disability support services (DSS) staff members must ensure that services and programs are provided on a fair and equitable basis. Facilities, programs and services must be accessible. Hours of operation and delivery of and access to programs must be responsive to the needs of all students and other constituents. Each program and service must adhere to the spirit and intent of equal opportunity laws.

DSS must be open and readily accessible to all students and must not discriminate except where sanctioned by law and institutional policy. Discrimination must be avoided on the bases of age; color; creed; cultural heritage; disability; ethnicity; gender identity; nationality; political affiliation; religious affiliation; sex; sexual orientation; or social, economic, marital, or veteran status.

Consistent with its mission and goals, DSS must take affirmative action to remedy significant imbalances in student participation and staffing patterns.

As the demographic profiles of campuses change and new instructional delivery methods are introduced, institutions must recognize the needs of students who participate in distance learning for access to programs and services offered on campus. ☐Institutions must provide appropriate services in ways that are accessible to distance learners and assist them in identifying and gaining access to other appropriate services in their geographic region.

DSS must educate the campus community about ensuring opportunities for individuals with disabilities in all facets of the institution. Additionally, as the demographic profiles of institutions of higher learning change and new instructional delivery methods are introduced, institutions of higher education must provide comparable distance education opportunities to students with disabilities.

## Part 10. CAMPUS and EXTERNAL RELATIONS

Disability support services (DSS) program must establish, maintain, and promote effective relations with campus offices and external agencies that provide direct support to persons with disabilities.
Such agencies would include vocational rehabilitation, the medical community, veterans administration, school districts, and social services agencies.

DSS must also work to maintain positive relations with students, faculty members, staff, the institutional legal counsel, the administration, all support offices, community agencies, the medical community, diagnosticians, and equal opportunity compliance officers.
DSS should take an active role in the coordination of the institution's response to the needs of persons with disabilities. This is essential to ensure the continuity of services, resource management, consistent institutional policies, and the integration of persons with disabilities into the total campus experience.
DSS should maintain a high degree of visibility with the academic units through the promotion and delivery of services, through involvement in determining what constitutes reasonable accommodations, and through promoting increased understanding of, and responsiveness to, the needs of persons with disabilities.
DSS should be informed about, and actively involved in, influencing and affecting the policies, practices and planning of other units, which directly affect persons with disabilities.

DSS staff members must be available to participate in appropriate campus-wide committees.
Disability support service staff members may act as liaisons between student services, academic services, and community services on the behalf of persons with disabilities.

## Part 11. DIVERSITY

Within the context of each institution's unique mission, diversity enriches the community and enhances the collegiate experience for all; therefore, programs and services must nurture environments where commonalties and differences among people are recognized and honored.

Disability support services (DSS) must promote education experiences that are characterized by open and continuous communication, that deepen the understanding of one's own identity, culture, and heritage, and that of others. DSS must educate and promote respect about commonalties and differences in their historical and cultural contexts.

DSS must address the characteristics and needs of a diverse population when establishing and implementing policies and procedures.

## Part. 12 ETHICS

All persons involved in the delivery of Disability Support Services (DSS) must adhere to the highest principles of ethical behavior.

DSS must develop or adopt and implement appropriate statements of ethical practice. Programs and services must publish these statements and insure their periodic review by relevant constituencies.
Ethical standards or other statements from relevant professional associations should also be considered.

Staff members must strive to insure the fair, objective, and impartial treatment of all persons with whom they deal. Staff members must not participate in nor condone any form of harassment that demeans persons or creates an intimidating, hostile, or offensive campus environment.

Staff members must use suitable means to confront and otherwise hold accountable other staff members who exhibit unethical behavior and must be knowledgeable about and practice ethical behavior in the use of technology.

Staff members must perform their duties within the limits of their training, expertise, and competence. When these limits are exceeded, individuals in need of further assistance must be referred to persons possessing appropriate qualifications.

Staff members must recognize and avoid personal conflict of interest or appearance thereof in their transactions with students and others.

Staff members must ensure that privacy and confidentiality are maintained with respect to all communications and records to the extent that such records are protected under the law and appropriate statements of ethical practice.

Information contained in students' education records must not be disclosed without written consent except as allowed by relevant laws and institutional policies.

Staff members must disclose to appropriate authorities information judged to be of an emergency nature, especially when the safety of the individual or others is involved, or when otherwise required by institutional policy or relevant law. All staff members must be aware of and comply with the provisions contained in the institution's human subjects research policy and in other relevant institutional policies addressing ethical practices and confidentiality of research data concerning individuals.

When handling institutional funds, all staff members must ensure that such funds are managed in accordance with established and responsible accounting procedures and the fiscal policies or processes of the institution.

## Part 13. ASSESSMENT and EVALUATION

Disability support services (DSS) regularly must conduct regular assessment and evaluations. Programs and services must employ effective qualitative and quantitative methodologies as appropriate, to determine whether and to what degree the stated mission, goals, and student learning and developmental outcomes are being met. The process must employ a sufficient and sound assessment measures to ensure comprehensiveness. Data collected must include responses from students and other affected constituencies.

Results of these evaluations must be used in revising and improving programs and services and in recognizing staff performance.

Comprehensive, systematic, and periodic assessments should be conducted to address the academic, social and physical needs of students as well as the psychological and physical environments of the campus. In turn, findings should be used to influence how present services should change for future development.

To determine the effectiveness of the organization and administration of the services a data collection system should be developed and implemented. Program evaluations should be obtained from designated staff members, students, faculty members and community.

Analyses of population characteristics and trends in the use of services should be performed regularly. Although not the sole measure of program's success, data may be compiled annually on attrition and graduation rates of students using the services.

DSS must evaluate periodically how well they complement and enhance the institution's stated mission and educational effectiveness.

# The ROLE of EDUCATIONAL SERVICES for DISTANCE LEARNERS
## *CAS* Standards Contextual Statement

Increasingly, *distance learning* has become a major educational issue in recent years. Although it has been defined in various ways by a number of educational authorities, the simplest definition is that "distance learning takes place when the instructor and student are not in the same room but instead are separated by physical distance" (Connick, 1999, p. 3). Distance learning often occurs when the student and instructor are separated by time as well.

*Distance education* refers to the various methods of instruction that have been intentionally designed to *result* in distance learning settings. Interestingly, distance education has its roots in the correspondence study movement, which began in Europe during the mid-1880s. By 1873, correspondence courses were being offered in the United States, and the University of Chicago had established a strong academic credit correspondence division by 1892 (Watkins, 1991).

Although higher education correspondence, sometimes referred to as "independent study programs," remain a viable alternative for many students today, developments in electronic communications have provided new technology-supported options for distance learners. In addition to correspondence study, the most common distance learning technologies include . . .

- Computer or online courses taught via the Internet or CD-ROM
- Interactive video systems in which two or more locations are connected, allowing student and instructor to see and hear one another from a distance
- Telecourses wherein instructional television courses are videotaped and broadcast over public or cable television stations

Many of these new teaching methods have gained recognition and acceptance throughout higher education including some of the most traditional academic institutions. Concurrently, regional accrediting bodies are awarding accreditation to both degree programs and institutions that offer instruction completely online. In the "Statement of Commitment by the Regional Accrediting Commissions for the Evaluation of Electronically Offered Degree and Certificate Programs" (Regional Accrediting, 2001b), the accrediting commissions collectively affirmed that although a growing number of colleges and universities are going online with academic programs, the "new delivery systems test conventional assumptions, raising fresh questions as to the essential nature and content of an educational experience and the resources required to support it" (p. 1). Not only are there questions about teaching and learning—distance education poses challenges to student affairs programs and related student support services to meet the needs of distance learners even though these students may never set foot on campus.

During the past century, student affairs practitioners have sought to learn how best to provide both resident and commuter students with effective programs and services designed to enhance student learning and personal development. As colleges and universities develop programs that implement distance education technologies, the entire campus community must find ways to serve the special needs of distance learners. In response to the growth of technologically mediated instruction, the Student Support section of the regional accrediting commissions"*Best Practices* (2001a) asserts that "the institution recognizes that appropriate services must be available for students of electronically offered programs, using the working assumption that these students will not be physically present on campus" (p 12).

The *Best Practices* were initially developed by the Western Cooperative for Educational Telecommunications <www.wiche.edu/telecom/> an organization widely recognized for its expertise in the field of distance learning. Staff members of this cooperative were consulted in the development of the CAS Standards for Educational Services for Distance Learners that follow.

### References, Readings, and Resources:

Connick, G. P. (Ed.) (1999). *The distance learner's guide.* Upper Saddle River, NJ.: Prentice Hall.

Regional Accrediting Commissions (2001a). *Best Practices for electronically offered degree and certificate programs.* <http://www.wiche.edu/telecom/Article1.htm>

Regional Accrediting Commissions (2001b). *Statement of commitment by the regional accrediting commissions for the evaluation of electronically offered degree and certificate programs* <http://www.wiche.edu/telecom/Article1.htm>.

Schwitzer, A.M., Ancis, J.R., & Brown, N. (2001). *Promoting student learning and student development at a distance.* lanham, MD: American College Personnel Association.

Watkins, B.L., & Wright, S.J. (eds.) (1991). *The Foundations of American Distance Education.* Dubuque, Iowa: Kendall/Hunt.

Western Cooperative for Educational Telecommunications (1999). *Guide to developing online student services.* http://www.wcet.info/resources/publications/guide/guide.htm

American Association for Collegiate Independent Study, http://www.aacis.org/

Western Cooperative for Educational Telecommu-nications, P.O. Box 9752, Boulder, CO 80301; 1540 30th Street, Boulder, CO 80303; (303)541-0231; (303)541-0291 (fax) <http://www.wiche.edu/telecom/>

# EDUCATIONAL SERVICES for DISTANCE LEARNERS
## *CAS* STANDARDS and GUIDELINES

## Part 1: MISSION and PROGRAM

Distance education, for purposes of these standards, refers to any formal educational process provided by or contracted for an institution of higher education in which the student and faculty member are separated by time and/or space.

Distance education may be delivered by a variety of methods including the Internet, radio and telecommunication, CD-ROM, television, video, and/or print. An institution may be a traditional higher education institution, a consortium of such institutions, or other education entity.

Distance Education Programs (DEP) must incorporate student learning and student development in its mission. DEP must enhance overall educational experiences. DEP must develop, record, disseminate, implement, and regularly review its mission and goals. Mission statements must be consistent with the mission and goals of the institution and with the standards in this document. DEP must operate as an integral part of the institution's overall mission.

Institutions providing DEP must offer commensurate educational services as outlined throughout this document to assist distance learners to achieve their goals. Such services must be comparable to educational services provided to conventional learners and they must meet standards comparable to those of other institutional offerings. Institutions must recognize, however, that the students who select distance education might have different needs than those enrolled in campus-based instruction.

Institutions must identify the characteristics of their distance students and adapt services to meetthe needs of the particular populations they serve.

## Part 2. CONGRUENCY of MISSION & PROGRAMS

The mission of distance education programs (DEP) must be clearly and explicitly stated. Institutional missions must be approved by appropriate governing bodies such as boards of trustees and state/provincial coordinating or governing agencies, and regularly reviewed by the institution and its regional and specialized accrediting agencies. The purposes or mission of distance education must be congruent with its host institution's purposes and must gain explicit approval of the relevant governance bodies of the

institution. Primary oversight of the compatibility of distance education purposes and those of the institution rests with the institution and its governance system.

Evidence of effective management must include use of comprehensive and accurate information for decisions, clear sources and channels of authority, effective communication practices, decision-making and conflict resolution procedures, responsiveness to changing conditions, accountability and evaluation systems, and recognition and reward processes. DEP must provide channels within the organization for regular review of administrative policies and procedures.

Guided by an overarching intent to ensure student learning and development, DEP must be structured purposefully and managed effectively to achieve stated goals. Evidence of appropriate structure must include current and accessible policies and procedures, written performance expectations for all employees, functional workflow graphics or organizational charts, and clearly stated service delivery expectations.

Authority over the distance education curriculum must be clearly articulated. Goals of DEP must be stated in terms of outcomes to be achieved by students in the program.

The formal education of students consists of the curriculum and the co-curriculum, and must promote student learning and development that is purposeful and holistic. DEP must identify relevant and desirable student learning and development outcomes and provide programs and services that encourage the achievement of those outcomes.

Relevant and desirable outcomes include: intellectual growth, effective communication, realistic self-appraisal, enhanced self-esteem, clarified values, career choices, leadership development, healthy behaviors, meaningful interpersonal relationships, independence, collaboration, social responsibility, satisfying and productive lifestyles, appreciation of diversity, spiritual awareness, and achievement of personal and educational goals.

DEP must provide evidence of its impact on the achievement of student learning and development outcomes.

The program may use the examples that follow or identify other more germane indicators.

## Student Learning & Development Outcome Domains

### Intellectual Growth

Examples of Achievement Indicators

Produces personal and educational goal statements; Employs critical thinking in problem solving; Uses complex information from a variety of sources including personal experience and observation to form a decision or opinion; Obtains a degree; Applies previously understood information and concepts to a new situation or setting; Expresses appreciation for literature, the fine arts, mathematics, sciences, and social sciences

### Effective Communication

Examples of Achievement Indicators

Writes and speaks coherently and effectively; Writes and speaks after reflection; Able to influence others through writing, speaking or artistic expression; Effectively articulates abstract ideas; Uses appropriate syntax; Makes presentations or gives performances

### Enhanced Self-Esteem

Examples of Achievement Indicators

Shows self-respect and respect for others; Initiates actions toward achievement of goals; Takes reasonable risks; Demonstrates assertive behavior; Functions without need for constant reassurance from others

### Realistic Self-Appraisal

Examples of Achievement Indicators

Articulates personal skills and abilities; Makes decisions and acts in congruence with personal values; Acknowledges personal strengths and weaknesses; Articulates rationale for personal behavior; Seeks feedback from others; Learns from past experiences

### Clarified Values

Examples of Achievement Indicators

Articulates personal values; Acts in congruence with personal values; Makes decisions that reflect personal values; Demonstrates willingness to scrutinize personal beliefs and values; Identifies personal, work and lifestyle values and explains how they influence decision-making

### Career Choices

Examples of Achievement Indicators

Articulate career choices based on assessment of interests, values, skills and abilities; Documents knowledge, skills and accomplishments resulting from formal education, work experience, community service and volunteer experiences; Makes the connections between classroom and out-of-classroom learning; Can construct a resume with clear job objectives and evidence of related knowledge, skills and accomplishments; Articulates the characteristics of a preferred work environment; Comprehends the world of work; Takes steps to initiate a job search or seek advanced education

### Leadership Development

Examples of Achievement Indicators

Articulates leadership philosophy or style; Serves in a leadership position in a student organization; Comprehends the dynamics of a group; Exhibits democratic principles as a leader; Exhibits ability to visualize a group purpose and desired outcomes

### Healthy Behavior

Examples of Achievement Indicators

Chooses behaviors and environments that promote health and reduce risk; Articulate the relationship between health and wellness and accomplishing life long goals; Exhibits behaviors that advance a healthy community

### Meaningful Interpersonal Relationships

Examples of Achievement Indicators

Develops and maintains satisfying interpersonal relationships; Establishes mutually rewarding relationships with friends and colleagues; Listens to and considers others' points of view; Treats others with respect

### Independence

Examples of Achievement Indicators

Exhibits self-reliant behaviors; Functions autonomously; Exhibits ability to function interdependently; Accepts supervision as needed; Manages time effectively

### Collaboration

Examples of Achievement Indicators

Works cooperatively with others; Seeks the involvement of others; Seeks feedback from others; Contributes to achievement of a group goal; Exhibits effective listening skills

### Social Responsibilit

Examples of Achievement Indicators

Understands and participates in relevant governance systems; Understands, abides by, and participates in the development, maintenance, and/or orderly change of community, social, and legal standards or norms; Appropriately challenges the unfair, unjust, or uncivil behavior of other individuals or groups; Participates in service/volunteer activities

### Satisfying and Productive Lifestyles

Examples of Achievement Indicators

Achieves balance between education, work and leisure time; Articulates and meets goals for work, leisure and education; Overcomes obstacles that hamper goal achievement; Functions on the basis of personal identity, ethical, spiritual and moral values; Articulates long-term goals and objectives

## Appreciating Diversity
Examples of Achievement Indicators

Understands ones own identity and culture. Seeks involvement with people different from oneself; Seeks involvement in diverse interests; Articulate the advantages and challenges of a diverse society; Challenges appropriately abusive use of stereotypes by others; Understands the impact of diversity on one's own society

## Spiritual Awareness
Examples of Achievement Indicators

Develops and articulates personal belief system; Understands roles of spirituality in personal and group values and behaviors

## Personal and Educational Goals
Examples of Achievement Indicators

Sets, articulates, and pursues individual goals; Articulate personal and educational goals and objectives; Uses personal and educational goals to guide decisions; Understands the effect of one's personal and education goals on others

DEP must be (a) intentional, (b) coherent, (c) based on theories and knowledge of learning and human development, (d) reflective of developmental and demographic profiles of the student population, and (e) responsive to needs of individuals, special populations, and communities.

## Part 3: Leadership
Effective and ethical leadership is essential to the success of all organizations. Institutions must appoint, position, and empower distance education program leaders within the administrative structure to accomplish stated missions. DEP leaders at various levels must be selected on the basis of formal education and training, relevant work experience, personal skills and competencies, relevant professional credentials, as well as potential for promoting learning and development in students, applying effective practices to educational processes, and enhancing institutional effectiveness. Institutions must determine expectations of accountability for leaders and fairly assess their performance.

Leaders of DEP must exercise authority over resources for which they are responsible to achieve their respective missions and must . . .
- articulate a vision for their organization
- set goals and objectives based on the needs and capabilities of the population served
- promote student learning and development
- prescribe and practice ethical behavior

- recruit, select, supervise, and develop others in the organization
- manage financial resources
- coordinate human resources
- plan, budget for, and evaluate personnel and programs
- apply effective practices to educational and administrative processes
- communicate effectively
- initiate collaborative interaction between individuals and agencies that possess legitimate concerns and interests in the functional area

DEP leaders must identify and find means to address individual, organizational, or environmental conditions that inhibit goal achievement.

DEP leaders must promote campus environments that result in multiple opportunities for student learning and development.

DEP leaders must continuously improve programs and services in response to changing needs of students and other constituents, and evolving institutional priorities.

## Part 4. FACULTY QUALITY and SUPPORT
The key ingredient of the quality of academic programs is the caliber of faculty members. The institution must provide adequate faculty support for distance education courses and programs.

Leaders must ensure that faculty members are competent in their disciplines and/or fields of study and capable of teaching students in using a variety of pedagogical methods consistent with qualifications required of non-distance education faculty.

Faculty members must possess demonstrable skill in the appropriate uses of the methods used to deliver instruction.
These methods may include the Internet, CD-ROM, television, video, and/or print.

To assure the quality of instruction, the institution must provide adequate support to faculty in the design and teaching of distance education courses and programs including training in the effective uses of the delivery methods to be used in providing instruction. This support must include access to individuals with special knowledge of the pedagogy of various forms of distance education and to technical personnel.

Faculty members must be educated about the special issues associated with teaching at a distance, including physical, emotional, social, and psychological issues.

In electronically delivered teaching, for example, teachers may need training in how to identify problems of distance students that interfere with learning and how to help students when there is little or no opportunity for face-to-face interaction. The distance education environment poses special challenges with respect to the manner in which educational materials are distributed and shared. Distance education faculty should receive special training on copyright laws and the use of copyrighted materials. Devising ways to assure academic integrity is another area of difficulty in the distance education environment. Institutions should regularly share best practices in this area with all faculty members teaching distance education courses.

Institutional policies concerning teaching load, class size, time needed for course preparation, and sharing of instructional responsibilities must be adapted to appropriately support distributed education models. Because the number of hours required for the preparation and delivery of electronic courses may exceed similar requirements for face-to-face delivery institutional policies must accommodate these requirements.

Faculty members are the primary contact between the institution and the distance student; therefore, they must be able to provide appropriate support and guidance. To accomplish this, the institution must provide faculty access to computer service technicians, advisors, counselors, disability services, student affairs professionals, site administrators, distribution clerks, and library resource personnel

## Part 5. RESOURCES FOR LEARNING

Distance education programs (DEP) must have adequate funding to accomplish its mission and goals. Funding priorities must be determined within the context of the stated mission, goals, objectives, and comprehensive analysis of the needs and capabilities of students, and the availability of internal or external resources.

DEP must demonstrate fiscal responsibility and cost effectiveness consistent with institutional protocols.

DEP must have adequate, suitably located facilities, adequate technology, and equipment to support its mission and goals efficiently and effectively. Facilities, technology, and equipment must be evaluated regularly and be in compliance with relevant federal, state, provincial, and local requirements to provide for access, health, safety, and security.

Facilities, equipment, and other resources associated with the viability and effectiveness of distance education programs should be reflected in the institution's long range planning, budgeting, and policy development processes.

DEP must have technical and support staff members adequate to accomplish its mission. Staff members must be technologically proficient and qualified to perform their job functions, be knowledgeable of ethical and legal uses of technology, and have access to training. The level of staffing and workloads must be adequate and appropriate for program and service demands.

DEP must be staffed adequately by individuals qualified to accomplish its mission and goals. Within established guidelines of the institution, DEP must establish procedures for staff selection, training, and evaluation; set expectations for supervision, and provide appropriate professional development opportunities. DEP must strive to improve the professional competence and skills of all personnel it employs.

DEP staff positions must be filled based on a defined set of qualifications such as level of education, work experience, and personal characteristics (for example, integrity, communication skills, and leadership ability).

Professional staff members must hold an earned graduate degree in a field relevant to the position they hold or must possess an appropriate combination of educational credentials and related work experience.

Degree or credential-seeking interns must be qualified by enrollment in an appropriate field of study and by relevant experience. These individuals must be trained and supervised adequately by professional staff members holding educational credentials and related work experience appropriate for supervision.

Student employees and volunteers must be carefully selected, trained, supervised, and evaluated. They must be trained on how and when to refer those in need of assistance to qualified staff members and have access to a supervisor for assistance in making these judgments. Student employees and volunteers must be provided clear and precise job descriptions, pre-service training based on assessed needs, and continuing staff development.

Salary levels and fringe benefits for all DEP staff members must be commensurate with those for comparable positions within the institution, in similar institutions, and in the relevant geographic area.

DEP must institute hiring and promotion practices that are fair, inclusive, and non-discriminatory. DEP must employ a diverse staff to provide readily identifiable role models for students and to enrich the campus community.

DEP must create and maintain position descriptions for all staff members and provide regular performance planning and appraisals.

DEP must have a system for regular staff evaluation and must provide access to continuing education and professional development opportunities, including in-service training programs and participation in professional conferences and workshops.

It is especially crucial that administrators, managers, and coordinators possess technical proficiency and a thorough understanding of how distance education programs are linked to institutional mission. These personnel also should be talented in communication skills to prepare them for effective involvement with other administrators, faculty, students, and staff of distance education programs. They also should be able to facilitate collaborative relationships among faculty and staff to achieve program goals and to enable program evaluation.

Adequate library resources must be available and accessible to distance students. Institutions must own the library/learning resources or have formal agreements with other institutions' library/learning resources to ensure adequate access to all distance education students.

## Part 6. LEGAL RESPONSIBILITIES

Distance education program (DEP) staff members must be knowledgeable about and responsive to laws and regulations that relate to their respective responsibilities. Staff members must inform users of programs and services and officials, as appropriate, of legal obligations and limitations including constitutional, statutory, regulatory, and case law; mandatory laws and orders emanating from federal, state/provincial and local governments; and the institution's policies.

DEP staff members must use reasonable and informed practices to limit the liability exposure of the institution, its officers, employees, and agents.

Staff members must be informed about institutional policies regarding personal liability and related insurance coverage options.

The institution must provide access to legal advice for DEP staff members as needed to carry out assigned responsibilities.

The institution must inform DEP staff and students in a timely and systematic fashion about extraordinary or changing legal obligations and potential liabilities.

## Part 7. EQUITY and ACCESS

Distance education program (DEP) staff members must ensure that services and programs are provided on a fair and equitable basis. Facilities, programs and services must be accessible. Hours of operation and delivery of and access to programs and services must be responsive to the needs of all students and other constituents. DEP must adhere to the spirit and intent of equal opportunity laws.

The DEP must be open and readily accessible to all students and must not discriminate except where sanctioned by law and institutional policy. Discrimination must especially be avoided on the bases of age; color; creed; cultural heritage; disability; ethnicity; gender identity; nationality; political affiliation, religious affiliation, sex, sexual orientation; or economic, marital, social, or veteran status.

Consistent with their mission and goals, DEP must take affirmative action to remedy significant imbalances in student participation and staffing patterns.

As the demographic profiles of campuses change and new instructional delivery methods are introduced, institutions must recognize the needs of students who participate in distance learning for access to programs and services offered on campus. ☐Institutions must provide appropriate services in ways that are accessible to distance learners and assist them in identifying and gaining access to other appropriate services in their geographic region.

## Part 8. CAMPUS and EXTERNAL RELATIONS

Distance education programs (DEP) must establish, maintain, and promote effective relations with relevant individuals, campus offices, and external agencies.

Leaders should pursue partnering opportunities with agencies, remote facility managers, and campus stakeholders to offer and improve distance education services.

## Part 9. DIVERSITY

Within the context of each institution's unique mission, diversity enriches the community and enhances the collegiate experience for all; therefore, distance education programs (DEP) must nurture environments where commonalties and differences among people are recognized and honored.

DEP must promote educational experiences that are characterized by open and continuous communication that deepens understanding of one's own identity, culture, and heritage, and that of others. DEP must educate and promote respect about commonalties and differences in their historical and cultural contexts.

DEP must address the characteristics and needs of a diverse population when establishing and implementing policies and procedures.

## Part 10. CURRICULUM, COURSE, and DEGREE REQUIREMENTS

Information about courses, programs, and degree requirements must be clear and understandable and accessible to all participants.

Preferably, this information should be published in written form and distributed widely, using a variety of media.

The institutional catalog must clearly state the distance education opportunities available to students. It must present a clear and accurate statement of the instructional delivery systems, learning formats, prerequisites, expected learning outcomes, completion requirements, and other relevant requirements.

Effective distance education programs should employ faculty teamwork, collaborative learning, focused outcomes and shared goals, active creation of knowledge and meaning, and meaningful interaction and feedback. Curriculum design should recognize these components of quality distance education experiences and provide for them intentionally and systematically.

## Part 11. FACULTY-STUDENT INTERACTIONS

Distance education programs must provide for appropriate and effective faculty and student interactions.

These interactions may use one or more media, but should be relevant to the course activities and accessible to all students.

Faculty members must provide for interchange among students, when possible, and with students in all cases.

These interactions must be learning-oriented and ideally should lead to a sense of community among learners and faculty members.

## Part 12. TECHNOLOGICAL COMPETENCE of STUDENTS

Distance students must be competent in appropriate technologies or instructional delivery approaches used in the distance education programs of the institution.

Students in distance education programs should possess attributes associated with their ability to succeed in educational programs equal to that of other students admitted elsewhere to the institution.

## Part 13. ACCESS TO STUDENT and ACADEMIC SERVICES

Institutions must provide appropriate student services for all students enrolled in distance education programs. These services must be sufficiently comprehensive to be responsive to the special needs of all distance students.

The needs of distance students should be carefully analyzed. Programs and services to aid these students should be carefully designed to meet their particular needs.

Institutions offering distance education programs must provide a fully functioning program of distributed education services.

Distributed educational services are those designed to be delivered in learning environments where student and teacher are separated by time and/or space. These services may be divided into three levels of service. The first level provides comprehensive and thorough information about the institution, programs, and services. The second level includes links to other relevant information sources, frequently asked questions about programs of study, and direct access to human resources including phone numbers and e-mail addresses. The third level should provide access to mechanisms to permit the formation of virtual communities of learners.

Services to students must be of comparable quality to services provided to on-campus students.

In many areas, the services to distance students are nearly identical to those provided to on-campus students. Services in admission, financial aid, and registration, for example, might be indistinguishable from those provided to on-campus students. Other services, however, such as advising, counseling, tutoring, career services, wellness programs, and opportunities to engage in aesthetic and culturally enriching activities, may require significant modification to services provided to on-campus students.

## Part 14. EDUCATIONAL SUPPORT SERVICES

The required program of distributed educational services must include at least the following.

146

## 14.A Information for Prospective Students

Information must be provided in anticipation that the prospective distance student will need to make decisions about whether to undertake study in this form. This information must include the following.

### Subpart 14.AA

*Pre-admission.* **Information must be no less comprehensive than that available to students during campus visits prior to admission. Information about what it is like to be a distance learner in general, and what it is like to be a distance learner specifically at the institution offering the services, must be accessible and effectively communicated.**

Web pages may be a good vehicle for making information available to distance learners.

### Subpart 14.AB

*Enrollment.* **Certain materials and processes must be described and provided through other suitable and readily accessible formats.**

Among these may be the catalog, academic advising, registration, the student handbook, and information related to services provided specifically for, and expectations of, distance learners.

**Policies applicable to all students, such as the academic dishonesty policy and other information mandated by law, must be distributed and include information concerning how the institution manages such issues for students studying via distance education.**

### Subpart 14.AC *Academic Program Information.*
**Prospective students must have access to full descriptive materials about all courses and programs. Requirements of students, including all course prerequisites and technical competence and equipment, must be stated clearly.**

Information should . . .

- be easily identified and highly visible and clearly organized on web pages
- provide a credible presentation of the institution and its distance learning programs
- provide prospective students with an opportunity to assess their personal readiness for distance learning
- provide students the tools to assess their hardware and software requirements and capabilities
- include costs, transferability, course sequencing, and equipment requirements
- contact sources

## 14.B Admission

**Applications for admission must be provided in a manner that is practical and that can be completed without undue assistance. These applications must be processed in a manner equitable with that of resident students. Application and admission counseling must be made available to distance learners.**

The admission process should be described in a detailed, step-by-step fashion. Admission requirements should be specified clearly. Criteria used in admission decisions should be specified clearly. Applications should be provided in several forms (e.g., printed, online), along with clear instructions. Deadlines should be specific and explicit.

## 14.C Financial Aid

**Information about financial aid must be provided to distance students and the application process must be described clearly. Eligibility requirements must be specifically outlined including all institutional financial aid policies. Deadlines for application for financial aid must be clearly stated. Student enrollment in multiple institutions must be recognized and applications for financial aid properly administered.**

Distance students applying for financial aid should be provided . . .

- General information about financial aid
- Clearly described types of financial aid available
- Specified costs of attendance
- Information about average percent of financial need met
- Other relevant forms
- Online information when appropriate, but also available in print form

## 14.D Registration

**Distance students must be provided registration services for each new term or course in a clear, timely, and user-friendly manner. Registration services must accommodate students enrolled in courses and programs taught asynchronously.**

Registration policies and processes should be clearly described. Alternative registration methods (e.g., online, print, fax, walk-in) should be identified and provided.

## 14.E Orientation Services

**Orientation to the institution and to the processes of learning required of new distance students must be offered.**

The orientation program should be interactive. As with the delivery of instructional services, orientation may employ a variety of methods of communication and should be accessible.

The orientation process should be interactive and must provide opportunities for student-to-student where possible and faculty (or other staff) member-to-student exchanges. Any qualified member of the faculty or staff may deliver this interactive orientation.

**All requirements for new distance students must be specified in the orientation program. All services available to new students must be specified.**

Prospective learners should be provided a sense of the nature of distance learning along with tips for success.

Academic integrity and related policy issues must be covered in orientation. All applicable student codes must be communicated.

### 14.F  Academic Advising

Academic advising must be readily available throughout the academic year and convenient to both students and advisors.

The academic advising program developed for distance students should be designed around their particular needs.

Advising services must be commensurate with services provided to on campus students in course selection and registration. Additional services to assist students in goal setting and educational and life planning must be provided as needed.

The academic advising services should include . . .
- One-on-one access to advisors by phone, Internet, or other communication tools
- All general education and major requirements
- Self-help pointers to educational planning and course selection
- Articulation information between programs and institutions
- Advising guidelines, such as curriculum guides
- Access to personal academic records (e.g., courses taken and completed, grades, GPA)

### 14.G  Technical Support

The institution must provide information concerning the equipment, software, and type of Internet service provider students will need to participate fully in their courses and programs.

The institution must take steps to insure that students have the technical skills necessary to participate fully in the academic program and must provide an introduction to the specific applications students will need.

Technical support must be available at times convenient to the students enrolled in distance education courses and programs.

Technical support should include:
- Eligibility for technical support;
- Tutorials for dealing with common technical difficulties;
- Self-help tools; and,
- A help line/help service.

### 14.H  Career Services

Career services must be provided for distance students appropriate to their needs. Their eligibility to receive them must be made clear.

Information about career service processes should be accessible to all students in a form consistent with the format of interaction.

These services may include, but are not limited to, self-exploration, self-assessment, goal setting, decision-making, educational planning, career planning, career information, co-op education, and job search services. Self-help tools for career decision-making and on-line searches for positions should be provided.

Opportunities for experiential learning, such as internships, service learning, cooperative education, and part-time jobs, should be effectively marketed and accessible for distance learners.

### 14.I  Library Services

The institution must provide an orientation to library services, which includes effective on-line search strategies geared to the programs of study offered at a distance. Service expectations must be defined.

Access to reference materials, periodicals, and books needed to fulfill course requirements must be readily available. Courses with unique or significant needs for library access must provide this information as part of the introduction to the course. Reference services must be available to individual students.

Library services should include . . .
- Reference support
- Convenient access to document delivery services
- Online tutorials on conducting library research
- Procedures that allow students to obtain necessary books and materials within a reasonable time period should be operable

### 14.J  Services for Students with Disabilities

Accessible services to distance students with disabilities must be provided. The institution's policies concerning reasonable and appropriate accommodations must be provided to the student.

Web pages should conform to World Wide Web (W3C) Content Accessibility Guidelines that explain how to make web pages content accessible to people with disabilities. These guidelines emphasize the importance of providing text equivalents of non-text content such as images, pre-recorded audio, and video.

Assistance in the availability and use of assistive technology must be provided.

### 14.K  Personal Counseling

Counseling services essential to assist distance students to achieve their goals must be provided.

Reasonable efforts should be made to extend comparable counseling services to distance education students. Counseling services, especially in their traditional forms that require face-to-face interaction, cannot be delivered in most distance education formats; however, services that effectively use electronic technologies should be offered when appropriate.

Counseling services for distance education students must be offered in accordance with applicable ethical standards, including ethical guidelines and standards for practice for counseling online. Counselors must develop or adopt ethical standards for their services.

These counseling services should include . . .
- descriptions of available counseling services
- for those experiencing a mental health crisis, contact with a personal counselor on campus, referrals to local emergency care resources, and phone numbers for crisis hotlines
- self-help tools, including online links to appropriate Internet sites and information about finding local referrals assistance

## 14.L  Academic Support Services
**Information concerning academic support services must be made available.**
Distance Learning students should have opportunities for developing learning strategies and getting assistance with content comprehension. Tutoring services, supplemental instruction, and other academic support services should be available to all distance education students. These services should conform to the CAS Standards for Learning Assistance Programs in terms of their quality.

## 14.M  Instructional Materials
**Convenient delivery of instructional materials must be provided to all distance students.**
Where campus bookstores are available, their services should include:
- Merchandise displayed visually
- Relevant policies about bookstore operations
- Online methods for locating course textbooks and materials
- Alternative methods for ordering books and supplies

## 14.N  Promoting Identity with the Institution
**Distance learners must be provided a reasonable opportunity to connect with other students and their instructors. Means of regular communication among students and their instructors must be provided.**
Regular communication with distance learners, such as in newsletters, should be offered. Frequent announcements to distance learners though such means as web pages should be provided. Efforts to create virtual communities among distance learners should be made, when appropriate.
Creative use of electronic or other messages that would likely promote an enhanced sense of community such as bulletin boards, special events, institutional news briefs, and opportunities in special interest groups or projects may be provided.

## 14.O  Other Student Services
**Additional student services deemed to be necessary or appropriate to the circumstances of each institution's distance education programs must be provided.**
Traditional campus services such as leadership development programs and housing services may not be necessarily appropriate or necessary to distance students. Where indicated, however, they should be provided in forms equivalent to those on campus.

Information about health and wellness programs should be made available to distance education students. Referrals to local health-care providers and prescriptions by mail may be examples of services to be provide Information about student activities, including organizations, leisure and recreational activities, and cultural and entertainment events may be provided to distance education students when possible.

## Part 15.  ETHICAL TEACHING and LEARNING
**All persons involved in the delivery of distance education programs (DEP) must adhere to the highest principles of ethical behavior. DEP must develop or adopt and implement appropriate statements of ethical practice. DEP must publish these statements and ensure their periodic review by relevant constituencies.**

**Students must be informed of the applicable ethical standards at the time of their initial enrollment.**

**Training on ethical principles and guidelines for professionals who deliver the instructional services must be provided. Training on principles and guidelines must be promulgated and enforced by the institution.**
Professional association statements of ethical principles and guidelines also are suitable.

**DEP staff members must ensure that privacy and confidentiality are maintained with respect to all communications and records to the extent that such records are protected under the law and appropriate statements of ethical practice. Information contained in students' education records must not be disclosed without written consent except as allowed by relevant laws and institutional policies. Staff members must disclose to appropriate authorities information judged to be of an emergency nature, especially when the safety of the individual or others is involved, or when otherwise required by institutional policy or relevant law.**

**All DEP staff members must be aware of and comply with the provisions contained in the institution's human subjects research policy and in other relevant institutional policies addressing ethical practices and confidentiality of research data concerning individuals.**

**DEP staff members must recognize and avoid personal conflict of interest or appearance thereof in their transactions with students and others.**

**DEP staff members must strive to insure the fair, objective, and impartial treatment of all persons with whom they deal. Staff members must not participate in nor condone any form of harassment**

that demeans persons or creates an intimidating, hostile, or offensive campus environment.

When handling institutional funds, all DEP staff members must ensure that such funds are managed in accordance with established and responsible accounting procedures and the fiscal policies or processes of the institution.

DEP staff members must perform their duties within the limits of their training, expertise, and competence. When these limits are exceeded, individuals in need of further assistance must be referred to persons possessing appropriate qualifications.

DEP staff members must use suitable means to confront and otherwise hold accountable other staff members who exhibit unethical behavior.

DEP staff members must be knowledgeable about and practice ethical behavior in the use of technology.

## Part 16. ASSESSMENT and EVALUATION

Distance education programs (DEP) must conduct regular assessment and evaluations. DEP must employ effective qualitative and quantitative methodologies as appropriate, to determine whether and to what degree the stated mission, goals, and student learning and development outcomes are being met. The process must employ sufficient and sound assessment measures to ensure comprehensiveness. Data collected must include responses from students and other affected constituencies.

DEP must evaluate periodically how well they complement and enhance the institution's stated mission and educational effectiveness. Results of these evaluations must be used in revising and improving programs and services and in recognizing staff performance. Program evaluation must address student retention and attrition of distance learners.

Evaluations should be clearly focused. Evaluations should include course content and quality of instruction apart from mode of delivery and use of technologies.

# THE ROLE of STUDENT FINANCIAL AID PROGRAMS
## *CAS* Standards Contextual Statement

Student aid from federal, state, and institutional sources increased by 75 percent in the last decade, topping $50 billion in 1995-96. This aid assisted some 8.5 million students—57 percent of those enrolled in postsecondary education—and most of the aid was administered by institutional personnel.

Concomitant with the tremendous growth of student aid has been growth in federal paperwork and reporting requirements for participating institutions. The number of pages of legislation governing the Title IV federal student aid programs alone has more than doubled in the last decade, and federal regulations promulgated to implement the law now contain more than 7,000 sections, according to a January 1995 study of— "Federal Regulations Affecting Higher Education" by the National Association of Independent Colleges and Universities. While states and institutions are important sources of aid, the federal government provides three-fourths of the total aid, and therefore imposes the strongest imperative for accountability.

The mission of the financial aid office focuses on service to students and stewardship of funds. Practically speaking, the financial aid office assumes primary responsibility on behalf of the institution for compliance with federal requirements. This responsibility is reflected in the Institutional Participation Agreement between the institution and the Department of Education. To uphold this agreement, federal regulations require specific standards of administrative capability (34 CFR 668.16):

"To begin and to continue to participate in any Title IV, HEA program, an institution shall demonstrate to the Secretary that the institution is capable of adequately administering that program under each of the standards established in this section. The Secretary considered an institution to have that administrative capability if the institution—

(a) Administers the Title IV, HEA programs in accordance with all statutory provisions of or applicable to Title IV of the HEA, all applicable regulatory provisions prescribed under that statutory authority, and all applicable special arrangements, agreements, and limitations entered into under the authority of statues applicable to Title IV of the HEA;

(b) (1) Designates a capable individual to be responsible for administering all the Title IV, HEA programs in which it participates and for coordinating those programs with the institution's other Federal and nonfederal programs of student financial assistance. The Secretary considered an individual to be "capable" under this paragraph if the individual is certified by the State I which the

institution is located, if the State requires certification of financial aid administrators. The Secretary may consider other factors in determining whether an individual is capable, including, but not limited to, the individual's successful completion of Title IV, HEA program training provided or approved by the Secretary, and previous experience and documented success in administering the Title IV, HEA programs properly;

(2) Uses an adequate number of qualified persons to administer the Title IV, HEA programs in which the institution participates. The Secretary considers the following factors to determine whether an institution uses an adequate number of qualified persons . . .

(i)     The number and types of programs in which the institution participates;

(ii)    The number of applications evaluated;

(iii)   The number of students who received any student financial assistance at the institution and the amount of funds administered;

(iv)    The financial aid delivery system used by the institution;

(v)     The degree of office automation used by the institution in the administration of the Title IV, HEA programs;

(vi)    The number and distribution of financial aid staff; and

(vii)   The use of third-party servicers to aid in the administration of the Title IV, HEA programs; . . . ."

An effective and comprehensive aid program must be supported by leaders at the institution who understand the increasing administrative and operational responsibilities and obligations and the potential liabilities that accompany participation in federal aid programs, and who are aware of the challenges and conflicts imposed on the administration of aid and the delivery of quality services to their students. Leaders can take several steps to ensure that the financial aid program advances the goals of the institution without compromising service quality or program integrity. The consistency between institutional goals and those of the aid program can be evaluated by examining the level of commitment of internal resources, the composition of aid packages, the levels of unmet need, and the extent of commitment to need-based aid.

The establishment and support of goals and measures that ensure high-quality financial aid operations should be a high priority for all institutions. Of equal importance is the leaders' responsibility for educating the institution's community about its goals and mission and the role of financial aid in defining and meeting them. Communicating the importance of financial aid to both internal and external constituencies is critical. Presidents, trustees, and others must understand and support the policies of their financial aid programs and serve as effective advocates at the institutional, state, and federal levels. These advocacy efforts should . . .

- Provide opportunities for representatives from all academic and administrative areas of the institution to discuss and help formulate institutional goals.
- Coordinate with the financial aid office to develop mission statements and strategic goals that consider its relationship with other offices and present its philosophy, purpose, goals, and strategies, and the principles governing financial aid awards; disseminate these statements to demonstrate the leadership's support of them and their complementary relationship to broader objectives of the institution.
- Provide forums to make known the impact of pending federal and state developments on the institution and the financial aid office.

- Communicate widely the criteria by which financial aid policies are defined and evaluated, and create opportunities to highlight program successes and the positive impact they have on students and the broader community.

Institutions committed to these strategies draw upon tools provided by the government, the National Association of Student Financial Aid Administrators, and other non-governmental entities. Regional and state associations of financial aid administrators support and augment the activities of national entities to provide the technical training and professional development needed to ensure the viability of financial aid operations.

**Recommended Readings and Resources**

National Association of Independent Colleges and Universities (1995). *Federal regulations affecting higher education*. Washington, DC: Author.

National Association of Student Financial Aid Administrators (NASFAA). 1920 L Street, NW, Suite 200, Washington, DC 20036-5020. (202) 785-0453; Fax (202) 785-1487.

# FINANCIAL AID PROGRAMS
## *CAS* STANDARDS and GUIDELINES

## Part 1. MISSION

Financial aid programs (FAP) must incorporate student learning and student development in its mission. The program must enhance overall educational experiences. FAP must develop, record, disseminate, implement and regularly review its mission and goals. Mission statements must be consistent with the mission and goals of the institution and with the standards in this document. FAP must operate as an integral part of the institution's overall mission.

FAP shall develop, review, and disseminate financial resources to students to assist them in achieving their educational goals from pre-enrollment through graduation. Many aspects of financial aid are mandated by federal and state entities that define the parameters within which institutional programs must operate. In a manner consistent with the goals of the institution the mission and goals of FAP must address the following . . .

### Students in Transition

Such students move from secondary to postsecondary education, from one postsecondary institution to another including undergraduate to graduate school, and return from a period of non-enrollment to formal learning or re-enrollment in the institution.

### Awarding Practices

Such practices establish, promulgate, and implement financial aid criteria that accurately represent the financial needs of the applicant pool, set priorities within this group, and respond with funding to the extent possible.

### Financial Counseling

Such counseling provides high quality services to students for (a) the purpose of providing better understanding of financial aid, (b) financial guidance, (c) individual review of situations that may require special consideration, and (d) guidance in academic and financial matters especially as they relates to satisfactory academic progress.

### Goal Integration

Goals should be consistent with the mission, goals, policies, procedures and characteristics of the institution and be compatible with the ability of the institution to provide adequate resources to meet the needs and educational goals of the students.

### Review of Goals

Institutional goals for financial aid should be developed and reviewed regularly. Such goals should be consistent with statements of good practices articulated by relevant and appropriate professional associations such as the National Association of Student Financial Aid Administrators and the Canadian Association of Student Financial Aid Administrators.

## Part 2. PROGRAM

The formal education of students consists of the curriculum and the co-curriculum, and must promote student learning and development that is purposeful and holistic. Financial aid programs (FAP) must identify relevant and desirable student learning and development outcomes and provide programs and services that encourage the achievement of those outcomes.

Relevant and desirable outcomes include: intellectual growth, effective communication, realistic self-appraisal, enhanced self-esteem, clarified values, career choices, leadership development, healthy behaviors, meaningful interpersonal relationships, independence, collaboration, social responsibility, satisfying and productive lifestyles, appreciation of diversity, spiritual awareness, and achievement of personal and educational goals.

The FAP must provide evidence of its impact on the achievement of student learning and development outcomes.
The program may use the examples that follow or identify other more germane indicators.

### Student Learning & Development Outcome Domains

### Intellectual Growth

Examples of Achievement Indicators
Produces personal and educational goal statements; Employs critical thinking in problem solving; Uses complex information from a variety of sources including personal experience and observation to form a decision or opinion; Obtains a degree; Applies previously understood information and concepts to a new situation or setting; Expresses appreciation for literature, the fine arts, mathematics, sciences, and social sciences

### Effective Communication

Examples of Achievement Indicators
Writes and speaks coherently and effectively; Writes and speaks after reflection; Able to influence others through writing, speaking or artistic expression; Effectively articulates abstract ideas; Uses appropriate syntax; Makes presentations or gives performances

## Enhanced Self-Esteem

Examples of Achievement Indicators

Shows self-respect and respect for others; Initiates actions toward achievement of goals; Takes reasonable risks; Demonstrates assertive behavior; Functions without need for constant reassurance from others

## Realistic Self-Appraisal

Examples of Achievement Indicators

Articulates personal skills and abilities; Makes decisions and acts in congruence with personal values; Acknowledges personal strengths and weaknesses; Articulates rationale for personal behavior; Seeks feedback from others; Learns from past experiences

## Clarified Values

Examples of Achievement Indicators

Articulates personal values; Acts in congruence with personal values; Makes decisions that reflect personal values; Demonstrates willingness to scrutinize personal beliefs and values; Identifies personal, work and lifestyle values and explains how they influence decision-making

## Career Choices

Examples of Achievement Indicators

Articulate career choices based on assessment of interests, values, skills and abilities; Documents knowledge, skills and accomplishments resulting from formal education, work experience, community service and volunteer experiences; Makes the connections between classroom and out-of-classroom learning; Can construct a resume with clear job objectives and evidence of related knowledge, skills and accomplishments; Articulates the characteristics of a preferred work environment; Comprehends the world of work; Takes steps to initiate a job search or seek advanced education

## Leadership Development

Examples of Achievement Indicators

Articulates leadership philosophy or style; Serves in a leadership position in a student organization; Comprehends the dynamics of a group; Exhibits democratic principles as a leader; Exhibits ability to visualize a group purpose and desired outcomes

## Healthy Behavior

Examples of Achievement Indicators

Chooses behaviors and environments that promote health and reduce risk; Articulate the relationship between health and wellness and accomplishing life long goals; Exhibits behaviors that advance a healthy community

## Meaningful Interpersonal Relationships

Examples of Achievement Indicators

Develops and maintains satisfying interpersonal relationships; Establishes mutually rewarding relationships with friends and colleagues; Listens to and considers others' points of view; Treats others with respect

## Independence

Examples of Achievement Indicators

Exhibits self-reliant behaviors; Functions autonomously; Exhibits ability to function interdependently; Accepts supervision as needed; Manages time effectively

## Collaboration

Examples of Achievement Indicators

Works cooperatively with others; Seeks the involvement of others; Seeks feedback from others; Contributes to achievement of a group goal; Exhibits effective listening skills

## Social Responsibility

Examples of Achievement Indicators

Understands and participates in relevant governance systems; Understands, abides by, and participates in the development, maintenance, and/or orderly change of community, social, and legal standards or norms; Appropriately challenges the unfair, unjust, or uncivil behavior of other individuals or groups; Participates in service/volunteer activities

## Satisfying and Productive Lifestyles

Examples of Achievement Indicators

Achieves balance between education, work and leisure time; Articulates and meets goals for work, leisure and education; Overcomes obstacles that hamper goal achievement; Functions on the basis of personal identity, ethical, spiritual and moral values; Articulates long-term goals and objectives

## Appreciating Diversity

Examples of Achievement Indicators

Understands ones own identity and culture. Seeks involvement with people different from oneself; Seeks involvement in diverse interests; Articulate the advantages and challenges of a diverse society; Challenges appropriately abusive use of stereotypes by others; Understands the impact of diversity on one's own society

## Spiritual Awareness

Examples of Achievement Indicators

Develops and articulates personal belief system; Understands roles of spirituality in personal and group values and behaviors

## Personal and Educational Goals

Examples of Achievement Indicators

Sets, articulates, and pursues individual goals; Articulate personal and educational goals and objectives; Uses personal and educational goals to guide decisions; Understands the effect of one's personal and education goals on others

**The FAP must be (a) intentional, (b) coherent, (c) based on theories and knowledge of learning and human development, (d) reflective of developmental and demographic profiles of the**

student population, and (e) responsive to needs of individuals, special populations, and communities. Further, the program must assist students by addressing financial issues that may serve as barriers to the achievement of educational goals.

The financial aid program must . . .
• comply with federal and state law, provincial statutes, and institutional policies
• promote and maintain integrity, accuracy, and timeliness in the delivery of financial aid
• provide adequate information for students and parents to make informed decisions regarding the financing of their education
• promote and provide equal access to eligible students interested in pursuing an education at the institution

## Part 3. LEADERSHIP

Effective and ethical leadership is essential to the success of all organizations. Institutions must appoint, position, and empower leaders within the administrative structure to accomplish stated missions. Financial aid program (FAP) leaders at various levels must be selected on the basis of formal education and training, relevant work experience, personal skills and competencies, relevant professional credentials, as well as potential for promoting learning and development in students, applying effective practices to educational processes, and enhancing institutional effectiveness. Institutions must determine expectations of accountability for leaders and fairly assess their performance.

FAP leaders must exercise authority over resources for which they are responsible to achieve their respective missions.

Program leaders must . . .
• articulate a vision for their organization
• set goals and objectives based on the needs and capabilities of the population served
• promote student learning and development
• prescribe and practice ethical behavior
• recruit, select, supervise, and develop others in the organization
• manage financial resources
• coordinate human resources
• plan, budget for, and evaluate personnel and programs
• apply effective practices to educational and administrative processes
• communicate effectively

• initiate collaborative interaction between individuals and agencies that possess legitimate concerns and interests in the functional area

The FAP leader must identify and find means to address individual, organizational, or environmental conditions that inhibit goal achievement. Program leaders must promote campus environments that result in multiple opportunities for student learning and development.

FAP leaders must continuously improve programs and services in response to changing needs of students and other constituents, and evolving institutional priorities.
The institution should designate a well-qualified senior administrator with appropriate financial aid experience and training to effectively lead the financial aid program staff.

The senior financial aid administrator must advocate for and represent the financial needs of students, the operation and staffing of the financial aid program, and the institution.

The senior financial aid administrator must ensure the development of . . .
• a set of policies and procedures that includes descriptions of the administrative processes
• clearly stated criteria used in the decision making process for financial aid and the source of authority for the criteria employed
• steps for appealing evaluating, or revising policies and procedures
• a statement of the institution's mission, goals, and objectives for the financial aid programs
• an effective system to manage the programs, services, and personnel of the financial aid program
• an assessment plan for its programs and services
• means for coordinating the financial aid program with other institutional agencies
• develop criteria for selecting qualified staff and ensuring adequate opportunities for staff development

## Part 4. ORGANIZATION and MANAGEMENT

Guided by an overarching intent to ensure student learning and development, financial aid programs (FAP) must be structured purposefully and managed effectively to achieve stated goals. Evidence of appropriate structure must include current and accessible policies and procedures, written performance expectations for all employees, functional workflow graphics or organizational charts, and clearly stated service delivery expectations.

Evidence of effective management must include use of comprehensive and accurate information for decisions, clear sources and channels of authority, effective communication practices, decision-making and conflict resolution procedures, responsiveness to changing conditions, accountability and evaluation systems, and recognition and reward processes. FAP must provide channels within the organization for regular review of administrative policies and procedures.

## Part 5. HUMAN RESOURCES

The financial aid program (FAP) must be staffed adequately by individuals qualified to accomplish its mission and goals. Within established guidelines of the institution, the program must establish procedures for staff selection, training, and evaluation; set expectations for supervision, and provide appropriate professional development opportunities. FAP must strive to improve the professional competence and skills of all personnel it employs.

Continued training is essential for all financial aid staff members. It is imperative to be alert to changes in the field and able to incorporate such changes into daily practice.

Every financial aid staff members should be . . .
- familiar with federal, state/provincial, and institutional regulations, policies, and practices regarding the awarding of financial aid funds
- willing to seek out and implement new ideas
- able to translate new ideas into practical methods for improving the overall operation of the financial aid program
- respectful of the confidential nature of the profession
- willing to seek out and use new conceptual frameworks and equipment that bring information to students more clearly and effectively
- aware of relevant developments in the higher education and be able to incorporate these developments

Financial aid staff members should have knowledge and understanding of the mission, programs and services of the institution. Institutional training should be provided for all staff members to include . . .
- a thorough tour of the campus
- familiarization with publications, academic programs, admission policies, and services of the institution
- rights and responsibilities as an employee of the institution

Job descriptions with the duties and responsibilities for each staff member should be developed.

Professional FAP staff members must hold an earned graduate degree in a field relevant to the position they hold or must possess an appropriate combination of educational credentials and related work experience.

Suggested formal training in preparation for professional financial aid employment include such fields as business administration, computer sciences, information systems, college student personnel, higher education administration, counseling and other human behavior disciplines; course work may include computer literacy, research and statistical methods, counseling, legal issues of higher education, and leadership and management.\

Professional staff members should be competent to provide assistance to students that may include but not be limited to, the following . . .
- careful and concerned analysis of each student's need
- knowledgeable guidance and counseling on all financial aid issues and concern
- explanation of federal and state, and, if appropriate, provincial statues of Canada
- interpretation of institutional policies and procedures

Degree or credential-seeking interns must be qualified by enrollment in an appropriate field of study and by relevant experience. These individuals must be trained and supervised adequately by professional staff members holding educational credentials and related work experience appropriate for supervision.

Student employees and volunteers must be carefully selected, trained, supervised, and evaluated. They must be trained on how and when to refer those in need of assistance to qualified staff members and have access to a supervisor for assistance in making these judgments. Student employees and volunteers must be provided clear and precise job descriptions, pre-service training based on assessed needs, and continuing staff development.

Student employees and volunteers should be trained in public relations, referral techniques, peer counseling, and dissemination of information. They should be knowledgeable in their individual job assignments and understand the confidential nature of their positions.

The FAP must have technical and support staff members adequate to accomplish its mission. Staff members must be technologically proficient and qualified to perform their job functions, be knowledgeable of ethical and legal uses of technology, and have access to training. The level of staffing and workloads must be adequate and appropriate for program and service demands.

Support staff members should be skilled in interpersonal communications, public relations, referral techniques and dissemination of information. support staff members with higher technical responsibilities should posses the academic background and experience for effective performance. support staff members should understand the confidential nature of their job.

Salary levels and fringe benefits for all FAP staff members must be commensurate with those for comparable positions within the institution, in similar institutions, and in the relevant geographic area.

The program must institute hiring and promotion practices that are fair, inclusive, and non-discriminatory and must employ a diverse staff to provide readily identifiable role models for students and to enrich the campus community.

The FAP must create and maintain position descriptions for all staff members and provide regular performance planning and appraisals. Likewise, the program must have a system for regular staff evaluation and must provide access to continuing education and professional development opportunities, including in-service training programs and participation in professional conferences and workshops.

## Part 6. FINANCIAL RESOURCES

The financial aid program (FAP) must have adequate funding to accomplish its mission and goals. Funding priorities must be determined within the context of the stated mission, goals, objectives, comprehensive analyses of student needs and capabilities, and the availability of internal or external resources.

The FAP must demonstrate fiscal responsibility and cost effectiveness consistent with institutional protocols.

Funding for the financial aid program should cover staff salaries; purchases and maintenance of office furnishings and equipment, including state of the art technology; purchases of supplies and materials; telephone, fax, electronic communication and postage costs; printing and media costs; institutional membership in appropriate professional organizations; relevant subscriptions and necessary library resources; attendance at professional association meetings, conferences, workshops and other professional development activities. In addition to institutional commitment of general funds, other funding sources maybe considered including state appropriations, federal resources, student fees, fines, donations and contributions.

The FAP budget must be properly prepared, clearly detailed and defined, continually monitored, and adequately funded for full program support.

## Part 7. FACILITIES, TECHNOLOGY, EQUIPMENT

Financial aid programs (FAP) must have adequate technology, suitably located facilities, and equipment to support its mission efficiently and effectively. Facilities, technology, and equipment must be evaluated regularly and be in compliance with relevant federal, state, provincial, and local requirements to provide for access, health, safety, and security.

The program should have ready access to facilities such as . . .
- private office or space for confidential counseling, interviewing, and other meetings
- office, reception, and storage space and security sufficient to accommodate assigned staff, supplies, equipment, library resources, and machinery
- conference room or meeting space

The FAP should be readily accessible, indicated on campus maps, and provided with highly visible signage.

## Part 8. LEGAL RESPONSIBILITIES

Financial aid program (FAP) staff members must be knowledgeable about and responsive to laws and regulations that relate to their respective responsibilities. Staff members must inform users of programs and services and officials, as appropriate, of legal obligations and limitations including constitutional, statutory, regulatory, and case law; mandatory laws and orders emanating from federal, state/provincial and local governments; and the institution's policies.

Program staff members must use reasonable and informed practices to limit the liability exposure of the institution, its officers, employees, and agents. Staff members must be informed about institutional policies regarding personal liability and related insurance coverage options.

The institution must provide access to legal advice for FAP staff members as needed to carry out assigned responsibilities. Further, the institution must inform staff and students in a timely and systematic fashion about extraordinary or changing legal obligations and potential liabilities.

## Part 9. EQUITY and ACCESS

Staff members must ensure that financial aid services are provided on a fair and equitable basis. Facilities must be accessible to all potential users with hours of operation and delivery of programs and services responsive to the needs of all students and other constituents. The financial aid program must adhere to the spirit and intent of equal opportunity laws.

The program should ensure that the needs of special populations such as traditionally under-represented, evening, part-time, and commuter students are considered when establishing programs, services, and office hours.

The FAP must be open and readily accessible to all students and must not discriminate except where sanctioned by law and institutional policy. Discrimination must especially be avoided on the bases of age; color, creed; cultural heritage; disability; ethnicity; gender identity; nationality; political affiliation, religious affiliation, sex, sexual orientation; or economic, marital, social, or veteran status.

Consistent with its mission and goals, the FAP must take affirmative action to remedy significant imbalances in student participation and staffing patterns.

As the demographic profiles of campuses change and new instructional delivery methods are introduced, institutions must recognize the needs of students who participate in distance learning for access to programs and services offered on campus. ☐Institutions must provide appropriate services in ways that are accessible to distance learners and assist them in identifying and gaining access to other appropriate services in their geographic region.

## Part 10. CAMPUS & EXTERNAL RELATIONS

The financial aid program (FAP) must establish, maintain, and promote effective relations with relevant individuals, campus offices, and external agencies.

Institutional functions and constituencies linked to financial aid typically include admissions, registration and records, athletics, business services, academic advising, counseling services, student affirmative action, outreach and educational opportunity programs, career services, institutional development, and faculty and alumni affairs.

Financial aid documents must be accurate and their confidentiality maintained by all institutional offices.

Financial aid and admission decisions should be made independently. However, the financial aid program should have access to appropriate information in the student's admission file to assure compliance with applicable rules and regulations.

The financial aid program should maintain relationships with interested groups within the community regarding general and institutional financial aid practices. The community may include grant and scholarship agencies, high schools, and other community outreach programs.

## Part 11. DIVERSITY

Within the context of each institution's unique mission, diversity enriches the community and enhances the collegiate experience for all.

Consequently, financial aid programs (FAP) must nurture environments where commonalties and differences among people are recognized and honored.

The FAP must promote educational experiences that are characterized by open and continuous communication that deepens understanding of one's own identity, culture, and heritage, and that of others. The program must educate and promote respect about commonalties and differences in their historical and cultural contexts.

The program must address the characteristics and needs of a diverse population when establishing and implementing policies and procedures.

Financial aid staff members should be particularly sensitive to the needs of traditionally under-represented students and students with special needs.

## Part 12. Ethics

Students must be provided access to financial aid programs (FAP) on a fair and equitable basis. All persons involved in the delivery of FAP must adhere to the highest principles of ethical behavior. The program must develop or adopt appropriate statements of ethical practice and publish and ensure their periodic review by relevant constituencies .

When formulating ethical standards, statements adopted by the profession at large or relevant professional associations may be of assistance and should be considered.

Staff members must ensure that privacy and confidentiality are maintained with respect to all communications and records to the extent that such records are protected under the law and appropriate statements of ethical practice. Information contained in students' education records must not be disclosed without written consent except as allowed by relevant laws and institutional policies. Staff members must disclose to appropriate authorities information judged to be of an emergency nature, especially when the safety of the individual or others is involved, or when otherwise required by institutional policy or relevant law.

All staff members must be aware of and comply with the provisions contained in the institution's human subjects research policy and in other relevant institutional policies addressing ethical practices and confidentiality of research data concerning individuals.

FAP staff members must recognize and avoid personal conflict of interest or appearance thereof in their transactions with students and others.

Staff members must strive to ensure the fair, objective, and impartial treatment of all persons with whom they deal. Staff members must not participate in nor condone any form of harassment that demeans persons or creates an intimidating, hostile, or offensive campus environment.

When handling institutional funds, all FAP staff members must ensure that such funds are managed in accordance with established and responsible accounting procedures and the fiscal policies or processes of the institution.

FAP staff members must perform their duties within the limits of their training, expertise, and competence. When these limits are exceeded, individuals in need of further assistance must be referred to persons possessing appropriate qualifications. Staff members must use suitable means to confront and otherwise hold accountable other staff members who exhibit unethical behavior.

FAP staff members must be knowledgeable about and practice ethical behavior in the use of technology.

Financial aid administrators must ensure timely and fair administration of policies regarding financial aid decisions and proper notification.
Publications and written communications should include a financial aid deadlines and information on opportunities for financial aid.

Financial aid must be awarded in compliance with applicable rules and regulations governing financial aid.
When appropriate, the senior financial aid administrator and professional staff members may need to exercise professional judgment in making exceptions to established financial aid policies. These decisions should be made in a fair and objective manner with supporting documentation.

## Part 13. ASSESSMENT and EVALUATION
The financial aid program (FAP) must conduct regular assessments and evaluations. The program must employ effective qualitative and quantitative methodologies as appropriate, to determine whether and to what degree the stated mission, goals, and student learning and development outcomes are being met. The process must employ sufficient and sound assessment measures to ensure comprehensiveness. Data collected must include responses from students and other affected constituencies.

The FAP must evaluate periodically how well it complements and enhances the institution's stated mission and educational effectiveness. Results of these evaluations must be used in revising and improving programs and services and in recognizing staff performance.
Publications such as the *Institutional Guide for Financial Aid Self-Evaluation*, published by the National Association of Student Financial Aid Administrators, have utility for evaluating programs and services.

# The Role of Fraternity and Sorority Advising
## *CAS* Standards Context and Statement

In the 1950s, the role of the campus fraternity and sorority professional began as a result of the burgeoning role fraternities and sororities were playing on college and university campuses. In 1976, a year which marked the bicentennial of the establishment of the nation's first Greek-letter society, Phi Beta Kappa, the Association of Fraternity Advisors (AFA) was established. As the profession has evolved, fraternity and sorority advising professionals have worked to solidify foundations and practices that further define their roles as administrators, advisors and educators.

Advising fraternities and sororities is a multi-dimensional experience for student affairs professionals. In most instances, the advisor acts as an external consultant whose ability to affect organizational progress depends significantly upon the involvement and leadership of undergraduate and alumni, as well as (inter)national headquarters and volunteers. The success of the fraternity and sorority community relies on its campus professionals to function as counselors, educational and leadership development programmers, and change agents. These individuals take responsibility for implementing educational and skill development programs addressing such topics as values clarification, ethical decision-making, academic success strategies, substance abuse awareness, and various areas of organizational management including leadership training, team building, and strategic planning.

In addition, the appreciation of a growing pluralistic society is pivotal for professionals in this field. As stated in *The Student Learning Imperative* (ACPA, 1994), "demographic shifts [are] resulting in increased numbers of people from historically underrepresented groups going to college." (p. 1). Consequently, advisors must facilitate establishment of multicultural, ethnic, and sexual orientation fraternities and sororities, Advisors must work to cultivate an inclusive community, as well as educate all members about the understanding of living in an increasingly diverse society.

The fraternity and sorority advisor is actively involved in the development and enforcement of institutional policy. He or she must be adept at managing resources, applying current technology, and building partnerships within the campus and larger communities.

Those who have studied student involvement theory and the overall student experience have repeatedly noted the potentially positive impact of co-curricular involvement and participation, including the undergraduate fraternity and sorority experience, on the student's overall educational development (Sanford, 1964; Astin, 1993; Whipple, 1998). As the 21st century has begun, the quest to determine success within the community of higher education has become focused upon the concept of improved student learning and development (ACPA, 1994; Toma, 1999). This includes not only the acquisition of knowledge, but the ability to apply and act upon that knowledge in the context of the larger society (Ehrlich, 2000). Increasingly, the call is for learning outcomes to include values-based aspects of competence, such as "consideration of judgment, the appreciation of ends as well as means, and the broad implications and consequences of one's actions and choices." (Ehrlich, 2000, p. xxix). This result of student learning and development occurs through a partnership with invested constituents of the fraternity and sorority movement as well as colleagues in the arena of Student Affairs.

Related to this movement to increase levels of student learning is a consensus among researchers that performance is positively linked to the establishment of high expectations (Kuh, 1999). Interestingly, demographic research indicates that this may be a most appropriate developmental context for the new generation of students coming to campus. Analysis of the data seems to indicate that students will thrive among conditions that foster exploration, dialogue, and experimentation within a context where expectations, systematic feedback, and protective boundaries afford a level of security (Newton, 2000).

Those involved in the advisement of undergraduate students should be well aware of the responsibility they have to facilitate a learning experience. In addition, they must take into account their own actions. The development of a Code of Ethics by AFA in 2001 reminds us of the obligation facing professionals and to lead by powerful examples. All who read these standards are encouraged to take into account this important document, a copy of which can be received through contacting the AFA Central Office or visiting the webpage listed below.

Fraternities and sororities have the capacity to exert significant influence related to these identified outcomes, and the campus fraternity and sorority professional may help foster remarkable levels of student learning and character development. He or she may facilitate all these potentially positive outcomes by helping the undergraduate fraternity and sorority leaders and members understand the values-based foundation of their organizations and the rights and responsibilities associated with the commitment to membership. By facilitating education and accountability, detailing services, and applying student development and current theory, professionals can create opportunities for quality education and student learning.

Challenges face campus professionals of which alcohol abuse and misuse and hazing are two of the more potent threats to the existence of fraternal organizations. The power of campus professionals to create meaningful opportunities to dialogue with constituent groups about the challenges they face and the development of a plan of action to tackle them head on cannot be overstated.

The standards that follow provide comprehensive guidance for institutions that include fraternity and sorority organizations in their campus cultures. These standards should be understood in the context of an evolving profession guided by the norms and policies of institutions, international headquarters, alumni/ae and other entities.

### References, Readings and Resources

American Association for Higher Education, American College Personnel Association, National Association of Student Personnel Administrators. (1998). *Powerful partnerships: A shared responsibility for learning.* Washington, DC: Authors.

American College Personnel Association. (1994). *The student learning imperative: implications for student affairs.* Washington, DC: Author.

Astin, A.W. (1998). What matters in college? *Liberal Education*, Fall 1998, pp. 4-15.

Ehrlich, T. (2000). *Civic responsibility and higher education.* Phoenix, AZ: The Onyx press.

Johnson, C. S. (1972). Fraternities in our colleges. New York: National Interfraternity Foundation.

Kuh, G. D. (1999). Setting the bar high to promote student learning. In G. S. Bliming, E. J. White & Associates. (Eds.). *Good practice in student affairs.* San Francisco: Jossey-Bass.

Newton, F. B. (2000). The new student. About Campus 5, November/December, 2000, pp. 8-15.

Sanford, N. (Ed.). (1964). College and Character. New York: Wiley & Sons.

Yonis, J. D., & A. J. Kazaar (Eds.). (1999). Reconceptualizing the collegiate ideal. *New Directions for Higher Education*, 105. San Francisco: Jossey-Bass.

Whipple, E. G. (Ed.) (1996). New challenges for Greek letter organizations: transforming fraternities and sororities into learning communities. *New Directors for Student Services*, 81, San Francisco: Jossey-Bass.

Winston, R. B., Jr.; W. R. Nettles, III. & J. H. Opper, Jr. (Eds.). (1987). Fraternities and sororities on the contemporary college campus. *New Directions for Student Services*, 40, San Francisco: Jossey-Bass.

Wingspread Group on Higher Education. (1993). *An American imperative: higher expectations for higher education.* Racine, WI: The Johnson Foundation.

Association of Fraternity Advisors web site: www.fraternityadvisors.org

# FRATERNITY and SORORITY ADVISING PROGRAM
## *CAS* STANDARDS and GUIDELINES

## Part 1. MISSION

The fraternity and sorority advising program (FSAP) must incorporate student learning and student development in its mission. The FSAP must enhance overall educational experiences. The FSAP must develop, record, disseminate, implement, and regularly review its mission and goals. Mission statements must be consistent with the mission and goals of the institution and with the standards in this document. The FSAP must operate as an integral part of the institution's overall mission.

The FSAP must promote academic and personal growth and development of students who affiliate with fraternities and sororities and promote the fraternity and sorority community as an integral and productive part of the institution.

To accomplish its mission, the program must . . .
• promote the intellectual, social, spiritual, moral, civic, and career development, and wellness of students
• provide education and experience in leadership, group dynamics, and organization development
• promote student involvement in co-curricular activities
• promote sponsorship of and participation in community service and philanthropic projects
• promote an appreciation for different lifestyles including cultural and religious heritages
• recognize and encourage the positive learning experiences that are possible in a fraternity and sorority community that has a diversified membership

Participation in a campus chapter represents one of several group affiliation options for college students. Fraternity and sorority affiliation may include: a recruitment process, new/ associate member education, initiation (formal induction into the organization), ongoing membership development programming, and lifelong affiliation. Professional staff members should promote student development in all affiliation processes.

Staff members should develop a comprehensive program to promote the education and welfare of participating students and coordinate resources and activities with others in the campus community.

**Participation in a fraternity or sorority must promote responsible membership in both the organization and the institution.**

## Part 2. PROGRAM

The formal education of students consists of the curriculum and the co-curriculum, and must promote student learning and development that is purposeful and holistic. The fraternity and sorority advising program (FSAP) must identify relevant and desirable student learning and development outcomes and provide programs and services that encourage the achievement of those outcomes.

Relevant and desirable outcomes include: intellectual growth, effective communication, realistic self-appraisal, enhanced self-esteem, clarified values, career choices, leadership development, healthy behaviors, meaningful interpersonal relationships, independence, collaboration, social responsibility, satisfying and productive lifestyles, appreciation of diversity, spiritual awareness, and achievement of personal and educational goals.

The FSAP must provide evidence of its impact on the achievement of student learning and development outcomes.

The fraternity and sorority advising program may use the examples that follow or identify other more germane indicators.

### Student Learning & Development Outcome Domains

### Leadership Development
Examples of Achievement Indicators
Articulates leadership philosophy or style; Serves in a leadership position in a student organization; Comprehends the dynamics of a group; Exhibits democratic principles as a leader; Exhibits ability to visualize a group purpose and desired outcomes

### Intellectual Growth
Examples of Achievement Indicators
Produces personal and educational goal statements; Articulates and uses personal and educational goals and objects to guide decisions; Employs critical thinking in problem solving; Uses complex information from a variety of sources including personal experience and observation to form a decision or opinion; Obtains a degree; Continuously open to learning opportunities; Applies previously understood information and concepts to a new situation or setting; Expresses appreciation for literature, the fine arts, mathematics, sciences, and social sciences

162

## Collaboration

Examples of Achievement Indicators

Works cooperatively with others; Seeks the involvement of others; Seeks feedback from others; Contributes to achievement of a group goal; Exhibits effective listening skills; Seeks the involvement of others in accomplishing tasks; Serves as a team member to accomplish common goals; Listens well

## Social Responsibility

Examples of Achievement Indicators

Understands and participates in relevant governance systems; Understands, abides by, and participates in the development, maintenance, and/or orderly change of community, social, and legal standards or norms; Appropriately challenges the unfair, unjust, or uncivil behavior of other individuals or groups; Participates in service/volunteer activities

## Effective Communication

Examples of Achievement Indicators

Writes and speaks coherently and effectively; Writes and speaks after reflection; Able to influence others through writing, speaking or artistic expression; Effectively articulates abstract ideas; Uses appropriate syntax; Makes presentations or gives performances

### Enhanced Self-Esteem

Examples of Achievement Indicators

Shows self-respect and respect for others; Initiates actions toward achievement of goals; Takes reasonable risks; Demonstrates assertive behavior; Functions without need for constant reassurance from others

## Realistic Self-Appraisal

Examples of Achievement Indicators

Articulates personal skills and abilities; Makes decisions and acts in congruence with personal values; Acknowledges personal strengths and weaknesses; Articulates rationale for personal behavior; Seeks feedback from others; Learns from past experiences

## Clarified Values

Examples of Achievement Indicators

Articulates personal values; Acts in congruence with personal values; Makes decisions that reflect personal values; Demonstrates willingness to scrutinize personal beliefs and values; Identifies personal, work and lifestyle values and explains how they influence decision-making

## Career Choices

Examples of Achievement Indicators

Articulates career choices based on assessment of interests, values, skills and abilities; Documents knowledge, skills and accomplishments resulting from formal education, work experience, community service and volunteer experiences; Makes the connections between classroom and out-of-classroom learning; Can construct a resume with clear job objectives and evidence of related knowledge, skills and accomplishments; Articulates the characteristics of a preferred work environment; Comprehends the world of work; Takes steps to initiate a job search or seek advanced education

## Healthy Behavior

Examples of Achievement Indicators

Chooses behaviors and environments that promote health and reduce risk; Articulate the relationship between health and wellness and accomplishing life long goals; Exhibits behaviors that advance a healthy community

## Meaningful Interpersonal Relationships

Examples of Achievement Indicators

Develops and maintains satisfying interpersonal relationships; Establishes mutually rewarding relationships with friends and colleagues; Listens to and considers others' points of view; Treats others with respect

## Independence

Examples of Achievement Indicators

Exhibits self-reliant behaviors; Functions autonomously; Exhibits ability to function interdependently; Accepts supervision as needed; Manages time effectively

## Satisfying and Productive Lifestyles

Examples of Achievement Indicators

Achieves balance between education, work and leisure time; Articulates and meets goals for work, leisure and education; Overcomes obstacles that hamper goal achievement; Functions on the basis of personal identity, ethical, spiritual and moral values; Articulates long-term goals and objectives

## Appreciating Diversity

Examples of Achievement Indicators

Understands ones own identity and culture. Seeks involvement with people different from oneself; Seeks involvement in diverse interests; Articulates the advantages and challenges of a diverse society; Challenges appropriately abusive use of stereotypes by others; Understands the impact of diversity on one's own society

## Spiritual Awareness

Examples of Achievement Indicators

Develops and articulates personal belief system; Understands roles of spirituality in personal and group values and behaviors

## Personal and Educational Goals

Examples of Achievement Indicators

Sets, articulates, and pursues individual goals; Articulates personal and educational goals and objectives; Uses personal and educational goals to guide decisions; Understands the effect of one's personal and education goals on others

**The FSAP must be (a) intentional, (b) coherent, (c) based on theories and knowledge of learning and**

human development, (d) reflective of developmental and demographic profiles of the student population, and (e) responsive to needs of individuals, special populations, and communities.

The FSAP must include the following elements . . .

- **Educational programming that enhances member knowledge, understanding, and competencies essential for academic success, personal development, and the exercise of leadership. Educational programming must complement the academic curriculum.**

Activities that improve the student's chances of academic success are particularly important. Programs should address the maturation and development of students and facilitate the application of knowledge and skills through experiential opportunities.

- **Staff members who provide programs that encourage faculty, staff, and administrator involvement and interaction with students.**

Leadership programs should help the individual effectively understand and manage group processes, particularly the relevant aspects of self-governance and accountability. Leadership programs also should enable students to gain knowledge about assessing leadership and management skills.

Good citizenship development programs, including opportunities for self-learning, should assist students in becoming responsible and involved community members.

- **Social and recreational programming that enhances the members' knowledge, understanding, and skills necessary for success and the productive use of leisure time.**

Social skills programs should assist individuals in developing more mature and satisfying interpersonal relationships.

Educational programs should promote wellness, teamwork, sportsmanship, and healthy competition.

- **Opportunities for recognition by the institution as appropriate.**
- **The institution and the fraternities and sororities must jointly define their relationship. The relationship statement must be formalized, documented, and disseminated.**

Campus chapters should participate in the same student organization registration and recognition process as other campus student groups. Additional statements regarding relationships between the institution and its chapters may be defined as appropriate for the campus. Areas of consideration may include:

- a description of the community
- historical relationships
- educational role of fraternities and sororities
- conditions and responsibilities of affiliation
- housing and other facilities

- support and program orientation
- governance and authority [e.g., national and international organization affiliation and expansion]
- reference to comprehensive policy documents
- expectations of the institution and the fraternity and sorority community
- accountability to other student governing bodies

- **Educational programming that addresses aspects of the fraternity and sorority community that are currently or historically problematic to the institution including housing safety, hazing, alcohol and other drug abuse, sexual harassment, racism, intolerance based on religion or sexual orientation, and other practices and attitudes that diminish human dignity or the physical and social security of the host institution or host community.**
- **Professional staff members who assist students to function productively within the institution and to fully understand the rights and responsibilities of individuals and groups.**

This may include such activities as interpreting institutional policies, administering a disciplinary system that safeguards due process, conducting performance evaluations, and providing outreach programming to familiarize other departments and community agencies with fraternity and sorority life. Staff members should avoid social situations or appearance of preferential treatment that may pose conflicts of interest.

The program may include awards for academic and service achievement as well as chapter/community monitoring.

- **Enforcement of applicable laws as well as institutional policies with particular attention paid to housing safety, hazing, the use and possession of alcohol and other drugs, sexual harassment, racism, intolerance based on religion or sexual orientation, and other practices and attitudes that diminish human dignity.**
- **Advising chapters, their individual members, their officers, and their alumni regarding leadership roles and responsibilities.**

Advising services to chapters may include . . .

- monitoring scholastic standing of chapter members individually and collectively and recommending programs for scholastic improvement
- meeting with chapter leaders to discuss individual and chapter goals and developmental needs;
- assisting student members to understand their responsibilities to the group and to the future of the organization
- attending chapter meetings on a periodic basis
- encouraging chapter members' attendance at regional, and national or international conferences
- evaluating chapter development and recommending programs for improvement
- providing assistance and advice in planning chapter programs (e.g., fund raising, and fiscal management)

Advising services for the fraternity and sorority system (e.g., chapter advisors, house corporation members, chapter presidents, and institutional administrators) may include . . .

- providing workshops, programs, retreats, and seminars on relevant topics (e.g., human relations, sexual responsibility, and eating disorders/body image)
- coordinating information gathering and dissemination regarding fraternity and sorority life via monthly meetings, newsletters, and/or information bulletins to the various entities involved in fraternity and sorority life
- acquiring resources for and promoting service projects
- advising governing bodies
- providing assistance and advice in the planning of fraternity and sorority community programs (e.g., Fraternity and Sorority Week)
- publishing documents that focus on current events, leadership opportunities, and other information regarding fraternity and sorority life
- developing and distributing a speakers' directory for distribution that focuses on educational programs
- coordinating annual fire prevention and energy conservation programs in conjunction with local agencies for housed organizations
- coordinating cooperative buying efforts in conjunction with local chapters and/or councils
- monitoring of membership statistics and academic retention by chapter and community

Advising services with other agencies may include . . .

- collaborating with national or international organizations when applicable/appropriate
- establishing and coordinating communication with local alumni volunteers
- serving as an immediate information resource for students, alumni, and administrators

## Part 3. LEADERSHIP

Effective and ethical leadership is essential to the success of all organizations. Institutions must appoint, position and empower fraternity and sorority advising program (FSAP) leaders within the administrative structure to accomplish stated missions. FSAP leaders at various levels must be selected on the basis of formal education and training, relevant work experience, personal skills and competencies, relevant professional credentials, as well as potential for promoting learning and development in students, applying effective practices to educational processes, and enhancing institutional effectiveness. Institutions must determine expectations of accountability for leaders and fairly assess their performance.

Leaders of the FSAP must exercise authority over resources for which they are responsible to achieve their respective missions.

FSAP leaders must . . .

- articulate a vision for their organization
- set goals and objectives based on the needs and capabilities of the population served

- promote student learning and development
- prescribe and practice ethical behavior
- recruit, select, supervise, and develop others in the organization
- manage financial resources
- coordinate human resources
- plan, budget for, and evaluate personnel and programs
- apply effective practices to educational and administrative processes
- communicate effectively
- initiate collaborative interaction between individuals and agencies that possess legitimate concerns and interests in the functional area

FSAP leaders must identify and find means to address individual, organizational, or environmental conditions that inhibit goal achievement. Leaders must promote campus environments that result in multiple opportunities for student learning and development.

FSAP leaders must continuously improve programs and services in response to changing needs of students and other constituents, and evolving institutional priorities.

## Part 4. ORGANIZATION and MANAGEMENT

Guided by an overarching intent to ensure student learning and development, the fraternity and sorority advising program (FSAP) must be structured purposefully and managed effectively to achieve stated goals. Evidence of appropriate structure must include current and accessible policies and procedures, written performance expectations for all employees, functional workflow graphics or organizational charts, and clearly stated service delivery expectations.

Evidence of effective management must include use of comprehensive and accurate information for decisions, clear sources and channels of authority, effective communication practices, decision-making and conflict resolution procedures, responsiveness to changing conditions, accountability and evaluation systems, and recognition and reward processes. The FSAP must provide channels within the organization for regular review of administrative policies and procedures.

The FSAP must be organized to encourage positive relationships with students.

The administrative organization of the fraternity and sorority advising program should organized by the size, nature, and mission of the institution. This may include special living arrangements for various levels of affiliation.

Fraternities and sororities should be a fully integrated institutional component provided with the necessary resources and support to effect the desired student outcomes. The program should be organized and administered in a manner that permits its stated mission to be fulfilled. The administrative leader of the program should be responsible to the chief student affairs officer or designee.

## Part 5. HUMAN RESOURCES

**The fraternity and sorority advising program (FSAP) must be staffed adequately by individuals qualified to accomplish its mission and goals. Within established guidelines of the institution, the FSAP must establish procedures for staff selection, training, and evaluation; set expectations for supervision, and provide appropriate professional development opportunities. The FSAP must strive to improve the professional competence and skills of all personnel it employs.**

**FSAP professional staff members must hold an earned graduate degree in a field relevant to the position they hold or must possess an appropriate combination of educational credentials and related work experience.**

Appropriate preparatory graduate level coursework may include organizational behavior and development, oral and written communication, research and evaluation, ethics, appraisal of educational practices, group dynamics, budgeting, counseling techniques, leadership development, learning and human development theories, higher education administration, performance appraisal and supervision, administrative uses of computers, legal issues in higher education, and student affairs functions.

Effective management is critical to the success of the program, with expertise often required in the areas of housing, dining, accounting, safety and risk management, alumni relations, and programming. In addition, professional staff members should have experience in the development and implementation of educational programs for students. Staff members should be qualified to work with various internal and external agencies in formulating goals and directions for the chapters and community that are consistent with institutional policies.

**Degree or credential-seeking interns must be qualified by enrollment in an appropriate field of study and by relevant experience. These individuals must be trained and supervised adequately by professional staff members holding educational credentials and related work experience appropriate for supervision.**

**Student employees and volunteers must be carefully selected, trained, supervised, and evaluated. They must be trained on how and when to refer those in need of assistance to qualified staff members and have access to a supervisor for assistance in making these judgments. Student employees and volunteers must be provided clear and precise job descriptions, pre-service training based on assessed needs, and continuing staff development.**

The use of graduate assistants and interns may be a way to expand staff capabilities and to provide valuable experience for professionals who have an interest in the field of fraternity and sorority advising.

When appropriate, student employees or volunteers may be utilized and assigned responsibilities for specific projects that are administered or coordinated within the program. Students can lend a valuable perspective to educational programming efforts.

**The fraternity and sorority advising program must have technical and support staff members adequate to accomplish its mission. Staff members must be technologically proficient and qualified to perform their job functions, be knowledgeable of ethical and legal uses of technology, and have access to training. The level of staffing and workloads must be adequate and appropriate for program and service demands.**

**Salary levels and fringe benefits for all FSAP staff members must be commensurate with those for comparable positions within the institution, in similar institutions, and in the relevant geographic area.**

**The FSAP must institute hiring and promotion practices that are fair, inclusive, and non-discriminatory. Programs and services must employ a diverse staff to provide readily identifiable role models for students and to enrich the campus community.**

**The FSAP must create and maintain position descriptions for all staff members and provide regular performance planning and appraisals.**

**The FSAP must have a system for regular staff evaluation and must provide access to continuing education and professional development opportunities, including in-service training programs and participation in professional conferences and workshops.**

**FSAP professional staff members must engage in professional development opportunities to keep abreast of research, theories, legislation, policies, and developments that affect fraternity and sorority advising.**

These activities may include in-service training programs, participation in professional conferences, workshops, and other continuing education activities.

The level of FSAP services must be established and reviewed regularly with regard to demands, enrollment, user surveys, diversity of services offered, institutional resources, and other services available on the campus and in the local community.

## Part 6. FINANCIAL RESOURCES
The fraternity and sorority advising program (FSAP) must have adequate funding to accomplish its mission and goals. Funding priorities must be determined within the context of the stated mission, goals, objectives and comprehensive analysis of the needs and capabilities of students and the availability of internal or external resources.

The FSAP must demonstrate fiscal responsibility and cost effectiveness consistent with institutional protocols.

When any special institutional or fraternity and sorority funding or expenditure accounts are used, professional staff members should provide for the collection and disbursement of funds and follow the institution's accounting procedures.

## Part 7. FACILITIES, TECHNOLOGY, & EQUIPMENT
The fraternity and sorority advising program (FSAP) must have adequate, suitably located facilities, adequate technology, and equipment to support its mission and goals efficiently and effectively. Facilities, technology, and equipment must be evaluated regularly and be in compliance with relevant federal, state, provincial, and local requirements to provide for access, health, safety, and security.

Contracts with outside vendors must include adherence to ethical and institutional policies. Houses or common rooms that are owned, rented, or otherwise assigned to fraternities and sororities for their use must be managed in accordance with all applicable regulatory and statutory requirements of the host institution and relevant government authorities.

To effectively carry out essential activities, services, and programs, adequate space should be provided for private consultation, work areas, equipment storage, and resource library. Any space should be accessible and integrated with other institutional student support services.

## Part 8. LEGAL RESPONSIBILITIES
Fraternity and sorority advising program (FSAP) staff members must be knowledgeable about and responsive to laws and regulations that relate to their respective responsibilities. FSAP staff members must inform users of programs and services and officials, as appropriate, of legal obligations and limitations including constitutional, statutory, regulatory, and case law; mandatory laws and orders emanating from federal, state/provincial and local governments; and the institution's policies.

Program staff members must use reasonable and informed practices to limit the liability exposure of the institution, its officers, employees, and agents. Staff members must be informed about institutional policies regarding personal liability and related insurance coverage options.

The institution must provide access to legal advice for FSAP staff members as needed to carry out assigned responsibilities. In addition, the institution must inform both staff and students in a timely and systematic fashion about extraordinary or changing legal obligations and potential liabilities.

## Part 9. EQUITY AND ACCESS
Fraternity and sorority advising program (FSAP) staff members must ensure that services and programs are provided on a fair and equitable basis. Facilities, programs and services must be accessible. Hours of operation and delivery of and access to programs and services must be responsive to the needs of all students and other constituents. The FSAP must adhere to the spirit and intent of equal opportunity laws.

The FSAP must be open and readily accessible to all students and must not discriminate except where sanctioned by law and institutional policy. Discrimination must especially be avoided on the bases of age; color, creed; cultural heritage; disability; ethnicity; gender identity; nationality; political affiliation, religious affiliation, sex, sexual orientation; or economic, marital, social, or veteran status.

Consistent with their mission and goals, the FSAP must take affirmative action to remedy significant imbalances in student participation and staffing patterns.

As the demographic profiles of campuses change and new instructional delivery methods are introduced, institutions must recognize the needs of students who participate in distance learning for access to programs and services offered on campus. Institutions must provide appropriate services in ways that are accessible to distance learners and assist them in identifying and gaining access to other appropriate services in their geographic region. The FSAP program must advocate for the needs of specific under-represented populations.

## Part 10. CAMPUS and EXTERNAL RELATIONS

The fraternity and sorority advising program (FSAP) must establish, maintain, and promote effective relations with relevant individuals, campus offices, and external stakeholders.

Program staff members must seek out and utilize multiple learning resource opportunities in the delivery of services and programs. These include the national or international headquarters staff, alumni, chapter officers and members, faculty members, institutional administrators, and community resources.

The FSAP must maintain effective contact with its local chapters' national and international representatives.

A team approach in working with students in the local chapters should be a common goal of advisors, alumni, and national or international representatives.

Faculty and staff members are valuable as chapter advisors and role models for students. They may serve on committees that focus on institutional issues affecting the fraternity and sorority community. Further, faculty members can help shape the institutional policy with regard to the fraternity and sorority community. Effective and consistent communications among faculty and staff members, fraternity and sorority chapter members, and chapter advisors can enhance the creation of meaningful learning experiences to improve academic success and increase understanding of educational goals.

Because alumni can serve as valuable resources, program staff members should encourage and enlist a productive level of alumni involvement and assist with information exchange and collaborative programming efforts.

The staff member is typically the principal representative of the administration to the fraternity and sorority community as well as the principal advocate for the fraternity and sorority community within the administration.

Particularly when houses are located in community neighborhoods, good working relationships with neighbors, merchants and community leaders must be maintained to promote cooperative solutions to problems that may arise.

Chapter houses may be governed by the local community and have access to its services and agencies.

The FSAP must assist students in maintaining responsible community living.

Attention should be paid to issues such as fire safety, noise control, parking, trash removal, security, facility and property maintenance and life safety and health code compliance.

Philanthropic activities and community volunteer involvement, which have been traditional components of fraternity and sorority programs, should be developed, maintained, and encouraged.

## Part 11. DIVERSITY

Within the context of each institution's unique mission, diversity enriches the community and enhances the collegiate experience for all; therefore, the fraternity and sorority advising program (FSAP) must nurture environments where commonalties and differences among people are recognized and honored.

The FSAP must promote educational experiences that are characterized by open and continuous communication that deepens understanding of one's own identity, culture, and heritage, and that of others. The FSAP must educate and promote respect about commonalties and differences in their historical and cultural contexts.

The FSAP must address the characteristics and needs of a diverse population when establishing and implementing policies and procedures.

The FSAP must enhance students' knowledge, understanding, skills, and responsibilities associated with being a member of a pluralistic society. The program must provide educational efforts that focus on awareness of cultural, religious, sexual orientation, and gender identity differences.

These efforts should also include assessment of possible prejudices and desirable behavioral changes.

The FSAP must include outreach to underrepresented populations in membership recruitment activities.

## Part 12. ETHICS

All persons involved in the delivery of the fraternity and sorority advising program (FSAP)) must adhere to the highest principles of ethical behavior. The FSAP must develop or adopt and implement appropriate statements of ethical practice. The FSAP must publish these statements and ensure their periodic review by relevant constituencies .

Staff members must ensure that privacy and confidentiality are maintained with respect to all communications and records to the extent that such records are protected under the law and appropriate statements of ethical practice. Information contained in students' education records must not be disclosed without written consent except as allowed by relevant laws and institutional policies. FSAP staff members must disclose to appropriate authorities information judged to be of an emergency nature, especially when the safety of the individual or others is involved, or when otherwise required by institutional policy or relevant law.

All FSAP staff members must be aware of and comply with the provisions contained in the institution's human subjects research policy and in other relevant institutional policies addressing ethical practices and confidentiality of research data concerning individuals.

FSAP staff members must recognize and avoid personal conflict of interest or appearance thereof in their transactions with students and others.

FSAP staff members must strive to insure the fair, objective, and impartial treatment of all persons with whom they deal. Staff members must not participate in nor condone any form of harassment that demeans persons or creates an intimidating, hostile, or offensive campus environment.

When handling institutional funds, all FSAP staff members must ensure that such funds are managed in accordance with established and responsible accounting procedures and the fiscal policies or processes of the institution.

FSAP staff members must perform their duties within the limits of their training, expertise, and competence. When these limits are exceeded, individuals in need of further assistance must be referred to persons possessing appropriate qualifications.

FSAP staff members must use suitable means to confront and otherwise hold accountable other staff members who exhibit unethical behavior.

FSAP staff members must be knowledgeable about and practice ethical behavior in the use of technology.

FSAP staff members must be familiar with, adhere to, advocate for, and model relevant ethical standards in the field.

FSAP staff members must demonstrate a high level of ethical conduct. The program must adopt a statement of ethics that strives to:
• treat fairly all students who wish to affiliate
• eliminate illegal discrimination associated with the selection of members
• uphold applicable standards of conduct expressed by the institution and by the respective national or international organizations

## Part 13. ASSESSMENT and EVALUATION

The fraternity and sorority advising program (FSAP) must conduct regular assessment and evaluations. The FSAP must employ effective qualitative and quantitative methodologies as appropriate, to determine whether and to what degree the stated mission, goals, and student learning and development outcomes are being met. The process must employ sufficient and sound assessment measures to ensure comprehensiveness. Data collected must include responses from students and other affected constituencies.

The FSAP must evaluate periodically how well they complement and enhance the institution's stated mission and educational effectiveness. Results of these evaluations must be used in revising and improving programs and services and in recognizing staff performance.

The program must seek evaluative feedback from relevant administrative units, community agencies, alumni, students, faculty, and national or international headquarters staff. Selected critical aspects of evaluations should be recorded and maintained by the institution.

Evaluations should address the fraternity and sorority community, programs, services, and activities.

Evaluations should be conducted to determine the strength of leadership, the fulfillment of the community's purposes and priorities, the effectiveness of self-governance procedures, individual chapter congruence with institutional and system purposes, the effectiveness of programs, and the availability and stability of resources.

Periodic assessment and evaluation of chapter needs, goals, and objectives should include chapter vitality and evaluation of each chapter's leadership, self-sufficiency, accountability to purpose, and productive activities.

The living environment of each chapter should be assessed including annual or as-needed safety, sanitation, and quality of life inspections of all housing facilities, kitchens, building electrical systems, heating systems, and fire control equipment.

Research also should be a part of the program. Relevant research topics include . . .
• how student development is influenced by fraternity or sorority membership
• influence of participation in members' values
• skill development among members at various stages of membership
* the effect of participation in fraternities and sororities on members' academic performance, retention, and matriculation

# THE ROLE of COLLEGE and UNIVERSITY STUDENT HOUSING
## *CAS* Standards Contextual Statement

Although American institutions of higher learning have provided student housing in one form or another since the first colleges were founded (Frederiksen, 1993), the professionalization of those employed in housing was greatly enhanced when the Association of College and University Housing Officers-International (ACUHO-I) held its first annual conference in 1949. This meeting marked a significant step forward in the development of college and university student housing programs as a profession.

Until the middle of this century, college and university residence halls were administered by "housemothers," often under the supervision of deans of men or women. These staff members assumed parental responsibility (*in loco parentis*) for the students housed in the residence halls. During the 1960s, dramatic changes in laws and education produced changes in the operation of residence halls. Housemothers were replaced by full-time staff with professional training in counseling and administration. These student affairs professionals focused on using the residence hall environment as a tool to complement formal classroom education. Since the 1960s, student housing has become increasingly more specialized and complex. However, the concept of utilizing residence halls as combined living-learning environments to enhance classroom learning has remained constant.

Many college and university student housing operations employ staff members with wide varieties of skills and functions. Areas administered by institutional housing and residence life programs include such functions as:

- Administration of various electronic media (residential cable TV channels, network access, internal movie and information channels, electronic access systems)
- Apartment housing
- Conference housing
- Education (e.g., leadership development, student government advising, student conduct, joint programs with faculty and academic departments, community and individual development)
- Facilities maintenance
- Financial and program planning and administration
- Food services (including catering and cash food operations)
- Marketing
- Off campus rental referral
- Planning and administration of the construction of new facilities
- Research, evaluation and assessment
- Safety and security

Most institutional student housing operations are self-supported auxiliaries that do not receive financial support from the institution or other public sources; In effect, student housing is an education "business." Because of the wide scope and function of student housing, planning is usually initiated institution-wide. Likewise, although housing encompasses many functions, most administrations agree that students are best served when all housing and residence life functions fall under the responsibility of a single administrator, usually the director of housing.

Group living influences maturation by exposing students to a variety of experiences. What distinguishes group living in campus residence from most other forms of housing is the involvement of both professional and paraprofessional staff members in providing intentional, as opposed to random, educational experiences for students. Students living in residence halls participate in more extracurricular, social, and cultural events; are more likely to graduate; and exhibit greater positive gains in psychosocial development, intellectual orientation, and self concept than students living at home or commuting. In addition, they demonstrate significantly greater increases in aesthetic, cultural, and intellectual values; social and political liberalism; and secularism (Schroeder & Mable, 1993).

Residence halls contribute significantly to a student's educational experience. The standards and guidelines that follow provide guidance to those who work in this field and accountability to the public they serve.

### Recommended Readings, and Resources

Association of College and University Housing Officers-International (ACUHO-I) (1992). *Ethical principles and standards for college and university housing Professionals.* Columbus, OH: Author.

Frederiksen, C. F. (1993). A brief history of collegiate housing. In R. B. Winston, Jr. & S. Anchors, *Student housing and residential life: A handbook for student affairs professionals committed to student development goals.* pp. 167-183. San Francisco: Jossey-Bass.

Schroeder, C. C., Mable, P., & Associates. (1993). *Realizing the educational potential of residence halls.* San Francisco: Jossey-Bass.

Winston, R. B, Jr., Anchors, S., & Associates (1993). *Student housing and residential life: A handbook for student affairs professionals committed to student development goals.* San Francisco: Jossey-Bass.

*The Journal of College and University Student Housing.* Published by the Association of College and University Housing Officers-International (ACUHO-I), 101 Curl Dr., Suite 140, Columbus, OH 43210. (614) 292-0099; Fax (614) 292-0305; gschwarz@magnus.acs.ohio-state.edu

American College Personnel Association. Commission on Housing and Residence Life. http://www.acpa.nche.edu/comms/comm03/index.html

# HOUSING and RESIDENTIAL LIFE PROGRAMS
## CAS STANDARDS and GUIDELINES

## Part 1. MISSION

The housing and residential life program (HRLP) must incorporate student learning and student development in its mission. HRLP must enhance overall educational experiences. The program must develop, record, disseminate, implement and regularly review its mission and goals. Mission statements must be consistent with the mission and goals of the institution and with the standards in this document. HRLP must operate as an integral part of the institution's overall mission.

HRLP mission must include provision for educational programs and services, residential facilities, management services, and, where appropriate, food services.

To accomplish the mission, the goals of the HRLP must provide . . .

• a residential community that encourages both individual and community development and learning

• reasonably priced safe and secure facilities that are clean, attractive, well maintained, and comfortable

• management services that ensure the orderly and effective administration and operation of all aspects of the program

• where appropriate, food, dining facilities, and related services that effectively meet institutional and residential life program goals

## Part 2. PROGRAM

The formal education of students consists of the curriculum and the co-curriculum, and must promote student learning and development that is purposeful and holistic. The housing and residential life program (HRLP) must identify relevant and desirable student learning and development outcomes and provide programs and services that encourage the achievement of those outcomes.

Relevant and desirable outcomes include: intellectual growth, effective communication, realistic self-appraisal, enhanced self-esteem, clarified values, career choices, leadership development, healthy behaviors, meaningful interpersonal relationships, independence, collaboration, social responsibility, satisfying and productive lifestyles, appreciation of diversity,

spiritual awareness, and achievement of personal and educational goals.

The housing and residential life program must provide evidence of its impact on the achievement of student learning and development outcomes.

The HRL program may use the examples that follow or identify other more germane indicators.

### Student Learning & Development Outcome Domains

### Intellectual Growth

Examples of Achievement Indicators

Acquires knowledge; Demonstrates critical thinking in problem solving; Uses complex information from a variety of sources including personal experience to form decisions or opinions; Applies previously understood information and concepts to a new situation or setting; Makes appropriate use of technology to enhance learning process; Expresses appreciation for the learning process.

### Effective Communication

Examples of Achievement Indicators

Writes and speaks coherently and effectively; Expresses themselves effectively through a variety of mediums; Able to respectfully disagree; Writes and speaks after reflection; Able to influence others through writing, speaking or artistic expression; Effectively articulates abstract ideas; Uses appropriate syntax; Makes presentations or gives performances.

### Enhanced Self-Esteem

Examples of Achievement Indicators

Shows self-respect and respect for others; Exercises initiative in community; Initiates actions toward the achievement of worthy personal goals; Takes reasonable risks; Demonstrates assertive behavior; Functions without need for constant reassurance from others.

### Realistic Self-Appraisal

Examples of Achievement Indicators

Develops and/or confirms a sense of identity; Articulates personal skills and abilities; Makes informed decisions and acts in congruence with personal values; Acknowledges personal strengths and weaknesses; Articulates rationale for personal behavior; Seeks feedback from others; Learns from past experiences

### Clarified Values

Examples of Achievement Indicators

Analyzes, develops, and/or confirms values through activities and opportunities; Acts in congruence with personal values; Makes decisions that reflect personal values; Demonstrates willingness to scrutinize personal beliefs and values; Identifies personal, work and lifestyle values and explains how they influence residential community development.

## Career Choices

Examples of Achievement Indicators

Explores career choices and interests based on educational activities and planned opportunities; Can construct a resume with clear job objectives that documents knowledge, skills and accomplishments resulting from the classroom, co-curricular activities, work experience, community service and volunteer experiences; Makes the connections between classroom and out-of-classroom learning; Able to develop and identify a career choice or direction; Articulates the characteristics of a preferred work environment.

## Leadership Development

Examples of Achievement Indicators

Participates in a student organization, intramurals, athletics, study group, learning community, or hall governance opportunities; Articulates leadership philosophy or style; Serves in a leadership position within a residential community or student organization; Comprehends the dynamics of a group; Exhibits democratic principles as a leader or participant; Develops/learns how to be an effective team member and work with others to accomplish a goal; Exhibits ability to visualize a group purpose and desired outcomes.

## Healthy Behavior

Examples of Achievement Indicators

Chooses activities, behaviors and environments that promote health and reduce risk with particular attention to alcohol and drugs; Recognizes mental health and/or substance abuse concerns and accesses resources; Engages in healthy choices with regard to exercise, recreation, nutrition, sexuality, and time management; Articulate the relationship between health and wellness and accomplishing long term goals; Chooses behaviors that advance a healthy residential community

## Meaningful Interpersonal Relationships

Examples of Achievement Indicators

Exhibits maturity in relating to others; Handles interpersonal and inter-group conflict constructively; Develops friendships; Presents and represents self honestly; Establishes mutually rewarding relationships with friends and colleagues; Listens to and considers others' points of view; Treats others with respect.

## Independence

Examples of Achievement Indicators

Exhibits self-reliant behaviors; Functions autonomously; Exhibits ability to function interdependently; Accepts supervision as needed; Manages time effectively; Achieves success in managing personal finances

## Collaboration

Examples of Achievement Indicators

Lives cooperatively with others; Seeks the involvement of others; Seeks feedback from others; Contributes to achievement of a community goal; Exhibits effective listening skills and feedback behaviors; Demonstrates reliability

## Social Responsibility

Examples of Achievement Indicators

Understands and participates in community governance; Abides by institutional, residential life policies/ procedures and local, municipal, state/provincial, and federal laws; Demonstrates respect for self, property, and others; Demonstrates responsible social behavior; Understands, abides by, and participates in the development, maintenance, and/or orderly change of community standards and expectations; Appropriately challenges the unfair, unjust, or uncivil behavior of other individuals or groups; Participates in service/volunteer / and community activities

## Satisfying and Productive Lifestyles

Examples of Achievement Indicators

Achieves balance between education, work and leisure time; Develops a plan for achieving goals; Reassesses goals and overcomes obstacles that hamper goal achievement; Functions on the basis of personal identity, ethical, spiritual and moral values; Articulates long-term goals and objectives

## Appreciating Diversity

Examples of Achievement Indicators

Understands the meaning of diversity including its application to race, color, gender, gender identity, religion, sexual orientation, national or ethnic origin, age, disability, marital status, or veteran status; .Understands own identity and culture and its impact on diversity issues; Appreciates new ideas, cultural, and lifestyle differences; Seeks involvement with people different from oneself; Seeks involvement in diverse interests; Articulates the advantages and challenges of a multicultural society; Challenges appropriately abusive use of stereotypes by others; Appropriately challenges abusive use of stereotypes by others; Understands the impact of diversity on society

## Spiritual Awareness

Examples of Achievement Indicators

Develops personal belief system; Understands roles of spirituality in personal and group values and behaviors

## Personal and Educational Goals

Examples of Achievement Indicators

Acquires knowledge and uses information and resources to make educated choices; Engages with faculty in the residential community; Sets, articulates, and pursues individual goals; Obtains a degree; Articulates personal and educational goals and objectives; Uses personal and educational goals to guide decisions; Understands the effect of one's personal and educational goals on others

**HRLP must be (a) intentional, (b) coherent, (c) based on theories and knowledge of learning and human development, (d) reflective of developmental and demographic profiles of the student population, and (e) responsive to needs of individuals, special populations, and communities. To fulfill its mission and goals effectively, HRLP must provide the following . . .**

• **Individual and group educational and developmental opportunities**

Opportunities should include activities and/or experiences in . . .

  • understanding and managing personal health, finances, and time
  • living cooperatively with other
  • improving interpersonal relationships and communication skills
  • promoting and demonstrating responsible social behavior such as avoiding participation in racial and sexual exploitation and discrimination
  • developing leadership skills
  • exploring and managing leisure time
  • promoting and demonstrating a proper understanding of the results of alcohol and other drug use and abuse
  • promoting a sense of responsibility for the security of the community environment

Educational programming, advising, and supervisory activities provided by the housing and residential life staff should address developmental objectives and should vary in accordance with local needs. Examples include . . .

  • introduction and orientation of students to facilities, services, staff members and functions, and community norms and expectations
  • education of students on safety, security, and emergency precautions and procedures and on taking responsibility for their safety and security
  • explanation of institutional and residential living policies, procedures, and expectations
  • development of an atmosphere conducive to educational pursuits
  • assessment of needs of both general and specific student populations including identified special interests
  • encouragement of student participation in institutional and residence hall programs, activities, groups, and organizations
  • encouragement of campus professionals' collaboration in conducing support activities such as learning strategies, time management, and study groups and workshops
  • provision of information to students about academics, institutional judicial system policies and procedures, and relevant civil and criminal laws
  • provision of training to aid staff members in recognizing problem behaviors, creating interventions, and making appropriate referrals
  • development of appropriate social, recreational, educational, cultural, and community service programs
  • provision of individual and group advising and counseling support
  • encouragement of students to develop a sense of community responsibility through exposure to education about inappropriate and disruptive behavior and participation activities such as (a) developing policies and making decisions, (b) mediating conflict within the community, (c) assessing fair charges to individuals responsible for damages, and (d) evaluating various aspects of the housing and residential life program.

• **Where applicable, specialized functions, such as conference administration, apartment housing, and off-campus housing services**

Any specialized functions should be effectively managed and administered in a manner consistent with the mission and goals of the institution. Such operations should be managed so as not to impair student housing operations when student residential facilities are used for conferences.

Off-campus housing services should include referrals to available housing opportunities, information about leases and landlord/tenant law, and other related information.

• **Where applicable, food services that provide high-quality, nutritious, and reasonably priced meals and support the programmatic and education mission of the institution**

Food services should include:

  • menu planning to provide optimum nutrition and variety
  • purchase of high quality food products
  • recipes and processes which ensure appetizing food preparation and presentation
  • safety features and sanitary conditions
  • attention to students' varied schedules, cultural differences, and special dietary needs
  • management policies and practices that ensure timely delivery of services and products
  • good customer relations
  • adequate space and a pleasant environment in dining areas
  • involvement in educational programming which supports program goals
  • materials which educate students about nutrition
  • solicitation of input from diners regarding menu selection and satisfaction with the dining program

## Part 3. LEADERSHIP

**Effective and ethical leadership is essential to the success of all organizations. Institutions must appoint, position and empower housing and residential life program (HRLP) leaders within the administrative structure to accomplish stated missions. HRLP leaders at various levels must be selected on the basis of formal education and training, relevant work experience, personal skills and competencies, relevant professional credentials, as well as potential for promoting learning and development in students, applying effective practices to educational processes, and enhancing institutional effectiveness. Institutions must determine expectations of accountability for HRLP leaders and fairly assess their performance.**

**HRLP leaders must exercise authority over resources for which they are responsible to achieve their respective missions.**

**HRLP leaders must . . .**
• **articulate a vision for their organization**
• **set goals and objectives based on the needs and capabilities of the population served**

173

- promote student learning and development
- prescribe and practice ethical behavior
- recruit, select, supervise, and develop others in the organization
- manage financial resources
- coordinate human resources
- plan, budget for, and evaluate personnel and programs
- apply effective practices to educational and administrative processes
- communicate effectively
- initiate collaborative interaction between individuals and agencies that possess legitimate concerns and interests in the functional area

HRLP leaders must identify and find means to address individual, organizational, or environmental conditions that inhibit goal achievement.

HRLP leaders must promote campus environments that result in multiple opportunities for student learning and development.

HRLP leaders must continuously improve programs and services in response to changing needs of students and other constituents, and evolving institutional priorities.

## Part 4. ORGANIZATION and MANAGEMENT

Guided by an overarching intent to ensure student learning and development, the housing and residential life program (HRLP) must be structured purposefully and managed effectively to achieve stated goals. Evidence of appropriate structure must include current and accessible policies and procedures, written performance expectations for all employees, functional workflow graphics or organizational charts, and clearly stated service delivery expectations.

Evidence of effective management must include use of comprehensive and accurate information for decisions, clear sources and channels of authority, effective communication practices, decision-making and conflict resolution procedures, responsiveness to changing conditions, accountability and evaluation systems, and recognition and reward processes. HRLP must provide channels within the organization for regular review of administrative policies and procedures.

Where the management of the HRLP is divided among different offices within the institution, it is the responsibility of institutional leaders and involved staff organizations to establish and maintain productive working relationships.

Ideally, a unified organizational structure, including all housing and residential life functions, should be employed. In this way, the organization can function to meet all the campus housing needs of students, rather than coordinating through multiple and separate organizational lines of communication and authority.

To fulfill its mission and goals effectively, HRLP must maintain well structured management functions, including planning, personnel, property management, purchasing, contract administration, financial control, and information systems.

Short- and long-range planning should be adequate to project and accommodate immediate and future needs. The management role should be defined to include adequate time for planning as well as program implementation.

Purchasing and property management procedures should be designed to ensure value for money spent, security for supplies and furnishings, and maintenance of proper inventories.

There should be a clear and complete written agreement between the resident and the institution, which conveys mutual commitments and responsibilities. There should be clear communication to students, other interested members of the campus community, and potential residents of the procedures and priorities for obtaining housing and/or meal options.

Procedures for canceling, subleasing, or being released from the housing and/or dining agreement should be written and distributed, if there is provision for such release.

## Part 5. HUMAN RESOURCES

The housing and residential life program (HRLP) must be staffed adequately by individuals qualified to accomplish its mission and goals. Within established guidelines of the institution, HRLP must establish procedures for staff selection, training, and evaluation; set expectations for supervision, and provide appropriate professional development opportunities. HRLP must strive to improve the professional competence and skills of all personnel it employs.

HRLP professional staff members must hold an earned graduate degree in a field relevant to the position they hold or must possess an appropriate combination of educational credentials and related work experience.

The chief housing officer should have attained a graduate degree in higher education, business administration, a behavioral science, or possess an appropriate combination of education and experience.

The chief housing officer should have knowledge of and experience with human behavior and business management. Recommended concentration areas for preparation are (a) human behavior (e.g., learning theory philosophical foundations, social psychology, the college student, contemporary issues, multicultural studies) and (b) business management (e.g., accounting, statistics, marketing, budgeting and report analysis, computers, and business management functions such as planning, organization, staffing, and supervision).

The administrator in charge of facilities should possess at least a bachelor's degree and/or related experience in engineering and maintenance. This officer should coordinate residential staff and students' interactions with all construction, maintenance, and custodial work. These functions should be carried out in support of educational goals. Recommended academic study related to preparation for this position includes (a) architecture and design principles, (b) construction and engineering principles, and (c) preventive maintenance theory and practice.

It is the responsibility of the food services administrator to manage those functions that are necessary to provide wholesome, appetizing, and nutritious meals. The functions should be carried out with food services staff and in support of educational goals. Preparation for this position may include courses in (a) dietetics and menu planning, (b) principles of public health and sanitation, (c) institutional food services management, and (d) employee training and supervision.

The administrator in charge of educational programming should possess the minimum of a master's degree in college student affairs, counseling, or a closely related field or should possess an appropriate combination of education and experience.

**Degree or credential-seeking interns must be qualified by enrollment in an appropriate field of study and by relevant experience. These individuals must be trained and supervised adequately by professional staff members holding educational credentials and related work experience appropriate for supervision.**

Desirable characteristics for both professional and paraprofessional staff members include demonstrated skills on leadership and communication, maturity, a well-developed sense of responsibility, sensitivity to individual differences, a positive self-concept, academic success, enthusiasm for working with students, and an understanding of issues facing students.

**Student employees and volunteers must be carefully selected, trained, supervised, and evaluated. They must be trained on how and when to refer those in need of assistance to qualified staff members and have access to a supervisor for assistance in making these judgments. Student employees and volunteers must be provided clear and precise job descriptions, pre-service training based on assessed needs, and continuing staff development.**

Residential life operations are highly dependent upon the use of part-time student employees (the most common

example being resident assistants) for the implementation of programs that affect student residents. Resident assistants and other paraprofessionals are expected to contribute to the accomplishment of the following functions: (a) educational programming, (b) administration, (c) group and activity advising, (d) leadership development, (e) discipline, (f) role modeling, (g) individual assistance and referral, and (h) providing information.

**HRLP must have technical and support staff members adequate to accomplish its mission. Staff members must be technologically proficient and qualified to perform their job functions, be knowledgeable of ethical and legal uses of technology, and have access to training. The level of staffing and workloads must be adequate and appropriate for program and service demands.**

**Salary levels and fringe benefits for all HRLP staff members must be commensurate with those for comparable positions within the institution, in similar institutions, and in the relevant geographic area.**

**HRLP must institute hiring and promotion practices that are fair, inclusive, and non-discriminatory. HRLP must employ a diverse staff to provide readily identifiable role models for students and to enrich the campus community.**

**HRLP must create and maintain position descriptions for all staff members and provide regular performance planning and appraisals.**

**HRLP must have a system for regular staff evaluation and must provide access to continuing education and professional development opportunities, including in-service training programs and participation in professional conferences and workshops.**

Housing professional staff members should strive to develop and maintain staff relations in a climate of mutual respect, support, trust, and interdependence, recognizing the strengths and limitations of each professional colleague.

**HRLP must provide procedures for filing, processing, and hearing employee grievances. All staff members must be aware of and support the goals, objectives, and philosophy of housing and residential life.**

The housing and residential life staff consists of professionally trained staff members, paraprofessionals, and technical, clerical, and other support staff members. Qualifications for housing and residential life officer positions may be gained through formal academic preparation, workshops, self-study, work experience, participation in professional organizations, and in-service training .

Educational programming should provide for interaction with faculty members so that students' living experiences complement and reinforce classroom learning. Recommended courses for preparation for programming positions may include: (a) developmental psychology, (b) group theory, (c) the college student, (d) contemporary issues, (e) multicultural studies, and (f) principles of management.

## Part 6. FINANCIAL RESOURCES

The housing and residential life programs (HRLP) must have adequate funding to accomplish its mission and goals. Funding priorities must be determined within the context of the stated mission, goals, objectives and comprehensive analysis of the needs and capabilities of students and the availability of internal or external resources.

HRLP must demonstrate fiscal responsibility and cost effectiveness consistent with institutional protocols.

HRLP fees must be dedicated to the support and improvement of housing and residential life programs and facilities.

It is not appropriate to use fees generated by an auxiliary to support operations not directly related to that auxiliary. Many campus housing and dining programs are auxiliary operations which are supported solely by fees charged to those using the service.

Financial reports must be available to appropriate offices, providing accurate and timely data. Information must be available to the campus community and to other appropriate constituencies.

Funding must be adequate to provide continuous upkeep of facilities, major maintenance and renovation of facilities, educational programming, and services to residents. Adequate reserves for essential repairs, replacements, and capital improvements must exist.

Student governance units (e.g., hall or campus-wide residential councils) should have access to accounting offices and services to effectively carry out their functions. Dues collected from students for programs and services should be managed within the institution.

Representatives of the residence hall and apartment housing communities should be given opportunities to comment on proposed rate increases and operating budgets. Rate increases should be announced and discussed well in advance of their effective date.

The budget should be used as a planning and goal-setting document which reflects commitment to the mission and goals of housing and residential life and of the institution.

## Part 7. FACILITIES, TECHNOLOGY, EQUIPMENT

The housing and residential life program (HRLP) must have adequate, suitably located facilities, adequate technology, and equipment to support its mission and goals efficiently and effectively. Facilities, technology, and equipment must be evaluated regularly and be in compliance with relevant federal, state, provincial, and local requirements to provide for access, health, safety, and security.

Facilities must provide sufficient and appropriate space to accommodate program goals and objectives and meet students needs for safety and security. Facilities must be maintained at optimal levels of cleanliness, repair, and decor.

Spaces provided must include adequate areas for study, office functions, lounging, recreation, and group meetings. Individual rooms must be adequately furnished to accommodate all assigned occupants.

All community bathrooms and other public areas should be cleaned at least daily on weekdays. Ramps, bathrooms, elevators, room fixtures, and other appropriate special provisions to accommodate mobility-impaired students should be well maintained and clearly marked and their availability thoroughly communicated to current and potential students. Public and common areas such as study rooms, exercise rooms, TV rooms, computer rooms, and kitchens should be adequately furnished. Sufficient space for maintenance work and storage should be available in close proximity to the assigned area of the maintenance and custodial staff. Laundry facilities should be provided within or in close proximity to living areas.

HRLP facilities must be accessible, clean, attractive, reasonably priced, properly designed, well-maintained, comfortable, and conducive to study, and must have safety and security features.

Functions associated with this goal should include new construction, maintenance and renovation, equipment replacement, custodial care, energy conservation, and grounds care . . .

• Any new construction projects should be responsive to the current and future needs of residents.

• Decisions about new construction should be based upon institutional need and consistent with the mission of the institution.

• Maintenance/renovation programs should be implemented in all housing operations and may include: (a) a preventive maintenance program designed to extend the life of the equipment and facilities, (b) a program designed to repair in a timely manner equipment and building systems as they become inoperable, and (c) a renovation program that modifies physical facilities and building systems to make them more effective, attractive, efficient, and safe.

- Systematically planned equipment replacement programs should exist for furnishings, mechanical and electrical systems, maintenance equipment, carpeting, draperies, and dining and kitchen equipment, where applicable.
- Regularly scheduled cleaning of public areas should be provided.
- Recycling and energy conservation efforts should be implemented through educational programs, as well as through timely renovation and replacement of inefficient equipment and obsolete facilities.
- Grounds, which may include streets, walks, and parking lots, should be clean and attractively maintained, with attention given to safety features. There should be planned maintenance and renewal procedures.

## Part 8. LEGAL RESPONSIBILITIES

Housing and residential life program (HRLP) staff members must be knowledgeable about and responsive to laws and regulations that relate to their respective responsibilities. Staff members must inform users of programs and services and officials, as appropriate, of legal obligations and limitations including constitutional, statutory, regulatory, and case law; mandatory laws and orders emanating from federal, state/provincial and local governments; and the institution's policies.

HRLP staff members must use reasonable and informed practices to limit the liability exposure of the institution, its officers, employees, and agents. Staff members must be informed about institutional policies regarding personal liability and related insurance coverage options.

The institution must provide access to legal advice for HRLP staff members as needed to carry out assigned responsibilities.

The institution must inform HRLP staff and students in a timely and systematic fashion about extraordinary or changing legal obligations and potential liabilities.

## Part 9. EQUITY and ACCESS

Housing and residential life program (HRLP) staff members must ensure that services and programs are provided on a fair and equitable basis. HRLP facilities, programs and services must be accessible. Hours of operation and delivery of and access to programs and services must be responsive to the needs of all students and other constituents. HRLP must adhere to the spirit and intent of equal opportunity laws.

The HRLP must be open and readily accessible to all students and must not discriminate except where sanctioned by law and institutional policy.

Discrimination must especially be avoided on the bases of age; color, creed; cultural heritage; disability; ethnicity; gender identity; nationality; political affiliation, religious affiliation, sex, sexual orientation; or economic, marital, social, or veteran status.
Consistent with its mission and goals, HRLP must take affirmative action to remedy significant imbalances in student participation and staffing patterns.

As the demographic profiles of campuses change and new instructional delivery methods are introduced, institutions must recognize the needs of students who participate in distance learning for access to programs and services offered on campus. □Institutions must provide appropriate services in ways that are accessible to distance learners and assist them in identifying and gaining access to other appropriate services in their geographic region.

## Part 10. CAMPUS & EXTERNAL RELATIONS

The housing and residential life program (HRLP) must establish, maintain, and promote effective relations with relevant individuals, campus offices, and external agencies.

Particular efforts should be made by the staff to develop positive relationships with campus and off-campus agencies responsible for judicial affairs, student counseling services, student health services, student activities, security and safety, academic advising, admissions, campus mail and telephone services, physical plant services, institutional budgeting and planning, computer center, vendors and suppliers of products used in residence and dining halls, and private and commercial housing operators.

HRLP staff members should be particularly aware of and supportive of the role of faculty. Faculty members should be encouraged to become involved in the residential program by presenting workshops, lectures, symposia, or by other means. Possibilities for faculty members to reside for a scheduled time in the residence halls as a community building activity or to accomplish a specific program objective should exist.

## Part 11. DIVERSITY

Within the context of each institution's unique mission, diversity enriches the community and enhances the collegiate experience for all; therefore, the housing and residential life program (HRLP) must nurture environments where commonalties and differences among people are recognized and honored.

HRLP must promote educational experiences that are characterized by open and continuous communication that deepens understanding of one's own identity, culture, and heritage, and that of others. HRLP must educate and promote respect about commonalties and differences in their historical and cultural contexts.

HRLP must address the characteristics and needs of a diverse population when establishing and implementing policies and procedures.

## Part 12. ETHICS

All persons involved in the delivery of housing and residential life programs (HRLP) must adhere to the highest principles of ethical behavior. HRLP must develop or adopt and implement appropriate statements of ethical practice. HRLP must publish these statements and ensure their periodic review by relevant constituencies .

HRLP staff members must ensure that privacy and confidentiality are maintained with respect to all communications and records to the extent that such records are protected under the law and appropriate statements of ethical practice. Information contained in students' education records must not be disclosed without written consent except as allowed by relevant laws and institutional policies. Staff members must disclose to appropriate authorities information judged to be of an emergency nature, especially when the safety of the individual or others is involved, or when otherwise required by institutional policy or relevant law.

HRLP staff members must be aware of and comply with the provisions contained in the institution's human subjects research policy and in other relevant institutional policies addressing ethical practices and confidentiality of research data concerning individuals.

HRLP staff members must recognize and avoid personal conflict of interest or appearance thereof in their transactions with students and others.

HRLP staff members must strive to insure the fair, objective, and impartial treatment of all persons with whom they deal. Staff members must not participate in nor condone any form of harassment that demeans persons or creates an intimidating, hostile, or offensive campus environment.

Each housing and residential life professional staff member should accept students as individuals, each with rights and responsibilities, each with goals and needs, and with this in mind, should seek to create and maintain a group living environment that enhances learning and personal development.

When handling institutional funds, HRLP staff members must ensure that such funds are managed in accordance with established and responsible accounting procedures and the fiscal policies or processes of the institution.

HRLP staff members must perform their duties within the limits of their training, expertise, and competence. When these limits are exceeded, individuals in need of further assistance must be referred to persons possessing appropriate qualifications.

HRLP staff members must use suitable means to confront and otherwise hold accountable other staff members who exhibit unethical behavior.

HRLP staff members must be knowledgeable about and practice ethical behavior in the use of technology.

## Part 13. ASSESSMENT and EVALUATION

The housing and residential life program (HRLP) must conduct regular assessment and evaluations. HRLP must employ effective qualitative and quantitative methodologies as appropriate, to determine whether and to what degree the stated mission, goals, and student learning and development outcomes are being met. The process must employ sufficient and sound assessment measures to ensure comprehensiveness. Data collected must include responses from students and other affected constituencies.

HRLP must evaluate periodically how well they complement and enhance the institution's stated mission and educational effectiveness.

Results of these evaluations must be used in revising and improving programs and services and in recognizing staff performance.

# THE ROLE of INTERNATIONAL STUDENT PROGRAMS
## *CAS* Standards Contextual Statement

In 1996, more than 450,000 international students from over 150 countries were studying at US colleges and universities. These students were pursuing undergraduate and graduate degrees as well as English-language training, and are drawn to this country because of the high quality programs and the wide range of academic options offered in the US. International students bring with them rich experiences and unique cross-cultural perspectives that help to internationalize the campus and give American students first-hand opportunities to learn about the world. International students face unique challenges as they attempt to adjust to American campus life and culture, master written and spoken English, comply with immigration regulations, meet the requirements of their academic programs, and prepare to return home to begin careers.

International student advisers work with these students providing information, advising, programs, and services designed to make their US experience as positive and productive as possible. They frequently serve as the liaison between international students and all those with whom these students come into contact, including American faculty, students, and staff; local citizens; officials of US and foreign government agencies; and the student's sponsor or family at home, representing the students' best interests and advising them accordingly.

International student advisers have a wide range of responsibilities, including advising on immigration, academic, and personal matters; orientation programming offered both at the beginning of the academic term and/or throughout the year; social and cultural programming to help international students learn more about American culture and develop friendships with American students; liaison and problem-solving with offices and groups on and off campus; crisis intervention in case of illness or serious legal, financial, or personal problems; and planning, budgeting, and office management.

International student advisers should be knowledgeable and articulate about American culture and how it differs from the cultures of other countries and should understand the social and psychological processes of cross-cultural adjustment. They should be familiar with the educational systems and political, economic, historical, and social issues and trends framing the contexts of the countries from which their students come. International student advisers must also be up to date on the intricacies of US immigration law and regulations, have good counseling and advising skills, understand how to develop effective and creative programming, and be good at setting priorities, managing time and resources, and communicating effectively with others. International student advisers must also enjoy helping people from diverse cultural backgrounds and learning about cultural differences.

### Recommended Readings and Resources
Althen, G. (Ed.) (1994). *Learning across cultures*. Cranberry Township, PA: NAFSA Publications.

Althen, G. (1983). *The handbook of foreign student advising*. Yarmouth, ME: Intercultural Press.

Althen, G. *Foreign student advising 101* [videotape]. Cranberry Township, PA: NAFSA Publications.

Gooding, J. (1995) *The faculty member's guide to immigration law*. . Cranberry Township, PA: NAFSA Publications.

Hall, E. T. (1976). *Beyond culture*. Yarmouth, ME: Intercultural Press.

Hall, E. T. (1981). *The dance of life*. Yarmouth, ME: Intercultural Press.

Hall, E. T. (1982). *The hidden dimension*. Yarmouth, ME: Intercultural Press.

Ogami, N. (1987). Cold water [videotape]. Yarmouth, ME: Intercultural Press.

Yenkin, A (Ed.) (1996). *Adviser's manual of federal regulations affecting international students and scholars*. Cranberry Township, PA: NAFSA-AIE Publications.

NAFSA-AIE Publications, P.O. Box 1604, Cranberry Township, PA 16066, (800) 836-4994

Intercultural Press, P.O. Box 700, Yarmouth, ME 04096, (207) 846-5168

# INTERNATIONAL STUDENT PROGRAMS and SERVICES
## *CAS* Standards and Guidelines

## Part 1. MISSION

International student programs and services (ISPS) must incorporate student learning and student development in its mission. The program and service must enhance overall educational experiences. The ISPS must develop, record, disseminate, implement, and regularly review its mission and goals. Mission statements must be consistent with the mission and goals of the institution and with the standards in this document. ISPS must operate as an integral part of the institution's overall mission.

The provision of international student programs and services should reflect a strong institutional commitment to the education of international students.

ISPS must promote the academic and personal growth and development of international students. To accomplish the mission, the program must:
- Assess the needs of international students, set priorities among those needs, and respond to the extent that the number of students, facilities, and resources permit
- Provide thorough information on immigration regulations and procedures to advise international students effectively, assure institutional adherence to those regulations and procedures, and interpret host country immigration policy to the campus community
- Provide professional services to students in the areas of counseling, advising, and assistance in complying with government regulations
- Orient international students to the policies and expectations of the institution, its culture, the host country educational system, and the host country in general
- Foster an international dimension within the institution and the community at large
- Promote positive interaction among international students, and between international and host country students, the academic community, and the community at large
- Facilitate the enrollment and retention of international students
- Facilitate re-entry and cultural re-adjustment related to the student's return home

International student programs and services should facilitate institutional sensitivity to the cultural needs of international community members (e.g., social, religious, dietary , and housing). Programs should be coordinated with academic units and other institutional functional areas that provide programs and services to students, faculty, and staff.

## Part 2. PROGRAM

The formal education of students consists of the curriculum and the co-curriculum, and must promote student learning and development that is purposeful and holistic. International student programs and services (ISPS) must identify relevant and desirable student learning and development outcomes and provide programs and services that encourage the achievement of those outcomes.

Relevant and desirable outcomes include: intellectual growth, effective communication, realistic self-appraisal, enhanced self-esteem, clarified values, career choices, leadership development, healthy behaviors, meaningful interpersonal relationships, independence, collaboration, social responsibility, satisfying and productive lifestyles, appreciation of diversity, spiritual awareness, and achievement of personal and educational goals.

ISPS must provide evidence of its impact on the achievement of student learning and development outcomes.

The program may use the examples that follow or identify other more germane indicators.

### Student Learning & Development Outcome Domains

**Intellectual Growth**
Examples of Achievement Indicators
Produces personal and educational goal statements; Employs critical thinking in problem solving; Uses complex information from a variety of sources including personal experience and observation to form a decision or opinion; Obtains a degree; Applies previously understood information and concepts to a new situation or setting; Expresses appreciation for literature, the fine arts, mathematics, sciences, and social sciences

**Effective Communication**
Examples of Achievement Indicators
Writes and speaks coherently and effectively; Writes and speaks after reflection; Able to influence others through writing, speaking or artistic expression; Effectively articulates abstract ideas; Uses appropriate syntax; Makes presentations or gives performances

**Enhanced Self-Esteem**
Examples of Achievement Indicators
Shows self-respect and respect for others; Initiates actions toward achievement of goals; Takes reasonable risks; Demonstrates assertive behavior; Functions without need for constant reassurance from others

## Realistic Self-Appraisal
Examples of Achievement Indicators
Articulates personal skills and abilities; Makes decisions and acts in congruence with personal values; Acknowledges personal strengths and weaknesses; Articulates rationale for personal behavior; Seeks feedback from others; Learns from past experiences

## Clarified Values
Examples of Achievement Indicators
Articulates personal values; Acts in congruence with personal values; Makes decisions that reflect personal values; Demonstrates willingness to scrutinize personal beliefs and values; Identifies personal, work and lifestyle values and explains how they influence decision-making

## Career Choices
Examples of Achievement Indicators
Articulate career choices based on assessment of interests, values, skills and abilities; Documents knowledge, skills and accomplishments resulting from formal education, work experience, community service and volunteer experiences; Makes the connections between classroom and out-of-classroom learning; Can construct a resume with clear job objectives and evidence of related knowledge, skills and accomplishments; Articulates the characteristics of a preferred work environment; Comprehends the world of work; Takes steps to initiate a job search or seek advanced education

## Leadership Development
Examples of Achievement Indicators
Articulates leadership philosophy or style; Serves in a leadership position in a student organization; Comprehends the dynamics of a group; Exhibits democratic principles as a leader; Exhibits ability to visualize a group purpose and desired outcomes

## Healthy Behavior
Examples of Achievement Indicators
Chooses behaviors and environments that promote health and reduce risk; Articulate the relationship between health and wellness and accomplishing life long goals; Exhibits behaviors that advance a healthy community

## Meaningful Interpersonal Relationships
Examples of Achievement Indicators
Develops and maintains satisfying interpersonal relationships; Establishes mutually rewarding relationships with friends and colleagues; Listens to and considers others' points of view; Treats others with respect

## Independence
Examples of Achievement Indicators
Exhibits self-reliant behaviors; Functions autonomously; Exhibits ability to function interdependently; Accepts supervision as needed; Manages time effectively

## Collaboration
Examples of Achievement Indicators
Works cooperatively with others; Seeks the involvement of others; Seeks feedback from others; Contributes to achievement of a group goal; Exhibits effective listening skills

## Social Responsibility
Examples of Achievement Indicators
Understands and participates in relevant governance systems; Understands, abides by, and participates in the development, maintenance, and/or orderly change of community, social, and legal standards or norms; Appropriately challenges the unfair, unjust, or uncivil behavior of other individuals or groups; Participates in service/volunteer activities

## Satisfying and Productive Lifestyles
Examples of Achievement Indicators
Achieves balance between education, work and leisure time; Articulates and meets goals for work, leisure and education; Overcomes obstacles that hamper goal achievement; Functions on the basis of personal identity, ethical, spiritual and moral values; Articulates long-term goals and objectives

## Appreciating Diversity
Examples of Achievement Indicators
Understands ones own identity and culture. Seeks involvement with people different from oneself; Seeks involvement in diverse interests; Articulate the advantages and challenges of a diverse society; Challenges appropriately abusive use of stereotypes by others; Understands the impact of diversity on one's own society

## Spiritual Awareness
Examples of Achievement Indicators
Develops and articulates personal belief system; Understands roles of spirituality in personal and group values and behaviors

## Personal and Educational Goals
Examples of Achievement Indicators
Sets, articulates, and pursues individual goals; Articulate personal and educational goals and objectives; Uses personal and educational goals to guide decisions; Understands the effect of one's personal and education goals on others

**ISPS must provide opportunities for discussion and understanding to minimize cultural conflict and to deal with conflict.**

**ISPS must include the following elements . . .**
- **Counseling and advising in immigration regulations, financial matters, employment, health insurance and health care, personal concerns, and English-language needs**

181

- Educational programs to enhance positive interaction between domestic and international students, to develop faculty and staff sensitivity to cultural differences and international student needs, and to assist in the understanding of and adjustment to a host country's educational system and culture
- Special orientation programs to enhance knowledge and understanding of the institution, the host country's educational system, and the culture of the host country in general, as well as programs to address issues related to re-entry to the student's home country
- Assessment of the educational goals; personal development levels; and social, emotional, and cultural needs of international students
- Appropriate and timely referrals to other service and program agencies
- Cross-cultural programs addressing cultural problems and issues for faculty, staff, teaching assistants, and students, and dependents of international students;
- Liaison with appropriate student organizations
- Advocacy within the institution for the needs of international students

## Part 3. LEADERSHIP

Effective and ethical leadership is essential to the success of all organizations. Institutions must appoint, position, and empower leaders within the administrative structure to accomplish stated missions. Leaders at various levels must be selected on the basis of formal education and training, relevant work experience, personal skills and competencies, relevant professional credentials, as well as potential for promoting learning and development in students, applying effective practices to educational processes, and enhancing institutional effectiveness. Institutions must determine expectations of accountability for leaders and fairly assess their performance.

International student program and services (ISPS) leaders must exercise authority over resources for which they are responsible to achieve their respective missions.

ISPS leaders must . . .
- articulate a vision for their organization
- set goals and objectives based on the needs and capabilities of the population served
- promote student learning and development
- prescribe and practice ethical behavior

- recruit, select, supervise, and develop others in the organization
- manage financial resources
- coordinate human resources
- plan, budget for, and evaluate personnel and programs
- apply effective practices to educational and administrative processes
- communicate effectively
- initiate collaborative interaction between individuals and agencies that possess legitimate concerns and interests in the functional area

ISPS leaders must identify and find means to address individual, organizational, or environmental conditions that inhibit goal achievement.

ISPS leaders must promote campus environments that result in multiple opportunities for student learning and development.

ISPS leaders must continuously improve programs and services in response to changing needs of students and other constituents, and evolving institutional priorities.

## Part 4. ORGANIZATION and MANAGEMENT

Guided by an overarching intent to ensure student learning and development, international programs and services (ISPS) must be structured purposefully and managed effectively to achieve stated goals. Evidence of appropriate structure must include current and accessible policies and procedures, written performance expectations for all employees, functional workflow graphics or organizational charts, and clearly stated service delivery expectations.

Evidence of effective management must include use of comprehensive and accurate information for decisions, clear sources and channels of authority, effective communication practices, decision-making and conflict resolution procedures, responsiveness to changing conditions, accountability and evaluation systems, and recognition and reward processes. ISPS must provide channels within the organization for regular review of administrative policies and procedures.

Institutions enrolling international students must designate a specific office or service unit to coordinate programs and services for this student population.

## Part 5. HUMAN RESOURCES

International programs and services (ISPS) must be staffed adequately by individuals qualified to accomplish its mission and goals. Within established guidelines of the institution, ISPS must establish procedures for staff selection, training, and evaluation; set expectations for supervision, and provide appropriate professional development opportunities. ISPS must strive to improve the professional competence and skills of all personnel it employs.

Wherever possible, staff members should be representative of the various cultures served in the student population.

ISPS professional staff members must hold an earned graduate degree in a field relevant to the position they hold or must possess an appropriate combination of educational credentials and related work experience. They must be knowledgeable about research and practice in areas related to international student programs and services and stay abreast of developments in policies, laws, and regulations affecting international students.

Professional staff members should be competent in skills such as group facilitation, leadership training and development, crisis intervention, workshop design, report writing, public speaking, social and interpersonal development, individual and group counseling and their cross-cultural aspects. Generally, these competencies are found in persons who graduate from student personnel, counseling, and other higher education graduate programs, as well as from programs such as cross-cultural communication, international studies, and anthropology.

Specific study in the following areas is desirable: multicultural theory, organizational development, counseling theory and practice, group dynamics, leadership development, human development, and research and evaluation. Proficiency in a language other than English and extended travel and/or living experience abroad are also helpful.

Degree or credential-seeking interns must be qualified by enrollment in an appropriate field of study and by relevant experience. These individuals must be trained and supervised adequately by professional staff members holding educational credentials and related work experience appropriate for supervision.

The use of graduate assistants and interns in international student programs and services should be encouraged. These individuals expand staff abilities, provide peer role models, and gain valuable pre-professional experience. Particular attention should be given to preparing assistants and interns to be especially sensitive to cultural differences and the special needs of international students.

Student employees and volunteers must be carefully selected, trained, supervised, and evaluated. They must be trained on how and when to refer those in need of assistance to qualified staff members and have access to a supervisor for assistance in making these judgments. Student employees and volunteers must be provided clear and precise job descriptions, pre-service training based on assessed needs, and continuing staff development.

ISPS must have technical and support staff members adequate to accomplish its mission. Staff members must be technologically proficient and qualified to perform their job functions, be knowledgeable of ethical and legal uses of technology, and have access to training. The level of staffing and workloads must be adequate and appropriate for program and service demands.

Salary levels and fringe benefits for all ISPS staff members must be commensurate with those for comparable positions within the institution, in similar institutions, and in the relevant geographic area.

ISPS must institute hiring and promotion practices that are fair, inclusive, and non-discriminatory. Programs and services must employ a diverse staff to provide readily identifiable role models for students and to enrich the campus community.

ISPS must create and maintain position descriptions for all staff members and provide regular performance planning and appraisals.

ISPS must have a system for regular staff evaluation and must provide access to continuing education and professional development opportunities, including in-service training programs and participation in professional conferences and workshops.

## Part 6. FINANCIAL RESOURCES

International student programs and services (ISPS) must have adequate funding to accomplish its mission and goals. Funding priorities must be determined within the context of the stated mission, goals, objectives and comprehensive analysis of the needs and capabilities of students and the availability of internal or external resources.

ISPS must demonstrate fiscal responsibility and cost effectiveness consistent with institutional protocols.

Institutions considering special student fees as a means of supporting international student services and programs should review carefully the ethical issues involved in implementing such fees.

## Part 7. FACILITIES, TECHNOLOGY, EQUIPMENT

International student programs and services (ISPS) must have adequate, suitably located facilities, adequate technology, and equipment to support its mission and goals efficiently and effectively. Facilities, technology, and equipment must be evaluated regularly and be in compliance with relevant federal, state, provincial, and local requirements to provide for access, health, safety, and security.

## Part 8. LEGAL RESPONSIBILITIES

International student program and services (ISPS) staff members must be knowledgeable about and responsive to laws and regulations that relate to their respective responsibilities. Staff members must inform users of programs and services and officials, as appropriate, of legal obligations and limitations including constitutional, statutory, regulatory, and case law; mandatory laws and orders emanating from federal, state/provincial and local governments; and the institution's policies. Further, staff should also be familiar with constitutional issues of due process and rights of freedom of expression as applicable to residents of the United States and Canada.

ISPS staff members must use reasonable and informed practices to limit the liability exposure of the institution, its officers, employees, and agents. Staff members must be informed about institutional policies regarding personal liability and related insurance coverage options.

The institution must provide access to legal advice for ISPS staff members as needed to carry out assigned responsibilities.

The institution must inform staff and students in a timely and systematic fashion about extraordinary or changing legal obligations and potential liabilities.

## Part 9. EQUITY and ACCESS

International student program and services (ISPS) staff members must ensure that services are provided on a fair and equitable basis. Facilities, programs and services must be accessible. Hours of operation and delivery of and access to programs and services must be responsive to the needs of all students and other constituents. ISPS must adhere to the spirit and intent of equal opportunity laws.

ISPS must be open and readily accessible to all students and must not discriminate except where sanctioned by law and institutional policy. Discrimination must especially be avoided on the bases of age; color, creed; cultural heritage; disability; ethnicity; gender identity; nationality; political affiliation, religious affiliation, sex, sexual orientation; or economic, marital, social, or veteran status.

Consistent with their mission and goals, ISPS must take affirmative action to remedy significant imbalances in student participation and staffing patterns.

As the demographic profiles of campuses change and new instructional delivery methods are introduced, institutions must recognize the needs of students who participate in distance learning for access to programs and services offered on campus. Institutions must provide appropriate services in ways that are accessible to distance learners and assist them in identifying and gaining access to other appropriate services in their geographic region.

## Part 10. CAMPUS & EXTERNAL RELATIONS

International Student Programs and Services (ISPS) must establish, maintain, and promote effective relations with relevant individuals, campus offices, and external agencies.

Professional staff members must coordinate, or where appropriate, collaborate with faculty and staff in providing services and programs for international students.

## Part 11. DIVERSITY

Within the context of the institution's unique mission, diversity enriches the community and enhances the collegiate experience for all; therefore, international student programs and services (ISPS) must nurture environments where similarities and differences among people are recognized and honored.

ISPS must promote educational experiences that are characterized by open and continuous communication that deepens understanding of one's own identity, culture, and heritage, and that of others. Programs and services must educate and promote respect about commonalties and differences in their historical and cultural contexts.

ISPS must address the characteristics and needs of a diverse population when establishing and implementing policies and procedures. ISPS must orient international students to the culture of the host country and promote and deepen international students' understanding of cross-cultural differences.

All institutional units that provide services to students should share responsibility for meeting the needs of international students. Coordinated efforts to promote multicultural sensitivity and the elimination of prejudicial behaviors in all functional areas on campus should be encouraged.

## Part 12. ETHICS

All persons involved in the delivery of programs and services for international students must adhere to the highest principles of ethical behavior. International student programs and services (ISPS) must develop or adopt and implement appropriate statements of ethical practice. ISPS must publish these statements and ensure their periodic review by relevant constituencies.

Staff members must ensure that privacy and confidentiality are maintained with respect to all communications and records to the extent that such records are protected under the law and appropriate statements of ethical practice. Information contained in students' education records must not be disclosed without written consent except as allowed by relevant laws and institutional policies, or as mandated by regulations from the US Immigration and Naturalization Service, or the US Information Agency. Staff members must disclose to appropriate authorities information judged to be of an emergency nature, especially when the safety of the individual or others is involved, or when otherwise required by institutional policy or relevant law.

All ISPS staff members must be aware of and comply with the provisions contained in the institution's human subjects research policy and in other relevant institutional policies addressing ethical practices and confidentiality of research data concerning individuals.

ISPS staff members must recognize and avoid personal conflict of interest or appearance thereof in their transactions with students and others.

ISPS staff members must strive to insure the fair, objective, and impartial treatment of all persons with whom they deal. Staff members must not participate in nor condone any form of harassment that demeans persons or creates an intimidating, hostile, or offensive campus environment.

When handling institutional funds, all ISPS staff members must ensure that such funds are managed in accordance with established and responsible accounting procedures and the fiscal policies or processes of the institution.

ISPS staff members must perform their duties within the limits of their training, expertise, and competence. When these limits are exceeded, individuals in need of further assistance must be referred to persons possessing appropriate qualifications.

ISPS staff members must use suitable means to confront and otherwise hold accountable other staff members who exhibit unethical behavior.

ISPS staff members must be knowledgeable about and practice ethical behavior in the use of technology.

ISPS staff members must balance the wants, needs, and requirements of students, institutional policies, laws, and sponsors, having as their ultimate concern the long-term well being of international educational exchange programs and the students participating in them.

ISPS staff members must demonstrate cross-cultural sensitivity, treating differences between value systems and cultures in non-judgmental ways. The use of pejorative stereotypical statements must be avoided. Staff members must maintain the highest principles of ethical behavior in the use of technology.

## Part 13. ASSESSMENT and EVALUATION

International students programs and services (ISPS) must conduct regular assessment and evaluations. ISPS must employ effective qualitative and quantitative methodologies as appropriate, to determine whether and to what degree the stated mission, goals, and student learning and development outcomes are being met. The process must employ sufficient and sound assessment measures to ensure comprehensiveness. Data collected must include responses from students and other affected constituencies.

ISPS must evaluate periodically how well they complement and enhance the institution's stated mission and educational effectiveness.

Results of these evaluations must be used in revising and improving programs and services and in recognizing staff performance.

# THE ROLE of STUDENT JUDICIAL PROGRAMS
## *CAS* Standards Contextual Statement

Throughout the history of American higher education, colleges have struggled with how to respond to student misconduct. In his letter to Thomas Cooper on November 2, 1822, Thomas Jefferson described the problem of student discipline as "a breaker ahead" which he was not sure that American higher education could weather. In recent years, issues related to student discipline, including sexual assault, use and abuse of alcohol and other drugs, and campus safety have come to the forefront.

Traditionally, the courts viewed the administration of student discipline as an internal institutional matter and did not become actively involved in the process through judicial rulings. However, this position changed in 1961, with the landmark case of *Dixon v. Alabama State Board of Education*, 294 F.2d 150 (5th Cir. 1961), the first of an ever-growing modern body of case law related to the administration of student discipline. The courts have held under the 14th Amendment to the Constitution that public colleges and universities must afford basic due process rights to students accused of violating student judicial codes. However, it is important to note the rights of due process described in this body of case law differ significantly from those observed in the criminal court system. The limitations placed upon private institutions are substantially less prescriptive. Although the Constitutional rights afforded to students at public institutions are not generally applicable to private institutions, several authors, including Kaplin and Lee (1996), and Cerminara and Stoner (1990), have encouraged private institutions to bear in mind the restrictions placed upon public institutions and accord their students the same general rights and protections.

In the early American colleges and universities, student discipline was primarily the responsibility of the faculty. As the positions of dean of men and women were established and the field of student affairs evolved, the responsibility for the administration of student discipline shifted. Barry and Wolf (1957) observed, "Despite all of their later disclaimers, most deans of men seem to have been appointed primarily to act as disciplinarians" (p.14). Only in the past twenty-five years has student discipline emerged as a distinct functional area within student affairs. Prior to that time, the responsibility for student discipline was one of a number of duties which fell to an individual or office such as the dean of men or the dean of women and later the dean of students.

In the early 1970s, the American College Personnel Association established Commission XV, Campus Judicial Affairs and Legal Issues, to meet the needs of this emerging profession. In 1988, the Association for Student Judicial Affairs (ASJA) was founded to facilitate the integration of student development concepts with principles of judicial practice in post-secondary education and to promote, encourage, and support student development professionals responsible for judicial affairs. ASJA now has a membership of over 1,000 and has sponsored conferences attended by more than 500 people annually. It has also sponsored a summer training institute for campus judicial affairs since 1993.

Over the past decade, the practice of student judicial affairs has been profoundly affected by the passage of federal legislation. While the Family Education Rights and Privacy Act of 1974 had implications for judicial affairs, the legislation passed more recently has differed significantly in that it directly targeted aspects of the campus judicial system. For example, the amendments to the Student Right-to-Know and Campus Security Act included in the Higher Education Amendments of 1998 required colleges and universities to include statistics for liquor law violations, drug law, and weapons law violations addressed through the campus judicial system. The Higher Education Amendments of 1998 also amended FERPA to allow the release of the final results of a campus disciplinary proceeding when a student was found responsible of a crime of violence or nonforcible sexual offense and to allow parental notification when the institution determined that a student under the age of 21 had violated alcohol or drug policies. In the years between the reauthorization, several pieces of legislation impacting student judicial affairs were being introduced into Congress annually as well. This increased governmental involvement demands that student judicial affairs professionals remain knowledgeable about legislative developments and actively work to address legislative proposals which would detrimentally impact the fundamental educational mission of the campus judicial system.

The Association for Student Judicial Affairs established three principles for the administration of judicial programs . . .

- The development and enforcement of standards of conduct for students is an educational endeavor which fosters students personal and social development; students must assume a significant role in developing and enforcing such regulations in order that they might be better prepared for the responsibilities of citizenship.

- Standards of conduct form the basis for behavioral expectations in the academic community; the enforcement of such standards must protect the rights, health, and safety of members of that community in order that they may pursue their educational goals without undue interference.

- Integrity, wisdom, and empathy are among the characteristics most important to the administration of student conduct standards; officials who have such responsibilities must exercise them impartially and fairly.

The primary role of student judicial affairs staff members is that of educator. The *ASJA Statement of Ethical Principles and Standards of Conduct* identifies the maintenance and enhancement of the ethical climate on campus and the promotion of academic integrity as the primary purposes for enforcing standards of student conduct. This document further states, "Clearly articulated and consistently administered standards of conduct form the basis for behavioral expectations within an academic community. These standards of conduct for students should be enforced in such manner as to protect the rights, health, and safety of the entire community. "

The student judicial programs standards and guidelines that follow represent the fundamental criteria by which programs can assess their quality and effectiveness.

## References, Readings, and Resources

Cerminara, K. L., & Stoner, E. N., II. (1990). Harnessing the "spirit of insubordination": A model student disciplinary code."*Journal of College and University Law, 17,* 89-121.

Dannells, M. (1997). *From discipline to development: Rethinking student conduct in higher education.* ASHE-ERIC Higher Education Report Vol. 25, No. 2. Washington, DC: The George Washington University, Graduate School of Education and Human Development.

Dixon v. Alabama State Board of Education, 294 F.2d 150 (5th Cir. 1961).

Hoekema, D. A. (1994). *Campus rules and moral community: In place of in loco parentis.* Lanham, MD: Rowman & Littlefield.

Kaplin, W. A., & Lee, B. (1996). *The law of higher education* (3rd ed.). San Francisco: Jossey-Bass.

Mercer, W. L. (Ed.). (1996). *Critical issues in judicial affairs: Current trends in practice.* San Francisco: Jossey-Bass.

Paterson, G. P., & Kibler, W. L. (Eds.). (1999). *The administration of student discipline: Student, organizational, and community issues.* Asheville, NC: College Administration Publications.

American College Personnel Association Commission XV, Campus Judicial Affairs and Legal Issues. One Dupont Circle Suite 300 Washington, DC 20036; (202) 835-2272. http://www.judprog.uga.edu/acpaxv.htm

Association for Student Judicial Affairs: P.O. Box 2237, College Station, TX 77841-2237; (409) 845-5262; Web Page: http://asja.tamu.edu/

# JUDICIAL PROGRAMS and SERVICES
## *CAS* STANDARDS and GUIDELINES

## Part 1. MISSION

Judicial programs and services (JPS) must incorporate student learning and student development in its mission. JPS must enhance overall educational experiences. JPS must develop, record, disseminate, implement and regularly review its mission and goals. Mission statements must be consistent with the mission and goals of the institution and with the standards in this document. JPS must operate as an integral part of the institution's overall mission.

The goals of JPS must address the institution's needs to . . .

- develop, disseminate, interpret, and enforce campus regulations
- protect relevant rights of students
- deal with student behavioral problems in a fair and reasonable manner
- facilitate and encourage respect for campus governance
- provide learning experiences for students who are found to be responsible for conduct which is determined to be in violation of institutional standards or who participate in the operations of the judicial system
- initiate and encourage educational activities that serve to prevent violations of campus regulations

JPS should support appropriate individual and group behavior as well as to protect the campus community from disruption and harm. The programs should be conducted in ways that will serve to foster the ethical development and personal integrity of students and the promotion of an environment that is in accord with the overall educational goals of the institution.

## Part 2. PROGRAM

The formal education of students consists of the curriculum and the co-curriculum, and must promote student learning and development that is purposeful and holistic. Judicial programs and services (JPS) must identify relevant and desirable student learning and development outcomes and provide programs and services that encourage the achievement of those outcomes.

Relevant and desirable outcomes include: intellectual growth, effective communication, realistic self-appraisal, enhanced self-esteem, clarified values, career choices, leadership development, healthy behaviors, meaningful

interpersonal relationships, independence, collaboration, social responsibility, satisfying and productive lifestyles, appreciation of diversity, spiritual awareness, and achievement of personal and educational goals.

JPS must provide evidence of its impact on the achievement of student learning and development outcomes.

The program may use the examples that follow or identify other more germane indicators.

### Student Learning & Development Outcome Domains

### Intellectual Growth
Examples of Achievement Indicators
Understands consequences of personal actions and institutional policies; Produces personal and educational goal statements; Employs critical thinking in problem solving; Uses complex information from a variety of sources including personal experience and observation to form a decision or opinion; Obtains a degree; Applies previously understood information and concepts to a new situation or setting; Expresses appreciation for literature, the fine arts, mathematics, sciences, and social sciences

### Clarified Values
Examples of Achievement Indicators
Does not commit additional violations of institutional policy; Understands the institutional values reflected in instructional policies; Understands the importance of personal and academic integrity; Articulates personal values; Acts in congruence with personal values; Makes decisions that reflect personal values; Demonstrates willingness to scrutinize personal beliefs and values; Identifies personal, work and lifestyle values and explains how they influence decision-making

### Social Responsibility
Examples of Achievement Indicators
Understands and participates in relevant governance systems; Understands, abides by, and participates in the development, maintenance, and/or orderly change of community, social, and legal standards or norms; Appropriately challenges the unfair, unjust, or uncivil behavior of other individuals or groups; Participates in service/volunteer activities

### Realistic Self-Appraisal
Examples of Achievement Indicators
Articulates personal skills and abilities; Makes decisions and acts in congruence with personal values; Acknowledges personal strengths and weaknesses; Articulates rationale for personal behavior; Seeks feedback from others; Learns from past experiences

## Healthy Behavior

Examples of Achievement Indicators

Chooses behaviors and environments that promote health and reduce risk; Articulate the relationship between health and wellness and accomplishing life long goals; Exhibits behaviors that advance a healthy community

## Enhanced Self-Esteem

Examples of Achievement Indicators

Shows self-respect and respect for others; Initiates actions toward achievement of goals; Takes reasonable risks; Demonstrates assertive behavior; Functions without need for constant reassurance from others

## Effective Communication

Examples of Achievement Indicators

Writes and speaks coherently and effectively; Writes and speaks after reflection; Able to influence others through writing, speaking or artistic expression; Effectively articulates abstract ideas; Uses appropriate syntax; Makes presentations or gives performances

## Career Choices

Examples of Achievement Indicators

Articulates career choices based on assessment of interests, values, skills and abilities; Documents knowledge, skills and accomplishments resulting from formal education, work experience, community service and volunteer experiences; Makes the connections between classroom and out-of-classroom learning; Can construct a resume with clear job objectives and evidence of related knowledge, skills and accomplishments; Articulates the characteristics of a preferred work environment; Comprehends the world of work; Takes steps to initiate a job search or seek advanced education

## Leadership Development

Examples of Achievement Indicators

Articulates leadership philosophy or style; Serves in a leadership position in a student organization; Comprehends the dynamics of a group; Exhibits democratic principles as a leader; Exhibits ability to visualize a group purpose and desired outcomes

## Meaningful Interpersonal Relationships

Examples of Achievement Indicators

Develops and maintains satisfying interpersonal relationships; Establishes mutually rewarding relationships with friends and colleagues; Listens to and considers others' points of view; Treats others with respect

## Independence

Examples of Achievement Indicators

Exhibits self-reliant behaviors; Functions autonomously; Exhibits ability to function interdependently; Accepts supervision as needed; Manages time effectively

## Collaboration

Examples of Achievement Indicators

Works cooperatively with others; Seeks the involvement of others; Seeks feedback from others; Contributes to achievement of a group goal; Exhibits effective listening skills

## Satisfying and Productive Lifestyles

Examples of Achievement Indicators

Achieves balance between education, work and leisure time; Articulates and meets goals for work, leisure and education; Overcomes obstacles that hamper goal achievement; Functions on the basis of personal identity, ethical, spiritual and moral values; Articulates long-term goals and objectives

## Appreciating Diversity

Examples of Achievement Indicators

Understands ones own identity and culture. Seeks involvement with people different from oneself; Seeks involvement in diverse interests; Articulates the advantages and challenges of a diverse society; Challenges appropriately abusive use of stereotypes by others; Understands the impact of diversity on one's own society

## Spiritual Awareness

Examples of Achievement Indicators

Develops and articulates personal belief system; Understands roles of spirituality in personal and group values and behaviors

## Personal and Educational Goals

Examples of Achievement Indicators

Sets, articulates, and pursues individual goals; Articulates personal and educational goals and objectives; Uses personal and educational goals to guide decisions; Understands the effect of one's personal and education goals on others

**JPS must be (a) intentional, (b) coherent, (c) based on theories and knowledge of learning and human development, (d) reflective of developmental and demographic profiles of the student population, and (e) responsive to needs of individuals, special populations, and communities.**

**JPS must establish the following within the context of its mission and purpose:**

*1. Authority*

**A written statement describing the authority, philosophy, jurisdiction and procedures of the campus judicial programs must be developed and disseminated to all members of the campus community.**

This statement should address (a) whether student academic or non academic misconduct are within the programs' jurisdiction, (b) which campus policies and regulations are enforced by these programs, (c) sanctions which may be imposed, (d) a clear description of the relationship between judicial programs and both campus and external law enforcement agencies, including guidelines if law enforcement authorities will be called in, (e) and information regarding the impact, if any, of decisions by the criminal courts on the outcome of corresponding campus judicial proceedings.

## 2. Components
**Selected components of a judicial system must be described in writing and include . . .**
- **hearing officer**
- **hearing bodies and their jurisdictions**
- **conduct regulations**
- **interim suspension**
- **pre-hearing procedures**
- **investigation procedures**
- **hearing procedures**
- **disciplinary sanctions**
- **appeals procedures**
- **confidentiality standards**
- **records policy/procedures**
- **statement of rights for accused, accusers and when appropriate, victims**

Generally, the judicial system should involve students on all boards; however, membership on boards need not be limited to students. The system should process complaints in a timely fashion, and yet allow sufficient time for an investigation of all allegations prior to a hearing.

**Procedures and processes must ensure timely, substantive, and procedural due process.**

JPS should provide students with ample opportunity to receive advice about the process, a general time frame for resolution, and a delineation of individual responsibilities in the process.

**Institutional disciplinary action against individual students or recognized student organizations must be administered in the context of a unified and coordinated set of regulations and processes in order to ensure fair and reasonable outcomes. Allegations of improper behavior originating from both instructional and non instructional components of the institution must be encompassed in a single comprehensive judicial system for students.**

The institution should be clear about which body or individual has jurisdiction over which conduct regulations. Students should be assisted in understanding the sources and lines of authority.

JPS should maintain written records to serve as referral materials, to document precedents, and to provide source material for identifying recurring problems or to use for appeals.

JPS should follow up on cases, including enforcement of sanctions, assessing the developmental processes that have been affected, and ensuring that students are directed to appropriate services for assistance.

The institution should be clear about how it defines student status and jurisdiction of the system to include whether students can be held responsible for behavior which takes place off the campus or between academic sessions.

The institution should clearly state the conduct regulations that apply to student organizations, the procedures that will be followed in the hearing of such cases, and the guidelines used to determine if the actions of individual members of an organization constitute action by the organization.

## 3. Information to Campus Community
**The institution must publish information about the campus judicial programs.**

Publications should contain (a) campus policies, such as those concerning legal representation, the maintenance of confidentiality, and the expunging of disciplinary records; (b) campus procedures, such as filing a disciplinary action, gathering information, conducting a hearing, and notifying a student of the hearing/appeal board's decision; (c) the composition, authority, and jurisdiction of all judicial bodies; (d) the types of advice that the complainant and others can receive about the process; (e) the types of disciplinary sanctions, including interim suspension procedures; and (f) a general explanation of how and when non-campus law enforcement officials are used.

Publications should be distributed through processes that reach all students. Students should not have to request such publications. Dissemination mechanisms may include electronic media, the institutional catalog, the orientation program, the student handbook, admissions and registration materials, and campus billing materials.

Published information should include not only descriptions about how the system works, but also the results of the system. By publishing the outcomes of campus judicial cases in a manner which protects the confidentiality of those involved, the institution demonstrates that the system does in fact work and encourages an open discussion of issues related to student conduct.

## 4. Hearing Authority
**In addition to a hearing officer, JPS must include a hearing or appellate body composed of representatives of the campus community and responsible for carrying out judicial functions delegated by the administration.**

Duties and responsibilities of judicial body members may include (a) reviewing disciplinary referrals and claims; (b) interpreting misconduct allegations and identifying specific charges to be brought against the student(s); (c) conducting preliminary hearings and gathering information pertinent to the charges; (d) advising students on their rights and responsibilities; (e) engaging in substantive discussions with students about relevant ethical issues; (f) scheduling, coordinating, and conducting hearings; (g) reviewing decisions from other hearing bodies, when applicable; (h) notifying the accused in writing about relevant decisions and the board's rationale for such; (i) maintaining accurate written records of the entire proceeding; (j) referring information to an appeal board when applicable; (k) following up on sanctions to ensure they have been implemented; (1) following up with students who have been sanctioned to ensure awareness of available counseling services; (m) establishing and implementing a procedure for maintenance and expunging of disciplinary records; and (n) assessing judicial procedures, policies and outcomes.

A staff judicial officer may be assigned responsibility for training judicial body members, scheduling and facilitating evaluations, and informing faculty, administration, and staff about legal and disciplinary matters.

Judicial body members may participate on campus government committees associated with student conduct, except when a conflict of interest will result.

### 5. Training of Judicial Body Members
Initial and in service training of all hearing body members must be provided.

In order for judicial board members to fulfill their duties, initial training should include (a) an overview of all judicial policies and procedures; (b) an explanation of the operation of the judicial process at all levels including authority and jurisdiction; (c) an overview of the institutions philosophy on student judicial affairs and its role in this process; (d) duties and responsibilities of all judicial bodies and their members; (e) review of constitutional and other relevant legal individual and institutional rights and responsibilities; (f) an explanation of sanctions; (g) an explanation of pertinent ethics, including particularly the importance of confidentiality and the prevention of bias and conflict of interest in the judicial process; (h) a description of available personal counseling programs and referral resources; (i) an outline of conditions and interactions which may involve external enforcement officials, attorneys, witnesses, parents of accused students, and the media; and (j) an overview of developmental and interpersonal issues likely to arise among college students.

In service training should include participation in relevant workshops, seminars, and conferences. A library containing current resources about the judicial system should be maintained and be accessible to judicial board members.

## Part 3. LEADERSHIP
Effective and ethical leadership is essential to the success of all organizations. Institutions must appoint, position, and empower judicial programs and services (JPS) leaders within the administrative structure to accomplish stated missions. JPS leaders at various levels must be selected on the basis of formal education and training, relevant work experience, personal skills and competencies, relevant professional credentials, as well as potential for promoting learning and development in students, applying effective practices to educational processes, and enhancing institutional effectiveness. Institutions must determine expectations of accountability for JPS leaders and fairly assess their performance.

JPS leaders of programs and services must exercise authority over resources for which they are responsible to achieve their respective missions.

JPS leaders must . . .
- **articulate a vision for their organization**
- **set goals and objectives based on the needs and capabilities of the population served**
- **promote student learning and development**
- **prescribe and practice ethical behavior**
- **recruit, select, supervise, and develop others in the organization**
- **manage financial resources**
- **coordinate human resources**
- **plan, budget for, and evaluate personnel and programs**
- **apply effective practices to educational and administrative processes**
- **communicate effectively**
- **initiate collaborative interaction between individuals and agencies that possess legitimate concerns and interests in the functional area**

JPS leaders must identify and find means to address individual, organizational, or environmental conditions that inhibit goal achievement.

JPS leaders must promote campus environments that result in multiple opportunities for student learning and development.

JPS leaders must continuously improve programs and services in response to changing needs of students and other constituents, and evolving institutional priorities.

## Part 4. ORGANIZATION and MANAGEMENT
Guided by an overarching intent to ensure student learning and development, judicial programs and services (JPS) must be structured purposefully and managed effectively to achieve stated goals. Evidence of appropriate structure must include current and accessible policies and procedures, written performance expectations for all employees, functional workflow graphics or organizational charts, and clearly stated service delivery expectations.

Evidence of effective management must include use of comprehensive and accurate information for decisions, clear sources and channels of authority, effective communication practices, decision-making and conflict resolution procedures, responsiveness to changing conditions, accountability and evaluation systems, and recognition and reward processes. Programs and services must provide channels within the organization for regular review of administrative policies and procedures.

## Part 5. HUMAN RESOURCES

Judicial programs and services (JPS) must be staffed adequately by individuals qualified to accomplish its mission and goals. Within established guidelines of the institution, JPS must establish procedures for staff selection, training, and evaluation; set expectations for supervision, and provide appropriate professional development opportunities. JPS must strive to improve the professional competence and skills of all personnel it employs.

JPS professional staff members must hold an earned graduate degree in a field relevant to the position they hold or must possess an appropriate combination of educational credentials and related work experience.

Degree or credential-seeking interns must be qualified by enrollment in an appropriate field of study and by relevant experience. These individuals must be trained and supervised adequately by professional staff members holding educational credentials and related work experience appropriate for supervision.

Student employees and volunteers must be carefully selected, trained, supervised, and evaluated. They must be trained on how and when to refer those in need of assistance to qualified staff members and have access to a supervisor for assistance in making these judgments. Student employees and volunteers must be provided clear and precise job descriptions, pre-service training based on assessed needs, and continuing staff development.

Students from graduate academic programs, particularly in areas such as counseling, student development, higher education administration, or criminology, may assist the judicial programs through practice, internships, and assistantships.

Students who participate on boards may be awarded academic credit for their participation in the system. Clear Teaming objectives and assignments should be outlined to ensure that a student's grade for this participation is in no way influenced by his/her decisions on a particular case.

Each organizational unit must have technical and support staff members adequate to accomplish its mission. JPS staff members must be technologically proficient and qualified to perform their job functions, be knowledgeable of ethical and legal uses of technology, and have access to training. The level of staffing and workloads must be adequate and appropriate for program and service demands.

Salary levels and fringe benefits for all JPS staff members must be commensurate with those for comparable positions within the institution, in similar institutions, and in the relevant geographic area.

JPS must institute hiring and promotion practices that are fair, inclusive, and non-discriminatory. Programs and services must employ a diverse staff to provide readily identifiable role models for students and to enrich the campus community.

JPS must create and maintain position descriptions for all staff members and provide regular performance planning and appraisals.

JPS must have a system for regular staff evaluation and must provide access to continuing education and professional development opportunities, including in-service training programs and participation in professional conferences and workshops.

A qualified member of the campus community must be designated as the person responsible for judicial programs.

The designee should have an educational background in the behavioral sciences (e.g., psychology, sociology, student development including moral and ethical development, higher education administration, counseling, law, criminology, or criminal justice).

The designee and any other professional staff member in the judicial programs should possess (a) a clear understanding of the legal requirements for substantive and procedural due process; (b) legal knowledge sufficient to confer with attorneys involved in student disciplinary proceedings and other aspects of the judicial services system; (c) a general interest in and commitment to the welfare and development of students who participate on boards or who are involved in cases; (d) demonstrated skills in working with decision making processes and conflict resolution; (e) teaching and consulting skills appropriate for the education, advising, and coordination of hearing bodies; (f) the ability to communicate and interact with students regardless of race, sex, disability, sexual orientation, and/or other personal characteristics; (g) understanding of the requirements relative to confidentiality and security of judicial programs files; and (h) the ability to create an atmosphere where students feel free to ask questions and obtain assistance.

## Part 6. FINANCIAL RESOURCES

Judicial programs and services (JPS) must have adequate funding to accomplish its mission and goals. Funding priorities must be determined within the context of the stated mission, goals, objectives and comprehensive analysis of the needs and capabilities of students and the availability of internal or external resources.

JPS must demonstrate fiscal responsibility and cost effectiveness consistent with institutional protocols.

## Part 7. FACILITIES, TECHNOLOGY, and EQUIPMENT

Judicial programs and services (JPS) must have adequate, suitably located facilities, adequate technology, and equipment to support its mission and goals efficiently and effectively. Facilities, technology, and equipment must be evaluated regularly and be in compliance with relevant federal, state, provincial, and local requirements to provide for access, health, safety, and security.

JPS must have access to facilities of sufficient size and arrangement to ensure confidentiality of records, meetings, and interviews.

The facilities should include a private office where individual consultations and pre-hearing conferences with those involved in disciplinary actions may be held, hearing room facilities, a meeting room for small groups, a library or resource area, and a secure location for confidential records.

## Part 8. LEGAL RESPONSIBILITIES

Judicial programs and services (JPS) staff members must be knowledgeable about and responsive to laws and regulations that relate to their respective responsibilities. JPS staff members must inform users of programs and services and officials, as appropriate, of legal obligations and limitations including constitutional, statutory, regulatory, and case law; mandatory laws and orders emanating from federal, state/provincial and local governments; and the institution's policies.

JPS staff members must use reasonable and informed practices to limit the liability exposure of the institution, its officers, employees, and agents. Staff members must be informed about institutional policies regarding personal liability and related insurance coverage options.

The institution must provide access to legal advice for JPS staff members as needed to carry out assigned responsibilities.

The institution must inform JPS staff and students in a timely and systematic fashion about extraordinary or changing legal obligations and potential liabilities.

Appropriate policies and practices to ensure compliance with regulations should include notification to all constituencies of their rights and responsibilities under the judicial system, a written description of all aspects of the judicial proceeding, accurate record keeping of judicial proceedings, and regular evaluations.

## Part 9. EQUITY and ACCESS

Judicial program and services (JPS) staff members must ensure that services and programs are provided on a fair and equitable basis. Facilities, programs and services must be accessible. Hours of operation and delivery of and access to programs and services must be responsive to the needs of all students and other constituents. JPS must adhere to the spirit and intent of equal opportunity laws.

The JPS must be open and readily accessible to all students and must not discriminate except where sanctioned by law and institutional policy. Discrimination must especially be avoided on the bases of age; color, creed; cultural heritage; disability; ethnicity; gender identity; nationality; political affiliation, religious affiliation, sex, sexual orientation; or economic, marital, social, or veteran status.

Consistent with their mission and goals, JPS must take affirmative action to remedy significant imbalances in student participation and staffing patterns.

As the demographic profiles of campuses change and new instructional delivery methods are introduced, institutions must recognize the needs of students who participate in distance learning for access to programs and services offered on campus. Institutions must provide appropriate services in ways that are accessible to distance learners and assist them in identifying and gaining access to other appropriate services in their geographic region.

## Part 10. CAMPUS and EXTERNAL RELATIONS

Judicial programs and services (JPS) must establish, maintain, and promote effective relations with relevant individuals, campus offices, and external agencies.

Representatives of the judicial system should meet regularly with pertinent campus constituencies (e.g., student government, student development agencies, staff, faculty, academic administrators, campus police, legal counsel) in order to exchange information concerning their respective operations and to identify ways to work together to prevent behavioral problems and to correct existing ones. Such collaborative efforts might include educational programs and joint publications.

Representatives should also meet periodically with relevant external agencies to ensure understanding about the judicial programs as well as to continually explore ways to utilize external agencies in dealing with student behavior problems in an effective manner.

## Part 11. DIVERSITY

Within the context of each institution's unique mission, diversity enriches the community and enhances the collegiate experience for all; therefore, judicial programs and services (JPS) must nurture environments where commonalties and differences among people are recognized and honored.

JPS must promote educational experiences that are characterized by open and continuous communication that deepens understanding of one's own identity, culture, and heritage, and that of others. JPS must educate and promote respect about commonalties and differences in their historical and cultural contexts.

JPS must address the characteristics and needs of a diverse population when establishing and implementing policies and procedures.

## Part 12. ETHICS

All persons involved in the delivery of judicial programs and services (JPS) must adhere to the highest principles of ethical behavior. JPS must develop or adopt and implement appropriate statements of ethical practice. JPS must publish these statements and ensure their periodic review by relevant constituencies .

JPS staff members must ensure that privacy and confidentiality are maintained with respect to all communications and records to the extent that such records are protected under the law and appropriate statements of ethical practice. Information contained in students' education records must not be disclosed without written consent except as allowed by relevant laws and institutional policies. Staff members must disclose to appropriate authorities information judged to be of an emergency nature, especially when the safety of the individual or others is involved, or when otherwise required by institutional policy or relevant law.

All JPS staff members must be aware of and comply with the provisions contained in the institution's human subjects research policy and in other relevant institutional policies addressing ethical practices and confidentiality of research data concerning individuals.

JPS staff members must recognize and avoid personal conflict of interest or appearance thereof in their transactions with students and others.

JPS staff members must strive to insure the fair, objective, and impartial treatment of all persons with whom they deal. Staff members must not participate in nor condone any form of harassment that demeans persons or creates an intimidating, hostile, or offensive campus environment.

When handling institutional funds, all JPS staff members must ensure that such funds are managed in accordance with established and responsible accounting procedures and the fiscal policies or processes of the institution.

JPS staff members must perform their duties within the limits of their training, expertise, and competence. When these limits are exceeded, individuals in need of further assistance must be referred to persons possessing appropriate qualifications.

JPS staff members must use suitable means to confront and otherwise hold accountable other staff members who exhibit unethical behavior.

JPS staff members must be knowledgeable about and practice ethical behavior in the use of technology.

## Part 13. ASSESSMENT and EVALUATION

Judicial programs and services (JPS) must conduct regular assessment and evaluations. Programs and services must employ effective qualitative and quantitative methodologies as appropriate, to determine whether and to what degree the stated mission, goals, and student learning and development outcomes are being met. The process must employ sufficient and sound assessment measures to ensure comprehensiveness. Data collected must include responses from students and other affected constituencies.

JPS must evaluate periodically how well they complement and enhance the institution's stated mission and educational effectiveness.

Results of these evaluations must be used in revising and improving programs and services and in recognizing staff performance.
Evaluation of JPS should include . . .

- performance evaluations of all staff members by their supervisors
- periodic performance evaluations of individual hearing boards
- on going evaluation of training programs and publications
- periodic review of applicable state and federal laws and current case law to ensure compliance.

Such an evaluation may include research inquiries into:

- whether judicial boards accurately follow the institution's procedural guidelines
- general impressions of the judicial system according to students, faculty, and staff members
- developmental effects on students and judicial board members
- annual trends in case load, rates of recidivism, types of offenses, and efficacy of sanctions
- effects of programming designed to prevent behavioral problems
- unique aspects of special function or special population judicial boards (e.g., traffic court or residence hall board)

# THE ROLE of LEADERSHIP PROGRAMS for STUDENTS
## *CAS* Standards Contextual Statement

Many college mission statements contain commitments to develop citizen leaders or prepare students for professional and community responsibilities in a global context. Throughout the history of higher education, however, leadership development has primarily been targeted toward students holding leadership positions, such as student government officials, officers in fraternities and sororities, and resident assistants. Consequently, only a handful of students had a genuine opportunity for focused experience in leadership development.

During the 1970s, many colleges refocused efforts on leadership development when events such as the Watergate scandal caused institutions to ponder how they taught ethics, leadership, and social responsibility. Subsequent initiatives such as the women's and African-American civil rights movements and adult reentry programs, increased access to college, and new forms of campus shared governance, coupled with a focus on intentional student development, led to new forms of leadership development through such programs as assertiveness training, emerging leaders' retreats, and leadership targeted toward special populations.

By the 1970s, professional associations were becoming increasingly interested in broad-based leadership efforts. Several associations, including the American College Personnel Association, National Association of Student Personnel Administrators, National Association for Campus Activities, and National Association for Women in Education, expanded projects and initiatives with a leadership focus. Burns' seminal book, *Leadership* (1978), brought new energy with its discussion of transformational leadership grounded in values and moral purpose. Thinking about leadership expanded in the 1980s and 1990s to include such perspectives as cultural influences, service learning, social change, and spirituality.

One college president noted that colleges need to develop not just better, but more leaders, and that efforts should be directed toward the entire student body. Because students experience leadership in many different settings—in and out of the classroom, on and off campus—virtually every student engages in some type of activity that involves the practice of leadership. Regardless of differences in academic discipline, organizational affiliation, cultural background, or geographical location, students must be better prepared to serve as citizen-leaders in a global community. The role of student affairs professionals

in this arena is to help students understand their experiences and to facilitate their learning, so they become effective contributors to their communities. While no specific models target leadership development of college students, the *CAS Student Leadership Program Standards* can be used to help professionals provide comprehensive leadership programs and enhance students' learning opportunities. Leadership for positional leaders will still occur within specific functional areas such as student activities and residence life; campuses that seek to develop a comprehensive leadership program will recognize the need to make intentional leadership development opportunities available to all students through coordinated campus-wide efforts.

Leadership is an inherently relational process of working with others to accomplish a goal or to promote change. Most leadership programs seek to empower students to enhance their self efficacy as leaders and understand how they can make a difference, whether as positional leaders or active participants in a group or community process. Leadership development involves self-awareness and understanding of others, values and diverse perspectives, organizations, and change. Leadership also requires competence in establishing purpose, working collaboratively, and managing conflict. Institutions can initiate opportunities to study leadership and to experience a range of leadership-related activities designed to intentionally promote desired outcomes of student leadership learning.

The Inter-Association Leadership Project brought student affairs leadership educators together in the early 1980s to create and sustain a leadership agenda. By the end of the decade, higher education's commitment to leadership was clear with over 600 campuses teaching leadership courses; creating special leadership centers such as the Jepson School of Leadership Studies at the University of Richmond and the McDonough Leadership Center at Marietta College; and establishing special programs, including the National LeaderShape Institute. In 1992 the National Clearinghouse for Leadership Programs was established at the University of Maryland-College Park, and a co-sponsored series of symposia encouraged leadership educators to identify a leadership agenda for the new millennium. Projects funded by the Kellogg, Pew, and Lilly Foundations; FIPSE; and the federal Eisenhower Leadership grant program have also focused broad-based attention on leadership development in recent years.

## References, Readings, and Resources

Boatman, S. (1987). *Student leadership development: Approaches, methods, and models.* Columbia, SC: National Association for Campus Activities.

Boatman, S. (1992). *Supporting student leadership: Selections from the student development series.* Columbia, SC: National Association for Campus Activities.

Komives, S. R., Lucas, N. , & McMahon, T. (1998) *Exploring leadership.* San Francisco: Jossey-Bass.

Murray, J. I. (1994). *Training for student leaders.* Dubuque:, IA: Kendall/Hunt.

Roberts, D. C. (1981). *Student leadership programs in higher education.* Carbondale, IL: American College Personnel Association.

Rogers, J. L. (2003). Leadership. In S. Komives & D. B. Woodard (Eds.), *Student Services: A handbook for the profession* (4th ed.)(pp. 447-465).

Center for Creative Leadership, One Leadership Place, P.O. Box 26300, Greensboro, NC 27438-6300. (910) 288-7210. Publisher of periodic sourcebooks

*Concepts & connections: A newsletter for leadership educators.* The National Clearinghouse for Leadership Programs, 1135 Stamp Student Union, University of Maryland at College Park, College Park, MD 20742-4631. (301) 314-7174

*Journal of Leadership Studies.* Baker College of Flint, 1050 W. Bristol Rd., Flint, MI 48507-9987. (313) 766-4105

*Leadership Quarterly.* JAI Press, 55 Old Post Road, # 2, P.O. Box 1678, Greenwich, CT 06836-1678. (203) 661-7602

# LEADERSHIP PROGRAMS for STUDENTS
## *CAS* STANDARDS and GUIDELINES

## Part 1. MISSION

Student leadership programs (SLP) must incorporate student learning and student development in its mission. SLP must enhance overall educational experiences. SLP must develop, record, disseminate, implement and regularly review its mission and goals. Mission statements must be consistent with the mission and goals of the institution and with the standards in this document. SLP must operate as an integral part of the institution's overall mission.

The mission of SLP must be to prepare students for leadership roles and responsibilities. To accomplish this mission, the program must:

- provide students with opportunities to develop and enhance a personal philosophy of leadership that includes understanding of self, others, and community, and acceptance of responsibilities inherent in community membership
- assist students in gaining varied leadership experience
- use multiple leadership techniques, theories, and models
- recognize and reward exemplary leadership behavior
- be inclusive and accessible

Student leadership development should be an integral part of the institution's educational mission.

SLP should include a commitment to student involvement in the institution's governance activities. SLP should seek an institution-wide commitment that transcends the boundaries of the units specifically charged with program delivery.

## Part 2. PROGRAM

The formal education of students consists of the curriculum and the co-curriculum, and must promote student learning and development that is purposeful and holistic. Student leadership programs (SLP) must identify relevant and desirable student learning and development outcomes and provide programs and services that encourage the achievement of those outcomes.

Relevant and desirable outcomes include: intellectual growth, effective communication, realistic self-appraisal, enhanced self-esteem, clarified values, career choices, leadership development, healthy behaviors, meaningful interpersonal relationships, independence,

collaboration, social responsibility, satisfying and productive lifestyles, appreciation of diversity, spiritual awareness, and achievement of personal and educational goals.

SLP must provide evidence of its impact on the achievement of student learning and development outcomes.

The SLP may use the examples that follow or identify other more germane indicators.

### Student Learning & Development Outcome Domains

**Intellectual Growth**

Examples of Achievement Indicators

Produces personal and educational goal statements; Employs critical thinking in problem solving; Uses complex information from a variety of sources including personal experience and observation to form a decision or opinion; Obtains a degree; Applies previously understood information and concepts to a new situation or setting; Expresses appreciation for literature, the fine arts, mathematics, sciences, and social sciences

**Effective Communication**

Examples of Achievement Indicators

Writes and speaks coherently; Writes, speaks, and listens effectively; Writes and speaks after reflection; Able to influence others through writing, speaking or artistic expression; Effectively articulates abstract ideas; Uses appropriate syntax; Makes presentations or gives performances

**Enhanced Self-Esteem**

Examples of Achievement Indicators

Shows self-respect and respect for others; Initiates actions toward achievement of goals; Takes reasonable risks; Demonstrates assertive behavior; Functions without need for constant reassurance from others

**Realistic Self-Appraisal**

Examples of Achievement Indicators

Articulates personal skills and abilities; Makes decisions and acts in congruence with personal values; Acknowledges personal strengths and weaknesses; Articulates rationale for personal behavior; Seeks feedback from others; Learns from past experiences

**Clarified Values**

Examples of Achievement Indicators

Articulates personal values; Acts in congruence with personal values; Makes decisions that reflect personal values; Demonstrates willingness to scrutinize personal beliefs and values; Identifies personal, work and lifestyle values and explains how they influence decision-making

## Career Choices
Examples of Achievement Indicators

Articulates career choices based on assessment of interests, values, skills and abilities; Documents knowledge, skills and accomplishments resulting from formal education, work experience, community service and volunteer experiences; Makes the connections between classroom and out-of-classroom learning; Can construct a resume with clear job objectives and evidence of related knowledge, skills and accomplishments; Articulates the characteristics of a preferred work environment; Comprehends the world of work; Takes steps to initiate a job search or seek advanced education

## Leadership Development
Examples of Achievement Indicators

Understands that leadership is a process rather than a position; Acknowledges that leadership is relational; Understands that everyone has a leadership capacity; Engages in the leadership process in increasing levels of quality and quantity; Analyzes contexts that influence the leadership process (i.e., characteristics of self and others, society, organizations); Relates insights to the application of the leadership process; Recognizes the ethical components of leadership;

## Healthy Behavior
Examples of Achievement Indicators

Chooses behaviors and environments that promote health and reduce risk; Articulate the relationship between health and wellness and accomplishing life long goals; Exhibits behaviors that advance a healthy community.

## Meaningful Interpersonal Relationships
Examples of Achievement Indicators

Develops and maintains satisfying interpersonal relationships; Establishes mutually rewarding relationships with friends and colleagues; Listens to and considers others' points of view; Treats others with respect

## Independence
Examples of Achievement Indicators

Exhibits self-reliant behaviors; Functions autonomously; Exhibits ability to function interdependently; Accepts supervision as needed; Manages time effectively

## Collaboration
Examples of Achievement Indicators

Works cooperatively with others; Seeks the involvement of others; Seeks feedback from others; Contributes to achievement of a group goal; Exhibits effective listening skills

## Social Responsibility
Examples of Achievement Indicators

Understands and participates in relevant governance systems; Understands, abides by, and participates in the development, maintenance, and/or orderly change of community, social, and legal standards or norms; Appropriately challenges the unfair, unjust, or uncivil behavior of other individuals or groups; Participates in service/volunteer activities

## Satisfying and Productive Lifestyles
Examples of Achievement Indicators

Achieves balance between education, work and leisure time; Articulates and meets goals for work, leisure and education; Overcomes obstacles that hamper goal achievement; Functions on the basis of personal identity, ethical, spiritual and moral values; Articulates long-term goals and objectives

## Appreciating Diversity
Examples of Achievement Indicators

Understands ones own identity and culture. Seeks involvement with people different from oneself; Seeks involvement in diverse interests; Articulates the advantages and challenges of a diverse society; Challenges appropriately abusive use of stereotypes by others; Understands the impact of diversity on one's own society

## Spiritual Awareness
Examples of Achievement Indicators

Develops and articulates personal belief system; Understands roles of spirituality in personal and group values and behaviors

## Personal and Educational Goals
Examples of Achievement Indicators

Sets, articulates, and pursues individual goals; Articulate personal and educational goals and objectives; Uses personal and educational goals to guide decisions; Understands the effect of one's personal and education goals on others

**The SLP must be (a) intentional, (b) coherent, (c) based on theories and knowledge of learning and human development, (d) reflective of developmental and demographic profiles of the student population, and (e) responsive to needs of individuals, special populations, and communities.**

**SLP must be comprehensive in nature and must include (1) opportunities to develop the competencies required for effective leadership; (2) training, education, and developmental activities; and (3) multiple delivery methods.**

*1. Opportunities to Develop*
**A comprehensive leadership program must be based on a broad philosophy of leadership upon which subsequent competencies are built. The program must contain components that assist the student in gaining self awareness, the relationship of self to others (differences and commonalties), the uniqueness of the institutional environment within which leadership is practiced, and the relationship to local and global communities. It must advance competencies in the categories of**

**foundations of leadership, individual development, and organizational development.**

Competencies should accrue from both cognitive and experiential development in the following areas:

Foundations of Leadership
- Historical perspectives and evaluation of leadership theory
- Theoretical, philosophical, and conceptual foundations of leadership of several cultures
- Cultural and gender influences on leadership
- Ethical practices in leadership
- Moral leadership
- Leadership and followership

*Personal Development*
- Awareness and understanding of various leadership styles and approaches
- Exploration and designing of personal leadership approaches
- Human development theories
- The intersections of human development theories, sexual orientation, national origin, and environment
- Personal management issues such as time management, stress reduction, development of relationships, problem solving, goal setting, and ethical decision-making
- Oral and written communication skills
- Critical thinking skills
- Risk taking
- Creativity
- Wellness lifestyle development
- Supervision
- Motivation

*Organizational Development*
- Team building
- Shared leadership
- Group dynamics and development
- Organizational communication
- Group problem-solving and decision making models
- Planning
- Conflict management and resolution
- Methods of assessing and evaluating organizational effectiveness
- Organizational culture, values and principles
- Community development
- Power and empowerment
- Collaboration
- Developing trust
- Organizational politics
- Leadership in diverse organizations

### 2. Training, Education, and Development Activities

*Leadership Training*

Training involves those activities designed to improve performance of the individual in the role presently occupied or that are concretely focused at helping the individual being trained to translate some newly learned skill, or information, to a real and immediate situation. Examples of training include programs for the preparation of residence hall student staff, student government, student judicial board members, community service volunteers, and employment.

*Leadership Education*

Education program elements are designed to enhance participants' knowledge and understanding of specific leadership theories, concepts, and models. Education occurs as students gain information in their present roles that serves ultimately to provide generalized theories, principles, and approaches to prepare them for future leadership responsibilities. The student leadership program should explore the processes by which decisions affecting students, faculty, and staff are made. Examples of education include a course on leadership and politics and a seminar on the evolution of leadership theories.

*Development Activities*

Development requires an environment which empowers students to mature and develop toward greater levels of leadership complexity, integration, and proficiency over a period of time. Developmental activities promote positive behavioral, cognitive, and affective outcomes. Examples of developmental activities include peer mentoring and peer leadership consultant programs.

### 3. Multiple delivery methods and contexts

**A comprehensive leadership program must involve a diverse range of faculty, students, and staff members in the delivery of programs and must recognize the diverse contexts of leadership. Regular assessment of the developmental levels and needs of participants must be conducted to implement multiple delivery strategies and contexts.**

Examples of delivery methods include internships, panel discussions, movies, lectures, mentor programs, adventure training, and participation in local, regional, and national associations. Examples of contexts for leadership include diverse academic and career fields, campus organizations and committees, employment setting, community involvement, family settings, international settings, and social and religious organizations in both formal and informal positions.

## Part 3. LEADERSHIP

**Effective and ethical leadership is essential to the success of all organizations. Institutions must appoint, position and empower student leadership program (SLP) leaders within the administrative structure to accomplish stated missions. SLP leaders at various levels must be selected on the basis of formal education and training, relevant work experience, personal skills and competencies, relevant professional credentials, as well as potential for promoting learning and development in students, applying effective practices to educational processes, and enhancing institutional effectiveness. Institutions must determine expectations of accountability for leaders and fairly assess their performance.**

**Leaders of SLP must exercise authority over resources for which they are responsible to achieve their respective missions.**

SLP leaders must . . .
- articulate a vision for their organization
- set goals and objectives based on the needs and capabilities of the population served
- promote student learning and development
- prescribe and practice ethical behavior
- recruit, select, supervise, and develop others in the organization
- manage financial resources
- coordinate human resources
- plan, budget for, and evaluate personnel and programs
- apply effective practices to educational and administrative processes
- communicate effectively
- initiate collaborative interaction between individuals and agencies that possess legitimate concerns and interests in the functional area

SLP leaders must identify and find means to address individual, organizational, or environmental conditions that inhibit goal achievement.

SLP leaders must promote campus environments that result in multiple opportunities for student learning and development.

SLP leaders must continuously improve programs and services in response to changing needs of students and other constituents, and evolving institutional priorities.

There should be a person or group of persons designated as responsible for the coordination of direction of the leadership program including allocation and maintenance of resources and developing student leadership opportunities.

## Part 4. ORGANIZATION and MANAGEMENT

Guided by an overarching intent to ensure student learning and development, student leadership programs (SLP) must be structured purposefully and managed effectively to achieve stated goals. Evidence of appropriate structure must include current and accessible policies and procedures, written performance expectations for all employees, functional workflow graphics or organizational charts, and clearly stated service delivery expectations.

Evidence of effective management must include use of comprehensive and accurate information for decisions, clear sources and channels of authority, effective communication practices, decision-making and conflict resolution procedures, responsiveness to changing conditions, accountability and evaluation systems, and recognition and reward processes. SLP must provide channels within the organization for regular review of administrative policies and procedures.

SLP are typically organized in a variety of offices and departments both in student services and in academic and other administrative areas. An advisory group with representatives from the involved areas should be established for the purpose of communication.

## Part 5. HUMAN RESOURCES

Student leadership programs (SLP) must be staffed adequately by individuals qualified to accomplish its mission and goals. Within established guidelines of the institution, programs and services must establish procedures for staff selection, training, and evaluation; set expectations for supervision, and provide appropriate professional development opportunities. The program and service must strive to improve the professional competence and skills of all personnel it employs.

SLP professional staff members must hold an earned graduate degree in a field relevant to the position they hold or must possess an appropriate combination of educational credentials and related work experience.

SLP should have adequate and qualified staff or faculty members to implement a comprehensive program.

Professional staff or faculty involved in leadership programs should possess:
- ability to work with diverse students
- knowledge of the history and current trends in leadership theories, models, and philosophies
- leadership experiences
- followership experiences
- knowledge of organizational development, group dynamics, strategies for change and principles of community
- knowledge of diversity issues related to leadership
- ability to evaluate leadership programs and assess outcomes
- effective oral and written communication skills
- ability to effectively organize learning opportunities that are consistent with students' stages of development
- ability to use reflection in helping students understand leadership concepts by processing critical incidents with students

Degree or credential-seeking interns must be qualified by enrollment in an appropriate field of study and by relevant experience. These individuals must be trained and supervised adequately by professional staff members holding educational credentials and related work experience appropriate for supervision.

Student employees and volunteers must be carefully selected, trained, supervised, and evaluated. They must be trained on how and when to refer those in need of assistance to qualified staff members and have access to a supervisor for assistance in making these judgments. Student employees and volunteers must be provided clear and precise job descriptions, pre-service training based on assessed needs, and continuing staff development.

SLP must have technical and support staff members adequate to accomplish its mission. Staff members must be technologically proficient and qualified to perform their job functions, be knowledgeable of ethical and legal uses of technology, and have access to training. The level of staffing and workloads must be adequate and appropriate for program and service demands.

Salary levels and fringe benefits for all SLP staff members must be commensurate with those for comparable positions within the institution, in similar institutions, and in the relevant geographic area.

SLP must institute hiring and promotion practices that are fair, inclusive, and non-discriminatory. Programs and services must employ a diverse staff to provide readily identifiable role models for students and to enrich the campus community.

SLP must create and maintain position descriptions for all staff members and provide regular performance planning and appraisals.

SLP must have a system for regular staff evaluation and must provide access to continuing education and professional development opportunities, including in-service training programs and participation in professional conferences and workshops.

Program staff should engage in continuous discovery and understanding of emerging leadership models, research, theories, and definitions through disciplined study and professional development activities.

Student organization advisors should be considered as resources to assist both formally and informally in student leadership programs. Advisors can provide information about issues that need to be addressed. The student leadership program staff should assist advisors in conducting leadership training, education, and development for their respective student groups.

## Part 6. FINANCIAL RESOURCES

Student leadership programs (SLP) must have adequate funding to accomplish its mission and goals. Funding priorities must be determined within the context of the stated mission, goals, objectives and comprehensive analysis of the needs and capabilities of students and the availability of internal or external resources.

SLP must demonstrate fiscal responsibility and cost effectiveness consistent with institutional protocols.

Funding for the student leadership program may come from a variety of sources, including institutional funds, grant money, student government funds, fees for services, and government contracts. Where possible, institutional funding should be allocated regularly for the operation of leadership programs.

## Part 7. FACILITIES, TECHNOLOGY, EQUIPMENT

Student leadership programs (SLP) must have adequate, suitably located facilities, adequate technology, and equipment to support its mission and goals efficiently and effectively. Facilities, technology, and equipment must be evaluated regularly and be in compliance with relevant federal, state, provincial, and local requirements to provide for access, health, safety, and security.

Leadership program facilities should be conveniently located on campus. Staff, faculty, and student space should be designed to encourage a maximum level of interaction among students, faculty, and staff.

## Part 8. LEGAL RESPONSIBILITIES

Student leadership program (SLP) staff members must be knowledgeable about and responsive to laws and regulations that relate to their respective responsibilities. Staff members must inform users of programs and services and officials, as appropriate, of legal obligations and limitations including constitutional, statutory, regulatory, and case law; mandatory laws and orders emanating from federal, state/provincial and local governments; and the institution's policies.

SLP staff members must use reasonable and informed practices to limit the liability exposure of the institution, its officers, employees, and agents. Staff members must be informed about institutional policies regarding personal liability and related insurance coverage options.

The institution must provide access to legal advice for SLP staff members as needed to carry out assigned responsibilities.

The institution must inform SLP staff and students in a timely and systematic fashion about extraordinary or changing legal obligations and potential liabilities.

## Part 9. EQUITY and ACCESS

Student leadership program (SLP) staff members must ensure that services and programs are provided on a fair and equitable basis. Facilities, programs and services must be accessible. Hours of operation and delivery of and access to programs and services must be responsive to the needs of all students and other constituents. SLP must adhere to the spirit and intent of equal opportunity laws.

The SLP must be open and readily accessible to all students and must not discriminate except where sanctioned by law and institutional policy. Discrimination must especially be avoided on the bases of age; color, creed; cultural heritage; disability; ethnicity; gender identity; nationality; political affiliation, religious affiliation, sex, sexual orientation; or economic, marital, social, or veteran status.

Consistent with their mission and goals, SLP must take affirmative action to remedy significant imbalances in student participation and staffing patterns.

As the demographic profiles of campuses change and new instructional delivery methods are introduced, institutions must recognize the needs of students who participate in distance learning for access to programs and services offered on campus. Institutions must provide appropriate services in ways that are accessible to distance learners and assist them in identifying and gaining access to other appropriate services in their geographic region.

## Part 10. CAMPUS and EXTERNAL RELATIONS

The student leadership program must establish, maintain, and promote effective relations with relevant individuals, campus offices, and external agencies.
SLP should maintain positive relations through effective communication and encourage participation with a variety of offices, departments, agencies, and constituencies both on and off campus for leadership involvement opportunities.

## Part 11. DIVERSITY

Within the context of each institution's unique mission, diversity enriches the community and enhances the collegiate experience for all; therefore, student leadership programs (SLP) must nurture environments where commonalties and differences among people are recognized and honored.

SLP must promote educational experiences that are characterized by open and continuous communication that deepens understanding of one's own identity, culture, and heritage, and that of others. SLP must educate and promote respect about commonalties and differences in their historical and cultural contexts.

SLP must address the characteristics and needs of a diverse population when establishing and implementing policies and procedures.

## Part 12. ETHICS

All persons involved in the delivery of student leadership programs (SLP) must adhere to the highest principles of ethical behavior. SLP must develop or adopt and implement appropriate statements of ethical practice. SLP must publish these statements and ensure their periodic review by relevant constituencies .

SLP staff members must ensure that privacy and confidentiality are maintained with respect to all communications and records to the extent that such records are protected under the law and appropriate statements of ethical practice. Information contained in students' education records must not be disclosed without written consent except as allowed by relevant laws and institutional policies. Staff members must disclose to appropriate authorities information judged to be of an emergency nature, especially when the safety of the individual or others is involved, or when otherwise required by institutional policy or relevant law.

All SLP staff members must be aware of and comply with the provisions contained in the institution's human subjects research policy and in other relevant institutional policies addressing ethical practices and confidentiality of research data concerning individuals.

SLP staff members must recognize and avoid personal conflict of interest or appearance thereof in their transactions with students and others.

SLP staff members must strive to insure the fair, objective, and impartial treatment of all persons with whom they deal. Staff members must not participate in nor condone any form of harassment that demeans persons or creates an intimidating, hostile, or offensive campus environment.

When handling institutional funds, all SLP staff members must ensure that such funds are managed in accordance with established and responsible accounting procedures and the fiscal policies or processes of the institution.

SLP staff members must perform their duties within the limits of their training, expertise, and competence. When these limits are exceeded, individuals in need of further assistance must be referred to persons possessing appropriate qualifications. Staff members must use suitable means to confront and otherwise hold accountable other staff members who exhibit unethical behavior.

SLP staff members must be knowledgeable about and practice ethical behavior in the use of technology.

Staff members must ensure that facilitators have appropriate training experience and credentials.

Expertise, training, and certification are essential in the administration and interpretation of personality, developmental, and leadership assessment instruments.

Where materials and instruments used in SLP are copyrighted, appropriate citations must be made and permission obtained.

## Part 13. ASSESSMENT and EVALUATION

Student leadership programs (SLP) must conduct regular assessment and evaluations. SLP must employ effective qualitative and quantitative methodologies as appropriate, to determine whether and to what degree the stated mission, goals, and student learning and development outcomes are being met. The process must employ sufficient and sound assessment measures to ensure comprehensiveness. Data collected must include responses from students and other affected constituencies.

SLP must evaluate periodically how well they complement and enhance the institution's stated mission and educational effectiveness.

Results of these evaluations must be used in revising and improving programs and services and in recognizing staff performance.

Areas to be assessed should include learning outcomes, student satisfaction, goal achievement, and effectiveness of teaching techniques. Particular efforts should be made to conduct longitudinal studies on program evaluations.

# THE ROLE of LEARNING ASSISTANCE PROGRAMS
## *CAS* Standards Contextual Statement

Learning assistance programs provide student-centered instruction and services for developing skills, strategies, and behaviors that increase the efficiency and effectiveness of the processes that improve learning outcomes. By helping students achieve their learning potential and succeed academically, learning assistance programs significantly influence student retention.

The history of learning assistance programs extends back to 1900, when "how to study books" were first published for underprepared entering freshmen. The reading clinics and study methods laboratories of the 1930s and 1940s and the self-help programs, learning modules, and programmed instruction of the reading and study skills laboratories of the 1950s and 1960s formed part of the historical foundation. By the 1970s, these programs had merged with educational technology and tutoring centers and offered services for the many new nontraditional students. At selective colleges and universities, these services were organized under the auspices of student affairs and typically were open to any student who requested help. At community colleges and institutions with open admissions policies, remedial courses and related services were usually offered under the auspices of either an academic department or a separate developmental education unit.

By the mid-1970s, professionals involved with learning assistance had initiated national organizations. One of these groups, Commission XVI: Learning Centers in Higher Education, was charged by its parent organization, the American College Personnel Association (ACPA), to participate in drafting the CAS Standards and Guidelines for Learning Assistance Programs. Conscious that Commission XVI represented primarily a student affairs-based learning center model, the leadership solicited input and involvement from constituents in other professional organizations to assure broad representation of institutional types and program models. The principle guiding the project was that standards for the profession must address aspects common to all quality programs, but be broad enough to encompass the various models for, and the multi-disciplinary nature of, learning assistance programs. After five years and numerous drafts, the CAS Standards and Guidelines for Learning Assistance Programs were completed and adopted in 1986. This first major document articulating universal concepts, beliefs, and practices

for learning assistance practitioners and their programs also confirmed that learning assistance programs had become permanent professional components in higher education.

The initial CAS Standards and Guidelines for Learning Assistance Programs had two major limitations. First, it did not contain a pedagogical component to directly address the teaching function of learning assistance programs. Second, its broad based purpose did not address standards for specific functions and content areas of learning assistance. Recognition of these limitations produced greater interest in standards and the movement gained momentum in professional organizations.

The National Association for Developmental Education (NADE), with help of other learning assistance associations including the College Reading and Learning Association (CRLA), Commission XVI of the American College Personnel Association (ACPA), the Midwest College Learning Center Association (MCLCA), and the New York College Learning Skills Association (NYCLSA), sponsored standards development initiatives that culminated in the 1995 publication of the *NADE Self-Evaluation Guides: Models for Assessing Learning Assistance/Developmental Education Programs*. Using the CAS Standards and Guidelines format as a template, this document applied the CAS process to specific programs, such as tutoring services, adjunct instructional programs, and developmental coursework. To address the profession's pedagogical component, it also included a section on program factors influencing the teaching/learning process. In 1989, CRLA had initiated the Tutor Certification Program to assure that minimum standards for tutor training were being met. As this and subsequent projects satisfy the profession's requirements for content and practice-specific standards, the CAS Standards for Learning Assistance Programs continue to provide a process for conducting a systematic self-study of the essential components of an entire learning assistance program.

In the early 1990s, both NADE and CRLA joined the CAS enterprise and committed to active participation in the revision of the CAS Standards and Guidelines for Learning Assistance Programs. The revision process was conducted over a two-year period and involved input from over 150 professional learning assistance practitioners representing numerous professional bodies. The document that follows is the product of that collaboration and represents professional consensus of the role and importance of learning assistance programs in higher education.

### References, Readings, and Resources

Casazza, M.E., & Silverman, S.L. (2000). *Learning & development: Making connections to enhance teaching.* San Francisco: Jossey-Bass.

Casazza, M. E., & Silverman, S. L. (1996). *Learning assistance and developmental education: A guide for effective practice.* San Francisco: Jossey-Bass.

Christ, F., Sheets, R., and Smith, K. (Eds). (2000) *Starting a learning assistance center: conversations with CRLA members who have been there and done that!.* Clearwater, FL: H&H Publishing Company.

Clark-Thayer, S. (Ed.) (1995). *NADE self-evaluation guides: Models for assessing learning assistance/developmental education programs.* Clearwater, FL: H&H Publishing Company.

Hashway, R. M. (Spring 1989). Developmental learning center designs. *Research and Teaching in Developmental Education*, 5(2), 25-38.

Lowenstein, S, (1993). Using advisory boards for learning assistance programs. New York College *Learning Skills Association: Perspectives on practice in Developmental Education.* 93-99.

Maxwell, M. (Ed.) (1994). *From access to success: A book of reading on college developmental education and learning assistance programs.* Clearwater, FL: H&H Publishing Co.

Maxwell, M. (1996). *Evaluating academic skills programs: A sourcebook* (3rd ed.). Kensington, MD: MM Associates.

Maxwell, M. (1997). *Improving student learning skills.* (2nd ed.) Clearwater, FL: H&H Publishing

New York College Learning Skills Association Ethics and Standards Committee. (revised, April 1994). *Statement of ethics and general guidelines for learning assistance programs.* New York: New York College Learning Skills Association.

Robert, E. R. & Thompson, G. (Spring 1994). Learning assistance and the success of underprepared students at Berkeley. *Journal of Developmental Education*, 17(3), 4-15.

Stahl, N. A., Brozo, W. G., & Gordon, B. (1984). The professional preparation of college reading and study-skills specialists. In G. McNinch (Ed.) *Reading teacher education: Yearbook of the 4th Annual conference of the American Reading Forum.* Carrollton, GA: West Georgia College. ERIC #248-761.

White, W. G., Jr., & Schnuth, M. L. (1990). College learning assistance centers: Places for learning. In R. M. Hashway (Ed.), *Handbook of developmental education.* New York: Praeger Press, 157-177.

White, W. G., Jr., Kyzar, B., & Lane, K. E. (1990). College learning assistance centers: Spaces for learning. In R. M. Hashway (Ed*.), Handbook of developmental education.* New York: Praeger Press, 179-195.

*Journal of College Reading and Learning*: College Reading and Learning Association.

*Journal of Developmental Education* and *Research in Developmental Education:* National Center for Developmental Education, Appalachian State University.

*The Learning Assistance Review*: National College Learning Center Association.

*NADE Monograph Series:* National Association of Developmental Education.

*Research & Teaching in Developmental Education:* New York College Learning Skills Association.

College Reading and Learning Association P.O. Box 6251, Auburn, CA 9560

http://www.crla.net/Welcome.htm
(530) 823-1076; Fax: (530) 823-6331

National Association of Developmental Education. 1234 Pembroke Drive, Warrensburg, MO 64093; http://www.nade@iland.net (1-877) 881-9876 (toll free); Fax: 660-747-3214

# LEARNING ASSISTANCE PROGRAMS
## *CAS* Standards and Guidelines

## Part 1. MISSION

The learning assistance program (LAP) must teach the skills and strategies to help students become independent and active learners and to achieve academic success.

The LAP must incorporate student learning and student development in its mission. The LAP must enhance overall educational experiences. The LAP must develop, record, disseminate, implement and regularly review its mission and goals. Mission statements must be consistent with the mission and goals of the institution and with the standards in this document. The LAP must operate as an integral part of the institution's overall mission.

The LAP must collaborate with faculty, staff, and administrators in addressing the learning needs, academic performance, and retention of students.
Models of learning assistance programs vary, but should share the following common goals . . .
  • to make students the central focus of the program
  • to assist members of the campus community in achieving their personal potential for learning
  • to provide instruction and services that address the cognitive, affective, and socio cultural dimensions of learning
  • to introduce students to the expectations of faculty and the culture of higher education
  • to help students develop positive attitudes towards learning and confidence in their ability to learn
  • to foster personal responsibility and accountability for one's own learning
  • to provide a variety of instructional approaches that are appropriate for the level of skills and learning styles of the student population
  • to assist students in transferring skills and strategies they have learned previously to their academic work;
  • to provide services and resources to faculty, staff, and administrators that enhance and support classroom instruction and professional development
  • to support the academic standards and requirements of the institution

## Part 2. PROGRAM

The formal education of students consists of the curriculum and the co-curriculum, and must promote student learning and development that is purposeful and holistic. The learning assistance program (LAP) must identify relevant and desirable student learning and development outcomes and provide programs and services that encourage the achievement of those outcomes.

Relevant and desirable outcomes include: intellectual growth, effective communication, realistic self-appraisal, enhanced self-esteem, clarified values, career choices, leadership development, healthy behaviors, meaningful interpersonal relationships, independence, collaboration, social responsibility, satisfying and productive lifestyles, appreciation of diversity, spiritual awareness, and achievement of personal and educational goals.

The LAP must provide evidence of its impact on the achievement of student learning and development outcomes.
The LAP may use the examples that follow or identify other more germane indicators.

### Student Learning & Development Outcome Domains

### Intellectual Growth
Examples of Achievement Indicators
  Produces personal and educational goal statements; Employs critical thinking in problem solving; Uses complex information from a variety of sources including personal experience and observation to form a decision or opinion; Obtains a degree; Applies previously understood information and concepts to a new situation or setting; Expresses appreciation for literature, the fine arts, mathematics, sciences, and social sciences

### Effective Communication
Examples of Achievement Indicators
  Writes and speaks coherently and effectively; Writes and speaks after reflection; Able to influence others through writing, speaking or artistic expression; Effectively articulates abstract ideas; Uses appropriate syntax; Makes presentations or gives performances

### Independence
Examples of Achievement Indicators
  Exhibits self-reliant behaviors; Functions autonomously; Exhibits ability to function interdependently; Accepts supervision as needed; Manages time effectively

### Personal and Educational Goals
Examples of Achievement Indicators
  Sets, articulates, and pursues individual goals; Articulates personal and educational goals and objectives; Uses personal and educational goals to guide decisions; Understands effects of one's personal and education goals on others

### Enhanced Self-Esteem

Examples of Achievement Indicators

Shows self-respect and respect for others; Initiates actions toward achievement of goals; Takes reasonable risks; Demonstrates assertive behavior; Functions without need for constant reassurance from others

### Realistic Self-Appraisal

Examples of Achievement Indicators

Articulates personal skills and abilities; Makes decisions and acts in congruence with personal values; Acknowledges personal strengths and weaknesses; Articulates rationale for personal behavior; Seeks feedback from others; Learns from past experiences

### Collaboration

Examples of Achievement Indicators

Works cooperatively with others; Seeks the involvement of others; Seeks feedback from others; Contributes to achievement of a group goal; Exhibits effective listening skills

### Satisfying and Productive Lifestyles

Examples of Achievement Indicators

Achieves balance between education, work and leisure time; Articulates and meets goals for work, leisure and education; Overcomes obstacles that hamper goal achievement; Functions on the basis of personal identity, ethical, spiritual and moral values; Articulates long-term goals and objectives

### Clarified Values

Examples of Achievement Indicators

Articulates personal values; Acts in congruence with personal values; Makes decisions that reflect personal values; Demonstrates willingness to scrutinize personal beliefs and values; Identifies personal, work and lifestyle values and explains how they influence decision-making

### Healthy Behavior

Examples of Achievement Indicators

Chooses behaviors and environments that promote health and reduce risk; Articulate the relationship between health and wellness and accomplishing life long goals; Exhibits behaviors that advance a healthy community.

### Career Choices

Examples of Achievement Indicators

Articulates career choices based on assessment of interests, values, skills and abilities; Documents knowledge, skills and accomplishments resulting from formal education, work experience, community service and volunteer experiences; Makes the connections between classroom and out-of-classroom learning; Can construct a resume with clear job objectives and evidence of related knowledge, skills and accomplishments; Articulates the characteristics of a preferred work environment; Comprehends the world of work; Takes steps to initiate a job search or seek advanced education

### Leadership Development

Examples of Achievement Indicators

Articulates leadership philosophy or style; Serves in a leadership position in a student organization; Comprehends the dynamics of a group; Exhibits democratic principles as a leader; Exhibits ability to visualize a group purpose and desired outcomes

### Meaningful Interpersonal Relationships

Examples of Achievement Indicators

Develops and maintains satisfying interpersonal relationships; Establishes mutually rewarding relationships with friends and colleagues; Listens to and considers others' points of view; Treats others with respect

### Appreciating Diversity

Examples of Achievement Indicators

Understands ones own identity and culture. Seeks involvement with people different from oneself; Seeks involvement in diverse interests; Articulates the advantages and challenges of a diverse society; Challenges appropriately abusive use of stereotypes by others; Understands the impact of diversity on one's own society

### Social Responsibility

Examples of Achievement Indicators

Understands and participates in relevant governance systems; Understands, abides by, and participates in the development, maintenance, and/or orderly change of community, social, and legal standards or norms; Appropriately challenges the unfair, unjust, or uncivil behavior of other individuals or groups; Participates in service/volunteer activities

### Spiritual Awareness

Examples of Achievement Indicators

Develops and articulates personal belief system; Understands roles of spirituality in personal and group values and behaviors

**The learning assistance programs must be (a) intentional, (b) coherent, (c) based on theories and knowledge of learning and human development, (d) reflective of developmental and demographic profiles of the student population, and (e) responsive to needs of individuals, special populations, and communities.**

**The LAP must promote, either directly of by referral, the affective skills that influence learning such as stress management, test anxiety reduction, assertiveness, power of concentration, and motivation.**

**The LAP must refer students to appropriate campus and community resources for assistance with personal problems, severe learning disabilities, financial difficulties, and other areas**

**of need that may be outside the purview or beyond the expertise of the learning assistance program.**

The scope of the LAP should be determined by the type and level of skills students require. The format utilized for strengthening academic skills may include mandatory credit-bearing developmental courses or non-credit elective workshops.

The scope of programs and services should also be determined by the needs of the student populations the learning assistance program is charged to serve. These can range from special populations (such as culturally and ethnically diverse students, international and English as a second language students, student athletes, returning students, and students with physical and learning disabilities) to the entire student population.

Formal and informal diagnostic procedures should be conducted to identify skills and strategies that the student should develop to achieve the level of proficiency prescribed or required by the institution or known to be necessary for college learning. Assessment results should be shared with the student to formulate recommendations and a plan of instruction.

The LAP should provide instruction and services for the development of reading, mathematics and quantitative reasoning, writing, critical thinking, problem solving, and study skills. Other programs may include: subject-matter tutoring, adjunct instructional programs and supplemental instruction groups, time management programs, freshman seminars, and preparation for graduate and professional school admissions tests and for professional certification requirements.

Modes of delivering learning assistance programs include individual and group instruction and instructional media such as print, video, audio, computers, and skills laboratories. Instruction and programs may be delivered on site or through distance learning programs.

The LAP should give systematic feedback to students concerning their progress in reaching cognitive and affective goals, teach self feedback methods utilizing self monitoring strategies, and give students practice in applying and transferring skills and strategies learned in the program to academic tasks across the curriculum.

The LAP should promote an understanding of the learning needs of the student population. Some of the ways in which learning assistance programs should educate the campus community:

• establishing advisory boards consisting of members from key segments of the campus community
• holding periodic informational meetings and consulting with staff, faculty, and administrators
• participating in staff and faculty development and in service programs on curriculum and instructional approaches that address the development of learning skills, attitudes, and behaviors
• encouraging the use of learning assistance program resources, materials, instruction and services as integral or adjunct classroom activities
• conducting in class workshops that demonstrate the application of learning strategies to the course content;
• disseminating information that describes the programs and services, hours of operation, procedures for

registering or scheduling appointments through publications, campus and local media announcements, and informational presentations
• training and supervising paraprofessionals and pre-professionals to work in such capacities as tutors, peer mentors, and advisors
• providing jobs, practica, courses, internships, and assistantships for graduate students interested in learning assistance and related careers

## Part 3. LEADERSHIP

**Effective and ethical leadership is essential to the success of all organizations. Institutions must appoint, position, and empower learning assistance program (LAP) leaders within the administrative structure to accomplish stated missions. LAP leaders at various levels must be selected on the basis of formal education and training, relevant work experience, personal skills and competencies, relevant professional credentials, as well as potential for promoting learning and development in students, applying effective practices to educational processes, and enhancing institutional effectiveness. Institutions must determine expectations of accountability for leaders and fairly assess their performance.**

**LAP leaders must exercise authority over resources for which they are responsible to achieve their respective missions.**

**LAP leaders must . . .**

• **articulate a vision for their organization**
• **set goals and objectives based on the needs and capabilities of the population served**
• **promote student learning and development**
• **prescribe and practice ethical behavior**
• **recruit, select, supervise, and develop others in the organization**
• **manage financial resources**
• **coordinate human resources**
• **plan, budget for, and evaluate personnel and programs**
• **apply effective practices to educational and administrative processes**
• **communicate effectively**
• **initiate collaborative interaction between individuals and agencies that possess legitimate concerns and interests in the functional area**

**LAP leaders must identify and find means to address individual, organizational, or environmental conditions that inhibit goal achievement.**

**LAP leaders must promote campus environments that result in multiple opportunities for student learning and development.**

**LAP leaders must continuously improve programs and services in response to changing needs of students and other constituents, and evolving institutional priorities.**

LAP administrators should:
- participate in institutional planning, policy, procedural, and fiscal decisions that affect learning support for students
- be informed about issues, trends, theories, and methodologies related to student learning and retention;
- represent the learning assistance program on institutional committees
- collaborate with leaders of academic departments and support services in addressing the learning needs and retention of students
- be involved in research, publication, presentations, consultation, and the activities of professional organizations
- communicate with professional constituents in the learning assistance field and related professions

## Part 4. ORGANIZATION and MANAGEMENT

**Guided by an overarching intent to ensure student learning and development, the learning assistance program (LAP) must be structured purposefully and managed effectively to achieve stated goals. Evidence of appropriate structure must include current and accessible policies and procedures, written performance expectations for all employees, functional workflow graphics or organizational charts, and clearly stated service delivery expectations.**

**Evidence of effective management must include use of comprehensive and accurate information for decisions, clear sources and channels of authority, effective communication practices, decision-making and conflict resolution procedures, responsiveness to changing conditions, accountability and evaluation systems, and recognition and reward processes. The LAP must provide channels within the organization for regular review of administrative policies and procedures.**

The mission and goals of the LAP, the needs and demographics of its clients, and its institutional role should determine where the unit is located in the organizational structure of the institution. Learning assistance programs are frequently organized as units in the academic affairs or the student affairs division. Regardless of where the learning assistance program is organized, it should communicate and collaborate with a network of key units across the institution to assure the coordination of related functions, programs, services, policies, procedures, and to expedite client referrals.

The LAP should have a broadly constituted advisory board to make suggestions, provide information, and give guidance.

The LAP should provide written goals, objectives, and anticipated outcomes for each program and service. Written procedures should exist for collecting, processing, and reporting student assessment and program data.

Regularly scheduled meetings should be held to share information; to coordinate the planning, scheduling, and delivery of programs and services; to identify and discuss potential and actual problems and concerns; and to collaborate on making decisions and solving problems.

## Part 5. HUMAN RESOURCES

**The learning assistance program (LAP) must be staffed adequately by individuals qualified to accomplish its mission and goals. Within established guidelines of the institution, the LAP must establish procedures for staff selection, training, and evaluation; set expectations for supervision, and provide appropriate professional development opportunities. The LAP must strive to improve the professional competence and skills of all personnel it employs.**

**Staff and faculty members who hold a joint appointment with the LAP must be committed to the mission, philosophy, goals, and priorities of the program and must possess the necessary expertise for assigned responsibilities.**

**LAP professional staff members must hold an earned graduate degree in a field relevant to the position they hold or must possess an appropriate combination of educational credentials and related work experience.**

Professional staff should have earned degrees from relevant disciplines such as reading, English, mathematics, student personnel and student development, guidance and counseling, psychology, or education. LAP professionals should be knowledgeable in learning theory and in the instruction, assessment, theory, and the professional standards of practice for their area of specialization and responsibility. In addition, they should understand the unique characteristics and needs of the populations they assist and teach. LAP professional staff should vary and adjust pedagogical approaches according to the learning needs and styles of their students, to the nature of the learning task, and to content of academic disciplines across the curriculum.

LAP professional staff should be competent and experienced in:
- teaching, advising, and counseling students at the college level
- written and oral communication skills
- working in a culturally and academically diverse environment
- consulting, collaborating, and negotiating with staff, faculty and administrators of academic and student affairs units
- designing and implementing instructional strategies and materials and utilizing instructional technologies

- training, supervising, and mentoring paraprofessionals and pre-professionals
- identifying and establishing lines of communication for student referral to other institutional and student support units

**Degree or credential-seeking interns must be qualified by enrollment in an appropriate field of study and by relevant experience. These individuals must be trained and supervised adequately by professional staff members holding educational credentials and related work experience appropriate for supervision.**

The LAP should be informed of the policies and procedures to be followed for internships and practica as required by the students' academic departments. The roles and responsibilities of the LAP and those of the academic department should be clearly defined and understood by all involved.

**Student employees and volunteers must be carefully selected, trained, supervised, and evaluated. They must be trained on how and when to refer those in need of assistance to qualified staff members and have access to a supervisor for assistance in making these judgments. Student employees and volunteers must be provided clear and precise job descriptions, pre-service training based on assessed needs, and continuing staff development.**

**The LAP must have technical and support staff members adequate to accomplish its mission. Staff members must be technologically proficient and qualified to perform their job functions, be knowledgeable of ethical and legal uses of technology, and have access to training. The level of staffing and workloads must be adequate and appropriate for program and service demands.**

Secretarial and technical staff should be updated on changes in programs, services, policies and procedures in order to expedite smooth and efficient assistance to clients. Appropriate staff development opportunities should be available.

**Salary levels and fringe benefits for all LAP staff members must be commensurate with those for comparable positions within the institution, in similar institutions, and in the relevant geographic area.**

**The LAP must institute hiring and promotion practices that are fair, inclusive, and non-discriminatory. Programs and services must employ a diverse staff to provide readily identifiable role models for students and to enrich the campus community.**

**The LAP must create and maintain position descriptions for all staff members and provide regular performance planning and appraisals.**

**The LAP must have a system for regular staff evaluation and must provide access to continuing education and professional development opportunities, including in-service training programs and participation in professional conferences and workshops.**

## Part 6.  FINANCIAL RESOURCES

**The learning assistance program (LAP) must have adequate funding to accomplish its mission and goals.  Funding priorities must be determined within the context of the stated mission, goals, objectives and comprehensive analysis of the needs and capabilities of students and the availability of internal or external resources.**

**The LAP must demonstrate fiscal responsibility and cost effectiveness consistent with institutional protocols.**

Prior to implementing a new program or service or to significantly expanding an existing program component, a financial analysis should be performed to determine the financial resources required to support the addition or expansion and the appropriate funds made available.

The LAP budget should support its instructional and student support service functions.  Adequate funds should be provided for the following budget categories: staff and student salaries, general office functions, student assessment and instructional activities, data management and program evaluation processes, research staff training and professional development activities, instructional materials and media, and instructional and office computing

## Part 7.  FACILITIES and EQUIPMENT

**The learning assistance program (LAP) must have adequate, suitably located facilities, adequate technology, and equipment to support its mission and goals efficiently and effectively.  Facilities, technology, and equipment must be evaluated regularly and be in compliance with relevant federal, state, provincial, and local requirements to provide for access, health, safety, and security.**

Facilities and equipment should support the instructional, service, and office functions of the learning assistance program.  Facility considerations should include flexible space that can be adapted to changes in the delivery of programs, services, and instructional modes; classrooms, labs, resource rooms, media and computer centers, group and one to one tutorial space to support instruction; private, sound proofed areas to support testing, counseling, and other activities that require confidentiality or concentration; adequate and secure storage for equipment, supplies, instructional and testing materials, and confidential records. Attention should be given to environmental conditions that influence learning such as appropriate acoustics, lighting, ventilation, heating and air-≠conditioning.

## Part 8. LEGAL RESPONSIBILITIES

Learning assistance program (LAP) staff members must be knowledgeable about and responsive to laws and regulations that relate to their respective responsibilities. Staff members must inform users of programs and services and officials, as appropriate, of legal obligations and limitations including constitutional, statutory, regulatory, and case law; mandatory laws and orders emanating from federal, state/provincial and local governments; and the institution's policies.

LAP staff members must use reasonable and informed practices to limit the liability exposure of the institution, its officers, employees, and agents. Staff members must be informed about institutional policies regarding personal liability and related insurance coverage options.

The institution must provide access to legal advice for LAP staff members as needed to carry out assigned responsibilities.

The institution must inform LAP staff and students in a timely and systematic fashion about extraordinary or changing legal obligations and potential liabilities.

Staff development programs should be available to educate learning assistance program staff of these changes.

## Part 9. EQUITY and ACCESS

Learning assistance program (LAP) staff members must ensure that services and programs are provided on a fair and equitable basis. Facilities, programs and services must be accessible. Hours of operation and delivery of and access to programs and services must be responsive to the needs of all students and other constituents. The LAP must adhere to the spirit and intent of equal opportunity laws.

The LAP must be open and readily accessible to all students and must not discriminate except where sanctioned by law and institutional policy. Discrimination must especially be avoided on the bases of age; color, creed; cultural heritage; disability; ethnicity; gender identity; nationality; political affiliation, religious affiliation, sex, sexual orientation; or economic, marital, social, or veteran status.

Consistent with their mission and goals, the LAP must take affirmative action to remedy significant imbalances in student participation and staffing patterns.

As the demographic profiles of campuses change and new instructional delivery methods are introduced, institutions must recognize the needs of students who participate in distance learning for access to programs and services offered on campus. □Institutions must provide appropriate services in ways that are accessible to distance learners and assist them in identifying and gaining access to other appropriate services in their geographic region.

## Part 10. CAMPUS and EXTERNAL RELATIONS

The learning assistance program (LAP) must establish, maintain, and promote effective relations with relevant individuals, campus offices, and external agencies.

The learning assistance program should:
- be an integral part of the academic offerings of the institution
- establish communication with academic and student services units
- to encourage the exchange of ideas, knowledge, and expertise
- to provide mutual consultation, as needed, on student cases
- to expedite student referrals to and from the learning assistance program
- to collaborate on programs and services that efficiently and effectively address the needs of students
- have representation on institutional committees relevant to the mission and goals of the program such as committees on retention, orientation, basic skills, learning communities, freshmen seminars, probation review, academic standards and requirements, curriculum design, assessment and placement, and faculty development
- solicit volunteers from the local community to contribute their skills and talents to the services of the learning assistance program
- provide training and consultation to community based organizations, e.g., literacy associations, corporate training, and school district based tutorial services

## Part 11. DIVERSITY

Within the context of each institution's unique mission, diversity enriches the community and enhances the collegiate experience for all; therefore, the learning assistance program (LAP) must nurture environments where commonalties and differences among people are recognized and honored.

The LAP must promote educational experiences that are characterized by open and continuous communication that deepens understanding of one's own identity, culture, and heritage, and that of others. The LAP must educate and promote respect about commonalties and differences in their historical and cultural contexts.

The LAP must address the characteristics and needs of a diverse population when establishing and implementing policies and procedures.

The program should facilitate student adjustment to the academic culture of the institution by orienting students to the practices, resources, responsibilities and behaviors that contribute to academic success.

The instructional content, materials, and activities of learning assistance programs should provide opportunities to increase awareness and appreciation of the individual and cultural differences of students.

## Part 12. ETHICS

All persons involved in the learning assistance program (LAP) must adhere to the highest principles of ethical behavior. The LAP must develop or adopt and implement appropriate statements of ethical practice. The LAP must publish these statements and ensure their periodic review by relevant constituencies.

LAP staff members must ensure that privacy and confidentiality are maintained with respect to all communications and records to the extent that such records are protected under the law and appropriate statements of ethical practice. Information contained in students' education records must not be disclosed without written consent except as allowed by relevant laws and institutional policies. Staff members must disclose to appropriate authorities information judged to be of an emergency nature, especially when the safety of the individual or others is involved, or when otherwise required by institutional policy or relevant law.

LAP staff members must be aware of and comply with the provisions contained in the institution's human subjects research policy and in other relevant institutional policies addressing ethical practices and confidentiality of research data concerning individuals.

LAP staff members must recognize and avoid personal conflict of interest or appearance thereof in their transactions with students and others.

Information and training should be made available regarding conflict of interest policies.

LAP staff members must strive to insure the fair, objective, and impartial treatment of all persons with whom they deal. Staff members must not participate in nor condone any form of harassment that demeans persons or creates an intimidating, hostile, or offensive campus environment.

When handling institutional funds, all LAP staff members must ensure that such funds are managed in accordance with established and responsible accounting procedures and the fiscal policies or processes of the institution.

LAP staff members must perform their duties within the limits of their training, expertise, and competence. When these limits are exceeded, individuals in need of further assistance must be referred to persons possessing appropriate qualifications.

With the prevalence of student paraprofessional and tutorial staff within learning assistance programs, specific attention should be given to properly orienting and advising student staff about matters of confidentiality. Clear statements should be distributed and reviewed with student staff as to what information is and is not appropriate for student staff to access or to communicate.

LAP staff members must use suitable means to confront and otherwise hold accountable other staff members who exhibit unethical behavior. Staff members must be knowledgeable about and practice ethical behavior in the use of technology.

Because LAP staff work with students' academic coursework, they must be knowledgeable of policies related to academic integrity, plagiarism, student code of conduct and other similar policies. All staff members must be cognizant of the implications of these policies.

Statements or claims made about outcomes that can be achieved from participating in learning assistance programs and services must be truthful and realistic.

LAP funds acquired through grants and other non institutional resources must be managed according to the regulations and guidelines of the funding source and the institution.

## Part 13. ASSESSMENT and EVALUATION

The learning assistance program (LAP) must conduct regular assessment and evaluations. The LAP must employ effective qualitative and quantitative methodologies as appropriate, to determine whether and to what degree the stated mission, goals, and student learning and development outcomes are being met. The process must employ sufficient and sound assessment measures to ensure comprehensiveness. Data collected must include responses from students and other affected constituencies.

Qualitative methods may include standard evaluation forms, questionnaires, interviews, observations, or case studies.

Quantitative measurements range from data on an individual student's performance to the impact on the campus' retention rate. Quantitative methods may include follow up studies on students' grades in mainstream courses, GPAs, graduation, re enrollment and retention figures. Comparative data of learning assistance program participants and non participants is also a measure of program effectiveness. Quantitative measures can include data on the size of the user population, numbers utilizing particular services, number of contact hours, the sources of student referrals to the program, numbers of students who may be on a waiting list or who have requested services not provided by the learning assistance program. Quantitative data should be collected within specific time periods and longitudinally to reveal trends.

**The LAP must evaluate periodically how well they complement and enhance the institution's stated mission and educational effectiveness.**

**Results of these evaluations must be used in revising and improving programs and services and in recognizing staff performance.**

The LAP should have the ability to collect and analyze data through its own resources and through access to appropriate data generated by the institution.

Periodic evaluations of the learning assistance program and services may be performed by on-campus experts and outside consultants and disseminated to appropriate administrators.

The LAP should conduct periodic self assessments, utilizing self study processes endorsed by professional organizations.

**Various means of assessment should be conducted for the purpose of identifying the learning needs of the students and guiding them to appropriate programs and services. Assessment results should be communicated to the student confidentially, honestly, and with sensitivity. Students should be advised directed to appropriate, alternative educational opportunities when there is reasonable cause to believe that students will not be able to meet requirements for academic success.**

The LAP should periodically review and revise its goals and services based on evaluation outcomes and based on changes in institutional goals, priorities, and plans. Data that reveals trends or changes in student demographics, characteristics and needs should be utilized for learning assistance program short and long term planning.

# The ROLE of LESBIAN, GAY, BISEXUAL, and TRANSGENDER SERVICES and PROGRAMS
## *CAS* Standards Contextual Statement

*History.* It is no longer a matter of whether to provide services for lesbian, gay, bisexual, and transgender (LGBT) college students; rather, it is a matter of when. The talent, energy, and hope with which LGBT students are entering college must be acknowledged and encouraged (Sanlo, 1998). Some students are declaring their bisexual or homosexual orientations in high school, then knocking on institutional doors with expectations of being fully appreciated for who they are in their entirety—including their sexual orientations. Many more students enter college questioning their sexual identities, not yet ready to make pronouncements nor embrace labels, but they deserve the institution's demonstrated acceptance and attention.

When LGBT people refused to allow police to raid the Stonewall Bar in New York City on June 27, 1969, one more time, a stunning message was heard throughout the United States. In response to this singular event, which occurred on the heels of the civil rights movement of the 1960s, numerous Gay Liberation Front groups sprang up on college campuses everywhere, challenging both administration and faculty alike. Marcus (1993) documented the role and involvement of lesbian and gay college students and the importance of these challenges. Sexual orientation issues had finally made their way into the academy.

*Public Policy.* Homosexuality was often described as a genetic defect, a mental disorder, or a learning disability in early scientific theories. However, Evelyn Hooker's (1963) research found no significant differences in the psychological adjustment of homosexual men when compared to a comparable group of heterosexual men. On the basis of further research by others demonstrating similar findings, the American Psychiatric Association removed homosexuality as a diagnostic mental disorder in 1973. Two years later, the American Psychological Association took the same action and also issued a statement that its member mental health providers must actively stop discrimination against lesbians and gay men. Concurrently, the National Education Association added sexual orientation to its non-discrimination policy. To date, over 200 professional organizations, including the American Educational Research Association, NASPA, ACPA, the American Federation of Teachers, the American Counseling Association, and the National Association of Social Workers, have done the same. The revised standards of the National Council for the Accreditation of Teacher Education (NCATE) now requires institutions to recruit and retain

a culturally diverse faculty and student body, including individuals with diverse sexual orientations.

However, despite statements of non-discrimination by professional organizations and by institutions, everyday life has not changed dramatically for LGBT people. Given the historical context, many LGBT people choose to remain invisible rather than face the consequences of campus intolerance and hostility (Sanlo, 1999).

*The Consortium.* The National Consortium of Directors of Lesbian, Gay, Bisexual, and Transgender Resources in Higher Education (the Consortium) was officially founded in San Diego in 1997 to provide support for the professionals in this growing new arena in student affairs. Beyond membership support, the Consortium seeks to assist colleges and universities in developing equity in every respect for lesbian, gay, bisexual, and transgender students, faculty, staff, administrators, and alumni. The Consortium also focuses on developing curricula to enhance its professional goals, to promote improved campus climates, and to advocate for policy change, program development, and the establishment of campus LGBT offices and centers. The Consortium's website—www.lgbtcampus.org—offers valuable information relating specifically to higher education.

*Recruitment, Retention, and Numbers of LGBT Students Unknown.* Minimal data are currently available as to the number of LGBT students on college campuses. Several reasons exist to explain this fact (Eyermann & Sanlo, 2001). First, some surveys regarding sexual behavior rely on people to self-disclose same-sex interactions, thoughts, or feelings. It is unlikely that people will answer such questions honestly or at all if they do not explicitly trust the anonymity of the process. Second, some surveys rely on people to identity themselves through labels such as homosexual, lesbian, gay, or bisexual. While some LGBT people may use these labels, many others, especially LGBT people of color, may not. Either they have decided to not attach a label to their non-heterosexual identity; or they have not journeyed through the "coming-out" process sufficiently to yet identify with a label; or they use different terminology, all of which are the experiences of LGBT college students. Finally, while some people may have strong feelings of same-sex attraction, it is likely that they remain in heterosexual relationships or become non-sexual and never act on their feelings of such same-sex attraction (Eyermann & Sanlo, 2001).

Consequently, limited empirical data exist to identify numbers of LGBT students. Three factors figure into college data-gathering. First, while surveys may elicit opinions about homosexual issues, few institutions or national polls ask respondents to identify their sexual orientation. For example, neither the General Social Survey (GSS), which surveys the population at large, nor the Annual Freshman Survey conducted by the Higher Education Research Institute (HERI), elicit sexual orientation demographics.

Second, no college or university has sexual orientation or gender identity boxes on admission forms, and retention studies related to LGBT students have not yet been conducted. Therefore, when administrators wish to ascertain the number of LGBT students on campuses, there are few, if any, data bases available to provide such information. Consequently, they find themselves resorting to asking an openly gay student or staff member or simply projecting numbers from LGBT college chat rooms.

Third, student survey respondents may not use the labels used by researchers. Of the few campuses that do ask about sexual identity on campus surveys, most use the traditional terms previously noted. These labels may be offensive to some or too graphic a description for others, depending upon the stage of sexual awareness and development. Either of these opinions may prompt LGB students to falsely answer or to ignore such questions, and few surveys and campuses even consider transgender students in any context.

*Violence.* Like racism, sexism, and other ideologies of oppression, heterosexism—that only heterosexuality is normal—is manifested in social customs, institutions, and in attitudes and behaviors of individuals. Preserved through the routine operation of institutions, the maintenance of heterosexism is possible because it is in keeping with prevalent social norms. Higher education contributes to the maintenance of institutionalized heterosexism as evidenced by hate crimes directed toward LGBT students, faculty, and staff members (Evans & Rankin, 1998). Given that heterosexism's values underlie higher education, the work involved in proactively addressing violence against LGBT individuals and building communities that are inclusive and welcoming of LGBT persons is both controversial and demanding.

Schuh (1998) noted that campuses are "no longer safe havens for students, faculty, or staff. Violence is a community and societal problem that has found its way into institutions of higher education" (p. 347). Institutions must make concerted efforts to create campus climates where every student is safe and every faculty and staff member is secure in knowing that there will never be another incident such as the one involving Matthew Shepard at the University of Wyoming.

*Services.* Over 40 higher education institutions currently have full-time professionally staffed offices or centers that provide services for and about LGBT students, faculty, and staff. Some such services include information and referral; advocacy; support/discussion groups; LGBT student organization advising; safe zones and ally projects; leadership programs; peer counseling; and Lavender Graduation celebrations (Sanlo, 2000). A similar number of campuses have LGBT offices staffed by part-time graduate students. In addition, some campuses with no actual LGBT office or center employ a person who is responsible for providing services to LGBT students (Sanlo, Rankin, & Schoenberg, in press).

## References, Reading, and Resources

Evans, N., & Rankin, S. (1998). Heterosexism and Campus Violence: Assessment and Intervention Strategies. In A. M. Hoffman, J. H., Schuh, & R. H. Fenske, (1998). Violence on campus: Defining the problems, strategies for action. Gaithersburg, MD: Aspen. pp. 169-186.

Eyermann, T., & Sanlo, R. (2002). Documenting Their Existence: Lesbian, Gay, and Bisexual Students in the Residence Halls In R. Sanlo, S. Rankin, & R. Schoenberg. *Our place on campus: Lesbian, gay, bisexual, and transgender services and programs in higher education* (pp.33-40). Westport, CT: Greenwood

Hooker, E. (1963). Male homosexuality. In N. L. Farberow (Ed.), Taboo topics. (pp. 44-55). New York: Atherton.

Marcus, E. (1993). Making history: The struggle for gay and lesbian equal rights, 1945-1990: An oral history. NY: HarperPerennial

Sanlo, R. (2000, Spring). The LGBT Campus Resource Center Director: The New Profession in Student Affairs. Washington, DC: NASPA Journal, 37(3). 485-495.

Sanlo, R. (Ed.) (1998). Working with lesbian, gay, bisexual, and transgender college students: A handbook for faculty and administrators. Westport, CT: Greenwood.

Sanlo, R. (1999). Unheard voices: The effects of silence on lesbian and gay educators. Westport, CT: G Bergin & Garvey.

Sanlo, R., Rankin, S., & Schoenberg, R. *Our place on campus: Lesbian, gay, bisexual, and transgender services and programs in higher education.* Westport, CT: Greenwood

Schuh, J. (1998). Conclusion. In A. M. Hoffman, J. H., Schuh, & R. H. Fenske, (1998). Violence on campus: Defining the problems, strategies for action. Gaithersburg, MD: Aspen. p. 347.

# LESBIAN, GAY, BISEXEXUAL, TRANSGENDER (LGBT) PROGRAMS and SERVICES
## *CAS* Standards and Guidelines

## Part 1. MISSION

The lesbian, gay, bisexual, transgender (LGBT) program must incorporate student learning and development in its mission. LGBT programs and services must enhance overall educational experiences. The program must develop, record, disseminate, implement and regularly review its mission and goals. Mission statements must be consistent with the mission and goals of the institution and with the standards in this document. The LGBT program must operate as an integral part of the institution's overall mission.

The scope and nature of the programs and services should be shaped by the mission of the institution.

The mission of the program must promote academic and personal growth and development of LGBT students, ensure unrestricted access to and full involvement in all aspects of the institution, and serve as a catalyst for the creation of a campus environment free from prejudice, bigotry, harassment and violence and be hospitable for all students.

To accomplish this mission, the goals of the program must be based on assessment of LGBT student needs and the campus climate they experience. The LGBT program must select priorities among those needs and respond to the extent that resources permit.

To respond to the presence of LGBT students, some institutions create a separate unit. When this is the case, standards outlined here apply. Whether there is a separate unit for LGBT students or not, institutional units share responsibility for meeting the needs of LGBT students. Coordinated efforts to promote the elimination of prejudicial behaviors should be made by all functional areas.

LGBT programs and services should not be the only organized agency to meet the needs of LGBT students. All institutional units share responsibility for meeting the needs of LGBT students in their areas of responsibility. Coordinated efforts to promote the elimination of prejudicial behaviors should be made at every institution by all functional areas.

## Part 2. PROGRAM

The formal education of students consists of the curriculum and the co-curriculum, and must promote student learning and development that is purposeful and holistic. The lesbian, gay, bisexual, transgender (LGBT) program must

identify relevant and desirable student learning and development outcomes and provide programs and services that encourage the achievement of those outcomes.

Relevant and desirable outcomes include: intellectual growth, effective communication, realistic self-appraisal, enhanced self-esteem, clarified values, career choices, leadership development, healthy behaviors, meaningful interpersonal relationships, independence, collaboration, social responsibility, satisfying and productive lifestyles, appreciation of diversity, spiritual awareness, and achievement of personal and educational goals.

The LGBT program must provide evidence of its impact on the achievement of student learning and development outcomes.

The program may use the examples that follow or identify other more germane indicators.

### Student Learning & Development

### Outcome Domains

### Intellectual Growth
Examples of Achievement Indicators

Produces personal and educational goal statements; Employs critical thinking in problem solving; Uses complex information from a variety of sources including personal experience and observation to form a decision or opinion; Obtains a degree; Applies previously understood information and concepts to a new situation or setting; Expresses appreciation for literature, the fine arts, mathematics, sciences, and social sciences

### Effective Communication
Examples of Achievement Indicators

Writes and speaks coherently and effectively; Writes and speaks after reflection; Able to influence others through writing, speaking or artistic expression; Effectively articulates abstract ideas; Uses appropriate syntax; Makes presentations or gives performances

### Enhanced Self-Esteem
Examples of Achievement Indicators

Shows self-respect and respect for others; Initiates actions toward achievement of goals; Takes reasonable risks; Demonstrates assertive behavior; Functions without need for constant reassurance from others

## Realistic Self-Appraisal

Examples of Achievement Indicators

Articulates personal skills and abilities; Makes decisions and acts in congruence with personal values; Acknowledges personal strengths and weaknesses; Articulates rationale for personal behavior; Seeks feedback from others; Learns from past experiences

## Clarified Values

Examples of Achievement Indicators

Articulates personal values; Acts in congruence with personal values; Makes decisions that reflect personal values; Demonstrates willingness to scrutinize personal beliefs and values; Identifies personal, work and lifestyle values and explains how they influence decision-making

## Career Choices

Examples of Achievement Indicators

Articulate career choices based on assessment of interests, values, skills and abilities; Documents knowledge, skills and accomplishments resulting from formal education, work experience, community service and volunteer experiences; Makes the connections between classroom and out-of-classroom learning; Can construct a resume with clear job objectives and evidence of related knowledge, skills and accomplishments; Articulates the characteristics of a preferred work environment; Comprehends the world of work; Takes steps to initiate a job search or seek advanced education

## Leadership Development

Examples of Achievement Indicators

Articulates leadership philosophy or style; Serves in a leadership position in a student organization; Comprehends the dynamics of a group; Exhibits democratic principles as a leader; Exhibits ability to visualize a group purpose and desired outcomes

## Healthy Behavior

Examples of Achievement Indicators

Chooses behaviors and environments that promote health and reduce risk; Articulate the relationship between health and wellness and accomplishing life long goals; Exhibits behaviors that advance a healthy community

## Meaningful Interpersonal Relationships

Examples of Achievement Indicators

Develops and maintains satisfying interpersonal relationships; Establishes mutually rewarding relationships with friends and colleagues; Listens to and considers others' points of view; Treats others with respect

## Independence

Examples of Achievement Indicators

Exhibits self-reliant behaviors; Functions autonomously; Exhibits ability to function interdependently; Accepts supervision as needed; Manages time effectively

## Collaboration

Examples of Achievement Indicators

Works cooperatively with others; Seeks the involvement of others; Seeks feedback from others; Contributes to achievement of a group goal; Exhibits effective listening skills

## Social Responsibility

Examples of Achievement Indicators

Understands and participates in relevant governance systems; Understands, abides by, and participates in the development, maintenance, and/or orderly change of community, social, and legal standards or norms; Appropriately challenges the unfair, unjust, or uncivil behavior of other individuals or groups; Participates in service/volunteer activities

## Satisfying and Productive Lifestyles

Examples of Achievement Indicators

Achieves balance between education, work and leisure time; Articulates and meets goals for work, leisure and education; Overcomes obstacles that hamper goal achievement; Functions on the basis of personal identity, ethical, spiritual and moral values; Articulates long-term goals and objectives

## Appreciating Diversity

Examples of Achievement Indicators

Understands ones own identity and culture. Seeks involvement with people different from oneself; Seeks involvement in diverse interests; Articulate the advantages and challenges of a diverse society; Challenges appropriately abusive use of stereotypes by others; Understands the impact of diversity on one's own society

## Spiritual Awareness

Examples of Achievement Indicators

Develops and articulates personal belief system; Understands roles of spirituality in personal and group values and behaviors

## Personal and Educational Goals

Examples of Achievement Indicators

Sets, articulates, and pursues individual goals; Articulate personal and educational goals and objectives; Uses personal and educational goals to guide decisions; Understands the effect of one's personal and education goals on others

**LGBT programs must be (a) intentional, (b) coherent, (c) based on theories and knowledge of learning and human development, (d) reflective of developmental and demographic profiles of the student population, and (e) responsive to needs of individuals, special populations, and communities.**

**LGBT programs and services must . . .**

- **advocate for the creation of a campus climate that is free from harassment and violence**
- **identity environmental conditions that negatively influence student welfare**

- advocate for solutions to be enacted that neutralize such condition
- work to create policies and procedures within the institution that promote and maintain a hospitable climate

**The LGBT program must ensure equitable access to and involvement in all educational programs.**
Particular attention should be given to financial aid, athletic scholarships, and employment opportunities on campus.

**LGBT programs and services must promote institutional understanding for the concerns of LGBT students, faculty, and staff; educating other campus programs and services to be responsive to the unique concerns of LGBT students. These programs and services must include:**

1. Individual and group psychological counseling such as . . .
   1a. coming out support
   1b. services for victims and perpetrators of homophobia
   1c. services to address family issues
   1d. services to address same sex dating issues
   1e. services to address same sex domestic violence
   1f. support for victims and perpetrators of hate crimes
2. Health services such as:
   2a. health forms with inclusive language
   2b. LGBT health issues brochures
   2c. safer sex information for same sex couples
3. Career services such as:
   3a. resume development
   3b. information on LGBT friendly employers
   3c. employer mentoring programs for LGBT students
   3d. information on LGBT issues in the workplace
4. academic advising such as the support of students' educational choices

**The LGBT program must provide educational opportunities that include . . .**
- examination of the intersection of sexual orientation with race, class, gender, disability, and age
- promotion of self awareness, self-esteem, and self-confidence
- promotion of leadership experiences
- identification of and networking with role models and mentors
- support of students and their families in achieving academic success

**The LGBT program must educate the campus community about decisions or policies that could affect the achievement of LGBT students; publicize** services, events, and issues of concern to LGBT students; and sponsor events that respond to the educational, personal, physical, and safety needs of LGBT students and their allies.

The LGBT program may . . .
- encourage awareness of off campus networks and other support systems for LGBT students including affiliation with state and national organizations
- improve campus awareness of the complex identity issues inherent in the lives of LGBT students
- publicize the accomplishments of LBGT students, faculty, and staff
- represent LGBT concerns and issues on campus-wide committees
- promote scholarship, research, and assessment on LGBT issues
- encourage campus-wide inclusion of LGBT students and avoidance of negative stereotyping in campus media.

LGBT programs and services should maintain or have ready access to resources regarding LGBT issues.

**The LGBT program must address the needs of all LGBT students regardless of their ethnicity, race, gender, religion, age, socioeconomic status, disability, and degree or enrollment status. In addition, The program must plan for and recognize the diversity among the LGBT student population.**
The LGBT program should advocate for the human rights of LGBT persons.

## Part 3. LEADERSHIP
**Effective and ethical leadership is essential to the success of all organizations. Institutions must appoint, position and empower lesbian, gay, bisexual, transgender ((LGBT) program leaders within the administrative structure to accomplish stated missions. Leaders at various levels must be selected on the basis of formal education and training, relevant work experience, personal skills and competencies, relevant professional credentials, as well as potential for promoting learning and development in students, applying effective practices to educational processes, and enhancing institutional effectiveness. Institutions must determine expectations of accountability for LGBT program and services leaders and fairly assess their performance.**

**LGBT program leaders must exercise authority over resources for which they are responsible to achieve their respective missions.**

The LGBT program leader must . . .
- articulate a vision for their organization
- set goals and objectives based on the needs and capabilities of the population served
- promote student learning and development
- prescribe and practice ethical behavior
- recruit, select, supervise, and develop others in the organization

- manage financial resources
- coordinate human resources
- plan, budget for, and evaluate personnel and programs
- apply effective practices to educational and administrative processes
- communicate effectively
- initiate collaborative interaction between individuals and agencies that possess legitimate concerns and interests in the functional area

Program leaders must identify and find means to address individual, organizational, or environmental conditions that inhibit goal achievement. Likewise, leaders must promote campus environments that result in multiple opportunities for student learning and development. Program leaders must continuously improve services in response to changing needs of students and other constituents, and evolving institutional priorities.

## Part 4. ORGANIZATION and MANAGEMENT

Guided by an overarching intent to ensure student learning and development, the lesbian, gay, bisexual, transgender (LGBT) program must be structured purposefully and managed effectively to achieve stated goals. Evidence of appropriate structure must include current and accessible policies and procedures, written performance expectations for all employees, functional workflow graphics or organizational charts, and clearly stated service delivery expectations.

Evidence of effective management must include use of comprehensive and accurate information for decisions, clear sources and channels of authority, effective communication practices, decision-making and conflict resolution procedures, responsiveness to changing conditions, accountability and evaluation systems, and recognition and reward processes. LGBT programs and services must provide channels within the organization for regular review of administrative policies and procedures.

LGBT programs should play a major role in implementing institutional programs developed in response to the assessed needs of LGBT students. Access to the policymakers of the institution should be readily available. The organization should be administered in a manner that permits the stated mission to be fulfilled. LGBT programs and services should be afforded the opportunity to organize in a manner that is efficient and best promotes equity concerns. Emphasis should be placed on achieving an organization in which services are not limited to a specific group of LGBT students (e.g. solely undergraduate students).

## Part 5. HUMAN RESOURCES

The lesbian, gay, bisexual, transgender (LGBT) program must be staffed adequately by individuals qualified to accomplish its mission and goals. Within established guidelines of the institution, programs and services must establish procedures for staff selection, training, and evaluation; set expectations for supervision, and provide appropriate professional development opportunities. LGBT programs and services must strive to improve the professional competence and skills of all personnel it employs.

Program leaders should possess the academic preparation, experience, abilities, professional interests, and competencies essential for the efficient operation of the office as charged, as well as the ability to identify additional areas of concern about LGBT students. Specific course work in organizational development, counseling, group dynamics, leadership development, human development, LGBT studies, multicultural education, women's studies, higher education, and research and assessment may be desirable.

LGBT program professional staff members must hold an earned graduate degree in a field relevant to the position they hold or must possess an appropriate combination of educational credentials and related work experience.

In addition to providing services, staff members should be provided time for advising and reporting, updating institutional information, research, faculty and staff contacts, staff meetings, training, supervision, personal and professional development, and consultation. Similarly, teaching, administration, research, and other responsibilities should be identified as relevant staff functions.

Staff members should have a combination of graduate course work, formal training (including gay/lesbian/ bisexual/ transgender issues), and supervised experience.

Degree or credential-seeking interns must be qualified by enrollment in an appropriate field of study and by relevant experience. These individuals must be trained and supervised adequately by professional staff members holding educational credentials and related work experience appropriate for supervision.

Student employees and volunteers must be carefully selected, trained, supervised, and evaluated. They must be trained on how and when to refer those in need of assistance to qualified staff members and have access to a supervisor for assistance in making these judgments. Student employees and volunteers must be provided clear and precise job descriptions, pre-service training based on assessed needs, and continuing staff development.

Student staff members should be provided with clear and precise job descriptions, pre-service training, and on-going staff development.

The LGBT program must have technical and support staff members adequate to accomplish its mission. Staff members must be technologically proficient and qualified to perform their job functions, be knowledgeable of ethical and legal uses of technology, and have access to training. The level of staffing and workloads must be adequate and appropriate for program and service demands.

Support staff should have a thorough knowledge of the institution and be able to perform office and administrative functions, including reception, information giving, problem identification, and referral. Special emphasis should be placed on skills in the areas of public relations, information dissemination, problem identification, and referral.

All LGBT staff members must be responsive to and knowledgeable about LGBT issues. Salary levels and fringe benefits for all LGBT program and services staff members must be commensurate with those for comparable positions within the institution, in similar institutions, and in the relevant geographic area.

The LGBT program must institute hiring and promotion practices that are fair, inclusive, and non-discriminatory. The program must employ a diverse staff to provide readily identifiable role models for students and to enrich the campus community. Further, the program must create and maintain position descriptions for all staff members and provide regular performance planning and appraisals.

The program must have a system for regular staff evaluation and must provide access to continuing education and professional development opportunities, including in-service training programs and participation in professional conferences and workshops.

Staff development is an essential activity. Additional credit courses, seminars, access to current research are examples of professional development activities that could be made available. Additionally, staff members should participate in appropriate professional organizations and should have the budgetary support to do so. Staff members should be encouraged to participate in community activities related to the student population being served.

Staff members must ensure that the confidentiality of students' sexual orientation and gender identity are protected when appropriate.

The level of services must be established and reviewed regularly with regard to service demands, enrollment, user surveys, diversity of services offered, institutional resources, and other student services available on the campus and in the local community. Staff members must be comfortable and interested in working with gay, lesbian, bisexual and transgender students.

## Part 6. FINANCIAL RESOURCES

The lesbian, gay, bisexual, transgender (LGBT) Program must have adequate funding to accomplish its mission and goals. Funding priorities must be determined within the context of the stated mission, goals, objectives and comprehensive analysis of the needs and capabilities of students and the availability of internal or external resources.

The LGBT program must demonstrate fiscal responsibility and cost effectiveness consistent with institutional protocols.

Funding for LGBT programs and devices may come from a composite of institutional funds, grant money, student government funds, and government contracts.

## Part 7. FACILITIES, TECHNOLOGY, EQUIPMENT

The lesbian, gay, bisexual, transgender (LGBT) Program must have adequate, suitably located facilities, adequate technology, and equipment to support its mission and goals efficiently and effectively. Facilities, technology, and equipment must be evaluated regularly and be in compliance with relevant federal, state, provincial, and local requirements to provide for access, health, safety, and security.

The LGBT program should maintain a physical and social environment that facilitates appropriate attention to safety factors. In addition, it should provide confidential individual and group meeting space and should have access to resources for research including access to private computer space.

## Part 8. LEGAL RESPONSIBILITIES

Lesbian, gay, bisexual, transgender (LGBT) program staff members must be knowledgeable about and responsive to laws and regulations that relate to their respective responsibilities. Staff members must inform users of LGBT programs and services and officials, as appropriate, of legal obligations and limitations including constitutional, statutory, regulatory, and case law; mandatory laws and orders emanating from federal, state/provincial and local governments; and the institution's policies.

LGBT staff members must use reasonable and informed practices to limit the liability exposure of the institution, its officers, employees, and agents. Staff members must be informed about

221

institutional policies regarding personal liability and related insurance coverage options.

The institution must provide access to legal advice for LGBT program staff members as needed to carry out assigned responsibilities and must inform staff and students in a timely and systematic fashion about extraordinary or changing legal obligations and potential liabilities.

## Part 9.  EQUITY and ACCESS

Lesbian, gay, bisexual, transgender (LGBT) program staff members must ensure that facilities and services are provided on a fair and equitable basis and must be accessible to all who seek them. Hours of operation and delivery of and access to services must be responsive to the needs of all students and other constituents.  The program must adhere to the spirit and intent of equal opportunity laws.

The LGBT must be open and readily accessible to all students and must not discriminate except where sanctioned by law and institutional policy. Discrimination must especially be avoided on the bases of age; color, creed; cultural heritage; disability; ethnicity; gender identity; nationality; political affiliation, religious affiliation, sex, sexual orientation; or economic, marital, social, or veteran status.

Consistent with its mission and goals, the LGBT program must take affirmative action to remedy significant imbalances in student participation and staffing patterns.

As the demographic profiles of campuses change and new instructional delivery methods are introduced, institutions must recognize the needs of students who participate in distance learning for access to programs and services offered on campus. Institutions must provide appropriate services in ways that are accessible to distance learners and assist them in identifying and gaining access to other appropriate services in their geographic region.

## Part 10. CAMPUS and EXTERNAL RELATIONS

The LGBT program must establish, maintain, and promote effective relations with relevant individuals, campus offices, and external agencies.
The success of the LGBT programs and services is dependent on the maintenance of good relationships with students, faculty, administrators, alumni, the community at large, contractors, and support agencies.
The program should collaborate with campus referral agencies for LGBT students (e.g., multicultural student affairs, women's centers, special academic support units,

campus security, health centers, counseling centers, religious programs and career services).
The LGBT program should establish relationships with a wide range of student groups (e.g., LGBT student association, student government association, fraternities and sororities) to promote visibility and to serve as a resource.
LGBT programs and services should foster relationships with academic units (especially in LGBT studies, ethnic studies, women's studies, higher education, and college student personnel) and with campus professionals (e.g. student activities, athletics, commuter affairs, and residential life.)  Staff should be an integral part of appropriate campus networks to effectively participate in the establishment of institution-wide policy and practices, and to collaborate with other staff and faculty in providing services.
The program should establish effective relations with institutional legal counsel and legal staff of relevant professional organizations in order to effectively respond to pertinent legal issues and precedents, which underlie the delivery components.
Where adequate LGBT resources are not available on campus, the program should establish and maintain close working relationships with off-campus community LGBT counseling and support agencies.
An advisory board made up of students, faculty, staff, alumni, and community members may be established to advise, support, and guide the LGBT programs.

## Part 11. DIVERSITY

Within the context of each institution's unique mission, diversity enriches the community and enhances the collegiate experience for all; therefore, the lesbian, gay, bisexual, transgender (LGBT) program and its services must nurture environments where commonalties and differences among people are recognized and honored.

The LGBT program must promote educational experiences that are characterized by open and continuous communication that deepens understanding of one's own identity, culture, and heritage, and that of others.  LGBT programs and services must educate and promote respect about commonalties and differences in their historical and cultural contexts. The program must address the characteristics and needs of a diverse population when establishing and implementing policies and procedures.

## Part 12. ETHICS

All persons involved in the delivery of the lesbian, gay, bisexual, transgender (LGBT) program and its services must adhere to the highest principles of ethical behavior.  The LGBT program must develop or adopt and implement appropriate statements of ethical practice.  The program must publish these statements and ensure their periodic review by relevant constituencies.

LGBT program staff members must ensure that privacy and confidentiality are maintained with respect to all communications and records to the extent that such records are protected under the law and appropriate statements of ethical practice. Information contained in students' education records must not be disclosed without written consent except as allowed by relevant laws and institutional policies. Staff members must disclose to appropriate authorities information judged to be of an emergency nature, especially when the safety of the individual or others is involved, or when otherwise required by institutional policy or relevant law.

Staff members must ensure that the confidentiality of individuals' sexual orientation and gender identity are protected.

Information should be released only at the written request of a student who has full knowledge of the nature of the information that is being released and of the parties to whom it is being released. Instances of limited confidentiality should be clearly articulated. The decision to release information without consent should occur only after careful consideration and under the conditions described above.

All LGBT programs and services staff members must be aware of and comply with the provisions contained in the institution's human subjects research policy and in other relevant institutional policies addressing ethical practices and confidentiality of research data concerning individuals.

LGBT programs and services staff members must recognize and avoid personal conflict of interest or appearance thereof in their transactions with students and others.

LGBT staff members must strive to ensure the fair, objective, and impartial treatment of all persons with whom they deal. Likewise, staff members must never participate in, nor condone, any form of harassment that demeans persons or creates an intimidating, hostile, or offensive campus environment.

When handling institutional funds, all LGBT staff members must ensure that such funds are managed in accordance with established and responsible accounting procedures and the fiscal policies or processes of the institution.

LGBT staff members must perform their duties within the limits of their training, expertise, and competence. When these limits are exceeded, individuals in need of further assistance must be referred to persons possessing appropriate qualifications. Staff members must use suitable means to confront and otherwise hold accountable other staff members who exhibit unethical behavior. LGBT program staff members must maintain the highest principles of ethical behavior in the use of technology.

## Part 13. ASSESSMENT and EVALUATION
The lesbian, gay, bisexual, transgender (LGBT) program must conduct regular assessment and evaluations. The program must employ effective qualitative and quantitative methodologies as appropriate, to determine whether and to what degree the stated mission, goals, and student learning and development outcomes are being met. The process must use sufficient and sound assessment measures to ensure comprehensiveness. Data collected must include responses from students and other affected constituencies.

The LGBT program must evaluate periodically how well it complements and enhances the institution's stated mission and educational effectiveness. Results of these evaluations must be used in revising and improving programs and services and in recognizing staff performance.

Evaluation of the LGBT program's facilities, staff, programs, services, and governance must be continuous and implemented within the context of the program's mission.

Both internal and external on-going evaluations are encouraged as part of a thoughtful plan of continuous evaluation of the LGBT program's mission and goals. Periodic reports, statistically valid research, external; reviews, and studies exploring student needs and opinions should be utilized.

# The Role of Minority Student Programs and Services
## *CAS* Standards and Guidelines

Minority Student Programs and Services are crucial to the retention and graduation of diverse student populations in higher education. The expansion of the civil rights movement begun in the 1960s promoted increased sensitivity to multicultural backgrounds, expansion of financial aid programs, and awareness of changing ethnic and racial demographics. Consequently, nontraditional enrollments have increased and the need for minority student services has expanded.

Although minority students are enrolling at ever-increasing rates, minority retention continues to be a challenge. The American Association of State Colleges and Universities reported a six-year graduation rate for minority students that ranged from 27 to 57 percent. To retain and graduate minority students requires support above and beyond the traditional student services typically provided college students. Minority students need advocates for changing campus environments and for adapting existing policies and academic curricula to reflect a wide array of cultures. Historically, although minority students were required to meet institutional expectations, little or no consideration was given to the existence of deficiencies or shortcomings in college readiness that may have resulted from pre-college entrance experiences.

Although minority student programs and services vary in structure from institution to institution, most provide advocacy for minority students. Some programs organize services to address specific ethnic populations while others seek to serve all minority students collectively. On campuses where academic departments for ethnic studies exist, the minority student program typically coordinates services with the programs in these departments. The additional support provided by minority student programs creates a campus climate that allows minority students to function within their unique cultural frameworks, instead of being pressured to assimilate into the predominant Eurocentric culture common to most US college campuses.

Minority programming often includes academic support services, such as tutoring, study skills training, supplemental instruction, and referral to learning assistance resources; minority student orientation; faculty and peer mentoring programs; minority student organizations; campus-wide programs for awareness and education; programs to prevent racial incidents and for crisis intervention; individualized academic advising and personal counseling; encouragement and mentoring for students entering graduate and professional programs; and advocacy for financial aid and administrative policies intended to facilitate retention of minority students.

Strong minority student programs and services are essential to the retention and graduation of minority students, and to increasing diversity on college and university campuses. Clearly, institutions exhibit their commitment to providing quality education for minority students through the level of support they provide to minority student programs and services. The CAS Standards for Minority Student Programs provide a relevant and viable model for the development and maintenance of minority student programs and services.

### Recommended Resources

Council for Opportunity in Educational (COE), 1025 Vermont Ave. NW, Suite 900, Washington, DC 20005. (202) 347-2218; Fax (202) 347-0786. www.trioprograms.org

# MINORITY STUDENT PROGRAMS
## *CAS* STANDARDS and GUIDELINES

## Part 1. MISSION

**Minority student programs (MSP) must incorporate student learning and student development in its mission. MSP must enhance overall educational experiences. MSP must develop, record, disseminate, implement, and regularly review its mission and goals. Mission statements must be consistent with the mission and goals of the institution and with the standards in this document. MSP must operate as an integral part of the institution's overall mission.**

The provision of minority student programs and services should presuppose a strong campus sense of a common community, serving all its citizens fairly and marked in the main by . . .

- access to, rather than exclusion from, academic, social, and recreational groups and activities
- shared goals
- intentional social intercourse, rather than passive social isolation or active social exclusion
- integration rather than segregation

**On those campuses with MSP, the program must promote the academic and personal growth and development of the various minority students served.**

**To accomplish this mission, the goals of the program must be to . . .**
- **assess the needs of minority students in selected areas, set priorities among those needs, and respond to the extent that the number of students, facilities, and resources permit**
- **orient minority students to the culture of the institution**
- **assist minority students to determine and assess their educational goals and academic skills**
- **provide support services to help minority students achieve educational goals and attain or refine academic skills necessary to perform adequately in the classroom**
- **promote the intellectual, career, social, and moral development of the students**
- **promote and deepen each minority student's understanding of his or her own culture and heritage**
- **promote and deepen majority students' understanding of their unique cultures and heritages**
- **provide training in leadership skills and other personal and social skills for minority students and those seeking to assist them**

- **offer or identify appropriate minority mentors and role models**

**In addition, the MSP must provide educational efforts for both majority and minority students that focus on . . .**
- **awareness of cultural differences**
- **self-assessment of cultural awareness and possible prejudices**
- **changing prejudicial attitudes or behaviors**

MSP may include efforts supplementary to other institutional functional areas such as recruitment, placement, academic advising, counseling, and alumni relations. Staff members in MSP should coordinate their efforts with academic units and other student affairs areas.

It is important not to look upon MSP as the only organized agency to meet the needs of minority students. All institutional units should be responsible for meeting the needs of minority students in their areas of responsibility.

Coordinated efforts to promote multicultural sensitivity and the elimination of prejudicial behaviors should be made at every institution by all functional areas.

## Part 2. PROGRAM

**The formal education of students consists of the curriculum and the co-curriculum, and must promote student learning and development that is purposeful and holistic. Minority student programs (MSP) must identify relevant and desirable student learning and development outcomes and provide programs and services that encourage the achievement of those outcomes.**

**Relevant and desirable outcomes include: intellectual growth, effective communication, realistic self-appraisal, enhanced self-esteem, clarified values, career choices, leadership development, healthy behaviors, meaningful interpersonal relationships, independence, collaboration, social responsibility, satisfying and productive lifestyles, appreciation of diversity, spiritual awareness, and achievement of personal and educational goals.**

**MSP must provide evidence of its impact on the achievement of student learning and development outcomes.**

The program may use the examples that follow or identify other more germane indicators.

**Student Learning & Development Outcome Domains**

## Intellectual Growth

Examples of Achievement Indicators

Produces personal and educational goal statements; Employs critical thinking in problem solving; Uses complex information from a variety of sources including personal experience and observation to form a decision or opinion; Obtains a degree; Applies previously understood information and concepts to a new situation or setting; Expresses appreciation for literature, the fine arts, mathematics, sciences, and social sciences

## Effective Communication

Examples of Achievement Indicators

Writes and speaks coherently and effectively; Writes and speaks after reflection; Able to influence others through writing, speaking or artistic expression; Effectively articulates abstract ideas; Uses appropriate syntax; Makes presentations or gives performances

## Enhanced Self-Esteem

Examples of Achievement Indicators

Shows self-respect and respect for others; Initiates actions toward achievement of goals; Takes reasonable risks; Demonstrates assertive behavior; Functions without need for constant reassurance from others

## Realistic Self-Appraisal

Examples of Achievement Indicators

Articulates personal skills and abilities; Makes decisions and acts in congruence with personal values; Acknowledges personal strengths and weaknesses; Articulates rationale for personal behavior; Seeks feedback from others; Learns from past experiences

## Clarified Values

Examples of Achievement Indicators

Articulates personal values; Acts in congruence with personal values; Makes decisions that reflect personal values; Demonstrates willingness to scrutinize personal beliefs and values; Identifies personal, work and lifestyle values and explains how they influence decision-making

## Career Choices

Examples of Achievement Indicators

Articulate career choices based on assessment of interests, values, skills and abilities; Documents knowledge, skills and accomplishments resulting from formal education, work experience, community service and volunteer experiences; Makes the connections between classroom and out-of-classroom learning; Can construct a resume with clear job objectives and evidence of related knowledge, skills and accomplishments; Articulates the characteristics of a preferred work environment; Comprehends the world of work; Takes steps to initiate a job search or seek advanced education

## Leadership Development

Examples of Achievement Indicators

Articulates leadership philosophy or style; Serves in a leadership position in a student organization; Comprehends the dynamics of a group; Exhibits democratic principles as a leader; Exhibits ability to visualize a group purpose and desired outcomes

## Healthy Behavior

Examples of Achievement Indicators

Chooses behaviors and environments that promote health and reduce risk; Articulate the relationship between health and wellness and accomplishing life long goals; Exhibits behaviors that advance a healthy community

## Meaningful Interpersonal Relationships

Examples of Achievement Indicators

Develops and maintains satisfying interpersonal relationships; Establishes mutually rewarding relationships with friends and colleagues; Listens to and considers others' points of view; Treats others with respect

## Independence

Examples of Achievement Indicators

Exhibits self-reliant behaviors; Functions autonomously; Exhibits ability to function interdependently; Accepts supervision as needed; Manages time effectively

## Collaboration

Examples of Achievement Indicators

Works cooperatively with others; Seeks the involvement of others; Seeks feedback from others; Contributes to achievement of a group goal; Exhibits effective listening skills

## Social Responsibility

Examples of Achievement Indicators

Understands and participates in relevant governance systems; Understands, abides by, and participates in the development, maintenance, and/or orderly change of community, social, and legal standards or norms; Appropriately challenges the unfair, unjust, or uncivil behavior of other individuals or groups; Participates in service/volunteer activities

## Satisfying and Productive Lifestyles

Examples of Achievement Indicators

Achieves balance between education, work and leisure time; Articulates and meets goals for work, leisure and education; Overcomes obstacles that hamper goal achievement; Functions on the basis of personal identity, ethical, spiritual and moral values; Articulates long-term goals and objectives

## Appreciating Diversity

Examples of Achievement Indicators

Understands ones own identity and culture. Seeks involvement with people different from oneself; Seeks involvement in diverse interests; Articulate the advantages and challenges of a diverse society; Challenges appropriately abusive use of stereotypes by others; Understands the impact of diversity on one's own society

## Spiritual Awareness

Examples of Achievement Indicators
Develops and articulates personal belief system; Understands roles of spirituality in personal and group values and behaviors

## Personal and Educational Goals
Examples of Achievement Indicators
Sets, articulates, and pursues individual goals; Articulate personal and educational goals and objectives; Uses personal and educational goals to guide decisions; Understands the effect of one's personal and education goals on others

**MSP must be (a) intentional, (b) coherent, (c) based on theories and knowledge of learning and human development, (d) reflective of developmental and demographic profiles of the student population, and (e) responsive to needs of individuals, special populations, and communities.**

## MSP components must include . . .
- **Assessment of the educational goals, academic skills, personal developmental levels, and social, recreational, and cultural needs of minority students**

Assessments may be carried out in many ways. Survey instruments, interviews, behavioral tests, observations, or some combination of these methods may be appropriate in a given institution.

- **Educational programs to enhance the knowledge, understanding, and skills necessary for academic success**

Educational programming should complement students' academic interests and be based upon assessment of students and demands of the institution's educational programs. It may be provided in collaboration with efforts by academic units and other support service offices.

- **Educational programs to enhance the knowledge, understanding, and skills necessary for personal development**

Activities that attempt to promote student's career, social, recreational, and moral development should be based upon assessments and should reflect unique dimensions of the minority student experience.
Social and recreational programs should enhance the knowledge, understanding, and skills necessary for social success, the productive use of leisure time, and the development of satisfying interpersonal relationships.
Recreational programs should be designed to promote physical health, leisure time enjoyment, and psychological well-being of students.
For both social skills and recreational programs, proper emphasis should be placed on any unique needs or cultural expressions of social relationships and recreational activities.

- **Educational programs to enhance the knowledge, understanding, and skills necessary for the**

**exercise of leadership**
Leadership programs should be designed to help individuals understand the components and styles of leadership.

- **Supplemental orientation programming to enhance knowledge and understanding of the purposes of the institution, its values, and predictable ways of behaving**

This program should help students assess the degree of congruence between their educational goals and skills and the culture of the institution. It also should emphasize institutional programs and services available to help students achieve the knowledge, understanding, and skills necessary to perform adequately, both in and out of the classroom.

- **Programming to enhance the knowledge and understanding of individual student's unique culture and heritage**

These programs should explore both the heritage and current expressions of the student's culture.
Various dimensions of the student's culture, such as history, philosophy, world view, literature, and various forms of artistic expression, should be explored.

- **Human relations programming to explore awareness of cultural differences, self-assessment of possible prejudices, and the facilitation of desired behavioral changes**

Human relations programs should be designed to assist both majority and minority students, faculty, and staff to develop more tolerance, understanding, and ability to relate to others.

- **Advocacy within the institution for minority student life experiences and organizations**

Tacit or overt prejudices or discriminations against minority students should be challenged.
Sometimes institutions espouse one point of view but practice knowingly or unknowingly another. If the practical effects of policies are prejudicial, then staff members should bring these facts to the attention of the proper authorities in the institution.
Impediments to the growth and development of minority students or full participation of minorities within the institution should be identified and addressed.

- **Advising of groups and individual students**

Advising services may include but are not limited to . . .
- monitoring scholastic standing of groups and individual students and recommending programs for improvement
- providing workshops, programs, retreats, and seminars on relevant topics and encouraging attendance at activities and services sponsored by other campus offices
- encouraging attendance at conferences, meetings, and programs
- advising formal groups such as editorial staffs of minority publications, fraternal groups, pre-professional clubs, and program councils

- providing assistance and advice in planning of minority student celebrations (e.g., Hispanic Week or Black History Month)
- assisting minority student groups or individuals in identifying and gaining access, where appropriate, to institutional services such as printing, bulk mailing, and computer services
- providing a directory of minority faculty and staff
- publishing a newsletter focusing on current events, leadership opportunities, and other relevant information

## Part 3. LEADERSHIP

Effective and ethical leadership is essential to the success of all organizations. Institutions must appoint, position, and empower minority student program (MSP) leaders within the administrative structure to accomplish stated missions. MSP leaders at various levels must be selected on the basis of formal education and training, relevant work experience, personal skills and competencies, relevant professional credentials, as well as potential for promoting learning and development in students, applying effective practices to educational processes, and enhancing institutional effectiveness. Institutions must determine expectations of accountability for leaders and fairly assess their performance.

Leaders of MSP must exercise authority over resources for which they are responsible to achieve their respective missions and must . . .

- articulate a vision for their organization
- set goals and objectives based on the needs and capabilities of the population served
- promote student learning and development
- prescribe and practice ethical behavior
- recruit, select, supervise, and develop others in the organization
- manage financial resources
- coordinate human resources
- plan, budget for, and evaluate personnel and programs
- apply effective practices to educational and administrative processes
- communicate effectively
- initiate collaborative interaction between individuals and agencies that possess legitimate concerns and interests in the functional area

MSP leaders must identify and find means to address individual, organizational, or environmental conditions that inhibit goal achievement. Leaders must promote campus environments that result in multiple opportunities for student learning and development.

MSP leaders must continuously improve programs and services in response to changing needs of students and other constituents, and evolving institutional priorities.

## Part 4. ORGANIZATION and MANAGEMENT

Guided by an overarching intent to ensure student learning and development, minority student programs (MSP) must be structured purposefully and managed effectively to achieve stated goals. Evidence of appropriate structure must include current and accessible policies and procedures, written performance expectations for all employees, functional workflow graphics or organizational charts, and clearly stated service delivery expectations.

Evidence of effective management must include use of comprehensive and accurate information for decisions, clear sources and channels of authority, effective communication practices, decision-making and conflict resolution procedures, responsiveness to changing conditions, accountability and evaluation systems, and recognition and reward processes. MSP must provide channels within the organization for regular review of administrative policies and procedures.

Many models exist for organizing MSP. The size and philosophy of the institution usually determine its organization. It is recommended that MSP be organized within the division of student affairs.

## Part 5. HUMAN RESOURCES

Minority student programs (MSP) must be staffed adequately by individuals qualified to accomplish its mission and goals. Within established guidelines of the institution, MSP must establish procedures for staff selection, training, and evaluation; set expectations for supervision, and provide appropriate professional development opportunities. MSP must strive to improve the professional competence and skills of all personnel it employs.

MSP professional staff members must hold an earned graduate degree in a field relevant to the position they hold or must possess an appropriate combination of educational credentials and related work experience.

Professional staff should be competent in career planning and development, group facilitation, leadership training and development, workshop design, social-interpersonal development, and individual and group counseling. Generally, these competencies are found in persons who graduate from graduate level college student affairs, higher education administration, or counseling programs. Specific coursework in organizational development, counseling theory and practice, group dynamics, leadership development, human development, and research and evaluation is desirable.

**Degree or credential-seeking interns must be qualified by enrollment in an appropriate field of study and by relevant experience. These individuals must be trained and supervised adequately by professional staff members holding educational credentials and related work experience appropriate for supervision.**

The use of graduate assistants and interns should be encouraged. Such assistants expand staff abilities, provide peer role models, and give valuable pre-professional experience. Particular attention should be given to preparing all pre-professional assistants to be especially sensitive to cultural differences and the special needs of minority students.

**Student employees and volunteers must be carefully selected, trained, supervised, and evaluated. They must be trained on how and when to refer those in need of assistance to qualified staff members and have access to a supervisor for assistance in making these judgments. Student employees and volunteers must be provided clear and precise job descriptions, pre-service training based on assessed needs, and continuing staff development.**

Student employees and volunteers from minority groups should be utilized and assigned responsibilities that are within their scope of competence. These paraprofessional helpers should be selected carefully, trained to do their assigned jobs, and regularly supervised by the professional staff members.

**MSP must have technical and support staff members adequate to accomplish its mission. Staff members must be technologically proficient and qualified to perform their job functions, be knowledgeable of ethical and legal uses of technology, and have access to training. The level of staffing and workloads must be adequate and appropriate for program and service demands.**

**Salary levels and fringe benefits for all MSP staff members must be commensurate with those for comparable positions within the institution, in similar institutions, and in the relevant geographic area.**

**MSP must institute hiring and promotion practices that are fair, inclusive, and non-discriminatory. Programs and services must employ a diverse staff to provide readily identifiable role models for students and to enrich the campus community.**

It is important that representatives of the various cultures involved be included on the professional staff.

**MSP must create and maintain position descriptions for all staff members and provide regular performance planning and appraisals.**

**MSP must have a system for regular staff evaluation and must provide access to continuing education and professional development opportunities, including in-service training programs and participation in professional conferences and workshops.**

## Part 6. FINANCIAL RESOURCES

**Minority student programs (MSP) must have adequate funding to accomplish its mission and goals. Funding priorities must be determined within the context of the stated mission, goals, objectives, and comprehensive analysis of the needs and capabilities of students and the availability of internal or external resources.**

**MSP must demonstrate fiscal responsibility and cost effectiveness consistent with institutional protocols.**

It is common in many institutions for some of the activities offered by MSP to be funded by grant resources. In these cases, the institution should make appropriate efforts to transfer funding from grants to the regular institutional budget when the programs have demonstrated effectiveness and efficiency, and are judged to be valuable.

## Part 7. FACILITIES, TECHNOLOGY, EQUIPMENT

**Minority student programs (MSP) must have adequate, suitably located facilities, adequate technology, and equipment to support its mission and goals efficiently and effectively. Facilities, technology, and equipment must be evaluated regularly and be in compliance with relevant federal, state, provincial, and local requirements to provide for access, health, safety, and security.**

Adequate space should be provided for a resource library, private individual consultations, group workshops, and work areas for support staff. Many of the activities offered by minority student programs and services require the same level of privacy as individual and group counseling. It is important, therefore, that the physical facilities be adequate for these purposes.

## Part 8. LEGAL RESPONSIBILITIES

**Minority student programs (MSP) staff members must be knowledgeable about and responsive to laws and regulations that relate to their respective responsibilities. MSP staff members must inform users of programs and services and officials, as**

appropriate, of legal obligations and limitations including constitutional, statutory, regulatory, and case law; mandatory laws and orders emanating from federal, state/provincial and local governments; and the institution's policies.

MSP staff members must use reasonable and informed practices to limit the liability exposure of the institution, its officers, employees, and agents. Staff members must be informed about institutional policies regarding personal liability and related insurance coverage options.

The institution must provide access to legal advice for MSP staff members as needed to carry out assigned responsibilities.

The institution must inform MSP staff and students in a timely and systematic fashion about extraordinary or changing legal obligations and potential liabilities.

## Part 9. EQUITY and ACCESS

Minority student programs (MSP) staff members must ensure that services and programs are provided on a fair and equitable basis. Facilities, programs and services must be accessible. Hours of operation and delivery of and access to programs and services must be responsive to the needs of all students and other constituents. MSP must adhere to the spirit and intent of equal opportunity laws.

The MSP must be open and readily accessible to all students and must not discriminate except where sanctioned by law and institutional policy. Discrimination must especially be avoided on the bases of age; color, creed; cultural heritage; disability; ethnicity; gender identity; nationality; political affiliation, religious affiliation, sex, sexual orientation; or economic, marital, social, or veteran status.

Consistent with their mission and goals, MSP must take affirmative action to remedy significant imbalances in student participation and staffing patterns.

As the demographic profiles of campuses change and new instructional delivery methods are introduced, institutions must recognize the needs of students who participate in distance learning for access to programs and services offered on campus. ☐Institutions must provide appropriate services in ways that are accessible to distance learners and assist them in identifying and gaining

access to other appropriate services in their geographic region.

## Part 10. CAMPUS and EXTERNAL RELATIONS

Minority student programs and services must establish, maintain, and promote effective relations with relevant individuals, campus offices, and external agencies.

Professional staff members must coordinate, or where appropriate, collaborate with faculty and other staff in providing services and programs for minority students.

Coordination and collaboration are important in order to minimize isolation of MSP and maximize the use of faculty and other staff resources in meeting the needs of minority students.

## Part 11. DIVERSITY

Within the context of each institution's unique mission, diversity enriches the community and enhances the collegiate experience for all; therefore, the minority student program (MSP) must nurture environments where commonalties and differences among people are recognized and honored.

MSP must promote educational experiences that are characterized by open and continuous communication that deepens understanding of one's own identity, culture, and heritage, and that of others. MSP must educate and promote respect about commonalties and differences in their historical and cultural contexts.

MSP must address the characteristics and needs of a diverse population when establishing and implementing policies and procedures.

## Part 12. ETHICS

All persons involved in the delivery of minority student programs (MSP) must adhere to the highest principles of ethical behavior. MSP must develop or adopt and implement appropriate statements of ethical practice. MSP must publish these statements and ensure their periodic review by relevant constituencies.

MSP staff members must ensure that privacy and confidentiality are maintained with respect to all communications and records to the extent that such records are protected under the law and appropriate statements of ethical practice. Information contained in students' education records must not be disclosed without written consent except as allowed by relevant laws and institutional policies. Staff members must disclose to appropriate authorities information judged to be of an emergency nature, especially when the safety of the individual or others is involved, or when otherwise required by institutional policy or relevant law.

All MSP staff members must be aware of and comply with the provisions contained in the institution's human subjects research policy and in other relevant institutional policies addressing ethical practices and confidentiality of research data concerning individuals.

MSP staff members must recognize and avoid personal conflict of interest or appearance thereof in their transactions with students and others.

MSP staff members must strive to insure the fair, objective, and impartial treatment of all persons with whom they deal. Staff members must not participate in nor condone any form of harassment that demeans persons or creates an intimidating, hostile, or offensive campus environment.

When handling institutional funds, all MSP staff members must ensure that such funds are managed in accordance with established and responsible accounting procedures and the fiscal policies or processes of the institution.

MSP staff members must perform their duties within the limits of their training, expertise, and competence. When these limits are exceeded, individuals in need of further assistance must be referred to persons possessing appropriate qualifications.

MSP staff members must use suitable means to confront and otherwise hold accountable other staff members who exhibit unethical behavior. Staff members must be knowledgeable about and practice ethical behavior in the use of technology.

MSP professional staff members must be knowledge-able about the research and practice in areas appropriate to their programming with minority students. Further, professional staff members must respond in some manner to formal requests by students for personal recommendations.

Recommendations made by minority student program staff members should reflect only the professional contacts and observations they have personally experienced with the students. The use of pejorative stereotypical statements should be carefully avoided.

Professional staff members should not initiate formal employment recommendations without the knowledge and consent of the student involved.

Professional staff members should inform students if they cannot make positive recommendations.

## Part 13. ASSESSMENT and EVALUATION

Minority student programs (MSP) must conduct regular assessment and evaluations. MSP must employ effective qualitative and quantitative methodologies as appropriate, to determine whether and to what degree the stated mission, goals, and student learning and development outcomes are being met. The process must employ sufficient and sound assessment measures to ensure comprehensiveness. Data collected must include responses from students and other affected constituencies.

Formative and summative evaluations are especially important when the development or operation of a program or service is funded by grants or other "soft" moneys. Accountability to granting agencies and data generated to support transfer of programs to the general budget both require careful evaluation.

General evaluation of the minority student programs and services should be conducted on a regularly scheduled basis. Evaluation data should be solicited from current minority students and alumni who have used the programs or services.

MSP must evaluate periodically how well they complement and enhance the institution's stated mission and educational effectiveness.

Periodic evaluation should be implemented for both developing and established programs.

Results of these evaluations must be used in revising and improving programs and services and in recognizing staff performance.

# THE ROLE of ORIENTATION PROGRAMS for Students
## *CAS* Standards Contextual Statement

To understand current trends in student orientation it is helpful to view today's practice within an historical context. The history of orientation programs in the United States is virtually as old as the history of the country's higher education. Harvard College was the first to formalize a system by which experienced students assisted new students in their transition to the institution. In addition to a personalized support system, students also experienced certain rites of passage which, from today's perspective, would likely be considered hazing. Clearly the system was flawed, but it was the beginning of the formalization of orientation as a process that includes support of students as they make the transition to the higher education.

Later in the 19th century, Harvard institutionalized faculty-student contact by assigning faculty members educational and administrative responsibilities outside the classroom. One of these responsibilities was the orientation of new students. Soon other colleges were taking an interest in those problems specific to freshman students.

Increases in the number and diversity of college students in the mid-1900s posed issues that many institutions had not previously considered. Today's orientation programs have responded to these demographics, recognizing that women, people of color, and nontraditional students have clearly changed institutional agendas across the nation. These programs have evolved from simply providing individualized faculty attention to focusing on a multitude of important issues while responding to the needs of an increasingly diverse student population.

Today, most orientation programs seek to provide a clear and cogent introduction to an institution's academic community. Orientation is viewed by most as an important tool for improving student retention. Many institutions have included academic advising in their orientation programs as an impetus for active participation. Many institutions are implementing continuing orientation programs via a freshman orientation course. Because of such changes, colleges and universities are taking steps to encourage student and parent attendance by formalizing and marketing orientation programs from a clearly academic perspective.

The most important change that has occurred in orientation programs in the last decade is that orientation is now viewed as a comprehensive process rather than as a simplistic program. Schools across the country are developing on-going orientation programs that truly address the transitional needs of students.

What trends will guide future approaches to student orientation? It is clear that retention will continue to be a major force in the development of orientation programs. Likewise, attempts to foster an environment responsive to the individual needs of students will also continue to have a profound effect on orientation programming. Very likely, funding for orientation programs will continue to be an issue of concern. Demographic changes in institutions of higher education and in the society at large will require institutional and programmatic accommodations. Simply maintaining current orientation programs by reacting to change will satisfy neither students, parents, or other constituents nor institutional leaders and the public in the years to come. New and creative programs must be assessed, planned, and ultimately implemented if the personal and educational needs of new and transfer students and their families are to be met.

The CAS Student Orientation Programs and Services Standards and Guidelines that follow have utility for institutions of all types and size and provide criteria to judge the quality and appropriateness of student orientation programs.

## References, Readings, and Resources

*National Orientation Directors Journal.* University of North Texas, P.O. Box 30538 Denton, Texas 76203

National Orientation Directors Data Bank. University of Maryland at College Park College Park, Md. 20742

National Orientation Directors Association Resource Web Site. http://www.nodaweb.org

# ORIENTATION PROGRAMS for STUDENTS
## CAS STANDARDS and GUIDELINES

## Part 1: MISSION

Student orientation programs (SOP) must incorporate student learning and student development in its mission. SOP must enhance overall educational experiences. SOP must develop, record, disseminate, implement and regularly review its mission and goals. Mission statements must be consistent with the mission and goals of the institution and with the standards in this document. SOP must operate as an integral part of the institution's overall mission.

The mission of the SOP must include . . .

• facilitating the transition of new students into the institution
• preparing new students for the institution's educational opportunities
• initiating the integration of new students into the intellectual, cultural, and social climate of the institution

## Part 2. PROGRAM

The formal education of students consists of the curriculum and the co-curriculum, and must promote student learning and development that is purposeful and holistic. Student orientation programs (SOP) must identify relevant and desirable student learning and development outcomes and provide programs and services that encourage the achievement of those outcomes.

Relevant and desirable outcomes include: intellectual growth, effective communication, realistic self-appraisal, enhanced self-esteem, clarified values, career choices, leadership development, healthy behaviors, meaningful interpersonal relationships, independence, collaboration, social responsibility, satisfying and productive lifestyles, appreciation of diversity, spiritual awareness, and achievement of personal and educational goals.

SOP must provide evidence of its impact on the achievement of student learning and development outcomes.

The program may use the examples that follow or identify other more germane indicators.

**Student Learning & Development**
**Outcome Domains**

### Intellectual Growth
Examples of Achievement Indicators
Produces personal and educational goal statements; Employs critical thinking in problem solving; Uses complex information from a variety of sources including personal experience and observation to form a decision or opinion; Obtains a degree; Applies previously understood information and concepts to a new situation or setting; Expresses appreciation for literature, the fine arts, mathematics, sciences, and social sciences

### Effective Communication
Examples of Achievement Indicators
Writes and speaks coherently and effectively; Writes and speaks after reflection; Able to influence others through writing, speaking or artistic expression; Effectively articulates abstract ideas; Uses appropriate syntax; Makes presentations or gives performances

### Enhanced Self-Esteem
Examples of Achievement Indicators
Shows self-respect and respect for others; Initiates actions toward achievement of goals; Takes reasonable risks; Demonstrates assertive behavior; Functions without need for constant reassurance from others

### Realistic Self-Appraisal
Examples of Achievement Indicators
Articulates personal skills and abilities; Makes decisions and acts in congruence with personal values; Acknowledges personal strengths and weaknesses; Articulates rationale for personal behavior; Seeks feedback from others; Learns from past experiences

### Clarified Values
Examples of Achievement Indicators
Articulates personal values; Acts in congruence with personal values; Makes decisions that reflect personal values; Demonstrates willingness to scrutinize personal beliefs and values; Identifies personal, work and lifestyle values and explains how they influence decision-making

### Career Choices
Examples of Achievement Indicators
Articulate career choices based on assessment of interests, values, skills and abilities; Documents knowledge, skills and accomplishments resulting from formal education, work experience, community service and volunteer experiences; Makes the connections between classroom and out-of-classroom learning; Can construct a resume with clear job objectives and evidence of related knowledge, skills and accomplishments; Articulates the characteristics of a preferred work environment; Comprehends the world of work; Takes steps to initiate a job search or seek advanced education

## Leadership Development

Examples of Achievement Indicators

Articulates leadership philosophy or style; Serves in a leadership position in a student organization; Comprehends the dynamics of a group; Exhibits democratic principles as a leader; Exhibits ability to visualize a group purpose and desired outcomes

## Healthy Behavior

Examples of Achievement Indicators

Chooses behaviors and environments that promote health and reduce risk; Articulate the relationship between health and wellness and accomplishing life long goals; Exhibits behaviors that advance a healthy community

## Meaningful Interpersonal Relationships

Examples of Achievement Indicators

Develops and maintains satisfying interpersonal relationships; Establishes mutually rewarding relationships with friends and colleagues; Listens to and considers others' points of view; Treats others with respect

## Independence

Examples of Achievement Indicators

Exhibits self-reliant behaviors; Functions autonomously; Exhibits ability to function interdependently; Accepts supervision as needed; Manages time effectively

## Collaboration

Examples of Achievement Indicators

Works cooperatively with others; Seeks the involvement of others; Seeks feedback from others; Contributes to achievement of a group goal; Exhibits effective listening skills

## Social Responsibility

Examples of Achievement Indicators

Understands and participates in relevant governance systems; Understands, abides by, and participates in the development, maintenance, and/or orderly change of community, social, and legal standards or norms; Appropriately challenges the unfair, unjust, or uncivil behavior of other individuals or groups; Participates in service/volunteer activities

## Satisfying and Productive Lifestyles

Examples of Achievement Indicators

Achieves balance between education, work and leisure time; Articulates and meets goals for work, leisure and education; Overcomes obstacles that hamper goal achievement; Functions on the basis of personal identity, ethical, spiritual and moral values; Articulates long-term goals and objectives

## Appreciating Diversity

Examples of Achievement Indicators

Understands ones own identity and culture. Seeks involvement with people different from oneself; Seeks involvement in diverse interests; Articulate the advantages and challenges of a diverse society; Challenges appropriately abusive use of stereotypes by others; Understands the impact of diversity on one's own society

## Spiritual Awareness

Examples of Achievement Indicators

Develops and articulates personal belief system; Understands roles of spirituality in personal and group values and behaviors

## Personal and Educational Goals

Examples of Achievement Indicators

Sets, articulates, and pursues individual goals; Articulate personal and educational goals and objectives; Uses personal and educational goals to guide decisions; Understands the effect of one's personal and education goals on others

**SOP must be (a) intentional, (b) coherent, (c) based on theories and knowledge of learning and human development, (d) reflective of developmental and demographic profiles of the student population, and (e) responsive to needs of individuals, special populations, and communities.**

Orientation is an ongoing process that begins when a student decides to attend a particular institution. The process should aid students in understanding the nature and purpose of the institution, their membership in the academic community, and their relationship to the intellectual, cultural, and social climate of the institution. The orientation process should include pre-enrollment, entry, and post-matriculation activities. Components may include credit and non-credit courses, comprehensive mailings, electronic communications, and campus visitations and may be administered through multiple institutional offices.

## The student orientation program must . . .

### • be based on stated goals and objectives

A comprehensive orientation program should be based on clearly defined and delineated goals and objectives that include service to both the student and the institution.

### • be coordinated with the relevant programs and activities of other institutional units

### • be available to all students new to the institution

First-year, transfer, and entering graduate students should be served as distinct population groups with specific attention given to the special needs of sub-groups (e.g., students with disabilities, athletes, adult learners, traditionally under-represented students, honor students, and international students).

- **assist new students in understanding the purposes of higher education and the mission of the institution**

New students should have a clear understanding of the overall purpose of higher education and how this general purpose translates to the institution they are attending. The roles, responsibilities, and expectations of faculty, staff, and students should be included.

- **assist new students in understanding their responsibilities within the educational setting**

The student orientation program should set forth the institution's expectations of students (e.g., scholarship, integrity, conduct, financial obligations, ethical use of technology) and should provide information that clearly identifies relevant administrative policies and procedures.

- **provide new students with information about academic policies, procedures, requirements, and programs sufficient to make well-reasoned and well- informed choices**

Class scheduling and registration processes should be explained and assistance should be provided by qualified faculty, staff, or peer academic advisors for developing educational plans.

- **inform new students about the availability of services and programs**

The student orientation program should identify appropriate referral resources (e.g., counselors and advisors) and provide information about relevant services and programs.

- **assist new students in becoming familiar with the campus and local environment**

The student orientation program should provide information about the physical layout of the campus, including the location and purposes of academic facilities, support services, co-curricular venues, and administrative offices. Information about personal health, safety and security should also be included.

- **provide intentional opportunities for new students to interact with faculty, staff, and continuing students**

The student orientation program should design and facilitate opportunities for new students to discuss their expectations and perceptions of the campus and to clarify their educational goals.

- **provide new students with information and opportunities for self-assessment**

Assist students in the selection of appropriate courses and course levels making use of placement examinations, career interest inventories, and study skills evaluations.

- **provide relevant orientation information and activities to the new students' primary support**

groups (e.g., parents, guardians, spouses, children)

## Part 3. LEADERSHIP

Effective and ethical leadership is essential to the success of all organizations. Institutions must appoint, position, and empower student orientation program (SOP) leaders within the administrative structure to accomplish stated missions. SOP leaders at various levels must be selected on the basis of formal education and training, relevant work experience, personal skills and competencies, relevant professional credentials, as well as potential for promoting learning and development in students, applying effective practices to educational processes, and enhancing institutional effectiveness. Institutions must determine expectations of accountability for leaders and fairly assess their performance.

Leaders of SOP must exercise authority over resources for which they are responsible to achieve their respective missions.

Program leaders must . . .
- articulate a vision for their organization
- set goals and objectives based on the needs and capabilities of the population served
- promote student learning and development
- prescribe and practice ethical behavior
- recruit, select, supervise, and develop others in the organization
- manage financial resources
- coordinate human resources
- plan, budget for, and evaluate personnel and programs
- apply effective practices to educational and administrative processes
- communicate effectively
- initiate collaborative interaction between individuals and agencies that possess legitimate concerns and interests in the functional area

SOP leaders must identify and find means to address individual, organizational, or environmental conditions that inhibit goal achievement. Leaders must promote campus environments that result in multiple opportunities for student learning and development.

SOP leaders must continuously improve programs and services in response to changing needs of students and other constituents, and evolving institutional priorities.

## Part 4. ORGANIZATION and MANAGEMENT

Guided by an overarching intent to ensure student learning and development, the student orientation program (SOP) must be structured purposefully and managed effectively to achieve stated goals. Evidence of appropriate structure must include current and accessible policies and procedures, written performance expectations for all employees, functional workflow graphics or organizational charts, and clearly stated service delivery expectations.

Evidence of effective management must include use of comprehensive and accurate information for decisions, clear sources and channels of authority, effective communication practices, decision-making and conflict resolution procedures, responsiveness to changing conditions, accountability and evaluation systems, and recognition and reward processes. SOP must provide channels within the organization for regular review of administrative policies and procedures.

All institutional offices involved in program delivery should be involved in the review. Coordination of the program should occur even though a number of offices may be involved in the delivery of structured activities. The size, nature, and complexity of the institution should guide the administrative scope and structure of SOP.

## Part 5. HUMAN RESOURCES

The student orientation program (SOP) must be staffed adequately by individuals qualified to accomplish its mission and goals. Within established guidelines of the institution, SOP must establish procedures for staff selection, training, and evaluation; set expectations for supervision, and provide appropriate professional development opportunities. SOP must strive to improve the professional competence and skills of all personnel it employs.

Faculty involvement in the development and delivery of SOP is essential to its success. Faculty members should be included as part of the overall staffing pattern.

Professional staff members must hold an earned graduate degree in a field relevant to the position they hold or must possess an appropriate combination of educational credentials and related work experience.

Degree or credential-seeking interns must be qualified by enrollment in an appropriate field of study and by relevant experience. These individuals must be trained and supervised adequately by professional staff members holding educational credentials and related work experience appropriate for supervision.

Student employees and volunteers must be carefully selected, trained, supervised, and evaluated. They must be trained on how and when to refer those in need of assistance to qualified staff members and have access to a supervisor for assistance in making these judgments. Student employees and volunteers must be provided clear and precise job descriptions, pre-service training based on assessed needs, and continuing staff development.

SOP must have technical and support staff members adequate to accomplish its mission. Staff members must be technologically proficient and qualified to perform their job functions, be knowledgeable of ethical and legal uses of technology, and have access to training. The level of staffing and workloads must be adequate and appropriate for program and service demands.

Salary levels and fringe benefits for all SOP staff members must be commensurate with those for comparable positions within the institution, in similar institutions, and in the relevant geographic area.

SOP must institute hiring and promotion practices that are fair, inclusive, and non-discriminatory. Programs and services must employ a diverse staff to provide readily identifiable role models for students and to enrich the campus community.

SAOP must create and maintain position descriptions for all staff members and provide regular performance planning and appraisals.

SOP must have a system for regular staff evaluation and must provide access to continuing education and professional development opportunities, including in-service training programs and participation in professional conferences and workshops.

## Part 6. FINANCIAL RESOURCES

Student orientation programs (SOP) must have adequate funding to accomplish its mission and goals. Funding priorities must be determined within the context of the stated mission, goals, objectives and comprehensive analysis of the needs and capabilities of students and the availability of internal or external resources.

**SOP must demonstrate fiscal responsibility and cost effectiveness consistent with institutional protocols.**

Money to underwrite expenses for SOP should be allocated on a permanent basis. In additional to institutional funding through general funds, other funding sources may be considered, including state appropriations, student fees, user fees, donations, contributions, fines, concession and store sales, rentals, and dues.

Overnight programs may require students and their families to stay on campus. Although recovering room and board costs directly from participants is an acceptable practice, SOP should be designed so as to impose as little financial burden on students and their families as possible.

## Part 7. FACILITIES, TECHNOLOGY, EQUIPMENT

**Student orientation programs (SOP) must have adequate, suitably located facilities, adequate technology, and equipment to support its mission and goals efficiently and effectively. Facilities, technology, and equipment must be evaluated regularly and be in compliance with relevant federal, state, provincial, and local requirements to provide for access, health, safety, and security.**

Cooperation from within the campus community is necessary to provide appropriate facilities. Whenever possible, a single office location to house personnel and provide adequate work space should be conveniently located and suitable for its high interaction with the public.

## Part 8. LEGAL RESPONSIBILITIES

**Student orientation programs (SOP) staff members must be knowledgeable about and responsive to laws and regulations that relate to their respective responsibilities. Staff members must inform users of programs and services and officials, as appropriate, of legal obligations and limitations including constitutional, statutory, regulatory, and case law; mandatory laws and orders emanating from federal, state/provincial and local governments; and the institution's policies.**

**SOP staff members must use reasonable and informed practices to limit the liability exposure of the institution, its officers, employees, and agents. Staff members must be informed about institutional policies regarding personal liability and related insurance coverage options.**

**The institution must provide access to legal advice for SOP staff members as needed to carry out assigned responsibilities.**

**The institution must inform SOP staff and students in a timely and systematic fashion about extraordinary or changing legal obligations and potential liabilities.**

## Part 9. EQUITY and ACCESS

**Student orientation program (SOP) staff members must ensure that services and programs are provided on a fair and equitable basis. Facilities, programs and services must be accessible. Hours of operation and delivery of and access to programs and services must be responsive to the needs of all students and other constituents. SOP must adhere to the spirit and intent of equal opportunity laws.**

**The SOP must be open and readily accessible to all students and must not discriminate except where sanctioned by law and institutional policy. Discrimination must especially be avoided on the bases of age; color, creed; cultural heritage; disability; ethnicity; gender identity; nationality; political affiliation, religious affiliation, sex, sexual orientation; or economic, marital, social, or veteran status.**

**Consistent with their mission and goals, SOP must take affirmative action to remedy significant imbalances in student participation and staffing patterns.**

**As the demographic profiles of campuses change and new instructional delivery methods are introduced, institutions must recognize the needs of students who participate in distance learning for access to programs and services offered on campus. □Institutions must provide appropriate services in ways that are accessible to distance learners and assist them in identifying and gaining access to other appropriate services in their geographic region.**

## Part 10. CAMPUS and EXTERNAL RELATIONS

**Student orientation programs (SOP) must establish, maintain, and promote effective relations with relevant individuals, campus offices, and external agencies.**

SOP should be an institution-wide process that systematically involves student affairs, academic affairs, and other administrative units, such as campus police, physical plant, and the business office.

SOP should disseminate information relating to other programs and services on campus. These services should, in turn, provide the media and human resources necessary to accomplish the transmission of information.

## Part 11. DIVERSITY

Within the context of each institution's unique mission, diversity enriches the community and enhances the collegiate experience for all; therefore, student orientation programs (SOP) must nurture environments where commonalties and differences among people are recognized and honored.

SOP must promote educational experiences that are characterized by open and continuous communication that deepens understanding of one's own identity, culture, and heritage, and that of others. SOP must educate and promote respect about commonalties and differences in their historical and cultural contexts.

SOP must address the characteristics and needs of a diverse population when establishing and implementing policies and procedures.

## Part 12. ETHICS

All persons involved in the delivery of student orientation programs (SOP) must adhere to the highest principles of ethical behavior. SOP must develop or adopt and implement appropriate statements of ethical practice. SOP must publish these statements and ensure their periodic review by relevant constituencies .

Ethical standards of relevant professional associations should be considered.

Program staff members must ensure that privacy and confidentiality are maintained with respect to all communications and records to the extent that such records are protected under the law and appropriate statements of ethical practice. Information contained in students' education records must not be disclosed without written consent except as allowed by relevant laws and institutional policies. Staff members must disclose to appropriate authorities information judged to be of an emergency nature, especially when the safety of the individual or others is involved, or when otherwise required by institutional policy or relevant law.

All staff members must be aware of and comply with the provisions contained in the institution's human subjects research policy and in other relevant institutional policies addressing ethical practices and confidentiality of research data concerning individuals.

SOP staff members must recognize and avoid personal conflict of interest or appearance thereof in their transactions with students and others. Staff members must strive to insure the fair, objective, and impartial treatment of all persons with whom they deal. Staff members must not participate in nor condone any form of harassment that demeans persons or creates an intimidating, hostile, or offensive campus environment.

When handling institutional funds, all SOP staff members must ensure that such funds are managed in accordance with established and responsible accounting procedures and the fiscal policies or processes of the institution.

SOP staff members must perform their duties within the limits of their training, expertise, and competence. When these limits are exceeded, individuals in need of further assistance must be referred to persons possessing appropriate qualifications.

SOP staff members must use suitable means to confront and otherwise hold accountable other staff members who exhibit unethical behavior and must be knowledgeable about and practice ethical behavior in the use of technology.

## Part 13. ASSESSMENT and EVALUATION

The student orientation program (SOP) must conduct regular assessment and evaluations. SOP must employ effective qualitative and quantitative methodologies as appropriate, to determine whether and to what degree the stated mission, goals, and student learning and development outcomes are being met. The process must employ sufficient and sound assessment measures to ensure comprehensiveness. Data collected must include responses from students and other affected constituencies.

SOP must evaluate periodically how well they complement and enhance the institution's stated mission and educational effectiveness.

Results of these evaluations must be used in revising and improving programs and services and in recognizing staff performance.

Evaluation of student and institutional needs, goals, objectives, and the effectiveness of the student orientation program should occur on a periodic basis. A representative cross-section of appropriate people from the campus community should be involved in reviews of the student orientation program.

# The ROLE of OUTCOMES ASSESSMENT and PROGRAM EVALUATION
## *CAS* Standards Contextual Statement

As early as 1899, William Rainey Harper, visionary President of the University of Chicago, called on colleges and universities to adopt a program of research with the college student as the subject. "In order that the student may receive the assistance so essential to his highest success, another step in the onward evolution will take place. This step will be the scientific study of the student himself; . . . provision must be made, either by the regular instructors or by those appointed for the purpose, to study in detail the men and women to whom instruction is offered" (quoted in Rentz, 1996, p. 38). The original Student Personnel Point of View (SPPV, 1937/1994), which responded to Harper's challenge, called for "studies designed to evaluate and improve . . . [the] functions and services" (p. 70) of the student affairs division. Later in the document, four specific kinds of studies were called for: student out-of-class life and its importance to the educational mission, faculty-student out-of-class relationships, financial aid to students, and follow-up study of college students to ascertain the effects of college on careers and personal adjustment.

The 1949 revision of the SPPV again stated that an adequate student affairs program *should* include "a continuing program of evaluation of student personnel services and of the educational program to insure the achievement by students of the objectives for which this program is designed" (SPPV, 1949/1994, p. 118). Wrenn (1951) in one of the pioneering texts in the field, proposed a guide for evaluating the effectiveness of student affairs programs. One of the""standards" in his evaluation reads: "carrying on research designed to evaluate and improve personnel functions and services" (p. 557).

These fundamental documents clearly mandate that institutions, primarily through student affairs divisions, have responsibility for systematic, continuing outcomes assessment and program evaluation. Yet, as Williamson and Biggs (1975) noted, while most agree about the importance of conducting research on students and programs, few student affairs divisions have considered it a vital part of their operations. A prominent exception to this caveat was Williamson's creation of the Student Life Studies Bureau, under the leadership of Ralph Berdie, in 1965, at the University of Minnesota.

Upcraft and Schuh (1996) identified five reasons why student affairs divisions can no longer ignore the necessity to assess student needs and evaluate programs and services. *First*, there is a widespread impression among important publics that higher education is not delivering on its promise to produce "educated persons." Consequently, there is an increased demand for accountability by governing boards, tax payers, parents, and legislative bodies."*Second*, there is rising dissatisfaction with steady increases in the cost of higher education. *Third*, there are questions about the quality of education, including instruction and programs and services available to students. *Fourth*, there is a discrepancy between the success rates of traditionally underrepresented groups and those of middle-class white students. Members of underrepresented groups want to know why. *Fifth*, regional accrediting agencies now require institutions to provide evidence that they are achieving the goals and objectives to which they aspire.

Adequate assessment programs should employ both qualitative and quantitative research methods and should include at least the following elements . . .

- Tracking of student use of services, programs, and facilities and determining their satisfaction with what is provided
- Assessing student needs and wants
- Assessing environments and their influences on student behavior
- Assessing student cultures and their influence on behavior
- Assessing individual and collective outcomes of programs and services
- Assessing developmental impact of individual programs and the total collegiate experience

Student affairs divisions currently beginning to implement programs to assess student outcomes and evaluate effects of programs should not be discouraged because of the enormity of the undertaking. The important thing is to begin, to be systematic, to use sound research methods, and to expand and improve operations incrementally. The standards and guidelines that follow provide a basis for such action

## References, Readings, and Resources

Beeler, K. J., & Hunter, D. E. (Eds.). (1991). *Puzzles and pieces in wonderland: The promise and practice of student affairs research.* Washington, DC: National Association of Student Personnel Administrators.

Erwin, T. D., & Sivo, S. A. (2001). Assessing student learning and development in student affairs: A nuts and bolts introduction. In R. B. Winston, Jr., D. G. Creamer, T. K. MIller, & Associates. *The professional student affairs administrator: Educator, leader, and manager. Philadelphia::* Taylor and Francis.

Pascarella, E. T., & Terenzini, P. T. (1991). *How college affects students: Findings and insights from twenty years of research.* San Francisco: Jossey-Bass.

Rentz, A. L. (1996). A history of student affairs. In A. L. Rentz (Ed.), *Student affairs practice in higher education* (2nd ed., pp. 28-55). Springfield, IL: Thomas.

Schuh, J. H., Upcraft, M. L., & Associates (2001) *Assessment practice in student affairs: An applications manual.* San Francisco: Jossey-Bass.

Stage, F. K. (Ed.). (1992). *Diverse methods for research and assessment of college students.* Washington, DC: American College Personnel Association.

*Student Personnel Point of View.* (1937/1994). In A. L. Rentz (Ed.),

*Student affairs: A profession's heritage* (2nd ed., pp. 66-78). Washington, DC: American College Personnel Association.

*Student Personnel Point of View.* (1949/1994). In A. L. Rentz (Ed.),

*Student affairs: A profession's heritage* (2nd ed., pp. 108-123). Washington, DC: American College Personnel Association.

Upcraft, M.L., & Schuh, J.H. (1996). *Assessment in student affairs: A guide for practitioners.* San Francisco: Jossey-Bass.

Upcraft, M. L., & Schuh, J. H. (1996). *Assessment in student affairs: A guide for practitioners.* San Francisco: Jossey-Bass.

Williamson, E. G., & Biggs, D. A. (1975). *Student personnel work: A program of developmental relationships.* New York: John Wiley & Sons.

Winston, R. B., Jr., & Miller, T. K. (1994). A model for assessing developmental outcomes related to student affairs programs and services. *NASPA Journal, 32,* 2-19.

Wrenn, C. G. (1951). *Student personnel work in college.* New York: Ronald Press.

# OUTCOMES ASSESSMENT and PROGRAM EVALUATION SERVICES
## *CAS* STANDARDS  and  GUIDELINES

## Part 1.  MISSION

Outcomes assessment and program evaluation service (OAPES) must incorporate student learning and student development in its mission. OAPES must enhance overall educational experiences. OAPES must develop, record, disseminate, implement and regularly review its mission and goals. Mission statements must be consistent with the mission and goals of the institution and with the standards in this document. OAPES must operate as an integral part of the institution's overall mission.

OAPES efforts must strive to improve student services and development programs, to expand the knowledge base about student development and student services work in general, and to assess the organizational effectiveness of student services. Most institutions do not have a separate student affairs assessment agency.  In such institutions the chief student affairs officer must be the advocate for student affairs assessment and program evaluation and must collaborate with, and otherwise provide support to, the institutional assessment efforts so as to accomplish the program.  More specifically, the OAPES must . . .

- describe students in terms of demographics, developmental characteristics, and personal behavior
- conduct periodic needs assessments for use in the design of programs
- study, or use available information about developmental changes of college students
- assess whether student services programs are consistent with and achieve their stated objectives
- assess in terms of behavior changes in students
- study the extent to which students are satisfied with their educational experiences

Student services professionals are responsible for translating a diverse set of service functions into an integrated series of programs and activities designed to encourage students' growth and development. The degree to which these programs and activities are necessary and successful should be measured through periodic assessment of both programs and students. Equally important is the responsibility for continually expanding the knowledge base about the relationship between student development theory and student services practices. The OAPES should seek to provide assessment and evaluation support for all institutional student support service programs. Further,

the assessment and evaluation program should strive to increase the institution's knowledge base about its student clientele.

## Part 2.  PROGRAM

The formal education of students consists of the curriculum and the co-curriculum, and must promote student learning and development that is purposeful and holistic. Outcomes assessment and program evaluation service (OAPES) must identify relevant and desirable student learning and development outcomes and provide programs and services that encourage the achievement of those outcomes.

Relevant and desirable outcomes include: intellectual growth, effective communication, realistic self-appraisal, enhanced self-esteem, clarified values, career choices, leadership development,  healthy behaviors, meaningful interpersonal relationships, independence, collaboration, social responsibility, satisfying and productive lifestyles, appreciation of diversity, spiritual awareness, and achievement of personal and educational goals.

OAPES must provide evidence of its impact on the achievement of student learning and development outcomes.

The program may use the examples that follow or identify other more germane indicators.

### Student Learning & Development Outcome Domains

### Intellectual Growth

Examples of Achievement Indicators

Produces personal and educational goal statements; Employs critical thinking in problem solving; Uses complex information from a variety of sources including personal experience and observation to form a decision or opinion; Obtains a degree; Applies previously understood information and concepts to a new situation or setting; Expresses appreciation for literature, the fine arts, mathematics, sciences, and social sciences

### Effective Communication

Examples of Achievement Indicators

Writes and speaks coherently and effectively;  Writes and speaks after reflection; Able to influence others through writing, speaking or artistic expression; Effectively articulates abstract ideas; Uses appropriate syntax; Makes presentations or gives performances

## Enhanced Self-Esteem

Examples of Achievement Indicators

Shows self-respect and respect for others; Initiates actions toward achievement of goals; Takes reasonable risks; Demonstrates assertive behavior; Functions without need for constant reassurance from others

## Realistic Self-Appraisal

Examples of Achievement Indicators

Articulates personal skills and abilities; Makes decisions and acts in congruence with personal values; Acknowledges personal strengths and weaknesses; Articulates rationale for personal behavior; Seeks feedback from others; Learns from past experiences

## Clarified Values

Examples of Achievement Indicators

Articulates personal values; Acts in congruence with personal values; Makes decisions that reflect personal values; Demonstrates willingness to scrutinize personal beliefs and values; Identifies personal, work and lifestyle values and explains how they influence decision-making

## Career Choices

Examples of Achievement Indicators

Articulate career choices based on assessment of interests, values, skills and abilities; Documents knowledge, skills and accomplishments resulting from formal education, work experience, community service and volunteer experiences; Makes the connections between classroom and out-of-classroom learning; Can construct a resume with clear job objectives and evidence of related knowledge, skills and accomplishments; Articulates the characteristics of a preferred work environment; Comprehends the world of work; Takes steps to initiate a job search or seek advanced education

## Leadership Development

Examples of Achievement Indicators

Articulates leadership philosophy or style; Serves in a leadership position in a student organization; Comprehends the dynamics of a group; Exhibits democratic principles as a leader; Exhibits ability to visualize a group purpose and desired outcomes

## Healthy Behavior

Examples of Achievement Indicators

Chooses behaviors and environments that promote health and reduce risk; Articulate the relationship between health and wellness and accomplishing life long goals; Exhibits behaviors that advance a healthy community

## Meaningful Interpersonal Relationships

Examples of Achievement Indicators

Develops and maintains satisfying interpersonal relationships; Establishes mutually rewarding relationships with friends and colleagues; Listens to and considers others' points of view; Treats others with respect

## Independence

Examples of Achievement Indicators

Exhibits self-reliant behaviors; Functions autonomously; Exhibits ability to function interdependently; Accepts supervision as needed; Manages time effectively

## Collaboration

Examples of Achievement Indicators

Works cooperatively with others; Seeks the involvement of others; Seeks feedback from others; Contributes to achievement of a group goal; Exhibits effective listening skills

## Social Responsibility

Examples of Achievement Indicators

Understands and participates in relevant governance systems; Understands, abides by, and participates in the development, maintenance, and/or orderly change of community, social, and legal standards or norms; Appropriately challenges the unfair, unjust, or uncivil behavior of other individuals or groups; Participates in service/volunteer activities

## Satisfying and Productive Lifestyles

Examples of Achievement Indicators

Achieves balance between education, work and leisure time; Articulates and meets goals for work, leisure and education; Overcomes obstacles that hamper goal achievement; Functions on the basis of personal identity, ethical, spiritual and moral values; Articulates long-term goals and objectives

## Appreciating Diversity

Examples of Achievement Indicators

Understands ones own identity and culture. Seeks involvement with people different from oneself; Seeks involvement in diverse interests; Articulate the advantages and challenges of a diverse society; Challenges appropriately abusive use of stereotypes by others; Understands the impact of diversity on one's own society

## Spiritual Awareness

Examples of Achievement Indicators

Develops and articulates personal belief system; Understands roles of spirituality in personal and group values and behaviors

## Personal and Educational Goals

Examples of Achievement Indicators

Sets, articulates, and pursues individual goals; Articulate personal and educational goals and objectives; Uses personal and educational goals to guide decisions; Understands the effect of one's personal and education goals on others

**OAPES must be (a) intentional, (b) coherent, (c) based on theories and knowledge of learning and human development, (d) reflective of developmental and demographic profiles of the**

student population, and (e) responsive to needs of individuals, special populations, and communities.

However organized, OAPES must include studies of students and their development and studies of student services program effectiveness. Furthermore, results of these studies must be disseminated throughout the institution.

Activities of OAPES should include . . .

- collecting and analyzing student data beginning with pre-enrollment characteristics of first year students and continuing through follow-up studies of former students
- planning, coordinating or conducting periodic studies of the characteristics of students and various student sub-groups
- students may be described in terms of their intellectual, emotional, social, moral, spiritual, and physical development and behavior; such data should be continually collected, updated, and disseminated
- regularly coordinating or conducting student needs assessments to guide program development
- analyzing data indicating trends in student behavior satisfaction retention, and attitudes in terms of the institution's purposes and interpreting the implications of these trends for institutional policies and practices
- assisting in collaborative assessments and planning of programs, activities, and services in the student services/ development division
- collecting and analyzing data to be used for making decisions about the continuation, modification, or termination of student services programs
- assessing on a systematic basis the professional contributions of staff members and providing feedback appropriate to professional development
- coordinating, conducting, or collaborating in accountability and cost effectiveness studies of student services/ development programs
- acting as a resource to faculty and staff regarding assessment and evaluation efforts
- regularly disseminating information about assessment and evaluation findings to concerned members of the campus community
- where appropriate, guiding and evaluating research efforts conducted by students

## Part 3. LEADERSHIP

Effective and ethical leadership is essential to the success of all organizations. Institutions must appoint, position and empower outcomes assessment and program evaluation service (OAPES) leaders within the administrative structure to accomplish stated missions. Leaders at various levels must be selected on the basis of formal education and training, relevant work experience, personal skills and competencies, relevant professional credentials, as well as potential for promoting learning and development

in students, applying effective practices to educational processes, and enhancing institutional effectiveness. Institutions must determine expectations of accountability for OAPES leaders and fairly assess their performance.

OAPES leaders must exercise authority over resources for which they are responsible to achieve their respective missions.

Leaders must . . .

- articulate a vision for their organization
- set goals and objectives based on the needs and capabilities of the population served
- promote student learning and development
- prescribe and practice ethical behavior
- recruit, select, supervise, and develop others in the organization
- manage financial resources
- coordinate human resources
- plan, budget for, and evaluate personnel and programs
- apply effective practices to educational and administrative processes
- communicate effectively
- initiate collaborative interaction between individuals and agencies that possess legitimate concerns and interests in the functional area

OAPES leaders must identify and find means to address individual, organizational, or environmental conditions that inhibit goal achievement. Leaders must promote campus environments that result in multiple opportunities for student learning and development and must continuously improve programs and services in response to changing needs of students and other constituents, and evolving institutional priorities.

## Part 4. ORGANIZATION and MANAGEMENT

Guided by an overarching intent to ensure student learning and development, outcomes assessment and program evaluation services (OAPES) must be structured purposefully and managed effectively to achieve stated goals. Evidence of appropriate structure must include current and accessible policies and procedures, written performance expectations for all employees, functional workflow graphics or organizational charts, and clearly stated service delivery expectations.

Evidence of effective management must include use of comprehensive and accurate information for decisions, clear sources and channels of authority, effective communication practices, decision-making and conflict resolution procedures, responsiveness to changing conditions, accountability and evaluation systems, and recognition and reward processes. OAPES must provide channels within the organization for regular review of administrative policies and procedures.

Because outcomes assessment and program evaluation efforts are conducted on most campuses in cooperation with other institutional research and evaluation efforts, the chief student affairs officer must be central to the establishment of specific objectives for student services research and evaluation.

Assessment and evaluation objectives should result from a collaborative effort between the chief student affairs officer, those responsible for the various student services programs and others responsible for institutional research evaluation efforts.

## Part 5. HUMAN RESOURCES

Outcomes assessment and program evaluation services (OAPES)) must be staffed adequately by individuals qualified to accomplish its mission and goals. Within established guidelines of the institution, OAPES must establish procedures for staff selection, training, and evaluation; set expectations for supervision, and provide appropriate professional development opportunities. OAPES must strive to improve the professional competence and skills of all personnel it employs.

Professional staff members must hold an earned graduate degree in a field relevant to the position they hold or must possess an appropriate combination of educational credentials and related work experience.

Degree or credential-seeking interns must be qualified by enrollment in an appropriate field of study and by relevant experience. These individuals must be trained and supervised adequately by professional staff members holding educational credentials and related work experience appropriate for supervision.

Student employees and volunteers must be carefully selected, trained, supervised, and evaluated. They must be trained on how and when to refer those in need of assistance to qualified staff members and have access to a supervisor for assistance in making these judgments. Student employees and volunteers must be provided clear and precise job descriptions, pre-service training

based on assessed needs, and continuing staff development.

OAPES must have technical and support staff members adequate to accomplish its mission. Staff members must be technologically proficient and qualified to perform their job functions, be knowledgeable of ethical and legal uses of technology, and have access to training. The level of staffing and workloads must be adequate and appropriate for program and service demands.

Salary levels and fringe benefits for all staff members must be commensurate with those for comparable positions within the institution, in similar institutions, and in the relevant geographic area.

OAPES must institute hiring and promotion practices that are fair, inclusive, and non-discriminatory. Programs and services must employ a diverse staff to provide readily identifiable role models for students and to enrich the campus community.

The program must create and maintain position descriptions for all staff members and provide regular performance planning and appraisals.

OAPES must have a system for regular staff evaluation and must provide access to continuing education and professional development opportunities, including in-service training programs and participation in professional conferences and workshops.

Within the institution, a qualified professional staff person must be designated to coordinate the outcomes assessment and program evaluation efforts and must work closely with or be responsible to the chief student affairs or academic affairs officer.

The number of staff members assigned to the assessment and evaluation effort will be a function of the size, complexity and purpose of the institution. Institutions unable to assign a full-time professional staff member should devote a portion of their research and evaluation program's resources to this effort.

Staff assigned responsibility for the assessment and evaluation effort should possess effective communication and consultation skills and have an appropriate combination of coursework, training, and experience in the following areas: statistics, research design, assessment, computer literacy, program planning and implementation strategies, human development theory, student subgroup cultures, and student affairs programs. When research staff lack adequate knowledge in any of these critical areas, they should seek expertise from appropriate campus officials.

## Part 6. FINANCIAL RESOURCES

The outcomes assessment and program evaluation service (OAPES) must have adequate funding to accomplish its mission and goals. Funding priorities must be determined within the context of the stated mission, goals, objectives and comprehensive analysis of the needs and capabilities of students and the availability of internal or external resources.

The services must demonstrate fiscal responsibility and cost effectiveness consistent with institutional protocols.

## Part 7. FACILITIES, TECHNOLOGY, and EQUIPMENT

Outcomes assessment and program evaluation services (OAPES) must have adequate, suitably located facilities, adequate technology, and equipment to support its mission and goals efficiently and effectively. Facilities, technology, and equipment must be evaluated regularly and be in compliance with relevant federal, state, provincial, and local requirements to provide for access, health, safety, and security.

It is important that the OAPES have secure storage facilities, computer support, sufficient work space, and ready access to appropriate institutional records. Financial resources should be sufficient to support research mailings and data collection, data entry and analysis and printing and distribution of research findings.

## Part 8. LEGAL RESPONSIBILITIES

Outcomes assessment and program evaluation services (OAPES) staff members must be knowledgeable about and responsive to laws and regulations that relate to their respective responsibilities. Staff members must inform users of programs and services and officials, as appropriate, of legal obligations and limitations including constitutional, statutory, regulatory, and case law; mandatory laws and orders emanating from federal, state/provincial and local governments; and the institution's policies.

Staff members must use reasonable and informed practices to limit the liability exposure of the institution, its officers, employees, and agents. Staff members must be informed about institutional policies regarding personal liability and related insurance coverage options.

The institution must provide access to legal advice for OAPES staff members as needed to carry out assigned responsibilities and must inform staff and students in a timely and systematic fashion about extraordinary or changing legal obligations and potential liabilities.

## Part 9. EQUITY and ACCESS

Outcomes assessment and program evaluation services (OAPES) staff members must ensure that services and programs are provided on a fair and equitable basis. Facilities, programs and services must be accessible. Hours of operation and delivery of and access to programs and services must be responsive to the needs of all students and other constituents. OAPES must adhere to the spirit and intent of equal opportunity laws.

The OAPES must be open and readily accessible to all students and must not discriminate except where sanctioned by law and institutional policy. Discrimination must especially be avoided on the bases of age; color, creed; cultural heritage; disability; ethnicity; gender identity; nationality; political affiliation, religious affiliation, sex, sexual orientation; or economic, marital, social, or veteran status. Consistent with its mission and goals, the program must take affirmative action to remedy significant imbalances in student participation and staffing patterns.

As the demographic profiles of campuses change and new instructional delivery methods are introduced, institutions must recognize the needs of students who participate in distance learning for access to programs and services offered on campus. □Institutions must provide appropriate services in ways that are accessible to distance learners and assist them in identifying and gaining access to other appropriate services in their geographic region.

## Part 10. CAMPUS and EXTERNAL RELATIONS

The outcomes assessment and program evaluation service (OAPES) must establish, maintain, and promote effective relations with relevant individuals, campus offices, and external agencies.

Regular and effective communication systems for the dissemination of results and procuring expertise are particularly important among the full range of academic and administrative offices, institutional governance bodies, and other appropriate constituencies.

## Part 11. DIVERSITY

Within the context of each institution's unique mission, diversity enriches the community and enhances the collegiate experience for all; therefore, outcomes assessment and program evaluation services (OAPES) must nurture environments where commonalties and differences among people are recognized and honored.

OAPES must promote educational experiences that are characterized by open and continuous communication that deepens understanding of one's own identity, culture, and heritage, and that of others. OAPES must educate and promote respect about commonalties and differences in their historical and cultural contexts.

The program must address the characteristics and needs of a diverse population when establishing and implementing policies and procedures.

## Part 12. ETHICS

All persons involved in the delivery of outcomes assessment and program evaluation services (OAPES) must adhere to the highest principles of ethical behavior. OAPES must develop or adopt and implement appropriate statements of ethical practice. OAPES must publish these statements and ensure their periodic review by relevant constituencies .

OAPES staff members must ensure that privacy and confidentiality are maintained with respect to all communications and records to the extent that such records are protected under the law and appropriate statements of ethical practice. Information contained in students' education records must not be disclosed without written consent except as allowed by relevant laws and institutional policies. Staff members must disclose to appropriate authorities information judged to be of an emergency nature, especially when the safety of the individual or others is involved, or when otherwise required by institutional policy or relevant law.

All staff members must be aware of and comply with the provisions contained in the institution's human subjects research policy and in other relevant institutional policies addressing ethical practices and confidentiality of research data concerning individuals. The privacy of study subjects and the confidential nature of data must not be breached.

Information on individuals should be purged regularly to protect the privacy of current and former students and other subjects.

OAPES staff members must recognize and avoid personal conflict of interest or appearance thereof in their transactions with students and others and must strive to ensure the fair, objective, and impartial treatment of all persons with whom they deal. Staff members must not participate in nor condone any form of harassment that demeans persons or creates an intimidating, hostile, or offensive campus environment.

When handling institutional funds, all OAPES staff members must ensure that such funds are managed in accordance with established and responsible accounting procedures and the fiscal policies or processes of the institution.

OAPES staff members must perform their duties within the limits of their training, expertise, and competence. When these limits are exceeded, individuals in need of further assistance must be referred to persons possessing appropriate qualifications.

Staff members must use suitable means to confront and otherwise hold accountable other staff members who exhibit unethical behavior and must be knowledgeable about and practice ethical behavior in the use of technology.

## Part 13. ASSESSMENT and EVALUATION

Outcomes assessment and program evaluation services (OAPES) must conduct regular assessment and evaluations. The program must employ effective qualitative and quantitative methodologies as appropriate, to determine whether and to what degree the stated mission, goals, and student learning and development outcomes are being met. The process must employ sufficient and sound assessment measures to ensure comprehensiveness. Data collected must include responses from students and other affected constituencies.

OAPES must evaluate periodically how well they complement and enhance the institution's stated mission and educational effectiveness.

Results of these evaluations must be used in revising and improving programs and services and in recognizing staff performance.

# THE ROLE OF RECREATIONAL SPORTS
## *CAS* Standards Contextual Statement

Recreational Sports programs are viewed as essential components of higher education, supplementing the educational process through enhancement of students' physical and mental development. Students who participate in recreational sports tend to develop positive self-images, awareness of strengths, increased tolerance and self-control, stronger social interaction skills, and maturity—all gleaned from recreational sports experiences. The field of recreational sports has grown into a dynamic, organized presence providing quality co-curricular opportunities for the majority of the student body.

The term "intramural" is derived from the Latin words "intra," meaning "within," and "muralis."

meaning "walls." Intramurals began in US colleges and universities during the 19th century as students developed leisure time sporting events. Throughout that century, intramural sports were almost exclusively the only form of athletic competition for college males. Originating from intramurals, interest in varsity athletics increased in popularity and the institutions assumed responsibility for organizing athletic events.

Until late in the 1800's, intramural sports were perceived by most to be of little instructional or educational value. Near the end of the century, however, colleges and universities began to administer intramural sports for men. In 1913, the first professional staff members were employed to direct intramural programs. Intramurals continued to grow in strength and gain support, until by the 1950's there was a general realization by institutional leaders of the intrinsic educational value of sports. Programs expanded and additional facilities were constructed in response to student-led initiatives, and campus facilities were established exclusively for recreational sports activities.

Over-time, intramural programs diversified and participation increased. The rise in popularity of aerobic exercise and a societal push toward greater gender equity in the workplace and on college campuses produced an influx of women into recreational sports, resulting in even higher levels of interest and participation. Consequently, the late 1980's witnessed a second period of rapid growth in programs and the advent of new and better campus facilities for physical activities.

As they evolved, recreational sports programs experienced changing perceptions about their institutional roles and the standards appropriate for their administration. The wide range of programming currently organized and managed by recreational sports personnel has resulted in a multiplicity of administrative structures. At a majority of institutions, recreational sports programs are placed under the administrative auspices of a division of student affairs. The National Intramural Recreational Sports Association (NIRSA) suggested that while organizational designs vary among institutions, the full realization for the contribution of recreational sports to any campus depends on institutional commitment to that endeavor.

NIRSA (1996) delineated seven primary goals of recreational sports programs . . .
1. To provide participation in a variety of activities that satisfy the diverse needs of students, faculty, and staff members and where appropriate guests, alumni, and public participants can become involved.
2. To provide value to participants by helping individuals develop and maintain a positive self-image, stronger social interactive skills, enhanced physical fitness, and good mental health.
3. To enhance college and university student and faculty recruitment and retention initiatives.
4. To coordinate the use of campus recreation facilities in cooperation with other administrative units such as athletics, physical education, and student activities.
5. To provide extracurricular education opportunities through participation in recreational sports and the provision of relevant leadership positions.
6. To contribute positively to institutional relations through significant and high-quality recreational sports programming.
7. To cooperate with academic units, focusing on the development of a recreational sports curricula and accompanying laboratory experiences.

Recreational sports programming significantly impacts student life, development and learning, as well as recruitment and retention. Hossler and Bean (1990, p.), in *The Strategic Management of College Enrollment,* wrote that "recreational sports (i.e., informal leisure time relaxation, games, intramurals) have been endorsed by institutions for their value in helping students maintain good physical health, enhancing their mental health by providing a respite from rigorous academic work, and teaching recreational skills with a carryover for leisure time exercise throughout life." Through participation in recreational sports, students are encouraged to develop critical thinking skills, create new problem-solving strategies, hone decision-making skills, enhance creativity, and more effectively synthesize and integrate this information into all aspects of their lives. In this way, students both perform more effectively in an academic environment and flourish throughout all phases of the co-curricular experience.

## References, Readings, and Resources

Hossler, D., Bean, P., & Associates. (1990). *The strategic management of college enrollment.* San Francisco: Jossey-Bass.

Mull, R.F., Bayless, K.G., & Ross, C.M. (1987). *Recreational sports programming.* North Palm Beach, FL: The Athletic Institute.

National Intramural Recreational Sports Association (1996). *General and Specialty Standards for collegiate recreational sports.* Corvallis, OR: Author.

*Recreational Sports & Fitness,* Executive Business Media Inc., Westbury, NY 11590.

National Intramural Recreational Sports Association, NIRSA National Center, 4185 SW Research Way, Corvallis, OR 97333-1067. (541) 766-8211; Fax (541) 766-8284.
e-mail: **nirsa@nirsa.org**
Web Page **www.nirsa.org**

# RECREATIONAL SPORTS
## CAS STANDARDS and GUIDELINES

## Part 1: MISSION

The recreational sports program (RSP) must incorporate student learning and student development in its mission. The program must enhance overall educational experiences. The RSP must develop, record, disseminate, implement and regularly review its mission and goals. Mission statements must be consistent with the mission and goals of the institution and with the standards in this document. The RSP must operate as an integral part of the institution's overall mission.

The mission of the RSP is to enhance students' fitness and wellness, knowledge, personal skills, and enjoyment by providing . . .
- **opportunities for a variety of activities that may contribute to individual physical fitness and wellness**
- **opportunities for cooperative and competitive play activity in the game form**
- **a medium through which students can learn and practice leadership, management, program planning and interpersonal skills**
- **access to quality facilities, equipment and programs**

To accomplish this mission recreational sports programs should:
- provide a variety of opportunities including informal programs (self-directed), intramural sports (structured), sports clubs (interest groups), instructional programs, special events, outdoor programs, fitness and wellness programs, extramural programs, family and youth programs and programs for people with disabilities
- coordinate effectively the scheduling of events and maintenance of campus sport facilities with other campus units
- provide extracurricular opportunities through participation and leadership roles designed to enhance social, psychological, and physiological development
- contribute positively to public relations efforts of the institution, including the recruitment and retention of students
- when appropriate, work in collaboration with academic units to help teach courses and facilitate laboratory experiences
- assist with the socialization of students into the campus environment

## Part 2. PROGRAM

The formal education of students consists of the curriculum and the co-curriculum, and must promote student learning and development that is purposeful and holistic. The recreational sports program (RSP) must identify relevant and desirable student learning and development outcomes and provide programs and services that encourage the achievement of those outcomes.

Relevant and desirable outcomes include: intellectual growth, effective communication, realistic self-appraisal, enhanced self-esteem, clarified values, career choices, leadership development, healthy behaviors, meaningful interpersonal relationships, independence, collaboration, social responsibility, satisfying and productive lifestyles, appreciation of diversity, spiritual awareness, and achievement of personal and educational goals.

The RSP must provide evidence of its impact on the achievement of student learning and development outcomes.

The program may use the examples that follow or identify other more germane indicators.

### Student Learning & Development Outcome Domains

#### Intellectual Growth
Examples of Achievement Indicators
Produces personal and educational goal statements; Employs critical thinking in problem solving; Uses complex information from a variety of sources including personal experience and observation to form a decision or opinion; Obtains a degree; Applies previously understood information and concepts to a new situation or setting; Expresses appreciation for literature, the fine arts, mathematics, sciences, and social sciences

#### Effective Communication
Examples of Achievement Indicators
Writes and speaks coherently and effectively; Writes and speaks after reflection; Able to influence others through writing, speaking or artistic expression; Effectively articulates abstract ideas; Uses appropriate syntax; Makes presentations or gives performances

#### Enhanced Self-Esteem
Examples of Achievement Indicators
Shows self-respect and respect for others; Initiates actions toward achievement of goals; Takes reasonable risks; Demonstrates assertive behavior; Functions without need for constant reassurance from others

#### Realistic Self-Appraisal
Examples of Achievement Indicators
Articulates personal skills and abilities; Makes decisions and acts in congruence with personal values; Acknowledges personal strengths and weaknesses; Articulates rationale for personal behavior; Seeks feedback from others; Learns from past experiences

## Clarified Values

Examples of Achievement Indicators

Articulates personal values; Acts in congruence with personal values; Makes decisions that reflect personal values; Demonstrates willingness to scrutinize personal beliefs and values; Identifies personal, work and lifestyle values and explains how they influence decision-making

## Career Choices

Examples of Achievement Indicators

Articulate career choices based on assessment of interests, values, skills and abilities; Documents knowledge, skills and accomplishments resulting from formal education, work experience, community service and volunteer experiences; Makes the connections between classroom and out-of-classroom learning; Can construct a resume with clear job objectives and evidence of related knowledge, skills and accomplishments; Articulates the characteristics of a preferred work environment; Comprehends the world of work; Takes steps to initiate a job search or seek advanced education

## Leadership Development

Examples of Achievement Indicators

Articulates leadership philosophy or style; Serves in a leadership position in a student organization; Comprehends the dynamics of a group; Exhibits democratic principles as a leader; Exhibits ability to visualize a group purpose and desired outcomes

## Healthy Behavior

Examples of Achievement Indicators

Chooses behaviors and environments that promote health and reduce risk; Articulate the relationship between health and wellness and accomplishing life long goals; Exhibits behaviors that advance a healthy community

## Meaningful Interpersonal Relationships

Examples of Achievement Indicators

Develops and maintains satisfying interpersonal relationships; Establishes mutually rewarding relationships with friends and colleagues; Listens to and considers others' points of view; Treats others with respect

## Independence

Examples of Achievement Indicators

Exhibits self-reliant behaviors; Functions autonomously; Exhibits ability to function interdependently; Accepts supervision as needed; Manages time effectively

## Collaboration

Examples of Achievement Indicators

Works cooperatively with others; Seeks the involvement of others; Seeks feedback from others; Contributes to achievement of a group goal; Exhibits effective listening skills

## Social Responsibility

Examples of Achievement Indicators

Understands and participates in relevant governance systems; Understands, abides by, and participates in the development, maintenance, and/or orderly change of community, social, and legal standards or norms; Appropriately challenges the unfair, unjust, or uncivil behavior of other individuals or groups; Participates in service/volunteer activities

## Satisfying and Productive Lifestyles

Examples of Achievement Indicators

Achieves balance between education, work and leisure time; Articulates and meets goals for work, leisure and education; Overcomes obstacles that hamper goal achievement; Functions on the basis of personal identity, ethical, spiritual and moral values; Articulates long-term goals and objectives

## Appreciating Diversity

Examples of Achievement Indicators

Understands ones own identity and culture. Seeks involvement with people different from oneself; Seeks involvement in diverse interests; Articulate the advantages and challenges of a diverse society; Challenges appropriately abusive use of stereotypes by others; Understands the impact of diversity on one's own society

## Spiritual Awareness

Examples of Achievement Indicators

Develops and articulates personal belief system; Understands roles of spirituality in personal and group values and behaviors

## Personal and Educational Goals

Examples of Achievement Indicators

Sets, articulates, and pursues individual goals; Articulate personal and educational goals and objectives; Uses personal and educational goals to guide decisions; Understands the effect of one's personal and education goals on others

**The RSP must be (a) intentional, (b) coherent, (c) based on theories and knowledge of learning and human development, (d) reflective of developmental and demographic profiles of the student population, and (e) responsive to special needs of individuals, special populations, and communities.**

**Recreational sports programs must reflect the needs and interests of students, faculty, staff, and other members of the campus community. The RSP must satisfy the particular needs of the campus by balancing team, dual, individual meet, and special event sport experiences.**

The overall recreational sports program should include . . .

- Informal programs to provide self-directed, individualized participation that accommodates the desire to participate in sport for fitness and enjoyment.
- Intramural sports to provide structured contests, meets, tournaments, and leagues limiting participation to the individuals within the institution. A variety of forms of tournaments should be available, including elimination, challenge, league, and meets. Equitable participation opportunities should be provided for men and women, and when appropriate, co-recreational activity should be offered. Opportunities to participate at various levels of ability should be made available to students (e.g., beginner, intermediate, and advanced).
- Sport clubs to provide opportunities for individuals to organize around a common interest. Opportunities should be available for a variety of interest focused on a sport within or outside the institution. Self-administered and self-regulated groups are normally coordinated and assisted by staff in such areas as governance, facilities, scheduling, safety, budgeting, and fund-raising through sport club coordination. Formation of clubs should be accomplished through appropriate and established channels.
- Instructional programs to provide learning opportunities, knowledge, and skills through lessons, clinics, and workshops. Depending on type, size, resources, and setting of the institution, the program may include extramural sports, outdoor recreation, fitness and wellness, and special events.
- Special events to introduce new sport or related activities that are unique in approach or nature from traditional programs. These events may be held within or outside the institution.
- Outdoor programs and activities to provide participants with opportunities to enjoy natural environments and experience new challenges.
- Fitness programs to provide opportunities and assistance in personal exercise programs. This voluntary program should motivate individuals to assess their levels of fitness and maintain a positive fitness lifestyle. Individual assessment should be available for participant feedback.
- Recreation and aquatic programs.
- Wellness programs to encourage achievement of one's full health potential. These programs should provide an opportunity to work cooperatively with professionals in health services including counselors and physicians and may be accomplished in concert with others who are similarly oriented.
- Extramural sports to provide structured tournaments, contests and meets among participants from other institutions. Champions from intramural sports are frequently chosen to represent the institution.
- Family and youth programs for members of the campus community. These activities may include special events, sports, games, instructional programs, fitness and wellness, and outdoor programs.
- Programs for people with disabilities to engage in activities designed to have a positive impact on mobility, socialization, independence, fitness, and community integration.

Program planning and implementation should include consideration of . . .
- proper facility coordination and scheduling
- rules and regulations that address participant safety
- an environment that minimizes the chance of injuries
- advice to groups and organizations
- accurate interpretation of institutional policies and procedures to program participants
- conflict management issues
- proper supervision of recreational sports activities
- inventory, maintenance, and procedures for participant use of equipment
- participant involvement in program content and procedures through committee structures
- recognition system for participants, employees, and volunteers
- cultural diversity issues
- accurate and adequate publicity and promotion
- volunteerism

## Part 3. LEADERSHIP

**Effective and ethical leadership is essential to the success of all organizations. Institutions must appoint, position, and empower leaders within the administrative structure to accomplish stated missions. Recreational sports program (RSP) leaders must be selected on the basis of formal education and training, relevant work experience, personal skills and competencies, relevant professional credentials, as well as potential for promoting learning and development in students, applying effective practices to educational processes, and enhancing institutional effectiveness. Institutions must determine expectations of accountability for leaders and fairly assess their performance.**

**RSP leaders of programs and services must exercise authority over resources for which they are responsible to achieve their respective missions.**

**RSP leaders must:**
- **articulate a vision for their organization**
- **set goals and objectives based on the needs and capabilities of the population served**
- **promote student learning and development**
- **prescribe and practice ethical behavior**
- **recruit, select, supervise, and develop others in the organization**
- **manage financial resources**
- **coordinate human resources**
- **plan, budget for, and evaluate personnel and programs**
- **apply effective practices to educational and administrative processes**
- **communicate effectively**

- initiate collaborative interaction between individuals and agencies that possess legitimate concerns and interests in the functional area

RSP leaders must identify and find means to address individual, organizational, or environmental conditions that inhibit goal achievement.

RSP leaders must promote campus environments that result in multiple opportunities for student learning and development.

RSP leaders must continuously improve programs and services in response to changing needs of students and other constituents, and evolving institutional priorities.

## Part 4. ORGANIZATION and MANAGEMENT

Guided by an overarching intent to ensure student learning and development, the recreational sports program (RSP) must be structured purposefully and managed effectively to achieve stated goals. Evidence of appropriate structure must include current and accessible policies and procedures, written performance expectations for all employees, functional workflow graphics or organizational charts, and clearly stated service delivery expectations.

Evidence of effective management must include use of comprehensive and accurate information for decisions, clear sources and channels of authority, effective communication practices, decision-making and conflict resolution procedures, responsiveness to changing conditions, accountability and evaluation systems, and recognition and reward processes. The RSP must provide channels within the organization for regular review of administrative policies and procedures.

> Institutional leaders should recognize the significant differences in mission among intercollegiate athletics, physical education and recreation academic units, and the recreational sports programs, and act accordingly. The organizational placement of recreational sports within the institution should ensure the accomplishment of the program's mission.

> Members of the campus community should be involved in the selection, design, governance, and administration of programs and facilities. Students, faculty and staff and members, and the public, when appropriate, may be involved through committees, councils, and boards.

## Part 5. HUMAN RESOURCES

The recreational sports program (RSP) must be staffed adequately by individuals qualified to accomplish its mission and goals. Within established guidelines of the institution, the RSP must establish procedures for staff selection, training, and evaluation; set expectations for supervision, and provide appropriate professional development opportunities. The program must strive to improve the professional competence and skills of all personnel it employs.

Professional staff members must hold an earned graduate degree in a field relevant to the position they hold or must possess an appropriate combination of educational credentials and related work experience.

Degree or credential-seeking interns must be qualified by enrollment in an appropriate field of study and by relevant experience. These individuals must be trained and supervised adequately by professional staff members holding educational credentials and related work experience appropriate for supervision.

Student employees and volunteers must be carefully selected, trained, supervised, and evaluated. They must be trained on how and when to refer those in need of assistance to qualified staff members and have access to a supervisor for assistance in making these judgments. Student employees and volunteers must be provided clear and precise job descriptions, pre-service training based on assessed needs, and continuing staff development.

The RSP must have technical and support staff members adequate to accomplish its mission. RSP staff members must be technologically proficient and qualified to perform their job functions, be knowledgeable of ethical and legal uses of technology, and have access to training. The level of staffing and workloads must be adequate and appropriate for program and service demands.

Salary levels and fringe benefits for all RSP staff members must be commensurate with those for comparable positions within the institution, in similar institutions, and in the relevant geographic area.

The RSP must institute hiring and promotion practices that are fair, inclusive, and non-discriminatory. The program must employ a diverse staff to provide readily identifiable role models for students and to enrich the campus community.

The RSP must create and maintain position descriptions for all staff members and provide regular performance planning and appraisals. Further, the program must have a system for regular staff evaluation and must provide access to continuing education and professional development opportunities, including in-service training programs and participation in professional conferences and workshops.

## Part 6: FINANCIAL RESOURCES

The recreational sports program (RSP) must have adequate funding to accomplish its mission and goals. Funding priorities must be determined within the context of the stated mission, goals, objectives and comprehensive analysis of the needs and capabilities of students and the viability of internal or external resources.

The RSP must demonstrate fiscal responsibility and cost effectiveness consistent with institutional protocols.

Institutional funds for the recreational sports program should be allocated on a permanent basis. In addition to institutional funding, other sources may be considered, including state appropriations, student fees, user fees, donations, contributions, fines, concession and store sales, rentals, and dues.

## Part 7. FACILITIES, TECHNOLOGY, EQUIPMENT

The recreational sports program (RSP) must have adequate, suitably located facilities, adequate technology, and equipment to support its mission and goals efficiently and effectively. Facilities, technology, and equipment must be evaluated regularly and be in compliance with relevant federal, state, provincial, and local requirements to provide for access, health, safety, and security.

The institution must provide adequate indoor and outdoor facilities, technology and equipment with prioritized blocks of time, for recreational sports programs to accommodate the diverse needs and interest of the campus community.

As a general rule, the larger the population and the more geographically isolated the institution, the greater the need for quality and diversity of facilities. Consideration should be given to a balance of facilities that would provide participation opportunities in team, dual, individual, and meet sports, as well as in fitness and conditioning. Examples of such facilities include swimming pools, gymnasiums, weight rooms and fitness facilities, and general use playing fields.

## Part 8. LEGAL RESPONSIBILITIES

Recreational sports program (RSP) staff members must be knowledgeable about and responsive to laws and regulations that relate to their respective responsibilities. Staff members must inform users of programs and services and officials, as appropriate, of legal obligations and limitations including constitutional, statutory, regulatory, and case law; mandatory laws and orders emanating from federal, state/provincial and local governments; and the institution's policies.

Staff members must use reasonable and informed practices to limit the liability exposure of the institution, its officers, employees, and agents. Staff members must be informed about institutional policies regarding personal liability and related insurance coverage options.

The institution must provide access to legal advice for RSP staff members as needed to carry out assigned responsibilities and must inform staff and students in a timely and systematic fashion about extraordinary or changing legal obligations and potential liabilities.

Recreational sports professionals should be fully aware of and understand legal areas such as due process, employment procedures, equal opportunity, and civil rights and liberties.

Although participation in recreational sports is a voluntary action, liability of wrongful or negligent acts should be a continuing concern.

Reasonable efforts must be made to insure a safe environment, properly maintained equipment, proper instruction, and adequate supervision.

## Part 9. EQUITY and ACCESS

Recreational sports program (RSP) staff members must ensure that services and programs are provided on a fair and equitable basis. Facilities, programs and services must be accessible. Hours of operation and delivery of and access to programs and services must be responsive to the needs of all students and other constituents. The RSP must adhere to the spirit and intent of equal opportunity laws.

The RSP must be open and readily accessible to all students and must not discriminate except where sanctioned by law and institutional policy. Discrimination must especially be avoided on the bases of age; color, creed; cultural heritage; disability; ethnicity; gender identity; nationality; political affiliation, religious affiliation, sex, sexual orientation; or economic, marital, social, or veteran status.

Consistent with its mission and goals, the RSP must take affirmative action to remedy significant imbalances in student participation and staffing patterns.

As the demographic profiles of campuses change and new instructional delivery methods are introduced, institutions must recognize the needs of students who participate in distance learning for access to programs and services offered on campus. ☐Institutions must provide appropriate services in ways that are accessible to distance learners and assist them in identifying and gaining access to other appropriate services in their geographic region.

## Part 10. CAMPUS and EXTERNAL RELATIONS

The recreational sports program (RSP) must establish, maintain, and promote effective relations with relevant individuals, campus offices, and external agencies.

The recreational sports program should be an institution-wide process that systematically involves student affairs, academic affairs, and other administrative units, such as campus police, physical plant, and the business office.

The recreational sports program should collaborate campus-wide to disseminate information abut their own and other programs and services on campus.

The program staff should serve as a resource to the community, providing expert advice on recreational issues and activities.

## Part 11. DIVERSITY

Within the context of each institution's unique mission, diversity enriches the community and enhances the collegiate experience for all; therefore, the recreational sports program (RSP) must nurture environments where commonalties and differences among people are recognized and honored.

The RSP must promote educational experiences that are characterized by open and continuous communication that deepens understanding of one's own identity, culture, and heritage, and that of others. The program must educate and promote respect about commonalties and differences in their historical and cultural contexts.

The RSP must address the characteristics and needs of a diverse population when establishing and implementing policies and procedures.

## Part 12. ETHICS

All persons involved in the delivery of the recreational sports program (RSP) must adhere to the highest principles of ethical behavior. The RSP must develop or adopt and implement appropriate statements of ethical practice. The RSP must publish these statements and ensure their periodic review by relevant constituencies .

Ethical standards of relevant professional associations should be considered.

RSP staff members must ensure that privacy and confidentiality are maintained with respect to all communications and records to the extent that such records are protected under the law and appropriate statements of ethical practice. Information contained in students' education records must not be disclosed without written consent except as allowed by relevant laws and institutional policies. Staff members must disclose to appropriate authorities information judged to be of an emergency nature, especially when the safety of the individual or others is involved, or when otherwise required by institutional policy or relevant law.

All RSP staff members must be aware of and comply with the provisions contained in the institution's human subjects research policy and in other relevant institutional policies addressing ethical practices and confidentiality of research data concerning individuals.

RSP staff members must recognize and avoid personal conflict of interest or appearance thereof in their transactions with students and others.

RSP staff members must strive to insure the fair, objective, and impartial treatment of all persons with whom they deal. Staff members must not participate in nor condone any form of harassment that demeans persons or creates an intimidating, hostile, or offensive campus environment.

When handling institutional funds, all RSP staff members must ensure that such funds are managed in accordance with established and responsible accounting procedures and the fiscal policies or processes of the institution.

RSP staff members must perform their duties within the limits of their training, expertise, and competence. When these limits are exceeded, individuals in need of further assistance must be referred to persons possessing appropriate qualifications.

RSP staff members must use suitable means to confront and otherwise hold accountable other staff members who exhibit unethical behavior.

RSP staff members must be knowledgeable about and practice ethical behavior in the use of technology.

## Part 13. ASSESSMENT and EVALUATION

The recreational sports program (RSP) must conduct regular assessment and evaluations. The program must employ effective qualitative and quantitative methodologies as appropriate, to determine whether and to what degree the stated mission, goals, and student learning and development outcomes are being met. The process must employ sufficient and sound assessment measures to ensure comprehensiveness. Data collected must include responses from students and other affected constituencies.

Evaluation of student and institutional needs, goals, objectives, and the effectiveness of the recreational sports program should occur on a periodic basis. A representative cross-section of appropriate people from the campus community should be involved in reviews of the recreational sports program.

The RSP must evaluate periodically how well they complement and enhance the institution's stated mission and educational effectiveness.

Results of these evaluations must be used in revising and improving programs and services and in recognizing staff performance.

# The Role of the Registrar
## *CAS* Standards and Guidelines

The position of registrar evolved from the position of "Bedel" in Europe, which appeared in the 12th century. As the position developed and the office changed, the "registrar" emerged in the 15th century. With the founding of Harvard, the position of registrar became an integral part of American higher education. In 1910, 15 registrars met in Detroit to discuss the need to share information and develop common practices, a meeting marked the birth of the American Association of Collegiate Registrars (AACR). That group added admissions officers in 1949 and changed its name to the American Association of Collegiate Registrars and Admissions Officers (AACRAO) (Quann, 1979). Over the years AACR and AACRAO and their more than 30 state and regional associations have provided linkages among registrars nationally and internationally, for the exchange of ideas and information that has led to a set of generally accepted policies and practices.

As the role of registrar evolved, it shifted from being essentially the number-two leadership position responsible for handling many aspects of administration, to filling a role more narrowly focused but vital to the life of all institutions of higher learning. Today's registrar usually reports to the vice president for academic affairs, student affairs, or enrollment management, and manages a staff that may vary from a few members to more than 100, depending on institution size. The registrar determines the organizational structure for the office; ensure the availability of adequate facilities, equipment, supplies, and services; develops position descriptions for and employs, trains, and supervises office staff; and oversees day-to-day activities.

The office of the registrar is a primary point of contact for students on the college campus. Through the registrars office, students obtain schedules of classes, register for courses, drop/add/withdraw, obtain grade reports and transcripts, and receive diplomas. Therefore, providing fast and efficient service to students and continuous quality improvement are major objectives for the registrar

The registrar's office is also a primary point of contact for faculty members for the scheduling of classes and assignment of classroom and laboratory space. In support of faculty members, who often assist in the advising and registration processes, the registrar's office provides class rosters and grade rolls, receives and processes grades, and produces grade reports and transcripts. Maintaining a close working relationship with faculty members, department heads, and academic deans is therefore an important role of the registrar.

While duties and responsibilities vary from institution to institution, the registrar is typically responsible for working with academic departments and faculty to determine which courses and sections are offered each term, assigning classroom facilities, and producing the catalog and schedule of classes students use to select courses.

The registrar oversees the registration process by which students select classes each academic term. When less sophisticated technological support was available, registration was usually conducted in an arena setting where students registered in person. Today, registration may be conducted on line, by touch tone telephone, and on the world wide web and students may register from campus or off-campus residences, workplaces, or elsewhere. as long as they have access to a telephone or on-line computer.

The registrar also is responsible for the maintenance of student records. While records are still maintained in paper or on microfilm, most institutions now store student records in electronic data bases. Imaging systems also are used increasingly to store former paper records in electronic form.

Other duties of most registrars include the production of class rosters, grade rosters, and grade reports; clearance of students for graduation, preparation of diplomas, and organization of graduation ceremonies; and publication of the college catalog. Registrars also play a vital role in developing and implementing policies and procedures, services, and systems to facilitate student enrollment, maintenance of student records, transfer of records to other institutions, and acceptance of transfer credit.

In addition, the registrar is the individual responsible for assuring that the Family Education Rights and Privacy Act (FERPA) requirements are met throughout the institution. Likewise, as student information systems increasingly are being implemented, responsibility for oversight of these technologies has gained greater importance as well.

Often, registrars are at the forefront of implementing new technologies on campus. Initially, student information systems were manual in design, but since mid-century they have involved increased levels of automation. Many, institutions now maintain student information systems that include on-line and/or touch-tone registration, on-line records, imaging systems, electronic interchange of records and data among institutions, and desktop publishing of class schedules and catalogs. Currently, increased levels of information are available through such on-line technology as the world wide web; once again, registrars are at the forefront by providing class schedules and other relevant information and making student registration available through the web.

The pace of change in higher education will increasingly affect the registrar's functions. The standards that follow, in addition to providing basic functional guidelines, are designed to help institutions address such challenges as distance learning; virtual universities; proficiency-based education; assessment; learning opportunities that are not constrained by time, location, or duration; and continuous rapid change in technology.

### Recommended Readings and Resources

Aucoin, P., & Associates (1996). *Academic record and transcript guide.* Washington, DC: American Association of Collegiate Registrars and Admissions Officers.

Bell, M. M. (1993). *Touchtone telephone/voice response registration: A guide for successful implementation.* Washington, DC: American Association of Collegiate Registrars and Admissions Officers.

Bilger, T. A., & Associates (1987). *Professional development guidelines for registrars: A self-audit.* Washington, DC: American Association of Collegiate Registrars and Admissions Officers.

Lonabocker, L., & Gwinn, D. (1996). *Breakthrough systems: Student access and registration.* Washington, DC: American Association of Collegiate Registrars and Admissions Officers.

Ockerman, E. & Legere, J. (1989). *The role of the registrar.* Washington, DC: American Association of Collegiate Registrars and Admissions Officers (AACRAO).

Perkins, H. L. (1996). *Electronic imaging in admissions, records and financial aid offices.* Washington, DC: American Association of Collegiate Registrars and Admissions Officers.

Peterson, E. D., & Associates (1987). *Retention of records: A guide for retention and disposal of student records.* Washington, DC: American Association of Collegiate Registrars and Admissions Officers.

Quann, C. J., & Associates (1979). *Admissions, academic records, and registrar services: A handbook of policies and procedures.* San Francisco: Jossey-Bass.

Rainsberger, R. A., & Associates. (1995). *Guidelines for postsecondary institutions for implementation of the Family Educational Rights and Privacy Act of 1974 as amended.* Washington, DC: American Association of Collegiate Registrars and Admissions Officers.

# REGISTRAR PROGRAMS AND SERVICES
## *CAS* STANDARDS and GUIDELINES

## Part 1. MISSION

Registrar programs and services (RPS) must incorporate student learning and student development in its mission. RPS enhance overall educational experiences. RPS must develop, record, disseminate, implement and regularly review its mission and goals. Mission statements must be consistent with the mission and goals of the institution and with the standards in this document. RPS must operate as an integral part of the institution's overall mission.

In support of the overall mission of the institution, and when responsibility is assigned, the mission of RPS must be to . . .

- develop institutional publications to provide information about courses, programs, policies, and procedures
- develop course schedules to provide information on courses and sections being offered in any given term with their day, time, and location
- schedule appropriate space for all classes
- provide information on regulations, policies and procedures
- develop forms and procedures as required
- provide a registration process for enrolling students in classes each term, which may include the assessment of tuition and fees
- certify student enrollment as required (e.g., veterans services, rehabilitation services, student loans, athletic eligibility)
- provide reports as required (e.g., class rosters, grade rosters, grade reports, transcripts);
- record properly evaluated transfer credit
- administer academic eligibility policies (e.g., graduation, honors, academic probation or dismissal)
- prepare and distribute diplomas
- maintain student record data base and archival files
- ensure that the security and confidentiality of student record data are maintained throughout the university/college
- prepare statistical reports (e.g., enrollment projections, retention, attrition, and graduation rates)

The registrar may also coordinate the arrangements for commencement and provide administrative support to the faculty senate or other governance bodies.

## Part 2. PROGRAM

The formal education of students consists of the curriculum and the co-curriculum, and must promote student learning and development that is purposeful and holistic. Registrar programs and services (RPS) must identify relevant and desirable student learning and development outcomes and provide programs and services that encourage the achievement of those outcomes.

Relevant and desirable outcomes include: intellectual growth, effective communication, realistic self-appraisal, enhanced self-esteem, clarified values, career choices, leadership development, healthy behaviors, meaningful interpersonal relationships, independence, collaboration, social responsibility, satisfying and productive lifestyles, appreciation of diversity, spiritual awareness, and achievement of personal and educational goals.

RPS must provide evidence of its impact on the achievement of student learning and development outcomes.

The program may use the examples that follow or identify other more germane indicators.

### Student Learning & Development Outcome Domains

**Intellectual Growth**
Examples of Achievement Indicators
    Produces personal and educational goal statements; Employs critical thinking in problem solving; Uses complex information from a variety of sources including personal experience and observation to form a decision or opinion; Obtains a degree; Applies previously understood information and concepts to a new situation or setting; Expresses appreciation for literature, the fine arts, mathematics, sciences, and social sciences

**Effective Communication**
Examples of Achievement Indicators
    Writes and speaks coherently and effectively; Writes and speaks after reflection; Able to influence others through writing, speaking or artistic expression; Effectively articulates abstract ideas; Uses appropriate syntax; Makes presentations or gives performances

**Enhanced Self-Esteem**
Examples of Achievement Indicators
    Shows self-respect and respect for others; Initiates actions toward achievement of goals; Takes reasonable risks; Demonstrates assertive behavior; Functions without need for constant reassurance from others

**Realistic Self-Appraisal**
Examples of Achievement Indicators
    Articulates personal skills and abilities; Makes decisions and acts in congruence with personal values; Acknowledges personal strengths and weaknesses;

Articulates rationale for personal behavior; Seeks feedback from others; Learns from past experiences

## Clarified Values

Examples of Achievement Indicators

Articulates personal values; Acts in congruence with personal values; Makes decisions that reflect personal values; Demonstrates willingness to scrutinize personal beliefs and values; Identifies personal, work and lifestyle values and explains how they influence decision-making

## Career Choices

Examples of Achievement Indicators

Articulate career choices based on assessment of interests, values, skills and abilities; Documents knowledge, skills and accomplishments resulting from formal education, work experience, community service and volunteer experiences; Makes the connections between classroom and out-of-classroom learning; Can construct a resume with clear job objectives and evidence of related knowledge, skills and accomplishments; Articulates the characteristics of a preferred work environment; Comprehends the world of work; Takes steps to initiate a job search or seek advanced education

## Leadership Development

Examples of Achievement Indicators

Articulates leadership philosophy or style; Serves in a leadership position in a student organization; Comprehends the dynamics of a group; Exhibits democratic principles as a leader; Exhibits ability to visualize a group purpose and desired outcomes

## Healthy Behavior

Examples of Achievement Indicators

Chooses behaviors and environments that promote health and reduce risk; Articulate the relationship between health and wellness and accomplishing life long goals; Exhibits behaviors that advance a healthy community

## Meaningful Interpersonal Relationships

Examples of Achievement Indicators

Develops and maintains satisfying interpersonal relationships; Establishes mutually rewarding relationships with friends and colleagues; Listens to and considers others' points of view; Treats others with respect

## Independence

Examples of Achievement Indicators

Exhibits self-reliant behaviors; Functions autonomously; Exhibits ability to function interdependently; Accepts supervision as needed; Manages time effectively

## Collaboration

Examples of Achievement Indicators

Works cooperatively with others; Seeks the involvement of others; Seeks feedback from others; Contributes to achievement of a group goal; Exhibits effective listening skills

## Social Responsibility

Examples of Achievement Indicators

Understands and participates in relevant governance systems; Understands, abides by, and participates in the development, maintenance, and/or orderly change of community, social, and legal standards or norms; Appropriately challenges the unfair, unjust, or uncivil behavior of other individuals or groups; Participates in service/volunteer activities

## Satisfying and Productive Lifestyles

Examples of Achievement Indicators

Achieves balance between education, work and leisure time; Articulates and meets goals for work, leisure and education; Overcomes obstacles that hamper goal achievement; Functions on the basis of personal identity, ethical, spiritual and moral values; Articulates long-term goals and objectives

## Appreciating Diversity

Examples of Achievement Indicators

Understands ones own identity and culture. Seeks involvement with people different from oneself; Seeks involvement in diverse interests; Articulate the advantages and challenges of a diverse society; Challenges appropriately abusive use of stereotypes by others; Understands the impact of diversity on one's own society

## Spiritual Awareness

Examples of Achievement Indicators

Develops and articulates personal belief system; Understands roles of spirituality in personal and group values and behaviors

## Personal and Educational Goals

Examples of Achievement Indicators

Sets, articulates, and pursues individual goals; Articulate personal and educational goals and objectives; Uses personal and educational goals to guide decisions; Understands the effect of one's personal and education goals on others

**RPS must be (a) intentional, (b) coherent, (c) based on theories and knowledge of learning and human development, (d) reflective of developmental and demographic profiles of the student population, and (e) responsive to needs of individuals, special populations, and communities.**

**The registrar must . . .**
- **have the authority to operate effectively in the academic community**
- **ensure that relevant policies and procedures are communicated widely**
- **ensure the accuracy and reliability of the data collected and distributed**
- **provide for the maintenance, upkeep, security, integrity and proper dissemination of academic records**

- develop a workable disaster recovery plan that will allow the registrar to function in the event of catastrophic circumstances
- educate the institutional community with regard to the security and release of student data

The Registrar should assist in institutional efforts to establish and maintain co-curricular transcripts or other records.

## Part 3. LEADERSHIP

Effective and ethical leadership is essential to the success of all organizations. Institutions must appoint, position, and empower registrar program and Service (RPS) leaders within the administrative structure to accomplish stated missions. RPS leaders at various levels must be selected on the basis of formal education and training, relevant work experience, personal skills and competencies, relevant professional credentials, as well as potential for promoting learning and development in students, applying effective practices to educational processes, and enhancing institutional effectiveness. Institutions must determine expectations of accountability for leaders and fairly assess their performance.

Leaders of RPS must exercise authority over resources for which they are responsible to achieve their respective missions.

RPS leaders must . . .
- articulate a vision for their organization
- set goals and objectives based on the needs and capabilities of the population served
- promote student learning and development
- prescribe and practice ethical behavior
- recruit, select, supervise, and develop others in the organization
- manage financial resources
- coordinate human resources
- plan, budget for, and evaluate personnel and programs
- apply effective practices to educational and administrative processes
- communicate effectively
- initiate collaborative interaction between individuals and agencies that possess legitimate concerns and interests in the functional area

RPS leaders must identify and find means to address individual, organizational, or environmental conditions that inhibit goal achievement.

RPS leaders must promote campus environments that result in multiple opportunities for student learning and development.

RPS leaders must continuously improve programs and services in response to changing needs of students and other constituents, and evolving institutional priorities.

The registrar's office should . . .
- develop, advocate, and implement a statement of the mission, goals, and objectives for the unit that is congruent with and complementary to the institutional mission
- be responsible for implementing services congruent with institutional mission, goals, and objectives
- provide accurate information and timely service to all constituencies
- be at the forefront of technological advancement
- be able to justify investment in hardware, by identifying time and cost efficiencies that will accrue to the institution
- be sensitive to the special needs of all students including evening students, commuting students, married students, single parents, students with disabilities, adult learners and students of various ethnic and cultural groups
- assess decision-making and problem-solving models and select those most appropriate to the institutional milieu
- serve as a catalyst in team building because the activities of the registrar impinge on most other institutional units

## Part 4. ORGANIZATION and MANAGEMENT

Guided by an overarching intent to ensure student learning and development, registrar programs and services (RPS) must be structured purposefully and managed effectively to achieve stated goals. Evidence of appropriate structure must include current and accessible policies and procedures, written performance expectations for all employees, functional workflow graphics or organizational charts, and clearly stated service delivery expectations.

Evidence of effective management must include use of comprehensive and accurate information for decisions, clear sources and channels of authority, effective communication practices, decision-making and conflict resolution procedures, responsiveness to changing conditions, accountability and evaluation systems, and recognition and reward processes. RPS must provide channels within the organization for regular review of administrative policies and procedures.

Registrar programs and services must provide channels within the organization for regular review of administrative policies and procedures and document such policies, practices, and procedures in a manual.

The registrar should . . .

- develop an organizational chart that describes the reporting lines within the office and identifies cooperative interrelationships with other institutional units
- coordinate programs and services with other institutional personnel, offices, functions, and activities;
- develop operational policies and procedures that include the detailed descriptions of responsibilities for each staff member
- ensure that staff responsibilities are consonant with the abilities of designated personnel
- provide for periodic review of policies, procedures, organizational structures, and currency of the office manual
- develop and maintain the office budget
- develop clear and concise criteria for decision making and establish primary responsibility when more than one unit is involved
- assume responsibility for establishing, updating, and evaluating staff training and professional development programs that also include skill improvement, interpersonal, organizational, and tine management components
- identify and be responsive to external constraints and requirements that impact on unit operation (e.g., implications of local, state, and federal regulations, union agreements, accreditation, professional, and athletic conference requirements); foster communication among the staff by scheduling regular staff meetings
- encourage staff members to participate in state, regional, and national professional activities
- expend significant effort for long-range planning for changes in technology, policy, procedure, and customer service

There should be an office manual that includes: organizational charts showing accountability and reporting lines; interrelationships with other institutional units; applicable operating policies, practices and procedures; unit-specific policies, practices and procedures; external constraints (union, state and federal requirements); ethical standards statements; grievance/appeal procedures; job descriptions and expectations; personnel policies; task and job evaluation forms; and procedures in case of an emergency, natural disaster, or school closure.

## Part 5. HUMAN RESOURCES

**Registrar programs and services (RPS) must be staffed adequately by individuals qualified to accomplish its mission and goals. Within established guidelines of the institution, RPS must establish procedures for staff selection, training, and evaluation; set expectations for supervision, and provide appropriate professional development opportunities. RPS must strive to improve the professional competence and skills of all personnel it employs.**

Staff members should be aware of the criteria on which they are to be evaluated at the beginning of each evaluation period. They should be properly trained and their performance monitored so that the evaluation at the end of the period does not contain judgment of criteria that have not been previously discussed.

**RPS professional staff members must hold an earned graduate degree in a field relevant to the position they hold or must possess an appropriate combination of educational credentials and related work experience.**

The chief administrator of the office should have the capacity to motivate, inspire, and help staff members develop a team atmosphere in the office. Attention should be paid to recognizing and rewarding the efforts of those who have accomplished expected and exceptional work.

Since the registrar works with all sectors of the institution, many of whom have terminal degrees, it would be advantageous if the registrar had a terminal degree as well. Other professional registrar staff may not require a terminal degree, but a master's or bachelor's degree is appropriate. Most degree programs do not specifically prepare individuals to become registrars. Courses of study relevant to the registrar area include: administration, education, business, counseling, curriculum, personnel, sociology, and psychology. Often professional staff are employed in the area after prior teaching or administrative experience. A demonstrated service-oriented philosophy is important since the office will be serving the entire campus population.

The registrar should possess an array of budget management skills: developing budgets, writing proposals for special projects, performing cost benefit analyses, amortizing the cost of major equipment purchases, and preparing analyses of future needs. Additionally, the registrar should be aware of the institution's personnel policies that could affect the budget, of accounting reports that track expenditures, and of policies governing unused funds.

The selection criteria for the registrar's position should include consideration of the match between a candidate's educational, personal, and experiential qualifications and the institution's mission, goals, and objectives. Staff member's selection should attempt to ensure the responsibilities are consonant with abilities.

Typically, the registrar reports to a vice president of academic affairs, student affairs, enrollment management, or comparable senior officer. Specific titles and reporting structures will necessarily reflect institutional mission, goals, and objectives.

**Degree or credential-seeking interns must be qualified by enrollment in an appropriate field of study and by relevant experience. These individuals must be trained and supervised adequately by professional staff members holding educational credentials and related work experience appropriate for supervision.**

Student employees and volunteers must be carefully selected, trained, supervised, and evaluated. They must be trained on how and when to refer those in need of assistance to qualified staff members and have access to a supervisor for assistance in making these judgments. Student employees and volunteers must be provided clear and precise job descriptions, pre-service training based on assessed needs, and continuing staff development.

RPS must have technical and support staff members adequate to accomplish its mission. Staff members must be technologically proficient and qualified to perform their job functions, be knowledgeable of ethical and legal uses of technology, and have access to training. The level of staffing and workloads must be adequate and appropriate for program and service demands.

The support staff should be skilled in interpersonal communications, public relations, and the dissemination of information. Personnel should be adept in handling complex and detailed activities and responsibilities. Accuracy is essential because the office is recording the academic history of students.

Development for the support staff should include adequate initial training to be able to represent the institution in their office function in a competent and professional manner. Ongoing training and staff development should be designed to enhance and broaden understanding of roles and responsibilities within the office and the institution.

Salary levels and fringe benefits for all RPS staff members must be commensurate with those for comparable positions within the institution, in similar institutions, and in the relevant geographic area.

RPS must institute hiring and promotion practices that are fair, inclusive, and non-discriminatory. Programs and services must employ a diverse staff to provide readily identifiable role models for students and to enrich the campus community.

RPS must create and maintain position descriptions for all staff members and provide regular performance planning and appraisals.

RPS must have a system for regular staff evaluation and must provide access to continuing education and professional development opportunities, including in-service training programs and participation in professional conferences and workshops.

Because the office often involves routine and repetitive work, special attention should be given to the accuracy of all work.

## Part 6. FINANCIAL RESOURCES

Registrar programs and services (RPS) must have adequate funding to accomplish its mission and goals. Funding priorities must be determined within the context of the stated mission, goals, objectives, and comprehensive analysis of the needs and capabilities of students, and the availability of internal or external resources.

RPS must demonstrate fiscal responsibility and cost effectiveness consistent with institutional protocols.

The registrar should have a clear understanding of the office's mission, sources of funding, and the budgeting process used by the institution.

Funds should be provided for salaries and benefits of staff and temporary or part time workers; professional development and staff training; office furnishings; communications and data processing equipment and software; postage, printing, and office supplies; subscriptions to professional and technical publications; membership in appropriate professional organizations; attendance at professional meetings, conferences, and workshops; special projects; and unexpected emergencies.

## Part 7. FACILITIES, TECHNOLOGY, EQUIPMENT

Registrar programs and services (RPS) must have adequate, suitably located facilities, adequate technology, and equipment to support its mission and goals efficiently and effectively. Facilities, technology, and equipment must be evaluated regularly and be in compliance with relevant federal, state, provincial, and local requirements to provide for access, health, safety, and security.

The design of the office must guarantee the security of the records and ensure the confidentiality of all sensitive information. The location and layout of the office must be sensitive to the special needs of students with disabilities as well as the needs of the general student population.

Facilities which produce a comfortable, functional, and pleasant work environment encourage staff members to be more productive. The administrative staff members should have private space in which to conduct their business. The offices should be equipped and furnished to support activities. All other employees should have work stations which are well equipped, adequate in size, as private as possible, and appropriately designed for their work.

Offices should be well lighted, properly ventilated, and heated or cooled to acceptable standards. Adequate space should be allocated for the secure storage of student records and supplies. Space should be provided for meetings with students, conferring with staff, and completing special projects. Ideally a comfortable area within the office or nearby should be available for staff breaks and lunches.

**When the Registrar is responsible for determining facilities usage outside the immediate office, policies and procedures must be developed and disseminated with respect to the assignment of such space.**

**Backup copies of important documentation such as transcripts and the student data base must be stored off site in the event of a natural disaster or damage to the records.**

## Part 8. LEGAL RESPONSIBILITIES

**The registrar program and services (RPS) staff members must be knowledgeable about and responsive to laws and regulations that relate to their respective responsibilities. Staff members must inform users of programs and services and officials, as appropriate, of legal obligations and limitations including constitutional, statutory, regulatory, and case law; mandatory laws and orders emanating from federal, state/provincial and local governments; and the institution's policies.**

**RPS staff members must use reasonable and informed practices to limit the liability exposure of the institution, its officers, employees, and agents. Staff members must be informed about institutional policies regarding personal liability and related insurance coverage options.**

**The institution must provide access to legal advice for RPS staff members as needed to carry out assigned responsibilities.**

**The institution must inform RPS staff and students in a timely and systematic fashion about extraordinary or changing legal obligations and potential liabilities.**

**The registrar must ensure that the institution has written policies on all office transactions which may have legal implications.**

**The registrar**
must have procedures to keep staff members informed of all requirements related to the maintenance of academic records. Forms used to implement regulations must be developed and reviewed to assure fulfillment of all institutional requirements.

The registrar should meet with the institution's legal counsel periodically to review all relevant documents for clarity and to determine that current regulations are being followed. Some of the relevant areas that should be reviewed include affirmative action policies; certification of diplomas, degrees, and dates of attendance; court orders; academic and disciplinary dismissals; degree requirements; tuition, fees, and refund policies; fraudulent records; name changes; personnel issues; record keeping practices; residency status determination; requests for information from law enforcement agencies; security procedures; social security number usage; and subpoenas.

**RPS must protect students' rights to privacy and access as defined in the legislative statute entitled Family Educational Rights and Privacy Act of 1974 (FERPA).**
FERPA, commonly known as the Buckley Amendment, protects the privacy of student records by requiring . . .
- institutions to limit the disclosure of information from student records to third persons
- notification to students or their parents, if dependency has been established, of their right to review student educational records
- institutions to inform students of their right to seek correction of information contained in their educational records

## Part 9. EQUITY and ACCESS

**Registrar program and services (RPS) staff members must ensure that services and programs are provided on a fair and equitable basis. Facilities, programs and services must be accessible. Hours of operation and delivery of and access to programs and services must be responsive to the needs of all students and other constituents. RPS must adhere to the spirit and intent of equal opportunity laws.**

**The RPS must be open and readily accessible to all students and must not discriminate except where sanctioned by law and institutional policy. Discrimination must especially be avoided on the bases of age; color, creed; cultural heritage; disability; ethnicity; gender identity; nationality; political affiliation, religious affiliation, sex, sexual orientation; or economic, marital, social, or veteran status.**

**Consistent with their mission and goals, RPS must take affirmative action to remedy significant imbalances in student participation and staffing patterns.**

**As the demographic profiles of campuses change and new instructional delivery methods are**

introduced, institutions must recognize the needs of students who participate in distance learning for access to programs and services offered on campus. □Institutions must provide appropriate services in ways that are accessible to distance learners and assist them in identifying and gaining access to other appropriate services in their geographic region.

## Part 10.  CAMPUS and EXTERNAL RELATIONS

Registrar programs and services (RPS) must establish, maintain, and promote effective relations with relevant individuals, campus offices, and external agencies. RPS staff members must relate effectively with administrators, faculty, students, alumni, and the public.

## Part 11.  DIVERSITY

Within the context of each institution's unique mission, diversity enriches the community and enhances the collegiate experience for all; therefore, the registrar program and services (RPS) must nurture environments where commonalties and differences among people are recognized and honored.

RPS must promote educational experiences that are characterized by open and continuous communication that deepens understanding of one's own identity, culture, and heritage, and that of others. RPS must educate and promote respect about commonalties and differences in their historical and cultural contexts.

RPS must address the characteristics and needs of a diverse population when establishing and implementing policies and procedures.

## Part 12.  ETHICS

All persons involved in delivering the registrar program and services (RPS) must adhere to the highest principles of ethical behavior. RPS must develop or adopt and implement appropriate statements of ethical practice. RPS must publish these statements and ensure their periodic review by relevant constituencies.

Standards of ethical practice that address the unique problems of managing the day to day maintenance of records and registration processes must be published. These standards must be made a part of the orientation program for each new employee and be routinely reviewed and updated.

Ethical standards statements previously used by the profession at large or relevant professional associations should be reviewed in the formulation of institutional standards.

RPS staff members must ensure that privacy and confidentiality are maintained with respect to all communications and records to the extent that such records are protected under the law and appropriate statements of ethical practice. Information contained in students' education records must not be disclosed without written consent except as allowed by relevant laws and institutional policies. Staff members must disclose to appropriate authorities information judged to be of an emergency nature, especially when the safety of the individual or others is involved, or when otherwise required by institutional policy or relevant law.

The institutional responsibilities of the registrar and records personnel in keeping and releasing student information demands conduct that consistently reflects fairness, common sense, honesty, and respect for the dignity of all persons.

RPS must ensure the institution has a written policy and published statement regarding confidentiality of records and procedures for access, release, and challenge of educational records. The same basic principles of confidentiality must govern electronic data as well as paper documents.

All RPS staff members must be aware of and comply with the provisions contained in the institution's human subjects research policy and in other relevant institutional policies addressing ethical practices and confidentiality of research data concerning individuals.

RPS staff members must recognize and avoid personal conflict of interest or appearance thereof in their transactions with students and others.

RPS staff members must strive to insure the fair, objective, and impartial treatment of all persons with whom they deal. Staff members must not participate in nor condone any form of harassment that demeans persons or creates an intimidating, hostile, or offensive campus environment.

When handling institutional funds, all RPS staff members must ensure that such funds are managed in accordance with established and responsible accounting procedures and the fiscal policies or processes of the institution.

RPS staff members must perform their duties within the limits of their training, expertise, and competence. When these limits are exceeded, individuals in need of further assistance must be referred to persons possessing appropriate qualifications.

RPS staff members must use suitable means to confront and otherwise hold accountable other staff members who exhibit unethical behavior.

The registrar should promote ethical awareness in the academic community as well as within the registrar's office. This can best be accomplished by developing a broad conceptual understanding of higher education, acquiring knowledge of the philosophy and values in the design and application of policies and practices, and implementing the philosophy and values developed for the registrar's office.

RPS staff members must be knowledgeable about and practice ethical behavior in the use of technology.

## Part 13. ASSESSMENT and EVALUATION

The registrar program and services (RPS) must conduct regular assessment and evaluations. RPS must employ effective qualitative and quantitative methodologies as appropriate, to determine whether and to what degree the stated mission, goals, and student learning and development outcomes are being met. The process must employ sufficient and sound assessment measures to ensure comprehensiveness. Data collected must include responses from students and other affected constituencies.

RPS must evaluate periodically how well they complement and enhance the institution's stated mission and educational effectiveness.

The evaluation of the operations of the registrar's office may be external or internal. In either case, the registrar's office should have a mechanism in effect that systematically reviews all of its activities and policies. As technology, laws, and regulations change, new activities or policies may need to be implemented. When developing new programs or activities, an evaluation should be a part of the plan to ensure effectiveness, efficiency, and/or appropriateness for future use.

Periodically, the entire office should undertake an extensive self-audit to determine if current activities and policies follow the standards in the profession. The registrar should continuously evaluate the activities of the office to determine if the services meet the needs of its constituents and continue to parallel the mission of the institution.

Results of these evaluations must be used in revising and improving programs and services and in recognizing staff performance.

# The Role of Religious Programs
## *CAS* Standards and Guidelines

The history of higher education in the United States and that of religious programs and services go hand in hand. Early colleges and universities were all established by some religious denomination, and education of the clergy was their primary goal. Religion permeated the entire campus, not only within the curriculum but also through all aspects of student life.

In the mid-1850s, the role of religion in higher education changed to "seek a broader public good through an increase in the number of professions for which students would be trained, more precision in the disciplines, less control by religion, and a democratic society" (Butler, 1989, p. 5). This trend continued with the passage of the Morrill Land-Grant Act of 1862 and the Morrill Act of 1890, which made public education more widely available. More areas of study became available outside of religious training and access to higher education generally was eased. Consequently, the numbers of citizens seeking advanced levels of education increased significantly.

With more students attending the new public institutions, various religious denominations began to establish student organizations to function on these campuses as student support services. Religious groups such as the Methodist Wesley Foundation, the Jewish Hillel programs, and the Catholic Newman Apostolate provided both religious support and social support for students. Subsequently, numerous independent religious organizations were established on college campuses, many of which are ecumenical in nature and not tied to any particular denomination (e.g., the Campus Crusade for Christ and the Fellowship of Christian Athletes).

Moving toward a more collaborative approach to providing campus religious programs and services was viewed as an important trend; however, as Butler (1989) pointed out, "major problems in level of funding, program direction and accountability, quality of professional training and placement, and the nature of relationships exist in practically every state" (p. 11). Through all of this, various faiths have sought to maintain their unique characteristics and traditions. Today, several ecumenical organizations exist to increase cooper-ation among religious groups on campus including the National Campus Ministries Association, National Association of College and University Chaplains, and Campus Ministry Women.

Today, religious groups on campus play an important role in the spiritual development of college students; they also provide safe havens for discussing personal issues and problems. Many campus clergy members provide personal and spiritual counseling. In addition, involvement with religiously affiliated student organizations or clubs can provide an avenue for students to develop leadership and interpersonal skills. Religious programs and services often provide significant out-of-classroom developmental opportunities for college students.

### References, Readings, and Resources

Butler, J. (1989). An overview of religion on campus. In J. Butler (ed.). Religion on campus. *New Directions for Student Services*, No. 46. San Francisco: Jossey-Bass.

Barker, V. L., & Voorhis, R. V. (1994). *An index for higher education programs and resources*. Charlotte, NC: United Ministries in Higher Education.

United Ministries in Education (1996). *Directory of ministries in higher education*. Charlotte, NC: Author.

The Resource Center (serving higher education campus ministries). Council for Higher Education Ministries/United Ministries in Higher Education. 7407 Steele Creek Road, Charlotte, NC 28217. (704) 588-2182. <linda_freeman@cunet.org>

# STUDENT RELIGIOUS PROGRAMS
## *CAS* STANDARDS and GUIDELINES

## Part 1. MISSION

**Student Religious Programs (SRP) must incorporate student learning and student development in its mission. SRP must enhance overall educational experiences. SRP must develop, record, disseminate, implement and regularly review its mission and goals. Mission statements must be consistent with the mission and goals of the institution and with the standards in this document. SRP must operate as an integral part of the institution's overall mission.**

A private or church related institution may state its preference for a particular faith or church and may directly use its own resources for this purpose.

**Public institutions must offer or provide access to programs that enable interested students to pursue full spiritual growth and development, and foster a campus atmosphere in which interested members of the college community may freely express their religion and faith.**

In this document "religion" is defined by function rather than substance. The courts have held that the First Amendment provides protection to religious believers and non-believers, and that the state shall be neutral in its relations with persons who profess a belief or disbelief in any religion. Everson v. Board of Education, 330 US 1 (1977).

A clear distinction should be made between two separate but related functions of an educational institution: providing for the academic study of religions, and for programs that promote the spiritual and moral development of its students.

A distinction should also be made between accommodation and promotion of religions and faiths by public institutions. The court has mandated an even handed accommodation of religious beliefs, whereas it has prohibited the promotion of a particular religious belief. Illinois ex rel. McCollum v. Board of Education, 333 US 203, S. Ct.; Zorach v. Causon, 343 US 306 (1952).

**According to the courts, any public institution's program must meet the following conditions to avoid violating the "establishment" clause of the US Constitution:**

- **It must have a secular purpose**
- **Its principal or primary effect must be one that neither advances nor inhibits religion**
- **It must not foster an excessive entanglement of the public institution with religion.** *Lemon v. Kurtzman, 403 US 602, 91 SC 2105, 29 L. Ed. 2d 745 (1071); Widmar v. Vincent, 454 US 263, Tol Ed. 2d 440, 102 S. Ct. 2 (1981)*

**Public institutions are prohibited from giving any preferential treatment to a particular religion or faith, to all religions or faiths, or to prefer one religion or faith over another. School District of Abington Township v. Schernpp, 374 US 203, (1963). The First Amendment mandates neutrality among religions, and between religion and non-religion. Epperson v. Arkansas, 393 US 97, (1968). The Constitution forbids the preference of a religious doctrine and the prohibition of a theory antagonistic to an individual dogma. Epperson v. Arkansas, 393 US 97, (1968).**

Public institutions should make provisions for religious programs indirectly, that is, through cooperation with off-campus agencies which provide religious services and programs.

The goals of any organized religious program or service should include:

- assisting interested students to achieve the religious development they seek
- the articulation of a personal philosophy of life
- the acquisition of skills and knowledge needed to address issues of values, ethics, and morality in life
- an understanding of the interaction of faith, intellectual inquiry, and social responsibility as bases for finding and affirming meaning and satisfaction in life
- providing a forum for dialogue between and among representatives of the religious and the secular
- providing interested members of the campus community with reasonable opportunity to express their faith(s)

## Part 2. PROGRAM

**The formal education of students consists of the curriculum and the co-curriculum, and must promote student learning and development that is purposeful and holistic. Student Religious Programs (SRP) must identify relevant and desirable student learning and development outcomes and provide programs and services that encourage the achievement of those outcomes.**

**Relevant and desirable outcomes include: intellectual growth, effective communication, realistic self-appraisal, enhanced self-esteem, clarified values, career choices, leadership development, healthy behaviors, meaningful interpersonal relationships, independence, collaboration, social responsibility, satisfying and productive lifestyles, appreciation of diversity, spiritual awareness, and achievement of personal and educational goals.**

**SRP must provide evidence of its impact on the achievement of student learning and development outcomes.**

The program may use the examples that follow or identify other more germane indicators.

## Student Learning & Development Outcome Domains

### Intellectual Growth
Examples of Achievement Indicators
Produces personal and educational goal statements; Employs critical thinking in problem solving; Uses complex information from a variety of sources including personal experience and observation to form a decision or opinion; Obtains a degree; Applies previously understood information and concepts to a new situation or setting; Expresses appreciation for literature, the fine arts, mathematics, sciences, and social sciences

### Effective Communication
Examples of Achievement Indicators
Writes and speaks coherently and effectively; Writes and speaks after reflection; Able to influence others through writing, speaking or artistic expression; Effectively articulates abstract ideas; Uses appropriate syntax; Makes presentations or gives performances

### Enhanced Self-Esteem
Examples of Achievement Indicators
Shows self-respect and respect for others; Initiates actions toward achievement of goals; Takes reasonable risks; Demonstrates assertive behavior; Functions without need for constant reassurance from others

### Realistic Self-Appraisal
Examples of Achievement Indicators
Articulates personal skills and abilities; Makes decisions and acts in congruence with personal values; Acknowledges personal strengths and weaknesses; Articulates rationale for personal behavior; Seeks feedback from others; Learns from past experiences

### Clarified Values
Examples of Achievement Indicators
Articulates personal values; Acts in congruence with personal values; Makes decisions that reflect personal values; Demonstrates willingness to scrutinize personal beliefs and values; Identifies personal, work and lifestyle values and explains how they influence decision-making

### Career Choices
Examples of Achievement Indicators
Articulate career choices based on assessment of interests, values, skills and abilities; Documents knowledge, skills and accomplishments resulting from formal education, work experience, community service and volunteer experiences; Makes the connections between classroom and out-of-classroom learning; Can construct a resume with clear job objectives and evidence of related knowledge, skills and accomplishments; Articulates the characteristics of a preferred work environment; Comprehends the world of work; Takes steps to initiate a job search or seek advanced education

### Leadership Development
Examples of Achievement Indicators
Articulates leadership philosophy or style; Serves in a leadership position in a student organization; Comprehends the dynamics of a group; Exhibits democratic principles as a leader; Exhibits ability to visualize a group purpose and desired outcomes

### Healthy Behavior
Examples of Achievement Indicators
Chooses behaviors and environments that promote health and reduce risk; Articulate the relationship between health and wellness and accomplishing life long goals; Exhibits behaviors that advance a healthy community

### Meaningful Interpersonal Relationships
Examples of Achievement Indicators
Develops and maintains satisfying interpersonal relationships; Establishes mutually rewarding relationships with friends and colleagues; Listens to and considers others' points of view; Treats others with respect

### Independence
Examples of Achievement Indicators
Exhibits self-reliant behaviors; Functions autonomously; Exhibits ability to function interdependently; Accepts supervision as needed; Manages time effectively

### Collaboration
Examples of Achievement Indicators
Works cooperatively with others; Seeks the involvement of others; Seeks feedback from others; Contributes to achievement of a group goal; Exhibits effective listening skills

### Social Responsibility
Examples of Achievement Indicators
Understands and participates in relevant governance systems; Understands, abides by, and participates in the development, maintenance, and/or orderly change of community, social, and legal standards or norms; Appropriately challenges the unfair, unjust, or uncivil behavior of other individuals or groups; Participates in service/volunteer activities

### Satisfying and Productive Lifestyles
Examples of Achievement Indicators
Achieves balance between education, work and leisure time; Articulates and meets goals for work, leisure and education; Overcomes obstacles that hamper goal achievement; Functions on the basis of personal identity, ethical, spiritual and moral values; Articulates long-term goals and objectives

### Appreciating Diversity
Examples of Achievement Indicators
Understands ones own identity and culture. Seeks involvement with people different from oneself; Seeks involvement in diverse interests; Articulate the advantages and challenges of a diverse society; Challenges appropriately abusive use of stereotypes by others; Understands the impact of diversity on one's own society

## Spiritual Awareness
Examples of Achievement Indicators
Develops and articulates personal belief system; Understands roles of spirituality in personal and group values and behaviors

## Personal and Educational Goals
Examples of Achievement Indicators
Sets, articulates, and pursues individual goals; Articulate personal and educational goals and objectives; Uses personal and educational goals to guide decisions; Understands the effect of one's personal and education goals on others

SRP must be (a) intentional, (b) coherent, (c) based on theories and knowledge of learning and human development, (d) reflective of developmental and demographic profiles of the student population, and (e) responsive to needs of individuals, special populations, and communities.

SRP will vary depending on the requirements and beliefs of specific denominations and faiths, as well as the needs and traditions of the particular institution.

To the extent either required or prohibited by constitutional, statutory, or regulatory provisions, institutions must provide reasonable opportunities for students to . . .
- question, explore, understand, affiliate with or avoid, and express or reject various religious faiths
- seek individual counseling and/or group associations for the examination and application of spiritual values and beliefs
- worship communally
- pray and meditate

In public institutions, staff members coordinate programs, while adjunct personnel associated with there religious groups provide the direct ministry.

In church related and private colleges, religious ministry and religious programs may be provided directly by staff members of the institution.

The types of religious programs and activities that may be offered are:
- religious studies
- opportunities for religious nurturance
- service opportunities
- where appropriate by law or regulation, opportunity to propagate specific faiths
- advocacy for particular ethical or moral policies in public life
- opportunities to relate religious beliefs to academic and professional programs through a variety of informational and experiential activities

In addition, institutions may provide counseling services to promote spiritual or religious growth. Co-curricular programs (e.g., lectures, discussions, or service projects) which are designed to help students understand their faiths and the faiths of others may also be offered.

## Part 3.  LEADERSHIP
Effective and ethical leadership is essential to the success of all organizations.  Institutions must appoint, position, and empower Student Religious Programs (SRP) leaders within the administrative structure to accomplish stated missions. SRP leaders at various levels must be selected on the basis of formal education and training, relevant work experience, personal skills and competencies, relevant professional credentials, as well as potential for promoting learning and development in students, applying effective practices to educational processes, and enhancing institutional effectiveness.  Institutions must determine expectations of accountability for leaders and fairly assess their performance.

Leaders of SRP must exercise authority over resources for which they are responsible to achieve their respective missions.

SRP leaders must:
- articulate a vision for their organization
- set goals and objectives based on the needs and capabilities of the  population served
- promote student learning and development
- prescribe and practice ethical behavior
- recruit, select, supervise, and develop others in the organization
- manage  financial resources
- coordinate human resources
- plan, budget for, and evaluate personnel and programs
- apply effective practices to educational and administrative processes
- communicate effectively
- initiate collaborative interaction between individuals and agencies that possess legitimate concerns and interests in the functional area

SRP leaders must identify and find means to address individual, organizational, or environmental conditions that inhibit goal achievement.

SRP leaders must promote campus environments that result in multiple opportunities for student learning and development.

SRP leaders must continuously improve programs and services in response to changing needs of students and other constituents, and evolving institutional priorities.

## Part 4. ORGANIZATION and MANAGEMENT

Guided by an overarching intent to ensure student learning and development, Student Religious Programs (SRP) must be structured purposefully and managed effectively to achieve stated goals. Evidence of appropriate structure must include current and accessible policies and procedures, written performance expectations for all employees, functional workflow graphics or organizational charts, and clearly stated service delivery expectations.

Evidence of effective management must include use of comprehensive and accurate information for decisions, clear sources and channels of authority, effective communication practices, decision-making and conflict resolution procedures, responsiveness to changing conditions, accountability and evaluation systems, and recognition and reward processes. SRP must provide channels within the organization for regular review of administrative policies and procedures.

Program activities, policies, and procedures should be scrutinized regularly in light of the growing body of constitutional law in the area of religion and higher education.

## Part 5. HUMAN RESOURCES

Student Religious Programs (SRP) must be staffed adequately by individuals qualified to accomplish its mission and goals. Within established guidelines of the institution, SRP must establish procedures for staff selection, training, and evaluation; set expectations for supervision, and provide appropriate professional development opportunities. SRP must strive to improve the professional competence and skills of all personnel it employs.

At public institutions, the title "director or "coordinator" of religious programs is more appropriate because of the predominantly educational and liaison functions of the position.

At public institutions, religious programs may be coordinated by a professional person and/or a committee. Adjunct professional or volunteer persons named (and paid) by the religious groups represented on the campus may carry out their respective religious activities.

Preferred titles for the chief coordinator at private institutions are "chaplain," "campus minister," or "director of religious life."

At private institutions, campus religious programs are typically coordinated by a professional person. Additional staff members may be employed by the institution. Religious groups may also provide additional staff for the institution. Church related institutions should permit on campus programs of religions other than those espoused by the institution.

SRP professional staff members must hold an earned graduate degree in a field relevant to the position they hold or must possess an appropriate combination of educational credentials and related work experience.

Any director or coordinator of religious programs should have an appropriate combination of graduate coursework, formal training, and experience. The director or coordinator of religious programs, or a professional staff member, should have a doctoral graduate theological degree, such as a Th.D. or Ph.D., and course work in theology, Bible, church history, religion in higher education, and pastoral counseling.

Any director or coordinator should have:
- an understanding of and a commitment to spiritual and religious development as a part of a student's human growth
- the ability to treat fairly all varieties of campus religious experience and personal faith

Depending upon the legal constraints of the institution, the responsibilities of the director or coordinator for religious programs may include . . .
- the development and communication of policies relating to religious programs which are educationally sound and legally acceptable
- the development of procedures whereby students may organize for religious or moral purposes and participate in programs and activities aimed at their spiritual and religious growth
- the provision of access to campus facilities for those responsible for religious programs; and the provision of opportunities for counseling in relation to students' religious needs

Degree or credential-seeking interns must be qualified by enrollment in an appropriate field of study and by relevant experience. These individuals must be trained and supervised adequately by professional staff members holding educational credentials and related work experience appropriate for supervision.

Student employees and volunteers must be carefully selected, trained, supervised, and evaluated. They must be trained on how and when to refer those in need of assistance to qualified staff members and have access to a supervisor for assistance in making these judgments. Student employees and volunteers must be provided clear and precise job descriptions, pre-service training based on assessed needs, and continuing staff development.

SRP must have technical and support staff members adequate to accomplish its mission. Staff members must be technologically proficient and qualified to perform their job functions, be knowledgeable of ethical and legal uses of technology, and have access to training. The level of staffing and workloads must be adequate and appropriate for program and service demands.

Salary levels and fringe benefits for all SRP staff members must be commensurate with those for comparable positions within the institution, in similar institutions, and in the relevant geographic area.

On a campus that is not church related, any employee responsible for coordinating the religious program should be paid by the institution. This official should be unbiased and neutral in his/her relationships to all agencies participating in the program.

SRP must institute hiring and promotion practices that are fair, inclusive, and non-discriminatory. Programs and services must employ a diverse staff to provide readily identifiable role models for students and to enrich the campus community.

SRP must create and maintain position descriptions for all staff members and provide regular performance planning and appraisals.

SRP must have a system for regular staff evaluation and must provide access to continuing education and professional development opportunities, including in-service training programs and participation in professional conferences and workshops.

Affiliation with appropriate professional organizations is encouraged.

Adjunct staff members should possess qualifications consistent with the particular religious body they represent and appropriate for a higher education setting.

## Part 6. FINANCIAL RESOURCES

Student Religious Programs (SRP) must have adequate funding to accomplish its mission and goals. Funding priorities must be determined within the context of the stated mission, goals, objectives, and comprehensive analysis of the needs and capabilities of students, and the availability of internal or external resources.

At a minimum the institution should provide sufficient funding for any institutional staff member(s) and the operational costs related to its religious programs. If this assignment accounts for only a part of an individual staff member's work load, the budget should clearly indicate the portion that is available for religious programs.

SRP must demonstrate fiscal responsibility and cost effectiveness consistent with institutional protocols.

Funding for personnel and programs of adjunct agencies (i.e., not directly provided by the institution) must be assumed by the sponsors of the adjunct agency.

## Part 7. FACILITIES, TECHNOLOGY, EQUIPMENT

Student Religious Programs (SRP) must have adequate, suitably located facilities, adequate technology, and equipment to support its mission and goals efficiently and effectively. Facilities, technology, and equipment must be evaluated regularly and be in compliance with relevant federal, state, provincial, and local requirements to provide for access, health, safety, and security.

Opportunity must be provided for all student religious groups to utilize campus facilities on the same basis as other student organizations.

In public institutions, whenever space is made permanently and/or exclusively available for specific religious personnel of adjunct agencies, arrangements should be made whereby the institution is appropriately reimbursed for expenses.

Public institutions should provide fair and equitable arrangements and facilities for specific religious groups' programming.

Private institutions may provide facilities specifically designed to suit the purpose of a preferred religious group.

Wherever possible, but especially in residential units, suitable areas for individual meditation and small group spiritual interaction are desirable.

## Part 8. LEGAL RESPONSIBILITIES

Student Religious Programs (SRP) staff members must be knowledgeable about and responsive to laws and regulations that relate to their respective responsibilities. SRP staff members must inform users of programs and services and officials, as appropriate, of legal obligations and limitations including constitutional, statutory, regulatory, and case law; mandatory laws and orders emanating from federal, state/provincial and local governments; and the institution's policies.

SRP staff members must use reasonable and informed practices to limit the liability exposure of the institution, its officers, employees, and agents. Staff members must be informed about institutional policies regarding personal liability and related insurance coverage options.

The institution must provide access to legal advice for SRP staff members as needed to carry out assigned responsibilities.

The institution must inform SRP staff and students in a timely and systematic fashion about extraordinary or changing legal obligations and potential liabilities.

## Part 9.  EQUITY and ACCESS

Student Religious Programs (SRP) staff members must ensure that services and programs are provided on a fair and equitable basis.  Facilities, programs and services must be accessible.  Hours of operation and delivery of and access to programs and services must be responsive to the needs of all students and other constituents.  SRP must adhere to the spirit and intent of equal opportunity laws.

Policies and practices of SRP must not discriminate on the basis of age, color, disability, sex, national origin, race, religious creed, sexual identity, and/or veteran status.  Exceptions are appropriate only where provided by relevant law and institutional policy.

Consistent with their mission and goals, SRP must take affirmative action to remedy significant imbalances in student participation and staffing patterns.

As the demographic profiles of campuses change and new instructional delivery methods are introduced, institutions must recognize the needs of students who participate in distance learning for access to programs and services offered on campus.  ☐Institutions must provide appropriate services in ways that are accessible to distance learners and assist them in identifying and gaining access to other appropriate services in their geographic region.

## Part 10.  CAMPUS and EXTERNAL RELATIONS

Student Religious Programs (SRP) must establish, maintain, and promote effective relations with relevant individuals, campus offices, and external agencies.

Because religion and spirituality may be concerns of many academic disciplines and may have an important impact on some aspects of student development activity, staff assigned to religious programs should consult with and coordinate their programs with interested colleagues.

The director/coordinator or chaplain may interact will faculty and staff formally through advisory councils or through informal contacts.

Continuing attention should be given to developing and improving relationships with both on campus and off campus publics. Specific programs and action projects may arise from many sources (e.g., academic departments, on campus groups such as residence halls and college students unions, and off campus organizations, whether local, regional, and/or national).

Institutional staff should meet with adjunct personnel from religious groups on a periodic basis.

## Part 11.  DIVERSITY

Within the context of each institution's unique mission, diversity enriches the community and enhances the collegiate experience for all; therefore, Student Religious Programs (SRP) must nurture environments where commonalties and differences among people are recognized and honored.

SRP must promote educational experiences that are characterized by open and continuous communication that deepens understanding of one's own identity, culture, and heritage, and that of others.  SRP must educate and promote respect about commonalties and differences in their historical and cultural contexts.

SRP must address the characteristics and needs of a diverse population when establishing and implementing policies and procedures.

## Part 12.  ETHICS

All persons involved in the delivery of Student Religious Programs (SRP) must adhere to the highest principles of ethical behavior.  SRP must develop or adopt and implement appropriate statements of ethical practice.  SRP must publish these statements and ensure their periodic review by relevant constituencies .

SRP staff members must ensure that privacy and confidentiality are maintained with respect to all communications and records to the extent that such records are protected under the law and appropriate statements of ethical practice. Information contained in students' education records must not be disclosed without written consent except as allowed by relevant laws and institutional policies.  Staff members must disclose to appropriate authorities information judged to be of an emergency nature, especially when the safety of the individual or others is involved, or when otherwise required by institutional policy or relevant law.

All SRP staff members must be aware of and comply with the provisions contained in the institution's human subjects research policy and in other relevant institutional policies addressing ethical practices and confidentiality of research data concerning individuals.

SRP staff members must recognize and avoid personal conflict of interest or appearance thereof in their transactions with students and others.

SRP staff members must strive to insure the fair, objective, and impartial treatment of all persons with whom they deal. Staff members must not participate in nor condone any form of harassment that demeans persons or creates an intimidating, hostile, or offensive campus environment.

Accommodation may be made in institutional class schedules so that students and staff from religious minorities may carry out the essential practices of their religion. Administrators should proceed with caution in such matters, however, due to the inevitable conflict of competing religious practices within any campus community.

When handling institutional funds, all SRP staff members must ensure that such funds are managed in accordance with established and responsible accounting procedures and the fiscal policies or processes of the institution.

SRP staff members must perform their duties within the limits of their training, expertise, and competence. When these limits are exceeded, individuals in need of further assistance must be referred to persons possessing appropriate qualifications.

SRP staff members must use suitable means to confront and otherwise hold accountable other staff members who exhibit unethical behavior.

SRP staff members must be knowledgeable about and practice ethical behavior in the use of technology.

The Constitutional rights of students and faculty and staff members of all religious beliefs must be respected.

Public institutions must avoid any policies or actions which favor one particular faith over another.

As the institution carries out its academic program, fair and reasonable consideration should be given to the need of campus members to participate in the basic activities of their faiths. Institutional policies and practices should be reviewed regularly so as to avoid undue interference with the free exercise of religion.

Private institutions which sponsor or require particular religious activities must clearly state so in their pre-admission literature, thus permitting a potential student to exercise free choice in this regard before admission. SRP staff members must work to provide reasonable access for all groups and points-of view to any public forums sponsored by the institution.

Membership requirements for on campus religious groups must be consistent with their stated purposes. No group can be required to participate in any extraordinary institutional arrangement or program that would violate a principle or tenet of their faith.

All religious groups must be accorded the same rights and privileges and be held accountable in the same manner as any other campus organization.

SRP staff members must attempt to protect students, through policy and practice, from undue influence or harassment from persons advocating particular religious positions or activities.

Accommodation may be made in institutional class schedules so that students and staff from religious minorities may carry out the essential practices of their religion. Administrators should proceed with caution in such matters, however, due to the inevitable conflict of competing religious practices within any campus community.

## Part 13. ASSESSMENT and EVALUATION

Student Religious Programs (SRP) must conduct regular assessment and evaluations. SRP must employ effective qualitative and quantitative methodologies as appropriate, to determine whether and to what degree the stated mission, goals, and student learning and development outcomes are being met. The process must employ sufficient and sound assessment measures to ensure comprehensiveness. Data collected must include responses from students and other affected constituencies.

Each institution should require evaluation of its religious program to determine the achievement of goals, the public being reached and its overall effectiveness.

This evaluation may be made in concert with the periodic examination of the diverse needs and interests of students and other members of the campus community.

SRP must evaluate periodically how well they complement and enhance the institution's stated mission and educational effectiveness.

Data should be collected from officers and advisors of campus religious organizations to determine the effectiveness of policies affecting religious activity.

In the case of church related institutions, policies and practices should be assessed to ensure consistency with theological and moral standards of sponsoring bodies.

Results of these evaluations must be used in revising and improving programs and services and in recognizing staff performance.

# The ROLE of TRIO* and OTHER EDUCATIONAL OPPORTUNITY PROGRAMS
## *CAS* Standards Contextual Statement

Students from low-income and first-generation backgrounds historically have had limited access to higher education. With the realization that the ideals of American higher education include access for all, both state and federal legislation have been enacted to mitigate some of these inequities. Since the 1960's, a variety of educational opportunity programs have been developed at the state and federal levels to increase access and persistence in higher education for students from disadvantaged backgrounds.

The TRIO Programs are federally funded educational opportunity programs designed to motivate and support students from disadvantaged backgrounds to attend and persist in post-secondary education. TRIO includes five outreach programs that target students who are from low-income families and who are the first generation college students. TRIO serves students from middle school to post-baccalaureate programs. In addition, TRIOs professional development component provides training opportunities for directors and staff of TRIO projects.

The TRIO programs are authorized under the Higher Education of 1965, Title IV, Part A, Subpart 2. FEDERAL TRIO PROGRAMS, as amended in 1998. Programs are administered by the US Department of Education, Office of Post-secondary Education, Division of Higher Education Preparation and Support Service (HEPS). TRIO projects are funded through competitive grant applications. In 2000, there were 2,341 TRIO projects at 1100 institutions of higher education or community agencies, serving approximately 724,735 students.

The Council for Opportunity in Education represents over 7,000 TRIO program staff; sponsors professional development activities including national conferences, symposia; workshops, and publications; sponsors TRIO and educational access research; advocates for TRIO programs and students; and acts as liaison with the US Department of Education.

The initial TRIO programs included Upward Bound, which emerged from the Economic Opportunity Act of 1964 as part of President Johnson's War on Poverty; Talent Search, created in 1965 as part of the Higher Education Act; and Student Support Services, in 1968. The term "TRIO" referred to these original federal programs. The Higher Education Amendments of 1972 added Educational Opportunity Centers and the 1986 Amendments authorized the Ronald E. McNair Post-

baccalaureate Achievement Program. The DOE established the Upward Bound Math/Science Program as a subset to Upward Bound in 1990.

Program Descriptions

Educational Opportunity Centers (EOC) provide counseling and information about college admissions and financial aid with the goal of increasing the number of adult participants who enroll in post-secondary education. Services include advising; counseling; provision of information about educational opportunities and financial assistance; help with completing applications for college admissions; testing, and financial aid; coordination with educational institutions and community partnerships; and provision of referrals, tutoring, and mentoring.

The Ronald E. McNair Post-baccalaureate Achievement program prepares undergraduates to enter doctoral studies. McNair participants are from disadvantaged backgrounds and have demonstrated strong academic potential. The goal of McNair is to increase graduate degree attainment by students from low-income, first-generation, and under-represented groups. Services include the provision of mentors; scholarly activities to prepare students for doctoral study; summer research internships; tutoring; counseling; assistance with securing graduate program admission and financial aid; preparation for GRE exams; and other activities that enhance successful entry to and persistence in doctoral programs.

The Student Support Services (SSS) program provides academic support for low-income, first-generation students and students with disabilities. Support is provided through academic development, assistance with college requirements, and activities that motivate students to complete post-secondary education. The goal of SSS is to increase college retention and graduation rates, and to facilitate two-year college student transition to four year institutions. Services include: basic skills instruction and tutoring,; academic, financial, and personal counseling; assistance with graduate or professional school admission and financial aid; mentoring; special services for students with limited English proficiency; cultural activities; and accommodations for students with disabilities.

The Talent Search program identifies, motivates and assists low-income, first generation youth to complete high school and enter and persist in higher education. Talent Search also serves high school dropouts by encouraging them to reenter the educational system and complete formal education. The goal of Talent Search is to increase the number of youth from disadvantaged backgrounds who complete high school and enroll in post-secondary education. Talent Search serves sixth to twelfth grade students by providing academic, financial, career, and personal counseling; tutoring; information about post-secondary education and college visits; procedures for completing college admissions and financial aid applications; preparation for college entrance exams; mentoring; and middle school student and family involvement activities.

Upward Bound is an intensive college preparatory support project designed to provide low-income, first-generation high school students with encouragement and the essential skills to complete high school and earn a post-secondary degree. The goal of Upward Bound is to increase post-secondary enrollment and graduation rates of participants. Upward Bound provides instruction and enrichment activities throughout the calendar year. Other services provided include study skill development; academic, financial, and personal counseling; tutoring; cultural and social activities; information about post-secondary education opportunities and college visits, assistance with college entrance and financial aid applications; and preparation for college entrance exams. The Veterans' Upward Bound program serves military veterans who are preparing to enter post-secondary education. The Upward Bound Math Science program authorizes the Department of Education to fund specialized Upward Bound Math and Science Centers designed to strengthen high school students' math and science skills and to encourage students to pursue post-secondary degrees in math and science. Services include intensive summer math and science experiences, counseling and advising, computer instruction, and research activities.

### References, Readings and Resources

Wolanin, T. (April, 1997). The history of TRIO: Three decades of success and counting. *NCEOA Journal*, pp. 2-4.

Council for Opportunity in Education, 1025 Vermont Avenue, N.W. Suite 900, Washington, DC 20005. (202) 347-7430; Fax: (202) 347-0786
Web Page: www.trioprograms.org

National TRIO Clearinghouse, Vermont Ave. N. W., Suite 900, Washington, DC 20005, Phone: (202) 347-2218, Fax: (202) 347-0786 www.trioprograms.org (clickon) TRIO Clearing-house

United States Department of Education, Office of Post-secondary Education, Higher Education Preparation and Support (TRIO Program Administration)
www.ed.gov/offices/OPE/HEP/hepss/index.html

# TRIO and OTHER EDUCATIONAL OPPORTUNITY PROGRAMS
## CAS STANDARDS and GUIDELINES

## Part 1. MISSION

The mission of TRIO and other educational opportunity programs is to encourage and assist people who are traditionally under-represented in post-secondary education because of income, family educational background, disability, or other relevant federal, state, provincial or institutional criteria, in the preparation for, entry to, and completion of a post-secondary education.

To accomplish this mission, TRIO programs must . . .
- serve as advocate for access to higher education
- provide services to assist individuals to achieve their educational goals
- facilitate the educational development of individuals served
- provide an environment that recognizes the diversity of backgrounds and learning styles of the individuals served
- develop collaborative relationships with institutions, organizations, and communities to promote an environment conducive to the completion of a post-secondary education

TRIO programs must incorporate student learning and student development in its mission. TRIO programs must enhance overall educational experiences. TRIO programs must develop, record, disseminate, implement and regularly review its mission and goals. Mission statements must be consistent with the mission and goals of the institution and with the standards in this document. TRIO programs must operate as an integral part of the institution's overall mission.

TRIO programs should address the developmental needs of the individuals served. Programs and services should enable the individual to acquire the necessary skills and attributes to complete a post-secondary education.

## Part 2. PROGRAM

The formal education of students consists of the curriculum and the co-curriculum, and must promote student learning and development that is purposeful and holistic. TRIO and other educational opportunity must identify relevant and desirable student learning and development outcomes and provide programs and services that encourage the achievement of those outcomes.

Relevant and desirable outcomes include: intellectual growth, effective communication,

realistic self-appraisal, enhanced self-esteem, clarified values, career choices, leadership development, healthy behaviors, meaningful interpersonal relationships, independence, collaboration, social responsibility, satisfying and productive lifestyles, appreciation of diversity, spiritual awareness, and achievement of personal and educational goals.

TRIO programs must provide evidence of its impact on the achievement of student learning and development outcomes.

The program may use the examples that follow or identify other more germane indicators.

### Student Learning & Development Outcome Domains

#### Intellectual Growth
Examples of Achievement Indicators
Produces personal and educational goal statements; Employs critical thinking in problem solving; Uses complex information from a variety of sources including personal experience and observation to form a decision or opinion; Obtains a degree; Applies previously understood information and concepts to a new situation or setting; Expresses appreciation for literature, the fine arts, mathematics, sciences, and social sciences

#### Effective Communication
Examples of Achievement Indicators
Writes and speaks coherently and effectively; Writes and speaks after reflection; Able to influence others through writing, speaking or artistic expression; Effectively articulates abstract ideas; Uses appropriate syntax; Makes presentations or gives performances

#### Enhanced Self-Esteem
Examples of Achievement Indicators
Shows self-respect and respect for others; Initiates actions toward achievement of goals; Takes reasonable risks; Demonstrates assertive behavior; Functions without need for constant reassurance from others

#### Realistic Self-Appraisal
Examples of Achievement Indicators
Articulates personal skills and abilities; Makes decisions and acts in congruence with personal values; Acknowledges personal strengths and weaknesses; Articulates rationale for personal behavior; Seeks feedback from others; Learns from past experiences

#### Clarified Values
Examples of Achievement Indicators
Articulates personal values; Acts in congruence with personal values; Makes decisions that reflect personal values; Demonstrates willingness to scrutinize personal beliefs and values; Identifies personal, work and lifestyle values and explains how they influence decision-making

## Career Choices
Examples of Achievement Indicators

Articulate career choices based on assessment of interests, values, skills and abilities; Documents knowledge, skills and accomplishments resulting from formal education, work experience, community service and volunteer experiences; Makes the connections between classroom and out-of-classroom learning; Can construct a resume with clear job objectives and evidence of related knowledge, skills and accomplishments; Articulates the characteristics of a preferred work environment; Comprehends the world of work; Takes steps to initiate a job search or seek advanced education

## Leadership Development
Examples of Achievement Indicators

Articulates leadership philosophy or style; Serves in a leadership position in a student organization; Comprehends the dynamics of a group; Exhibits democratic principles as a leader; Exhibits ability to visualize a group purpose and desired outcomes

## Healthy Behavior
Examples of Achievement Indicators

Chooses behaviors and environments that promote health and reduce risk; Articulate the relationship between health and wellness and accomplishing life long goals; Exhibits behaviors that advance a healthy community

## Meaningful Interpersonal Relationships
Examples of Achievement Indicators

Develops and maintains satisfying interpersonal relationships; Establishes mutually rewarding relationships with friends and colleagues; Listens to and considers others' points of view; Treats others with respect

## Independence
Examples of Achievement Indicators

Exhibits self-reliant behaviors; Functions autonomously; Exhibits ability to function interdependently; Accepts supervision as needed; Manages time effectively

## Collaboration
Examples of Achievement Indicators

Works cooperatively with others; Seeks the involvement of others; Seeks feedback from others; Contributes to achievement of a group goal; Exhibits effective listening skills

## Social Responsibility
Examples of Achievement Indicators

Understands and participates in relevant governance systems; Understands, abides by, and participates in the development, maintenance, and/or orderly change of community, social, and legal standards or norms; Appropriately challenges the unfair, unjust, or uncivil behavior of other individuals or groups; Participates in service/volunteer activities

## Satisfying and Productive Lifestyles
Examples of Achievement Indicators

Achieves balance between education, work and leisure time; Articulates and meets goals for work, leisure and education; Overcomes obstacles that hamper goal achievement; Functions on the basis of personal identity, ethical, spiritual and moral values; Articulates long-term goals and objectives

## Appreciating Diversity
Examples of Achievement Indicators

Understands ones own identity and culture. Seeks involvement with people different from oneself; Seeks involvement in diverse interests; Articulate the advantages and challenges of a diverse society; Challenges appropriately abusive use of stereotypes by others; Understands the impact of diversity on one's own society

## Spiritual Awareness
Examples of Achievement Indicators

Develops and articulates personal belief system; Understands roles of spirituality in personal and group values and behaviors

## Personal and Educational Goals
Examples of Achievement Indicators

Sets, articulates, and pursues individual goals; Articulate personal and educational goals and objectives; Uses personal and educational goals to guide decisions; Understands the effect of one's personal and education goals on others

**TRIO programs must be (a) intentional, (b) coherent, (c) based on theories and knowledge of learning and human development, (d) reflective of developmental and demographic profiles of the student population, and (e) responsive to needs of individuals, special populations, and communities.**

**All TRIO programs must support the retention and graduation of their students.**

**Activities and services must address the specific objectives of each TRIO programs.**
Programs, services, and activities for students involved in specific TRIO programs should include academic support services such as academic instruction; tutoring; English as a Second Language (ESL) activities; collaborative learning opportunities; supplemental instruction; development of oral and written communication skills; assessment of academic needs, skills and individual plans to provide appropriate interventions; monitoring of academic progress; preparation for proficiency and entrance exams; academic advising; opportunities for national and international study exchange; research internships; and opportunities to present and publish research.

Programming should also include a variety of mentoring experiences; career development and work internship activities; activities to assist with college admissions and financial aid; activities to prepare students for matriculation into graduate education; coordination with clubs and school activities; academic and cultural field trips; social activities; activities to encourage appreciation of cultural and ethnic diversity; athletic and physical development; leadership development; and other activities that promote matriculation into post-secondary or graduate schools, and support retention, persistence, and graduation.

TRIO programs should also implement programming with their own institution or agency, and with schools, community, and student families to accomplish their mission.

## Part 3. LEADERSHIP

Effective and ethical leadership is essential to the success of all organizations. Institutions must appoint, position, and empower TRIO and other educational opportunity leaders within the administrative structure to accomplish stated missions. TRIO program leaders at various levels must be selected on the basis of formal education and training, relevant work experience, personal skills and competencies, relevant professional credentials, as well as potential for promoting learning and development in students, applying effective practices to educational processes, and enhancing institutional effectiveness. Institutions must determine expectations of accountability for leaders and fairly assess their performance.

TRIO program leaders must exercise authority over resources for which they are responsible to achieve their respective missions.

TRIO program leaders must . . .
- articulate a vision for their organization
- set goals and objectives based on the needs and capabilities of the population served
- promote student learning and development
- prescribe and practice ethical behavior
- recruit, select, supervise, and develop others in the organization
- manage financial resources
- coordinate human resources
- plan, budget for, and evaluate personnel and programs
- apply effective practices to educational and administrative processes
- communicate effectively
- initiate collaborative interaction between individuals and agencies that possess legitimate concerns and interests in the functional area

TRIO program leaders must identify and find means to address individual, organizational, or environmental conditions that inhibit goal achievement.

Program leaders must promote campus environments that result in multiple opportunities for student learning and development. TRIO program leaders must continuously improve programs and services in response to changing needs of students and other constituents, and evolving institutional priorities.

## Part 4. ORGANIZATION and MANAGEMENT

Guided by an overarching intent to ensure student learning and development, TRIO and other educational opportunity programs must be structured purposefully and managed effectively to achieve stated goals. Evidence of appropriate structure must include current and accessible policies and procedures, written performance expectations for all employees, functional workflow graphics or organizational charts, and clearly stated service delivery expectations.

Evidence of effective management must include use of comprehensive and accurate information for decisions, clear sources and channels of authority, effective communication practices, decision-making and conflict resolution procedures, responsiveness to changing conditions, accountability and evaluation systems, and recognition and reward processes. TRIO programs must provide channels within the organization for regular review of administrative policies and procedures.

TRIO programs must be placed in the institution's organizational structure to promote cooperative interaction with appropriate campus or community entities and to develop the support of senior administrators.

TRIO programs should be positioned to assure appropriate recognition and visibility.

## Part 5. HUMAN RESOURCES

TRIO and other educational opportunity programs must be staffed adequately by individuals qualified to accomplish its mission and goals. Within established guidelines of the institution, programs and services must establish procedures for staff selection, training, and evaluation; set expectations for supervision, and provide appropriate professional development opportunities. TRIO programs must strive to improve the professional competence and skills of all personnel it employs.

TRIO program professional staff members must hold an earned graduate degree in a field relevant to the position they hold or must possess an appropriate combination of educational credentials and related work experience.

Degree or credential-seeking interns must be qualified by enrollment in an appropriate field of study and by relevant experience. These individuals must be trained and supervised adequately by professional staff members holding educational credentials and related work experience appropriate for supervision.

Student employees and volunteers must be carefully selected, trained, supervised, and evaluated. They must be trained on how and when to refer those in need of assistance to qualified staff members and have access to a supervisor for assistance in making these judgments. Student employees and volunteers must be provided clear and precise job descriptions, pre-service training based on assessed needs, and continuing staff development.

TRIO programs must have technical and support staff members adequate to accomplish its mission. Staff members must be technologically proficient and qualified to perform their job functions, be knowledgeable of ethical and legal uses of technology, and have access to training. The level of staffing and workloads must be adequate and appropriate for program and service demands.

Salary levels and fringe benefits for all TRIO program staff members must be commensurate with those for comparable positions within the institution, in similar institutions, and in the relevant geographic area.

TRIO programs must institute hiring and promotion practices that are fair, inclusive, and non-discriminatory. Programs must employ a diverse staff to provide readily identifiable role models for students and to enrich the campus community.

TRIO programs must create and maintain position descriptions for all staff members and provide regular performance planning and appraisals. Hiring and promotion practices must ensure diverse staffing profiles.

TRIO programs must have a system for regular staff evaluation and must provide access to continuing education and professional development opportunities, including in-service training

programs and participation in professional conferences and workshops.

TRIO program professional staff members must possess a combination of knowledge and experience in working with individuals who are traditionally under-represented in post-secondary education.

Professional staff members should possess . . .
- effective oral and written communication skills
- an understanding of the culture, heritage, and learning styles of the persons served by the program
- leadership, management, organizational, and human relations skills

Student employees and volunteers from groups traditionally under-represented in higher education should be used and assigned responsibilities that are within the scope of their competencies.

The size, scope, and role of the program staff depend on the mission of TRIO programs and the populations served. Staffing should be based on the needs of the students or participants and the resources available. When possible, the staff should reflect the characteristics of the population being served.

TRIO programs should provide continuing professional development opportunities for staff such as in-service training programs, TRIO professional training seminars, participation in professional conferences, workshops, or other continuing education activities.

TRIO program staff members should contribute to the knowledge and practice of the profession through research and publications.

## Part 6. FINANCIAL RESOURCES

TRIO and other educational opportunity programs must have adequate funding to accomplish its mission and goals. Funding priorities must be determined within the context of the stated mission, goals, objectives and comprehensive analysis of the needs and capabilities of students and the availability of internal or external resources.

TRIO programs must demonstrate fiscal responsibility and cost effectiveness consistent with institutional protocols.

## Part 7. FACILITIES, TECHNOLOGY, EQUIPMENT

TRIO and other educational opportunity programs must have adequate, suitably located facilities, adequate technology, and equipment to support its mission and goals efficiently and effectively. Facilities, technology, and equipment must be evaluated regularly and be in compliance with relevant federal, state, provincial, and local requirements to provide for access, health, safety, and security.

As applicable, the facilities must include, or the staff must have access to, private offices or spaces for counseling, advising, tutoring, interviewing, or meetings of a confidential nature. Facilities must be accessible to persons with disabilities.

TRIO programs facilities should be physically located to promote visibility of the programs and to ensure coordination with other campus programs and services.

TRIO programs should have equal access to the institution's technological resources.

TRIO programs should advocate for and facilitate access to technology for their students and families. Technology should be employed to promote and provide academic and other student services, and to communicate with students including those at outreach locations. Programs should intentionally model for their students the use of technology.

## Part 8. LEGAL RESPONSIBILITIES

TRIO and other educational opportunity program staff members must be knowledgeable about and responsive to laws and regulations that relate to their respective responsibilities. Staff members must inform users of programs and services and officials, as appropriate, of legal obligations and limitations including constitutional, statutory, regulatory, and case law; mandatory laws and orders emanating from federal, state/provincial and local governments; and the institution's policies.

TRIO staff members must use reasonable and informed practices to limit the liability exposure of the institution, its officers, employees, and agents. Staff members must be informed about institutional policies regarding personal liability and related insurance coverage options.

The institution must provide access to legal advice for TRIO staff members as needed to carry out assigned responsibilities and must inform staff and students in a timely and systematic fashion about extraordinary or changing legal obligations and potential liabilities.

## Part 9. EQUITY and ACCESS

TRIO and other educational opportunity program staff members must ensure that services and programs are provided on a fair and equitable basis. Facilities, programs, and services must be accessible. Hours of operation and delivery of and access to programs and services must be responsive to the needs of all students and other constituents. TRIO programs must adhere to the spirit and intent of equal opportunity laws.

TRIO programs must be open and readily accessible to all students and must not discriminate except where sanctioned by law and institutional policy. Discrimination must especially be avoided on the bases of age; color, creed; cultural heritage; disability; ethnicity; gender identity; nationality; political affiliation, religious affiliation, sex, sexual orientation; or economic, marital, social, or veteran status.

Consistent with their mission and goals, TRIO programs must take affirmative action to remedy significant imbalances in student participation and staffing patterns.

As the demographic profiles of campuses change and new instructional delivery methods are introduced, institutions must recognize the needs of students who participate in distance learning for access to programs and services offered on campus. Institutions must provide appropriate services in ways that are accessible to distance learners and assist them in identifying and gaining access to other appropriate services in their geographic region.

## Part 10. CAMPUS and EXTERNAL RELATIONS

TRIO and other educational opportunity programs must establish, maintain, and promote collaborative relations with relevant individuals, campus offices, external agencies, project area schools, community organizations, and students' families.

TRIO programs must include a public relations component to regularly inform the institutions, communities, agencies, and schools about their mission and services.

## Part 11. DIVERSITY

Within the context of each institution's unique mission, diversity enriches the community and enhances the collegiate experience for all; therefore, TRIO and other educational opportunity programs must nurture environments where commonalties and differences among people are recognized and honored.

TRIO programs must promote educational experiences that are characterized by open and continuous communication that deepens understanding of one's own identity, culture, and heritage, and that of others. Programs must educate and promote respect about commonalties and differences in their historical and cultural contexts.

TRIO programs must address the characteristics and needs of a diverse population when establishing and implementing policies and procedures.

## Part 12. ETHICS

All persons involved in the delivery of TRIO and other educational opportunity programs must adhere to the highest principles of ethical behavior. Programs must develop or adopt and implement appropriate statements of ethical practice. TRIO programs must publish these statements and ensure their periodic review by relevant constituencies.

TRIO staff members must ensure that privacy and confidentiality are maintained with respect to all communications and records to the extent that such records are protected under the law and appropriate statements of ethical practice. Information contained in students' education records must not be disclosed without written consent except as allowed by relevant laws and institutional policies. Staff members must disclose to appropriate authorities information judged to be of an emergency nature, especially when the safety of the individual or others is involved, or when otherwise required by institutional policy or relevant law.

All TRIO staff members must be aware of and comply with the provisions contained in the institution's human subjects research policy and in other relevant institutional policies addressing ethical practices and confidentiality of research data concerning individuals.

TRIO staff members must recognize and avoid personal conflict of interest or appearance thereof in their transactions with students and others.

Program staff members must strive to insure the fair, objective, and impartial treatment of all persons with whom they deal. Staff members must not participate in nor condone any form of harassment that demeans persons or creates an intimidating, hostile, or offensive campus environment.

When handling institutional funds, all TRIO staff members must ensure that such funds are managed in accordance with established and responsible accounting procedures and the fiscal policies or processes of the institution.

TRIO staff members must perform their duties within the limits of their training, expertise, and competence. When these limits are exceeded, individuals in need of further assistance must be referred to persons possessing appropriate qualifications.

TRIO program staff members must use suitable means to confront and otherwise hold accountable other staff members who exhibit unethical behavior. Staff members also must be knowledge-able about and practice ethical behavior in the use of technology.

## Part 13. ASSESSMENT and EVALUATION

TRIO and other educational opportunity programs must conduct regular assessment and evaluations. TRIO programs must employ effective qualitative and quantitative methodologies as appropriate, to determine whether and to what degree the stated mission, goals, and student learning and development outcomes are being met. The process must employ sufficient and sound assessment measures to ensure comprehensiveness. Data collected must include responses from students and other affected constituencies.

TRIO programs must evaluate periodically how well they complement and enhance the institution's stated mission and educational effectiveness. Results of these evaluations must be used in revising and improving programs and services and in recognizing staff performance.

Annual program performance reports must be conducted in accordance with federal project guidelines.
Annual evaluation reports should be made available, when appropriate, to the program's various stakeholders, such as relevant campus offices, external agencies, area schools, and community organizations.

# The ROLE OF WOMEN STUDENT PROGRAMS and SERVICES
## *CAS* Standards Contextual Statement

With the appointment of the first Dean of Women, Lois Kimball Mathews, at the University of Wisconsin in 1910, female college students began to receive more systematic institutional attention. In comparison to their male counterparts, however, women were not as highly valued nor did deans of women have much authority. Consequently, it was no surprise when the women deans caucused soon after their positions came into being and the National Association for Deans of Women (NADW) was established. This organization actually preceded the establishment of its counterpart for deans of men, the National Association for Deans of Men (NADM) by two years, in 1916. Even with the existence of these professional associations, it took half a century for institution and association politics to evolve to a point where equality and integration of men and women in the academic community became a reality.

The American College Personnel Association (ACPA), established in 1924, was from the outset open to both men and women. Although it initially joined forces with NADW under the auspices of the National Education Association (NEA), immediately following WW2, ACPA chose to become Division I of the American Personnel and Guidance Association (APGA), while NADW remained autonomous. NADM became the National Association of Student Personnel Administrators (NASPA), which women joined in large numbers after they were accepted for membership. NADW evolved into the National Association for Women in Education (NAWE) and, although open to male members, it has remained an overwhelmingly female association committed to the advancement of both women students and professionals. Its members and leaders have been highly involved in the development of programs and services for women students during the past two decades.

Women students currently represent over 50 percent of all college and university students and an increasing number of women are returning to campus after years in the workforce or at home raising families. With the passage of Title IX of the Education Amendments of 1972, which prohibits discrimination on the basis of gender, women programs and services were established for women to better assure institutional access by removing barriers that had developed over the years. These programs also provide support for women students who need help in achieving their personal and educational goals, many of which are unclear after a hiatus of several years from higher education.

Women student programs and services typically include personal and career counseling, developmental workshops and classes, small weekly programs, and large campus events. These support services provide both individual and comprehensive campus-wide advocacy for women, often centering on empowerment, violence, and safety issues. Programs also focus on political and personal issues that assist women students in decision-making in accordance with their values and beliefs. Provision of these support activities is designed to help women students achieve success in their chosen careers and better understand the changing roles of women in society.

Because women student programs and services are an essential and integral part of any comprehensive institution of higher learning, there is a continuing need for creating and maintaining well-managed and adequately financed programs designed to meet the special educational and developmental needs of women students. The *CAS Standards and Guidelines for Women Student Programs and Services* have been created to enhance this important educational need.

### Recommended Readings and Resources

Aburdene, P., & Naisbitt, J., (1992). *Megatrends for women.* New York: Villard Books.

Astin, H. S., & Leland, C.(1991). *Women of influence, women of vision: A cross-generational study of leaders and social change.* San Francisco: Jossey-Bass.

Pearson, C. S., Shavlik, D. L. & Touchton, J. G. (1989). *Educating the majority: Women challenge tradition in higher education.* New York: American Council on Education, Macmillan.

Sagaria, M. A., (Ed.). (1989*). Empowering women: Leadership development strategies on campus.* New Directions for Student Services, No. 44. San Francisco: Jossey-Bass.

### Special Note:

In August 2000, the National Association of Women in Education (NAWE) was dissolved with some of its programs being transferred to Higher Education Resource Services (HERS) Mid-America at the University of Denver. NAWE was a founding member of CAS in 1979..

# WOMEN STUDENT PROGRAMS and SERVICES
## *CAS* STANDARDS and GUIDELINES

## Part 1. MISSION

Women student programs and services (WSPS) must incorporate student learning and student development in its mission. WSPS must enhance overall educational experiences. WSPS must develop, record, disseminate, implement, and regularly review its mission and goals. Mission statements must be consistent with the mission and goals of the institution and with the standards in this document. Programs must operate as an integral part of the institution's overall mission.

The mission of WSPS is to promote unrestricted access and full involvement of women students in all aspects of the college or university experience. WSPS must consider and respond to the diverse needs of women students and must help these students benefit from the institution's total educational process.

To accomplish this mission, the goals of WSPS must be to . . .

- assist women in achieving full potential in education, personal lives and work through personal empowerment, expansion of opportunities, and professional development
- provide programs, services and facilities to meet educational, personal, physical, and safety needs of women students
- ensure that the institution provides women students equal access to educational opportunities, services, and facilities
- encourage the development of self-awareness, self esteem, and self-confidence of women students and promote leadership opportunities for them
- recognize and plan for diversity among the women student population, e.g., ethnicity, race, religion, disability, sexual orientation, age, and socioeconomic status
- act as an advocate for women students
- serve as a catalyst for change to enhance the education of women on campus
- offer or identify appropriate mentors and role models for women students

Women students in any institution of higher education are entitled to the full benefits of the curricular and co-curricular programs and services offered. Each woman student is entitled to fair and reasonable access to institutional resources and full administrative support.

Women student services and programs should address . . .

- needs of women students that are special in such areas as health services, child care, safety, and protection from sexual harassment
- developmental opportunities, such as tutoring for reentry women students, assessment of prior experience, social programs, and support groups for those experiencing major life transitions
- provision of demographic data to the campus community such as: head of household status, dependents, marital status, age, employment status, and financial aid
- dissemination of information to the campus community regarding societal trends and conditions that affect socialization patterns, cultural expectations, stereotypic behaviors, various lifestyle characteristics, "chilly climate," institutional sexism, and sexual harassment
- provision of adequate financial aid

To respond to the woman student and her special needs, many colleges and universities create a separate women's center or women students' area within the institution or on campus. When no specific office is identified for women students, then all areas of the institution should be evaluated to ensure that women students have equal access to quality programs and services.

## Part 2. PROGRAM

The formal education of students consists of the curriculum and the co-curriculum, and must promote student learning and development that is purposeful and holistic. Women student programs and services (WSPS) must identify relevant and desirable student learning and development outcomes and provide programs and services that encourage the achievement of those outcomes.

Relevant and desirable outcomes include: intellectual growth, effective communication, realistic self-appraisal, enhanced self-esteem, clarified values, career choices, leadership development, healthy behaviors, meaningful interpersonal relationships, independence, collaboration, social responsibility, satisfying and productive lifestyles, appreciation of diversity, spiritual awareness, and achievement of personal and educational goals.

WSPS must provide evidence of its impact on the achievement of student learning and development outcomes.

The program may use the examples that follow or identify other more germane indicators.

### Student Learning & Development Outcome Domains

283

## Intellectual Growth

Examples of Achievement Indicators

Produces personal and educational goal statements; Employs critical thinking in problem solving; Uses complex information from a variety of sources including personal experience and observation to form a decision or opinion; Obtains a degree; Applies previously understood information and concepts to a new situation or setting; Expresses appreciation for literature, the fine arts, mathematics, sciences, and social sciences

## Effective Communication

Examples of Achievement Indicators

Writes and speaks coherently and effectively; Writes and speaks after reflection; Able to influence others through writing, speaking or artistic expression; Effectively articulates abstract ideas; Uses appropriate syntax; Makes presentations or gives performances

## Enhanced Self-Esteem

Examples of Achievement Indicators

Shows self-respect and respect for others; Initiates actions toward achievement of goals; Takes reasonable risks; Demonstrates assertive behavior; Functions without need for constant reassurance from others

## Realistic Self-Appraisal

Examples of Achievement Indicators

Articulates personal skills and abilities; Makes decisions and acts in congruence with personal values; Acknowledges personal strengths and weaknesses; Articulates rationale for personal behavior; Seeks feedback from others; Learns from past experiences

## Clarified Values

Examples of Achievement Indicators

Articulates personal values; Acts in congruence with personal values; Makes decisions that reflect personal values; Demonstrates willingness to scrutinize personal beliefs and values; Identifies personal, work and lifestyle values and explains how they influence decision-making

## Career Choices

Examples of Achievement Indicators

Articulate career choices based on assessment of interests, values, skills and abilities; Documents knowledge, skills and accomplishments resulting from formal education, work experience, community service and volunteer experiences; Makes the connections between classroom and out-of-classroom learning; Can construct a resume with clear job objectives and evidence of related knowledge, skills and accomplishments; Articulates the characteristics of a preferred work environment; Comprehends the world of work; Takes steps to initiate a job search or seek advanced education

## Leadership Development

Examples of Achievement Indicators

Articulates leadership philosophy or style; Serves in a leadership position in a student organization; Comprehends the dynamics of a group; Exhibits democratic principles as a leader; Exhibits ability to visualize a group purpose and desired outcomes

## Healthy Behavior

Examples of Achievement Indicators

Chooses behaviors and environments that promote health and reduce risk; Articulate the relationship between health and wellness and accomplishing life long goals; Exhibits behaviors that advance a healthy community

## Meaningful Interpersonal Relationships

Examples of Achievement Indicators

Develops and maintains satisfying interpersonal relationships; Establishes mutually rewarding relationships with friends and colleagues; Listens to and considers others' points of view; Treats others with respect

## Independence

Examples of Achievement Indicators

Exhibits self-reliant behaviors; Functions autonomously; Exhibits ability to function interdependently; Accepts supervision as needed; Manages time effectively

## Collaboration

Examples of Achievement Indicators

Works cooperatively with others; Seeks the involvement of others; Seeks feedback from others; Contributes to achievement of a group goal; Exhibits effective listening skills

## Social Responsibility

Examples of Achievement Indicators

Understands and participates in relevant governance systems; Understands, abides by, and participates in the development, maintenance, and/or orderly change of community, social, and legal standards or norms; Appropriately challenges the unfair, unjust, or uncivil behavior of other individuals or groups; Participates in service/volunteer activities

## Satisfying and Productive Lifestyles

Examples of Achievement Indicators

Achieves balance between education, work and leisure time; Articulates and meets goals for work, leisure and education; Overcomes obstacles that hamper goal achievement; Functions on the basis of personal identity, ethical, spiritual and moral values; Articulates long-term goals and objectives

## Appreciating Diversity

Examples of Achievement Indicators

Understands ones own identity and culture. Seeks involvement with people different from oneself; Seeks involvement in diverse interests; Articulate the advantages and challenges of a diverse society; Challenges appropriately abusive use of stereotypes by others; Understands the impact of diversity on one's own society

## Spiritual Awareness

Examples of Achievement Indicators

Develops and articulates personal belief system; Understands roles of spirituality in personal and group values and behaviors

## Personal and Educational Goals

Examples of Achievement Indicators

Sets, articulates, and pursues individual goals; Articulate personal and educational goals and objectives; Uses personal and educational goals to guide decisions; Understands the effect of one's personal and education goals on others

WSPS must be (a) intentional, (b) coherent, (c) based on theories and knowledge of learning and human development, (d) reflective of developmental and demographic profiles of the student population, and (e) responsive to needs of individuals, special populations, and communities.

WSPS must assist students in overcoming specific personal, physical, or educational problems, or skill deficiencies and must likewise identify environmental conditions that may negatively influence welfare and propose interventions that may neutralize such conditions.

Staff members must address the needs of all undergraduate and graduate women students regardless of ethnicity, race, religion, disability, sexual orientation, age, socioeconomic status, degree and enrollment status.

**WSPS must include the following elements . . .**
- **promotion of an institutional commitment for understanding and addressing the concerns of women students on campus**
- **services to women students to assure equitable access to and involvement in all educational programs**

WSPS should address the provision of . . .
- adequate, accessible, affordable, and flexible-time child care
- flexible scheduling of classes, academic support, and extra- curricular activities
- psychological counseling and career services both for groups and individuals that are sensitive to special needs of women students
- referral for individual women students who need expertise on a specific issue

- **creation and nurturance of a campus environment which dominates barriers, diminishes prejudice and bigotry, and extends a hospitable climate to all women students**

Awareness of cultural differences and prejudices or discrimination against racial or ethnic groups or other minority women students should be identified and addressed.

WSPS should monitor campus-based publications and publicity and encourage strategies to increase the visibility of women students on campus, with particular attention to how publications affect the recruitment and retention of women students.

- **research and assessment of the status of women students with regard to educational programs and services, financial aid and awards such as fellowships and athletic scholarships, and lack of enrollment or over enrollment of women in particular disciplines**
- **advocacy for assessment of the campus environment for the presence of gender bias in the areas of employment, educational opportunities, classroom climate, and other issues facing women students**
- **monitoring of the campus climate for women students in areas of sexual harassment and sexual violence, and creating systematic procedures to institutionalize appropriate policies, education, and programs to work toward the elimination of violence against women**
- **publicizing of services, events, and issues of concern to women students on campus**
- **sponsorship of events which address women students' needs and issues, and maintenance of contact with the campus and community to increase awareness of the status of women students on campus**

WSPS should seek to enhance awareness of the roles of women students in the multiple aspects of campus life, appreciating the positive and seeking to improve upon the negative.

- **encouragement of support systems and communication networks for women students on campus**

WSPS should provide opportunities for women on campus to . . .
- participate in campus activities which provide an opportunity for women students to meet appropriate role models
- publicize services, events, and issues of concern to women students on campus
- sponsor events which address women's needs and issues
- maintain contact with the community to enrich the flow of communication to and from the campus
- organize activities around specific issues and needs

- **development of structures which encourage liaisons between women's organizations in the state and nation and the campus based women student programs and services, to focus campus attention on emerging critical issues outside the institution**
- **identification of role models by the sharing and publicizing of the accomplishments of women faculty, staff, and students**

WSPS should create liaisons with campus offices and organizations which have an impact on women.

- **education of women students and the campus community at large when institutional decisions affect or have the potential to affect the status and/or achievement of women students**

WSPS should particularly focus attention on those institutional policies which result in an inequitable impact on women as students or employees, or on a particular subgroup of women students.

- **promotion of new scholarship and research on women through a women studies program if available or through traditional departments if no program exists**
- **education of women students through understanding and practical experiences to use campus organizational systems, political influences, and other sources of power effectively to contribute productively to the construction and maintenance of a campus climate that is responsive to their needs**

## Part 3. LEADERSHIP

Effective and ethical leadership is essential to the success of all organizations. Institutions must appoint, position, and empower women student programs and services (WSPS) leaders within the administrative structure to accomplish stated missions. WSPS leaders at various levels must be selected on the basis of formal education and training, relevant work experience, personal skills and competencies, relevant professional credentials, as well as potential for promoting learning and development in students, applying effective practices to educational processes, and enhancing institutional effectiveness. Institutions must determine expectations of accountability for leaders and fairly assess their performance.

Leaders of WSPS must exercise authority over resources for which they are responsible to achieve their respective missions.

WSPS leaders must . . .
- **articulate a vision for their organization**
- **set goals and objectives based on the needs and capabilities of the population served**
- **promote student learning and development**
- **prescribe and practice ethical behavior**
- **recruit, select, supervise, and develop others in the organization**
- **manage financial resources**
- **coordinate human resources**

- **plan, budget for, and evaluate personnel and programs**
- **apply effective practices to educational and administrative processes**
- **communicate effectively**
- **initiate collaborative interaction between individuals and agencies that possess legitimate concerns and interests in the functional area**

WSPS leaders must identify and find means to address individual, organizational, or environmental conditions that inhibit goal achievement.

WSPS leaders must promote campus environments that result in multiple opportunities for student learning and development.

WSPS leaders must continuously improve programs and services in response to changing needs of students and other constituents, and evolving institutional priorities.

## Part 4. ORGANIZATION and MANAGEMENT

Guided by an overarching intent to ensure student learning and development, women student programs and services (WSPS) must be structured purposefully and managed effectively to achieve stated goals. Evidence of appropriate structure must include current and accessible policies and procedures, written performance expectations for all employees, functional workflow graphics or organizational charts, and clearly stated service delivery expectations.

Evidence of effective management must include use of comprehensive and accurate information for decisions, clear sources and channels of authority, effective communication practices, decision-making and conflict resolution procedures, responsiveness to changing conditions, accountability and evaluation systems, and recognition and reward processes. WSPS must provide channels within the organization for regular review of administrative policies and procedures.

WSPS should play a principal role in implementing institutional programs developed in response to the assessed needs of women students. Access to the policy makers of the institution should be readily available. The administrative organization of WSPS should be governed by the size, nature, and mission of the institution. WSPS may function as autonomous units or may be housed as components of other units on campus. In either instance, women student programs and services should be organized and administered in a manner that permits the stated mission to be fulfilled.

Many models for organizing WSPS exist in higher education. Individual units should be afforded the opportunity to organize in a manner that is efficient and best promotes equity concerns on campus. Emphasis should be placed on achieving an organizational placement so that activities of WSPS are not limited to a specific group of women students (e.g., solely undergraduate women) or specific service (e.g., solely counseling services).

## Part 5. HUMAN RESOURCES

**The women student program and services (WSPS) must be staffed adequately by individuals qualified to accomplish its mission and goals. Within established guidelines of the institution, WSPS must establish procedures for staff selection, training, and evaluation; set expectations for supervision, and provide appropriate professional development opportunities. WSPS must strive to improve the professional competence and skills of all personnel it employs.**

Leadership of the program by persons with the credentials and ability to forge gender equity on campus is important to promoting the integrity of the unit. Professionals working within the program should represent the diversity of women students on the campus. It is important that the leadership position be evaluated and scaled within the administration of the institution on a level commensurate with its institution-wide mission.

**WSPS professional staff members must hold an earned graduate degree in a field relevant to the position they hold or must possess an appropriate combination of educational credentials and related work experience.**

The professional staff should possess the academic preparation, experience, abilities, professional interests, and competencies essential for the efficient operation of the office as charged, as well as the ability to identify additional areas of concern about the female student population. Specific coursework in organizational development, counseling (theory and practice), group dynamics, leadership development, human development, and research and evaluation may be desirable. It is important that the leadership have knowledge of and preferably experience with gender issues and their impact on development. Coursework in and/or a relationship with women studies courses and/or a program is desirable.

Professional staff should: (a) develop and implement programs and services; (b) conduct assessment, research, and evaluation; (c) advocate for the improvement of the quality of life for women as students; and (d) perform developmental educational functions.

**Degree or credential-seeking interns must be qualified by enrollment in an appropriate field of study and by relevant experience. These individuals must be trained and supervised adequately by professional staff members holding educational credentials and related work experience appropriate for supervision.**

Pre-professional, practicum, or intern student staff members may come from academic programs in a variety of disciplines.

**Student employees and volunteers must be carefully selected, trained, supervised, and evaluated. They must be trained on how and when to refer those in need of assistance to qualified staff members and have access to a supervisor for assistance in making these judgments. Student employees and volunteers must be provided clear and precise job descriptions, pre-service training based on assessed needs, and continuing staff development.**

Where student staff members are employed, they should be provided with clear and precise job descriptions, pre-service training which including an understanding of gender issues, and adequate supervision.

**WSPS must have technical and support staff members adequate to accomplish its mission. Staff members must be technologically proficient and qualified to perform their job functions, be knowledgeable of ethical and legal uses of technology, and have access to training. The level of staffing and workloads must be adequate and appropriate for program and service demands.**

Technical and support staff should be sufficient to perform office and administrative functions, including reception, information-giving, problem identification, and referral. In the selection and training of technical and support staff members, special emphasis should be placed on skills in the areas of public relations, information dissemination, problem identification, and referral. A thorough knowledge of the institution and its various offices is important.

**Salary levels and fringe benefits for all WSPS staff members must be commensurate with those for comparable positions within the institution, in similar institutions, and in the relevant geographic area.**

Women working within WSPS should be afforded the same professional opportunities and institutional commitment to advancement as other employees of the institution. The use of appropriate professional support staff and professional consultant staff is to be encouraged. The use of paid and supervised graduate and undergraduate student interns may be encouraged. Paraprofessionals and volunteers should be trained in the mission of the program and should be assigned duties commensurate with their abilities. Supervision by the professional staff is essential to their role.

**WSPS must institute hiring and promotion practices that are fair, inclusive, and non-discriminatory. WSPS must employ a diverse staff**

to provide readily identifiable role models for students and to enrich the campus community.

WSPS must create and maintain position descriptions for all staff members and provide regular performance planning and appraisals.

WSPS must have a system for regular staff evaluation and must provide access to continuing education and professional development opportunities, including in-service training programs and participation in professional conferences and workshops.

Staff development is an essential activity if staff members are to remain current and effective in an educational setting. Additional credit courses, seminars, professional conferences, and access to published research and opinion and relevant other media are examples of staff development activities.

## Part 6. FINANCIAL RESOURCES

Women student programs and services (WSPS) must have adequate funding to accomplish its mission and goals. Funding priorities must be determined within the context of the stated mission, goals, objectives, and comprehensive analysis of the needs and capabilities of students, and the availability of internal or external resources.

WSPS must demonstrate fiscal responsibility and cost effectiveness consistent with institutional protocols.

Funding for WSPS may come from a composite of institutional funds, grant money, student government funds, fees for services, and government contracts. It is important that permanent institutional funding be allocated for the operation of women student programs and services.

## Part 7. FACILITIES, TECHNOLOGY, and EQUIPMENT

Women student programs and services (WSPS) must have adequate, suitably located facilities, adequate technology, and equipment to support its mission and goals efficiently and effectively. Facilities, technology, and equipment must be evaluated regularly and be in compliance with relevant federal, state, provincial, and local requirements to provide for access, health, safety, and security.

Facilities must be located in an area determined to be easily accessible by women students.

The location of facilities should give special accommodation to safety factors and the diversity of women students as such relates to scheduling, availability, and use of facilities.

## Part 8. LEGAL RESPONSIBILITIES

Women student program and services (WSPS) staff members must be knowledgeable about and responsive to laws and regulations that relate to their respective responsibilities. WSPS staff members must inform users of programs and services and officials, as appropriate, of legal obligations and limitations including constitutional, statutory, regulatory, and case law; mandatory laws and orders emanating from federal, state/provincial and local governments; and the institution's policies.

WSPS staff members must use reasonable and informed practices to limit the liability exposure of the institution, its officers, employees, and agents. Staff members must be informed about institutional policies regarding personal liability and related insurance coverage options.

The institution must provide access to legal advice for WSPS staff members as needed to carry out assigned responsibilities and must inform WSPS staff and students in a timely and systematic fashion about extraordinary or changing legal obligations and potential liabilities.

WSPS should play a major role in seeing that the institution, as a whole, is knowledgeable about and in compliance with legal requirements of Title IX of The Education Amendments of 1972.

## Part 9. EQUITY and ACCESS

Women student programs and services (WSPS) staff members must ensure that services and programs are provided on a fair and equitable basis. Facilities, programs and services must be accessible. Hours of operation and delivery of and access to programs and services must be responsive to the needs of all students and other constituents. WSPS must adhere to the spirit and intent of equal opportunity laws.

The WSPS must be open and readily accessible to all students and must not discriminate except where sanctioned by law and institutional policy. Discrimination must especially be avoided on the bases of age; color, creed; cultural heritage; disability; ethnicity; gender identity; nationality; political affiliation, religious affiliation, sex, sexual orientation; or economic, marital, social, or veteran status.

Consistent with their mission and goals, WSPS must take affirmative action to remedy significant imbalances in student participation and staffing patterns.

As the demographic profiles of campuses change and new instructional delivery methods are introduced, institutions must recognize the needs of students who participate in distance learning for access to programs and services offered on campus. ☐Institutions must provide appropriate services in ways that are accessible to distance learners and assist them in identifying and gaining access to other appropriate services in their geographic region.

## Part 10. CAMPUS and EXTERNAL RELATIONS

Women student programs and services must establish, maintain, and promote effective relations with relevant individuals, campus offices, and external agencies.

WSPS should maintain good working relationships with such agencies as counseling, financial aid, health services, recreational sports and athletics, residential life, and campus security. WSPS should maintain a high degree of visibility with academic units through direct promotion and delivery of services, through involvement with co-curricular programs, and through staff efforts to increase understanding of the needs of women students.

Program staff should be an integral part of appropriate campus networks in order to effectively participate in the establishment of institution-wide policy and practices, and to effectively collaborate with other staff and faculty in providing services. In addition, WSPS should provide effective liaisons between the community and the institution to assist each group in articulation of common concerns and in using each other as resources.

## Part 11. DIVERSITY

Within the context of each institution's unique mission, diversity enriches the community and enhances the collegiate experience for all; therefore, women student programs and services (WSPS) must nurture environments where commonalties and differences among people are recognized and honored.

WSPS must promote educational experiences that are characterized by open and continuous communication that deepens understanding of one's own identity, culture, and heritage, and that of others. WSPS must educate and promote respect about commonalties and differences in their historical and cultural contexts.

WSPS must address the characteristics and needs of a diverse population when establishing and implementing policies and procedures.

## Part 12. ETHICS

All persons involved in the delivery of women student programs and services (WSPS) must adhere to the highest principles of ethical behavior. WSPS must develop or adopt and implement appropriate statements of ethical practice. WSPS must publish these statements and ensure their periodic review by relevant constituencies.

WSPS staff members must ensure that privacy and confidentiality are maintained with respect to all communications and records to the extent that such records are protected under the law and appropriate statements of ethical practice. Information contained in students' education records must not be disclosed without written consent except as allowed by relevant laws and institutional policies. Staff members must disclose to appropriate authorities information judged to be of an emergency nature, especially when the safety of the individual or others is involved, or when otherwise required by institutional policy or relevant law.

All WSPS staff members must be aware of and comply with the provisions contained in the institution's human subjects research policy and in other relevant institutional policies addressing ethical practices and confidentiality of research data concerning individuals.

WSPS staff members must recognize and avoid personal conflict of interest or appearance thereof in their transactions with students and others.

WSPS staff members must strive to insure the fair, objective, and impartial treatment of all persons with whom they deal. Staff members must not participate in nor condone any form of harassment that demeans persons or creates an intimidating, hostile, or offensive campus environment.

When handling institutional funds, all WSPS staff members must ensure that such funds are managed in accordance with established and responsible accounting procedures and the fiscal policies or processes of the institution.

WSPS staff members must perform their duties within the limits of their training, expertise, and competence. When these limits are exceeded, individuals in need of further assistance must be referred to persons possessing appropriate qualifications. Staff members must use suitable means to confront and otherwise hold accountable other staff members who exhibit unethical behavior.

WSPS staff members must be knowledgeable about and practice ethical behavior in the use of technology.

## Part 13. ASSESSMENT and EVALUATION

Women student programs and services (WSPS) must conduct regular assessment and evaluations. WSPS must employ effective qualitative and quantitative methodologies as appropriate, to determine whether and to what degree the stated mission, goals, and student learning and development outcomes are being met. The process must employ sufficient and sound assessment measures to ensure comprehensiveness. Data collected must include responses from students and other affected constituencies.

WSPS must evaluate periodically how well they complement and enhance the institution's stated mission and educational effectiveness.

A comprehensive evaluation of the ongoing program should be carried out in accordance with the general practice of program review for other units of the institution. To assist staff in planning and program formation, an ongoing evaluation process of WSPS should be established.

Results of these evaluations must be used in revising and improving programs and services and in recognizing staff performance.

# PROFESSIONAL STUDENT AFFAIRS PREPARATION
## *CAS* Standards Contextual Statement

Standards for the professional education of student affairs practitioners are of relatively recent vintage, having largely been developed during the past two decades. Although the philosophical foundations of formal student affairs practice have been and continue to be of interest (NASPA, 1987; Whitt et al., 1990), documents that identify and postulate basic principles of student affairs practice are not adequate to the task of guiding the academic preparation of student affairs practitioners. In 1964 the Council of Student Personnel Associations in Higher Education (COSPA) drafted "A Proposal for Professional Preparation in College Student Personnel Work," which subsequently evolved into a statement drafted by COSPA in collaboration with the Inter-divisional Committee of the American Personnel and Guidance Association, entitled "Guidelines for Graduate Programs in the Preparation of Student Personnel Workers in Higher Education," dated March 5, 1967. The change in title from "proposal for" in the 1964 version to "guidelines for" in this fourth draft revision exemplifies the movement from a rather tentative statement of what professional preparation should entail to one asserting specific guidelines that should be followed in graduate education programs. A final statement, popularly recognized as the COSPA Report, was actually published some time after the dissolution of the Council (1975).

During this period, others concerned with the graduate education of counselors and other helping professionals were busy developing counselor education standards and exploring the possibilities for accrediting graduate academic programs. A moving force in this effort was the Association of Counselor Educators and Supervisors (ACES), a division of the American Personnel and Guidance Association (APGA), now the American Counseling Association (ACA). In 1978, ACES published a set of professional standards to be used to accredit counseling and personnel services education programs. APGA had recognized ACES as its official counselor education accrediting body and moved to establish an inter-association committee to guide counselor education program accreditation activity and the review and revision of the ACES/APGA preparation standards. In response to this initiative, the American College Personnel Association (ACPA) established an ad hoc Preparation Standards Drafting Committee to develop a set of standards designed to focus on the special concerns of student affairs graduate education. At its March 1979 meetings, the ACPA Executive Council adopted the committee's statement entitled"Standards for the Preparation of Counselors and College Student Affairs Specialists at the Master's Degree Level" as the official ACPA preparation standards. ACPA then initiated a two-pronged effort in the area of professional standards. One was a collaborative effort with NASPA to establish a profession-wide program of standards development and the other was a concerted effort to work under the then-APGA organizational umbrella to establish an agency for the accreditation of counseling and student affairs preparation programs. The former initiative resulted in the creation of the Council for the Advancement of Standards in Higher Education (CAS) and the latter in the establishment of the Council for the Accreditation of Counseling and Other Related Educational Programs (CACREP), an academic program accrediting agency. Both the CAS and CACREP preparation standards reflected the influence of the ACPA standards for student affairs preparation.

The forgoing process was prelude to *the CAS Masters Level Student Affairs Graduate Program Standards and Guidelines*, which follow. A major value of graduate standards is that they provide criteria by which an academic program of professional preparation can judge its educational effectiveness. Whether used for accreditation or program development purposes, standards provide faculty, staff, administrators, and students alike a tool to measure a program's characteristics against a set of well-conceived criteria designed to ensure educational quality and effectiveness.

The CAS standards for student affairs graduate programs were revised in 2001 and offer standards and guidelines based on profession-wide inter-association collaboration. Topics addressed in the standards include the program's mission; recruitment and admission policies and procedures; curriculum policies; pedagogy; the curriculum; equal opportunity access and affirmative action; academic and student support; professional ethics and legal responsibilities; and program evaluation.

Curriculum standards are organized around Foundation Studies, Professional Studies, and Supervised Practice. Foundation Studies pertain to the historical and philosophical foundations of higher education and student affairs. This includes historical documents of the profession such as the *Student Personnel Point of View* (ACE, 1937), *Re-*

*turn to the Academy* (Brown, 1972), the *Student Learning Imperative* (ACPA, 1996), *Principles of Good Practice* (Blimling & Whitt, 1999), *Powerful Partnerships* (Joint Task Force, 1998), and *Reasonable Expectations* (Kuh et al, 1994) among others. Professional Studies pertains to student development theory, student characteristics, the effects of college on students, individual and group interventions, the organization and administration of student affairs, and assessment, evaluation and research. Supervised Practice includes practica, internships, and externships under professionally supervised work conditions.

The single best way to assure that an academic program is accomplishing its educational objectives is to document with reasonable evidence that the instruction provided and the learning obtained merit recognition as being of academic worth and social value. That is the primary value of the CAS preparation standards.

### References, Readings, and Resources

American College Personnel Association (1996). The student learning imperative: Implications for student affairs. *Journal of College Student Development, 37,* 118-122.

American Council on Education (ACE) (1937). *The student personnel point of view* (Ser. 1, Vol. 1, No. 3,). Washington, DC: Author. [revised in 1949 and 1989].

Association of Counselor Educators and Supervisors (ACES). (1978). Standards for the preparation of counselors and other personnel services specialists at the master's degree level. Washington, DC: Author.

Blimling, G. S. & Whitt, E. J. (1999). *Good Practice in student affairs.* San Francisco: Jossey Bass.

Brown, R. D. (1972). Student development in tomorrow's higher education - A return to the academy. *Student Personnel Series, 16.* Washington, D.C.: American College Personnel Association.

Bryant, W. A., Winston, R. B. Jr., & Miller, T. K. (Eds.) (1991). *Using professional standards in student affairs,* No. 53. New Directions for Student Affairs. San Francisco: Jossey-Bass.

Council of Student Personnel Associations (COSPA). (1964). A proposal for professional preparation in college student personnel work. Unpublished manuscript, Indianapolis: Author.

Council of Student Personnel Associations (COSPA). (March, 1967). Guidelines for graduate programs in the preparation of student personnel workers in higher education. Unpublished manuscript, Washington, DC: Author.

Council of Student Personnel Associations (COSPA). (1975). Student development services in post-secondary education. *Journal of College Student Personnel, 16* (6), 524-528.

Joint Task Force of Student Learning. (1998). *Powerful partnerships: A shared responsibility for learning. Washington, D. C.* American Association for Higher Education, American College Personnel Association, and National Association of Student Personnel Administrators.

Kuh, G. D. (1994). *Reasonable expectations: Renewing the educational compact between institutions and students.* Washington, D.C.: National Association of Student Personnel Administrators.

National Association of Student Personnel Administrators (NASPA). (1987). *A perspective on student affairs: A statement issued on the 50th anniversary of the student personnel point of view.* Washington, DC: Author. Also at www.naspa.org/resources/stulearn.cfm or www.acpa.nche.edu/pubs.powpart.html

Whitt, E. J., Carnaghi, J. E., Matkin, J., Scalese-Love, P., & Nestor, D. (1990). Believing is seeing: Alternative perspectives on a statement of professional philosophy for student affairs. *NASPA Journal, 27* (3), 178-184.

Winston, R. B. Jr., Creamer, D. G., Miller, T. K., & Associates (2001). *The professional student affairs administrator: Educator, leader, and manager.* Philadelphia: Taylor and Francis.

American College Personnel Association [ACPA]. Commission on Professional Preparation. ACPA National Office, One Dupont Circle, N.W., Suite 300. Washington, DC 20036-1110. (202) 835-2272; Fax (202) 296-3286.http//www.acpa.nche.edu

# Council for the Advancement of Standards in Higher Education
## Masters-Level Graduate Program for Student Affairs Professionals
## Standards and Guidelines

### Part 1: Mission and Objectives

The mission of professional preparation programs shall be to prepare persons through graduate education for professional positions in student affairs in schools, colleges, and universities. Each program mission must be consistent with the mission of the institution offering the program.

Program missions should reflect a particular emphasis, such as administration, counseling, student learning and development, student cultures, or other appropriate emphases as long as the standards herein are met.

The program's mission may include providing in-service education, professional development, research, and consultation for student affairs professional staff members at the institution.

Each professional preparation program must publish a clear statement of mission and objectives prepared by the program faculty in consultation with collaborating student affairs professionals and relevant advisory committees. The statement must be readily available to current and prospective students and to appropriate faculty and staff members and agencies. It must be written to allow accurate assessment of student learning and program effectiveness. The statement must be reviewed periodically.

This review may be conducted with the assistance of current students and faculty, graduates of the program, student affairs professionals, and personnel in cooperating agencies.

The program faculty should consider recommendations of local, state/provincial, regional, and national legislative bodies and professional groups concerned with student affairs when developing, revising, and publishing the program's mission and objectives. The mission and objectives should reflect consideration of the current issues and needs of society, of higher education, and of the student populations served. Personnel in cooperating agencies and faculty members with primary assignments in other disciplines should be aware of and encouraged to support and work toward the achievement of the program's mission and stated objectives.

The mission and objectives should specify both mandatory and optional areas of study and should include a plan for assessing student progress throughout the program of study. The mission and objectives may address recruitment, selection, retention, employment recommendations, curriculum, instructional methods, research activities, administrative policies, governance, and program evaluation.

### Part 2: Recruitment and Admission

Accurate descriptions of the graduate program including the qualifications of its faculty and records of its students' persistence, degree completion, and subsequent study and employment must be made readily available for review by both current and prospective students.

Students selected for admission to the program must meet the institution's criteria for admission to graduate study. Program faculty members must make admission decisions using written criteria that are disseminated to all faculty members and to prospective students.

Admissions materials must be clear about preferences for particular student status, such as full-time students, currently employed students or students seeking learning opportunities by distance, and the manner in which such preferences may affect admissions decisions.

Students admitted to the program should have ample intellectual capacities, strong interpersonal skills, serious interest in the program, commitment to pursuing a career in student affairs, the potential to serve a wide range of students of varying developmental levels and backgrounds, and the capacity to be open to self-assessment and growth. Criteria known to predict success in the program for students of various backgrounds and characteristics should be used in their selection. Students from diverse backgrounds should be encouraged to apply.

Students from diverse backgrounds must be given equal opportunity for entry into the program.

### Part 3: Curriculum Policies

The preparation program must specify in writing and distribute to prospective students its curriculum and graduation requirements. The program must conform to institutional policy and must be fully approved by the institution's administrative unit responsible for graduate programs. The institution must employ only faculty members with credentials that clearly reflect professional knowledge, ability, and skill to teach, advise, or supervise in the program.

Any revisions to the publicized program of studies must be published and distributed to students in a timely fashion. Course syllabi must be available that reflect purposes, teaching/learning methods, and outcome objectives.

All prerequisite studies and experiences should be identified clearly in course descriptions and syllabi.

The equivalent of two years full-time academic study must be required for the Masters degree.

Ordinarily, to accomplish the goals of the curriculum as outlined later in this document, a program should include a total 42-48 semester credit hours.

Programs must demonstrate that the full curriculum, as outlined in Part 5 of these standards and guidelines, is covered and that graduates reflect relevant proficiency.

Because of the benefits of immersion-like educational experiences characterized by full-time study, full-time enrollment should be encouraged. However to serve those students for whom full-time study is not possible, programs may provide opportunities for part-time study. Part-time enrollment will result in a program of more than two academic years of study.

Appropriate consideration and provisions for admission and curriculum decisions should be made for students with extensive student affairs experience.

Distance learning options may be used in the program.

There must be a sequence of basic to advanced studies. Any required associated learning experiences must be included in the required program of studies.

Associated learning experiences may include comprehensive examinations, degree candidacy, and research requirements.

Opportunity for students to develop understandings and skills beyond minimum program requirements must be provided through elective course options, supervised individual study, and/or enrichment opportunities.

Programs should encourage students to take advantage of special enrichment opportunities and education that encourages learning beyond the formal curriculum, such as experiences in student affairs organizations, professional associations and conferences, and outreach projects.

An essential feature of the preparation program must be to foster an appreciation of spirit of inquiry, in faculty members and students, as evidenced by active involvement in producing and using research, evaluation, and assessment information in student affairs.

Research, program evaluation, and assessment findings should be used frequently in instructional and supervised practical experience offerings. The study of methods of inquiry should be provided in context of elected program emphasis, such as administration, counseling, student learning and development, student cultures, or other program options.

## Part 4: Pedagogy

Each program must indicate its pedagogical philosophy in the program literature. In addition, the individual faculty member must identify his or her pedagogical strategies. Faculty members must accommodate multiple student learning styles. Teaching approaches must be employed that lead to the accomplishment of course objectives, achievement of student learning outcomes, and are subject to evaluation by academic peers for the purpose of program improvement.

Such teaching approaches include active collaboration, service learning, problem-based learning, experiential, and constructivist learning. Faculty members should elect to use multiple teaching strategies. Recognition of the student's role in learning should play a significant role in choice of teaching approach.

## Part 5: The Curriculum

All programs of study must include 1) foundational studies, 2) professional studies, and 3) supervised practice. Foundational studies must include the study of the historical and philosophical foundations of higher education and student affairs. Professional studies must include (a) student development theory, (b) student characteristics and the effects of college on students, (c) individual and group interventions, (d) organization and administration of student affairs, and (e) assessment, evaluation, and research. Supervised practice must include practica and/or internships consisting of supervised work involving at least two distinct experiences. Demonstration of minimum knowledge and skill in each area is required of all program graduates.

The curriculum described above represents areas of study and should not be interpreted as specific course titles. The precise nature of courses should be determined by a variety of factors, including institutional mission, policies and practices, faculty judgment, current issues, and student needs. It is important that appropriate courses be available within the institution or from another institution, but it is not necessary that all be provided directly within the department or college in which the program is located administratively. Although all areas of study must be incorporated into the academic program, the precise nature of study may vary by institution, program emphasis, and student preference. The requirements for demonstration of competence and minimum knowledge in each area should be established by the faculty and regularly reviewed to assure that students are learning the essentials that underlie successful student affairs practice. A formal comprehensive examination or other culminating assessment project designed to provide students the opportunity to exhibit their knowledge and competence toward the end of their programs of study is encouraged.

Programs of study may be designed to emphasize one or more distinctive perspectives on student affairs such as educational program design, implementation, and evaluation; individual and group counseling and advising; student learning and human development; and/or administration of student affairs in higher education. Such program designs should include the most essential forms of knowledge and groupings of skills and competencies needed by practicing professionals and should be fashioned consistent with basic curriculum requirements. The wide range of expertise and interest of program faculty members and other involved and qualified contributors to curriculum content should be taken into account when designing distinctive perspectives in programs of study.

**Each program must specify the structure of its degree options including which courses are considered core, which are considered thematic, which are required, and which are elective.**

A "core" course is one that is principal to the student affairs preparation program. Theme courses are those that center around a common content area (such as introduction to student development theory, the application of student development theory, and using student development theory for environmental assessment).

Programs may structure their curriculum according to their distinctive perspectives and the nature of their students insuring adequacy of knowledge in foundation, professional, and supervised experience studies.

## Part 5a: Foundation Studies

**This component of the curriculum must include study in the historical, philosophical, ethical, cultural, and research foundations of higher education that inform student affairs practice. The study of the history and philosophy of student affairs are essential components of this standard.**

**Graduates must be able to reference historical and current documents that state the philosophical, foundations of the profession and to communicate their relevance to current student affairs practice**

**Graduates must also be able to articulate the inherent values of the profession that are stipulated in these documents in a manner that indicates how these values guide practice.**

These values may include educating the whole student, treating each student as a unique individual, offering seamless learning opportunities, and ensuring the basic rights of all students.

This standard encompasses studies in other disciplines that inform student affairs practice, such as cultural contexts of higher education; governance, public policy, and finance of higher education; the impact of environments on behavior, especially learning; and international education and global understanding. Studies in this area should emphasize the diverse character of higher education environments. The foundational studies

curriculum component should be designed to enhance students' understanding of higher education systems and exhibit how student affairs programs are infused into the larger educational picture.

**Graduates must be knowledgeable about and be able to apply a code of ethics or ethical principles sanctioned by a recognized professional organization that provides ethical guidance for their work.**

## Part 5b: Professional Studies

**This component of the curriculum must include studies of basic knowledge for practice and all programs must encompass at least five related areas of study including (a) student development theory; (b) student characteristics and effects of college on students; (c) individual and group interventions; (d) organization and administration of student affairs; and (e) assessment, evaluation, and research.**

Other areas of study, especially when used as enrichment or cognate experiences, are encouraged. Studies in disciplines such as sociology, psychology, political science, and ethnic studies, for example, may be helpful to students depending upon the particular program emphasis. Communication skills and using technology as a learning tool should be emphasized in all the professional studies areas listed above.

## Part 5b.1: Student Development Theory

**This component of the curriculum must include studies of student development theories and research relevant to student learning and personal development. There must be extensive examination of theoretical perspectives that describe students' growth in the areas of intellectual, moral, ego, psychosocial, career, and spiritual development; racial, cultural, ethnic, gender, and sexual identity; the intersection of multiple identities; and learning styles throughout the late adolescent and adult lifespan. Study of collegiate environments and how person-environment interactions affect student development is also required.**

**Graduates must be able to demonstrate the ability to use appropriate development theory to understand, support, and advocate for student learning and development by assessing learning and developmental needs and creating learning and developmental opportunities.**

This component should include studies of and research about human development from late adolescence through the adult life span and models and processes for translating theory and research into practice. Studies should stress differential strengths and applications of student development theories relative to student age, gender, ethnicity, race, culture, sexual identity, disability, spirituality, national origin, socioeconomic status, and resident/commuter status. Studies should also include specialized theories of development particular to certain populations or groups.

## Subpart 5b.2: Student Characteristics and Effects of College on Students

This component of the curriculum must include studies of student characteristics, how such attributes influence student educational and developmental needs, and effects of the college experience on student learning and development.

Graduates must be able to demonstrate knowledge of how student learning and learning opportunities are influenced by student characteristics and by collegiate environments so that graduates can design and evaluate learning experiences for students.

This area should include studies of the effects of college on students, satisfaction with the college experience, student involvement in college, and factors that correlate with student persistence and attrition. This curriculum component should include, but is not limited to, student characteristics such as age, gender, ethnicity, race, religion, sexual identity, academic ability and preparation, learning styles, socioeconomic status, national origin, immigrant status, disability, developmental status, cultural background and orientation, transfer status, and family situation. Also included should be the study of specific student populations such as resident, commuter, and distance learners, part-time and full-time students, student athletes, members of fraternities and sororities, adult learners, first generation students and international students.

## Subpart 5b.3: Individual and Group Interventions

This component of the curriculum must include studies of techniques and methods of interviewing; helping skills; and assessing, designing, and implementing developmentally appropriate interventions with individuals and organizations.

Graduates must be able to demonstrate knowledge and skills necessary to design and evaluate effective educational interventions for individuals and groups. Graduates must be able to identify and appropriately refer persons who need additional resources.

This curriculum component should include opportunities for study, skill building, and strategies for the implementation of advising, counseling, disciplining, instructing, mediating, and facilitating to assist individuals and groups. The program of study should include substantial instruction in counseling and group dynamics. Students should be exposed to a variety of theoretical perspectives, provided opportunities to practice individual and group interventions, and receive extensive supervision and feedback. Intervention skills are complex and require periods of time to practice under supervised conditions.

In addition to exposure to intervention theory, programs of study should include instruction in individual and group techniques and practices for addressing personal crises as well as problem solving, self-examination, and growth needs. Further, studies should include problem analyses, intervention design, and subsequent evaluation. Studies should emphasize theory plus individual and group interventions that are appropriate for and applicable to diverse populations.

## Subpart 5b.4: Organization and Administration of Student Affairs

This component of the curriculum must include studies of organizational, management, and leadership theory and practice; student affairs functions; legal issues in higher education; and professional issues, ethics, and standards of practice.

Graduates must be able to identify and apply leadership, organizational, and management practices that assist institutions in accomplishing their mission.

This curriculum component should include opportunities for the study of student affairs programs and services including but not limited those for which CAS has developed standards and guidelines such as admissions, financial aid, orientation, counseling, academic advising, residence life, judicial services, campus activities, commuter student programs, recreational sports, career services, fraternity and sorority advising, religious programs, service learning, disability services, academic support services, education opportunity programs, multicultural student affairs international student affairs, and health services among others. Studies of organizational culture, budgeting and finance, planning, technology as applied to organizations, and the selection, supervision, development, and evaluation of personnel should be included as well.

## Subpart 5b.5: Assessment, Evaluation, and Research

This component of the curriculum must include the study of assessment, evaluation, and research. Studies must include both qualitative and quantitative research methodologies, measuring learning processes and outcomes, assessing environments and organizations, measuring program and environment effectiveness, and critiques of published studies.

Graduates must be able to critique a sound study or evaluation, and be able to design, conduct, and report on a sound research study, assessment study, or program evaluation, grounded in the appropriate literature.

Graduates must be aware of research ethics and legal implications of research including the necessity of adhering to a human subjects review.

This curriculum component should include studies of the assessment of student needs and developmental attributes, the assessment of educational environments that influence student learning, and the assessment of student outcomes of the educational experience particular to student affairs work. This curriculum component also should include studies of program evaluation models and processes suitable for use in making judgments about the value of a wide range of programs and services. Students should be introduced to methodologies and techniques of quantitative and qualitative research, plus the philosophical foundations, assumptions, methodologies, methods, and criteria of worthiness of both. Students should be familiar with prominent research in student affairs that has greatly influenced the profession.

## Part 5c: Supervised Practice

A minimum of 300 hours of supervised practice, consisting of at least two distinct experiences, must be required. Students must gain exposure to both the breadth and depth of student affairs work. Students must gain experience in developmental work with individual students and groups of students in: program planning, implementation, or evaluation; staff training, advising, or supervision; and administration functions or processes.

Supervision must be provided on-site by competent professionals working in cooperation with qualified program faculty members. On-site supervisors must provide direct regular supervision and evaluation of students' experiences and comply with all ethical principles and standards of the American College Personnel Association, the National Association of Student Personnel Administrators, and other recognized professional associations.

Qualified student affairs professionals possessing appropriate student affairs education and experience should be invited to sponsor and supervise students for practicum and internship experiences. Typical qualifications include at least a master's degree in student affairs or a related area of professional study, several years of successful professional experience, and experience at that institution. Student affairs professionals serving as on-site supervisors and evaluators of students in training should be approved by the responsible faculty member as competent to accomplish this task.

Site supervisors must be approved in advance by program faculty. Program faculty must offer clear expectations of learning goals and supervision practices to site supervisors.

Supervised practice includes practica and internships consisting of supervised work completed for academic credit in student programs and services in higher education. The exposure of students to diverse settings and work with diverse clientele or populations should be encouraged.

Because individual supervision of students in practica and internships is labor intensive for faculty with this instructional responsibility, supervision must be limited to a small group to enable close regular supervision. Students must be supervised closely by faculty individually, in groups, or both.

When determining practicum and internship course loads, faculty members who provide direct practicum or internship supervision during any academic term should receive instructional credit for the equivalent of one academic course for each small group. Likewise, students enrolled in such internships should receive academic credit.

A graduate assistantship in programs and services in higher education, which provides both substantive experience and professional supervision, may be used in lieu of a practicum or internship. For this to be effective, faculty members responsible for assuring quality learning outcomes should work closely with graduate assistantship supervisors in students' assignment and evaluation processes. Appropriate consideration and provisions should be made for students with extensive experience in student affairs.

Preparation of students for practica and internships is required. Practica and internship experiences must be reserved for students who have successfully completed a sequence of courses pertaining to basic foundational knowledge of professional practice. This must include basic knowledge and skills in interpersonal communication, consultation, and referral skills. Students must comply with all ethical principles and standards of appropriate professional associations.

Preparation of students for supervised practice may be accomplished through special prepractica seminars, laboratory experiences, and faculty tutorials as well as coursework.

Student membership in professional associations should be expected. Attendance at professional conferences, meetings, or other professional development opportunities should also be encouraged.

## Part 6: Equity and Access

A graduate program must adhere to the spirit and intent of equal opportunity in all activities. The program must encourage establishment of an ethical community in which diversity is viewed as an ethical obligation. The program must ensure that its services and facilities are programmatically and physically accessible. Programs that indicate in their admissions materials convenience and encouragement for working students must provide services, classes, and resources that respond to the needs of evening, part-time, and commuter students.

Institutional personnel policies must not discriminate on the basis of race, gender, color, veteran status, religion, age, sexual identity, national origin, and/or disability. In hiring and promotion policies, faculty and administrators must take affirmative action that strives to remedy significant staffing imbalance, particularly when resulting from past discriminatory practices; and must seek to identify, prevent, and remedy existing discriminatory practices.

The program should recognize the important educational opportunities that diversity among its students and faculty brings to student affairs preparation. Therefore, programs should encourage the recognition of and adherence to the spirit of multiculturalism by all who are allied with the program's educational enterprise.

## Part 7: ACADEMIC and STUDENT SUPPORT

Institutions must provide sufficient faculty and staff members, resource materials, advising, career services, student financial support, facilities, and funding resources for the program.

Outcome indicators to determine whether a program has adequate resources could include student retention.

## Part 7a: Faculty and Staff Members

The institution must provide adequate faculty and support staff members for the various aspects of the student affairs graduate program.

The institution must provide an academic program coordinator who is qualified by preparation and experience to manage the program.

The program coordinator or administrative director should have responsibility for managing the program's day to day operations, convening the program faculty as required, developing curriculum, and generally administering the preparation program within the context of the academic unit to which it is assigned. This individual should be the person responsible for guiding faculty teaching assignments, establishing and maintaining connections with student affairs staff members who serve as practicum/internship site

supervisors, guiding general program activities, and representing the program to external constituencies.

Faculty assignments must demonstrate a serious commitment to the preparation of student affairs professionals. Sufficient full-time core faculty members must be devoted to teaching and administering the program to graduate not only employable students but also students capable of designing, creating, and implementing learning opportunities. At least one faculty member must be designated full-time to the program.

Faculty members should be available according to a reasonable faculty-student ratio that permits quality teaching, advising, supervision, research, and professional service. A core faculty member is one who identifies principally with the preparation program. Primary teaching responsibility in the program is recognized when core faculty member's instructional responsibilities are dedicated halftime or greater to teaching the program's curriculum. Devoted full-time to the program is defined as a faculty member whose institutional responsibilities are fully dedicated to the program. Teaching loads should be established on the basis of institutional policy and faculty assignments for service, research, and supervision. A system within the program and the institution should exist for involving professional practitioners who are qualified to assist with faculty responsibilities. Collaboration between full-time faculty members and student affairs practitioners is recommended for the instruction, advisement, and practicum and internship supervision of students in the preparation program. Student affairs practitioners should be consulted in the design, implementation, and evaluation of the preparation program, particularly regarding practicum and internship requirements.

Faculty members must be skilled as teachers and knowledgeable about student affairs in general plus current theory, research, and practice in areas appropriate to their teaching or supervision assignments. Faculty members must also have current knowledge and skills appropriate for designing, conducting, and evaluating learning experiences using multiple pedagogies.

Faculty must maintain regular office hours that are clearly listed on course syllabi and in other prominent locations.

Faculty must act in accordance with ethical principals and standards of good practice disseminated by recognized professional organizations.

The institution must provide opportunity and resources for the continuing professional development of program faculty members. To ensure that faculty members can devote adequate time to professional duties, the academic program must have sufficient clerical and technical support staff.

**Technical support must be of sufficient quality and quantity to accomplish word processing, data management, scheduling, electronic instructional material development, and distance learning. Equipment sufficient for electronic communications and Internet use is essential.**

For more information on distance education standards refer to the CAS Standards and Guidelines for Educational Services for Distant Learners.

Technical support should include regular training in software upgrades and new hardware developments, hardware and software repairs, virus protection, access to the web, on-line journals, courseware, and presentation software.

Classroom facilities should have the capacity to offer classes using electronic technologies.

**Adjunct and part-time faculty must be fully qualified and adequately trained to serve as teachers, advisors, and internship supervisors.**

Adjuncts and part-time faculty should be provided with information about institutional policies and procedures, access to program resources and faculty, and feedback about their performance.

## Part 7b: Resource Materials

**Adequate resource materials must be provided to support the curriculum.**

Resources may include career information; standardized tests and technical manuals; and materials for simulations, structured group experiences, human relations training, and data-based interventions for human and organization development. In addition, resources may include instruments and assessment tools that measure development and leadership from various theoretical points of view and materials that facilitate leadership, organizational design, management style, conflict management, and time management development. Resources should include software that allows for the analysis of qualitative and quantitative data.

**Library resources must be provided for the program including current and historical books, periodicals, on-line journals, search mechanisms, and other media for the teaching and research aspects of the program. Library resources must be accessible to students and must be selected carefully, reviewed, and updated periodically by the program faculty.**

The library resources should be available days, evenings, and weekends and should include adequate interlibrary loan services, ERIC and similar data sources, computerized search capabilities, and photocopy services.

Research support must be adequate for both program faculty and students.

Computing services, data collection and storage services, research design consultation services, and adequate equipment should be available in support of research activities of both students and faculty members. The program should provide students with individualized research project development and implementation.

## Part 7c: Advising

**Faculty members must provide high quality academic and professional advising.**

Academic advising should be viewed as a continuous process of clarification and evaluation. High quality academic advising should include, but is not limited to, development of suitable educational plans; selection of appropriate courses and other educational experiences; clarification of professional and career goals; knowledge of and interpretation of institutional and program policies, procedures, and requirements; knowledge of course contents, sequences, and support resources; evaluation of student progress; referrals to and use of institutional and community support services; support for and evaluation of scholarly endeavors including research and assessment; and knowledge and interpretation of professional ethics and standards. Advisors should be readily available to students and should possess abilities to facilitate a student's career exploration, self-assessment, decision-making, and responsible behavior in interactions with others. Advisors should be able to interpret the scores of assessment tools used in the advising process. These might include the Graduate Record Examination, Myers Briggs Type Indicator, and Learning Styles Inventory. The number of faculty advisees should be monitored and adjusted as necessary to ensure that faculty can give adequate attention to all advisees.

## Part 7d: Career Services

**The institution must provide professional career assistance, either by institutional career services or by the program faculty.**

Students should be assisted in clarifying objectives and establishing goals; exploring the full range of career possibilities; preparing for the job search including presenting oneself effectively as a candidate for employment; and making the transition from graduate student to professional practitioner. Faculty members should collaborate with campus career service providers to develop an active program of assistance including acquiring job listings; the preparation of credentials such as recommending applications, correspondence, and resumes; development of employment interview skills; identification of appropriate job search networks including professional associations; selection of suitable positions; and communication of ethical obligations of those involved in the employment process. Ideally, these services should be available to graduates throughout their professional careers.

## Part 7e: Student Financial Support

**Information must be provided to students about the availability of graduate assistantships, fellowships, work-study, research funding, travel support, and other financial aid opportunities.**

Graduate assistantships should be made available to students to provide both financial assistance and opportunities for supervised work experience.

## Part 7f: Facilities and Funding Resources

**The institution must provide facilities accessible to all students and a budget that ensures continuous operation of all aspects of the program.**

A program office should be located in reasonable proximity to faculty offices, classrooms, and laboratory facilities. Adequate and appropriate space, equipment, and supplies should be provided for faculty, staff members, and graduate assistants. There should be facilities for advising, counseling, and student development activities that are private, adequate in size, and properly equipped. Special facilities and equipment may include audio and video recording devices, one-way observation rooms, small group rooms, and computer labs. Adequate classroom, seminar, and laboratory facilities to meet program needs also should be available. Adequate office and technical equipment should be provided including access to e-mail and other relevant technological resources.

## Part 8: Professional Ethics and Legal Responsibilities

**Faculty members must comply with institutional policies and ethical principles and standards of the American College Personnel Association, the National Association of Student Personnel Administrators, American Association of University Professors, and the CAS functional area ethical standards. Faculty members must demonstrate the highest standards of ethical behavior and academic integrity in all forms of teaching, research, publications, and professional service and must instruct students in ethical practice and in the principles and standards of conduct of the profession.**

**Ethical expectations of graduate students must be disseminated in writing on a regular basis to all students.**

Ethical principles and standards of all relevant professional organizations should be consulted and used as appropriate. An ethical climate should prevail throughout the preparation program wherein faculty members model appropriate ethical behavior at all times for students to experience, observe, and emulate. Faculty members should present various theoretical positions and encourage students to make comparisons and to develop personally meaningful theoretical positions. Faculty members are expected to ensure that educational experiences focusing on self-understanding and personal growth are voluntary or, if such experiences are program requirements, that reasonable effort is made to inform prospective students of them prior to admission to the program. Students should be held accountable for appropriate ethical behavior at all times with special attention paid to the ethics components of the various CAS functional area standards when students participate in related practicum and internship assignments.

**Faculty must strive to ensure the fair and impartial treatment of students and others.**

**Faculty must maintain ethical relationships with students exemplifying respect and the ideals of pedagogy.**

**Faculty must not teach, supervise, or advise any student with whom they have an intimate relationship. When a student enters an academic program having a pre-existing intimate relationship with a faculty member, both must notify a third party, such as a department chair, to monitor the pedagogical relationship and assign appropriate teaching, supervisory, and advising responsibilities.**

**Graduate program faculty members must evaluate annually all students' progress and suitability for entry into the student affairs profession. Evaluation of students' ethical behaviors must be included. Faculty members must keep students informed about their progress toward successful program completion.**

Through continual evaluation and appraisal of students, faculty members are expected to be aware of ethically problematic student behaviors, inadequate academic progress, and other behaviors or characteristics that may make a student unsuitable for the profession. Appropriate responses leading to remediation of the behaviors related to students' academic progress or professional suitability should be identified, monitored, evaluated, and shared with individual students as needed. Faculty members are expected in cases of significant problematic behaviors to communicate to the student the problems identified and the remediation required to avoid being terminated from the preparation program. After appropriate remediation has been proposed and evaluated, students who continue to be evaluated as being unsuitable for the profession, making poor academic progress, or having ethically problematic behaviors should be dismissed from the preparation program following appropriate due process procedures. If termination is enforced, faculty members are expected to explain to the student the grounds for the decision.

Faculty must ensure that privacy is maintained with respect to all communication and records considered to be educational records unless written permission is given by the student or when the disclosure is allowable under the law and institution policy.

Faculty must respond to requests for employment-related recommendations by students. When endorsement cannot be provided for a particular position, the student must be informed of the reason for non-endorsement.

Faculty members should base endorsements on knowledge of the student's competencies, skills, and personal characteristics.

Each candidate should be informed of procedures for endorsement, certification, registry, and licensure, if applicable.

Faculty must inform all students of the institutional and program policies regarding graduate student liability.

Program policy should be established to ensure that all students are periodically informed of their liabilities and options for protection. Programs may wish to establish policies requiring students to hold membership in particular professional associations and to purchase liability insurance prior to entering into practica or internships.

## Part 9: Program Evaluation

Planned procedures for continuing evaluation of the program must be established and implemented, and the evaluation information must be used for appropriate program enhancements.

Criteria for program evaluation should include knowledge and competencies learned by students, employment rates of graduates, professional contributions to the field made by graduates, and quality of faculty teaching, advising, and research. Evaluation of program effectiveness should reflect evidence obtained from former students; course evaluations; supervisors from institutions and agencies employing graduates of the program; personnel in state/provincial, regional, and national accrediting agencies during formal reviews; and clientele served by graduates.

Review of policies and procedures relating to recruitment, selection, retention, and career services should be included in program evaluations. The timing and regularity of evaluations should be determined in accordance with institutional policy. Generally, the length of time between comprehensive program evaluations by the program faculty should not exceed five years.

# TABLE OF APPENDICES

A. *CAS* Member Associations as of July 2003

B. *CAS* Standards and Guidelines

C. *CAS* Member Representatives to *CAS* Board of Directors

D. *CAS* Functional Area Contextual Statement Authors

E. *CAS* Protocols for the Review and Revision of Standards

F. Glossary of Terms

G. Frequently Asked Questions

# Appendix A

## *CAS* Member Associations—July 2003

| Association | Member Since |
|---|---|
| American Association for Employment In Education (AAEE) | 1979 |
| American College Counseling Association (ACCA) | 1993 |
| American College Health Association (ACHA) | 1995 |
| American College Personnel Association (ACPA) | 1979 |
| American Counseling Association (ACA) | 1983 |
| Association of College and University Housing Officers-International (ACUHO-I) | 1979 |
| Association of College Unions International (ACUI) | 1979 |
| Association of Collegiate Conference and Events Directors-International (ACCED-I) | 1999 |
| Association of Fraternity Advisors (AFA) | 1981 |
| Association for Student Judicial Affairs (ASJA) | 1990 |
| Association on Higher Education and Disability (AHEAD) | 1981 |
| Canadian Association of College and University Student Services (CACUSS) | 1994 |
| College Information and Visitor Services Association (CIVSA) | 1998 |
| College Reading and Learning Association (CRLA) | 1993 |
| NAFSA: Association of International Educators (NAFSA) | 1989 |
| National Academic Advising Association (NACADA) | 1981 |
| National Association of Campus Activities (NACA) | 1979 |
| National Association of College Admission Counselors (NACAC) | 1979 |
| National Association of College Auxiliary Services (NACAS) | 1998 |
| National Association of Colleges and Employers [NACE] | 1979 |
| National Association of Developmental Educators (NADE) | 1992 |
| National Association of Student Financial Aid Administrators (NASFAA) | 1991 |
| National Association of Student Personnel Administrators (NASPA) | 1979 |
| National Clearinghouse for Commuter Programs (NCCP) | 1980 |
| National Council of Lesbian, Gay, Bisexual, and Transgender Resources in Higher Education (LGBT) | 1999 |
| National Council of Educational Opportunity Associations (NCEOA) | 1994 |
| National Council on Student Development (NCSD: AACC Council) | 1979 |
| National Intramural Recreational Sports Association (NIRSA) | 1981 |
| National Network for the Elimination of Drug and Alcohol Abuse (NNEDAA) | 1999 |
| National Orientation Directors Association (NODA | 1979 |
| National Society for Experiential Education  (NSEE) | 2003 |
| Southern Association for College Student Affairs (SACSA) | 1982 |

# Appendix B

## CAS Standards and Guidelines†

1. Academic Advising [1986, 1997, 2002]

2. Admission Programs and Services [1987,1997, 2002]

3. Alcohol, Tobacco and Other Drug Programs [1990, 1997, 2003]

4. Campus Activities [1986, 1997, 2002]

5. Campus Information and Visitor Services [2000, 2002]

6. Career Services [1986, 1997, 2000, 2002]

7. College Health Programs [2001, 2002]

8. College Unions [1986, 1997, 1998, 2002]

9. Commuter Student Programs [1986,1997, 2002]

10. Conference and Events Programs [2002]

11. Counseling Services [1986, 1997, 1999, 2002]

12. Disability Support Services [1986, 1997, 2003]

13. Educational Services for Distance Learners [2000, 2002]

14. Financial Aid Programs [1996, 2002]

15. Fraternity and Sorority Advising [1986, 1996, 2002]

16. Housing and Residential Life Programs [1986, 1992, 1997, 2002]

17. International Student Programs and Services [1996, 2002]

18. Judicial Programs and Services [1986, 1996, 2002]

19. Leadership Programs [1996, 2002]

20. Learning Assistance Programs [1986, 1996, 2002]

21. Lesbian, Gay, Bisexual, and Transgender Programs and Services [2000, 2002]

22. Minority Student Programs and Services [1986, 1997, 2002]

23. Orientation Programs [1986, 1996, 2002]

24. Outcome Assessment and Program Evaluation [1986, 1997, 2002]

25. Recreational Sports [1986, 1996, 2002]

26. Registrar Programs and Services [1995, 2002]

27. Religious Programs [1986, 1997, 2002]

28. TRIO and Other Educational Opportunity Programs [1999, 2002]

29. Women Student Programs and Services [1992, 1997, 2002]

30. Master's Student Affairs Preparation Programs [1979, 1986, 1997, 2002]

† [Dates of Origin and Revisions]

# Appendix C

## *CAS* Member Associations
## Representatives on CAS Board of Directors
## July 2003

| DIRECTOR | ALTERNATE DIRECTOR |
|---|---|

American Association For Employment In Education (AAEE)
Alison R. Angell, Lesley University [1999-]

B.J. Bryant, AAEE National Office

American College Counseling Association (ACCA)
Laura A. Dean, Pfeiffer U. [1997-]

Michelle Stefanisko, Western Carolina University (2002)

American College Health Association (ACHA)
Paula L. Swinford, U. of Southern California [2000-]

E. Victor Leino, ACHA [1998-]

American College Personnel Association (ACPA)
Don G. Creamer, Virginia Tech [2001-]

John W. Lowery, U of South Carolina [2001-]

American Counseling Association (ACA)
Michelle Stefanisko, Western Carolina University [1999-]

Association of College and University Housing Officers-International (ACUHO-I)
Carol Henry, University of Connecticut [1999-]

Jill Eckardt, Mesa State College [2002-]

Association of College Unions International (ACUI)
Bob Rodda, College of Wooster [2002-]

Brett Perozzi ACUI [2001-]

Association of Collegiate Conference and Events Directors-International (ACCED-I)
Patrick Perfetto, University of Maryland [1999-]

Tom Arkell, Brock University [2000-]
Thomas Flynn, Univ. of Maryland [1999-2000]

Association of Fraternity Advisors (AFA)
Douglas K. Lange, MRT Multimedia, Inc. [1982-]

Association for Student Judicial Affairs (ASJA)
John W. Lowery, Univ. of South Carolina [2001-]

Association on Higher Education & Disability (AHEAD)
Peggy Hayeslip, Johns Hopkins University [2000-] Beth Hunsinger, Com. College of Baltimore County-Essex [2002-].

Canadian Association of College & University Student Services [CACUSS]
Peggy Patterson, University of Calgary [1994-96; 1999-]

College Reading & Learning Association (CRLA)
Becky Johnen, Mt. de Chantal Visitation Acad. [1998-]

Georgine Materniak, University of Pittsburgh [1997-]

Collegiate Information and Visitor Services Association (CIVSA)
Matthew Weismantel, Rutgers University [1998-]

Denise Wellman, University of South Carolina [2000-]

Council for Opportunity in Education [The Council]
Andrea Reeve, The Council [1994-]

Sally Burge, Eastern Washington University [2002]
Dan Connell, Morehead State U. [1994-2000]

National Academic Advising Association (NACADA)
Charlie L. Nutt, NACADA [2001]

Eric White, Penn State University [1999-]

National Association for Campus Activities (NACA)
Jan Arminio, Shippensburg University [1988-]

Dawn Thomas, NACA [1999-]

National Association for College Admission Counseling (NACAC)
Kerry Cunningham, NACAC [2002-]

National Association for Developmental Education (NADE)
Dee Bost, Harding University [2002-]    Susan Clark-Thayer, Suffolk University [2002-]

National Association of College Auxiliary Services (NACAS)
Willie J. Nichols, Bowie State University [1998-]

National Association of Colleges & Employers [NACE]
Patricia Carretta, George Mason University [2001-]    Marilyn Mackes, NACE [2001-]

NAFSA - Association of International Educators (NAFSA)
Betty Soppelsa, NAFSA [2003-]    Judith Green NAFSA [2003-]

National Association of Student Financial Aid Administrators (NASFAA)
A. Dallas Martin, Jr., NASFAA [1989-]    Joan Holland Crissman, NASFAA [1989-]

National Association of Student Personnel Administrators (NASPA)
William L. Thomas, Jr., University of Maryland [1979-]

National Clearinghouse for Commuter Programs (NCCP)
Barbara Jacoby, University of Maryland [1980-]    Martha B. Wilmes, University of Maryland[1980-]

National Consortium of Lesbian, Gay, Bisexual, & Transgender Resources in Higher Education  (Consortium)
Luke Jensen, U. Maryland-College Park (2002-]    Gwendolyn Alden Dean, Cornell University [2002-]

National Council On Student Development (NCSD)
Deborah Garrett, Ivy Tech State College [2001-]    Rosemary Woolley, St Louis Community College-Forest Park

National Intramural-Recreational Sports Association (NIRSA)
Kent J. Blumenthal, NIRSA [1996-]    Dixie Bennett, Loyola University of Chicago [1996-]

National Orientation Directors Association (NODA)
Ralph Busby, Stephen F. Austin State University (2003-)

National Society for Experiential Education (NSEE)
Linda Goff, Marymount University (2003-) Eugene J. Alpert, Washington Center for Internships & Academic Seminars (2003-)

Southern Association for College Student Affairs (SACSA)
Merrily Dunn, The University of Georgia [1999-]    Ted K. Miller, The University of Georgia [1996-]

The Network: Addressing Collegiate Alcohol & Other Drug Issues (The Network)
Carol Middlebrooks, The University of Georgia [1999-]

CAS Public Directors:
Carmen G. Neuberger, ACPA Executive Director Emeritus [2000-]
Marianne R. Phelps, US Department of Education [1997-]

Council for the Advancement of Standards in Higher Education (CAS)
Phyllis Mable, Executive Director
CAS, One Dupont Circle, NW. Suite 300. Washington, DC 20036-1188
Web Page:  WWW.CAS.EDU; Phone (202) 862-1400; Fax (202) 296-3286

The Council for the Advancement of Standards in Higher Education [CAS] is a not-for-profit consortium of 32 International, national professional associations established to develop, disseminate, and promote professional standards for the practice and preparation of student support service providers in higher education settings.

# Appendix D

## *CAS* Functional Area Standards
## Contextual Statement Authors

| | | |
|---|---|---|
| Academic Advising | Linda Higginson [NACADA] | Pennsylvania State University |
| | Eric White [NACADA] | Pennsylvania State University |
| Admission Programs | Joyce Smith [NACAC] | NACAC National Office |
| Alcohol & Other Drug Programs | Carole Middlebrooks [The Network] | The University of Georgia |
| CAS General Standards | Ted K. Miller [SACSA] | The University of Georgia |
| Campus Activities | Jan Arminio [NACA] | Shippensburg University |
| Campus Information & Visitor Services | Matthew J. Weismantel (CIVSA) | Rutgers University |
| Career Services | Denise Dwight Smith [NACE] | UNC-Charlotte |
| | Alison R. Angell [AAEE] | Lesley University |
| College Health Programs | Paula L.Swinford [ACHA] | University of Southern California |
| | E. Victor E. Leino | American College Health Assoc. |
| College Unions | Nancy Davis Metz [ACUI] | ACUI National Office |
| Commuter Student Programs | Barbara Jacoby [NCCP] | University of Maryland |
| | Martha Baer Wilmes [NCCP] | University of Maryland |
| Conference and Events Programs | Pat Perfetto [ACCED-I] | University of Maryland |
| Counseling Services | Michelle C. Stefanisko [ACA] | Western Carolina University |
| | Laura A. Dean [ACCA] | Pfeiffer University |
| Disability Support Services | Peggy Hayeslip, | Johns Hopkins University |
| Educational Services-Distance Learners | Nancy Thompson (AACIS) | The University of Georgia |
| Financial Aid Programs | Joan H. Crissman  [NASFAA] | NASFAA National Office |
| | A. Dallas Martin, Jr. | NASFAA National Office |
| Fraternity and Sorority Advising | Daniel Bureau | University of Illinois at Urbana-Champaign |
| Housing and Residential Life | Mike Eyster [ACUHO-I] | University of Oregon |
| International Student Programs | Bill Carroll [NAFSA] | NAFSA National Office |
| Judicial Programs | John Wesley Lowery [ASJA] | University of South Carolina. |
| Learning Assistance Programs | Becky Johnen [CRLA] | Mt. de Chantal Visitation Academy |
| | Susan Clark-Thayer [NADE] | Suffolk University |
| | Georgine Materniak [CRLA] | University of Pittsburg |
| Leadership Programs | Jan Arminio [NACA] | Shippensburg University |
| Lesbian, Gay, Bisexual & Transgender | Ronni Sanlo (LGBT) | University of California at Los Angeles |
| Minority Student Programs | Andrea Reeve | The Council National Office |
| | Christopher Davis | The Council National Office |
| Orientation Prorams | Gerry Strumpf [NODA] | University of Maryland |
| | Chris Boyer [NODA] | |
| Outcomes Assessment & | Roger B. Winston, Jr. | The University of Georgia |
| Program Evaluation | | |
| Recreational Sports | Dixie Bennett [NIRSA] | Loyola University Chicago |
| Registrar Programs | Wayne Becraft [AACRAO] | AACRAO National Office |
| Religious Programs | Diane L. Cooper | The University of Georgia |
| TRIO & Other Educational | Andrea Reeve [The Council] | The Council National Office |
| Opportunity Programs | | |
| Women Student Programs | Kathryn Brooks | University of Utah |
| | Carmen G. Neuberger [Public] | ACPA National Office |
| Masters Level Preparation | Jan Arminio [NACA] | Shippensburg University |

## Appendix E

### PROTOCOL for DEVELOPING NEW STANDARDS

1. The CAS Board of Directors identifies and defines the functional area for which a CAS standard is to be written. Functional areas for which standards are developed may be proposed by any professional entity or group of concerned professional practitioners. If a standard currently exists, CAS will identify its source and seek its sponsoring agency's cooperation on developing CAS standards and guidelines for that functional area. The CAS Board of Directors must agree by majority vote to sponsor development of a new professional standard.

2. When the CAS Board determines that a new CAS Functional Area Standard needs to be developed, a Drafting Committee of three to five CAS Directors will be formed to guide the development process. The committee is encouraged to use every available method of electronic communication to facilitate the process of soliciting and receiving input and feedback

3. The Drafting Committee will initially identify all CAS member associations at a Directors meeting to establish which associations have a significant interest in the functional area for which standards are being developed. The Committee will also identify other non-CAS professional organizations that might have a significant interest in the functional area for which standards are to be developed. The CAS General Standards will be used as the foundation for any newly developed functional area standard. A request will be sent to CAS Directors of identified organizations (and leaders of non-CAS professional organizations) for their personal review and to share with colleagues who can provide timely and substantive recommendations for the new standards and, if they wish, rough draft copies of proposed standards. A minimum of two months return time should be allowed for response if facilitated by traditional mail, or six weeks via electronic communications

4. Non-CAS member organizations with interest in the functional area under consideration will be invited to join the CAS consortium. Failure of such an association to join CAS will not deter CAS from moving forward on developing the new standards.

5. The Drafting Committee will evaluate all substantive recommendations and provide its own well-considered ideas to the standards development process.

6. The Drafting Committee will prepare an initial draft of the functional area standards and guidelines, using the CAS standards and guideline format, for review and comment by CAS Directors, CAS member association leaders who had participated actively during the request for opinions and comments. If several proposed standards were developed by the associations involved, the Committee will unify them into one draft. This draft should be prepared within 6 months after initiation of the process.

7. Following a minimum of six-week critique and comment review time, the Drafting Committee will revise the draft as appropriate based upon critiques received.

8. The Drafting Committee chairperson and/or functional areas expert who participated in the Drafting Committee will present its final draft proposal to the CAS Executive Committee in person or by phone conference as needed.

9. The CAS Executive Committee reviews the draft and formulates a penultimate draft for consideration by the CAS Board of Directors.

10. The CAS Board of Directors takes required action to adopt the standards and guidelines.

11. The newly developed standards, upon adoption by the Board, are then put into the CAS *Self Assessment Guide* format for distribution to the profession at large.

12. Upon completion, the Standards and Guidelines will be published in the Blue Book along with the appropriate contextual statement.

### PROTOCOL for REVISING CAS STANDARDS

1. The CAS Board of Directors will systematically review approximately six or more CAS Functional Area Standards and Guidelines per year on a five year staggered basis to determine if there is a need for revision. Member associations with interests in the functional area(s) under review will be called upon to help assess the need for revision as well.

2. When the CAS periodic review identifies a CAS Functional Area Standard that requires revision, a Review Committee of three to five CAS Directors will be formed to guide the revision process. The Committee is encouraged to use every available method of electronic communication to facilitate the process of soliciting and receiving input and feedback.

3. The Review Committee will initially poll all CAS member associations at a Directors Meeting to establish which associations have a significant interest in the functional area for which standards are under consideration. The Committee will also identify other non-CAS professional organizations that might have a significant interest in the functional area for which standards are under consideration. Copies of the current functional standards will be sent to CAS Directors of identified organizations (and leaders of non-CAS professional organizations) for their personal review and to share with colleagues who can provide timely and substantive recommendations for revision. A minimum of two months return time should be allowed for response if facilitated by traditional mail, or six weeks via electronic communications.

4. The Review Committee will also concurrently identify a minimum of five recognized expert practitioners in the functional area under consideration and request critical comment and suggested revisions. These expert practitioners should represent institutions of varied sizes, types and geographic locations. A minimum of two months return time should be allowed for response if facilitated by traditional mail, or six weeks via electronic communications.

5. The Review Committee will evaluate all recommendations for revision and provide its own well-considered ideas to the revision process.

6. The Review Committee will prepare an initial draft of the revised functional area standards and guidelines for review and comment from CAS Directors, CAS member association leaders, and identified experts who had participated actively in the first request for review. These expert practitioners should represent institutions of varied sizes, types, and geographic locations. This draft should be prepared within six months after initiation of the process.

7. Following a minimum of six-week critique and comment review time, the Review Committee will revise the draft as appropriate based upon critiques received.

8. The Review Committee chairperson and/or functional area expert who participated in the Review Committee will present the Committee's final draft proposal to the CAS Executive Committee in person or by phone conference as needed.

9. The CAS Executive Committee reviews the draft and formulates a penultimate draft for consideration by the CAS Board of Directors.

10. The CAS Board of Directors takes required action to adopt the standards and guidelines.

11. The revised standards, upon adoption by the Board, is then put into the CAS *Self Assessment Guide* format for distribution to the profession at large.

12. Upon completion, the functional area standards and guidelines will be published in the Blue Book along with its appropriate contextual statement.

# Appendix F

## Glossary of Terms

**accreditation.** A voluntary process conducted by peers through non-governmental agencies for purposes of improving educational quality and assuring the public that programs and services meet established standards. In higher education, accreditation is divided into two types—institutional and specialized. Although both are designed to assure fundamental levels of quality, the former focuses on the institution as a whole while the latter focuses on academic pre-professional or specialty professional programs such as law, business, psychology, and education; or services such as counseling centers within the institution. Although the CAS Standards have utility for accreditation self-study, CAS is not an accrediting body.

**affirmative action.** Policies and/or programs designed to redress historic injustices committed against racial minorities and other specified groups by making special efforts to provide members of these groups with access to educational and employment opportunities. This may apply to students as well as to faculty and staff members.

**best practice.** A level of professional conduct or practice identified as being necessary for college and university personnel to exhibit in their daily work for the host program or service to be judged satisfactory, sufficient and of acceptable quality. CAS Standards and Guidelines represent best practice.

**CAS.** The Council for the Advancement of Standards in Higher Education. A consortium of professional associations concerned with the development and promulgation of professional standards and guidelines for student support programs and services in institutions of higher learning. The Council's Board of Directors is composed of representatives from member associations and meets semiannually in the spring and fall. Prior to 1992, the consortium's name was the Council for the Advancement of Standards for Student Services/Development Programs.

**CAS Blue Book.** The informal name of the publication entitled *The CAS Book of Professional Standards for Higher Education* that presents the CAS standards and guidelines. The first iteration of the CAS standards was published in 1986. Revised editions were published in 1997, 1999, 2001, and 2003. CAS policy calls for an updated revision to be published biannually.

**CAS Board of Directors.** A body of representatives from professional higher education associations in the U.S. and Canada that have joined the CAS consortium, pay annual dues, and keep their memberships informed about CAS standards and related initiatives. Each member association may designate two official representatives [Director and Alternate] to act on its behalf at CAS Board meetings; each association has one vote on the Council.

**CAS consortium.** An alliance of professional U.S. and Canadian higher education associations established in 1979 to develop and promulgate professional standards that guide and enhance the quality of student life, learning, and development through support programs and to educate practitioners in this regard.

**CAS Executive Committee.** A body of elected CAS officers, including president, secretary, treasurer, members at large, and others elected at the discretion of the Board of Directors. This body meets periodically to deal with CAS governance issues and to review penultimate standard statements prior to final review and adoption by the Board of Directors.

**CAS functional area standard.** A statement that presents criteria describing the fundamental essential expectations of practice agreed upon by the profession at large for a given institutional function. Standards are presented in **bold** type and use auxiliary verbs "must" and "shall." Currently there are 29 sets of CAS functional area standards (see Appendix B).

**CAS general standards.** Statements presenting criteria that represent the most fundamental essential expectations agreed on by the profession at large for all higher education support programs and services. These "boilerplate" criteria are presented in **bold** type and use the auxiliary verbs "must" and "shall" as do all CAS standards. The most recent revision of the General Standards was adopted in 2002.

**CAS Internet URL.** http://www.cas.edu The CAS web site at which various CAS initiatives and resources are described, publications may be ordered, and links to CAS member associations are listed.

**CAS member association.** One of the professional higher education associations that has joined the CAS consortium and is committed to the development and promulgation of professional standards for college student learning and development support services.

**CAS preparation program standards.** A set of professional standards developed and promulgated for purposes of providing student affairs administration master's level programs with criteria to guide the professional education and preparation of entry-level practitioners in student affairs.

**CAS Public Director.** An individual appointed to the CAS Board of Directors to represent the public at large. CAS by-laws call for the appointment of two public directors who do not represent a specific functional area or professional association.

**CAS Self-Assessment Guide (SAG).** An operational version of the *CAS Standards and Guidelines* designed to provide users with an assessment tool that can be used for self-study or self-assessment purposes. A SAG is available for each functional area for which a CAS standard exists.

**CAS Standards and Guidelines.** Published criteria and related statements designed to provide college and university support service providers with established measures against which to evaluate programs and services. A standard uses the auxiliary verbs "must" and "shall" while a guideline uses the verbs "should" and "may." Standards are essentials, guidelines are not.

**certification.** Official recognition by a governmental or professional body attesting that an individual practitioner meets established standards or criteria. Criteria usually include formal academic preparation in prescribed content areas and a period of supervised practice, and may also include a systematic evaluation (that is, standardized test) of the practitioner's knowledge.

**compliance.** Adherence to a standard of practice or preparation. Compliance with the CAS standards implies that an institution or program meets or exceeds the fundamental essential criteria established for a given functional area program and service or for an academic student affairs administration preparation program.

**guideline.** A statement that clarifies or amplifies professional standards. Although not required for acceptable practice, a guideline is designed to provide institutions with suggestions and illustrations that can assist in establishing programs and services that more fully address the needs of students than those mandated by a standard. Guidelines may be thought of as providing guidance in ways to exceed fundamental requirements, to approach excellence, or to function at a more optimal level. CAS Guidelines use the auxiliary verbs "should" and "may."

**learning and development outcomes.** Change occurring in students as a direct result of their interaction with an educational institution and its programs and services. Part 2 of the CAS standards identifies 16 learning and development outcomes that students should accomplish as a result of their higher education experiences. A number of outcome indicators are also included to guide assessing the outcomes.

**in-service (or inservice) education.** Educational skill building activities provided by an institution to staff members within the context of their work responsibilities. A form of staff development designed to strengthen the ability of practitioners to carry out their duties more effectively.

**licensure.** Official recognition, usually by a government entity, that authorizes practice in the public arena. A license is usually granted only upon the presentation of compelling evidence that the individual is well qualified to practice in a given profession. Granting of a professional license typically authorizes holders to announce their qualifications to provide selected services to the public and attach professional titles to their names. Insurance companies often require individuals to be licensed to qualify for third-party payments.

**paraprofessional.** An individual who has received an adequate level of training and supervision to work in support of professional practitioners, their offices, and programs. Paraprofessionals may be students, staff members, or volunteers who have not undertaken formal or graduate level professional preparation or earned credentials to function as a professional practitioner.

**personal development.** Closely related to student development, this term refers to the processes associated with human maturation, especially those concerned with evolving psychosocial, morale, relational, and self-concept changes that influence an individual's quality of life.

**pre-professional.** An individual who is in the process of obtaining professional education that will qualify her or him for professional practice (e.g., graduate student, intern).

**program.** Refers to one of two types. (a) organizational, a departmental level administrative unit or sub-unit; (b) activity, an institutional support service such as an invited lecture, a workshop, a social event, or a series of organized presentations over time (e.g., a "lunch and learn" program).

**quality assurance.** The *raison d'être* for the CAS standards and virtually all types of credentialing activities devised to assure the public that educational institutions, programs, and services and those providing them exhibit high levels of competence leading to excellence. Quality assurance initiatives are intended to ensure that those accessing available programs and services will truly benefit from them.

**registry.** An official record of the names and qualifications of individuals who meet preestablished criteria to function as professional practitioners. The names of professionally licensed and/or certified practitioners are typically listed in a registry. In some instances a professional "register" may be maintained for purposes of providing individuals, institutions, and organizations with the names of those who meet an established level of competence for employment or other activity such as consulting or lecturing. A registry may also be used to identify those judged to possess relevant knowledge or skill outside the context of licensure.

**self-study.** An internal process by which institutions and programs evaluate their quality and effectiveness in reference to established criteria such as the CAS standards. This process, often used for institutional and specialty accreditation purposes, results in a formal report presenting the findings of the internal evaluation implemented by institutional employees. For accreditation purposes, this report is then validated by a visiting, external committee of peers from comparable institutions or programs. CAS SAGs have great utility for this purpose.

**self-regulation.** The recommended process by which the *CAS Standards and Guid*elines can best be used to evaluate and assess institutional support programs and services. This approach calls for institutions and programs to establish, maintain, and enhance the quality of their offerings and environments by using the standards to evaluate themselves. From the CAS perspective, each institution and its programs can and should seek to identify and regulate its own best practices rather than relying on external agencies to do so.

**staff development.** Refers to the programs, workshops, conferences, and other training related activities offered by institutions, professional associations, and corporate agencies for purposes of increasing effectiveness in accomplishing work responsibilities of staff members.

**standard.** A statement framed within the context of a professional arena designed to provide practitioners with criteria against which to judge the quality of the programs and services offered. A standard reflects an essential level of practice that, when met, represents quality performance. CAS standards use auxiliary verbs "**must**" and "shall" presented in **bold** print.

**student development.** Refers to those learning outcomes that occur as a result of students being exposed to higher education environments designed to enhance academic, intellectual, psychosocial, psychomotor, moral, and, for some institutions, spiritual development. This concept is based on applying human development theories within the context of higher education. In some instances, the term has also been applied to administrative units (e.g., center for student development).

**student learning and development.** Refers to the outcomes students realize when exposed to new experiences, concepts, information, and ideas; the knowledge and understanding gleaned from interactions with higher education learning environments. Learning means acquiring knowledge and applying it to life, appreciating human differences, and approaching an integrated sense of self.

# Appendix G

## FAQ
## Frequently Asked Questions
### About *CAS* and Its Initiatives

1. **What is CAS?**

   CAS, the acronym used for the Council for the Advancement of Standards in Higher Education established in 1979, is a consortium of 32 professional associations concerned with the development and promulgation of professional standards and guidelines for student learning and development support programs and services in institutions of higher learning. The Council's Board of Directors is composed of representatives from member associations and meets semi-annually in the Spring and the Fall. Prior to 1992, the consortium's name was the Council for the Advancement of Standards for Student Services/Development Programs.

2. **Why does CAS write standards?**

   One criterion for the existence of a profession is the existence of professional standards to guide and judge practice. Without standards there would be few if any criteria established that institutions and their programs and services could use to judge their educational quality and assure constituents that they are provided high quality education. CAS was established to develop and promulgate the standards necessary to achieve educational excellence.

3. **What CAS Standards and Guidelines are currently in place?**

   As of July 2003, CAS had developed 29 sets of functional area standards and guidelines and one set of student affairs master's level preparation standards. Functional areas for which standards have been developed include programs and services concerned with: 1. Academic Advising, 2. Admission, 3. Alcohol, Tobacco, and Other Drug Programs, 4. Campus Activities, 5. Campus Information and Visitor Services, 6. Career Services, 7. College Health Services, 8. College Union, 9. Collegiate Conferences and Events, 10. Commuter Students, 11. Counseling, 12. Disability, 13. Educational Services for Distance Learners, 14. Financial Aid, 15. Fraternity and Sorority, 16. Housing, 17. International Student, 18. Judicial Affairs, 19. Leadership Programs, 20. Learning Assistance, 21. Lesbian, Gay, Bisexual, & Transgender, 22. Minority Student, 23. Orientation, 24. Outcomes Assessment and Program Evaluation, 25. Recreational Sports, 26. Registrar, 27. Religious, 28. TRIO and Other Educational Opportunity, and 29. Women Student.

4. **What other CAS Standards are currently being developed?**

   Additional functional areas for which standards are in the process of development include Campus Auxiliary Services, Food Services, and Service Learning.

5. **What is the difference between a CAS standard and a CAS guideline?**

   A CAS standard, which is printed in **BOLD TYPE**, is considered to be essential to successful professional practice and uses the auxiliary verbs "**must**" and "shall." Compliance with the CAS standards indicates that a program meets essential criteria as described in each standard statement and that there is tangible evidence available to support that fact. A CAS guideline, printed in Light-Face Type, is a statement that clarifies or amplifies a CAS standard. Although not required for achieving compliance, CAS guidelines are designed to offer suggestions and illustrations that can assist programs and services to more fully address the learning and development needs of students. CAS guidelines provide guidance for exceeding the criteria established by the CAS standards so as to approach excellence or to function at a more optimal level. CAS guidelines use the auxiliary verbs "should" and "may."

6. **Are institutions in jeopardy if they fail to meet the CAS *Standards and Guidelines*?**

   CAS Standards are provided primarily for institutions to use within the context of a "self-regulation" process. That is, although compliance with the standards evidences "good practice" that is recognized profession-wide, there are no external sanctions for non-compliance. However, institutions that do not meet the CAS standards will likely discover that their student support programs and services fail to meet the manifest needs of their students. Further, institutions that evidence compliance with the CAS standards are virtually assured of receiving "high grades" from regional or specialized accrediting bodies.

7. **What utility do the *CAS Standards and Guidelines* have for practitioners?**

   The CAS standards are multi-purpose in nature. They can be used to study and evaluate institutional divisions of student affairs and the various functional student support areas common to contemporary institutions of higher learning. Likewise, they can be used for staff professional development purposes to ensure that staff members comprehend their roles and functions and develop the level of knowledge and skill essential for good practice. Also, the CAS standards can be used to guide the development of new or enhanced functional areas designed to provide students with additional learning and development opportunities.

8. **Where will I find the *CAS Standards and Guidelines*?**

   CAS publishes two versions of its standards, one in text format and another in workbook format. The CAS Blue Book (*The CAS Book of Professional Standards for higher education*, 2003) provides an introduction to CAS, its mission, initiatives, and the principles upon which it was founded. Also, individual functional area standards accompanied by introductory contextual statements are included. In addition, for use with programmatic self-studies, there is a CAS Self-Assessment Guide (SAG) for each set of standards. These assessment workbooks include the standards and guidelines along with a series of "criterion measure" statements used to judge the level of program compliance with the standard. The criterion measures scale to rate the criteria, provide a vehicle for program assessment and evaluation. The CAS SAGs are also available electronically via the CAS internet web site and in Compact Disk (CD ROM) format.

9. **How can I obtain the CAS publications and what are their costs?**

   All available CAS publications are listed on the CAS internet web site and in the back of the CAS blue book and may be purchased from the CAS national office, One Dupont Circle, NW, Suite 300, Washington, DC 20036-1188. The 2003 edition of the CAS Blue Book is priced at $45.00 (10 or more copies at $35.00 each) and international orders are $50.00 each. Functional Area Self-Assessment Guides (SAGs) are available for $15.00 each. The CD-ROM version of CAS SAGs is available for $150.00 for the full set. Although CAS cannot accept institutional purchase orders, VISA, MasterCard, and American Express credit cards are accepted and prices include shipping. The CAS Federal ID Number is 52-122-8597.

10. **Where will I find information about using the**
    ***CAS Standards and Guidelines*?**

    An outline of how to put the CAS standards to work is included in the blue book and each functional area SAG has an introductory section that describes HOW TO APPLY the SAG for self-study purposes. It is strongly recommended that these descriptive application materials be reviewed prior to initiating a self-study assessment and evaluation.

11. **Can a partial program self-study using less than a full functional area standard be implemented?**

    Each CAS standard is organized into 13 parts. These individual program components can be used on stand-alone bases for program self-studies or for program development purposes. That is, a partial self-study using selected components may be desirable for some programs to consider. Likewise, each component has utility for staff development purposes. One recommended training approach is to hold a series of training sessions in which individual parts are examined in detail.

12. **How long does a typical division or individual program self-study take to complete?**

    The time required to complete the self-study process varies with size and complexity of institutions and programs. In most instances, it will take from 6 to 9 months to complete a comprehensive division or campus-wide self-study while a single administrative unit functional area program self-study may well be completed in approximately 3 months. One of the major time-consuming factors of any self-study is the data collection process wherein documentary evidence is obtained and organized into a usable format. If several campus-wide surveys are required to obtain data, more time will be required than if the documentary evidence has already been collected, compiled, and analyzed.

13. **Does CAS offer certification or accreditation?**

    CAS does not function as a certification or accreditation agency. Rather, CAS encourages institutions and their functional area programs to follow a "self-regulation" approach wherein program evaluation self-studies are implemented for internal assessment purposes.

14. **Do the CAS Standards have utility for regional or other accreditation purposes?**

    Institutions undergoing accreditation self-studies will find the CAS standards most useful. Because CAS functional area standards are invariably more comprehensive than regional accreditation criteria, a self-study using the CAS standards will provide ample documentation that can be used as evidence of compliance with accreditation criteria.

15. **How does one become a member of CAS?**

    Because CAS is a consortium of professional organizations concerned with student support services designed to enhance student learning and personal development, there are no individual memberships available. The CAS Board of Directors is composed of representatives from member organizations and each member association has one vote on Council business. Organizational membership information is available from the CAS national office.

16. **Does CAS have a presence at national association meetings?**

    Because CAS is a consortium of professional associations, each member association is responsible for providing its membership with information about the nature and availability of CAS standards. Most member associations include CAS related presentations at their conventions. Several CAS officers and directors are available upon request to provide CAS workshops or programs sponsored by professional organizations. CAS oriented programs have been offered at numerous international conferences in recent years including the European Association of Institutional Research in Prague, the Hong Kong Student Services Association, the Asia-Pacific Student Services Association in the Philippines, and the National Student Services in the 21st Century Conference in Taiwan.

**17. Does CAS provide institutional staff training programs and workshops?**

The CAS national office can provide information about CAS officers and board members who are well qualified to provide staff development training workshops and programs for institutions.

**19. How often are CAS Functional Area Standards and Guidelines revised?**

CAS policy calls for every functional area standard to be reviewed periodically on a 5-year basis for purposes of determining whether a revision is needed. Individuals or organizations who believe a given standard is in need of revision are invited to contact CAS to make such recommendations.

**19. My association has written professional standards, what can CAS provide that we don't already have?**

Several professional associations have established standards for their constituent members, some of which are quite comparable to CAS standards and some of which are not. In general, CAS standards are designed to be used in every type and size of higher educational institution and were created for this broad user base. A primary benefit of the CAS standards is the fact that CAS represents a profession-wide effort to develop, promulgate, and encourage use of its professional standards in institutions of higher education throughout the United States and Canada and increasingly on a global basis. CAS represents some 32 professional associations and over 100,000 professional constituents. Consequently, the professional credibility of the *CAS Standards and Guidelines* tends to exceed those proffered by a single organization. Further, The CAS approach to standards development assures profession-wide input into the development and periodic review process.

**20. How are CAS projects funded?**

CAS membership dues have been maintained at a low annual fee since the Council's inception in 1979. Consequently, CAS has come to rely upon sale of professional publications as its primary source of funding. As a non-profit organization, CAS can accept tax-exempt contributions from individuals as well as grants from philanthropic foundations.

**21. Does CAS have a web site?**

Yes, the CAS web site URL is:  www.cas.edu. The site provides links to the web sites of many CAS member organizations. In addition, CAS publications and related resources may be purchased via the web site and American Express, VISA, and MasterCard credit cards may be used to purchase over the secured site.

**22. Who uses the CAS Standards and how are they typically put to use?**

This important question was studied through a comprehensive, CAS sponsored nation-wide research project. Results are included in Part I of the CAS blue book and full results will be provided on the CAS web site.

**23. Why do CAS SAG criterion measures focus only on standards and not on guidelines?**

CAS SAGs were designed for self-study purposes for programs to compare themselves to the CAS standards. Consequently, only standards are rated for determining compliance because guidelines are presented to clarify and amplify the standards only.

**24. Why use CAS  standards to evaluate my program rather than using another form (e.g., benchmarks)?**

The CAS standards were developed and adopted by knowledgeable representatives from a wide range of higher education organizations. They represent a profession-wide perspective.

# *CAS* PUBLICATIONS PURCHASE INFORMATION

**Easy Order via www.cas.edu using VISA or MasterCard**

*CAS* publications and related resources may be purchased using order information that follows.
**CAS Blue Book Prices:'**
**Domestic Orders**:     1 to 9 copies, priced at $45.00 per book including postage and handling.
        10 or more copies, priced at $35.00 each including postage & handling.
**International Orders:**  1 to 9 copies, priced at $50.00 per book including postage and handling.
        10 or more copies, priced at $40.00 each including postage & handling..

**CAS Self-Assessment Guides:**
        A full set of 30 *CAS* Self-Assessment Guides (SAGs) is available in three formats,
        (1) Hard copy, (2) CD ROM format; (3) PDF download format from www.cas.edu
        SAGs are operational versions of *CAS* standards and guidelines designed for self-study purposes.
        A complimentary e-learning course on conducting self-assessments with Power Point slides useful
        for staff training purposes is included in the Assessment CD.

**Self-Assessment Guide Prices:**

**Domestic Orders:**     Complete set of 30 SAGs in CD ROM format at $150.00 each.
        Individual SAGs available on download from www.cas.edu
        Individual SAGs available in hard copy at $20.00 each.

**Shipped Postage Paid**: Additional charge for expedited hard copy shipping available on request.

**International Orders:**  Complete set of 30 SAGs in the Assessment CD ROM format at $160.00 each.
        Individual SAGs available on download from www.cas.edu
        Individual SAGs available in hard copy at $25.00 each.
**Shipped Surface Mail** Additional charge for expedited shipping available upon request.

**Payment:**          By check or money order, in US dollars only made payable to *CAS*.
        *CAS* Federal ID #: 52-122-8597  Purchase Orders cannot be honored.

        By credit card using VISA or MasterCard. Include card type, account number, expiration
        date, full name of card holder, and card holder's signature.

**Shipping Address:**   Include with order the recipient's name, street/building mailing address [no P.O.
        Boxes please], city, state, zip code, and country if other than US.
        Please include phone number and e-mail address for follow-up purposes.

**Orders by mail:**     *CAS*
        One Dupont Circle, NW
        Suite 300
        Washington, DC 20036-1188

**Phone orders:**      (202) 835-2272; Fax: (202) 296-3286
        **CAS Web Site URL**     www.cas.edu

        **CAS Information:**       PhyllisMable@aol.com

# *CAS* PUBLICATIONS ORDER FORM

**Easy Order via**
**www.cas.edu using VISA or MasterCard**

## Shipping and Handling Costs are Included in Prices Listed

Send me ____ (Quantity) copies of the 2003 revised edition of the *CAS* "Blue Book"
          Domestic Order:     $45.00 per book; 10 or more books at $35.00 each

          International Order: $50.00 per book; 10 or more books at $40.00 each

Send me the number of hard copy *CAS* Self-assessment Guides (SAG) as noted below..

          Domestic Order: $20.00 per SAG;  International Order: $25.00 per SAG

| | |
|---|---|
| ____ Academic Advising | ____ Admission Programs |
| ____ Alcohol, Tobacco, and Other Drug Programs | ____ Campus Activities |
| ____ Campus Information and Visitor Services | ____ Career Services |
| ____ College Health Programs | ____ College Unions |
| ____ Commuter Student Programs | ____ Conference and Events Programs |
| ____ Counseling Services | ____ Disability Services |
| ____ Educational Services for Distance Learners | ____ Financial Aid Programs |
| ____ Fraternity and Sorority Advising | ____ Housing and Residential Life |
| ____ International Student Programs | ____ Judicial Programs and Services |
| ____ Learning Assistance Programs | ____ Lesbian, Gay, Bisexual, and Transgender Programs |
| ____ Minority Student Programs | ____ Outcome Assessment and Program Evaluation |
| ____ Recreational Sports | ____ Registrar Programs |
| ____ Religious Programs | ____ Student Leadership Programs |
| ____ Student Orientation Programs | ____ TRIO & Other Educational Opportunity Programs |
| ____ Women Student Programs | ____ Master's Student Affairs Preparation Programs |

Send me ___ (Quantity) Interactive Assessment Compact Disks that include a full set of 30 CAS

SAGs and e-learning course on conducting self-assessments at $150.00 per disk

          Payment in the amount of $_____ Total is enclosed (U.S. Dollars only)
          Make checks payable to: *CAS* or The Council for the Advancement of Standards
          in Higher Education

### — NO PURCHASE ORDERS PLEASE—

Credit Card Order:     __ MasterCard          __ Visa

Account Number: _____

Name of cardholder (please print): _____

Expiration date: Month _____, Year _____    Amount to be charged: $_____

Signature: _____

Send to (please type or print):

Name: _____

Address: _____

           _____

           _____

e-mail address: _____

Phone:   (_____) _____

**SEND ORDER FORM WITH PAYMENT TO:**

*CAS*
**One Dupont Circle, NW, Suite 300**
**Washington, DC 20036-1188**
Credit card phone orders:  (202) 862-1400;  Fax: (202) 296-3286

*CAS* Federal ID Number is 52-122-8597